FINE ARTS, MUSIC AND LITERATURE

A HISTORY OF ROMAN CLASSICAL LITERATURE

FINE ARTS, MUSIC AND LITERATURE

Additional books and e-books in this series can be found
on Nova's website under the Series tab.

FINE ARTS, MUSIC AND LITERATURE

A HISTORY OF ROMAN CLASSICAL LITERATURE

R. W. BROWNE

Copyright © 2019 by Nova Science Publishers, Inc.

All rights reserved. No part of this book may be reproduced, stored in a retrieval system or transmitted in any form or by any means: electronic, electrostatic, magnetic, tape, mechanical photocopying, recording or otherwise without the written permission of the Publisher.

We have partnered with Copyright Clearance Center to make it easy for you to obtain permissions to reuse content from this publication. Simply navigate to this publication's page on Nova's website and locate the "Get Permission" button below the title description. This button is linked directly to the title's permission page on copyright.com. Alternatively, you can visit copyright.com and search by title, ISBN, or ISSN.

For further questions about using the service on copyright.com, please contact:
Copyright Clearance Center
Phone: +1-(978) 750-8400   Fax: +1-(978) 750-4470   E-mail: info@copyright.com.

NOTICE TO THE READER

The Publisher has taken reasonable care in the preparation of this book, but makes no expressed or implied warranty of any kind and assumes no responsibility for any errors or omissions. No liability is assumed for incidental or consequential damages in connection with or arising out of information contained in this book. The Publisher shall not be liable for any special, consequential, or exemplary damages resulting, in whole or in part, from the readers' use of, or reliance upon, this material. Any parts of this book based on government reports are so indicated and copyright is claimed for those parts to the extent applicable to compilations of such works.

Independent verification should be sought for any data, advice or recommendations contained in this book. In addition, no responsibility is assumed by the Publisher for any injury and/or damage to persons or property arising from any methods, products, instructions, ideas or otherwise contained in this publication.

This publication is designed to provide accurate and authoritative information with regard to the subject matter covered herein. It is sold with the clear understanding that the Publisher is not engaged in rendering legal or any other professional services. If legal or any other expert assistance is required, the services of a competent person should be sought. FROM A DECLARATION OF PARTICIPANTS JOINTLY ADOPTED BY A COMMITTEE OF THE AMERICAN BAR ASSOCIATION AND A COMMITTEE OF PUBLISHERS.

Additional color graphics may be available in the e-book version of this book.

Library of Congress Cataloging-in-Publication Data

ISBN: 978-1-53615-963-9

Published by Nova Science Publishers, Inc. † New York

Contents

Preface		xi
Section I.	**First Era**	1
Chapter 1	Comparison of the Latin Language with the Greek—Eras of Latinity—Origin of the Romans—Elements of the Latin Language—Etruscan Influence	3
Chapter 2	The Eugubine Tables—Existence of Oscan in Italy—Bantine Table—Perugian Inscription—Etruscan Alphabet and Words—Chant of Fratres Arvales—Salian Hymn—Other Monuments of Old Latin—Latin and Greek Alphabets Compared	11
Chapter 3	Saturnian Metre—Opinions Respecting Its Origin—Early Examples of This Metre—Saturnian Ballads in Livy—Structure of the Verse—Instances of Rhythmical Poetry	25
Chapter 4	Three Periods of Roman Classical Literature—Its Elements Rude—Roman Religion—Etruscan Influence—Early Historical Monuments—Fescennine Verses—Fabulæ Atellanæ—Introduction of Stage Players—Derivation of Satire	31
Chapter 5	Emancipation of Livius Andronicus—His Imitation of the Odyssey—New Kind of Scenic Exhibitions—First Exhibition of His Dramas—Nævius A Political Partisan—His Bitterness—His Punic War—His Nationality—His Versification	37
Chapter 6	Nævius Stood Between Two Ages—Life of Ennius—Epitaphs Written by Him—His Taste, Learning, and Character—His Fitness for Being a Literary Reformer—His Influence on the Language—His Versification—the Annals—Difficulties of the Subject—Tragedies and Comedies—Satiræ—Minor Works	47

Chapter 7	The New Comedy of the Greeks the Model of the Roman—the Morality of Roman Comedy—Want of Variety in the Plots of Roman Comedy—Dramatis Personæ—Costume—Characters—Music—Latin Pronunciation—Metrical Licenses— Criticism of Volcatius—Life of Plautus—Character of His Comedies—Analysis of His Plots	**53**
Chapter 8	Statius Compared with Menander—Criticism of Cicero—Hypotheses Respecting the Early Life of Terence—Anecdote Belated by Donatus—Style And Morality of Terence—Anecdote of Him Related by Cornelius Nepos—His Pecuniary Circumstances and Death—Plots and Criticism of His Comedies—the Remaining Comic Poets	**65**
Chapter 9	Why Tragedy Did Not Flourish at Rome—National Legends Not Influential with the People—Fabulæ Prætextatæ—Roman Religion Not Ideal—Roman Love for Scenes of Real Action and Gorgeous Spectacle—Tragedy Not Patronised by the People—Pacuvius—His Dulorestes and Paulus	**81**
Chapter 10	L. Attius—His Tragedies and Fragments—Other Works—Tragedy Disappeared with Him—Roman Theatres—Traces of the Satiric Spirit in Greece—Roman Satire—Lucilius—Criticisms of Horace, Cicero, and Quintilian—Passage Quoted by Lactantius—Lævius, a Lyric Poet	**89**
Chapter 11	Prose Literature—Prose Suitable to Roman Genius—History, Jurisprudence, and Oratory—Prevalence of Greek—Q. Fabius Pictor—L. Cincius Alimentus—C. Acilius Glabrio—Value of the Annalists—Important Literary Period, During Which Cato Censorius Flourished—Sketch of His Life—His Character, Genius, and Style	**97**
Chapter 12	The Origines of Cato—Passage Quoted by Gellius—Treatise De Re Rustica—Orations—L. Cassius Hemina—Historians in the Days of the Gracchi—Traditional Anecdote of Romulus—Autobiographers—Fragment of Quadrigarius—Falsehoods of Antias—Sisenna—Tubero	**107**
Chapter 13	Early Roman Oratory—Eloquence of Appius Claudius Cæcus—Funeral Orations—Defence of Scipio Africanus Major—Scipio Africanus Minor Æmilianus—Era of the Gracchi—Their Characters—Interval Between the Gracchi and Cicero—M. Antonius—L. Licinius Crassus—Q. Hortensius—Causes of His Early Popularity and Subsequent Failure	**115**

Chapter 14	Study of Jurisprudence—Earliest Systematic Works on Roman Law—Groundwork of the Roman Civil Law—Eminent Jurists—the Scævolæ—Ælius Gallus—C. Aquilius Gallus, a Law Reformer—Other Jurists—Grammarians	127
Section II.	**The Era of Cicero and Augustus**	133
Chapter 15	Prose the Test of the Condition of a Language—Dramatic Literature Extinct—Mimes—Difference Between Romanand Greek Mimes—Laberius—Passages from His Poetry—Matius Calvena—Mimiambi—Publius Syrus—Roman Pantomime—Its Licentiousness—Principal Actors of Pantomime	135
Chapter 16	Lucretius a Poet Rather Than a Philosopher—His Life—Epic Structure of His Poem—Variety of His Poetry—Extracts from His Poem—Argument of It—the Epicurean Doctrines Contained in It—Morality of Epicurus and Lucretius—Testimonies of Virgil and Ovid—Catullus: His Life, Character, and Poetry—Other Poets of This Period	143
Chapter 17	Age of Virgil Favourable to Poetry—His Birth, Education, Habits, Illness, and Death—His Popularity and Character—His Minor Poems, the Culex Ciris Moretum Copa and Catalecta—His Bucolics—Italian Manners Not Suited to Pastoral Poetry—Idylls of Theocritus—Classification of the Bucolics—Subject of The Pollio—Heyne's Theory Respecting It	157
Chapter 18	Beauty of Didactic Poetry—Elaborate Finish of the Georgics—Roman Love of Rural Pursuits—Hesiod Suitable as a Model—Condition of Italy—Subjects Treated of in the Georgics—Some Striking Passages Enumerated—Influence of Roman Literature on English Poetry—Sources from Which the Incidents of the Æneid Are Derived—Character of Æneas—Criticism of Niebuhr	167
Chapter 19	The Libertini—Roman Feelings as to Commerce—Birth and Infancyof Horace—His Early Education at Rome—His Military Career—He Returns to Rome—Is Introduced to Mæcenas—Commences the Satires—Mæcenas Gives Him His Sabine Farm—His Country Life—the Epodes—Epistles—Carmen Seculare—Illness and Death	177
Chapter 20	Character of Horace—Descriptions of His Villa at Tivoli, and His Sabine Farm—Site of the Bandusian Fountain—the Neighbouring Scenery—Subjects of His Satires and Epistles—Beauty of His Odes—Imitations of Greek Poets—Spurious Odes—Chronological Arrangement	187

Chapter 21	Biography of Mæcenas—His Intimacy and Influence with Augustus—His Character—Valgius Rufus—Varius—Cornelius Gallus—Biography of Tibullus—His Style—Criticism of Muretus—Propertius—Imitated the Alexandrian Poets—Æmilius Macer	201
Chapter 22	Birth and Education of Ovid—His Rhetorical Powers—Anecdote Related by Seneca—His Poetical Genius—Self-Indulgent Life—Popularity—Banishment—Place of His Exile—Epistles and Other Works—Gratius Faliscus—Pedo Albinovanus—Aulus Sabinus—Marcus Manilius	211
Chapter 23	Prose Writers—Influence of Cicero Upon the Language—His Converse with His Friends—His Early Life—Pleads His First Cause—Is Quæstor, Ædile, Prætor and Consul—His Exile, Return, and Provincial Administration—His Vacillating Conduct—He Delivers His Philippics—Is Proscribed and Assassinated—His Character	221
Chapter 24	Cicero No Historian—His Oratorical Style Defended—Its Principal Charm—Observations on His Forensic Oration—His Oratory Essentially Judicial—Political Orations—Rhetorical Treatises—the Object of His Philosophical Works—Characteristics of Roman Philosophical Literature—Philosophy of Cicero—His Political Works—Letters—His Correspondents—Varro	229
Chapter 25	Roman Historical Literature—Principal Historians—Lucceius—Lucullus—Cornelius Nepos—Opinions of the Genuineness of the Works Which Bear His Name—Biography of J. Cæsar—His Commentaries—Their Style and Language—His Modesty Overrated—Other Works—Character of Cæsar	245
Chapter 26	Life of Sallust—His Insincerity—His Historical Works—He Was A Bitter Opponent of the New Aristocracy—Profligacy of That Order—His Style Compared with That of Thucydides—His Value as an Historian—Trogus Pompeius—His Historiæ Philippicæ	255
Chapter 27	Life of Livy—His Object in Writing His History—Its Spirit and Character—Livy Precisely Suited to His Age—Not Wilfully Inaccurate—His Political Bias Accounted for—Materials Which He Might Have Used—Sources of His History—His Defects as an Historian—His Style—Grammarians—Vitruvius Pollio an Augustan Writer—Contents of His Work	261

Section III.	**Era of the Decline**	271
Chapter 28	Decline of Roman Literature—It Became Declamatory—Biography of Phædrus—Genuineness of His Fables—Moral and Political Lessons Inculcated in Them—Specimens of Fables—Fables Suggested by Historical Events—Sejanus and Tiberius—Epoch Unfavourable to Literature—Ingenuity of Phædrus—Superiority of Æsop—the Style of Phædrus Classical	273
Chapter 29	Dramatic Literature in the Augustan Age—Revival Under Nero—Defects of the Tragedies Attributed to Seneca—Internal Evidence of Their Authorship—Seneca the Philosopher a Stoic—Inconsistent and Unstable—the Sentiments of His Philosophical Works Found in His Tragedies—Parallel Passages Compared—French School of Tragic Poets	283
Chapter 30	Biography of Persius—His Schoolboy Days—His Friends—His Purity and Modesty—His Defects as a Satirist—Subjects of His Satires—Obscurity of His Style—Compared with Horace—Biography of Juvenal—Corruption of Roman Morals—Critical Observations of the Satires—Their Historical Value—Style of Juvenal—He Was the Last of Roman Satirists	291
Chapter 31	Biography of Lucan—Inscription to His Memory—Sentiments Expressed in the Pharsalia—Lucan An Unequal Poet—Faults and Merits of the Pharsalia—Characteristics of His Age—Difficulties of Historical Poetry—Lucan a Descriptive Poet—Specimens of His Poetry—Biography of Silius Italicus—His Character by Pliny—His Poem Dull and Tedious—His Description of the Alps	303
Chapter 32	C. Valerius Flaccus—Faults of the Argonautica—Papinius Statius—Beauty of His Minor Poems—Incapable of Epic Poetry—Domitian—Epigram—Martial—His Biography—Profligacy of the Age in Which He Lived—Impurity of His Writings—Favourable Specimens of His Poetry	313
Chapter 33	Aufidius Bassus and Cremutius Cordus—Velleius Paterculus—Character of His Works—Valerius Maximus—Cornelius Tacitus—Age of Trajan—Biography of Tacitus—His Extant Works Enumerated—Agricola—Germany—Histories—Traditions Respecting the Jews—Annals—Object of Tacitus—His Character—His Style	323
Chapter 34	C. Suetonius Tranquillus—His Biography—Sources of His History—His Great Fault—Q. Curtius Rufus—Time When He Flourished Doubtful—His Biography of Alexander—Epitomes of L. Annæus Florus—Sources Whence He Derived Them	333

Chapter 35	M. Annæus Seneca—His Controversy and Suasoriæ—L. Annæus Seneca—Tutor to Nero—His Enormous Fortune—His Death and Character—Inconsistencies in His Philosophy—a Favourite With Early Christian Writers—His Epistles—Work on Natural Phenomena—Apocolocyntosis—His Style	339
Chapter 36	Pliny the Elder—His Habits Described by His Nephew—His Industry and Application—His Death in the Eruption of Vesuvius—the Eruption Described in Two Letters of Pliny the Younger—the Natural History of Pliny—Its Subjects Described—Pliny the Younger—His Affection for His Guardian—His Panegyric, Letters, and Despatches—That Concerning the Christians—the Answer	345
Chapter 37	M. Fabius Quintilianus—His Biography—His Institutiones Oratoriæ—His Views on Education—Division of His Subjects into Five Parts—Review of Greek and Roman Literature—Completeness of His Great Work—His Other Works—His Disposition—Grief for the Loss of His Son	355
Chapter 38	A. Cornelius Celsus—His Merits—Cicero Medicorum—Scribonius Largus Designatianus—Pomponius Mela—L. Junius Moderatus Columella—S. Julius Frontinus—Decline of Taste in the Silver Age—Foreign Influence on Roman Literature—Conclusion	361
Chronological Table		367
Index		373
Related Nova Publications		379

PREFACE*

The history of Roman Classical Literature, although it comprehends the names of many illustrious writers and many voluminous works, is, chronologically speaking, contained within narrow limits. Dating from its earliest infancy, until the epoch when it ceased to deserve the title of classical, its existence occupies a period of less than four centuries.

The imperial city had been founded for upwards of five hundred years without exhibiting more than those rudest germs of literary taste which are common to the most uncivilized nations, without producing a single author either in poetry or prose.

The Roman mind, naturally vigorous and active, was still uncultivated, when, about two centuries and a half before the Christian era,[1] conquest made the inhabitants of the capital acquainted, for the first time, with Greek science, art, and literature; and the last rays of classic taste and learning ceased to illumine the Roman world before the accession of the Antonines.[2]

Such a history, however, must be introduced by a reference to times of much higher antiquity. The language itself must be examined historically, that is, its progress and its formation from its primitive elements, must be traced with reference to the influences exercised upon it from without by the natives who spoke the dialects out of which it was composed; and the earliest indications of a taste for poetry, and a desire to cultivate the intellectual powers, must be marked and followed out in their successive stages of development. In this investigation, it will be seen how great the difficulties were with which literary men had to struggle under the Republic—difficulties principally arising from the physical activity of the people, and the practical character of the Roman mind, which led the majority to undervalue and despise devotion to sedentary and contemplative pursuits.

The Roman, in the olden times, had a high and self-denying sense of duty—he was ambitious, but his ambition was for the glory, not of himself, but his country; he thus lived for conquest: his motive, however, was not self-aggrandizement but the extension of the domination of Rome. When the state came to be merged in the individual, generals and statesmen sought to heap up wealth and to acquire power; but it was not so in the Republican times. Owing to these characteristic features, the Roman citizen conceived it to be his duty to devote his energies to the public service: he concentrated all his powers, mental and bodily,

---

* This is an edited, augmented and reformatted version of "A History of Roman Classical Literature" by R. W. Browne, originally published by London R. Bentley, dated 1884.
[1] B.C. 210; A. U. C. 514.
[2] A.D. 138; A. U. C. 891.

upon war and politics; he despised all other occupations and sources of fame; for he was conscious that his country owed her position amongst nations to her military prowess, and her liberties at home to the wise administration of her constitution.

Hence it will be seen, that there never was a period in which literature did not require to be fostered and protected by the patronage of the wealthy and powerful. Even tragedy never captivated the feelings or acquired an influence over the minds of the people at large as it did in Greece; it degenerated into mere recitations in a dramatic form, addressed like any other poetry to a *coterie*. Comedy formed the only exception to this rule. It was the only species of literature which the masses thoroughly enjoyed. Learning was a sickly plant: patronage was the artificial heat which brought it to maturity. Accius was patronized by D. Brutus; Ennius by Lucilius and the Scipios; Terence by Africanus and Lælius; Lucretius by the Memmii; Tibullus by Messala; Propertius by Ælius Gallus; Virgil and his friends by Augustus, Mæcenas, and Pollio; Martial and Quintilian by Domitian.

As the conquest of Magna Græcia, Sicily, and, finally, of Greece itself, first directed to the pursuit of intellectual cultivation a people whose national literature, even if it deserved to be so called, was of the rudest and most meager description, Roman literature was, as might be expected, the offspring of the Greek, and its beauties a reflection of the Greek mind; and although some portions were more original than others, as being more congenial to the national character—such, for example, as satire, oratory, and history—it was, upon the whole, never anything more than an imitation. It had, therefore, all the faults of an imitation. As in painting, those that study the old masters, and neglect nature, are nothing more than copyists, however high the finish and elaborate the polish of their works may be; so in the literature of Rome, we are delighted with the execution, and charmed with the genius, wit, and ingenuity, but we seek in vain for the enthusiasm and inspiration which breathes in every part of the original.

One faculty of the greatest importance to literary eminence was possessed by the Romans in the highest perfection, because it may be acquired as well as innate, and is always improved and polished by education: that faculty is taste—the ability, as Addison defines it, to discern the beauties of an author with pleasure, and his imperfections with dislike.

Of the three periods into which this history is divided, the first may be considered as *dramatic*. Eloquence, indeed, made rapid strides, and C. Gracchus may be considered as the father of Latin prose; but the language was not sufficiently smoothed and polished; the sentiments of the orator were far superior to the diction in which they were conveyed. Jurisprudence also was studied with thoughtfulness and accuracy; history, however, was nothing more than annals, and epic poetry rugged and monotonous. But the acting tragedy of the Romans is almost exclusively confined to this period; and the comedies of Plautus and Terence were then written, which have survived to command the admiration of modern times. Although, at this epoch, the language was elaborately polished and embellished with the utmost variety of graceful forms and expressions, it was simple and unconstrained: it flowed easily and naturally, and was therefore full and copious; brevity and epigrammatic terseness are acquired qualities, and the result of art, although that art may be skillfully concealed.

The second period consists of two subdivisions, of which the first was the era of *prose*, and, consequently, the period at which the language attained its greatest perfection; for the structure, power, and genius of a language must be judged of by its prose, and not by its poetry. Cicero is the representative of this era as an orator and philosopher—Cæsar and Sallust as historians. The second subdivision, or the Augustan age, is the era of poetry, for in it poetry arrived at the same eminence which prose had attained in the preceding generation. But the age of Cicero and that of Augustus can only be made subdivisions of one great period; they are not separated from each other by a strong line of demarkation; they are blended together, and gradually melt into one another. In the former, Lucretius and Catullus were the harbingers of Virgil, Horace, and Ovid; and, in the latter, the sun of Cicero, Cæsar, and Sallust, seems to set in the sweet narrative of Livy.

The last period is *rhetorical*: it has been called "the silver age." It produced Rome's only fabulist, Phædrus; the greatest satirist, Juvenal; the wittiest epigrammatist, Martial; the most philosophical historian, Tacitus; the most judicious critic, Quintilian; and a letter-writer, scarcely inferior to Cicero himself, the younger Pliny; and yet, notwithstanding these illustrious names, this is the period of the decline. These great names shed a lustre over their generation; but they did not influence their taste or arrest the approaching decay of the national genius: causes were at work which were rapidly producing this effect, and they were beyond their control. A new and false standard of taste was now set up, which was inconsistent with original genius and independent thought. Rome was persuaded, to accept a declamatory rhetoric as a substitute for that fervid eloquence in which she had delighted, and which was now deprived of its use, and was driven from the Forum to the lecture-room. This taste infected every species of composition. Seneca abused his fine talents to teach men to admire nothing so much as glitter, novelty, and affectation; and, at length, all became constrained, hollow, and artificial. With the national liberty, the national intellect lapsed into a state of inactivity: a period of intellectual darkness succeeded, the influence which the capital had lost was taken up by the provinces, and thus the way was paved for the inroad of barbarism.

Such is the outline of this work; and if the reader finds some features, which he considers of great importance, rapidly touched upon, the extent of the subject, and the wish to compress it within a moderate compass, must be offered as the author's apology. In conclusion, the author acknowledges his deep obligations to those historians and biographers whose works he has consulted during the composition of this history. He feels that it would have been presumptuous to offer such a work to the public without having profited by the laborious investigations of Wolf, Bayle, Hermann, Grotefend, Bernhardy, Bähr, Schlegel, Lachmann, Dunlop, Matthiæ, Schoell, Krause, Ritter, Nisard, Pierron, Niebuhr, Milman, Arnold, Merivale, Donaldson, Smith, and the authors of the "*Biographie Universelle.*"

Section I. First Era

Chapter 1

COMPARISON OF THE LATIN LANGUAGE WITH THE GREEK—ERAS OF LATINITY—ORIGIN OF THE ROMANS—ELEMENTS OF THE LATIN LANGUAGE—ETRUSCAN INFLUENCE

The various races which, from very remote antiquity, inhabited the peninsula of Italy, necessarily gave a composite character to the Latin language. But as all of them sprang from one common origin, the great Indo-European stock to which also the Hellenic family belonged, a relation of the most intimate kind is visible between the languages of ancient Greece and Rome. Not only are their alphabets and grammatical constructions identical, but the genius of the one is so similar to that of the other, that the Romans readily adopted the principles of Greek literary taste, and Latin, without losing its own characteristic features, moulded itself after the Greek model.

Latin, however, has not the plastic property which the Greek possesses—the natural faculty of transforming itself into every variety of shape conceived by the fancy and imagination. It is a harder material, it readily takes a polish, but the process by which it receives it is laborious and artificial. Greek, like a liquid or a soft substance, seems to crystallize as it were spontaneously into the most beautiful forms: Latin, whether poetry or prose, derives only from consummate art and skill that graceful beauty which is the natural property of the kindred language.

Latin, also, to continue the same metaphor, has other characteristic features of hard substances—gravity, solidity, and momentum or energy. It is a fit language for embodying and expressing the thoughts of an active and practical but not an imaginative and speculative people.

But the Latin language, notwithstanding its nervous energy and constitutional vigour, has, by no means, exhibited the permanency and vitality of the Greek. The Greek language, reckoning from the earliest works extant to the present day, boasts of an existence measured by nearly one-half the duration of the human race, and yet how gradual were the changes during the classical periods, and how small, when compared with those of other European languages, the sum and result of them all! Setting aside the differences due to race and physical organization, there are no abrupt chasms, no broad lines of demarkation, between one literary period and another. The transition is gentle, slow, and gradual. The successive steps can be traced and followed out. The literary style of one period melts and is absorbed into that of the following one, just like the successive tints and colours of the prism. The Greek of the Homeric poems is not so different from that of Herodotus and Thucydides, or the tragedians or the orators, or even the authors of the later debased ages, but that the same scholar who understands the one can analyze the rest. Though separated by so many ages, the contemporaries of Demosthenes could appreciate the beauties of Homer; and the Byzantines and early Christian fathers wrote and spoke the language of the ancient Greek philosophers.

The Greek language long outlived Greek nationality. The earliest Roman historians wrote in Greek because they had as yet no native language fitter to express their thoughts. The Romans, in the time of Cicero, made Greek the foundation of a liberal education, and frequented Athens as a University for the purpose of studying Greek literature and philosophy. The great orator, in his defence of the poet Archias, informs us that Greek literature was read by almost all nations of the world, whilst Latin was still confined within very narrow boundaries. At the commencement of the Christian era Greek was so prevalent throughout the civilized world, that it was the language chosen by the Evangelists for recording the doctrines of the gospel. In the time of Hadrian, Greek was the favourite language of literary men. The Princess Anna Comnena, daughter of the Emperor Alexis, and Eustathius, the commentator on Homer, both of whom nourished in the twelfth century after the birth of Christ, are celebrated for the singular purity of their style; and, lastly, Philelphus, who lived in the fifteenth century, and had visited Constantinople, states, in a letter dated A.D. 1451, that although much bad Greek was spoken in that capital, the court, and especially the ladies, retained the dignity and elegance which characterize the purest writers of the classical ages. "Græci quibus lingua depravata non sit, et quos ipsi tum sequimur tum imitamur ita loquuntur vulgo etiam hac tempestate ut Aristophanes comicus ut Euripides tragicus, ut oratores omnes ut historiographi ut philosophi etiam ipsi et Plato et Aristoteles. Viri aulici veterem sermonis dignitatem atque elegantiam retinebant."[3]

Such was the wonderful vitality of Greek in its ancient form; and yet, strange to say, notwithstanding it clung so to existence, it seems as though it was a plant of such delicate nature, that it could only flourish under a combination of favourable circumstances. It pined and withered when separated from the living Greek intellect. It lived only where Greeks themselves lived, in their fatherland or in their colonies. It refused to take root elsewhere. Whenever in any part of the world a Greek settlement decayed, and the population became extinct, even although Greek art and science, and literature and philosophy, had found there a temporary home, the language perished also.

The Greek language could not exist when the fostering care of native genius was withdrawn: it then shrunk back again into its original dimensions, and was confined within the boundaries of its original home. When the Greeks in any place passed away, their language did not influence or amalgamate with that of the people which succeeded them. Latin, on the other hand, was propagated like the dominion of Rome by conquest; it either took the place of the language of the conquered nation, or became engrafted upon it and gradually pervaded its composition. Hence its presence is discernible in all European languages. In Spain it became united with the Celtic and Iberian as early as the period of the Gracchi: it was planted in Gaul by the conquests of Julius Cæsar, and in Britain (so far as the

---

[3] See Forster's Essay on Greek Quantity, c. vi.

names of localities are concerned) by his transient expeditions; and lastly, in the reign of Trajan, it became permanently fixed in the distant regions of Dacia and Pannonia.

It is scarcely correct to term Greek a dead language. It has degenerated, but has never perished or disappeared. Its harmonious modulations are forgotten, and its delicate pronunciation is no longer heard, but Greek is still spoken at Athens. The language, of course, exhibits those features which constitute the principal difference between ancient and modern languages; prepositions and particles have supplanted affixes and inflexions, auxiliary verbs supply the gaps caused by the crumbling away of the old conjugations, and literal translations of modern modes of speech give an air of incongruity and barbarism; but still the language is upon the whole wonderfully preserved. A well-educated modern Greek would find less difficulty in understanding the writings of Xenophon than an Englishman would experience in reading Chaucer, or perhaps Spenser.

Greek has evinced not only vitality, but individuality likewise. Compared with other languages, its stream flowed pure through barbarous lands, and was but little tinged or polluted by the soil through which it passed. There is nothing of this in Latin, neither the vitality nor the power of resistance to change. Strange to say, although partially derived from the same source, its properties appear to be totally different. Latin seems to have a strong disposition to change; it readily became polished, and as readily barbarized; it had no difficulty in enriching itself with new expressions borrowed from the Greek, and conforming itself to Greek rules of taste and grammar. When it came in contact with the languages of other nations, the affinity which it had for them was so strong that it speedily amalgamated with them, but it did not so much influence them as itself receive an impress from them. It did not supersede, but it became absorbed in and was corrupted by, other tongues. Probably, as it was originally made up of many European elements, it recognised a relationship with all other languages, and therefore readily admitted of fusion together with them into a composite form. Its existence is confined within the limits of less than eight centuries. It assumed a form adapted for literary composition less than two centuries and a half before the Christian era, and it ceased to be a spoken language in the sixth century.

As long as the Roman empire existed in its integrity, and the capital city retained its influence as the patron to whom all literary men must look for support, and as the model of refinement and civilization, the language maintained its dominion. Provincial writers endeavoured to rid themselves of their provincialisms. At Rome they formed their taste and received their education. The rule of language was the usage of the capital; but when the empire was dismembered, and language was thus set free from its former restrictions, each section of it felt itself at liberty to have an independent language and literature of its own, the classical standard was neglected, Latin rapidly became barbarized. Again, Latin has interpenetrated or become the nucleus of every language of civilized Europe; it has shown great facilities of adaptation, but no individuality or power to supersede; but the relation which it bears to them is totally unlike that which ancient Greek bears to modern. The best Latin scholar would not understand Dante or Tasso, nor would a knowledge of Italian enable one to read Horace and Virgil.

The old Roman language, as it existed previous to coming in contact with Greek influences, has almost entirely perished. It will be shown hereafter that only a few records of it remain; and the language of these fragments is very different from that of the classical period. Nor did the old language grow into the new like the Greek of two successive ages by a process of development, but it was remoulded by external and foreign influences. So different was the old Roman from classical Latin, that although the investigations of modern scholars have enabled us to decipher the fragments which remain, and to point out the analogies which exist between old and new forms, some of them were with difficulty intelligible to the cleverest and best educated of the Augustan age. The treaty which Rome made with Carthage in the first year of the Republic was engraved on brazen tablets, and preserved in the archives of the Capitol. Polybius had learning enough to translate it into Greek, but he tells us that the language of it was too archaic for the Romans of his day.[4]

A wide gap separates this old Latin from the Latin of Ennius, whose style was formed by Greek taste; another not so wide is interposed between the age of Ennius and that of Plautus and Terence, both of whom wrote in the language of their adopted city, but confessedly copied Greek models; and, lastly, Cicero and the Augustan poets mark another age, to which from the preceding one, the only transition with which we are acquainted is the style of oratory of Caius Gracchus, which tradition informs us was free from ancient rudeness, although it had not acquired the smoothness and polish of Hortensius or Cicero.

In order to arrive at the origin of the Latin language it will be necessary to trace that of the Romans themselves. In the most distant ages to which tradition extends, the peninsula of Italy appears to have been inhabited by three stocks or tribes of the great Indo-Germanic family. One of these is commonly known by the name of Oscans; another consisted of two branches, the Sabellians, or Sabines, and the Umbrians; the third were called Sikeli, sometimes Vituli and Itali. What affinities there were between these and the other Indo-European tribes out of Italy, or by what route they came from the original cradle of the human race is wrapped in obscurity. Donaldson considers that all the so-called aboriginal inhabitants of Italy were of the same race as the Lithuanians or old Prussians. The Oscans evidently, from the name which tradition assigns to them, claimed to be the aboriginal inhabitants. The name Osci, or Opici, which is a longer form of it, is etymologically connected with Ops, the goddess Earth, and consequently their national appellation is equivalent to the Greek terms αυτοχθονες, or γηγενεις, the "children of the soil." That the Sabellians and Umbrians are branches of the same stock is proved by the similarity which has been discovered to exist between the languages spoken by them. The Umbrians also claimed great antiquity, for the Greeks are said to have given them their name from ομβρος, rain; implying that they were an antediluvian race, and had survived the storms of rain which deluged the world. Pliny likewise considers them the most ancient race in Italy.[5]

The original settlements of the Umbrians extended over the district bounded on one side by the Tiber, on the other by the Po. All the country to the south was in the possession of the Oscans, with the exception of Latium, which was inhabited by the Sikeli. But in process of time, the Oscans, pressed upon by the Sabellians, invaded the abodes of this peaceful and rural people, some of whom submitted and amalgamated with their conquerors, the rest were driven across the narrow sea into Sicily, and gave the name to that island.[6] These native tribes were not left in undisturbed possession of their rich inheritance. There arrived in the north of Italy that enterprising race, famed alike for their warlike spirit and their skill in the arts of peace, the Pelasgians (or dark Asiatics,) and became the civilizers of Italy. Historical research has failed to discover what settlements this wonderful race inhabited immediately previous to

---

[4] Pol. Hist. iii. 22; see Donaldson's Varron.
[5] Plin. N. H. iii. 14.
[6] See Thucyd. ii. 6.

their occupation of Etruria. According to Livy's account[7] they must have arrived in Italy by sea, for he asserts that their first settlements were south of the Apennines, that thence they spread northwards, and that the Rhæti were a portion of them, and spoke their language in a barbarous and corrupt form. His testimony ought to have some weight, because, as a native of the neighbourhood, he probably knew the Rhætian language. Their immigration must have taken place more than one thousand years before Christ,[8] and yet they were far advanced in the arts of civilization and refinement, and the science of politics and social life. They enriched their newly-acquired country with commerce, and filled it with strongly-fortified and populous cities; their dominion rapidly spread over the whole of Italy from sea to sea, from the Alps to Vesuvius and Salerno, and even penetrated into the islands of Elba and Corsica.[9] Herodotus[10] asserts that they migrated from Lydia; and this tradition was adopted by the Romans and by themselves.[11] Dionysius[12] rejects this theory on the grounds that there is no similarity between the Lydian and Etruscan language, religion, or institutions, and that Xanthus, a native Lydian historian, makes no mention of this migration. Doubtless the language is unique, nor can a connection be traced between it and any family; but their alphabet is Phœnician, their theology and polity oriental, their national dress and national symbol, the eagle, was Lydian, and a remarkable custom alluded to both by Herodotus[13] and Plautus[14] was Lydian likewise.

Entering the territory of the Umbrians, they drove them before them into the rugged and mountainous districts, and themselves occupied the rich and fertile plains. The head-quarters of the invaders was Etruria; the conquered Umbrians lived amongst them as a subject people, like the Peloponnesians under their Dorian conquerors, or the Saxons under the Norman nobility. This portion of the Pelasgians called themselves Rasena, the Greeks spoke of them as Tyrseni, a name evidently connected with the Greek τυρρις or τυρσις (Latin, Turris,) and which remarkably confirms the assertion of Herodotus, since the only Pelasgians who were famed for architecture or tower-building, were those who claimed a Lydian extraction, namely, the Argives and Etruscans.[15] This theory of the Pelasgian origin of the Etruscans is due to Lepsius,[16] and has been adopted by Donaldson;[17] and if it be correct, the language of Etruria was probably Pelasgian amalgamated with, and to a certain extent corrupted by, the native Umbrian.

Pelasgian supremacy on the left bank of the Tiber found no one to dispute it. Let us now turn our attention to the influence of these invaders in lower Italy. As they marched southwards, they vanquished the Oscans and occupied the plains of Latium. They did not, however, remain long at peace in the districts which they had conquered. The old inhabitants returned from the neighbouring highlands to which they had been driven, and subjugated the northern part of Latium.

---

[7] Lib. v. 33.
[8] Müller, Etrusk. iv. 7, 8.
[9] See authorities quoted by Dennis, Cities of Etruria, i. xxiv.
[10] Lib. i. 94.
[11] Tac. Ann. iv. 55.
[12] Lib. i. p. 22, 24.
[13] Lib. i. 93.
[14] Cistell. II. iii. 20.
[15] A Cyclopean or Pelasgian wall, built of polygonal stones, without mortar, exists so far north as Düsternbrook, near Kiel, in Schleswig-Holstein.
[16] Ueber die Tyr. Pel. in Etr. Leips. 1842.
[17] Varronianus, i. sec. 10.

The history of the occupation of Etruria, which has been already related, was here acted over again, with only the following alteration, that here the Oscan was the dominant tribe, and the subject people amongst whom they took up their abode were Pelasgians and Sikeli, by whom the rest of the low country of Latium were still occupied. The towns of the north formed a federal union, of which Alba was the capital, whilst of the southern or Pelasgian confederacy the chief city was Lavinium, or Latinium. The conquering Oscans were a nation of warriors and hunters, and consequently, as Niebuhr remarked, in the language of this district the terms belonging to war and hunting are Oscan, whilst those which relate to peace and the occupations of rural life are Pelasgian. As, therefore, the language of Etruria was Pelasgian, corrupted by Umbrian, so Pelasgian + Oscan is the formula which presents the language of Latium.

But the Roman or Latin language is still more composite in its nature, and consists of more than these two elements. This phenomenon is also to be accounted for by the origin of the Roman people. The septi-montium upon which old Rome was built was occupied by different Italian tribes. A Latin tribe belonging, if we may trust the mythical tradition, to the Alban confederacy, had their settlement upon the Mount Palatine, and a Sabine or Sabellian community occupied the neighbouring heights of the Quirinal and Capitoline. Mutual jealousy of race kept them for some time separate from each other; but at length the privilege of intermarriage was conceded, and the two communities became one people.

The Tyrrhene Pelasgians, however, separated only by a small river from this new state, rapidly rising to power and prosperity, were not likely to view its existence without distrust and jealousy. Accordingly, the early Roman historical traditions evidently point to a period during which Rome was subject to Etruscan rule. When the Etruscan dynasty passed away, its influence in many respects still remained. The religion and mythology of Etruria left an indelible stamp on the rites and ceremonies of the Roman people. The Etruscan deities were the natural gods of Rome before the influence of Greek poetry introduced the mythology of Homer and Hesiod into her Pantheon. The characters and attributes of these deities were totally different from those of Greece. No licentious orgies disgraced their worship; they were defiled by none of their vices[18] Saturn, Janus, Sylvanus, Faunus, and other Etruscan deities, were grave, venerable, pure, and delighted in the simple occupations of rural life. It was only general features of resemblance which enabled the poets in later ages to identify Saturn with Kronos, Sylvanus with Pan, the prophetic Camenæ of the Janiculum with the muses of Parnassus.[19] The point, however, most important for the present consideration is that their language was likewise permanently affected.

The ethnical affinities which have been here briefly stated, and which may be considered as satisfactorily established by the investigations of Niebuhr, Müller, Lepsius, Donaldson, and others, are a guide to the affinities of the Latin language, and point out the elements of which

---

[18] Heyne, Exc. Virg. Æn. iii.
[19] The religion of Rome furnishes many other traces of Etruscan influence:—ex. gr., the ceremonies of the augurs and haruspices were Etruscan, and the lituus, or augur's staff, may be seen on old Etruscan monuments. The Tuscan Fortune, Nortia, the etymology of whose name (ne-verto) coincides with that of the Greek Ἄτροπος (the unchangeable,) had the nails, the emblem of necessity, as her device; and hence the consul marked the commencement of the year by driving a nail. The Roman Hymen, the god of marriage, was Talassius; a fact which illustrates one of the incidents in the tradition which Livy (book i. c. ix.) adopts respecting the rape of the Sabine virgins.
The name Talassius was evidently derived from the Tuscan name Thalna, or Talana, by which was designated the Juno Pronuba of the Romans, and the Ἥρη τελεία of the Greeks.

it is composed. These elements, then, are Umbrian, Oscan, Etruscan, Sabine, and Pelasgian; but, as has been stated, the Etruscan language was a compound of Oscan and Pelasgian, and the Sabine was the link between the Umbrian and Oscan, therefore the elements of the Latin are reduced to three, namely, Umbrian, Oscan and Pelasgian. These may again be classified under two heads, the one which has, the other which has not, a resemblance to the Greek. All Latin words which resemble Greek are Pelasgian,[20] all which do not are Oscan and Umbrian. From the first of these classes must of course be excepted those words—such, for example, as Triclinium, &c.,—which are directly derived from the Greek, the origin of which dates partly from the time when Rome began to have intercourse with the Greek colonies of Magna Græcia, partly since Greek exercised an influence on Roman literature. It is clear from the testimony of Horace that the enriching of the language by the adoption of such foreign words was defended and encouraged by the literary men of the Augustan age:—

—— Si forte necesse est
Indiciis monstrare recentibus abdita rerum
Fingere cinctutis non exaudita Cethegis
Continget; dabiturque licentia sumta pudenter,
Et nova fictaque nuper habebunt verba fidem, si
Græco fonte cadant, parce detorta.
Hor. Ep. ad Pis. 48.

---

[20] Owing to the existence of the Pelasgian element in Latin, as well as in Greek, an affinity can be traced between these languages and the Sanscrit in no fewer than 339 Greek and 319 Latin words.

Chapter 2

The Eugubine Tables—Existence of Oscan in Italy—Bantine Table—Perugian Inscription—Etruscan Alphabet and Words—Chant of Fratres Arvales—Salian Hymn—Other Monuments of Old Latin—Latin and Greek Alphabets Compared

The Umbrian Language

In the neighbourhood of Ugubio,[21] at the foot of the Apennines (the ancient Iguvium,) were discovered, in A. D. 1444, seven tables, commonly called the Eugubine Tables. They were in good preservation, and contained prayers and rules for religious ceremonies. Some of them were engraved in the Etruscan or Umbrian characters, others in Latin letters. Lepsius[22] has determined, from philological considerations, that the date of them must be as early as from A. U. C. 400,[23] and that the letters were engraved about two centuries later. A comparison of the two shows, in the Umbrian character, the letter *s* standing in the place occupied by *r* in the Latin, and *k* in the place of *g*, because the Etruscan alphabet, with which the Umbrian is the same, did not contain the medial letters *B*, *G*, *D*. An analogous substitute is seen in the transition from the old to the more modern Latin. The names Furius and Caius, for example, were originally written Fusius and Gaius. *H* is also introduced between two vowels, as stahito for stato, in the same way that in Latin aheneus is derived from *aes*. It also appears that the termination of the masculine singular was *o*: thus, orto = ortus; whilst that of the plural was or; e. g., subator = subacti; screhitor = scripti. This mode of inflexion illustrates the form amaminor for amamini, which was itself a participle used for amamini estis, an idiom analogous to the Greek τετυμμενοι εισι.

---

[21] See Donaldson's Varron., c. iii.
[22] Leps. de Tab. Eug., p. 86.
[23] B. C. 354.

The following extract, with the translation by Donaldson,[24] together with a few words which present the greatest resemblance to the Latin, will suffice to give a general notion of the relation which the Umbrian bears to it:—

Teio subokau suboko, Dei Grabovi, okriper Fisiu, totaper Jiovina, erer nomne-per, erar, nomne-per; fos sei, paker sei, okre Fisei, Tote Jiovine, erer nomne, erar nomne: Tab. VI. (*Lepsius.*) Te invocavi invoco, Jupiter Grabovi, pro monte Fisio, pro urbe Iguvina, pro illius nomine, pro hujus nomine, bonus sis, propitius sis, monti Fisio, urbi Iguvinæ, illius nomine, hujus nomine.

Alfu	albus	white
Asa	ara	altar
Aveis	aves	birds
Buf	boves	oxen
Ferine	farina	meal
Nep	nec	nor
Nome	nomen	name
Parfa	parra	owl
Peica	picus	pie
Periklum	preculum	prayer (dim.)
Poplus	populus	people
Puni	panis	bread
Rehte	recte	rightly
Skrehto	scriptus	written
Suboko	sub-voco	invoke
Subra	supra	above
Taflle	tabula	table
Tuplu	duplus	double
Tripler	triplus	triple
Tota (analogous to)	totus	a city (a whole or collection)
Vas	fas	law
Vinu	vinum	wine
Uve	ovis	sheep
Vitlu	vitulus	calf.[25]

---

[24] Varronianus, c. iii.
[25] See Grotefend, Rud. Ling. Umbr. Hanov. 1835; and Lassen. Beitrage zur Eug. Tafeln. Rhein. Mus. 1833.

THE OSCAN LANGUAGE

The remains which have come down to us of this language belong, in fact, to a composite idiom made up of the Sabine and Oscan. Although its literature has entirely perished, inscriptions fortunately still survive; but as they must have been engraved long subsequently to the settlement of the Sabellians in Southern Italy, the language in which they are written must necessarily be compounded of those spoken both by the conquerors and the conquered. Although Livy[26] makes mention of an Oscan dramatic literature, for he tells us that the "Fabulæ Atellanæ" of the Oscans were introduced when a pestilence raged at Rome,[27] together with other theatrical entertainments, he only speaks of the Oscan language in one passage.[28] This, however, is an important one, because it proves that Oscan was the vernacular tongue of the Samnites at that period. He relates that Volumnius sent spies into the Samnite camp who understood Oscan: "Gnaros Oscæ linguæ exploratum quid agatur mittit."

It is clear that the reason why the Oscan language prevailed amongst this people is, that the dominant orders in Samnium were Sabines. But there is evidence of the existence of Oscan in Italy at a still later period. Niebuhr[29] asserts that in the Social War[30] the Marsi spoke Oscan, although in writing they used the Latin characters. Some denarii still exist struck by the confederate Italian Government established in that war at Corfinium, on which the word *Italia* is inscribed, whilst others bear the word Viteliu. The latter is the old Oscan orthography, the former the Latin. One class of these coins, therefore, was struck for the use of the Sabine, the other of the Marsian allies. It is said also that Oscan was spoken even after the establishment of the empire.

The principal monument of the Sabello-Oscan is a brass plate which was discovered A. D. 1793. As the word *Bansæ* occurs in the 23d line of the inscription, it has been supposed to refer to the town of Bantia, which was situated not far from the spot where the tablet was found, and it is therefore called the Bantine Table. In consequence of the perfect state of the central portion, much of this inscription has been interpreted with tolerable certainty and correctness. The affinity may be traced between most of the words and their corresponding Latin; and it is perfectly clear that the variations from the Latin follow certain definite rules, and that the grammatical inflexions were the same as in the oldest Latin. A copy of the Table may be found in the collection of Orellius, and also in Donaldson's "*Varronianus.*"[31] The following are a few specimens of words in which a resemblance to the Latin will be readily recognised, and also, in some instances, the relation of the Oscan to the other ancient languages of Italy:—

Licitud	Liceto
Multam	Mulctam,
Maimas	Maximas,
Carneis	Carnes

---

[26] Liv. vii. 11.
[27] A. U. C. 361; B. C. 393.
[28] Liv. x. 20.
[29] Lect. on Rom. Hist. l. xxxiii.
[30] A. U. C. 664; B. C. 90.
[31] Pp. 86–89.

Senateis	Senatus
Pis	quis
Hipid	habeat
Pruhipid	præhibeat
Pruhipust	præhibuent
Censtur	censor
Censazet	censapit
Censaum, &c.	censum, &c.
Comonei	Communis
Perum dolum mallom siom	Per dolum malum suum
Iok—Ionc	hoc—hunc
Pod	quod
Valæmon	Valetudinem
Fust	fuerit
Poizad	penset (Anglicè, poize.)
Fuid	fuit
Tarpinius	Tarquinius
Ampus	Ancus

To these other well-known words may be added, which all philologers allow to be originally Oscan, but which have been incorporated with the Latin—such as, for example, Brutus, Cascus, Catus, Fœdus, Idus, Porcus, Trabea; and names of deities, such as Fides, Terminus, Vertumnus, Fors, Flora, Lares, Mamers, Quirinus, &c.

THE ETRUSCAN LANGUAGE

The difficulty and obscurity in which the Etruscan language is involved are owing to the nature of the inscriptions and monuments which have been discovered. Those records, to which reference has already been made when speaking of the Umbrian and Sabello-Oscan, were of a ceremonial or legal character; they therefore contained connected phrases and sentences, varied modes of thought and expression. Monuments such as the Eugubine or Bantine Tables contribute not a little towards a vocabulary of the languages, and still more to a knowledge of their structure and analogies. This, however, is not the case with the Etruscan monuments of antiquity which have been hitherto discovered. They are, indeed, numerous, but they exhibit little variety. They are sepulchral records of a complimentary kind, or titles inscribed on statues and votive offerings. Hence the same brief phraseology continually recurs, and the principal portions of the inscriptions are occupied by proper names.

The most important, because the largest, Etruscan record which has been hitherto discovered, is one which was found near Perugia, A. D. 1822.[32] This inscription contains one

---

[32] Micali, Tav. cxx.

hundred and thirty-one words and abbreviations of words, and of these no fewer than thirty-eight are proper names. Of the rest, a vast number are either frequently repeated, or are etymologically connected. These have not proved sufficient to enable any philologist (although many have attempted it) to give a satisfactory and trustworthy explanation of its contents.

A comparison of the Perugian with the Eugubine inscription shows the existence of similarity between some of the words found in both of them; and this is exactly what we should *à priori* expect to result from the theory of the Etruscan being a compound of the Pelasgian and Umbrian. In the Perugian inscription, words which resemble the Umbrian forms are more numerous than those which seem to have an affinity for the Pelasgian. Indeed, the language in which it is written appears almost entirely to have lost the Pelasgian element. The same observation may be made with respect to the Cortonian inscription:[33]—

Arses verses Sethlanl tephral ape termnu pisest estu; i. e., Avertas ignem Vulcane victimarum carne post terminum piatus esto; Avertas ignem Vulcane in cinerem redigens qui apud terminum piatus esto.

Probably, therefore, both these belong to a period at which the old Umbrian of the conquered tribes had been exercising a long-continued influence in corrupting the pure Pelasgian of the conquerors.

One example of the Etruscan alphabet is extant. It was discovered in a tomb at Bomarzo, by Mr. Dennis,[34] inscribed round the foot of a cup, and probably had been a present for a child. The letters ran from left to right, and are as follows:—

ph ch th u t s r s p n m l i th h z v e c a [35]

It will be seen from this specimen that the Etruscan language was deficient in the letters B Γ Δ Ξ Ψ H O Ω.

The following is a catalogue of those Etruscan words which have been handed down to us, together with their Latin interpretation. The list is but a meager one, but valuable as containing some which have been admitted into the Latin, and as exhibiting many affinities to the Pelasgian:—

Æsar	Deus
Agalletor	Puer
Andar	Boreas
Anhelos	Aurora
Antar	Aquila
Aracos	Accipiter
Arimos	Simia
Arse Verse	Averte ignem

---
[33] Orellii Inscr. 1384.
[34] Cities of Etruria, i. p. 225.
[35] See Etrusc. Alphabet. Lanzi, Saggio di L. E. i. 208.

Ataison		Vitis
Burros		Poculum
Balteus		
Capra	}	The same as in the Latin.
Cassis		
Celer		
Capys		Falco
Damnus		Equus
Drouna		Principium
Falandum		Cœlum
Gapos		Currus
Hister		Ludio
Iduare		Dividere
Idulus		Ovis
Itus		Idus
Læna		Vestimentum
Lanista		Carnifex
Lar		Dominus
Lucumo		Princeps
Mantisa		Additamentum
Nanos		Vagabundus
Nepos		Luxuriosus
Rasena		Etrusci
Subulo		Tibicen
Slan		Filius
Sec		Filia
Ril avil		Vixit annos
Toga		Toga

The discoveries of General Galassi and Mr. Dennis at the Etruscan city of Cervetri have shown to what an extent the Pelasgian element prevailed in the old Etruscan. Cervetri was the old Cære or Agylla, which was founded by Pelasgians, maintained a religious connection with the Greeks as a kindred race,[36] and remained Pelasgian to a late period.[37] In the royal tomb discovered in this place the name of Tarquin—

---

[36] Herod. i. 167.
[37] Virg. Æn. viii. 597.

TAPXNAS

occurs no less than thirty-five times.[38] On a little cruet-shaped vase, like an ink-bottle, was found inscribed the syllables Bi, Ba, Bu, &c., as in a horn-book, and also an alphabet in the Pelasgian character.[39] These characters are almost identical with the Etruscan. Again, General Galassi found here a small black pot, with letters legibly scratched, and filled with red paint.[40] Lepsius pronounced them to be Pelasgian, divided them into words, and arranged them in the following lines, which are evidently hexametrical:—

> Mi ni kethu ma mi mathu maram lisiai thipurenai
> Ethe erai sic epana mi nethu nastav helephu.

Mr. Donaldson[41] has offered some suggestions, with a view to explaining this inscription, and has clearly shown many close affinities to the Greek; but there is another which he quotes, and which is pronounced by Müller[42] to be pure Pelasgian, which even in its Pelasgian form is almost Greek:—

> Mi kalairu fuius.
> ἐιμι Καλαιροῦ Fυιός.

It would be impossible in this work to attempt the analysis of all the known Etruscan words, and to point out their affinities to the Pelasgian, the Greek, or the Latin; but a few examples may be given, whilst the reader, who wishes to pursue the subject further, is referred to the investigations of the learned author of the "*Varronianus.*"

Aifil, age, is evidently from the same root as the Greek αἰων, the digamma, which is the characteristic of the Pelasgian, as it was of the derivative dialect, the Æolic, being inserted between the vowels. Aruns, an agriculturist, contains the root of ἀρόω, to plough. Capys, a falcon, that of capio, to catch. Cassis (originally capsis,) that of caput, the head. Lituus, a curved staff, that of obliquus. Toga, that of tego, the dress, which was originally as much the Etruscan costume as it subsequently became characteristic of the Roman. Lastly, it is well known that, whereas the Greeks denoted numbers by the letters of the alphabet, the Romans had a system of numeral signs. This was a great improvement. The Greek system of notation was clumsy, because in reality it only pointed out the order in which each number stands. The Roman notation, on the other hand, represented arithmetical quantity, and even the addition and subtraction of quantities; and this elegant contrivance the Romans owed to the Etruscans. Their numerals were as follows:—

---

[38] Dennis, ii. 44.
[39] Ibid. ii. 53.
[40] Ibid. ii. 53.
[41] Varron., p. 127.
[42] Etrusk. i. p. 451.

I. II. III. IIII. Λ. ΛI. ΛII. ΛIII. IX. X. . . ↑. ↑. . .
1. 2. 3.   4.   5. 6. 7.   8.   9. 10.   40. 50.

100. 500. 1000.

This system is identical with the Roman, for Λ inverted became V, and

↑ ⊕ ᗞ
,   ,

and

became respectively L, C, D, and CIƆ, for which M was substituted in later times.

From the few examples which have been here given, it is evident that the Pelasgian element of the Etruscan was most influential in the formation of the Latin language, as the Pelasgian art and science of that wonderful people contributed to the advancement and improvement of the Roman character.

THE OLD LATIN LANGUAGE

The above observations, and the materials out of which the old Latin was composed, have prepared the way for some illustrations of its structure and character. The monuments from which all our information is derived are few in number: the conflagration of Rome destroyed the majority; the common accidents of a long series of years completed the mischief. Almost the only records which remain are laws, ceremonials, epitaphs, and honorary inscriptions.

An example of the oldest Latin extant is contained in the sacred chant of the Fratres Arvales. The inscription which embodied this Litany was discovered A. D. 1778,[43] whilst digging out the foundations of the sacristy of St. Peter's at Rome. The monument belongs to the reign of Heliogabalus;[44] but although the date is so recent, the permanence of religious formulæ renders it probable that the inscription contains the exact words sung by this priesthood in the earliest times.

---

[43] Schoell. Hist. de Lit. Rom. i. p. 42; Orell. Insc. 2270.
[44] Circ. A. D. 218.

The Fratres Arvales were a college of priests, founded, according to the tradition, by Romulus himself. The symbolical ensign of their office was a chaplet of ears of corn (spicea corona,) and their function was to offer prayers in solemn dances and processions at the opening of spring for plenteous harvests. Their song was chanted in the temple with closed doors, accompanied by that peculiar dance which was termed the tripudium, from its containing three beats. To this rhythm the Saturnian measure of the hymn corresponds; and for this reason each verse was thrice repeated. The hymn contains sixteen letters: *s* is sometimes put for *r*, *ei* for *i*, and *p* for *f* or *ph*. The following is a transcription of it, as given by Orellius, to which an interpretation is subjoined:—

>Enos Lases juvate.
>Nos Lares juvate.
>Us O Lares help.
>Neve luaerve Marmer sins incurrere in pleoris.
>Neve luem Mars sinas incurrere plus.
>Nor the pestilence O Mars permit to invade more.
>Satur fufere Mars limen Salista berber.
>Satiatus furendo Mars lumen Solis sta fervere.
>Satiated with fury, O Mars, the light of the sun stop from burning.
>Semunis alternei advocapit conctos.
>Semihemones alterni ad vos capite cunctos.
>Us half-men in your turns to you take all.
>Enos Marmer juvato.
>Nos Mars juvato.
>Us Mars help.
>Triumpe, triumpe, triumpe, triumpe, triumpe.
>Triumph, &c.

Of the Salian hymn (Carmen Saliare,) another monument of ancient Latin, the following fragments, preserved by Varro,[45] are all that remain, with the exception of a few isolated words:—

>(1.) Cozeulodoizesa, omina vero ad patula coemisse
>Jam cusiones; duonus ceruses dunzianus vevet.[45]

This has been corrected, arranged in the Saturnian metre, and translated into Latin by Donaldson,[46] as follows:—

>Choroi-aulōdos eso, omina enim vero
>Ad patula' ose misse Jani cariones.
>Duonus Cerus esit dunque Janus vevet.
>Choroio-aulodus ero, omina enim vero ad patulas aures
>Miserunt Jani curiones. Bonus Cerus erit donec Janus vivet.

---

[45] De L. L. vii. 26, 27, or vi. 1–3.
[46] Varronianus, vi. 4.

I will be a flute-player in the chorus, for the priests of Janus have sent omens to open ears. Cerus (the Creator) will be propitious so long as Janus shall live.

> (2.) Divum empta cante, divum deo supplicante.
> i. e., Deorum impetu canite, deorum deo suppliciter canite.

Sing by the inspiration of the gods, sing as suppliants to the god of gods.

The *Leges Regiæ* are generally considered as furnishing the next examples, in point of antiquity, of the old Latin language; but there can be little doubt that, although they were assumed by the metrical traditions to belong to the period of the kings,[47] they belong to a later historical period than the laws of the Twelve Tables. Some fragments of laws, attributed to Numa and Servius Tullius, are preserved by Festus[48] in a restored and corrected form, and, therefore, it is to be feared that they have been modernized in accordance with the orthographical rules of a later age.

One of these laws is quoted by Livy[49] as put in force in the trial of the surviving Horatius for the murder of his sister when he returned, as the tradition relates, from his victory over the Curatii. Another is alluded to by Pliny,[50] which forbids the sacrificing all fish which have not scales; but they are given in modern Latin, and can only be restored to their old form by conjecture.

We may, therefore, proceed at once to a consideration of the Latin of the Twelve Tables, of which fragments have been preserved by Cicero, Aulus Gellius, Festus, Gaius, Ulpian, and others. These fragments are to be found collected together in Haubold's "*Institutionum Juris Romani privati lineamenta*" and Donaldson's "*Varronianus.*"[51] The laws of the Twelve Tables were engraven on tablets of brass, and publicly set up in the Comitium, and were first made public in B. C. 449.[52] Nor had the Romans any other digested code of laws until the time of Justinian.[53] The following are a few examples of the words and phrases contained in them:—

Ni	nec
Em	eum
Endo jacito	injicito
Ævitas	ætas
Fuat	sit
Sonticus	nocens
Hostis	Hospes
Diffensus esto	differatur
Se	sine
Venom-dint	venum det
Estod	esto

---

[47] See *ex. gr.* Liv. i. 26.
[48] S. V. V. Plorare, Occisum, Pellices, Parricidi, Quæstores, &c.
[49] Lib. i. 26.
[50] H. N. xxxii. 2.
[51] Ch. vi.
[52] Dionys. x. 57.
[53] Dionys. x. 57.

Escit	est
Legassit, &c.	legaverit.

The next example of the old Latin is contained in the Tiburtine inscription, which was discovered in the sixteenth century at Tivoli, the ancient Tibur. It came into the possession of the Barberini family; but it was afterwards lost, and has never been recovered. Niebuhr[54] considers (and his conjecture is probably correct) that this monument is a Senatus-consultum, belonging to the period of the second Samnite war.[55] The inscription is given at length in the collection of Gruter,[56] and also by Niebuhr[57] and Donaldson.[58] The Latin in which it is written may be considered almost classical, the variations from that of a later age being principally orthographical. For example:—

Tiburtes	is written Teiburtes
Castoris	is written Kastorus
Advertit	is written advortit
Dixistis	is written deixsistis
Publicæ	is written poplicæ
Utile	is written oitile
Inducimus	is written indoucimus
A or ab before v	is written af.

This document is followed very closely, in point of time, by the well-known inscription on the sarcophagus of L. Cornelius Scipio[59] Barbatus, and the epitaph on his son,[60] which are both written in the old Saturnian metre. Scipio Barbatus was the great-grandfather of the conqueror of Hannibal, and was consul in A. U. C. 456, the first year of the third Samnite war. His sarcophagus was found A. D. 1780 in a tomb near the Appian Way, whence it was removed to the Vatican. The epitaph is as follows:—

> Cornelius Lucius Scipio Barbatus Gnaivod
> Patre prognatus fortis vir sapiensque
> Quoius forma virtutei parisuma fuit
> Consol Censor Aidilis quei fuit apud vos
> Taurasia Cisauna Samnio cepit
> Subigit omne Loucana opsidesque abdoucit.

"Cornelius L. Scipio Barbatus, son of Cnæus, a brave and wise man, whose beauty was equal to his virtue. He was amongst you Consul, Censor, Ædile. He took Taurasia, Cisauna, and Samnium; he subjugated all Lucania, and led away hostages."

---

[54] Dionys. x. 57.
[55] A. U. C. 428–50, Arnold; 423–44, Niebuhr.
[56] Page 499.
[57] Rom. Hist.
[58] Varron. vi. 20.
[59] Orell. No. 550.
[60] Ibid. No. 552. Meyer's Anth. Nos. 1, 2; where see also No. 5.

His son was Consul A. U. C. 495.[61] The following inscription is on a slab which was found near the Porta Capona. The title is painted red (rubricatus:)—

>   L. Cornelio L. F. Scipio, Aidiles, Consol, Censor.
>   Honc oino ploirume cosentiunt R.
>   Duonoro optimo fuise viro
>   Luciom Scipionem. Filios Barbati
>   Consol Censor Aidiles hic fuet
>   Hic cepit Corsica Aleria que urbe
>   Dedet tempestatebus aide mereto.

"Romans for the most part agree, that this one man, Lucius Scipio, was the best of good men. He was the son of Barbatus, Consul, Censor, Ædile. He took Corsica and the city Aleria. He dedicated a temple to the Storms as a just return."

It is not a little remarkable that the style of this epitaph is more archaic than that of the preceding.

The consul of the year B. C. 260 was C. Duilius, who in that year gained his celebrated naval victory over the Carthaginians; the inscription, therefore, engraved on the pedestal of the Columna Rostrata, which was erected in commemoration of that event, may be considered as a contemporary monument of the language.[62] Some alterations were probably made in its orthography at a period subsequent to its erection, for it was rent asunder from top to bottom by lightning A. U. C. 580,[63] and is supposed not to have been repaired until the reign of Augustus, for the restoration of a temple built by Duilius was begun by that emperor and completed by Tiberius.[64] The principal peculiarities to be observed in this inscription are, that the ablatives singular end in *d*, as in the words Siceliad, obsidioned; *c* is put for *g*, as in *macistratos, leciones*; *e* for *i*, as in *navebos, ornavet*; *o* for *u*, as in *Duilios, aurom*; *classes, nummi*, &c., are spelt clases, numei, and *quinqueremos, triremos, quinresmos, triesmos*. This monument was discovered A. D. 1565, in a very imperfect state, but its numerous *lacunæ* were supplied by Grotefend.

About sixty years after the date of this epitaph,[65] the Senatus-consultum, respecting the Bacchanals, was passed.[66] This monument was discovered A. D. 1692, in the Calabrian village of Terra di Feriolo, and is now preserved in the Imperial Museum of Vienna.[67]

There is scarcely any difference between the Latinity of this inscription and that of the classical period except in the orthography and some of the grammatical inflexions. The expressions are in accordance with the usage of good authors, and the construction is not without elegance. Nor is this to be wondered at when it is remembered that, at the period when this decree was published, Rome already possessed a written literature. Ennius was now known as a poet and an historian, and many of the comedies of Plautus had been acted on the public stage.

---

[61] B. C. 259.
[62] Orellius, No. 549.
[63] Liv. xlii. 20.
[64] Tac. Ann. ii. 49.
[65] A. U. C. 568; B. C. 186.
[66] Livy, xxxix. 18.
[67] Schoell, i. 52.

Having thus enumerated the existing monuments of the old Roman language and its constituent elements, it remains to compare the Latin and Greek alphabets, for the purpose of exhibiting the variations which the Latin letters have severally undergone.

The letters then may be arranged according to the following classification:—

			Soft	P	C K or Q,	T.
		Mutes {	Medial	B	G	D.
Consonants	{		Aspirates	F (V)	H	
		Liquids		L, M, N, R.		
		Sibilants		S, X.		
Vowels				A, E, I, O, U.		

Owing to the relation which subsists between P, B, and F or V, as the soft medial and aspirated pronunciation of the same letters, P and B, as well as F and V, in Latin, are the representatives or equivalents of the Greek F sound (φ and F,) and V also sometimes stands in the place of β. For example (1,) the Latin *fama, fero, fugio, vir*, &c., correspond to the Greek φημή, φέρω, φεύγω (F)Ἄρης. (2.) *Nebula, caput, albus, ambo*, to νεφέλη, κεφαλή, ἀλφός, ἄμφω. Similarly, *duonus* and *duellum* become *bonus* and *bellum*; the transition being from *du* to a sound like the English *w*, thence to *v*, and lastly to *b*. The old Latin *c* was used as the representative of its corresponding medial G, as well as K; for example, magistratus, legiones, Carthaginienses were written on the Columna Rostrata, *leciones, macistratus, Cartacinienses*. The representative of the Greek κ was c; thus caput stands for κεφαλή: the sound *qu* also, as might be expected, from its answering to the Greek koppa (Q,) and the Hebrew koph (ק,) had undoubtedly in the old Latin the same sound as C or K, and, therefore, quatio becomes, in composition, cutio; and quojus, quoi, quolonia, become, in classical Latin, *cujus, cui, colonia*. This pronunciation has descended to the modern French language, although it has become lost in the Italian. A passage from the "*Aulularia*"[68] of Plautus illustrates this assertion, and Quintilian[69] also bears testimony to the existence of the same pronunciation in the time of Cicero.

The aspirate H is in Latin the representative of the Greek X, as, for example, *hiems, hortus*, and *humi* correspond to χείμων, χόρτος, χάμαι, whilst the third Greek aspirated mute Θ becomes a tenuis in the mouths of the early Latins, as in *Cartaginienses*, and the *h* sound was afterwards restored when Greek exercised an influence over the language as well as the literature of Rome.

The absence of the *th* sound in the old Latin is compensated for in a variety of ways; sometimes by an *f*, as fera, fores, for θήρ and θύρα.

The interchanges which take place between the T and D, and the liquids L, N, R, can be accounted for on the grammatical principle,[70] which is so constantly exemplified in the literal changes of the Semitic languages, that letters articulated by the same organ are frequently put one for the other. Now D, T, L, N are all palatals, and in the pronunciation of R also some use is made of the palate. Hence we find a commutation of *r* and *n* in δωρον, donum; *æreus*,

---

[68] Ver. 276.
[69] Lib. vi. 3, 47.
[70] See Bythner's Lyra Prophet.

æneus; of *t* and *l* in θώρηξ and *lorica*; *d* and *l* in olfacio and odere facio, Ulysses and Ὀδυσσεύς; *r* and *d* in *auris* and *audio*, *arfuise*, and *adfuisse*.

To the remaining liquid, *m*, little value seems to have been attached in Latin. In verse it was elided before a vowel; in verbs it was universally omitted from the first person of the present tense, although it was originally its characteristic, and was only retained in *sum* and *inquam*: it was also omitted in other words, as *omne* for *omnem*;[71] and Cato the Censor was in the habit of putting *dice* and *facie* for *dicam* (or *dicem*) and *faciam* (*faciem*.)

As the Roman *x* was nothing more than a double letter compounded of *g* or *c* and *s*, as *rego*, *regsi*, *rexi*; *dico*, *dicsi*, *dixi*, the only consonant now remaining for consideration is the sibilant *s*. The principal position which it occupies in Latin is as corresponding to the aspirate in Greek words derived from the same Pelasgic roots. Thus ὗς, ἕξ, ὕλη, &c., are represented by *sus*, *sex*, *silva*. This may possibly be accounted for by the fact that S is in reality a very powerful aspirate. It is only necessary to try the experiment, in order to prove that a strong expiration produces a hissing sound. Those words which in classical Greek are written without an aspirate, such as εἰ, ἄναξ, &c., which, nevertheless, have an *s* in Latin, as si, senex, &c., may possibly have been at one period pronounced with the stronger breathing. The most remarkable change, however, which has taken place with respect to this letter, in the transition from the old to the classical Latin, is the substitution of *r* for *s*. Thus *Fusius*, *Papisius*, *eso*, *arbos*, &c., become *Furius*, *Papirius*, *ero*, *arbor*, &c.

The following table exhibits the principal changes undergone by the vowels and diphthongs:—

In modern Latin.	In ancient Latin.
E was represented by i, sometimes u, as	luci, condumnari,
I was represented by u, ei, e, o	optume, nominus, preivatus, dedit, senatuos.
U was represented by oi, ou, o	quoius, ploirume, douco, honc.
Æ was represented by ai	Aidiles.
Œ was represented by oi	proilium.

The vowels were sometimes doubled, as leegi, luuci, haace.[72]

In the grammatical inflexions, the principal difference between the old and the new Latin is, that in nouns the old forms were longer, and assumed their modern form by a process of contraction, and that the ablative ended in *d*, as *Gnaivod*, *sententiad*; consequently the adverbial termination was the same as *suprad*, *bonod*, *malod*. The same termination appears in the form of *tod* in the singular number of the imperative mood.

---

[71] See epitaph on L. C. Scipio.
[72] See Bant. Table.

Chapter 3

Saturnian Metre—Opinions Respecting Its Origin—Early Examples of This Metre—Saturnian Ballads in Livy—Structure of the Verse—Instances of Rhythmical Poetry

The origin and progress of the Roman language have now been briefly traced, by the help of existing monuments, from the earliest dawn of its existence, when the fusion of its discordant elements was so incomplete as to be scarcely intelligible, to the period when even in the unadorned form of public records it began to assume a classical shape. But such an analysis will not be complete without some account of the verse in which the earliest national poetry was composed.

The oldest measure used by the Latin poets was the Saturnian. According to Hermann,[73] there is no doubt that it was derived from the Etruscans, and that long before the fountains of Greek literature were opened; the strains of the Italian bards flowed in this metre, until Ennius introduced the heroic hexameter. The grammarian Diomedes[74] attributed the invention of it to Nævius, and seems to imply that the Roman poet derived the idea from the Greeks, for his theory is, that he formed the verse by adding a syllable to the Iambic trimeter. Terentianus Maurus, as well as Atilius, professed to find verses of this kind in the tragedies of Euripides and the odes of Callimachus, and Servius and Censorinus attempted to analyze the Saturnian according to the strict rules of Greek prosody; but they were obliged to permit every conceivable license, and to make Roman rudeness an excuse for a violation of those rules which they themselves had arbitrarily imposed. The opinion of Bentley was, that it was a Greek metre introduced into Italy by Nævius.[75] The only argument in favour of the latter theory is the fact that the Saturnian is found amongst the verses of Archilochus; but many circumstances, which shall hereafter be pointed out, combine to make it far more probable that the use of it by the Greek poet is an accidental coincidence, than that the old Roman bards copied it from him.

Whatever be its history, there can be no doubt that, if it did not originate in Italy, its rhythm in very early times recommended itself to the Italian ear, and became the recognised

---

[73] Elem. Doc. Met. iii. 9.
[74] P. 212.
[75] Ep. Phal. xi.

vehicle of their national poetry. A rude resemblance of it is discernible in the Eugubine tables; it had obtained a more advanced degree of perfection in the Arvalian chants, and the *axamenta*[76] or Salian hymns. Examples of it are found in fragments of Roman laws, which Livy[77] refers to the reign of Tullus Hostilius, and Cicero[78] to that of Tarquinius Priscus. The epitaphs of the Scipios are in fact Saturnian næniæ. Ennius, whose era was sufficiently early for him to know that Nævius, instead of being the inventor of a new verse, or the introducer of a Greek one, followed the example of his predecessors, finds fault with the antiquated rudeness of his Saturnians.

> Scripsere alii rem
> Versibus quos olim Fauni Vatesque canebant
> Quom neque Musarum scopulos quisquam superarat,
> Nec dicti studiosus erat.
> Some in such verses wrote,
> As sung the Fauns and Bards in olden times,
> When none had scaled the Muses' rocky heights
> Or studied graceful diction.

Had the Saturnian been introduced from Greece, Ennius would not have denied to it the inspiration of the Muses, or have doubted that its birthplace was on the rocky peaks of Parnassus, nor would his ear, attuned to the varied melody of Greek poetry, have been unconscious of its simple and natural rhythm, and have entirely rejected it for the more ponderous and grandiloquent hexameter. The truth is, the taste which was formed by the study of Greek letters created a prejudice against the old national verse. As it was not Greek, it was pronounced rough and unmusical, and was exploded as old-fashioned. The well-known passage of Horace represents the prevailing feeling, although he says that the Saturnian remained long after the introduction of the hexameter, and that, even in his own day, when Virgil had brought the Latin hexameter to the highest degree of perfection, a few traces of that old long-lost poetry, which Cicero[79] wished for back again, might still be discovered:—

> Græcia capta ferum victorem cepit et artes
> Intulit agresti Latio. Sic horridus ille
> Defluxit numerus Saturnius, et grave virus
> Munditiæ pepulere: sed in longum tamen ævum
> Manserunt, hodieque manent vestigia ruris.
> *Ep.* II., ii. 156.

Some passages of Livy bear evident marks of having been originally portions of Saturnian ballads, although the historian has mutilated the metre by the process of translating them into more modern Latin. The prophetic warning of C. Marcius[80] has been thus restored by Hermann with but slight alteration of the words of Livy:

---

[76] The term *axamenta* is derived from the old Latin word *axo*, to name.
[77] Lib. i. 26.
[78] Pro Rab. 4, 13.
[79] Brutus, xix.
[80] Liv. xxv. 12.

> Amnén, Trojúgena, Cánnam fuge, ne te alienigenæ
> Cogánt in cámpo Díomedéi manús consérere;
> Sed nec credes tu mihi, donec complessis sangui
> Campum, miliaque multa occisa tua tetulerit
> Is amnis in portum magnum ex terra frugifera.
> Piscibus avibus ferisque quæ incolunt terras, eis
> Fuat esca carnis tua; ita Juppiter mihi fatus.

The oracle which tradition recorded as having been brought from Delphi respecting the waters of the Alban lake[81] was evidently embodied in a Saturnian poem, probably the composition of the same Marcius, or one of his contemporaries, such as Fabius Pictor, Cincius Alimentus, or Acilius. This lay has also been conjecturally restored by Hermann.

> Romane aquam Albanam lacu cave contineri,
> Cave in mare immanare suopte flumine siris;
> Missam manu per agros rigassis, dissipatam
> Rivis extinxis, tum tu insistito hostium audax
> Muris memor, quam per tot annos circum obsides
> Urbem, ex ea tibi his, quæ nunc panduntur fatis,
> Victoriam datam; bello perfecto donum
> Amplum ad mea victor templa portato; sacra patria
> Nec curata instaurato, utique adsolitum, facito.

In later times Livius Andronicus translated the whole Odyssey into Saturnians, and Nævius wrote in the same metre a poem consisting of seven books, the subject of which was the first Punic war. Detached fragments of both these have been preserved by Aulus Gellius, Priscian, Festus, and others, which have been collected together by Hermann.[82]

The structure of the Saturnian is very simple, and its rhythmical arrangement is found in the poetry of every age and country. Macaulay[83] quotes the following Saturnians from the poem of the Cid and from the Nibelungen-Lied—

> Estás nuevás a mío | Cíd erán venídas
> A mí lo dían; á ti | dán las órejádas.
> Man móhte míchel wúnder | vón Sifríde ságen
> Wa ích den kúnic vínde | dás sol mán mir ságen.

He adds, also, an example of a perfect Saturnian, the following line from the well known nursery song—

> The quéen was ín her párlour | eáting breád and hóney.

---

[81] Liv. v. 16.
[82] Elem. Doc. Metr. iii. 9.
[83] Lays of Rome, Preface, p. 19.

It was the metre naturally adapted to the national mode of dancing, in which each alternate step strongly marked the time,[84] and the rhythmical beat was repeated in a series of three bars, which gave to the dance the appellation of tripudium.

The Saturnian consists of two parts, each containing three feet, which fall upon the ear with the same effect as Greek trochees. The whole is preceded by a syllable in thesis technically called an anacrusis. For example—

> Sum|más o|pés qui | régum ‖ régi|ás re|frégit ‖

The metre in its original form was perfectly independent of the rules of Greek prosody; its only essential requisite was the beat or ictus on the alternate syllable or its representative. The only law to regulate the stress was that of the common popular pronunciation. In fact, stress occupied the place of quantity. Two or three syllables, which, according to the rules of prosody would be long by position, might be slurred over or pronounced rapidly in the time of one, as in the following line:—

> Amném Trojúgena Cánnam | fúge ne té alienígenæ.

Thus it is clear that the principles which regulated it were those of modern versification, without any of the niceties and delicacies of Greek quantity.

The anacrusis resembles the introductory note to a musical air, and does not interfere with the essential quality of the verse, namely, the three beats twice repeated, any more than it does in English poems, in which octosyllabic lines, having the stress on the even places, are intermingled with verses of seven syllables, as in the following passage of Milton's L'Allegro:—

> Come and trip it as you go
> On the light fantastic toe,
> And in thy right hand lead with thee
> The mountain nymph, sweet Liberty;
> And if I give thee honour due,
> Mirth, admit me of thy crew.

It is remarkable that in the degenerate periods of Latin literature, there was a return to the same old rhythmical principles which gave birth to the Saturnian verse: ictus was again substituted for quantity, and the Greek rules of prosody were neglected for a rhythm consisting of alternate beats, which pervades most modern poetry.

The empire had become so extensive, that the taste of the people, especially of the provincials, was no longer regulated by that of the capital, and emphasis and accent became, instead of metrical quantity, the general rule of pronunciation. This was the origin of rhythmical poetry. Traces of it may be found as early as the satirical verses of Suetonius on J. Cæsar.

It is the metre of the little jeu d'esprit addressed by the emperor Hadrian to Florus—[85]

---

[84] Alterno terram quatiunt pede.—*Hor. Od.*
[85] See Meyer, Anthol. Lat. 207, 212.

> Ego nolo Florus esse
> Ambulare per tabernas
> Latitare per popinas
> Culices pati rotundos;

and also of the historian's repartee—

> Ego nolo Cæsar esse
> Ambulare per Britannos
> Scythicas pati pruinas.

The simple grandeur of such strains as—

> Dies iræ, dies illa,
> Solvet sæclum in favilla, &c.

and other monkish hymns, go far to rescue the old Saturnian from the charge of ruggedness and rusticity ascribed to it by Horace and others, whose taste was formed by Greek poetry, and whose fastidious ears could not brook any harmony but that which had been consecrated to the outpourings of Greek genius.

From this species of verse, which probably prevailed among the natives of Provence (the Roman Provincia) the Troubadours derived the metre of their ballad poetry, and thence introduced it into the rest of Europe. But whatever phases the external form of ancient poetry underwent, the classical writers both of Greece and Rome eschewed rhyme. Even to a modern ear the beautiful effect of the ancient metres is entirely destroyed by it. It was a false taste and a less refined ear which could accept it as a compensation for the imperfections of prosody.

Although rhyme was introduced as an embellishment of verses framed on the principle of ictus, and not of quantity, at a very early period of Christian Latin literature, it is not quite certain when it came to be added as a new difficulty to the metres of classical antiquity. It is recorded by Gray[86] that when the children educated in the monastery of St. Gall addressed a Bishop of Constance on his first visitation with expostulatory orations, the younger ones recited the following doggerel rhymes:—

> Quid tibi fecimus tale ut nobis facias male
> Appellamus regem quia nostram fecimus legem.
> The elder and more advanced students spoke in rhyming hexameters:—
> Non nobis pia spes fuerat cum sis novus hospes
> Ut vetus in pejus transvertere tute velis jus.

---

[86] Gray's Works, ii. 30–54.

Chapter 4

Three Periods of Roman Classical Literature—Its Elements Rude—Roman Religion—Etruscan Influence—Early Historical Monuments—Fescennine Verses—Fabulæ Atellanæ—Introduction of Stage Players—Derivation of Satire

The era during which Roman classical literature commenced, arrived at perfection, and declined, may be conveniently divided into three periods. The first of these embraces its rise and progress, such traces as are discoverable of oral and traditional compositions, the rude elements of the drama, the introduction of Greek literature, and the cultivation of the national taste in accordance with this model, the infancy of eloquence, and the construction and perfection of comedy.

To this period the first five centuries of the republic may be considered as introductory; the groundwork and foundation were then being gradually laid on which the superstructure was built up; for, properly speaking, Rome had no literature until the conclusion of the first Punic war.[87]

Independently therefore of these 500 years, this period consists of 160 years extending from the time when Livius Andronicus flourished[88] to the first appearance of Cicero in public life.[89]

The second period ends with the death of Augustus.[90] It comprehends the age of which Cicero is the representative, as the most accomplished orator, philosopher, and prose writer of his times, as well as that of Augustus, which is commonly called the golden age of Latin poetry.

The third and last period of Roman classical literature terminates with the death of Hadrian.[91] Notwithstanding the numerous excellencies which will be seen to distinguish the literature of this period, its decline had evidently commenced. It missed the patronage of

---

[87] A. U. C. 513; B. C. 241.
[88] B. C. 240; A. U. C. 514.
[89] B. C. 81; A. U. C. 673.
[90] A. D. 14.
[91] A. D. 138.

Augustus and his refined court, and was chilled by the baneful influence of his tyrannical successors. As the age of Augustus has been distinguished by the epithet "golden," so the succeeding period has been, on account of its comparative inferiority, designated as "the silver age."

The Romans, like all other nations, had oral poetical compositions before they possessed any written literature. Cicero, in three places,[92] speaks of the banquet being enlivened by the songs of bards, in which the exploits of heroes were recited and celebrated. By these lays national pride and family vanity were gratified, and the anecdotes thus preserved by memory furnished the sources of early legendary history.

But these lays and legends must not be compared to those of Greece, which had probably taken an epic form long before they furnished the groundwork of the Iliad and the Odyssey. In Roman tradition there are no traces of elevated genius or poetical inspiration. The religious sentiment was the fertile source of Greek fancy, which gave a supernatural glory to the effusions of the bard, painted men as heroes, and heroes as deities; and, whilst it was the natural growth of the Greek intellect, twined itself round the affections of the whole people.

Roman religion was a ceremonial for the priests, not for the people; and its poetry was merely formulæ in verse, and soared no higher than the semi-barbarous ejaculations of the Salian priests or the Arvalian brotherhood. Fabulous legends doubtless formed the groundwork of history, and therefore probably constituted the festive entertainments to which Cicero alludes; but they were rude and simple, and the narratives founded upon them, which are embodied in the pages of Livy and others, are as much improved by the embellishments of the historian, as these in their turn have been expanded by the poetic talent of Macaulay.

It is scarcely possible to conceive that the uncouth literature which was contemporary with such rude relics as have come down to modern times should have displayed a higher degree of imaginative power. A few simple descriptive lines, one or two animating and heart-stirring sentiments, and no more, would be tolerated as an interruption to the grosser pleasures of the table amongst a rude and boisterous people. The Romans were men of actions, not of words; their intellect, though vigorous, was essentially of a practical character: it was such as to form warriors, statesmen, jurists, orators, but not poets; in the highest sense of the word, i. e. if by poetic talent is meant the creative faculty of the imagination. The Roman mind possessed the germs of those faculties which admit of cultivation and improvement, such as taste and genius, and the appreciation of the beautiful, and their endowments rendered them capable of attaining literary excellence; it did not possess the natural gifts of fancy and imagination, which were part and parcel of the Greek mind, and which made them in a state of infancy, almost of barbarism, a poetical people.

With the Romans literature was not of spontaneous growth: it was the result of external influence. It is impossible to fix the period at which they first became subject to this influence, but it is clear that in everything mental and spiritual their neighbours the Etruscans were their teachers. The influence exercised by this remarkable people was not only religious, but moral: its primary object was discipline, its secondary one refinement. If it cultivated the intellectual powers, it was with a view to disciplining the moral faculties. To this pure culture the old Roman character owed its vigour, its honesty, its incorruptible sternness, and those virtues which are summed up in the comprehensive and truly Roman word "gravitas." History proves that these qualities had a real existence—that they were not the mere ideal phantasies

---

[92] Brut. 19; Tusc. Dis. i. 2; iv. 2.

of those who loved to praise times gone by. The error into which those fell who mourned over the loss of the old Roman discipline, and lamented the degeneracy of their own times, was, that they attributed this degeneracy to the onward march of refinement and civilization, and not to the accidental circumstance that this march was accompanied by profligacy and effeminacy, and that the race which was the dispensers of these blessings was a corrupt and degenerate one. They could not separate the causes and the effects; they did not see that Rome was intellectually advanced by Greek literature, but that unfortunately it was degraded at the same time by Greek profligacy.

For centuries the Roman mind was imbued with Etruscan literature; and Livy[93] asserts that, just as Greek was in his own day, it continued to be the instrument of Roman education during five centuries after the foundation of the city.

The tendency of the Roman mind was essentially utilitarian. Even Cicero, with all his varied accomplishments, will recognise but one end and object of all study, namely, those sciences which will render a man useful to his country:—"Quid esse igitur censes discendum nobis?... Eas artes quæ efficiunt ut usui civitati simus; id enim esse præclarissimum sapientiæ munus maximumque virtutis vel documentum vel officium puto."[94] We must, therefore, expect to find the law of literary development modified in accordance with this ruling principle. From the very beginning, the final cause of Roman literature will be found to have been a view to utility, and not the satisfaction of an impulsive feeling.

In other nations poetry has been the first spontaneous production. With the Romans the first literary effort was history. But their early history consisted simply of annals and memorials—records of facts, not of ideas or sentiments. It was calculated to form a storehouse of valuable materials for future ages, but it had no impress of genius or thought; its merits were truth and accuracy; its very facts were often frivolous and unimportant, neither rendered interesting as narratives, nor illustrated by reflections. These original documents were elements of literature rather than deserving the name of literature itself—antiquarian rather than historical. The earliest records of this kind were the Libri Lintei—manuscripts written on rolls of linen cloth, to which Livy refers as containing the first treaty between Rome and Carthage, and the truce made with Ardea and Gabii.[95] To these may be added the Annales Maximi, or Commentarii Pontificum, of the minute accuracy of which, the following account is given by Servius.[96] "Every year the chief pontiff inscribed on a white tablet, at the head of which were the names of the consuls and other magistrates, a daily record of all memorable events both at home and abroad. These commentaries or registers were afterwards collected into eighty books, which were entitled by their authors Annales Maximi."

Similar notes of the year were kept regularly from the earliest periods by the civil magistrates, and are spoken of by Latin authors under the titles of Commentarii Consulares, Libri Prætorum, and Tabulæ Censoriæ. All these records, however, which were anterior to the capture of Rome by the Gauls, perished in the conflagration of the city.

Each patrician house, also, had its private family history, and the laudatory orations said to have been recited at the funerals of illustrious members, were carefully preserved, as adorning and illustrating their nobility; but this heraldic literature obscured instead of

---

[93] Lib. ix. 36.
[94] De Rep. i. 20.
[95] Lib. iv. 7, 13, 20.
[96] In Virg. Æn. i. 372. See also Cic. Or. ii. 12; and Quinct, Ins. Or. x. 2, 7.

throwing a light upon history: it was filled with false triumphs, imaginary consulships, and forged genealogies.[97]

The earliest attempt at poetry, or rather versification, for it was simply the outward form and not the inward spirit which the rude inhabitants of Latium attained, was satire in somewhat of a dramatic form. The Fescennine songs were metrical, for the accompaniments of music and dancing necessarily subjected their extemporaneous effusions to the restrictions of a rude measure. Like the first theatrical exhibitions of the Greeks, they had their origin, not in towns, but amongst the rural population. They were not, like Greek tragedy, performed in honour of a deity, nor did they form a portion of a religious ceremonial. Still, however, they were the accompaniment of it, the pastime of the village festival. Religion was the excuse for the holiday sport, and amusement its natural occupation. At first they were innocent and gay, their mirth overflowed in boisterous but good-humoured repartee; but liberty at length degenerated into license, and gave birth to malicious and libellous attacks on persons of irreproachable character.[98] As the licentiousness of Greek comedy provoked the interference of the legislature, so the laws of the Twelve Tables forbade the personalities of the Fescennine verses.

This infancy of song illustrates the character of the Romans in its rudest and coarsest form. They loved strife, both bodily and mental: with them the highest exercise of the intellect was in legal conflict and political debate; and, on the same principle, the pleasure which the spectators in the rural theatre derived from this species of attack and defence, approached somewhat nearly to the enthusiasm with which they would have witnessed an exhibition of gladiatorial skill. The rustic delighted in the strife of words as he would in the wrestling matches which also formed a portion of his day's sports, and thus early displayed that taste, which, in more polished ages, and in the hands of cultivated poets, was developed in the sharp cutting wit, the lively but piercing points of Roman satire.

The Fescennine verses show that the Romans possessed a natural aptitude for satire. The pleasure derived from this species of writing, as well as the moral influence exercised by it, depends not upon an æsthetic appreciation of the beautiful, but on a high sense of moral duty; and such a sense displays itself in a stern and indignant abhorrence of vice rather than a disposition to be attracted by the charms and loveliness of virtue. The Romans were a stern, not an æsthetic people, consequently satire is the most original of all Roman literature, and the perfect and polished form which it afterwards assumed was entirely their own. They did, indeed, afterwards acutely observe and readily seize upon those parts of Greek literature which were subservient to this end, and hence Lucilius, the founder of Roman satire, eagerly adopted the models and materials which Greek comedy placed at his disposal, and thus became, as Horace[99] writes, a disciple of Eupolis, Cratinus, and Aristophanes.

So permanent was the popularity of these entertainments that they even survived the introduction of Greek letters, and received a polish and refinement from the change which then took place in the spirit of the national poetry.[100] It has been said, that in these rude elements of the drama, Etruria was the first teacher of Latium, and that the epithet, Fescennine, perpetuates the name of an Etrurian village, Fescennia, from which the

---

[97] Cic. Brut. 16.
[98] Hor. Ep. II. i. 139, &c.
[99] Sermon. i. 4, 6.
[100] Virg. Georg. II. 385; Tibull. II. i. 55; Catull. 61, 27.

amusement derived its origin; but Niebuhr has shown that Fescennia was not an Etruscan village, and, therefore, that this etymology is untenable.

The most probable etymology of the word Fescennine is one given by Festus.[101] Fascinium was the Greek Phallus, the emblem of fertility; and as the origin of Greek comedy was derived from the rustic Phallic songs, so he considers that the same ceremonial may be, in some way, connected with the Fescennine verses. If this be the true account, the Etruscans furnished the spectacle—all that which addresses itself to the eye, whilst the habits of Italian rural life supplied the sarcastic humour and ready extemporaneous gibe, which are the essence of the true comic; and these combined elements having migrated from the country to the capital, and being enthusiastically adopted by young men of more refined taste and more liberal education, afterwards paved the way for the introduction and adaptation of Greek comedy.

If in these improvisatory dialogues may be discerned the germ of the Roman Comic Drama, the next advance in point of art must be attributed to the Oscans. Their quasi-dramatic entertainments were most popular amongst the Italian nations. They represented in broad caricature national peculiarities: the language of the dialogue was, of course, originally Oscan, the characters of the drama were Oscan likewise.[102] The principal one was called Macchus, whose part was that of the Clown in the modern pantomime. Another was termed Bucco, who was a kind of Pantaloon, or charlatan. Much of the wit consisted in practical jokes like that of the Italian Polichinello. These entertainments were sometimes called Ludi Osci, but they are more commonly known by the title of Fabulæ Atellanæ, from Aderla,[103] or, as the Romans pronounced it, Atella, a town in Campania, where they were very popular, or perhaps first performed. After their introduction at Rome they underwent great modifications and received important improvements. They lost their native rusticity; their satire was good natured; their jests were seemly, and kept in check by the laws of good taste, and were free from scurrility or obscenity.[104] They seem in later times to have been divided, like comedies, into five acts, with exodia,[105] i. e., farcical interludes in verse, interspersed between them. Nor were they acted by the common professional performers. The Atellan actors[106] formed a peculiar class; they were not considered infamous, nor were they excluded from the tribes, but enjoyed the privilege of immunity from military service. Even a private Roman citizen might take a part in them without disgrace or disfranchisement, although these were the social penalties imposed upon the regular histrio. The Fabulæ Atellanæ introduced thus early remained in favour for centuries. The dictator Sylla is said to have amused his leisure hours in writing them; and Suetonius bears testimony to their having been a popular amusement under the empire.

As early, however, as the close of the fourth century, the drama took a more artificial form. In the consulship of C. Sulpicius Peticus and C. Dicinius Stolo,[107] a pestilence devastated Rome. In order to deprecate the anger of the gods, a solemn lectisternium was proclaimed; couches of marble were prepared, with cushions and coverlets of tapestry, on which were placed the statues of the deities in a reclining posture. Before them were placed

---

[101] Sub voc.
[102] Bernhardy's Grundriss, 379; Diomedes, Gr. iii. 487; Val. Max. ii. 4; Festus v. person. fab.
[103] Now St. Arpino.
[104] Cic. Ep. ad Pap.
[105] Juv. Sat. iii. 172.
[106] V. Schlegel, lect. viii.
[107] B. C. 364; A. U. C. 390.

well-spread tables, as though they were able to partake of the feast. On this occasion a company of stage-players (histriones) were sent for from Etruria, as a means, according to Livy[108] of propitiating the favour of Heaven; but probably also for the wiser purpose of diverting the popular mind from the contemplation of their own suffering. These entertainments were a novelty to a people whose only recognised public sports, up to that time, with the exception of the rural drama already described, had been trials of bodily strength and skill. The exhibitions of the Etruscan histriones consisted of graceful national dances, accompanied with the music of the flute, but without either songs or dramatic action. They were, therefore, simply ballets, and not dramas.

Thus the Etruscans furnished the suggestion: the Romans improved upon it, and invested it with a dramatic character. They combined the old Fescennine songs with the newly introduced dances. The varied metres which the unrestrained nature of their rude verse permitted to the vocal parts, gave to this mixed entertainment the name of satura (a hodge-podge or pot-pourri,) from which in after times the word satire was derived. The actors in these quasi-dramas were professed histriones, and no further alteration took place until that introduced by Livius Andronicus.

---

[108] Livy, vii. 2.

Chapter 5

Emancipation of Livius Andronicus—His Imitation of the Odyssey—New Kind of Scenic Exhibitions—First Exhibition of His Dramas—Nævius A Political Partisan—His Bitterness—His Punic War—His Nationality—His Versification

Livius Andronicus (Flourished About B. C. 240.)

The events already related had by this time prepared the Roman people for the reception of a more regular drama, when, at the conclusion of the first Punic War, the influence of Greek intellect, which had already long been felt in Italy, extended to the capital. But not only did the Romans owe to Greece the principles of literary taste, and the original models from which the elements of that taste were derived, but their first and earliest poet was one of that nation. Livius Andronicus, although born in Italy, educated in the Latin tongue at Rome, and subsequently a naturalized Roman, is generally supposed to have been a native of the Greek colony of Tarentum. He was a man of cultivated mind, and well versed in the literature of his nation, especially in dramatic poetry. How he came to be at Rome in the condition of a slave, it is impossible to say. Attius stated that he was taken prisoner at Tarentum by Q. Fabius Maximus, when he recovered that city, in the tenth year of the second Punic War. But Cicero shows, on the authority of Atticus, that this date is thirty years later than the period at which he first exhibited at Rome, and Niebuhr[109] considers that the reason why he is called a Tarentine captive is, from being confounded with one M. Livius Macatus, mentioned by Livy.[110] He may perhaps have owed his change of fortune to being made a prisoner of 77war; at any rate, he became one of the household of M. Livius Salinator, and occupied the confidential position of instructor to his children. The employment as tutors of Greek slaves, who, being men of education and refinement, had fallen into this position by the fortune of war, was customary with the wealthy Romans. By this means there was rapidly introduced

---

[109] Lect. R. H. lxx.
[110] Lib. xxvii. 34: xxiv. 20.

amongst the rising generation of the higher classes a knowledge of that language and learning which the Romans so eagerly embraced and so enthusiastically admired.

Fidelity in so important a situation generally gained the esteem and affection of the patron. The generous Roman became a protector of the man of genius rather than his master, and conferred upon him the gift of freedom. Andronicus was emancipated under such circumstances as these, and according to custom received the name of his former master, Livius, and his civil and political rank became that of an ærarius. He wrote a translation, or perhaps an imitation of the Odyssey, in the old Saturnian metre, and also a few hymns. Niebuhr supposes that the reason why he has translated or epitomized the Odyssey in preference to the Iliad is, that it would have greater attractions for the Romans, in consequence of the relation which it bore to the ancient legends of Italy. The sea which washes the coast of Italy was the scene of many of the most marvellous adventures of Ulysses. Sicily, in which, owing to the wars with Hiero and the Carthaginians, the Romans now began to take a lively interest, was represented in the Odyssey as abounding in the elements of poetry. Circe's fairy abode was within sight of land—a promontory of Latium bore her name, and one of Ulysses' sons by her was, according to the legend of Hesiod, Latinus, the patriarch of the Latin name. His principal works, however, were tragedies. The passion of the Romans for shows and exhibitions, the love of action, and of stirring business-like occupation, which characterizes them, would make the drama popular, and it would harmonize with the public entertainments, in which they had been accustomed to take pleasure from the earliest times, when tradition informs us that the founder of their race instituted the solemn games to the equestrian Neptune, and 78invited all the neighbours to the spectacle;[111] and when Ancus celebrated with unwonted splendour the Great Games, and appointed separate seats and boxes for the knights and senators.[112] It was probable that Livius Andronicus, coming forward as the introducer of a new era in literature, would study the character as well as the language of his newly-adopted countrymen, and endeavour to please them as well as teach them. In order to become eventually a leader of the public taste, he would at first fall in with it to a certain degree. The process by which he moulded it after the model which he considered the true one, would be gentle and gradual, not sudden and abrupt. The paucity and brevity of the fragments which are extant furnish but little opportunity for forming an accurate estimate of his ability as a poet, and his competency to guide and form the taste of a people. Hermann[113] has collected together the fragments of the Latin Odyssey which are scattered through the works of Gellius, Priscian, Festus, Nonius, and others, and has compared them with the Homeric passages of which they are the translations. Few of these, however, are longer than a single line; and, therefore, the only opinion which can be formed respecting them is, that although the versification is rough and rhythmical rather than metrical, the language is vigorous and expressive, and conveys, as far as a translation can, the force and meaning of the original.

Nor do the criticisms of the ancient classical authors furnish much assistance in coming to a decision. Their tastes were so completely Greek, and the prejudices of their education so strong, that they could scarcely confess the existence of excellence in a poet so old as Andronicus. Cicero says in the Brutus,[114] that his Latin Odyssey was as old-fashioned and

---

[111] Liv. i. 9, 35.
[112] Ibid. i. 35.
[113] Elem. Doctr. Metr. iii. 9.
[114] 71.

rude as would have been the sculptures of Dædalus, and that his dramas would not bear a second perusal. Horace, however, is not quite so sweeping in his strictures. He confesses that he would not condemn the poems of Livius[115] to utter oblivion, although he remembers them in connexion with the floggings of his schoolmaster; but he is surprised that any one should consider them polished and beautiful, and not falling far short of critical exactness.

A passage in the history of Livy seems to imply that Andronicus ventured upon some deviations from the ancient plan of scenic exhibitions.[116] According to him, Livius was the first who substituted, for the rude extemporaneous effusions of the Fescennine verse, plays with a regular plot and fable. He adds, that in consequence of losing his voice from being frequently encored, he obtained permission to introduce a boy to sing the ode, or air, to the accompaniment of the flute, whilst he himself represented the action of the song by his gestures and dancing. He was thus enabled to depict the subject with greater vigour and freedom of pantomimic action, because he was unimpeded by the obligation to use his voice. Hence the custom began of the actor responding by his gesticulation to the song and music of another, whilst the dialogue between the odes was delivered without any musical accompaniment.

The passage of which the above is a paraphrase, is as follows:—"Livius post aliquot annos qui ab saturis ausus est primus argumento fabulam serere (idem scilicet, id quod omnes tum erant, suorum carminum actor) dicitur, quum sæpius revocatus vocem obtudisset, veniâ petitâ, puerum ad canendum ante tibicinem quum statuisset, canticum egisse aliquanto magis vigente motu, quia nihil vocis usus impediebat. Inde ad manum cantari histrionibus cæptum, diverbiaque tantum ipsorum voci relicta." It is evident that this description points out the introduction of the principles of Greek art. We are reminded of the hyporchemes in honour of Apollo, in which the gestures of certain members of the chorus represented the incidents related or sentiments expressed by the singer, and also the separation of the choral or musical part from the dialogue of a Greek tragedy. Nevertheless, the choral or lyrical portion of the drama to which alone this novel practice introduced by Livius applies, found but a small part in a Latin tragedy, if compared with those of the Greeks. In this alone the poet himself sustained a part, whilst the whole of the dialogue (diverbia) was recited by professional performers.

This new style of dramatic performances, however, does not appear at first to have taken such hold upon the affections of the people as to supersede their old amusements. They admitted them, and witnessed them with pleasure and applause, but they would not give up the old. The young men wished their amusements to be really games and sports; they were not content to be merely quiet spectators. Extemporaneous effusions were more convenient for amateurs than regular plays, and joke and jest than tragic earnest. The new custom introduced by Livius elevated the drama above the region of ribaldry and laughter, but the art and skill requisite confined the work to the professional performer. The young Romans, therefore, left to the stage-player the regular drama, restored their old amusement as an exodium or after-piece, and did not suffer it, as Livy says, to be "polluted" by the interference of *histriones*. According to the testimony of Cicero,[117] who makes his statement on the authority of Atticus, Livius first exhibited his dramas in the year before the birth of Ennius, in

---

[115] Ep. II. i. 69.
[116] Liv. vii. 2.
[117] Brut. 72.

the consulship of C. Clodius and M. Tuditanus, A. U. C. 514.[118] This date is also adopted by Aulus Gellius,[119] who places his first dramatic representations about a hundred and sixty years after the death of Sophocles, and fifty-two years after that of Menander. The titles of his tragedies which are extant show that they were translations or adaptations from the Greek. Amongst them are those of Egisthus, Hermione, Tereus, Ajax, and Helena. From each of the last two one line is preserved, and four lines are quoted by Terentianus Maurus from his tragedy of Ino;[120] but the language and metre render it far more probable that they were written by some more modern poet. Two of his tragedies, the Clytemnestra and the Trojan Horse, were acted in the second consulship of Pompey the Great, at the inauguration of the splendid stone theatre[121] which he built. No expense was spared in putting them upon the stage, for Cicero writes, in a letter to M. Marius,[122] that three thousand bucklers, the spoils of foreign nations, were exhibited in the latter, and a procession of six hundred mules, probably richly caparisoned, were introduced in the former, whilst cavalry and infantry, clad in various armour, mingled in mimic combat on the scene. He considers, however, that this splendour was an offence against good taste, and that the enjoyment was spoilt by the gorgeousness of the spectacle. The taste of his patrons, the Roman people, as well as the testimony of antiquity, render it highly probable that he was the author of comedies[123] as well as tragedies. Festus speaks of one, of which he quotes a single line, for the sake of its philological value.

CN. NÆVIUS

Nævius was the first poet who really deserves the name of Roman. His countrymen in all ages, as well as his contemporaries, looked upon him as one of themselves. The probability is, that he was not actually born at Rome, though even this has been maintained with some show of plausibility.[124] He was, at any rate, by birth entitled to the municipal franchise, and from his earliest boyhood was a resident in the capital. Nor was he a mere servile imitator, but applied Greek taste and cultivation to the development of Roman sentiments. A true Roman in heart and spirit in his fearless attachment to liberty; his stern opposition to all who dared invade the rights of his fellow-citizens; he was unsparing in his censure of immorality, and his admiration for heroic self-devotion. He was a soldier, and imbibed the free and martial enthusiasm which breathes in his poems when he fought the battles of his country in the first Punic War. His honest principles cemented, in his later years, a strong friendship between him and the upright and unbending Cato,[125]—a friendship which probably contributed to form the political and literary character of that stern old Roman.

---

[118] B. C. 240.
[119] Noct. Att. See also Quinct. I. O. x. 2, 7.
[120] See Bothe, Poetæ Scen. Roman. Trag.
[121] For the slight differences between a Greek and Roman theatre, the reader is referred to Smith's Dictionary of Antiquities, *sub voce*.
[122] Ep. ad Fam. vii. 1.
[123] Roman critics divide comedy into *Comœdia Palliata*, in which the characters, and therefore the costume, were Greek; and *Togata*, in which they were Roman. Comœdia Togata was again subdivided into Trabeata, or genteel comedy, and Tabernaria, or low comedy. The Fabulæ Prætextatæ were historical plays, like those of Shakspeare.
[124] Klussman, Frag. Næv.
[125] Cic. Cat. 14.

It is generally assumed that Nævius was a Campanian; but the only reason for this assumption is, that A. Gellius[126] criticises his epitaph, of which Nævius himself was the author, as full of Campanian pride.

The time of his birth is unknown, but it is probable that his public career commenced within a very few years after that of Livius. Gellius fixes the exhibition of his first drama in B. C. 235,[127] and Cicero places his death in the consulship of M. Cornelius Cethegus and P. Sempronius Tuditanus,[128] although he allows that Varro, who places it somewhat later, is the most pains-taking of Roman antiquarians. It is also certain that he died at an advanced age, for, according to Cicero, he was an old man when he wrote one of his poems. He was the author of an epic poem, the title of which was the Punic War; but, owing to the popularity of dramatic literature, his earliest literary productions were tragedies and comedies. The titles of most of these show that their subjects were Greek legends or stories. It was, therefore, in his epic poem that the acknowledged originality of his talents was mainly displayed. Nævius was a strong political partisan, a warm supporter of the people against the encroachments of the nobility. In consequence of the expenditure during the war, great part of the population was reduced to poverty, and a strong line of demarkation was drawn between the rich and the poor. The estrangement and want of sympathy between those two classes were daily increasing. The barrier of *caste* was indeed almost destroyed, but that of *class* was beginning to be erected in its stead. The passing of the Licinian bills[129] had led to the gradual rise of a plebeian nobility. The Ogulnian law[130] had admitted patrician and plebeian to a religious as well as political equality, and more than three-quarters of a century had passed away since Appius Claudius the blind[131] had given political existence to the freedmen by admitting them into the tribes, and had even raised some whose fathers had been freedmen to the rank of senators, to the exclusion of many distinguished plebeians who had filled curule offices. The object which he proposed to himself by this policy was undoubtedly the depression of the rising plebeian nobility, and this object was for a time attained; but the ultimate result was a vast increase in the numbers and the power of those who were opposed to the old patrician nobility, by the formation of a higher class, the only qualification for admission into which was wealth and intelligence. According to the old distinctions of rank it was necessary that even a plebeian should have a pedigree; his father and grandfather must have been born free. Appius, when chosen for the first time, waived this, and introduced a new principle of political party. Of this anti-aristocratic party Nævius was the literary representative, and the vehement opponent of privileges derived from the accident of birth. His position, too, was calculated to provoke a man of better temper. He was a Roman citizen, but, as a native of a municipal town, he did not possess the full franchise which he saw enjoyed by others around him who were intellectually inferior to himself, and the sense of his political inferiority was galling to him. Accordingly he used literature as a new and powerful instrument to foster the jealousy which existed between the orders of the state. He attacked the principle of an aristocracy of birth in the persons of some members of the most distinguished families. He held up Scipio Africanus to ridicule by making him the hero of a tale of scandal.

---

[126] Noct. Att. i. 24; xvii. 21.
[127] A. U. C. 519.
[128] A. U. C. 550; B. C. 204.
[129] B. C. 367.
[130] B. C. 300.
[131] B. C. 312.

> Etiam qui res magnas manu gessit sæpe gloriose,
> Cujus facta viva nunc vigent, qui apud gentes solas
> Præstat, eum suus pater cum pallio una ab amica abduxit.

The public services of the two Metelli could not shield them from the poet's bitterness, which attributed their consulships not to their own merits, but to the mere will of fate.[132] One bitter sentence, "Fato Metelli Romæ fiunt consules." made that powerful family his enemies. The Metellus, who at that time held the office of consul, threatened him with vengeance for his slander in the following verse:—"Dabunt malum Metelli Nævio poetæ." and the offending poet was indicted for a libel, in pursuance of a law of the Twelve Tables,[133] and thrown into prison. Whilst there he composed two pieces, in which he expressed contrition; and Plautus[134] describes him as watched by two jailers, pensively resting his head upon his hands:—

> Nam os columnatum poetæ esse inaudivi barbaro,
> Quoi bini custodes semper totis horis accubant.

Through the influence of the tribunes he was set at liberty.[135] As, however, is frequently the case, he could not resist indulging again in his satiric vein, and he was exiled to Utica, where he died,[136] having employed the last years of his life in writing his epic poem. The following laudatory epitaph was written by himself:—

> Mortales immortales flere si foret fas,
> Flerent Divæ Camenæ Nævium poetam.
> Itaque postquam est Orcino traditus thesauro
> Obliti sunt Romani loquier Latinâ linguâ.
> If gods might to a mortal pay the tribute of a tear,
> The Muses would shed one upon the poet Nævius' bier;
> For when he was transferred unto the regions of the tomb,
> The people soon forgot to speak the native tongue of Rome.

The best and most admired writers have paid their homage to his excellence. Ennius and Virgil discovered in him such a freshness and power that they unscrupulously copied and imitated him, and transferred his thoughts into their own poems as they did those of Homer. Horace writes that in his day the poems of Nævius were universally read, and were in the hands and hearts of everybody, and Cicero[137] praises him, although he had no taste for the old national literature.

We cannot be surprised at the universal popularity of Nævius. His stern love of liberty, his unsparing opposition to aristocratic exclusiveness, was identical with the old Roman republicanism. His taste for satire exactly fell in with the spirit of the earliest Roman literature, whilst he depicted with life and vigour and graphic skill the scenes of heroism in which the soldier-poet of the first Punic War was himself an actor. His tragedies were

---

[132] Cic. Verres, i. 10.
[133] See Arnold's Rome, l. 289.
[134] Miles Glorios. II., ii. 56.
[135] A. Gell. iii. 3.
[136] B. C. 204. See Cic. Brut. 15.
[137] Ep. ii. 153; Brutus, 19.

probably entirely taken from the Greek, but his comedies had undoubted pretensions to originality. The titles of many of them plainly show a Greek origin; but probably all more or less presented pictures of Roman life and manners, and therefore went home to the hearts of the people. This is essential to the complete effectiveness of comedy. Tragedy appeals to higher feelings: it depicts passions and principles of action which are recognised by the whole human race; it may, therefore, enlist the sympathies on the side of those whose habits and manners differ from our own, as it does in favour of those characters which are of a heroic and superhuman mould. Comedy professes to describe real life, and to paint men as they are; it therefore loses part of its power unless it deals with scenes which the experience of the audience can realize. Thus it is with painting. The high art of the Italian school, which selected for its subjects the holy scenes of religion, the heroism of history, and the creatures of classical poetry, was fostered by the taste of the rich and noble amongst a highly cultivated and imaginative people. The homely realities of the Flemish painters, with their accurate and lifelike delineations, were the delight of a rude prosaic nation, who could not appreciate a more elevated style or understand ideal beauties unless brought down to the level of everyday life.

The new form with which Nævius invested comedy gave him scope for holding up to public scorn the prevailing vices and follies of the day. He had also another vehicle for personality in his Ludi or Satiræ, as they were termed by Cicero. These were comic scenes, and not regular dramas, somewhat resembling the Atellan farces, without their extemporaneous character. But his great work was his poem on the first Punic War. We cannot judge of its merits by the few fragments which remain; but the testimony borne to it by Cicero, and the use which was made of it by Ennius and Virgil, prove that it fully deserved the title of an epic poem. The idea was original, the plot and characters Roman. The author, although Greek literature taught him how to be a poet, drew his inspiration from the scenes of his native Italy and the exploits of his countrymen. To this poem Virgil owed that beautiful allegorical representation of the undying enmity between Rome and Carthage, and the disastrous love of Æneas and Dido. Here was first painted in such touching colours the self-devoted patriotism of Regulus, whom (although love of historic truth refuses to believe the legend) the poet represents as sacrificing home and wife and children to a sense of honour, and as submitting to a torturing death for the sake of his country. Probably many other heart-stirring legends and tales of prowess which had cheered the nightly bivouac of the soldiers and inspirited them in the field, were embodied in this popular epic. Not that he disdained any more than Virgil the aid of Homer.[138] The second book of the Iliad suggested to him the enumeration of the opposing forces at the commencement of the struggle, and the description of the storm, from which Virgil, in his turn, copied in the Æneid,[139] owes much of its energy to the eighth book of the Odyssey. The expostulation of Venus with the father of gods and men,[140] respecting the perils of her son, and the promise of future prosperity to the descendants of Æneas, with which Jupiter consoles her, as well as the address of Æneas to his companions, are imitations of passages from this poem of Nævius; and Ennius copied so much from him and his predecessors as to have provoked the following rebuke from Cicero:[141]—"They have written well, if not with all thy elegance, and so oughtest thou to

---

[138] Pierron, Hist. de la R. 42.
[139] Lib. i. 198.
[140] Cic. Brut. 19; Macr. vi. 2.
[141] Brutus, 76.

think who have borrowed so much from Nævius, if you confess that you have done so, or, if you deny it, have stolen so much from him."

The fragments of Nævius extant are not more numerous than those of Livius, but some are rather longer. The two following may be quoted as examples of simplicity and power:—

> Amborum
> Uxores noctu Troiad exibant capitibus
> Opertis, flentes ambæ, abeuntes lacrymis multis.[142]

These few words tell their tale with as much pathos as that admired line in the Andrian of Terence—

> Rejecit se in eum flens quam familiariter.

The following lines describe the panic of the Carthaginians; nor could any Roman poet have sketched the picture in fewer strokes or with more suggestive power:—

> Sic Poinei contremiscunt artibus universim;
> Magnei metus tumultus pectora possidet
> Cæsum funera agitant, exequias ititant,
> Temulentiamque tollunt festam.[143]

Whoever can forgive roughness of expression for the sake of vigorous thought, would, if more had remained, have read with delight the inartificial although unpolished poetry of Nævius. Without that elaborate workmanship which was to the Roman the only substitute for the spontaneous grace and beauty of all that proceeded from the Greek mind, and was expressed in the Greek tongue, there is no doubt that Nævius displayed genius, originality, and dignity. The prejudices of Horace in favour of Greek taste were too strong for him to value what was old in poetry, or to sympathize with the admiration of that which the goddess of death had consecrated.[144] But Cicero, whilst he attributed to Livius only the mechanic skill and barbaric art of Dædalus, gave to Nævius the creative talent and plastic power of Myron.

Even when Roman critics were not unanimous in assigning him a niche amongst the greatest bards, the Roman people loved him as their national poet, and were grateful to him for his nationality. They paid him the highest compliment possible by retaining him as the educator of their youth. Orbilius flogged his sentiments into his pupil's memories; and, whilst the niceties of grammar were taught through the instrumentality of Greek by Greek instructors, and poetic taste was formed by a study of the Homeric poems, Nævius still had the formation of the character of the young Roman gentlemen, and his epic was in the hands and hearts of every one.

One more subject remains to be treated of with reference to the literary productions of Nævius, and that is, the metrical character of his poetry. He appreciated that important element of Greek poetic beauty. The varied versification by means of which it appeals at once to the ear, just as physical beauty charms long before we are attracted by the hidden power of

---

[142] Meyer's Anthol. Lat.
[143] Meyer's Anthol. Lat.
[144] II. Epist. i. 49.

moral excellence, and external form creates a prejudice in favour of that which is of more intrinsic value, but cannot so readily be perceived, so the melody of verse more readily pleases than the beauty of the imagery and sentiments which the verses convey. Nævius, therefore, did not disdain to recommend his original genius by a study of the principles of Greek versification, and by clothing his thoughts in those which his ear suggested as being most appropriate to the occasion. He does not seem to have overcome the difficulties of the heroic metre, although he studied the Homeric poems.

Probably as the Saturnian, the only natural Italian measure which he found existing, was a triple time, the Roman ear could not at once adapt itself to the common time of the dactylic measures. The versification of our own country furnishes an analogous example. The usual metres of English poetry consist of an alternation of long and short syllables; dactyles and anapæsts are of less frequent occurrence and are of more modern introduction, and the English ear is even yet not quite accustomed to the hexametrical rhythm. The dignity of the epic is expressed in the grave march of the iambus; the ballad tells its story in the same metre, though in shorter lines; the joyous Anacreontic adopts the dancing step of the trochee. For this reason, perhaps, Nævius, as a matter of taste, limited himself to the introduction of iambic and trochaic metres, and the irregular features of Greek lyric poetry to the exclusion of the heroic hexameter.

It was long before the Romans could arrive at perfection in this metre. Ennius was unsuccessful. His hexameters are rough and unmusical; he seems never to have perfectly understood the nature and beauty of the *cæsura* or pause. The failure of Cicero, notwithstanding his natural musical ear, is proverbial. No one previous to Virgil seems to have overcome the difficulty. Versification seems always to have been somewhat of a labour to the Romans. In the structure of their poetry they worked by rule; their finish was artistic, but it was artificial. Hence the Latin poet allowed himself less metrical liberty than the Greek, whom he made his model. He seemed to feel that the Greek metres, which the education of his taste had compelled him to adopt, were not precisely the form into which Latin words naturally fell; that this deficiency must be supplied by the care with which he moulded his verse, according to the strictest possible standard. One can imagine the extemporaneous effusions of a Homeric bard; but to Roman taste which, in every literary work, especially in poetry, looked for elaborate finish, the power of the improvisator, who could pour forth a hundred verses standing on one foot, was a ridiculous pretension.[145]

As a general rule, no Roman poet attained facility in versification; Ovid was perhaps the only exception. In the early period, when Roman poetry was extemporaneous, their national verse was only rhythmical, and now that modern Italy can boast of the faculty of improvisation, verse has become rhythmical again. But although Nævius introduced a variety of Greek metres to the Romans, the principal part of his poems, and especially his national epic, were written in the old Saturnian measure: its structure was indeed less rude, and its metre more regular and scientific, but still he did not permit the new rules of Greek poetry to banish entirely the favourite verses "in which in olden times Fauns and bards sung," and which would most acceptably convey to the national ear the achievements of Roman arms.

---

[145] Horace, 1 Serm. iv. 10.

Chapter 6

NÆVIUS STOOD BETWEEN TWO AGES—LIFE OF ENNIUS—EPITAPHS WRITTEN BY HIM—HIS TASTE, LEARNING, AND CHARACTER—HIS FITNESS FOR BEING A LITERARY REFORMER—HIS INFLUENCE ON THE LANGUAGE—HIS VERSIFICATION—THE ANNALS—DIFFICULTIES OF THE SUBJECT—TRAGEDIES AND COMEDIES—SATIRÆ—MINOR WORKS

ENNIUS (BORN B. C. 239.)

Nævius appears to have occupied a position between two successive ages; he was the last of the oldest school of writers, and prepared the way for a new one. Although a true Roman in sentiment, he admired Greek cultivation. He saw with regret the old literature of his country fading away, although he had himself introduced new principles of taste to his countrymen. He was not prepared for the shock of seeing the old school superseded by the new. But still the period for this had arrived, and in his epitaph, as we have seen, he deplored that Latin had died with him. A love for old Roman literature remained amongst the goatherds of the hills and the husbandmen of the valleys and plains, in whose memories lived the old songs which had been the delight of their infancy: it survived amongst the few who could discern merit in undisciplined genius; but the rising generation, who owed their taste to education, admired only those productions by which their taste had been formed. Greek literature had now an open field in which to flourish: it had driven out its predecessor, although as yet it had not struck its roots deeply into the Roman mind; a new school of poetry arose, and of that school Ennius was the founder. The principal events in the life of Ennius are as follows:—he was born at the little village of Rudiæ, in the wild and mountainous Calabria, B. C. 239.[146] Of ancient and honourable descent,[147] he is said[148] to have begun life in a military career, and to

---

[146] A. U. C. 515.
[147] Claudian, xxiii. 7.
[148] Silius It.

have risen to the rank of a centurion or captain. The anonymous author of the life of Cato, which is generally attributed to Cornelius Nepos, relates that Cato in his voyage from Africa to Rome[149] visited Sardinia, and finding Ennius in that island took him home with him. But no reason can be assigned why Ennius should have been there, or why Cato should have gone so far out of his way. If the Censor did really introduce the poet to public notice at Rome, he may have made his acquaintance during his quæstorship in Africa, if Ennius was with Scipio in that province; or during his prætorship[150] in Sardinia, if the poet was a resident in that island. There exist, however, no sufficient data to clear up these difficulties.

It seems, moreover, strange that Cato should have been his patron, and yet that he should have reproached M. Fulvius Nobilior for taking the poet with him as his companion throughout his Ætolian expedition.[151] With the exception of this campaign, Ennius resided during the remainder of his long life at Rome. Greek and Greek literature were now eagerly sought after by the higher classes, and Ennius earned a subsistence sufficient for his moderate wants by tuition. He enjoyed the friendship and esteem of the leading literary societies at Rome; and at his death, at the age of seventy, he was buried in the family tomb of the Scipios, at the request of the great conqueror of Hannibal, whose fame he contributed to hand down to posterity. His statue was honoured with a niche amongst the images of that illustrious race. The following epitaph was written by himself:—[152]

> Adspicite, O cives, senis Enni imagini' formam
> Hic vostrum panxit maxima facta patrum.
> Nemo me lacrymis decoret, nec funera fletu
> Faxit. cur? volito vivu' per ora virum.

The epitaph which he wrote in honour of Scipio Africanus has also been preserved:—[153]

> Hic est ille situs, cui nemo civi' neque hostis
> Quivit pro factis reddere operæ pretium.

It is probable that death alone put a period to his career as a poet, and that his last work was completed but a short time before his decease. So popular was he for centuries, and with such care were his poems preserved, that his whole works are said to have existed as late as the thirteenth century.[154]

Literature, as represented by Ennius, attained a higher social and political position than it had hitherto enjoyed. Livius Andronicus was, as we have seen, a freedman, and probably a prisoner of war. Nævius never arrived at the full civic franchise, nor became anything more than the native of a municipality, resident at Rome. Hitherto the Romans, although they had begun to admire learning, had not learned to respect its professors. Ennius was evidently a gentleman; he was the first to obtain for literature its due influence. Thus he achieved for himself the much-coveted privileges of a Roman citizen, to which Livius had never aspired, and which Nævius was never able to attain. Hence Cicero always speaks of him with

---

[149] B. C. 204.
[150] B. C. 198.
[151] B. C. 189.
[152] Meyer, Anthol. Vet. Rom. No. 19.
[153] Meyer, No. 16.
[154] Smith's Dict. of Biograph. s. v. Ennius.

affection as a fellow-countryman. "Our own Ennius" is the appellation which he uses when he quotes his poetry. Horace also calls him "Father Ennius," a term implying not only that he was the founder of Latin poetry, but also reverence and regard.

To discriminating taste and extensive learning he added that versatility of talent which is displayed in the great variety of his compositions. He was acquainted with all the best existing sources of poetic lore, the ancient legends of the Roman people, and the best works of the Greek writers; he had critical judgment to select beautiful and interesting portions, ingenuity to imitate them, and at the same time genius and fancy to clothe them with originality. It was not to be expected that he could be entirely freed from the antiquated style of the old school. The process of remodelling a national literature, including the very language in which it is expressed, and the metrical harmonies in which it falls upon the ear, is almost like reforming the modes of thought, and reconstructing the character of a people. Such a work must be gradual and gentle: a nation's mind will not bend at once to new principles of taste and new rules of art. To attempt a violent revolution would be absurd, and argue ignorance of human nature. The poet who attempted it would fail in gaining sympathy, which is an essential element of success. To cause such a revolution at all requires a strong will and a vigorous manly mind; and these are precisely the characteristic features of the Ennian poetry.

If we were to paint the character best adapted to act the part of a literary reformer to a nation such as the Romans were, it would be exactly that of Ennius. He was, like his friends Cato the Censor and Scipio Africanus the elder, a man of action as well as philosophical thought. He was not only a poet, but he was a brave and stout-hearted soldier. He had all the singleness of heart and unostentatious simplicity of manners which marked the old times of Roman virtue; he lived the life of the Cincinnati, the Curii, and Fabricii, which the poets of the luxurious Augustan age professed to admire, but did not imitate. Rome was now beginning to be wealthy, and wealth to be the badge of rank; yet the noble poet was respected by the rich and great, even in his lowly cottage on the Aventine, and found it no discredit to be employed as an instructor of youth, although it had been up to his time only the occupation of servants and freedmen. He was the founder of a new school, and was leading his admirers forward to a new career; but his imagination could revel in the recollections and traditions of the past. To him the glorious exploits of the patriarchs of his race furnished as rich a mine of fable as the heroic strains of Homer, the marvellous mythologies of Hesiod, and the tragic heroes of Argos, Mycenæ and Thebes. His early training in Greek philosophy and poetry, and in the midst of Greek habits in his native village, had not polished and refined away his natural freshness. He was a child of art, but a child of nature still. He had a firm belief in his mission as a poet, an abiding conviction of his inspiration. He thought he was not metaphorically, but really, what Horace calls him, a second Homer,[155] for that the soul of the great Greek bard now animated his mortal body. He had all the enthusiasm and boldness necessary for accomplishing a great task, together with a consciousness that his task was a great and honourable one.

Owing to this rare union of the best points of Roman character with Greek refinement and civilization, he rendered himself as well as his works acceptable to the most distinguished men of his day, and his intimacy and friendship influenced the minds of Porcius Cato, Lælius, Fulvius Nobilior, and the great Scipio.

---

[155] Ep. ii. 50.

A comparison of the extant specimens of the old Latin with the numerous fragments[156] of the poems of Ennius which have been preserved, will show how deeply they were indebted to him for the improvement of their language, not only in the harmony of its numbers and the convenience of its grammatical forms, but also in its copiousness and power.

It must not, however, be supposed that Ennius is to be praised, not only because he did so much, but because he refrained from doing more, as though he designedly left an antiquated rudeness, redolent of the old Roman spirit and simplicity. A language in the condition or phase of improvement to which he brought it is valuable in an antiquarian point of view; but it is not to be admired as if it were then in a higher state of perfection than it afterwards attained. Elaborate polish may, perhaps, overcome life and freshness, but no one who possesses any correctness of ear or appreciation of beauty can prefer the limping hexameters of Ennius to the musical lines of Virgil, or his later style to the refined eloquence of the Augustan age. As Quintilian says, we value Ennius, not for the beauty of his style, but for his picturesqueness, and for the holiness, as it were, which consecrates antiquity, just as we feel a reverential awe when we contemplate the huge gnarled fathers of the forest. "Ennium sicut sacros vetustate lucos adoremus in quibus grandia et antiqua robora, jam non tantam habent speciem, quantam religionem."

His predecessors had done little to remould the rude and undigested mass which, as has been shown, was made up of several elements, thrown together by the chance of war and conquest, and left to be amalgamated together by the natural genius of the people. Ennius naturally possessed great power over words, and wielded that power skilfully. In reconstructing the edifice he did the most important and most difficult part, although the result of his labours does not strike the eye as perfect and consummate. He laid the foundation strongly and safely. What he did was improved upon, but was never undone. The taste of succeeding ages erected on his basement an elegant and beautiful superstructure. To Ennius we owe the fact that after his time Latin literature was always advancing until it reached its perfection. It never went back, because the groundwork on which it was built was sound.

Ennius imitated most of the Greek metrical forms; but he wrote verses like a learner, and not like one imbued with the spirit of the metres which he imitated. He attended to the prosodiac rules of quantity, so far as his observation deduced them from the analogies of the two languages, instead of the old Roman principle of ictus or stress; but, provided the number of feet were correct, and the long and short syllables followed each other in proper order, his ear was satisfied: it was not as yet sufficiently in tune to appreciate those minuter accessaries which embellish later Latin versification. This is the principal cause of that ruggedness with which even the admirers of Ennius justly find fault. But notwithstanding these defects, there are amongst his verses some as musical and harmonious as those of the best poets in the Augustan age.

His great epic poem, entitled "*The Annals*," gained him the attachment as well as the admiration of his countrymen. This poem, written in hexameters, a metre now first introduced to the notice of the Romans, detailed in eighteen books the rise and progress of their national glory, from the earliest legendary periods down to his own times. The only portion of history which he omitted was the first Punic war; and the reason which he gives for the omission is that others have anticipated him[157]—alluding to his predecessors Livius and Nævius.

---

[156] Meyer, Anthol. 515–585.
[157] Cic. Brut. 76.

The subject which he proposed to himself was one of considerable difficulty. The title and scope of his work compelled him to adopt a strict chronological order instead of the principles of epic arrangement, and to invest the truths which the course of history forced upon his acceptance with the interest of fiction. His subject could have no unity, no hero upon whose fortunes the principal interest should be concentrated, and around whom the leading events should group themselves. But still no history could be better adapted to his purpose than that of his own country. Its early legends form a long series of poetical romances, fit to be sung in heroic numbers, although from being originally unconnected with each other, incapable of being woven into one epic story. Ennius had to unite in himself the characters of the historian and the poet—to teach what he believed to be truth, and yet to move the feelings and delight the fancy by the embellishments of fiction. The poetical merit in which he must necessarily have been deficient was the conduct of the plot; but the fragments of his poem are not sufficiently numerous for us to discover this deficiency. They are, however, amply sufficient to show that he possessed picturesque power both in sketching his narratives and in portraying his characters. His scenes are full of activity and animation; his characters seem to live and breathe; his sentiments are noble, and full of a healthful enthusiasm. His language is what that of an old Roman ought to be, such as we might have expected from Cato and Scipio had they been poets: dignified, chaste, severe, it rises as high as the most majestic eloquence, although it does not soar to the sublimity of poetry.

The parts in which he approaches most nearly to his great model, or, as he believed, the source of his inspiration, were in his descriptions of battles. Here the martial spirit of the Roman warrior shines forth; the old soldier seems to revel in the scenes of his youth. The poem which occupied his declining years shows that it was his greatest pleasure to record the triumphs of his countrymen, and to teach posterity how their ancestors had won so many glorious fields. His similes are simply imitations; they show that he had taste to appreciate the peculiar features of the Homeric Poem; but as must be the case with mere imitations, they have not the energy which characterizes his battles.

As a dramatic poet, Ennius does not deserve a high reputation. A tragic drama must be of native growth, it will not bear transplanting. The Romans did not possess the elements of tragedy; the genius of Ennius was not able to remedy that defect, and he could do no more than select, with the taste and judgment which he possessed, such Greek dramas as were likely to be interesting. Probably, however, his tragedies never became popular; they were admired by the narrow literary circle in which his private life was passed. Those who were familiar with the Greek originals were delighted to see their favourites transferred into their native language; those who were not, had their curiosity gratified, and welcomed even these reflections of the glorious minds of Æschylus, Sophocles, and Euripides.

But the tribute of admiration which the ancient classical authors paid to Ennius, was paid to him as an epic not as a dramatic poet. Cicero when he speaks in his praise generally quotes from the Annals, only once from a tragedy.[158] Virgil borrows lines and thoughts, together with the commencement and conclusion of the same poem; and, although the fame of Ennius survived the decline of Roman tragedy, and flourished even in the age of the Antonines,[159] and his verses were heard in the theatre of Puteoli (Pozzuoli,) the entertainment did not consist of one of his tragedies, but of recitations from his epic poem. Nevertheless his

---

[158] Andromache.
[159] A. Gellius.

tragedies were very numerous, and the titles and some fragments of twenty-three remain. They are all close imitations, or even translations, of the Greek. Of fifteen fragments of his Medea which are extant, there is not one which does not correspond with some passage in the Medea of Euripides: the little which we have of his Eumenides is a transcript from the tragedy of Æschylus;[160] and, according to A. Gellius, his Hecuba is a clever translation likewise.

His favourite model was Euripides: nor is it surprising that he should have been better able to appreciate the inferior excellencies of this dramatic poet, when we remember that the birth of Latin literature was coincident with the decay of that of Greece. Callimachus died just as Livius began to write.[161] Theocritus expired when Ennius was twenty-five years old;[162] and by this decaying living literature his taste must have been partially educated and formed.

In comedy, as in tragedy, he never emancipated himself from the trammels of the Greek originals. His comedies were *palliatæ*; and Terence when accused of plagiarism defends himself by an appeal to the example of Ennius. Fragments are preserved of four only.

The poems which he wrote in various metres, and on miscellaneous subjects, were, for that reason, entitled *Satiræ* or *Saturæ*. Ennius does not, indeed, anticipate the claim of Lucilius to be considered the father of Roman satire in its proper sense; but still there can be little doubt that the scope of these minor poems was the chastisement of vice. The degeneracy of Roman virtue, even in his days, provoked language of Archilochian bitterness from so stern a moralist, although he would not libellously attack those who were undeserving of censure. The salutation which he addresses to himself expresses the burning indignation which he felt against wickedness:—

> Enni poeta salve qui mortalibus
> *Versus* propinas flammeos medullitus.

Amongst his minor works were epitaphs on Scipio and on himself, a didactic poem, entitled Epicharmus, a collection of moral precepts, an encomium on his friend Scipio Africanus, a translation in hexameters of a poem on edible fishes and their localities, by Archestratus (Phagetica,) and a work entitled Asotus, the existence of which is only known from its being mentioned by Varro and Festus for the sake of etymological illustration; by some it is thought to have been a comedy. The idea that he was the author of a piece called "*Sabinæ*" is without foundation.

Cicero[163] mentions a mythological work (Evemerus,) a translation in trochaics of the Ἱερα Ἀναγραφη of the Sicilian writer who bore that name. It was a work well adapted to the talent which Ennius possessed of relating mythical traditions, in the form of poetical history. The theory embodied in the original was one which is often adopted by Livy in his early history, and therefore most probably entered into the ancient legends, namely, that the gods were originally mighty warriors and benefactors of mankind, who, as their reward, were deified and worshipped.

---

[160] Pierron, Rom. Lit. p. 74.
[161] B. C. 280.
[162] B. C. 214.
[163] De Nat. Deor. i. 42.

Chapter 7

THE NEW COMEDY OF THE GREEKS THE MODEL OF THE ROMAN—THE MORALITY OF ROMAN COMEDY—WANT OF VARIETY IN THE PLOTS OF ROMAN COMEDY—DRAMATIS PERSONÆ—COSTUME—CHARACTERS—MUSIC—LATIN PRONUNCIATION—METRICAL LICENSES—CRITICISM OF VOLCATIUS—LIFE OF PLAUTUS—CHARACTER OF HIS COMEDIES—ANALYSIS OF HIS PLOTS

It has already been shown that the dramatic taste of the Romans first displayed itself in the rudest species of comedy. The entertainment was extemporaneous, and performed by amateurs, and rhythmical only so far as to be consistent with these conditions. It was satirical, personal, full of burlesque extravagances, practical jokes, and licentious jesting. When it put on a more systematic form, by the introduction of music, and singing, and dancing, and professional actors, still the Roman youth would not give up their national amusement, and a marked distinction was made in the social and political condition of the actor and the amateur. Italian comedy made no further progress, but on it was engrafted the Greek comedy, and hence arose that phase of the drama, the representatives of which were Plautus, Cæcilius Statius, and Terence.

Now the old Attic comedy consisted of either political or literary criticism. In Italy, however, the Fescennine verses, and the farces of Atella, were not political, neither was there any literature to criticise or to parody. But the personalities in which the people had taken pleasure prepared them to enjoy the comedy of manners, embodying as it did pictures of social life. The new comedy, therefore, of the Greeks furnished a suitable model; and the comedies of Menander, Diphilus, Apollodorus, and others formed a rich mine of materials for adaptation or imitation.

From them the Roman poet could derive much more than the "vis comica," in which Cæsar complained that they were still so deficient. In the extant fragments of Menander may be found powerful delineations of human passions, especially of the pains and pleasures of love, melancholy but true views of the vanity of human hopes, elevated moral sentiments, and noble ideas of the divine nature. A vein of temperate and placid gentleness, intermingled with amiable pleasantry, pervaded the comedies of Philemon, and his sentiments are tender and serious, without being gloomy. These good qualities recommended them to Chrysostom, Eustathius, and other early Christians, by whom so many of their fragments have been preserved.

There is no doubt that the comic, as well as the tragic poet of Greece, considered himself as a public instructor; but it is difficult to say how far the Roman author recognised a moral object, because it cannot be determined what moral sentiments were designedly introduced, and what were merely transcriptions from the original. It is plain, however, that Roman comedy was calculated to produce a moral result, although the morality which it inculcated was extremely low: its standard was merely worldly prudence, its lessons utilitarian, its philosophy, like that of Menander himself, Epicurean, and therefore it did not inculcate an unbending sense of honour, the self-denying heroism of the Stoic school, or that rigid Roman virtue which was akin to it—it contented itself with encouraging the benevolent affections.

It did not profess to reform the knave, except by showing him that knavery was not always successful. It taught that cunning must be met with its own weapons, and that the qualities necessary for the conflict were wit and sharpness. The union between the moral and the comic element was exhibited in making intrigue successful wherever the victim was deserving of it, and in representing him as foiled by accidents and cross-purposes, because the prudence and caution of the knave are not always on a par with his cunning. It also had its sentimental side, and the sympathies of the audience were enlisted in favour of good temper, affection, and generosity.

But the new Attic comedy presented a truthful portraiture of real native life. This was scarcely ever the case with the Romans; the plots, characters, localities, and political institutions, were all Greek, and therefore it can only be said that the whole was in perfect harmony and consistency with Roman modes of thinking and acting. The comedies of Plautus probably, as will be seen hereafter, form the only exception.

It cannot be denied that there is a want of variety in the plots of Roman comedy;[164] but this defect is owing to the political and social condition of ancient Greece. Greece and the neighbouring countries were divided into numerous independent states; its narrow seas were, even more than they are now, infested with pirates, who had their nests and lurking-places in the various unfrequented coasts and islands; and slaves were an article of merchandise. Many a romantic incident therefore occurred, such as is found in comedy. A child would be stolen, sold as a slave, educated in all the accomplishments which would fit her to be a *Hetæra*, engage the affections of some young Athenian, and eventually, from some jewels or personal marks, be recognised by her parents, and restored to the rank of an Athenian citizen.

Again, in order to confine the privilege of citizenship, marriages with foreigners were invalid, and this restriction on marriage caused the *Hetæra* to occupy so prominent a part in comedy; besides, love was little more than sensual passion, and marriage generally a matter of convenience: the Hetæræ, too, were often clever and accomplished, whilst the virtuous matron was fitter for the duties of domestic life than for society. The regulations of the Greek theatre also, which were adopted by the Romans, caused some restrictions upon the variety of plots. In comedy the scene represented the public street, in which Greek females of good

---

[164] See Lecture vii. of A. W. V. Schlegel.

character did not usually appear unveiled: matrons, nurses, and women of light character alone are introduced upon the stage, and in all the plays of Terence, except the Eunuch, the heroine is never seen.

As the range of subjects is small, so there is a sameness in the dramatis personæ: the principal characters are a morose and parsimonious, or a gentle and easy father, who is sometimes, also, the henpecked husband of a rich wife, an affectionate or domineering wife, a young man who is frank and good-natured but profligate, a grasping or benevolent Hetæra, a roguish servant, a fawning favourite, a hectoring coward, an unscrupulous procuress, and a cold calculating slave-dealer.

The actors wore appropriate masks, sometimes partial, sometimes covering the whole face, the features of which were not only grotesque, but much exaggerated and magnified. This was rendered absolutely necessary by the immense size of the theatre, the stage of which sometimes measured sixty yards, and which would contain many thousands of spectators; the mouth, also, answered the purpose of a sounding board, or speaking-trumpet to assist in conveying the voice to every part of the vast building. The characters, too, were made known by a conventional costume: old men wore ample robes of white; young men were attired in gay parti-coloured clothes; rich men in purple; soldiers in scarlet; poor men and slaves in dark-coloured and scanty dresses.

The names assigned to the characters of the Roman comedy have always an appropriate meaning. Young men, for example, are Pamphilus, "dear to all;" Charinus, "gracious;" Phædria, "joyous:" old men are Simo, "flat-nosed," such a physiognomy being considered indicative of a cross-grained disposition: Chremes, from a word signifying troubled with phlegm. Slaves generally bear the name of their native country, as Syrus, Phrygia; Davus, a Dacian; Byrrhia, a native of Pyrrha in Caria; Dorias, a Dorian girl; a vain-glorious soldier is Thraso, from θρασος, boldness; a parasite, Gnatho, from γναθος, the jaw; a nurse, Sophrona (discreet;) a freedman, Sosia, as having been spared in war; a young girl is Glycerium, from γλυκυς, sweet; a judge is Crito; a courtesan, Chrysis, from χρυσος, gold. These examples will be sufficient to illustrate the practice adopted by the comic writers.

It is very difficult to understand the relation which music bore to the exhibition of Roman comedy. It is clear that there was always a musical accompaniment, and that the instruments used were flutes; the lyre was only used in tragedy, because in comedy there was no chorus or lyric portion. The flutes were at first small and simple; but in the time of Horace were much larger and more powerful, as well as constructed with more numerous stops and greater compass.[165]

Flutes were of two kinds. Those played with the right hand (tibiæ dextræ) were made of the upper part of the reed, and like the modern fife or octave flute emitted a high sound: they were therefore suitable to lively and cheerful melodies; and this kind of music, known by the name of the Lydian mode, was performed upon a pair of tibiæ dextræ. The left-handed flutes (tibiæ sinistræ) were pitched an octave lower: their tones were grave and fit for solemn music. The mode denominated Tyrian, or Sarrane,[166] was executed with a pair of tibiæ sinistræ. If the subject of the play was serio-comic, the music was in the Phrygian mode, and the flutes used

---

[165] Ep. ad Pison. 202.
[166] From Tzur, צור.

were *impares* (unequal,) *i. e.*, one for the right, the other for the left hand.[167] In tragedy the lyrical portion was sung to music and the dialogue declaimed. But if that were the case in comedy, it is difficult to imagine what corresponded to the lyrical portion, and therefore where music was used. Quintilian informs us that scenic modulation was a simple, easy chant,[168] resembling probably intonation in our cathedrals. Such a practice would aid the voice considerably; and if so, the theory of Colman is probably correct, that there was throughout some accompaniment, but that the music arranged for the soliloquies (in which Terence especially abounds) was more laboured and complicated than that of the dialogue.[169]

In order to understand the principles which regulated the Roman comic metres, some remarks must be made on the manner in which the language itself was affected by the common conversational pronunciation. In most languages there is a natural tendency to abbreviation and contraction. As the object of language is the expression of thought, few are inclined to take more trouble or to expend more time than is absolutely necessary for conveying their meaning: this attention to practical utility and convenience is the reason for all elliptical forms in grammatical constructions, and also for all abbreviated methods of pronunciation by slurring or clipping, or, to use the language of grammarians, by apocope, syncope, synæresis, or crasis.

The experience of every one proves how different is the impression which the sound of a foreign language makes upon the ear, when spoken by another, from what it makes upon the eye when read even by one who is perfectly acquainted with the theory of pronunciation. Until the ear is habituated, it is easier for an Englishman to speak French than to understand it when spoken. If we consider attentively the manner in which we speak our own language, it is astonishing how many letters and even syllables are slurred over and omitted: the accented syllable is strongly and firmly enunciated, the rest, especially in long words, are left to take care of themselves, and the experience of the hearer and his acquaintance with the language find no difficulty in supplying the deficiency. This is universally the case, except in careful and deliberate reading, and in measured and stately declamation.

With regard to the classical languages, the foregoing observations hold good; in a slighter degree, indeed, with respect to the Greek, for the delicacy of their ear, their attention to accent and quantity, not only in poetry but in oratory, and even in conversation, caused them to give greater effect to every syllable, and especially to the vowel sounds. But even in Greek poetry elision sometimes prevents the disagreeable effect of a hiatus, and in the transition from the one dialect to the other, the numerous vowels of the Ionic assume the contracted form of the Attic.

The resemblance between the practice of the Romans and that of modern nations is very remarkable; with them the mark of good taste was ease—the absence of effort, pedantry, and affectation. As they principally admired facility in versification, so they sought it in pronunciation likewise. To speak with mouthing (hiulce,) with a broad accent (late, vaste,) was to speak like a clown and not like a gentleman (rustice et inurbaniter.) Cicero[170] admired the soft, gentle, equable tones of the female voice, and considered the pronunciation of the

---

[167] Colman illustrates the preface to his translation of Terence with an engraving from a bas-relief in the Farnese Palace, in which these flutes are introduced. The original represents a scene in the Andria, and contains Simo, Davus, Chremes, and Dromo, with a knotted cord.

[168] I. O. ii. 10.

[169] Donatus says, "Diverbia (*the dialogues*) histriones pronuntiabant; cantica (*the soliloquies*) vero temperabantur modis non a poetâ sed a perito artis musicæ factis."

[170] Cic. de Orat. iii. 45.

eloquent and cultivated Lælia as the model of purity and perfection: he thought that she spoke as Plautus or Nævius might have spoken. Again, he speaks of the habit which Cotta had of omitting the iota; pronouncing, for example, dominus, dom'nus, as a prevalent fashion; and although he says,[171] that such an *obscuration* argues negligence, he, on the other hand, applies to the opposite fault a term (putidius) which implies the most offensive affectation. From these observations, we must expect to find that Latin as it was pronounced was very different from Latin as it is written; that this difference consisted in abbreviation either by the omission of sounds altogether, or by contraction of two sounds into one; and that these processes would take place especially in those syllables which in poetry are not marked by the ictus or beat, or in common conversation by the stress or emphasis. Even in the more artificial poetry and oratory of the Augustan age, in which quantity was more rigidly observed by the Roman imitators than by the Greek originals, we find traces of this tendency; and Virgil does not hesitate to use in his stately heroics such forms as aspris, for asperis, semustum for semiustum, oraclum for oraculum, maniplus for manipulus; and, like Terence, to make rejicere (rēīcĕrĕ) a dactyle.[172] A number of the most common words, sanctioned by general usage, and incorporated into the language when in its most perfect state, were contractions—such as amassent for amavissent, concio for conventio, cogo from con and ago, surgo from sub and rego, malla for maxilla, pomeridianus from post-mediam-diem, and other instances too numerous to mention.

But in the earlier periods, when literature was addressed still more to the ear than to the eye, when the Greek metres were as yet unknown, and even when, after their introduction, exact observation of Greek rules was not yet necessary, we find, as might be expected, these principles of the language carried still further. They pervade the poems of Livius and Ennius, and the Roman tragedies, even although their style is necessarily more declamatory than that of the comic writers; but in the latter we have a complete representation of Latin as it was commonly pronounced and spoken, and but little trammelled or confined by a rigid adhesion to the Greek metrical laws. In the prologues, indeed, which are of the nature of declamation, and not of free and natural conversation, more care is visible; the iambic trimeters in which they are written fall upon the ear with a cadence similar to those of the Greek, with scarcely any license except an occasional spondee in the even places. But in the scenes little more seems to have been attended to, than that the verse should have the required number of feet, and the syllables pronounced the right quantity, in accordance with the widest license which the rules of Greek prosody allowed. What syllables should be slurred, was left to be decided by the common custom of pronunciation.

Besides the licenses commonly met with in the poets of the Augustan age, the following mutilations are the most usual in the poetical language of the age of which we are treating:—

1. The final *s* might be elided even before a consonant, and hence the preceding vowel was made short: thus mălīs became mali, on the same principle that in Augustan poetry aūdīsnĕ was contracted into audīn'. Thus the short vowel would suffer elision before another, and the following line of Terence would consequently be thus scanned:—

Ut mă | līs gaū | dēat ălĭ | ēn' ātq'. | ēx ĭn | cōmmŏ | dīs.

---

[171] Ibid. 41.
[172] Phorm. Prol. 18; Ecl. iii. 96.

2. Vowels and even consonants were slurred over; hence Liberius became Lib'rius; Adolescens, Ad'lescens; Vehemens, Vemens; Voluptas, V'luptas (like the French voila, v'la;) meum, eum, suum, siet, fuit, Deos, ego, ille, tace, became monosyllables; and facio, sequere, &c., dissyllables.

3. *M* and *D* were syncopated in the middle of words: thus enimvero became en'vero; quidem and modo qu'en and mo'o, circumventus, circ'ventus.

4. Conversely *d* was added to me, te, and se, when followed by a vowel, as Reliquit med homo, &c., and in Plautus, med erga.

Observations of such principles as these enable us to reduce all the metres of Terence, and nearly all of Plautus, to iambic and trochaic, especially to iambic senarii and trochaic tetrameters. Many of those which defy the attempt have become, by the injudicious treatment of transcribers or commentators, wrongly arranged: for example, one of four lines in the Andria of Terence, which has always proved a difficulty, might be thus arranged:—

Innā | tă cuī | quām tānt' | ūt siēt | vēcōr | dĭa;

instead of the usual unmanageable form—

Tanta vecordia innata cuiquam ut siet.
Andr. iv. 1.

Volcatius Sedigitus, a critic and grammarian, assigns an order of merit to the authors of Roman comedy in the following passage:—

Multos incertos certare hanc rem vidimus
Palmam poetæ comico cui deferant.
Eum, me judice, errorem dissolvam tibi;
Ut contra si quis sentiat, nihil sentiat.
Cæcilio palmam Statio do comico.
Plautus secundus facile exsuperat cæteros.
Dein Nævius qui servet pretium, tertius est.
Si erit, quod quarto dabitur Licinio.
Post insequi Licinium facio Atilium.
In sexto sequitur hos loco Terentius.
Turpilius septimum, Trabea octavum obtinet;
Nono loco esse facile facio Luscium.
Decimum addo causa antiquitatis Ennium.
Volc. Sedig. ap. Gel. lib. xv. 24.

However correct this judgment may be, Plautus is the oldest, if not the most celebrated of those who have not as yet been mentioned.

PLAUTUS

T. Maccius Plautus was a contemporary of Ennius, for it is generally supposed that he was born twelve years later,[173] and died fifteen years earlier[174] than the founder of the new school of Latin poetry. The flourishing period, therefore, of both coincide. He was a native of Sarsina, in Umbria, but was very young when he removed to Rome. Very little is known respecting his life; but it is universally admitted that he was of humble origin, and owing to the prevalence of this tradition we find *Plautinæ prosapiæ homo*, used as a proverbial expression. The numerous examples in his comedies of vulgar taste and low humour are in favour of this supposition.

He had no early gentlemanlike associations to interfere with his delineations of Roman character in low life. His contemporary, Ennius, was a gentleman; Plautus was not: education did not overcome his vulgarity, although it produced a great effect upon his language and style, which were more refined and cultivated than those of his predecessors. Plautus must have lived and associated with the class whose manners he describes; hence his pictures are correct and truthful.

The class from which his representations of Roman life was taken is that of the *ærarii*, who consisted of clients, the sons of freedmen, and the half-enfranchised natives of Italian towns. His plots are Greek, his personages Greek, and the scene is laid in Greece and her colonies; but the morality, manners, sentiments, wit, and humour, were those of that mixed, half-foreign, class of the inhabitants of the capital, which stood between the slave and the free-born citizen. One of his characters is, as was observed by Niebuhr,[175] not Roman, for the parasite is a Greek, not a Roman character; but then a flatterer is by profession a citizen of the world, and his business is to conform himself to the manners of every society. How readily that character became naturalized, we are informed by some of the most amusing passages in the satires of Horace and Juvenal.

The humble occupation which his poverty compelled him to follow was calculated to draw out and foster the comic talent for which he was afterwards distinguished, for Varro[176] tells us that he acted as a stage-carpenter (*operarius*) to a theatrical company; he adds, also, that he was subsequently engaged in some trade in which he was unsuccessful, and was reduced to the necessity of earning his daily bread by grinding in a mill. To this degrading labour, which was not usually performed by men, except as a punishment for refractory slaves, it has been supposed that he owed his cognomen, Asinius, which is sometimes appended to his other names. Ritzschl, however, has most ingeniously and satisfactorily proved that the name of Asinius is a corruption of Sarsinas (native of Sarsina:) he supposes that Sarsinas became Arsinas, that this was afterwards written Arsin, then Asin, and that this was finally considered as the representative of Asinius.

This view is further supported by the fact that, in all cases in which the name Asinius is used, the poet is called not Asinius Plautus, but Plautus Asinius, like Livius Patavinus, this being the proper position for the ethnic name. Another error respecting the poet's name has been perpetuated throughout all the editions of his works, although it is not found in any

---

[173] A. U. C. 527; B. C. 227.
[174] A. U. C. 570; B. C. 184. See Cic. Brut. 15.
[175] Lect. lxx.
[176] A. Gell. iii. 3.

manuscript. It was discovered by Ritzschl[177] whilst examining the palimpsest MS. in the Ambrosian Library at Milan. He thus found that his real names were Titus Maccius, and not Marcus Accius. The name Plautus was given him because he had flat feet, this being the signification of the word in the Umbrian language. Niebuhr,[178] although he does not deny his poverty, gives no credit to the story of his working at a mill.

The earliest comedies which he wrote are said to have been entitled "*Addictus*," and "*Saturio*," but they are not contained amongst the twenty which are now extant. As soon as he became an author there can be no doubt that he emerged from his state of poverty and obscurity, for he had no rival during his whole career, unless Cæcilius Statius, a man of very inferior talent, can be considered one. Comedies began now to be in great demand: the taste for the comic drama was awakened; it was precisely the sort of literature likely to be acceptable to an active, bustling, observant people like the Romans. They liked shows of every kind, and public speaking, and had always their eyes and their ears open, loved jokes and rude satire and boisterous mirth, and would appreciate bold and fearless delineations of character, which they met with in their every-day life. The demand for the public games, therefore, began to be quite as great as the supply, and the theatrical managers would take care always to have a new play in rehearsal, in case they should be called upon for a public representation.

Plautus had no aristocratic patrons, like Ennius and Terence—probably his humour was too broad, and his taste not refined enough, to please the Scipios and Lælii, and their fastidious associates. Horace finds fault with Plautus because his wit was not sufficiently gentlemanlike, as well as his numbers not sufficiently harmonious. Probably the higher classes might have observed similar deficiencies; with the masses, however, the comedies of Plautus, notwithstanding their faults, retained their original popularity even in the Augustan age. The Roman public were his patrons. His very coarseness would recommend him to the rude admirers of the Fescennine songs and the Atellan *Fabulæ*. His careless prosody and inharmonious verses would either escape the not over-refined ears of his audience, or be forgiven for the sake of the fun which they contained. Life, bustle, surprise, unexpected situations, sharp, sprightly, brilliant, sparkling raillery, that knew no restraint nor bounds, carried the audience with him. He allowed no respite, no time for dulness or weariness. To use an expression of Horace, he hurried on from scene to scene, from incident to incident, from jest to jest, so that his auditors had no opportunity for feeling fatigue.

Another cause of his popularity was, that although Greek was the fountain from which he drew his stores, and the metres of Greek poetry the framework in which he set them, his wit, his mode of thought, his language, were purely Roman. He had lived so long amongst Romans that he had caught their national spirit, and this spirit was reflected throughout his comedies. The incidents of them might have taken place in the streets of Rome, so skilful was he in investing them with a Roman dress.

His style too was truly Latin, and Latin of the very purest and most elegant kind.[179] He did not, like Cato and Ennius, carry his admiration for Greek so far as to "enrich" his native tongue with new and foreign words. Nor would this feature be without some effect in gaining him the sympathy of the masses. They admire elegance of language if it is elegant simplicity.

---

[177] See Smith's Biog. Dict. s. v.
[178] Lect. on Rom. Hist. lxx.
[179] Quint. x. 1, 99.

They appreciate well-chosen and well-arranged sentences, if the words are such as fall familiarly, and, therefore, intelligibly on their ears.

The coarseness of Plautus, however, was the coarseness of innuendo, and even if the allusion was indelicate, it was veiled in decent language. This quality of his wit called forth the approbation of Cicero.[180] But it is difficult to conceive how he could compare him, in this particular, with the old Athenian comedy, the obscenity of which is so gross and palpable, as to constitute the sole blemish of those delightful compositions.

The following laudatory epigram written by Varro is found in the Noctes Atticæ of A. Gellius:[181]—

> Postquam est mortem aptus Plautus, comœdia luget,
> Scena est deserta dein risus ludu, jocusque,
> Et numeri innumeri simul omnes collacrumarunt.

The same grammarian paid to his style a compliment similar to that which had been paid to Plato, by saying, that if the Muses spoke in Latin they would borrow the language of Plautus.[182] Whatever might have been the faults of the Plautian comedy, it maintained its position on the Roman stage for at least five centuries, and was acted as late as the reign of Dioclesian.

It does not appear that Plautus ever attained the full privileges of a Roman citizen. Probably he had no powerful friends to press his claims, and therefore enjoyed no more than the Italian franchise to the end of his days. No fewer than one hundred and thirty comedies have been attributed to him, but of these many were spurious. Varro considers the twenty which are now extant genuine, together with the Vidularia, of which only a few lines remain, and those only in the palimpsest MS. already mentioned. The rest, the titles of which alone survive, are of doubtful authority.

All the comedies of Plautus, except the *Amphitruo*, were adapted from the new comedy of the Greeks. The statement that he imitated the Sicilian Epicharmus,[183] and founded the *Menæchmi* on one of his comedies, rests only on a vague tradition. There can be no doubt that he studied also both the old and the middle comedy; but still Menander, Diphilus, and Philemon furnished him the originals of his plots. The popularity of Plautus was not confined to Rome, either republican or imperial. Dramatic writers of modern times have recognised the effectiveness of his plots, and, therefore, have adopted or imitated them, and they have been translated into most of the European languages.

The following is a brief sketch of the subjects of his extant comedies.

I. Amphitruo. This is the only piece which Plautus borrowed from the middle Attic comedy; the plot is founded on the well-known story of Jupiter and Alcmena, and has been imitated both by Molière and Dryden.

II, III, IV. The Asinaria, Casina, and Mercator, depict a state of morals so revolting that it is impossible to dwell upon them.

V. In the Aulularia, a very amusing play, a miser finds a pot of gold (aulula,) and hides it with the greatest care. His daughter is demanded in marriage by an old man named

---
[180] De Off. i. 29.
[181] Lib. i. 24.
[182] Quint. x. 1, 90.
[183] Hor. Ep. ii. 1, 58.

Megadorus, the principal recommendation to whose suit is, that he is willing to take her without a dowry. Meanwhile the slave of her young lover steals the gold, and, as may be conjectured, for no more of the play is preserved, the lover restores the gold, and the old man, in the joy of his heart, gives him his daughter.

This comedy suggested to Molière the plot of L'Avare, the best play which he ever wrote, and one in which he far surpasses the original. Two attempts have been made to supply the lost scenes, which may be found in the Delphin and Variorum edition.

VI. The Bacchides are two twin sisters, one of whom is beloved by her sister's lover. He does not know that there are two, and, misled by the similarity of the name, thinks himself betrayed. Hence arise amusing situations and incidents, but at length an éclaircissement takes place.

VII. The Captivi, for its style, sentiments, moral, and the structure of the plot, is incomparably the best comedy of Plautus. In a war between the Ætolians and Eleians, Philopolemus, an Ætolian, the son of Hegio, is taken prisoner, whilst Philocrates is captured by the Ætolians. Philocrates and his slave Tyndarus are purchased by Hegio, with a view to recover his son by an exchange of prisoners. The master and slave, however, agree to change places; and thus Philocrates is sent back to his country, valued only as a slave. Hegio discovers the trick, and condemns Tyndarus to fetters and hard labour. Philocrates, however, returns, and brings back Philopolemus with him, and it also turns out that Tyndarus is a son of Hegio whom he had lost in his infancy.

VIII. The Curculio derives its name from a parasite, who is the hero, and who acts his part in a plot full of fraud and forgery; the only satisfactory point in the comedy being the deserved punishment of an infamous pander.

IX. In the Cistellaria, Demipho, a Lemnian, promises his daughter to Alcesimarchus, who is in love with Silenium. The young lady has fallen into the hands of a courtesan, who endeavours to force her into a vicious course of life; she, however, steadily refuses; and it is at length discovered, by means of a box of toys (cistella,) that she is the illegitimate daughter of Demipho, and had been exposed as an infant. Her virtue is rewarded by her being happily married to her lover.

X. The Epidicus was evidently a favourite play with the author, for he makes one of the characters in another comedy say that he loves it as dearly as himself.[184] The plot turns on the common story of a lost child recognised. The intrigue, which is remarkably clever, is managed by Epidicus, a cunning slave, who gives the name to the play.

XI. The Mostellaria is exceedingly lively and amusing. A young man, in his father's absence, makes the paternal mansion a scene of noisy and extravagant revelry. In the midst of it the father returns, and in order to prevent discovery, a slave persuades him that the house is haunted. When he discovers the trick he is very angry, but ultimately pardons both his son and the slave. The name is derived from Mostellum, the diminutive of Monstrum, a prodigy, or supernatural visitor.

XII. The Menæchmi is a Comedy of Errors, arising out of the exact likeness between two brothers, one of whom was stolen in infancy, and the other wanders in search of him, and at last finds him in great affluence at Epidamnus. It furnished the plot to Shakspeare's play, and likewise to the comedy of Regnard, which bears the name of the original.

---

[184] Bacch. ii. 2.

XIII. The Miles Gloriosus was taken from the Ἀλαζων (Boaster) of the Greek comic drama. Its hero, Pyrgopolinices, is the model of all the blustering, swaggering captains of ancient and modern comedy. The braggadocio carries off the mistress of a young Athenian, who follows him, and takes up his abode in the next house to that in which the girl is concealed. Like Pyramus and Thisbe the lovers have secret interviews through a hole in the party-wall. (The device being borrowed from the "*Phantom*" of Menander.)[185] When they are discovered, the soldier is induced to resign the lady by being persuaded that another is desperately in love with him, but the only reward which he gets is a good beating for his pains.

XIV. In the Pseudolus, a cunning slave of that name procures, by a false memorandum, a female slave for his young master; and when the fraud is discovered the matter is settled by the payment of the price by a complaisant father. Notwithstanding the simplicity of the plot, the action is bustling and full of intrigue; and from a passage of Cicero,[186] it appears that this play and Truculentus were favourites with the author himself. The procurer in this comedy was one of the characters in which Roscius especially excelled.

XV. The Pœnulus derives its name from its romantic plot. A young Carthaginian slave is adopted by an old bachelor, who leaves him a good inheritance. He falls in love with a girl, a Carthaginian like himself, who had been kidnapped with her sister, and now belonged to a procurer. The arrival of the father leads to a discovery that they are free-born, and that they are the first cousins of the young man. Thus it comes to pass that the girls are rescued, and the lovers united. The most curious portion of this comedy is that in which Hanno, the father, is represented as talking Punic;[187] and his words bear so close a resemblance to the Hebrew that commentators have expressed them in Hebrew characters, and rendered them, after a few emendations, capable of translation.[188]

XVI. The tricks played upon a procurer by a slave, aided by a Persian parasite, furnish the slender plot of the Persa.

XVII. The Rudens derives its name from the rope of a fishing-net, and, with the exception perhaps of the Captivi, is the most affecting and pleasing of all the twenty plays. The morality is pure, the sentiments elevated, the poetic justice complete. A female child has fallen into the hands of a procurer. Her lover in vain endeavours to ransom her, and being shipwrecked, the toys with which she played in infancy are lost in the waves, but are eventually brought to shore by the net of a fisherman. She is thus recognised by her father, and is married to her lover, whilst the procurer is utterly ruined by the loss of his property in the wreck.

XVIII. Stichus is the name of the slave on whom the intrigue of the play which bears this name mainly depends. The plot is very simple. Two brothers marry two sisters, and are ruined by extravagant living; they determine therefore to go abroad and repair their fortunes. After they have been many years absent the ladies' father wishes them to marry again. They,

---

[185] The plot of the Phasma of Menander is as follows:—A woman who has married a second husband has a daughter concealed in the next house, with whom she has secret interviews by means of a communication through the party-wall. In order the better to carry on her clandestine plan, she pretends that she has intercourse with a supernatural being, who visits her in answer to her invocations. Her step-son by accident sees the maiden, and is at first awe-struck, thinking that he had beheld a goddess; but, discovering the truth, he is captivated with her beauty. A happy marriage, with the consent of all parties, concludes the play.
[186] De Sen. 50.
[187] Act v. scene i.
[188] See Plaut. Ed. Var. pp. 1320 and 2095.

however, steadily refuse, and their constancy is rewarded by the return of their husbands with large fortunes.

XIX. The Trinummus is a translation from the Thesaurus of the Greek comic poet Philemon.[189] It derived its Latin title from the incident of the informer being bribed with three *nummi*.[190] An old merchant on leaving home places his son and daughter, together with a treasure which he has buried in his house, under the guardianship of his friend Callicles. The son squanders his father's property, and is even forced to sell his house, which Callicles purchases. Soon a young man of good family and fortune makes proposals for the daughter's hand, and Callicles is at a loss to know how to give her a dowry without saying something about the treasure. At length he hires a man to pretend that he has come from the absent father, and has brought one thousand pieces of gold. The return of the father interferes with the plan; but everything is explained, the daughter is married, and the son forgiven.

XX. The Truculentus, although the moral picture which it presents is detestable, is remarkably clever, both for the variety of incidents and the graphic delineations of character which it contains. The artful courtesan who dupes and ruins her lovers; the three lovers themselves—one a man of the town, another an unpolished but generous rustic, the third a stupid and conceited soldier; and, lastly, the slave, whose rude sagacity and bluff hatred of courtesans expose him to the imputation of being actually savage (truculentus,) are powerfully drawn; but notwithstanding its merits, it is not a play which can possibly please the tastes and sentiments of modern times.

Plautus must not be dismissed without some notice of his prologues. The prologue of the Greek drama prepared the audience for the action of the play, by narrating all the previous events of the story which were necessary in order to understand the plot. That of the modern stage is an address of the poet to the spectators, praying for indulgence, deprecating severe criticism, enlivened frequently by characteristic sketches and satirical observations on the manners and habits of the age. In these features it sometimes resembles the parabasis of the old Attic comedy. The prologues of Plautus united all these objects; and whilst they introduced the comedy, their amusing gayety was calculated to put the audience in good humour and secure their applause. The shrewd knowledge which the author displayed in them of the character of his fellow-countrymen claimed their sympathies, and called forth their prejudices in his favour; whilst their polish and finish must have been appreciated by an assembly whose attention had not begun to flag or to weary. Some are long pieces. That of the Amphitruo, which is the longest, extends to upwards of one hundred and fifty lines. That of the Trinummus takes the unusual form of a brief allegorical dialogue between Luxury and her daughter Poverty.

---

[189] See Prol. 18.
[190] See act iv. scene ii.

Chapter 8

STATIUS COMPARED WITH MENANDER—CRITICISM OF CICERO—HYPOTHESES RESPECTING THE EARLY LIFE OF TERENCE—ANECDOTE BELATED BY DONATUS—STYLE AND MORALITY OF TERENCE—ANECDOTE OF HIM RELATED BY CORNELIUS NEPOS—HIS PECUNIARY CIRCUMSTANCES AND DEATH—PLOTS AND CRITICISM OF HIS COMEDIES—THE REMAINING COMIC POETS

CÆCILIUS STATIUS

Between Plautus and Terence flourished Cæcilius Statius, whom Volcatius, as well as Cicero,[191] places at the head of the list of Roman comic poets. He was an emancipated slave, and was born at Milan. The time of his birth is unknown, but he died A. U. C. 586, and was therefore a contemporary of Ennius. He did not depart from the established custom of transferring the comedy of the Greek stage to that of Rome, and as far as a judgment can be formed from the titles of his forty-five comedies which are extant, they were all "*Palliatæ*." The collection of fragments remaining of his works is a large one, but they are not sufficiently long or connected to test the favourable opinion entertained by the critics of ancient times.

Aulus Gellius[192] enables us to estimate the powers of C. Statius as a translator by a comparison of two passages taken from his "*Plocius*" with the original of Menander. The result is, that the usual fault of translations is too plainly manifest, namely, the loss of the spirit and vigour. "Our comedies," he remarks, "are written in an elegant and graceful style, and may be read with pleasure; but if compared with the Greek originals, they fall so far short that the arms of Glaucus could not have been more inferior to those of Diomede: the Greek is full of emotion, wit, and liveliness; the Latin dull and uninteresting." Cicero, likewise, and Varro have pronounced judgment upon his merits and demerits. The sum and substance of

---
[191] De Opt. Gen. Dic. i.
[192] Noct. Att. ii. 33.

their criticisms appear to be that his excellencies consisted in the conduct of the plot,[193] dignity,[194] and in pathos,[195] whilst his fault was not sufficient care in preserving the purity of the Latin style.

Cicero,[196] though not without hesitation, assigns the palm to him amongst the writers of Latin comedy, as he awards that of epic poetry to Ennius, and that of tragedy to Pacuvius.[196] He says, on the other hand,[197] that the bad Latin of Cæcilius and Pacuvius formed exceptions to the usual style of their age, which was as commendable for its Latinity as for its innocence. And in a letter to Atticus,[198] he writes:—"I said, not as Cæcilius, *Mane ut ex portu in Piræum*, but as Terence, whose plays, on account of their elegant Latinity, were thought to have been written by C. Lælius, Heri aliquot adolescentuli coimus in Piræum." Horace,[199] without stating his own opinion, gives, as that commonly received in his day, that Cæcilius is superior in dignity (*gravitate,*) Terence in skill (*arte*.)

The prologue of Terence's comedy of the Hecyra proves that the earlier plays of Cæcilius had a great struggle to achieve success. The actor who delivers it, an old favourite with the public, and probably the manager, apologizes for bringing forward a play which had been once rejected (*exacta,*) on the ground that by perseverance in a similar course he had caused the reception and approval of not one but many of the comedies of Cæcilius which had been unsuccessful, and adds, that of those which did succeed, some had a narrow escape.

P. TERENTIUS AFER

P. Terentius Afer was a slave in the family of a Roman senator, P. Terentius Lucanus. His early history is involved in obscurity, but he is generally supposed to have been born A. U. C. 561.[200] His cognomen, Afer, points to an African origin, for it was a common custom to distinguish slaves by an ethnical name. Whether there is any sufficient authority for the tradition that he was a native of Carthage is uncertain. He could not, as was rightly observed by Fenestella,[201] have been actually a prisoner of war, because he was both born and died in the interval between the first and second Punic Wars; nor, if he had been captured by the Numidians or Gætulians in any war which these tribes carried on with Carthage, could he have come into the possession of a Roman general by purchase, for there was no commercial intercourse between these nations and Rome until after the destruction of Carthage.

Another hypothesis has been suggested, which is by no means improbable.[202] During the interval which elapsed between the first and second Punic Wars, the Carthaginians were involved in wars with their own mercenaries, the Numidians, and the southern Iberians. Some embassies from Rome also visited Carthage. Terence, therefore, may possibly have been taken prisoner in one of these wars, have been purchased by a Roman in the Carthaginian

---

[193] Varro.
[194] Horace.
[195] Varro.
[196] De Opt. Gen. Orat. i.
[197] Brut. 258.
[198] Lib. vii. 3.
[199] Ep. ii. 1.
[200] B. C. 193.
[201] See Life of Ter. in Ed. Varior.
[202] See Smith's Dict. of Ant. s. v.

slave-market, and so have been carried to Rome. What his condition was in the house of Lucanus is not known; but it is clear that he had opportunities of cultivating his natural talents, and acquiring that refined and masterly acquaintance with all the niceties and elegancies of the Latin language which his comedies exhibited, and it is probable, also, that very early in life he obtained his freedom.

His first essay as a dramatic author was the "*Andrian*," perhaps the most interesting, certainly the most affecting of all his comedies. Terence, an unknown and obscure young man, offered his play to the Curule Ædiles. They, accordingly, we are told, referred the new candidate to the experienced judgment of Cæcilius Statius, then at the height of his popularity. Terence, in humble garb, was introduced to the poet whilst he was at supper, and seated on a low stool near the couch on which Cæcilius was reclining, he commenced reading. He had finished but a few lines when Cæcilius invited him to sit by him and sup with him. He rapidly ran through the rest of his play, and gained the unqualified admiration of his hearer. This story is related by Donatus, but whether there is any truth in it is very doubtful. It is, at any rate, certain that "*The Andrian*" was not brought forward immediately after obtaining this decision in its favour, for the date of its first representation[203] is two years subsequent to the death of Cæcilius.

Talents of so popular a kind as those of Terence, and a genius presenting the rare combination of all the fine and delicate touches which characterize true Attic sentiment, without corrupting the native ingenuous purity of the Latin language, could not long remain in obscurity. He was soon eagerly sought for as a guest and a companion by those who could appreciate his powers. The great Roman nobility, such as the Scipiones, the Lælii, the Scavolæ, and the Metelli, had a taste for literature. Like the *Tyranni* in Sicily and Greece, and like some of the Italian princes in the middle ages, they assembled around them circles of literary men, of whom the polite and hospitable host himself formed the nucleus and centre.

The purity and gracefulness of the style of Terence, "*per quam dulces Latini leporis facetiæ nituerunt,*"[204] show that the conversation of his accomplished friends was not lost upon his correct ear and quick intuition. To these habits of good society may also be attributed the leading moral characteristics of his comedies. He invariably exhibits the humanity and benevolence of a cultivated mind. He cannot bear loathsome and disgusting vice: he deters the young from the unlawful indulgence of their passions by painting such indulgence as inconsistent with the refined habits and tastes of a gentleman.

His truthfulness compels him to depict habits and practices which were recognised and allowed, as well by the manners of the Athenians, from whom his comedies were taken, as by the lax morality of Roman fashionable society. Nor can we expect from a heathen writer of comedy so high a tone of morality as to lash vice with the severe censure which the Christian feels it deserves, however venial society may pronounce it to be. It is as much as can be hoped for, if we find the principles of good taste brought forward on the stage to influence public morals. Even the code of Christian society too often contents itself with rebuking such vice as interferes with its own comfort or safety, and stigmatizes conduct, not for its immorality, but for its being unbecoming a gentleman. It is a standard which has its use, but it is not higher than the Terentian.

---

[203] B. C. 166; A. U. C. 588.
[204] Valerius Paterc.

And if the plays of Terence are compared with those of authors professing to be Christians, which form part of the classical literature of the English nation, and were unblushingly witnessed on their representation by some of both sexes, who, nevertheless, professed a regard for character, how immeasurably superior are the comedies of the heathen poet! Point out to the young the greater light and knowledge which the Christian enjoys, and the plays of Terence may be read without moral danger. No amount of colouring and caution would be sufficient to shield the mind of an ingenuous youth from the imminent peril of being corrupted by those of Wycherly and Congreve. Pictures of Roman manners must represent them as corrupt, or they would not be truthful; but often a good lesson is elicited from them. When the deceived wife reproachfully asks her offending husband with what face he can rebuke his son because he has a mistress when he himself has two wives,[205] one is far more struck with the honour which the strictness of Roman virtue paid to the nuptial tie, than offended at the lenient view which is taken of the young man's fault. The knaveries and tricks of Davus[206] meet with sufficient poetical justice in his fright and his flogging. The very dress in which the Meretrix, or woman of abandoned morals, was costumed, kept constantly before the eyes of the Roman youth their grasping avarice, and therefore warned them of the ruin which awaited their victims; and the well-known passage,[207] in which the loathsome habits of this class are described, must have been, as Terence himself says, a preservative of youthful virtue:—

Nosse omnia hæc saluti est adolescentulis.

The Pander, who basely, for the sake of filthy lucre, ministers to the passions of the young, is represented as the most degraded and contemptible of mortals. The Parasite, who earns his meal by flattering and fawning on his rich patron, is made the butt of unsparing ridicule. And the timid, simple maiden, confiding too implicitly in the affections of her lover, and sacrificing her interests to that love, and not to lust or love of gain, is painted in such colours as to command the spectator's pity and sympathy, and to call forth his approbation when she is deservedly reinstated in her position as an honourable matron. Lastly, her lover is not represented as a profligate, revelling in the indiscriminate indulgence of his passions, and rendering vice seductive by engaging manners and fascinating qualities: but we feel that his sin necessarily results from the absence of a high tone of public morality to protect the young against temptation; and in all cases the reality and permanency of his affection for the victim of his wrongdoing is proved by his readiness and anxiety to become her husband.

So far as it can be so, comedy was in the hands of Terence an instrument of moral teaching, for it can only be so indirectly by painting men and manners as they are, and not as they ought to be.

It is said that the patrons of Terence assisted him in the composition of his comedies, or, at least, corrected their language and style, and embellished them by the insertion of scenes and passages. An anecdote is related by Cornelius Nepos,[208] which, if true, at once proves the point. He says that Lælius was at his villa near Puteoli during the festival of the Matronalia. On this holiday the power of the Roman ladies was absolute.

---

[205] Phorm. v. viii.
[206] Andr. v. ii.
[207] Eunuchus, v. iv.
[208] Fr. Incert. 6.

Lælius was ordered by his wife to come to supper early. He excused himself on the ground that he was occupied, and begged not to be disturbed. When he appeared in the supper-room, he said he had never been so well satisfied with his compositions. He was asked for a specimen of what he had written, and immediately repeated a scene in the "*Self-Tormentor*"[209] of Terence. Terence, however, gently refutes this story in the prologue to the "*Adelphi*," and gives it a positive contradiction in the prologue to the comedy in which the passage occurs. Perhaps he may at first have permitted the report to be credited for the sake of paying a compliment to his patron.

There is a tradition that he lived and died in poverty, and this tale is perpetuated in the following lines by Porcius Licinius:——

> Nil Publius
> Scipio profuit, nihil ei Lælius, nil Furius,
> Tres per idem tempus qui agitabant nobiles facillume,
> Eorum ille opere ne domum quidem habuit conductitium
> Saltem ut esset quo referret obitum domini servulus.
> Nothing did Publius Scipio profit him;
> Nothing did Lælius, nothing Furius;
> At once the three great patrons of our bard.
> And yet so niggard of their bounty to him,
> He had not even wherewithal to hire
> A house in Rome to which a faithful slave
> Might bring the tidings of his master's death. *Colman.*

The patrons of Terence, however, never deserved the reproach of meanness. Nor could the comic poet have been very poor. He received large sums for his comedies; he had funds sufficient to reside for some time in Greece; and at his death he possessed gardens on the Appian Way twenty jugera in extent.

A mystery hangs over his death, which took place B. C. 158.[210] It is not known whether he died in Greece, or was lost at sea, together with all the comedies of Menander, which he had translated whilst in Greece, or whether, after embarking for Asia, he was, as Volcatius writes, never seen more:——

> Ut Afer sex populo edidit comœdias
> Iter hinc in Asiam fecit, navim cum semel
> Conscendit visus nunquam est. Sic vitâ vacat.

One daughter married to a Roman knight survived him.

Six comedies by Terence remain, and it is probable that these are all that he ever wrote; they belong to the class technically denominated *Palliatæ*.

---

[209] Satis pol, &c., iv. 4, 1.
[210] Hier. Chron. Ol. clv. 3.

"The Andrian"

"*The Andrian*" was exhibited at the Magalensian games, A. U. C. 588,[211] when the poet was in his twenty-seventh year. The musical accompaniment was performed on equal flutes, right-handed and left-handed (*tibiis paribus dextris et sinistris;*) i. e., as the action was of a serio-comic character, the lively music of the *tibiæ dextræ* was used in the comic scenes; the solemn sounds of the *tibiæ sinistræ* accompanied the serious portion. The manners are Greek, and the scene is laid at Athens.

The plot is as follows:—Glycerium, a young Athenian girl, is placed under the care of an Andrian, who educates her with his daughter Chrysis. On his death Chrysis migrates to Athens, taking Glycerium with her as her sister, and is driven by distress to become a courtesan. Pamphilus, the son of Simo, falls in love with Glycerium, and promises her marriage. Simo accidentally discovers his son's attachment in the following manner:— Chrysis dies, and at her funeral Glycerium imprudently approaches too near to the burning pile. Her lover rushes forward and embraces her, and affectionately expostulates with her for thus risking her life. "Dearest Glycerium!" he exclaims, "what are you doing? Why do you rush to destruction?" Upon this the girl burst into a flood of tears, and threw herself into his arms. Simo had meanwhile betrothed Pamphilus to Philumena, the daughter of Chremes; and although he had discovered his son's passion, and Chremes had heard of the promise of marriage, he pretends that the marriage with Philumena shall still take place, in order that he may discover what his son's real sentiments are. In this difficulty, Pamphilus applies to Davus, a cunning and clever slave, who advises him to offer no opposition. At this crisis Glycerium is delivered of a child, which Davus causes to be laid at the door of Simo. Chremes sees the infant, and, understanding that Pamphilus is the father, refuses to give him his daughter. The opportune arrival of Crito, an Andrian, discovers to Chremes that Glycerium is his own daughter, whom on a former absence from Athens he had intrusted to his brother Phania, now dead. Consequently Glycerium is married to Pamphilus, and Philumena is given to a young lover, named Charinus, who had hitherto pressed his suit in vain.

"*The Andrian*" was, as it deserved to be, eminently successful, and encouraged the young author to persevere in the career which he had chosen. The interest is well sustained, the action is natural, and many scenes touching and pathetic, whilst the serious parts are skilfully relieved by the adroitness of Davus, and his cleverness in getting out of the scrapes in which his cunning involves him. Cicero[212] praises the funeral scene[213] as an example of that talent for narrative which Terence constantly displays. The substance of his criticism is, that the poet has attained conciseness without the sacrifice of beauty; and whilst he has avoided wearisome affectation, has not omitted any details which are agreeable and interesting. Nothing can be more beautiful than the struggle between the love and filial duty of Pamphilus,[214] which ends with his determination to yield to his father's will; nothing more candid than his confession, or more upright than his earnest desire not to be suspected of suborning Crito.

---

[211] B. C. 166.
[212] De Orat. ii. 81.
[213] Act i. scene i.
[214] Act v. scene iii. 25.

"*The Andrian*" has been closely imitated in the comedy of "*The Conscious Lovers*," by Sir Richard Steele; but in natural and graceful wit, as well as ingenuity, the English play is far inferior to the Roman original.

"Eunuchus"

"*The Eunuch*" is a transcript of a comedy by Menander. Even the characters are the same, except that Gnatho and Thraso together occupy the place of Colax (the flatterer) in the original Greek. It was represented in the consulship of M. Valerius Messala and C. Fannius Strabo.[215] The musical accompaniment was Lydian. It was the most popular of all Terence's plays, and brought the author the largest sum of money that had ever been paid for a comedy previously, namely, 8,000 sestertii, a sum equivalent to about 65*l*. sterling. In vain Lavinius, Terence's most bitter rival, endeavoured to interrupt the performance, and to accuse the author of plagiarism. His defence was perfectly successful, and Suetonius states[216] that it was called for twice in one day.

"*The Eunuch*" is not equal to some of Terence's plays in wit and humour; but the plot is bustling and animated, and the dialogue gay and sparkling: it is also unquestionably the best acting play of the whole. There is no play in which there is a greater individuality of character, or more effect of histrionic contrast. The lovesick and somewhat effeminate Phædria contrasts well with the ardent and passionate Chærea, the swaggering, bullying Thraso with the pompous, philosophical parasite, who proposes to found a Gnathonic School. Parmeno is quite as crafty, but far more clever, than Davus, and his description of the evils of love is the perfection of shrewd wisdom.

The plot is as follows:—Pamphila, the daughter of an Athenian citizen, was kidnapped in her infancy, and sold to a Rhodian. He gave her to a courtesan, who educated her with her own daughter Thais. Subsequently Thais removes to Athens; and on the mother's death Pamphila is sold to a soldier, named Thraso. The soldier, being in love with Thais, resolves to make her a present of his purchase; but Thais has got another lover, Phædria, and Thraso refuses to give Pamphila to Thais unless Phædria is first turned off. She, thinking that she has discovered Pamphila's relations, and anxious to restore her to them, persuades Phædria to absent himself for two days, in order that Thraso may present her with the maiden. Meanwhile Chærea, Phædria's younger brother, sees Pamphila accidentally, and falls desperately in love with her. He, therefore, persuades his brother's slave, Parmeno, to introduce him into Thais' house in the disguise of a eunuch, whom Phædria has intrusted him to convey to her during his absence. This leads to an *éclaircissement*. Pamphila is discovered to be an Athenian citizen, and her brother Chremes gives her in marriage to Chærea.

The most skilful part of this play is the method by which Terence has connected the underplot between Parmeno and Pythias, the waiting-maid of Thais, with the main action, their quarrels being entirely instrumental in bringing about the *dénouement*. Of all the comedies of Terence, the moral tone of this is the lowest and most degrading. The connivance of Laches the father of Chærea, at his son's illicit amour with Thais, presents a sad picture of

---

[215] A. U. C. 592; B. C. 167.
[216] In Vita Ter.

moral corruption, as the arrangement coolly made between Phædria and Gnatho[217] displays the meanness, which evidently was not considered inconsistent with the habits of Roman society.

Grievous as are these blemishes, this comedy must always be a favourite. There are in it passages of which the lapse of ages has not diminished the pungency: take, for example, the quiet satire contained in the contrast which Chærea draws between the healthful and natural beauty of his mistress and the "every-day forms of which his eyes are weary:"—

>Ch.
>Haud similis virgo est virginum nostrarum; quas matres student
>Demissis humeris esse, vincto pectore, ut graciles sient;
>Si qua est habitior paulo, pugilem esse aiunt; deducunt cibum,
>Tametsi bona est natura, reddunt curatura junceas:
>Itaque ergo amantur.
>Pa.
>Quid tua istæc.
>Ch.
>Nova figura oris.
>Pa.
>Papæ!
>Ch.
>Color verus, corpus solidum et succi plenum.[218]

"*The Eunuch*" suggested the plot of Sir Charles Sedley's "*Bellamira*," was translated by Lafontaine, and imitated in "*Le Muet*" of Brueys.

"Heautontimorumenos"

"*The Self-Punisher*" is a translation from Menander. It was acted the first time with Phrygian music, the second time with Lydian, in the consulship of the celebrated Ti. Sempronius Gracchus and M. Juventius Thalna.[219] This play may be considered as the masterpiece of Terence; it was a great favourite, notwithstanding its seriousness, and the absence of comic drollery throughout. Steele[220] remarks with truth, that it is a picture of human life; but there is not in the whole one passage which could raise a laugh. It is a good specimen of the refined taste of Terence, who, unlike Plautus, abhorred vulgarity and ribaldry, and did not often condescend even to humour. Its favourable reception, moreover, proves that, notwithstanding the preference which the Roman people were inclined to give to gladiatorial shows, and the more innocent amusements of buffoons and rope-dancers, and the noisy mirth with which theatrical entertainments were frequently interrupted, they could appreciate and enjoy a skilfully-constructed plot, and that quality which Terence especially claims for this comedy,[221] purity of style. The noble sentiment,

---

[217] Act v. scene ix.
[218] Act ii. scene iii.
[219] A. U. C. 590; B. C. 163.
[220] Spect. No. 502.
[221] Prol. 46.

> Homo sum, nihil humanum a me alienum puto,

was received by the whole audience with a burst of applause.

Plot.——Clinia, the son of Menedemus, falls in love with Antiphila, supposed to be the daughter of a poor Corinthian woman, and, to avoid his father's anger, enters the service of the king of Persia. Menedemus, repenting of his severity, punishes himself by purchasing a farm, and, giving up all the luxuries of a town life, works hard from morning to night. Like Laertes, in the Odyssey, he seeks by occupation to divert his mind from the contemplation of his son's absence:—

> The mournful hour that tore his son away
> Sent the sad sire in solitude to stray;
> Yet, busied with his slaves, to ease his wo
> He drest the vine, and bade the garden blow.
> *Odys.* xvi. 145.

Clinia returns from Asia, and takes up his abode at the house of his friend Clitipho, the son of Chremes. This Clitipho has fallen in love with Bacchis, an extravagant courtesan; and Syrus, an artful slave, persuades him to pass off Bacchis as the object of Clinia's affection, and Antiphila as her waiting-maid. Chremes, next day, to whom Menedemus had communicated his grief and remorse, acquaints him with the return of his son, and recommends him to pretend ignorance of his amour. By the intrigues and knavery of Syrus, Chremes is induced to pay 10 minæ (40*l.*) to Clitipho for the support of Bacchis. Sostrata, the wife of Chremes, has mean while discovered, by a ring in her possession, that Antiphila is her daughter. She had, according to the cruel Athenian practice, given her to the Corinthian in infancy that she might not be exposed; she had given the ring, the means of her discovery, at the same time. Clinia, therefore, marries Antiphila; and Chremes, although enraged at the imposition of Syrus, forgives him and his son, and Clitipho promises that he will give up Bacchis and marry a neighbour's daughter.

This play abounds in amiable and generous sentiments and passages of simple and graphic beauty. The whole scene, in which the habits of the poor girl whom Clinia loves is described, is exquisitely true to nature. Her occupation is like that of the chaste Lucretia in the legend:—

> Texentem telam studiose ipsam offendimus,
> Mediocriter vestitam veste lugubri,
> Ejus anuis causa, opinor, quæ erat mortua;
> Sine auro, tum ornatam, ita uti quæ ornantur sibi;
> Nulla mala re esse expolitam muliebri;
> Capillus passus, prolixus, circum caput
> Rejectus negligenter.
> *Heaut.* II. iii.
> Busily plying of the web we found her,
> Decently clad in mourning, I suppose,
> For the deceased old woman. She had on
> No gold, or trinkets, but was plain and neat,
> And dressed like those who dress but for themselves.

> No female varnish to set off her beauty;
> Her hair dishevelled, long, and flowing loose
> About her shoulders.

The reader cannot but sympathize with the remark of Clitipho, when he has heard this description of virtuous poverty,—"If all this is true, as I believe it is, you are the most fortunate of men."

The degraded Bacchis also reads a valuable lesson to her sex, when she shows the blessings of the path of virtue from which she has strayed:—

> Nam expedit bonas esse vobis: nos, quibuscum est res, non sinunt;
> Quippe forma impulsi nostra, nos amatores colunt:
> Hæc ubi immutata est, illi suum animum alio conferunt.
> Nisi si prospectum interea aliquid est, desertæ vivimus.
> Vobis cum uno semel ubi ætatem agere decretum 'st viro,
> Cujus mos maxume 'st consimilis vostrum, hi se ad vos applicant.
> Hoc beneficio utrique ab utrisque vero devincimini,
> Ut nunquam ulla amori vestro incidere possit calamitas.
> *Heaut.* II. iv.
> Virtue's your interest: those with whom we deal
> Forbid it to be ours; for our gallants,
> Charmed by our beauty, court us but for that;
> Which, fading, they transfer their love to others.
> If, then, mean while we look not to ourselves,
> We live forlorn, deserted, and distressed.
> You, when you've once agreed to pass your life
> Bound to one man whose temper suits with yours,
> He too attaches his whole heart to you.
> Thus mutual friendship draws you each to each;
> Nothing can part you, nothing shake your love.

How beautiful, too, is the unselfish devotion of Antiphila, when she artlessly professes to know nothing of other women's feelings, but to know this one thing only, that her happiness is wrapped up in that of her lover!——

> Nescio alias; me quidem semper scio fecisse sedulo
> Ut ex illius commodo meum compararem commodum.
> II. iv. 16.

Phormio

The Phormio is a translation or adaptation of the Epidicazomene (*the subject of the law suit*) of Apollodorus: it was entitled Phormio.

> Quia primas partes qui aget, is erit Phormio
> Parasitus, per quem res geretur maxume.[222]

It was acted four times; on the last occasion, in the consulship of C. Fannius Strabo and M. Valerius Messala,[223] at the Roman or Circensian games.

Plot.——Chremes, an Athenian, although he has a wife at Athens, (Nausistrata,) marries another at Lemnos under the feigned name of Stilpho. By her he has a daughter, Phanium. When she has attained a marriageable age, Chremes arranges with his brother Demipho, that she shall become the wife of his son Antipho. After this, the two old men leave Athens; and in their absence Demipho's son, Phædria, falls in love with a minstrel-girl, and the Lemnian wife arrives at Athens, together with her daughter Phanium. There she dies; and Antipho, seeing Phanium at the funeral, becomes enamoured of her. Not knowing what to do, he takes the advice of Phormio. In the case of a destitute orphan, the Athenian law compelled the nearest of kin to marry her or to give a portion. Phormio brings an action against Antipho; the case is proved, and he marries Phanium. The old men return, and Chremes, not knowing that Phanium is his own daughter, is desperately angry. Mean while, Dorio, the owner of Pamphila, threatens to sell her to some one else unless Phædria will immediately pay him thirty minæ. Geta, a knavish servant of Demipho, procures this money by telling the old gentleman that Phormio is willing to take Antipho's wife off his hands on condition of receiving thirty minæ. Phanium is eventually discovered and acknowledged, and thus matters are happily concluded. Nausistrata is at first very angry, but relents on the submission of the repentant Chremes.

This comedy supplied Molière with a large portion of the materials for "*Les Fourberies de Scapin.*"

Hecyra

This comedy, which, if the inscription may be trusted, is a translation or adaptation from one by Menander, was the least successful of all the plays of Terence. Twice it was rejected; on the first occasion, as the prologue to its second representation informs us, owing to "an unheard-of calamity and impediment."[224] The thoughts of the public were so occupied by a rope-dancer that they would not hear a word. Terence feared to risk a second representation on the same day; but such confidence had he in the merits of the play, that he offered it a second time for sale to the ædiles, and it was acted again in the consulship of Cn. Octavius and T. Manlius.[225] It was acted a third time at the funeral games of L. Æmilius Paulus, when it was again rejected. On its next representation, it was successful; and Ambivius Turpio, by whose theatrical company it was performed, and whose popularity had already caused the revival of some unsuccessful plays,[226] undertook to plead its cause in a new prologue. This prologue enters fully into the circumstances which caused its rejection. It states that some renowned boxers and expected performances of a rope-dancer caused a great tumult and

---

[222] Prol. 27.
[223] A. U. C. 592; B. C. 161.
[224] See Prol. i.
[225] B. C. 165; A. U. C. 588.
[226] See Prol. ii.

disturbance, especially among the female part of the audience; that, at the next representation, the first act went off with applause, but a rumour spread of a gladiatorial combat, the people flocked to a show which was more congenial to their taste, and the theatre was deserted. In conclusion, for the sake of the art of poetry, for the encouragement of himself to buy new plays, and for the protection of the poet from malicious critics, Ambivio entreated the patient attention of the audience; and the appeal of the old favourite servant of the public was successful.

The Hecyra is, without doubt, inferior to the other plays of Terence, and probably for that reason has never been imitated in modern literature. It is a drama of domestic life, and yet the plot is deficient in interest, and the scenes want life and variety.

Plot.—Pamphilus, at the desire of his father, Laches, marries Philumena, the daughter of Phidippus and Myrrhina, but being involved in an amour with Bacchis, has no affection for his wife, and avoids all intercourse with her. Meanwhile, Bacchis offended at his marriage, shows such an ill-temper, that his affection is weaned from her and transferred to Philumena. Pamphilus then goes to Imbrus, and on his return is surprised with the news that Philumena has left his father's house, and subsequently discovers that she has given birth to a son. He refuses, consequently, to receive her as his wife; but as he loves her to distraction, he promises her mother that he will keep her shame secret. As he will neither live with his wife nor assign any reason, Bacchis is suspected of being the cause. But she clears herself from the suspicion. Myrrhina, however, recognises upon her finger a ring belonging to her daughter. This leads to the *dénouement*. Pamphilus had one night when intoxicated met Philumena, and offered her violence. He had forced a ring from her finger and given it to Bacchis. He, therefore, with joy, acknowledges the child as his own, and restores his injured wife to his affections.

The comedy derives its title, Hecyra (the mother-in-law,) from the part taken by Sostrata, the mother of Pamphilus. Laches, unable to account for the conduct of Philumena and his son, is firmly persuaded that his wife Sostrata had taken a prejudice against her daughter-in-law, and Pamphilus, notwithstanding his dutiful affection for his mother, cannot avoid being under a similar impression. Sostrata, in order to remove this suspicion, offers with noble generosity to leave the house in order that Philumena may return.

This amiable rivalry of maternal devotion on the one hand, and filial respect on the other, constitutes the most interesting portion of the comedy; and Terence has thus endeavoured to rescue the relation of mother-in-law from the prejudice which, too often deservedly, attached to it.

Adelphi

This comedy was acted at the funeral games of L. Æmilius Paulus Macedonius, the conqueror of Perseus, in the consulship of L. Anicius Gallus and M. Cornelius Cethegus.[227] The music was Sarrane or Tyrian, the grave character of which was suitable to the solemnity of the occasion. The cost of the representation was borne by Q. Fabius Maximus, and P. C. Scipio Africanus, the sons of the deceased.

---

[227] A. U. C. 593; B. C. 161.

Plot.—Demea, a country gentleman and a strict disciplinarian, has two sons, Æschinus and Ctesipho. Æschinus, the elder, is adopted by his uncle Micio, a bachelor of indulgent temper and somewhat loose principles, who lives a town life at Athens. Whilst Ctesipho is brought up strictly in the country, Æschinus is educated with too great indulgence, and pursues a course of riot and extravagance. One night, in a moment of drunken passion, he offers violence to Pamphila, a young maiden, well born but poor; for which outrage he makes amends by a promise of marriage. Ctesipho soon after falls in love with a minstrel girl whom he accidentally meets; and Æschinus, to save his brother from his father's anger, conceals his amour and takes the discredit of it upon himself. At last he assaults the pander to whom the girl belongs, takes her away by force, and gives her to his brother. The affair comes to Demea's ears, who severely reproves Micio for ruining his son by injudicious indulgence. Matters are at length explained, and the marriage between Æschinus and Pamphila takes place, the minstrel girl is assigned to Ctesipho, and the price for her paid. The old bachelor, Micio, marries Sostrata, the mother of Pamphila, and, according to the usual rule of comedy, all the inferior persons of the drama are made happy.

Lax as the morals are which Micio refrains from correcting, his conduct illustrates a valuable principle in education; that——

> There is a way of winning more by love
> And urging of the modesty than fear.
> Force works on servile humours, not the free.
> Ben Jonson.

Nor are the evils likely to arise from indifference to moral principle left entirely without an antidote. A wise and not indiscriminate indulgence is upheld by Demea; and, at the conclusion of the play, he announces his deliberate change of character, but, at the same time, points out the pernicious errors of that kindness and indulgence which proceeds from impulse and not from principle.

> Dicam tibi:
> Ut id ostenderem, quod te isti facilem et festivum putant,
> Id non fieri ex vera vita, neque adeo ex æquo et bono;
> Sed assentando atque indulgendo et largiendo, Micio.
> Nunc adeo, si ob eam rem vobis mea vita invisa, Æschine, est,
> Quia non justa, injusta, prorsus omnia omnino obsequor;
> Missa facio; effundite, emite, facite, quod vobis lubet.
> Sed si id voltis potius, quæ vos propter adulescentiam
> Minus videtis, magis impense cupitis, consulitis parum,
> Hæc reprehendere et corrigere quam, obsecundare in loco;
> Ecce me qui id faciam vobis.
> Now, therefore, if I'm odious to you, son,
> Because I'm not subservient to your humour
> In all things, right or wrong; away with care:
> Spend, squander, and do what you will. But if,
> In those affairs where youth has made you blind,
> Eager, and thoughtless, you will suffer me

> To counsel and correct you, and in due season
> Indulge you, I am at your service. *Colman.*

This twofold lesson is by no means a useless one to parents, not to purchase the affection of their children by injudicious indulgence like Micio, nor, on the other hand, like Demea, to strain the cord too tight, and thus tempt their children to pursue a course of deceit, and to refuse their confidence to their natural advisers and guardians. The most beautiful feature, however, of the play is the picture which it gives of fraternal affection. This was the last comedy of the author. It furnished Molière with the idea of his "*Ecole des Maris*," and Baron with great part of the plot of "*L'Ecole de Pères.*" Shadwell was also indebted to it for his "*Squire of Alsatia*," and Garrick for his comedy of "*The Guardian.*"

The following comparison of the two great Roman comic poets by a French critic is a just one:——

> "Ce poète (Térence) a beaucoup plus d'art, mais il me semble que l'autre a plus d'esprit. Terence fait beaucoup plus parler qu'agir; l'autre fait plus agir que parler: et c'est le véritable caractère de la comédie, qui est beaucoup plus dans l'action que dans le discours. Cette vivacité me paroît donner encore un grand avantage à Plaute; c'est que ses intrigues sont bien variées, et ont toujours quelque chose qui surprend agréablement; au lieu que le théâtre semble languir quelquefois dans Térence, à qui la vivacité de l'action et les nœuds des incidens et des intrigues manquent manifestement."

If Terence was inferior to Plautus in life and bustle and intrigue, and in the powerful delineation of national character, he is superior in elegance of language and refinement of taste; he far more rarely offends against decency, and he substitutes delicacy of sentiment for vulgarity. The justness of his reflections more than compensates for the absence of his predecessor's humour: he touches the heart as well as gratifies the intellect.

If he was deficient in *vis comica*, it is only the defect which Cæsar attributed to Roman comedy generally; and Cicero, who thought that Roman wit was even more piquant than Attic salt itself, paid him a merited compliment in the following line:——

> Quicquid come loquens atque omnia dulcia dicens.

It has been objected to Terence that he superabounds in soliloquies;[228] but it is not surprising that he should have delighted in them, since no author ever surpassed him in narrative. His natural and unaffected simplicity renders him the best possible teller of a story: he never indulges in a display of forced wit or in attempts at epigrammatic sharpness; there are no superfluous touches, although his pictures are enlivened by sufficient minuteness; his moral lessons are conveyed in familiar proverb-like suggestions, not in dull and pedantic dogmatism.

The remaining comic poets will require but brief notice. L. Afranius was a contemporary of Terence, and flourished about B. C. 150. His comedies were all of the lowest class of *fabulæ togatæ* (tabernariæ;) and he was generally allowed by the critics to possess great skill in accommodating the Greek comedy to the representation of Roman manners:——

---

[228] Warton, in the Adventurer.

> Dicitur Afrani *toga* convenisse Menandro.
> Hor. Ep. II. i. 57.

His style was short and eloquent (*perargutus et disertus*,)[229] but he was a man of low tastes and profligate morals;[230] and, therefore, although, from living amidst the scenes of vulgar vice which he delighted to paint, his characters were true to nature, they were revolting and disgusting. His immorality, probably, as much as his talent, caused him to continue a favourite under the most corrupt times of the empire. Fragments and titles of many of his comedies have been preserved.

The name of Atilius is made known to us by Cicero, who mentions him three times. In a letter to Atticus,[231] he calls him a most crabbed poet (*poeta durissimus*,) and quotes the following line from one of his comedies:—

> Suam cuique sponsam, mihi meam; suum cuique amorem, mihi meum.

In the treatise "*De Finibus*,"[232] he speaks of him as the author of a bad translation of the Electra of Sophocles, and refers to the testimony of Licinius, who pronounces him as "hard as iron"——

> Ferreum scriptorem; verum opinor; scriptorem tamen
> Ut legendus sit;

and, lastly, in the "*Tusculan Disputations*,"[233] he gives the title of one of his plays—Μισογυνος (the Woman-hater.) Of his birth and private history nothing has been recorded.

P. Licinius Tegula is generally supposed to have been one of the oldest of the Latin comic writers, having flourished as early as the beginning of the second century B. C. The few fragments which remain of his works afford no opportunity of determining how far he deserved the place assigned to him in the epigram of Volcatius.

Lavinius Luscius is severely criticised by Terence in his prologues to the Eunuchus, Heautontimorumenos, and Phormio, although he is not mentioned by name. Terence, however, defends the severity of his strictures, on the ground that Luscius was the first aggressor. In the first of the above-mentioned prologues, we are informed that he translated well; but, by unskilful alterations and adaptations of the plots, made bad Latin comedies out of good Greek ones:—

> —— bene vertendo et describendo male
> Ex Græcis bonis Latinas fecit non bonas.

Two plays of Menander are mentioned as having been thus ill-treated—the Phasma (Phantom,) and the Thesaurus (Treasure.) How he spoilt the plot of the former is not stated;

---

[229] Cic. Brut. 167.
[230] Quint. x. i. 100.
[231] Lib. xiv. 20.
[232] Lib. i. 2.
[233] Lib. iv. ii.

but in the version of the Thesaurus, Terence convicts Luscius of a legal blunder. A young prodigal has sold his inheritance, on which his father's tomb stands, to an old miser. The father, foreseeing the consequence of his son's extravagance, had, before his death, bid him open the tomb after the expiration of ten years. He does so, and finds a treasure. The old man claims the treasure as his own, and the young man brings an action to recover it. The mistake of which Luscius was guilty, was, that in the conduct of the cause he made the defendant open the pleadings instead of the plaintiff.

Of the works of Q. Trabea no fragments remain except the short passages quoted by Cicero,[234] and the time at which he flourished is unknown. There is an anecdote which relates that Muretus presented to Jos. Scaliger a translation in Latin verse from a poem of Philemon, preserved by Stobæus, which he pretended was by Trabea. Scaliger was imposed upon; and in his notes on Varro, quoted the verses of Muretus as the work of Trabea. When he discovered the trick, he suppressed them in the Latin editions of his notes, and revenged himself on Muretus by a libellous epigram.[235]

The last of these dramatic writers who remains to be mentioned is Sextus Turpilius. A few fragments, as well as the titles of some of his plays, are still extant. All the titles are Greek, and, therefore, probably his comedies were *Fabulæ Palliatæ*. He flourished during the second century B. C., and died, according to the Eusebian Chronicle, at the commencement of the first century.[236]

---

[234] De Fin. ii. 4; Tusc. Dis. iv. 31.
[235] Dict. Univ. s. v.
[236] See Smith's Dict. of Antiq. s. v.

Chapter 9

Why Tragedy Did Not Flourish at Rome— National Legends Not Influential with the People—Fabulæ Prætextatæ—Roman Religion Not Ideal—Roman Love for Scenes of Real Action and Gorgeous Spectacle— Tragedy Not Patronised by the People— Pacuvius—His Dulorestes and Paulus

From what has been already said, it is sufficiently clear that the Italians, like all other Indo-European races, had some taste for the drama, but that this taste developed itself in a love for scenes of humorous satire. Whilst, therefore, Roman comedy originated in Italy, and was brought to perfection by the influence of Greek literature, Roman tragedy,[237] on the other hand, was transplanted from Athens, and with the exception of a very few cases, was never anything more than translation or imitation.

In the century, during which, together with comedy, it flourished and decayed, it boasted of five distinguished writers—Livius, Nævius, Ennius, Pacuvius, and Attius. The only claim of Atilius to be considered as a tragic poet is his having been the translator of one Greek tragedy. But, in after ages, Rome did not produce one tragic poet unless Varius can be considered an exception. His tragedy, *Thyestes*, which enjoyed so high a reputation amongst the critics of the Augustan age, that Quintilian, whose judgment generally agrees with them, pronounces it as able to bear comparison with the productions of the Greek tragic poets. It was acted on one occasion, namely, after the return of Octavius from the battle of Actium, and the poet received for it 1,000,000 sesterces (about 8,000*l.*)[238] The tragedies attributed to Seneca were never acted, and were only composed for reading and recitation.

Some account has already been given of Livius, Nævius, and Ennius, because their poetical reputation rests rather on other grounds than on their talents for dramatic poetry. But, before proceeding with the lives and writings of Pacuvius and Attius, it will be necessary to examine the causes which prevented tragedy from flourishing at Rome.

---

[237] See on this subject Lange, Vind. Trag. Rom. Leips. 1823.
[238] Hor. Serm. i. 9, 23; Ep. Pis. 55; Mart. Ep. viii. 18.

In endeavouring to account for this phenomenon, it is not sufficient to say, that in the national legends of the Hellenic race were imbodied subjects essentially of a dramatic character, and that epic poetry contained incidents, characters, sentiments, and even dramatic machinery, which only required to be put upon the stage. Doubtless the Greek epics and legends were an inexhaustible source of inspiration to the tragic poets. But it is also true that the Romans had national legends which formed the groundwork of their history, and were interwoven in their early literature. These legends, however, were private, not public property; they were preserved in the records and pedigrees of private families, and ministered to their glory, and were therefore more interesting to the members of these houses than to the people at large: they were not preserved as a national treasure by priestly families, like those of the Attic Eumolpidæ, nor did they twine themselves around the hearts of the Roman people, as the venerable traditions of Greece did around those of that nation. The Romans did not live in them—they were embalmed in their poets as curious records of antiquity or acknowledged fictions—they did not furnish occasions for awakening national enthusiasm. Although, therefore, they existed, they were comparatively powerless over the popular mind as elements of dramatic effect.

They were jealously preserved by illustrious houses, furnished materials in a dry and unadorned form to the annalists, and were embellished by the graphic power of the historian; but it is not probable that they ever constituted, in the same sense as the Greek legends, the folklore of the Roman people. In themselves, the lays of Horatius and of the lake Regillus were sufficiently stirring, and those of Lucretia, Coriolanus, and Virginia sufficiently moving, for tragedy, but they were not familiar to the masses of the people.

A period at length arrived in which there was a still further reason why Roman national legends, however adapted for tragedy they might be abstractedly, had not power to move the affections of the Roman populace. It ceased to have a personal interest in them. The masses had undergone a complete change. The Roman people of the most flourishing literary eras were not the descendants of those who maintained the national glory in the legendary period. Not only were almost all the patrician families then extinct, but war and poverty had extinguished the middle classes, and miserably thinned the lower orders. The old veterans of pure Roman blood who survived were settled at a distance from Rome in the different military colonies. Into the vacancy thus caused had poured thousands of slaves, captives in the bloody wars of Gaul and Spain, and Greece and Africa. These and their descendants replaced the ancient people. Many of them received liberty and franchise, and some by their talents and energy arrived at wealth and station. But they could not possibly be Romans at heart, or consider the past glories of their adopted country as their own. They were bound by no ties of old associations to it. The ancient legends had no especial interest in their eyes. It mattered little whether the incidents and characters of the tragedy which they witnessed were Greek or Roman. It was to the rise of this new element of population, and the displacement or absorption of the old race, that the decline of patriotism was owing—the careless disregard of everything except daily sustenance and daily amusement,[239] which paved the way for the empire, and marked the downfall of liberty. From this cause, also, resulted in some degree the non-influential position which national traditions occupied at Rome; and tragedy, though for a time popular, could not maintain its popularity. Thus it entirely disappeared; and, when it revived, it came forth, not as the favourite of the people, but under the patronage of select

---

[239] Juv. Sat. x. 80.

circles, and took its place, not like Athenian tragedy, as the leading literature of the age, but simply as one species of literary composition.

A people made up of these elements held out no temptation to the poet to leave the beaten track of his predecessor, the imitations of Greek tragedy. They were step-sons of Rome, as Scipio Æmilianus called the mob, who clamoured at his saying that the death of Tiberius Gracchus was just:—

> Mercedibus emptæ
> Et viles operæ quibus est mea Roma noverca.
> *Petron.* v. 164.

The poet's real patrons had been educated on Greek principles; and hence Greek taste was completely triumphant over national legend, and the heroes of Roman tragedy were those who were celebrated in Hellenic story. The Roman historical plays, (prætextatæ,) which approached most nearly towards realizing the idea of a national tragedy, were graceful compliments to distinguished individuals. They were usually performed at public funerals; and as, in the procession, masks representing the features of the deceased were borne by persons of similar stature, so incidents in his life formed the subject of the drama which was exhibited on the occasion.

The list of *Fabulæ Prætextatæ*, even if it were perfect, would occupy but narrow limits; nor had they sufficient merits to stand the test of time. They survive but in name, and the titles extant are but nine in number:——

> The Paulus of Pacuvius, which represented an incident in the life of L. Æmilius Paulus.[240]
> The Brutus, Æneadæ, and Marcellus of Attius.[241]
> Iter ad Lentulum, a passage in the life of Balbus.[242]
> Cato.
> Domitius Nero, by Maternus, in the time of Vespasian.
> Vescio, by the Satirist (?) Persius.
> Octavian, by Seneca, in the reign of Trajan.

Nor must it be forgotten, in comparing the influence which tragedy exercised upon the people of Athens and Rome, that with the former it was a part and parcel of the national religion. By it not only were the people taught to sympathize with their heroic ancestors, but their sympathies were hallowed. In Greece, the poet was held to be inspired—poetry was the voice of deified nature—the tongue in which the natural held communion with the supernatural, the visible with the invisible. With the Romans, poetry was nothing more than an amusement of the fancy; with the Greeks, it was a divinely originating emotion of the soul.

Hence, in Athens, the drama was, as it were, an act of worship,—it formed an integral part of a joyous, yet serious, religious festival. The theatre was a temple; the altar of a deity was its central point; and a band of choristers moved in solemn march and song in honour of the god, and, in the didactic spirit which sanctified their office, taught men lessons of virtue.

---

[240] Liv. xxii. 49.
[241] Cic. Att. xvi. 2, 5.
[242] Cic. Fam. x. 32.

Not that the audience entered the precincts with their hearts imbued with holy feelings, or with the thoughts of worshippers; but this is always the case when religious ceremonials become sensuous. The real object of the worship is by the majority forgotten. But still the Greeks were habituated unconsciously to be affected by the drama, as by a development of religious sentiments. With the Romans, the theatre was merely a place of secular amusement. The thymele existed no longer as a memorial of the sacrifice to the god. The orchestra, formerly consecrated to the chorus, was to them nothing more than stalls occupied by the dignitaries of the state. Dramas were certainly exhibited at the great Megalensian games, but they were only accessories to the religious character of the festival. A holy season implies rest and relaxation—a *holiday* in the popular sense of the word—and theatrical representations were considered a fit and proper species of pastime; but as religion itself did not exercise the same influence over the popular mind of the Romans which it did over that of the Greeks, so neither with the Romans did the drama stand in the place of the handmaid of religion.

Again, their religion, though purer and chaster, was not ideal like that of the Greeks. Its freedom from human passions removed it out of the sphere of poetry, and, therefore, it was neither calculated to move terror nor pity. The moral attributes of the Deity were displayed in stern severity; but neither the belief nor the ceremonial sought to inflame the heart of the worshipper with enthusiasm. Rome had no priestly caste uniting in one and the same person the character of the bard and of the minister of religion. In after ages, she learned from the Greeks to call the poet sacred, but the holiness which she attributed to his character was not the earnest belief of the heart. The Roman priests were civil magistrates; religion, therefore, became a part of the civil administration, and a political engine. It mattered little what was believed as true. The old national faith of Italy, not being firmly rooted in the heart, soon became obsolete: it readily admitted the engrafting of foreign superstitions. The old deities assumed the names of the Greek mythology: they exchanged their attributes and histories for those of Greek legend, and a host of strange gods filled their Pantheon. They had, however, no hold either on the belief or the love of the people: they were mythological and unreal characters, fit only to furnish subjects and embellishments for poetry.

Nor was the genius of the Roman people such as to sympathize with the legends of the past. The Romans lived in the present and the future, rather than in the past. The poet might call the age in which he lived degenerate, and look forward with mournful anticipations to a still lower degradation, whilst he looked back admiringly to bygone times. Through the vista of past years, Roman virtue and greatness seemed to his imagination magnified: he could lament, as Horace did, a gradual decay, which had not as yet reached its worst point:——

> Ætas parentum pejor avis tulit
> Nos nequiores mox daturos
> Progeniem vitiosiorem.
> *Od.* III. vi. 46.

But the people did not sympathize with these feelings: they delighted in action, not in contemplation and reflection. They did not look back upon their national heroes as demigods, or dream over their glories: they were pressing forward and extending the frontiers of their empire, bringing under their yoke tribes and nations which their forefathers had not known. If they regarded their ancestors at all, it was not in the light of men of heroic stature, as compared with themselves, but as those whom they could equal or even surpass: they lived in hope and not in memory.

These are not the elements of character which would lead a people to realize to themselves the ideal of tragedy. The tragic poet at Athens would have been sure that the same subject which inspired him would also interest his audience—that if his genius rose to the height which their critical taste demanded, he could reckon up the sympathy of a theatre crowded with ten thousand of his countrymen. A Roman tragic poet would have been deserted for any spectacle of a more stirring nature—his most affecting scenes and noble sentiments, for scenes of real action and real life. The bloody combats of the gladiators, the miserable captives and malefactors stretched on crosses, expiring in excruciating agonies, or mangled by wild beasts, were real tragedies—the sham fights and Naumachiæ, though only imitations, were real dramas, in which those pursuits which most deeply interested the spectators, which constituted their chief duties and highest glories, were visibly represented. Even gorgeous spectacles fed their personal vanity and pride in their national greatness. The spoil of conquered nations, borne in procession across the stage, reminded them of their triumphs and their victories; and the magnificent dress of the actors—the model of the captured city, preceded and followed by its sculptures in marble and ivory—represented in mimic grandeur the ovation or the triumph of some successful general, whose return from a distant expedition, laden with wealth, realized the rumours which had already arrived at the gates of Rome; whilst the scene, glittering with glass, and gold, and silver, and adorned with variegated pillars of foreign marble, told ostentatiously of their wealth and splendour.[243]

Again, the Romans were a rough, turbulent people, full of physical rather than intellectual energy, loving antagonism, courting peril, setting no value on human life or suffering. Their very virtues were stern and severe. The unrelenting justice of a Brutus, representing as it did the victory of principle over feeling, was to them the height of virtue. They were ready to undergo the extreme of physical torture with Regulus, and to devote themselves to death, like Curtius and the Decii. Hard and pitiless to themselves, they were, as might be expected, the same towards others. They were, in fact, strangers to both the passions, which it was the object of tragedy to excite and to purify, Pity and Terror.[244] They were too stern to pity, too unimaginative to be moved by the tales of wonder and deeds of horror which affected the tender and marvel-loving imagination of the Greeks. Being an active, and not a sentimental people, they did not appreciate moral suffering and the struggles of a sensitive spirit. They were moved only by scenes of physical suffering and agony.

The public games of Greece at Olympia, or the Isthmus, were bloodless and peaceful, and the refinements of poetry mingled with those which were calculated to invigorate the physical powers and develop manly beauty. Those of Rome were exhibitions, not of moral, but of physical courage and endurance: they were sanguinary and brutalizing,—the amusements of a nation to whom war was not a necessary evil or a struggle for national existence, for hearths and altars, but a pleasure and a pastime—the means of gratifying an aggressive ambition. The tragic feeling of Greece is represented by the sculptured grief of Niobe, that of Rome by the death-struggles which distort the features and muscles of the Laocoon. It was, if the expression is allowable, *amphitheatrical*, not *theatrical*.

---

[243] See Cic. de Off. ii. 16; Plin. H. N. 36, 3, &c.
[244] Arist. Poet.

To such a people the moral woes of tragedy were powerless; and yet it is to the people that the drama, if it is to flourish, must look for patronage. A refined and educated society, such as always existed at Rome during its literary period, might applaud a happy adaptation from the Greek tragedians, and encourage a poet in his task—for it is only an educated and refined taste which can appreciate such talent as skilful imitation displays; but a tragic drama under such circumstances could hardly hope to be national. Nor must it be forgotten, with reference to their taste for spectacle, that the artistic accessories of the drama would have a better chance of success with a people like the Romans than literary merit, because the pleasures of art are of a lower and more sensuous kind. Hence, in the popular eye, the decoration of the theatre and the costume of the performers naturally became the principal requisites, whilst the poet's office was considered subordinate to the manner in which the play was put upon the stage; and thus the degenerate theatrical taste which prevailed in the days of Horace called forth the poet's well-known and well-deserved criticism.[245]

It cannot, indeed, be asserted that tragedy was never, to a certain extent, an acceptable entertainment at Rome, but only that it never flourished at Rome as it did at Athens—that no Roman tragedies can, notwithstanding all that has been said in their praise and their defence, be compared with those of Greece, and that the tragic drama never maintained such a hold on the popular mind as not to be liable to be displaced by amusements of a more material and less intellectual kind. It was imitative and destitute of originality. It was introduced from without as one portion of the new literature; it did not grow spontaneously by a process of natural development out of preceding eras of epic and lyric poetry, and start into being, as it did at Athens, at the very moment when the public mind and taste was ready to receive and appreciate it.

Three eras, separated from one another by chasms, the second wider than the first, produced tragic poets. In the first of these flourished Livius Andronicus, Nævius, and Ennius; in the second Pacuvius and Attius; in the third Asinius Pollio[246] wrote tragedies, the plots of which, as the words of Virgil seem to imply, were taken from Roman history.[247] Varius either wrote, or, as some of the Scholiasts assert, stole, the "*Thyestes*" from Cassius or Virgil. Ovid attempted a "*Medea*," of which Quintilian speaks, as being, to say the least, a promising performance; and even the Emperor Augustus himself, together with other men of genius, tried their hands, though unsuccessfully, at tragedy. The epistle of Horace to the Pisos shows at once the prevalence of this taste, and that general ignorance of the rules and principles of art required instruction. Ten rhetorical dramas, attributed with good reason to the philosopher Seneca, complete the catalogue of tragedies belonging to this era, but with the exception of these, no specimens remain; most probably they did not merit preservation. The tragedies of the older school were of a higher stamp, and they kept their place in the public estimation long enough to give birth to the newer and inferior school. Passages from the old Latin tragedies quoted by Cicero well deserve the admiration with which he regarded them; and a fragment of the "*Prometheus*" of Attius is marked by a grandeur and sublimity which makes us regret the almost total loss of this branch of Roman literature.

---

[245] Epist. II. i. 182.
[246] Asinius Pollio is said by Seneca (Controv. iv. Præf.) to have introduced the practice of poets reading their works to a circle of friends.
[247] Ecl. iii. 86.

PACUVIUS (BORN B. C. 220.)

The era at which Roman tragedy reached its highest degree of perfection was the second of those mentioned, and was simultaneous with that of comedy. Both nourished together; for, whilst Terence was so successfully reproducing the wit and manners of the new Attic comedy, M. Pacuvius was enriching the Roman drama with free imitations of the Greek tragedians. He was a native of Brundisium, and nephew,[248] or, according to St. Jerome, grandson of the poet Ennius. Although born as early as B. C. 220, he does not appear to have attained the height of his popularity until B. C.[249] During his residence at Rome, where he remained until after his 80th year,[250] he distinguished himself as a painter as well as a dramatic poet; and one of his pictures in the temple of Hercules was thought only to be surpassed by the work of Fabius Pictor.[251] He formed one of that literary circle of which Lælius was so great an ornament. The close of his long life was passed in the retirement of Tarentum, where he died in the ninetieth year of his age. A simple and unpretending epigram is preserved by Aulus Gellius,[252] which may probably have been written by himself:——

> Adulescens, etsi properas, te hoc saxum rogat
> Uti ad se aspicias, deinde quod scriptum est, legas.
> Hic sunt poetæ Pacuvi Marci sita
> Ossa. Hoc volebam, nescius ne esses. Vale!

Pacuvius was a great favourite with those who could make allowances for the faults, and appreciate the merits, of the great writers of antiquity, and his verses were popular in the time of J. Cæsar;[253] and that lover of the old Roman literature, Cicero, though not blind to his faults, is warm in his commendations. He was not without admirers in the Augustan age, and even his defects had zealous defenders in the time of Persius amongst those who could scarcely discover a fault in any work which savoured of antiquity.[254] The archaic ruggedness of his language, his uncouth forms, such as *axim*, *tetinerim*, *egregiissimus*, and his unauthorized constructions, like *mihi piget*, were due to the unsettled state of the Latin language in his days. His strange combinations, such as *repandirostrum* and *incurvicervicum*, may possibly have been suggested by the study of Greek, and by his overweening admiration for its facility of composition. But his polish, pathos, and learning,[255] the harmony of his periods,[256] his eloquence,[257] his fluency, his word-painting,[258] are peculiarly his own.

The tragedies of Pacuvius were not mere translations, but adaptations of Greek tragedies to the Roman stage. The fragments which are extant are full of new and original thoughts. His plots were borrowed from the Greek, but the plan and treatment were his own. The lyric portion appears to have occupied an important place in his tragedies, and displays

---

[248] Math. Hist. of Class. Lit.; Bernhardy, Grund. 366.
[249] Hier. in Eus. Chron. Ol. 156, 3.
[250] Cic. Brut. 64.
[251] Plin. N. H. xxxv. 1, 4.
[252] N. A. i. 24; Meyer, Anth. xxiv.
[253] Cic. de Am. 7.
[254] Pers. Sat. i. 77.
[255] Hor. Ep. II. i. 55.
[256] Ad Heren. iv. 4 and 11, 23.
[257] Varro ap. Gel. vii. 14.
[258] Cic. de Div. i. 14; Orat. iii. 39.

considerable imaginative power. It is evident that his mind only required suggestions, and was sufficiently original, to form new combinations. The titles of thirteen of his tragedies are preserved,[259] of which the most celebrated were the "*Antiopa*" and "*Dulorestes*" (Orestes in Slavery.) Of the former, the only fragment extant is one severely criticised by Persius. The latter was principally founded on the "*Iphigenia in Tauris*" of Euripides,[260] although the author was evidently inspired with the poetical conceptions of Æschylus. In fact, Pacuvius is less Euripidean than the other Roman tragic poets. The very roughness of his style and audacity of his expressions have somewhat of the solemn grandeur and picturesque boldness which distinguish the father of Attic tragedy.

The subject of the "*Dulorestes*" was the adventures of the son of Agamemnon. When driven from the palace of his ancestors, he was in exile and in slavery.[261] On the first representation of this play, the generous friendship of Orestes and Pylades called forth the most enthusiastic applause from the audience, who then probably heard the legend for the first time. "What acclamations," says Lælius,[262] "resounded through the theatre at the representation of the new play of my guest and friend, M. Pacuvius, when the king, being ignorant which of the two was Orestes, Pylades affirmed that he was Orestes, that he might be put to death in his place, whilst Orestes persevered in asserting that he was the man!"

One of his plays, "*Paulus*," was a *fabula prætextata*: its subject was taken entirely from Roman history, the hero being L. Æm. Paulus, the conqueror of Perseus. Besides tragedies, the grammarians have attributed to him one satura.[263] He is said also to have written comedies; but there is no evidence in favour of any, with the exception of one, entitled "*Mercator*."

---

[259] See Smith's Dict.
[260] De Pac. Dul. A. Steigl. Leips. 1826.
[261] Pierron, p. 162.
[262] Cic. de Am. vii.
[263] Diom. iii.

Chapter 10

L. ATTIUS—HIS TRAGEDIES AND FRAGMENTS—OTHER WORKS—TRAGEDY DISAPPEARED WITH HIM—ROMAN THEATRES—TRACES OF THE SATIRIC SPIRIT IN GREECE—ROMAN SATIRE—LUCILIUS—CRITICISMS OF HORACE, CICERO, AND QUINTILIAN—PASSAGE QUOTED BY LACTANTIUS—LÆVIUS, A LYRIC POET

L. ATTIUS (BORN ABOUT B. C. 170.)

Although born about fifty years later than Pacuvius,[264] Attius was almost his contemporary, and a competitor for popular applause. The amiable old poet lived on the most friendly terms with his young rival; and A. Gellius tells us that after he withdrew from the literary society of Rome to retirement at Tarentum, he on one occasion invited the rising poet to be his guest for some days, and made him read his tragedy of "*Atreus.*" Pacuvius criticised it kindly, fairly praised the grandeur of the poetry, but said that it was somewhat harsh and hard. "You are right," replied Attius, "but I hope to improve. Fruits which are at first hard and sour, become soft and mellow, but those which begin by being soft, end in being rotten." Valerius Maximus[265] relates that in the assemblies of the poets he refused to rise at the entrance of J. Cæsar, because he felt that in the republic of letters he was the superior. If this anecdote is genuine, it does not prove that the aged poet was guilty of unwarrantable self-esteem, for Cæsar must then have been quite a youth, and if he had any claim to reputation as a poet, he was, at any rate, not yet distinguished as a warrior or a statesman. Amongst the great men whose friendship the poet enjoyed was Dec. Brutus, who was consul A. U. C. 616.[266] Nothing more is known respecting his private history, except that his parents were freedmen, and that he was one of the colonists settled at Pisaurum, where, in after times, a farm or estate (fundus Attianus) continued to bear his name. His tragedies were very

---
[264] Cic. Brut. 64.
[265] Lib. iii. 7, 11.
[266] Cic. Brut. 64; Gell. xiii. 2; Brut. 28.

numerous. He is said to have written more than fifty. Three at least were *prætextatæ*, their titles being "*Brutus*," "*The Æneadæ*," or "*Decius*,"[267] and "*Marcellus*." His "*Trachiniæ*" and "*Phœnissæ*" were almost translations, the one from Sophocles, the other from Euripides; the rest were free imitations of Greek tragedies. They were distinguished both for sublimity and pathos; and although he was warmed by the fiery spirit and tragic grandeur of Æschylus, he evidently evinced a predilection for Sophocles.[268] His taste is chastened, his sentiments noble, his versification elegant. His language is almost classical, and was deservedly admired by the ancients for its polish as well as its vigour. The "*Brutus*" was written at the suggestion of his friend Decimus. The plot was the expulsion of the Tarquins, the hero Brutus, the heroine Lucretia. He had chosen one of the noblest romances in Roman history. Two passages,[269] quoted by Cicero, are all that remain of this national tragedy. In them the tyrant relates to the augurs a dream which had haunted him, and they, at his request, give their interpretation of it. Varro has also preserved the soliloquy of Hercules in the agonies of death, from the Trachiniæ,[270] a noble paraphrase of Sophocles. This fine specimen of his genius extends to the length of forty-five lines. In another passage, Philoctetes pours forth his sufferings in language as touching as the original Greek; and in a third, Prometheus, now delivered from the tyranny of Jupiter, addresses to his assembled Titans a strain of indignant eloquence not unworthy of Æschylus.[271] The following lines from the "*Phœnissæ*" and the "*Complaint of Philoctetes*," are, though brief, fair examples of his language and versification:——

> Sol, qui micantem candido curru atque equis
> Flammam citatis fervido ardore explicas,
> Quianam tam adverso augurio et inimico omine
> Thebis radiatum lumen ostendis tuum![272]
> Heu! quis salsis fluctibus mandet
> Me ex sublimi vertice saxi,
> Jamjam absumor; conficit animam
> Vis volneris, ulceris æstus.[273]

These are the most important of the numerous fragments which are extant of the various tragedies of the lofty Attius.[274] He has been considered by some as the founder of the *Tragœdia Prætextatæ*. This, however, is not true, for there is no doubt that such dramas were written by his predecessors. Nevertheless, he brought the natural tragedy to its highest state of perfection.

The time was now evidently approaching when the Romans were beginning to show, that although they did not possess the inventive genius of the Greeks, they were capable of stripping their native language of its rudeness, and of transferring into it the beauties of Greek thought; that they were no longer mere servile copyists, but could use Greek poetry as furnishing suggestions for original efforts. They could not quarry for themselves, but they

---

[267] Cic. de Leg. ii. 21; Pro Arch. ii.
[268] Bernhardy, 367; Hor. Ep. II. i. 56; Quint, x. i. 97
[269] De Divin. i. 22; Bothe, Poet. Scen. fr. p. 191.
[270] Bothe, p. 246.
[271] Tusc. Disp. ii. 10; Bothe, p. 239.
[272] Bothe, p. 238.
[273] Ibid. p. 231.
[274] Hor. Ep. II. i. 55.

could now build up Greek materials into a glowing and polished edifice, of which the details were new and the effect original.

The metres which Attius used were chiefly the iambic trimeter and the anapæstic dimeter, but his *prætextatæ* were written in trochaic and iambic tetrameters, the rhythm of which proves that his ear was more refined than that of his predecessors.[275]

It is not known whether he was the author of any comedies, but he was a historian, an antiquarian, and a critic, as well as a poet. He left behind him a review of dramatic poetry, entitled "*Libri Didascalion*," "*Roman Annals*," in verse, and two other works—"*Libri Pragmaticon*," and "*Parerga*." The former of these is quoted by Nonius, and A. Gellius. He died at an advanced age, probably about A. U. C. 670, and is thus a link, as it were, which connects the first literary period with the age of Cicero; for the great orator was personally acquainted with him, and at his death must have been about twenty-two years of age.

With Attius Latin tragedy disappeared. The tragedies of the third period were written expressly for reading and recitation, and not for the stage. They may have deserved the commendations which they obtained, but the merit and talent which they displayed were simply rhetorical, and not dramatic; they were dramatic poems, not dramas.

The state of political affairs, which synchronized with the death of Attius, was less congenial than ever to the tragic muse. Real and bloody tragedies were being enacted, and there was no room in the heart of the Roman people for fictitious woes. If it was improbable that a people who delighted in the sanguinary scenes of the amphitheatre should sympathize with the sorrows of a hero in tragedy, it was almost impossible that tragedy should flourish when Rome itself was a theatre in which scenes of horror were daily enacted.

Either then, or not long before, the terrible domination of Cinna and Marius had begun. Massacre and violence raged through the streets of Rome. The best and noblest fell victims to the raging thirst for blood. The aged Marius, distracted by unscrupulous ambition and savage passions, died amidst the delirious ravings of remorse, and thus made way for the tyranny of his perjured accomplice Cinna. Still there was no respite or interruption. The cruel Sulla sent his orders from Antemnæ to slaughter 8,000 prisoners in cold blood. The massacre had hardly begun when he himself arrived, had taken his place in the Senate; and the shrieks of his murdered victims were audible in the house whilst he was coolly speaking. This was the beginning of horrors: the notorious proscription followed. Besides other victims, 5,600 Roman knights perished.

Amidst such scenes as these, the voice of the tragic muse was hushed. Depending for her very existence on the breath of popular favour, she necessarily could not find supporters, and so languished and was silenced. It might appear surprising that literature of any kind should have lived through such times of savage barbarism. But other literature is not dependent upon public patronage: it finds a refuge beneath the shelter of the private dwelling. The literary man finds friends and patrons amongst those who, devoted to the humanities of intellectual pursuits, shuns the scenes of revolutionary strife and the struggles of selfish ambition. Even Sulla himself had a polished and refined taste; and, when he resigned the Dictatorship, passed those hours of retirement in literary studies which were not devoted to depravity and licentiousness.

The style in which the Roman theatres were built, indicate that whatever taste for tragedy the Roman people possessed had now decayed. The huge edifice erected by Pompey was too

---

[275] See Nieb. Lect. 88.

vast for the exhibition of tragedy. The forty thousand spectators which it contained could scarcely hear the actor, still less could they see the expression of human passions and emotions. The two theatres, placed on pivots, back to back, so that they could be wheeled round and form one vast amphitheatre, show how an interest in the drama was shared with the passion for spectacle; and provision was thus publicly made for gratifying that corrupt taste which had arrived at its zenith in the time of Horace, and, as we have seen, interrupted even comedy so early as the times of Terence.

Satire

The invention of satire is universally attributed to the Romans, and this assertion is true as far as the external form is concerned; but the spirit of satire is found in many parts of the literature of Greece. It animated the Homeric Margites, the poem on woman by Simonides, the bitter lyrical iambics of Archilochus, Stesichorus' attack on Helen, and especially, as Horace says, the old comedy of Eupolis, Cratinus, and Aristophanes. Some resemblance may also be discerned between Roman satire and the Greek Silli, poems belonging to the declining period of Greek literature,[276] the design of which was to attack vice and folly with severe ridicule.[277]

Satire is, in fact, if Horace may be believed, the form which comedy took amongst the people with whom the drama did not flourish. Ennius was the inventor of the name, but Lucilius[278] was the father of satire, in the proper sense, and was at Rome what the writers of the old comedy were at Athens. It subsequently occupied a wider field: Persius and Juvenal confined themselves to its didactic purpose, but Horace made it a vehicle for the narration of amusing adventure, and picturesque descriptions of human life.

The Satires of Lucilius mark an era in Roman literature, and prove that a love for this species of poetry had already made great progress. Hitherto, science, literature, and art, had been considered the province of slaves and freedmen. The stern old Roman virtue despised such sedentary and inactive employment as intellectual cultivation, and thought it unworthy of the warrior and statesman. Some of the higher classes loved literature and patronised it, but did not make it their pursuit. Cato blamed M. Fulvius Nobilior for being accompanied by poets when he proceeded to his provincial government,[279] and did not until advanced in years undertake to study Greek.[280] C. Lucilius was by birth of equestrian rank, the first Roman knight who was himself a poet.[281] He was born at Suessa Aurunca, B. C. 148,[282] and lived to

---

[276] B. C. 279.
[277] The etymology of σίλλοι is unknown. Casaubon derived the word from συλλαίνειν, to scoff. The probability, however, is that the substantive is the root of the verb. The invention of the *Silli* has been ascribed by some to Xenophanes, the philosopher of Colophon. He was the author of a didactic poem, and his invectives were directed against the absurd and erroneous doctrines of his predecessors. Timon, a skeptical philosopher, who lived in the reign of Ptolemy Philadelphus, was undoubtedly the author of Silli. Some of these are dialogues, in which one of the persons is Xenophanes, whence perhaps he was erroneously considered the inventor of this kind of poetry. All the Silli of Timon are epic parodies, and their subject a ludicrous and skeptical attack on philosophy of every kind. Fragments of Silli are preserved by Diogenes, Lucilius, and Chrysostom.—Ad. Alex. Orat. See also Brunck's Analecta, and Suidas *s. vv.* συλλαίνειν, Τίμων.
[278] Hor. Sat. i. 4, 10.
[279] Cic. Tusc. i. 2.
[280] Aurelius Victor states (De Vit. Illust. xlvii.) that Cato took lessons in Greek from Ennius.
[281] Juv. Sat. i. 20.

the age of forty-six years.[283] At fourteen, he served under Scipio at the siege of Numantia.[284] He was the maternal great-uncle of Pompey, and numbered amongst his friends and patrons, Africanus and Lælius. His Satires were comprised in thirty books, of which the first twenty and the thirtieth were written in hexameters, the rest in iambics or trochaics. Numerous fragments are still extant, some of considerable length. The Satires were probably arranged according to their subject-matter; for those in the first book are on topics connected with religion, whilst those in the ninth treat of literary and grammatical criticism. His versification is careless and unrefined; very inferior in this respect to that of his predecessors. He sets at defiance the laws of prosody, and almost returns to the usage of that period in which the ear was the only judge.

The prejudices of Horace[285] against the ancient Roman literature render him an unsafe guide in criticism. Even in his own time his attacks were considered by some indefensible; but his strictures on the style of Lucilius are not undeserved; it was unmusical, affected, and incorrect. His sentences are frequently ill-arranged, and therefore deficient in perspicuity. His mixture of Greek and Latin expressions, without that skill and art with which Horace considered it allowable to enrich the vernacular language, is itself offensive to good taste, and is rendered still more disagreeable by unnecessary diminutives and forced alliteration. On these grounds, and on these alone, he merits the contemptuous criticism of Horace.

His real defect was want of facility; and it is not improbable that, if prose had been considered a legitimate vehicle, he would have preferred pouring forth in that unrestricted form his indignant eloquence, rather than that, as Horace says, every verse should have cost him many scratchings of the head, and biting his nails to the quick. Whilst the criticism of Horace errs on the side of severity, that of Cicero[286] is somewhat too partial: firstly, because he himself was deficient in poetical facility; secondly, because in his time there were no models of perfection wherewith to compare the works of Lucilius. The judgment of Quintilian[287] is moderate; and although the taste for poetry was then corrupted by a love of quietness and rhetorical affectation, the praise is well merited which he bestows on the frank honesty and biting wit of the Satires of Lucilius. As he took the writers of old Attic comedy for his models, it cannot be a matter of surprise that he occasionally added force to his attacks on vice by coarseness and personality. Like them, if Lucilius found any one who deserved rebuke for his crimes, he did not trouble himself to make general remarks, and to attack vice in the abstract, but to illustrate his principles by living examples.

The education of Lucilius had probably been desultory, and his course of study not sufficiently strict to give the rich young Roman knight the accurate training, the critical knowledge, necessary to make him a poet as well as a satirist. It had given him learning and erudition—it had furnished him with the wealth of two languages, both of which he used whenever he thought they supplied him with a two-edged weapon—but it had not sufficiently cultivated his ear and refined his taste. On the other hand, his Satires must have possessed nobler qualities than those of style.

---

[282] Hieron. Chron. Euseb.
[283] In defence of the chronology of Lucilius' life, see Smith's Dictionary of Biography, *s. v.* Lucilius.
[284] Vell. Paterc. ii. 9.
[285] See Sat. I. iv.; I. x.; I. i. 29, &c.
[286] De Orat. ii. 6; De Fin. i. 3.
[287] Inst. Or. x. i.

He was evidently a man of high moral principle, though stern and stoical, devotedly attached to the cause of virtue, a relentless enemy of vice and profligacy, a gallant and fearless defender of truth and honesty. He must have felt with Juvenal, "difficile est satiram non scribere." He was under an obligation which he could not avoid. What cared he for correct tetrameters, or heroics, or senarii, so that he could crush effeminacy, and gluttony, and self-indulgence, and restore the standard of ancient morals, to which he looked back with admiration?

This chivalrous devotion inspired him with eloquence, and gave a dignity to his rude verses, although it did not invest them with the graces and charms of poetry. Nor is it only when he declares open war against corruption that he must have made his adversaries tremble, or his victims, conscience-stricken, writhe beneath his knife. His encomiums upon virtue form as striking pictures; but in both it is the masterly outline of the drawing which amazes and instructs, not the mere accessory of the colouring. See, for example, the following noble passage, with its unselfish conclusion, preserved by Lactantius:[288]—

> Virtus, Albine, est pretium persolvere verum
> Queis in versamur, queis vivimu' rebu' potesse.
> Virtus est homini scire id quod quæque habeat res.
> Virtus, scire homini rectum, utile, quid sit honestum,
> Quæ bona, quæ mala item quid inutile turpe inhonestum.
> Virtus, quærendæ finem rei scire modumque;
> Virtus, divitiis pretium persolvere posse.
> Virtus, id dare quod reipsa debetur honori,
> Hostem esse atque inimicum hominum morumque malorum;
> Contra, defensorem hominum morumque bonorum;
> Magnificare hos, his bene velle, his vivere amicum;
> Commoda præterea patriai prima putare,
> Deinde parentum, tertia jam postremaque nostra.

Had they been extant, we should have found useful information and instruction in his faithful pictures of Roman life and manners in their state of moral transition—amusement in such pieces as his journal of a progress from Rome to Capua, from which Horace borrowed the idea of his journey to Brundisium, whilst in his love poems, addressed to his mistress, Collyra, we should have traced the tender sympathies of human nature, which the sternness of stoicism was unable to overcome.

Besides satire, Lucilius is said to have attempted lyric poetry: if this be the case, it is by no means surprising that no specimens have stood the test of time, for he possessed none of the qualifications of a lyric poet.

After the death of Lucilius, satire languished. Varro Atacinus attempted it and failed.[289] Half a century subsequently it assumed a new garb in the descriptive scenes of Horace, and put forth its original vigour in the burning thoughts of Persius and Juvenal.

---

[288] Inst. Div. vi. 5.
[289] Hor. Sat. I. x. 46.

Lævius

This literary period was entirely destitute of lyric poetry, unless Niebuhr is correct in supposing that Lævius flourished contemporaneously with Lucilius.[290] Nothing is known of his history; and such uncertainty prevails respecting him that his name is constantly confounded with those of Livius and Nævius. It is not improbable, that some passages attributed to them, which appear to belong to a later literary age, are, in reality, the work of Lævius—for example, the hexameters which are found in the Latin Odyssey of Livius. He translated the Cyprian poems, and wrote some fugitive amatory pieces entitled Erotopægnia. They seem to have possessed neither the graceful simplicity nor the tender warmth which are essential to lyric poetry, although they perhaps attained as great elegance of expression as the state of the language then admitted. Short fragments are preserved by Apuleius and in the *Noctes Atticæ* of A. Gellius.[291]

---

[290] Nieb. Lect. lxxxviii.
[291] Lib. ii. 24; xix. 9.

Chapter 11

PROSE LITERATURE—PROSE SUITABLE TO ROMAN GENIUS—HISTORY, JURISPRUDENCE, AND ORATORY—PREVALENCE OF GREEK— Q. FABIUS PICTOR—L. CINCIUS ALIMENTUS—C. ACILIUS GLABRIO—VALUE OF THE ANNALISTS—IMPORTANT LITERARY PERIOD, DURING WHICH CATO CENSORIUS FLOURISHED—SKETCH OF HIS LIFE— HIS CHARACTER, GENIUS, AND STYLE

Prose was far more in accordance with the genius of the Romans than poetry. As a nation they had little or no ideality or imaginative power, no enthusiastic love of natural beauty, no acute perception of the sympathy and relation existing between man and the external world. In the Greek mind a love of country and a love of nature held a divided empire—they were poets as well as patriots. Roman patriotism had indeed its dark side—an unbounded lust of dominion, an unscrupulous ambition to extend the power and glory of the republic; but, nevertheless, it prompted a zealous devotion to whatever would promote national independence and social advancement. Statesmanship, therefore, and the subjects akin to it, constituted the favourite civil pursuit of an enlightened Roman, who sought a distinguished career of public usefulness; and, therefore, that literature which tended to advance the science of social life had a charm for him which no other literature possessed.

The branches of knowledge which would engage his attention were History, Jurisprudence, and Oratory. They would be studied with a view to utility, and in a practical spirit they would require a scientific and not an artistic treatment; and, therefore, their natural language would be prose and not poetry. As matter was more valued than manner by this utilitarian people, it was long before it was thought necessary to embellish prose literature with the graces of composition. The earliest orators spoke with a rude and vigorous eloquence which is always captivating: they wrote but little; their style was stiff and dry, and very inferior to their speaking. Cato's prose was less rugged than that of his contemporaries or even his immediate successors. Sisenna was the first historian to whom gracefulness and polish have been attributed; and C. Gracchus is spoken of as a single exception to the orators of his age, on account of the rhythmical modulation of his prose sentences—a quality which he probably owed not more to a delicate ear than to the softening influence of a mother's education. Even the prose of that celebrated model of refinement and good taste, C. Lælius, was harsh and unmusical.[292]

Besides the influence which the practical character of the Roman mind exercised upon prose writing, it must not be forgotten that Roman literature was imitative: its end and object, therefore, were not invention, but erudition; it depended for its existence on learning, and was almost synonymous with it. This principle gave a decidedly historical bias to the Roman intellect: an historical taste pervades a great portion of the national literature. There is a manifest tendency to study subjects in an historical point of view. It will be seen hereafter that it is not like the Greek, original and inventive, but erudite and eclectic. The historic principle is the great characteristic feature of the Roman mind; consequently, in this branch of literature, the Romans attained the highest reputation, and may fairly stand forth as competitors with their Greek instructors. Not that they ever entirely equalled them; for though they were practical, vigorous, and just thinkers, they never attained that comprehensive and philosophical spirit which distinguished the Greek historians.

The work of an historian was, in the earliest times, recognised as not unworthy of a Roman. It was not like the other branches of literature, in which the example was first set by slaves and freedmen. Those who first devoted themselves to the pursuit were also eminent in the public service of their country. Fabius Pictor was of an illustrious patrician family. Cincius Alimentus, Fulvius Nobilior, and others, were of free and honourable birth. Such were Roman historians until the time of Sulla; for L. Otacilius Pilitus, who flourished at that period, was the first freedman who began to write history.[293] [294]

Again, the science of jurisprudence formed an indispensable part of statesmanship. It was a study which recommended itself by its practical nature: it could not be stigmatized even by the busiest as an idle and frivolous pursuit, whilst the constitutional relation which subsisted between patron and client, rendered the knowledge of its principles, to a certain extent, absolutely necessary. Protection from wrong was the greatest boon which the strong could confer upon the weak, the learned on the unlearned. It was, therefore, the most efficacious method of gaining grateful and attached friends; and by their support, the direct path was opened to the highest political positions. It is not, therefore, to be wondered at that, even when elegant literature was in its infancy, so many names are found of men illustrious as jurists and lawyers.

Practical statesmanship, in like manner, gave an early encouragement to oratory. It is peculiarly the literature of active life. The possession of eloquence rendered a man more efficient as a soldier and as a citizen. Great as is the force of native, unadorned eloquence, vigorous common sense, honest truthfulness, and indignant passion, nature would give way to art as taste became more cultivated. Nor could the Romans long have the finished models of Greek eloquence before their eyes, without transferring to the forum or the senate-house somewhat of their simple grandeur and majestic beauty.

The first efforts of the Roman historians were devoted to the transfer of the records of poetry into prose, as their more appropriate and popular vehicle. The national lays which

---

[292] See Nieb. Lect. lxxix. and Schol. in Cic. Orell. ii. p. 283.
[293] Suet. de Clar. Rhet. iii.
[294] The fragments of the ancient Roman historians have been collected by Augustus Krause, and published at Berlin in 1833.

tradition had handed down were the storehouses which they ransacked to furnish a supply of materials. As far as the records of authentic history are concerned, they performed the functions of simple annalists: they related events almost in the style of public monuments, without any attempt at ornament, without picturesque detail or political reflection. When Cicero compares the style of Fabius Pictor, Cato, and Piso, to that of the old Greek logographers,[295] Pherecydes, Hellanicus, and Acusilaus, the points of resemblance which he instances are, that both neglected ornament, were careful only that their statements should be intelligible, and thought the chief excellence of a writer was brevity. Probably the subject-matter of the Roman annalists was the more valuable, whilst the Greeks had the advantage in liveliness and skill. Some of the earliest historians wrote in Greek instead of Latin. Even, in later times, such men as Sulla and Lucullus, and also Cn. Aufidius, who flourished during the boyhood of Cicero, wrote their memoirs in a foreign tongue. There was some reason for this. The language in which the higher classes received their education was Greek—the tutors, even the nurses, were Greek, as well as the librarians, secretaries, and confidential servants in most distinguished families. Such was the humanizing spirit of literature that these distinguished foreigners found an asylum in the households of noble Romans, notwithstanding the severity with which the law treated prisoners of war. Fashionable conversation, moreover, was interlarded with Greek phrases, and, in some houses, Greek was habitually spoken. Even so late as the times of Cicero,[296] Greek literature was read and studied in almost every part of the civilized world, while the works of Latin writers were only known within the circumscribed limits of Italy.

Q. FABIUS PICTOR

The most ancient prose writer of Roman history was Q. Fabius Pictor, the contemporary of Nævius. He belonged to that branch of the noble house of the Fabii, which derived its distinguishing appellation from the eminence of its founder as a painter. The temple of Salus, which he painted, was dedicated B. C. 302, by the dictator, C. Junius Bubulcus; and this oldest known specimen of Roman fine art remained until the conflagration of the temple in the reign of Claudius. It must, therefore, have been subjected to the criticisms of an age capable of forming a correct judgment respecting its merits; and it appears from the testimony of antiquity to have possessed the two essentials of accurate drawing and truthful colouring, and to have been free from the fault of conventional treatment.[297]

The Fabii were an intellectual family as well as a distinguished one: perhaps the numerous records of their exploits which exist were, in some degree, owing to their learning. The grandson of the eminent artist was Fabius Pictor the historian. Livy[298] continually refers to him, and throughout his narrative of the Hannibalian war, he professes implicit confidence in him on the grounds of his being a contemporary historian,[299] (*æqualem temporibus hujusce belli;*) he is likewise the authority on whom the greatest reliance was placed by Dion Cassius

---

[295] De Orat. ii. 12.
[296] Pro Arch. x.
[297] Dion. xvi. 6; Nieb. H. R. iii. 356.
[298] Lib. i. 44, 45; ii. 40; viii. 30, &c.
[299] Lib. xxii. 7.

and Appian. Nor did the accurate and faithful Polybius consider him otherwise than trustworthy upon the whole, although he accuses him of partiality towards his countrymen.[300] Niebuhr[301] attributes to Fabius Pictor the accurate knowledge of constitutional history displayed by Dion Cassius, and acknowledges how deeply we are indebted to him for the information which we possess concerning the changes which took place in the Roman constitution. It is to his care that we owe the faithfulness of Dion, whilst Dionysius and Livy too often lead us astray. It constitutes some justification of his partiality as an historian, that Philinus of Agrigentum had also written a history of the first Punic war in a spirit hostile to Rome, and that this provoked Pictor to a defence of his country's honour. His work was written in Greek, and its principal subject was a history of the first and second Punic wars, especially that against Hannibal. It has been held by some, on the authority of a passage in the "*De Oratore*" of Cicero,[302] that he wrote in Latin as well as in Greek; but Niebuhr believes that Cicero is in error, and has confused him with a Latin annalist, named F. Max. Servilianus. The period to which his work extended is uncertain; but the last event alluded to by Livy, on his authority, is the battle of Trasymenus,[303] and the last occasion on which he mentions his name is when he records his return from an embassy to Delphi in the following year.[304] The earlier history of Rome was prefixed by way of introduction; for his object was not merely to assist in constructing the rising edifice of Roman literature, but to spread the glory of his country throughout that other great nation of antiquity, which now, for the first time, came in contact with a worthy rival. The pontifical annals, the national ballads, the annals of his own house, so rich in legendary tales of heroism, furnished him with ample materials; but he is also said to have drawn largely on the stores of a Greek author, named Diocles, a native of Peparethus, who had preceded him in the work of research and accumulation.

L. CINCIUS ALIMENTUS

Contemporary with Fabius was the other annalist of the second Punic war, L. Cincius Alimentus. He was prætor in Sicily[305] in the ninth year of the war, and took a prominent part in it.[306] The soldiers who fought at Cannæ[307] were placed at his disposal, his period of command was prolonged, and after his return home he was sent as *legatus* to the consul Crispinus, on the occasion of the melancholy death of his colleague, Marcellus.[308] Sometime after this, he was taken prisoner by Hannibal.[309] Like Fabius, he wrote his work in Greek, and prefixed to it a brief abstract of early Roman history.[310]

---

[300] Pol. i. 14.
[301] Lect. R. H. iii. xxvi.
[302] Lib. ii. 12.
[303] Liv. xxii. 7.
[304] Lib. xxiii. ii.; B. C. 216; A. U. C. 538.
[305] A. U. C. 544; B. C. 210.
[306] Liv. xxvi. 23.
[307] Ibid. 28.
[308] Ibid. xxvii. 29.
[309] Ibid. xxi. 31.
[310] Dionys. i. 6.

Livy speaks of him as a diligent antiquarian, and appeals to his authority to establish the Etruscan origin of the custom of the dictator driving a nail into the temple of Jupiter Optimus Maximus.[311] As his accurate investigation of original monuments gives a credibility to his early history, so his being personally engaged in the war in a high position, renders him trustworthy in the later periods. It is also said that, when he was a prisoner of war, Hannibal, who delighted in the society of literary men, treated him with great kindness and consideration, and himself communicated to him the details of his passage across the Alps into Italy.

To him, therefore, and to the opportunities which he enjoyed of gaining information, we owe the credibility of this portion of Livy's history[312] on a point on which authors were at variance, namely, the number of Hannibal's forces at this time. Livy appeals to the statement of Cincius as settling the question, and says, Hannibal himself informed Cincius how many troops he had lost between the passage of the Rhone and his descent into Italy.

His accurate habit of mind must have made his annals a most valuable work; and, therefore, it was most important that the variation of his early chronology from that which is commonly received should be explained and reconciled. This task Niebuhr has satisfactorily accomplished. He supposes that Cincius took cyclical years of ten months, which were used previous to the reign of Tarquinius Priscus, in the place of common years of twelve months. The time which had elapsed between the building of Rome and this epoch was, according to the pontifical annals, 132 years. The error, therefore, due to this miscalculation would be 132 - 132 + 10⁄12 = 22 years. If this be added to the common date of the building of Rome, B. C. 753 = Ol. vii. 2, the result is the date given by Cincius, namely Ol. vii. 4.[313]

C. ACILIUS GLABRIO

A few words may be devoted to C. Acilius Glabrio, the third representative of the Græco-Roman historic literature. Very little is known respecting him. He was quæstor A. U. C. 551, tribune A. U. C. 557, and subsequently attained senatorial rank; for Gellius[314] relates that, when the three Athenian philosophers visited Rome as ambassadors, Acilius introduced them to the senate and acted as interpreter. His story was considered worthy of translation by an author named Claudius, and to this translation reference is twice made by Livy.[315]

Valuable though the works of these annalists must have been as historical records, and as furnishing materials for more thoughtful and philosophical minds, they are only such as could have existed in the infancy of a national literature. They were a bare compilation of facts, the mere scaffolding and framework of history; they were diversified by no critical remarks or political reflections. The authors made no use of their facts, either to deduce or to illustrate principles. With respect to style, they were meager, insipid, and jejune.

---

[311] Liv. vii. 3.
[312] See, on this subject, Lachmann de Font. Hist. Ti. Liv.
[313] See Dr. Smith's Dict. of Antiq. *s. v.*
[314] N. A. vii. 14.
[315] Lib. xxv. 39; xxxv. 14.

M. Porcius Cato Censorius

The versatility and variety of talent displayed by Cato claim for him a place amongst orators, jurists, economists, and historians. It is, however, amongst the latter, as representatives of the highest branch of prose literature, that we must speak of the author of the "*Origines.*" His life extends over a wide and important period of literary history: everything was in a state of change—morals, social habits, literary taste. Not only the influence of Greek literature, but also that of the moral and metaphysical creed of Greek philosophy, was beginning to be felt when Cato's manly and powerful intellect was flourishing. When he filled the second public office to which the Roman citizen aspired, Nævius was still living. He was censor when Plautus died; and, before his own life ended, the comedies of Terence had been exhibited on the Roman stage.

Three political events took place during his lifetime, which must have exercised an important influence on the mental condition of the Roman people. When Macedonia, at the defeat of Perseus,[316] was reduced to the condition of a Roman province, nearly a thousand Achæans, amongst whom was the historian Polybius, were sent to Rome, and detained in Italy as hostages during nearly seventeen years. The thirteenth year from that event witnessed the dawn of philosophy at Rome, for previously to this epoch, the philosophical schools of Magna Græcia appear to have been unnoticed and disregarded. But now[317] Carneades the academic, Critolaus the peripatetic, and Diogenes the stoic,[318] came to Rome as ambassadors from Athens, and delivered philosophical lectures, which attracted the attention of the leading statesmen, whilst the doctrines which they taught excited universal alarm. The following year Crates arrived as ambassador from Attalus, king of Pergamus, and during his stay delighted the literary society of the capital with commentaries on the Greek poets.[319] It is not surprising that one who lived through a period during which Greek literature had such favourable opportunities of being propagated by some of its most distinguished professors, sufficiently overcame his prejudices as to learn in his old age the language of a people whom he both hated and despised.

M. Porcius Cato Censorius was born at Tusculum, B. C. 234.[320] His family was of great antiquity, and numbered amongst its members many who were distinguished for their courage in war and their integrity in peace. His boyhood was passed in the healthy pursuits of rural life, at a small Sabine farm belonging to his father; and his mind, invigorated by stern and hardy training, was early directed to the study as well as the practice of agriculture. To this rugged yet honest discipline may be traced the features of his character as displayed in after life, his prejudices as well as his virtues.

He became a soldier at a very early age, B. C. 217, served in the Hannibalian war, was under the command of Fabius Maximus both in Campania and Tarentum, and did good service at the decisive battle of the Metaurus. Between his campaigns he did not seek to exhibit his laurels in the society of the capital, but, like Curius Dentatus and Quintius Cincinnatus, employed himself in the rural labours of his Sabine retirement.

---

[316] A. U. C. 586; B. C. 168.
[317] A. U. C. 599; B. C. 155.
[318] Cic. de Orat. ii. 37; Quint. xii. 1.
[319] Suet. de Gram. Ill. 2.
[320] De Senec. 4.

His shrewd remarks and easy conversation, as well as the skill with which he pleaded the causes of his clients before the rural magistracy, soon made his abilities known, and his reputation attracted the notice of one of his country neighbours, L. Valerius Flaccus, who invited him to his town-house at Rome. Owing to the patronage of his noble friend, and his own merits, his rise to eminence as a pleader was rapid. He was a quæstor in B. C. 206, ædile in B. C. 199, prætor the following year, and in B. C. 195 he obtained the consulship, his patron Flaccus being now his colleague. His province was Spain;[321] and, whilst stern and pitiless towards his foes, he exhibited a noble example of self-denying endurance in order to minister to the welfare of his army. At the conclusion of his consulship, he served as legatus in Thrace and Greece; and in B. C. 189 was sent on a civil mission to Fulvius Nobilior in Ætolia.

After experiencing one failure, he was elected censor in B. C. 184; and he had now an opportunity of making a return for the obligations which his earliest patron had conferred upon him; for, by his influence, Flaccus was appointed his colleague. This office was, above all others, suited to his talents; and to his remarkable activity in the discharge of his duties, he owes his fame and his surname.

He had now full scope for displaying his habits of business, his talents for administration, his uncompromising resistance to all luxury and extravagance, his fearlessness in the reformation of abuses: and though he was severe, public opinion bore testimony to his integrity, for he was rewarded with a statue and an inscription. He had now served his country in every capacity, but still he gave himself no rest; advancing age did not weaken his energies; he was always ready as the champion of the oppressed, the advocate of virtue, the punisher of vice. He prosecuted the extortionate governors of his old province, Spain.[322] He pleaded before the senate the cause of the loyal Rhodians.

He caused the courteous dismissal of the three Greek philosophers, because the arguments of Carneades made it difficult to discern what was truth.[323] Although his prejudice against Greeks prevented him sympathizing with the sorrows of the Achæan exiles, he supported the vote for their restoration to their native land. Neither his enemies nor his country would allow him rest. In his eighty-sixth year, he had to defend himself against a capital charge. In his eighty-ninth, he was sent to Africa as one of the arbitrators between the Carthaginians and Massinissa,[324] and in his ninetieth, the year in which he died,[325] his last public act was the prosecution of Galba for his perfidious treatment of the conquered Lusitanians.[326]

Cato loved strife, and his long life was one continued combat. He never found a task too difficult, because difficulty called forth all his energies, and his strong will and invincible perseverance insured success. His inherent love of truth made him hate anything conventional. As a politician, he considered rank valueless, except it depended upon personal

---

[321] Liv. xxxiv.
[322] B. C. 171.
[323] Plin. H. N. vii. 31.
[324] A. U. C. 605.
[325] Livy (xxxix. 40) and Niebuhr (Lect. lxix.) state that Cato died at the age of ninety; Cicero (Brut. 15, 20, 23) and Pliny, at the age of eighty-five.
[326] Valerius Maximus relates the following anecdote of the respect in which this virtuous Roman was held by his countrymen:—At the Floralia, the people were accustomed to call for the exhibition of dances, accompanied with acts of great indecency. Cato on one of these occasions happened to be present, and the spectators were ashamed to make their usual demand until he had left the theatre. Martial also alludes to this anecdote in one of his epigrams.

merit; and therefore he was an unrelenting enemy of the aristocracy. As a moralist, he indignantly rejected that false gloss of modern fashion which was superseding the old plainness, and which was, in his opinion, the foundation of his country's glory. In literature, he distrusted and condemned everything Greek, because he confounded the sentiments of its noblest periods as a nation with those of the degenerate Greeks with whom he came in contact. But, at length, his candid and truthful disposition discovered and confessed his error on this point, and his prejudices gave way before conviction.

Cato, with all his virtues, was a hard-hearted man.[327] He had no amiability, no love, no affection; he did not love right, for he loved nothing; but he had a burning indignation against wrong. This was the mainspring of his conduct. He did not feel for the oppressed, but he declared war against the oppressor. He never could sympathize with living men. In his youth, all his admiration was for the past generation. In his old age, his feeling was that his life had been spent with the past, and he had nothing in common with the present.

As is usually the case with those who live during a period of transition, his feelings were so interested in that past by which his character was formed, that he was incapable of discerning any good whatever in change and progress. For this reason he dreaded the invasion of refinement and civilization. Accustomed to connect virtue and purity with the absence of temptations, he was prepared to take an exaggerated view of the relation between polish and effeminacy, between a taste for the beautiful and luxury.

He was a bitter hater of those who opposed his prejudices. His enmity to Carthage sprung much more from his antagonism to Scipio, as the leader of the Greek or movement party, than from fears for the safety of Rome. Scipio said, Let Carthage be; therefore Cato's will was, let Carthage be destroyed. When his hatred of injustice was aroused, as, for example, by the perfidy of S. Sulpicius Galba towards the Lusitanians, he could support the cause of foreigners against a fellow-countryman. His character is full of apparent inconsistencies. Although he hated oppression, he was cruel to his slaves; tyrannical and implacable, simply because he would not brook opposition to his will. His integrity was incorruptible, and yet he was a grinding usurer; frugal in his habits, and notwithstanding his few wants, grasping and avaricious; but it was his love of business that he was gratifying, rather than a love of money. Trade was with him a combat in which he would not allow an advantage to be gained by his adversary. Virtue did not present itself to Cato in an amiable form. He had but one idea of it—austerity; and, as his hatred of wrong was not counterbalanced by a love of right, the intensity of his hatred was only kept in check by the practical good sense and utilitarian views which occupy so prominent a place in the Roman character. Being himself reserved and undemonstrative, he expected others to be so likewise, and thought it unbecoming the dignity of a Roman to exhibit tenderness of feeling. On one occasion we are told that he degraded a Roman knight for embracing his wife in the presence of his daughter. His personal appearance was not more prepossessing than his manners, as we learn from the following severe epigram:—[328]

Πυρρὸν, πανδακέτην, γλαυκόμματον, οὐδὲ θανόντα
Πόρκιον εἰς ἀΐδην Περσεφόνη δέχεται.

---

[327] Hor. Od. ii. i.
[328] Plut. Life of Cato.

With his red hair, constant snarl, and gray eyes, Proserpine would not receive Porcius, even after death, into Hades.

As, notwithstanding his defects, Cato was morally the greatest man ever Rome produced, so he was one of the greatest intellectually. His genius was perfectly original; his character was not moulded by other men; he had no education except self-education. He had immense power of acquiring learning, and he ransacked every source to increase his stores; but he was indebted to no man for his opinions—they were self-formed, except those which he inherited, and in which his own independent convictions led him to acquiesce. He had the ability and the determination to excel in everything which he undertook, politics, war, rural economy, oratory, history. His style is rude, unpolished, ungraceful, because to him wit was artifice, and polish superficial, and therefore unreal. For this reason he did not profit by the inconceivably rapid change which was then taking place in the Latin language, and which is evident from the comparison of the fragments of Cato's works with the polished comedies of Terence.

His statements, however, were clear and transparent; his illustrations, though quaint, were striking; the words with which he enriched his native tongue were full of meaning; his wit was keen and lively, although he never would permit it to offend against gravity, or partake of irreverence.[329] His arguments went straight to the intellect, and carried conviction with them.

The character of Cato forms one of the most beautiful passages in the works of Livy:[330] "In hoc viro tanta vis animi ingeniique fuit, ut, quocunque loco natus esset, fortunam sibi ipse facturus fuisse videretur. Nulla ars, neque privatæ, neque publicæ rei gerendæ, ei defuit. Urbanas rusticasque res pariter callebat. Ad summos honores alios scientia juris, alios eloquentia, alios gloria militaris provexit. Huic versatile ingenium sic pariter ad omnia fuit, ut natum ad id unum diceres, quodcunque ageret. In bello manu fortissimus, multisque insignibus clarus pugnis; idem, postquam ad magnos honores pervenit, summus imperator: idem in pace, si jus consuleres, peritissimus; si causa oranda esset, eloquentissimus. Nec is tantum, cujus lingua vivo eo viguerit, monumentum eloquentiæ nullum exstet: vivit immo vigetque eloquentia ejus, sacrata scriptis omnis generis. Orationes et pro se multæ, et pro aliis et in alios; nam non solum accusando, sed etiam causam dicendo, fatigavit inimicos. Simultates nimio plures et exercuerunt eum, et ipse exercuit eas; nec facile dixeris, utrum magis presserit eum nobilitas, an ille agitaverit nobilitatem. Asperi proculdubio animi, et linguæ acerbæ, et immodice liberæ fuit; sed invicti a cupiditatibus animi, et rigidæ innocentiæ; contemptor gratiæ divitiarum. In parsimonia, in patientia laboris, periculi, ferrei prope corporis animique; quam neque senectus quidem, quæ solvit omnia, fregerit. Qui sextum et octogesimum annum agens causam dixerit, ipse pro se oraverit, scripseritque; nonagesimo anno Ser. Galbam ad populi adduxerit judicium."

---

[329] Cicero tells us (De Orat. ii. 64) that, when censor, he degraded L. Nasica for an unseasonable jest.
[330] Lib. xxxix. 40.

Chapter 12

The Origines of Cato—Passage Quoted by Gellius—Treatise De Re Rustica—Orations—L. Cassius Hemina—Historians in the Days of the Gracchi—Traditional Anecdote of Romulus—Autobiographers—Fragment of Quadrigarius—Falsehoods of Antias—Sisenna—Tubero

Cato's great historical and antiquarian work, "*The Origines*," was written in his old age.[331] Its title would seem to imply that it was merely an inquiry into the ancient history of his country; but in reality it comprehended far more than this—it was a history of Italy and Rome from the earliest times to the latest events which occurred in his own lifetime. The contents of the work are thus described by Cornelius Nepos.[332] It is divided into seven books. The first treats of the history of the kings; the second and third of the rise and progress of the Italian states; the fourth contains the first Punic war; the fifth the war with Hannibal; the remaining two the history of the subsequent wars down to the prætorship of Servius Galba.

It was a work of great research and originality. For his archæological information, he had consulted the records and documents, not only of Rome, but of the principal Italian towns. It is probable that their constitutional history was introduced incidentally to the main narrative; and that the rise and progress of the Roman constitution was illustrated by the political principles of the Italian nations. The "*Origines*" also contained valuable notices respecting the history and constitution of Carthage,[333] his embassy having furnished him with full opportunity for collecting materials. It was, in fact, a unique work: no other Roman historian wrote in the same spirit, or was equally laborious in the work of original investigation.

The truthfulness and honesty of Cato must have rendered the contemporary part of the history equally valuable with the antiquarian portion. He could not have been guilty of flattery, he had no regard for the feelings of individuals. Not only he never mentions himself,

---

[331] About A. U. C. 600.
[332] Cato, iii.
[333] See frag. of book iv. Krause.

but, except in times long gone by, he never names any one.[334] The glory of a victory, or of a gallant exploit, belongs to the general, or consul, or tribune, as the representative of the republic. He does not allow either individual or family to participate in that which he considered the exclusive property of his country.

Sufficient fragments of the "*Origines*" remain to make us regret that more have not been preserved; but though very numerous, they are, with the exception of two, excessively brief. One of these is a portion of his own speech in favour of the Rhodians;[335] the other a simple and affecting narrative of an act of self-devoted heroism. A consular army was surprised and surrounded by the Carthaginians in a defile, from which there was no escape. The tribune, whom Cato does not name, but who, as A. Gellius informs us, was Cædicius, went to the consul and recommended him to send four hundred men to occupy a neighbouring height. The enemy, he added, will attack them, and without doubt they will be slain to a man. Nevertheless, whilst the enemy is thus occupied, the army will escape. But, replied the consul, who will be the leader of this band? I will, said the tribune; I devote my life to you, and to my country. The tribune and four hundred men set forth to die. They sold their lives dearly, but all fell. "The immortal gods," adds Cato, for Gellius is here quoting his very words, "granted the tribune a lot according to his valour. For thus it came to pass. Though he had received many wounds, none proved mortal; and when his comrades recognised him amongst the dead, faint from loss of blood, they took him up, and he recovered. But it makes a vast difference in what country a generous action is performed. Leonidas, of Lacedæmon, is praised, who performed a similar exploit at Thermopylæ. On account of his valour united Greece testified her gratitude in every possible way, and adorned his exploit with monumental records, pictures, statues, eulogies, histories. The Roman tribune gained but faint praise, and yet he had done the same, and saved the republic." The most pathetic writer could not have told the tale more effectively than the stern Cato.

Circumstances invest his treatise "*De Re Rustica*" with great interest. The population of Rome, both patrician and plebeian, was necessarily agricultural. For centuries they had little commerce: their wealth consisted in flocks and herds, and in the conquered territories of nations as poor as themselves. The *ager Romanus*, and subsequently as they gained fresh acquisitions, the fertile plains, and valleys, and mountain sides of Italy, supplied them with maintenance. The statesman and the general, in the intervals of civil war or military service, returned, like Cincinnatus and Cato, to the cultivation of their fields and gardens. The Roman armies were recruited from the peasantry; and when the war was over, the soldier returned to his daily labour; and, in later times, the veteran, when his period of service was completed, became a small farmer in a military colony. To a restless nation, who could not exist in a state of inactivity, a change of labour was relaxation; and the pleasures of rural life, which were so often sung by the Augustan poets, were heartily enjoyed by the same man whose natural atmosphere seemed to be either politics or war.

Besides the possession of these rural tastes the Romans were essentially a domestic people. The Greeks were social; they lived in public; they had no idea of home. Woman did not with them occupy a position favourable to the existence of home-feeling. The Roman matron was the centre of the domestic circle; she was her husband's equal, sometimes his counsellor, and generally the educator of his children in their early years. Hundreds of

---

[334] C. Nepos in Vita.
[335] Lib. v. Krause, p. 114.

sepulchral inscriptions bear testimony to the sweet charities of home-life, to the dutiful obedience of children, the devoted affection of parents, the fidelity of wives, the attachments of husbands. Hence, home and all its pursuits and occupations had an interest in the eyes of a Roman. For this reason there were so many writers on rural and domestic economy. From Cato to Columella we have a list of authors whose object was instruction in the various branches of the subject. They were thus enumerated by Columella himself:[336] "Cato was the first who taught the art of agriculture to speak in Latin; after him it was improved by the diligence of the two Sasernæ, father and son; next it acquired eloquence from Scrofa Tremellius; polish from M. Terentius, (Varro;) poetic power from Virgil." To their illustrious names he adds those of J. Hyginus, the Carthaginian Mago, Corn. Celsus, J. Atticus, and his disciple J. Græcinus.

The work of Cato, "*De Re Rustica*," has come down to us almost in form and substance as it was written. It has not the method of a regular treatise. It is a commonplace-book of agriculture and domestic economy under one hundred and sixty-three heads. The subjects are connected, but not regularly arranged; they form a collection of useful instructions, hints, and receipts. Its object is utility, not science. It serves the purposes of a farmers' and gardeners' manual; a domestic medicine, an herbal, and cookery-book; prudential maxims are interspersed, and some favourite charms for the cure of diseases in man and beast. Cato teaches his readers, for example, how to plant ozier-beds, to cultivate vegetables, to preserve the health of cattle, to pickle pork, and to make savoury dishes. He is shrewd and economical, but he never allows humanity to interfere with profits; for he recommends his readers to sell everything which they do not want, even old horses and old slaves. He is a great conjurer, for he informs us that the most potent cure for a sprain is the repetition of the following hocus-pocus:[337] "Daries dardaries, astataries dissunapitea;" or, "Huat hanat, huat hista, pista sista, domiabo damnaustra;" or, "Huat huat, huat, ista sis tar sis, ordannabon damnaustra." This miscellaneous collection is preceded by an introduction, in which is maintained the superiority of agriculture over other modes of gaining a livelihood, especially over that of trade and money-lending.

Cato was a conscientious father. He could not trust Greeks, but undertook the education of his son himself. As a part of his system, he addressed to him, in the form of letters, instruction on various topics—historical, philosophical, and moral. A very few fragments of this work, unfortunately, remain. In one of them he recommends a cursory view of Greek literature, but not a profound study of it. He evidently considered Greek writings morally dangerous; but he entertained a still greater horror of their medicine. He had confidence in his own old-fashioned charms and rural pharmacopeia; but he firmly believed, as he would the voice of an oracle, that all the Greek physicians were banded together to destroy the Romans as barbarians.

Of the orations of Cato, ninety titles are extant, together with numerous fragments.[338] Some of these were evidently judicial, but the majority deliberative. After what has been said of his works it is scarcely necessary to describe the style of his eloquence. Unless a man is a mere actor, his character is generally exemplified in his speaking. This is especially true of Cato. He despised art. He was too fearless and upright, too confident in the justice of his

---

[336] Lib. i. 12.
[337] The hocus-pocus of Cato resembles Latin about as nearly as did the gibberish of the Spanish witches in the days of witch-finding. "In nomine Patricâ Aragueaco Petrica agora agora valentia jouando goure gaito goustra."
[338] Meyer, Frag. Rom. Orat.

cause, to be a rhetorician; too much wrapt up in his subject to be careful of the language in which he conveyed his thoughts. He imitated no one, and no one was ever able to imitate him. His style was abrupt, concise, witty, full of contrast; its beauty that of nature, namely, the rapid alternations of light and shade. Now it was rude and harsh, now pathetic and affecting. It was the language of debate—antagonistic, gladiatorial, elenchtic.

Plutarch compares him to Socrates; but he omits the principal point of resemblance, namely, that he always speaks as if he was hand to hand with an adversary. Even amidst the glitter and polish of the Augustan age, old Cato had some admirers.[339] But this was not the general feeling. The intrinsic value of the rough gem was not appreciated. Cicero[340] tells us that, to his astonishment, Cato was almost entirely unknown. The time afterwards arrived when criticism became a science, and he was estimated as he deserved to be; but this admiration for the antique form was not a revival of the antique spirit; it was only an attempt to compensate for its loss; it was an imitation, not a reality.

Such was the literary position occupied by him whom Niebuhr pronounces to be the only great man in his generation, and one of the greatest and most honourable characters in Roman history.[341]

L. Cassius Hemina

There was no one worthy to follow Cato as an historian but L. Cassius Hemina. A. Postumius Albinus, consul B. C. 151, was, according to Cicero,[342] a learned and eloquent man, and wrote a history of Rome in Greek;[343] but it was so inelegant that he apologized on the ground that he was a Roman writing in a foreign language.[344] It is probable, also, that he was inaccurate and puerile. He tells us, for example, that Baiæ was so named after Boia, the nurse of one of Æneas' friends, and that Brutus used to eat green figs and honey.[345]

Hemina wrote Roman annals in five or six books, and published them about the time of the fall of Carthage:[346] a considerable number of fragments are extant. He was the last writer of this period who investigated the original sources of history. His researches went back to very early times; and he appears to have attempted, at least, a comparison of Greek and Italian chronology, for he fixes the age of Homer and Hesiod in the dynasty of the Silvii, more than 160 years after the siege of Troy. He relates the original legend of Cacus and the oxen of Hercules, the finding of Numa's coffin, and the celebration of the fourth sæcular games in the consulship of Lentulus and Mummius.[347] This was probably the last event of importance previous to the publication of his work. Only two fragments are of sufficient length to enable us to form any judgment respecting his style. Many of his expressions are very archaic, but the story of Cacus is told in a simple and pleasing manner.

---

[339] See, *ex. gr.* Liv. xxxix. 40.
[340] Brutus.
[341] Lect. R. H. lxix.
[342] Brut.
[343] Gell. xi. 8.
[344] Serv. Æn. ix. 70.
[345] Macrob. ii. 16.
[346] A. U. C. 608.
[347] A. U. C. 608.

After Hemina, Roman history was, for some years, nothing more than a compilation from the old chronicles, and from the labours and investigations of previous authors. Q. Fabius Maximus Servilianus was consul A. U. C. 612. His Latin style must have been very deficient in euphony, if he frequently indulged in such words as *litterosissimum*, which occurs in one of the fragments extant. C. Fannius, prætor A. U. C. 617, wrote a meager history[348] in not inelegant Latin. Vennonius, his contemporary, was the author of annals which are referred to by Dionysius. To this list of historians may be added C. Sempronius Tuditanus, a polished gentleman as well as an elegant writer.[349]

The days of the Gracchi were very fruitful in historians and autobiographers. At the head of them stands L. Cælius Antipater,[350] a Roman freedman, an eloquent orator, and skilful jurist. His work consisted of seven books, and many fragments are preserved by the grammarians. He seems to have delighted in the marvellous; for Cicero quotes from two remarkable dreams in his treatise on divination. He is also frequently referred to by Livy in his history of the Punic wars.

Contemporaneously with Cælius lived Cn. Gellius, whose voluminous history extended to the length of ninety-seven books at least. Livy seldom refers to him. Probably, in this instance, he acted wisely; for he seems to have been an historian of little or no authority. Two other Gellii, Sextus and Aulus, flourished at the same time.

Publius Sempronius Asellio wrote, about the middle of the seventh century of Rome, a memoir of the Numantian war. He was an eye-witness of the scenes which he describes, for he was tribune at Numantia under Scipio Africanus.[351]

The only constitutional history of Rome was the work of C. Junius, who was surnamed Gracchanus, in consequence of his intimacy with C. Gracchus. It is certain that this work must have been the result of original research, as there are no remains extant of any history which could have furnished the materials. The legal and political knowledge which it contained was evidently considerable, for it is quoted by the jurists as a trustworthy authority.[352]

Servius Fabius Pictor[353] wrote annals; but his principal work was a treatise on the pontifical law, an antiquarian record of rites and ceremonies. L. Calpurnius Piso Frugi Censorius was consul in the year in which Ti. Sempronius Gracchus was killed, and censor the year after the murder of C. Gracchus:[354] he is occasionally quoted by Dionysius, and twice by Livy, who, on the points in question, consider his authority less trustworthy than that of Fabius Pictor.[355] Gellius[356] quotes from him the following traditional anecdote of Romulus. Once upon a time the king was invited out to supper. He drank very little, because he had business to transact on the following day. Someone at table remarked, if everybody did so, wine would be cheaper. "Nay," replied Romulus, "I have drank as much as I wished; if everybody did so, it would be dear."

---

[348] Cic. de Leg. ii. 2; Brut. 26.
[349] Cic. Brut. 25.
[350] Ibid. 26.
[351] Gell. ii. 13.
[352] See Nieb. Lect. V. on Rom. Lit.
[353] Brut. 21.
[354] B. C. 133.
[355] Liv. i. 55.
[356] Lib. xi. 14.

Piso was an honest man, but not an honest historian. He acquired the surname Frugi by his strict integrity and simple habits; but his ingenuity tempted him to disregard historical truth. Niebuhr considers him the first who introduced systematic forgeries into Roman history. Seeing the discrepancies and consistencies between the accounts given by previous annalists, instead of weighing them together, and adopting those which were best supported by the testimony of antiquity, he either invented theories, in order to reconcile conflicting statements, or substituted some narrative which he thought might have been the groundwork of the marvellous legend. Niebuhr observes, that he treated history precisely in the same way in which the rationalists endeavoured to divest the scripture of its miraculous character.

M. Æmilius Scaurus, P. Rutilius Rufus, and Q. Lutatius Catulus, were the first Roman autobiographers; and their example was afterwards followed by Sulla, who employed his retirement in writing his own memoir in twenty-two books. Scaurus was the son of a charcoal-dealer, who, by his military talents, twice raised himself to the consulship, and once enjoyed the honour of a triumph. A few unimportant fragments of his personal memoirs are preserved by the grammarians. Rutilius was consul A. U. C. 649: he wrote his own life in Latin, and a history of Rome in Greek.[357] Catulus is praised by Cicero for his Latinity, who compares his style to that of Xenophon.[358]

The other historians, who flourished immediately before the literary period of Cicero, were C. Licinius Macer, Q. Claudius Quadrigarius, and Q. Valerius Antias.

Macer[359] was a prolix and gossiping writer: he was not deficient in industry; he spared no pains in collecting traditions; but he had no judgment in selection, and accepted all the Greek fables respecting Italy without discrimination. Hence he makes some statements which were rejected by annalists of greater authority. Niebuhr[360] defends him, and regrets deeply the loss of his annals. He thinks it not improbable that Cicero's unfavourable criticism may have been owing to political prejudice. His work was voluminous, and probably traced the Roman history from the commencement to his own times.

Quadrigarius is much quoted both by Livy and the grammarians. From the fragments extant it is clear that his history commenced with the Gallic wars; and from a passage in Plutarch's Life of Numa,[361] he appears to have been actuated by a motive indicative of his truthfulness as an historian. He was not content with fabulous legends; and there were no documents in existence anterior to the capture of Rome by the Gauls. His work consisted of twenty-three books: it carried the history, as is generally supposed, as far as the death of Sulla,[362] or, as Niebuhr believed, down to the consulship of Cicero.[363] The longest fragment extant has been preserved by Gellius, and relates the combat of Manlius Torquatus with the gigantic Gaul.

The style is abrupt and sententious, and the structure of the sentences loose; but the story is told in a naïve and spirited manner. One can realize the scene as the historian describes it—the awe of the Roman host at the unwonted sight—the gigantic stature, the truculent countenance of the Goliath-like youth—the unbroken silence, in the midst of which his voice of thunder uttered his defiance—the scorn with which he sneered and put out his tongue when

---

[357] Athenæus, iv. 168.
[358] Brut. 35.
[359] See Cic. de Leg. i. 2; Brut. 67.
[360] Lect. iii. xliv.
[361] Numa, c. i. See Niebuhr, Lect. III. xli.
[362] A. U. C. 678.
[363] A. U. C. 691.

no one accepted his challenge—the shame and grief of the noble Manlius—the struggle—the cutting off the monster's head, and the wreathing his own neck with the collar still reeking with blood.

It has been suggested that this historian received the surname Quadrigarius because, in the games of the circus, celebrated after the victory of Sulla, he won the prize in the chariot-race.

No Roman historian ever made greater pretensions to accuracy than Valerius Antias, and no one was less trustworthy. Livy, on one occasion,[364] accuses him of either negligence or impudent exaggeration; but there is no doubt that he was guilty of the latter fault. Almost all the places in which he is quoted by Livy have reference to numbers, and in all he not only goes far beyond all other historians,[365] but even transgresses the bounds of possibility. Livy never hesitates to call him a liar. In all cases he is guilty of falsehood; the only question is whether his falsehood is more or less moderate. The following examples are sufficient to convict him. He undertakes to assert that the exact number of the Sabine virgins was 527.[366] If one historian states that 60 engines of war were taken, he makes the number 6,000;[367] when all authors, Greek and Latin, unite in asserting that in A. U. C. 553, there was no memorable campaign, he says a battle was fought in which 12,000 of the enemy were slain and 1,200 taken prisoners.[368] In another place 10,000 slain become 40,000;[369] and a fine which Quadrigarius states was to be paid by instalments in thirty years, he distributes only over the space of ten.[370] With matter of this unauthentic kind, he filled no less than seventy-five books, of which a large portion of passages have been preserved, especially by Livy.

Hitherto, with one doubtful exception, Latin historical composition was in the hands of the great and noble; the first historian belonging to the order of the libertinei was L. Otacilius Pilitus. Suetonius[371] says, that he was not only originally a slave, but that he acted as porter, and, as was the custom, was chained to his master's door. Nothing is known of his works; it is probable, therefore, that they were of no merit.

Two more important names remain to be mentioned amongst the annalists of this period—L. Cornelius Sisenna and Q. Ælius Tubero. Sisenna, according to the testimony of Cicero,[372] was born between B. C. 640 and B. C. 680, and filled the office of quæstor B. C. 676. He was, according to the same authority, a man of learning and taste, wrote pure Latin, was well acquainted with public business, and, although deficient in industry, surpassed all his predecessors and contemporaries in his talents as an historian. Probably his style of writing approached more nearly to that of the new school, although still below the Ciceronian standard. The testimony of Sallust is not so favourable, as he considers him not sufficiently impartial to fulfil adequately the duties of a contemporary historian.[373]

No fragments are extant of sufficient length to enable us to form any estimate of his merits, although, on account of the numerous unusual words which occur in his writings, no

---

[364] Lib. xxx. 19.
[365] There is one instance to the contrary, (Liv. xxxviii. 23,) in which Quadrigarius makes the number of the slain 40,000, Antias only 10,000.
[366] Plut. Romulus, 14.
[367] Liv. xxvi. 49.
[368] Lib. xxxii. 6.
[369] Lib. xxxiii. 10.
[370] Lib. xxxiii. 30.
[371] De Clar. Rhet. 3.
[372] Brut. 64 and 88.
[373] Jug. 95.

historian of this period has been more frequently quoted by the grammarians. The probability is that his twenty-three books are of little or no value, as they are never referred to in order to illustrate matters of historical or antiquarian interest.

Tubero was the contemporary of Cicero, and did not write his annals until after Cicero's consulship. Nevertheless he must be considered as belonging to the old school, and its last as well as one of its most worthy representatives. He was the father of L. Tubero, the legate of Q. Cicero, in Asia. Like Piso, he was a stout opponent of the Gracchic policy, and a firm supporter of the aristocracy. A stoic in philosophy, his life was in strict accordance with his creed, and his style of writing is said to have been marked with Catonian rudeness. He describes, in his history, the cruel tortures of Regulus by the Carthaginians, and relates the story of the wonderful serpent at Bagrada.[374] He is once quoted by Dionysius and twice by Livy.

---

[374] Gell. vi. 3, 4.

Chapter 13

Early Roman Oratory—Eloquence of Appius Claudius Cæcus—Funeral Orations—Defence of Scipio Africanus Major—Scipio Africanus Minor Æmilianus—Era of the Gracchi—Their Characters—Interval Between the Gracchi and Cicero—M. Antonius—L. Licinius Crassus—Q. Hortensius—Causes of His Early Popularity and Subsequent Failure

Eloquence, though of a rude, unpolished kind, must have been in the very earliest times a characteristic of the Roman people. It is a plant indigenous to a free soil. Its infancy was nurtured in the schools of Tisias and Corax, when, on the dethronement of the tyrants, the dawn of freedom brightened upon Sicily; and, just as in modern times it has flourished, especially in England and America, fostered by the unfettered freedom of debate, so it found a congenial home in free Greece and republican Rome. He who could contrast in the most glowing colours the cruelty of the pitiless creditor, with the sufferings of the ruined debtor—who could ingeniously connect those patent evils with some defects in the constitution, some inequalities in political rights hitherto hidden and unobserved—would wield at will the affections of the people, and become the master-spirit amongst his fellow-citizens.

Occasions would not be wanting in a state where, from the earliest times, a struggle was continually maintained between a dominant and a subject race, for the use of those arts of eloquence which nature, the mistress of all art, suggests. The plebeians, in their conflicts with the patricians, must have had some leader, and eloquence, probably to a great extent, directed the selection, even though there was, in reality, no Menenius Agrippa to lead them back from the sacred mountain with his homely wisdom. Cases of oppression, doubtless, inspired some Icilius or Virginius with words of burning indignation, and many a Siccius Dentatus, though he had never learnt technical rhetoric, used the rhetorical artifice of appealing to his honourable wounds and scars in front, which he had received in the service of his country, and to disgraceful weals with which his back was lacerated by the lash of the torturer. In an army where the personal influence of the general was more productive of heroism than the rules of a long-established discipline, a short harangue often led the soldiers to victory. And, lastly, the relation subsisting between the two orders of patron and client taught a milder and more business-like eloquence—that of explaining with facility common civil rights, and unravelling the knotty points of the constitutional law. Oratory, in fact, was the unwritten literature of active life, and recommended itself by its antagonistic spirit and its utility to a warlike and utilitarian people. Long, therefore, before the art of the historian was sufficiently advanced to record a speech, or to insert a fictitious one, as an embellishment or illustration of its pages, the forum, senate, the battle-field, the threshold of the jurisconsult, had been nurseries of Roman eloquence, or schools in which oratory attained a vigorous youth, and prepared for its subsequent maturity.

Tradition speaks of a speech recorded even before the poetry of Nævius was written, and this speech was known to Cicero. It was delivered against Pyrrhus by Appius Claudius the blind.[375] He belonged to a house, every member of which, from the decemvir to the emperor, was born to bow down their fellow-men beneath their strong wills. Such a character, united with a poetical genius, implies the very elements of that oratory which would curb a nation accustomed to be restrained by force as much as by reason. On this celebrated occasion,[376] the blind old man caused himself to be borne into the senate-house on a litter, that he might confront the wily Cineas whom Pyrrhus had sent to negotiate peace. The Macedonian minister was an accomplished speaker, and his memory, that important auxiliary to eloquence, was so powerful, that in one day he learnt to address all the senators and knights by name, yet it is said that he was no match for the energy of Appius, and was obliged to quit Rome.

Whilst the legal and political constitution of the Roman people gave direct encouragement to deliberative and judicial oratory, respect to the illustrious dead furnished opportunities for panegyric. The song of the bard in honour of the departed warrior gave place to the funeral oration, (*laudatio*.)

Before the commencement of the second Punic war,[377] Q. Metellus pronounced the funeral harangue over his father, the conqueror of Hasdrubal; history also speaks of him as a debator in the senate, and his address to the censors is found in the fourth decade of Livy.[378] This funeral oration was admired even in the time of J. Cæsar, and Pliny[379] has recorded the substance of one remarkable passage which it contained. The period of the second Punic war produced Corn. Cethegus. Cicero mentions him in his list of Roman orators;[380] and although he had never seen a specimen of his style, he states that he retained his force and vigour even in his old age. Ennius also bears testimony to his eloquence in the following line:—

> Flos delibatus populi, suaviloquenti ore.

---

[375] Appius Claudius Cæcus was also author of a moral poem on Pythagorean principles, which was extant in the time of Cicero, (Brutus, 16.)
[376] B. C. 280.
[377] About B. C. 221.
[378] Lib. xxxv. 8; xl. 46.
[379] H. N. vii. 43, 44.
[380] Brut. 14, 19, de Sen.

At the conclusion of the second war, Fabius Cunctator pronounced the eulogium[381] of his elder son; and Cicero, although he denies him the praise of eloquence, states that he was a fluent and correct speaker.

Scipio Africanus Major, on that memorable day when his enemies called upon him to render an account of the moneys received from Antiochus, proved himself a consummate orator: he disdained to refute the malignant charges of his opponents, but spoke till dusk of the benefits which he had conferred upon his country. Thus it came to pass that the adjourned meeting was held on the anniversary of Zama. Livy has adorned the simple words of the great soldier with his graceful language, but A. Gellius[382] has preserved the peroration almost in his own words. "I call to remembrance, Romans," said he, "that this is the very day on which I vanquished in a bloody battle on the plains of Africa the Carthaginian Hannibal, the most formidable enemy Rome ever encountered. I obtained for you a peace and an unlooked-for victory. Let us then not be ungrateful to heaven, but let us leave this knave, and at once offer our grateful thanksgivings to Jove, supremely good and great."

The people obeyed his summons—the forum was deserted, and crowds followed him with acclamations to the Capitol.

Mention has already been made of the stern eloquence of his adversary Cato. He was equally laborious as a speaker and a writer. No fewer than one hundred and fifty of his orations were extant in Cicero's time, most of which were on subjects of public and political interest.

The father of the Gracchi was distinguished amongst his contemporaries for a plain and nervous eloquence, but no specimens of his oratory have survived.

Scipio Africanus Minor (Æmilianus) was precisely qualified to be the link between the new and the old school of oratory. His soldier-like character displayed all the vigour and somewhat of the sternness of the old Roman, but the harder outlines were modified by an ardent love of learning. His first campaign was in Greece, under his father Æmilius Paulus. His first literary friendship was formed there with the historian Polybius, which ripened into the closest intimacy when Polybius came as a hostage to Rome. Subsequently he became acquainted with Panætius, who was his instructor in the principles of philosophy. His taste was gratified with Greek refinement, although he abhorred the effeminacy and profligacy of the Greeks themselves. In the spirit of Cato, for whom he entertained the warmest admiration, he indignantly remonstrated against the inroad of Greek manners. In his speech in opposition to the law of C. Gracchus, he warned his hearers of the corruptions which were already insinuating themselves amongst the Roman youth. "I did not believe what I heard," he says, "until I witnessed it with my own eyes: at the dancing-school I saw more than five hundred of the youth of both sexes. I saw a boy, of at least twelve years old, wearing the badge of noble birth, who performed a castanet dance, which an immodest slave could not have danced without disgrace."

The degeneracy of Greek manners had not corrupted his moral nature, or rendered him averse to the active duties of a citizen; it had not destroyed the frankness, whilst it had humanized the rough honesty, of the Roman, and taught him to love the beautiful as well as the good, and to believe that the former was the proper external development of the latter.

---

[381] Cic. Cat. 4, 12; de Sen. 4; Brut. 14, 18.
[382] Noct. Attic. iv. 18.

One friend, whose influence contributed to form the mind of Scipio, was the wise and gentle Lælius. In other places, as well as in the "*de Amicitia*," Cicero associates their names together. These distinguished friends were well suited to each other. The sentiments of both were noble and elevated. "Both," as Cicero[383] says, "were '*imprimis eloquentes.*'" Their discrepancies were such as draw men of similar tastes more closely together, in those hours which they can devote to their favourite pursuits. Scipio was an active man of business—Lælius, a contemplative philosopher: Scipio, a Roman in heart and soul—Lælius, a citizen of the world: Scipio was rather inclined to ostentatious display—Lælius was retiring. The former had a correct taste, spoke Latin with great purity, and had an extensive acquaintance with the literature both of Greece and his own country. The attainments of the latter were more solid, and his acquaintance with the mind of Greece more profound. But Lælius was not equally calculated to occupy a place in history; and hence, perhaps, although a few fragments of the eloquence of Scipio are extant,[384] the remains of that of Lælius extend only to as many lines. Cheerfulness, (hilaritas,) smoothness, (lenitas,) and learning distinguished the speeches of Lælius, whilst spirit, genius, and natural power marked those of Scipio.

Servius Sulpicius Galba, whom Cato[385] prosecuted for his treachery to the Lusitanians, obtained from Cicero the praise of having been the first Roman who really understood how to apply the theoretical principles of Greek rhetoric. He is said likewise to have carried away with him the feelings of his auditors by his animated and vehement delivery. How skilful he was in the use of rhetorical artifice is shown by his parading before the assembly of the people, when brought to trial, his two infant sons, and the orphan of his friend Sulpicius Gallus. His tears and embraces touched the hearts of his judges, and the cold-blooded perjurer was acquitted. External artifice, however, probably constituted his whole merit. He had the tact thus to cover a dry and antique style, destitute of nerve and muscle, of which no specimen except only a few words remain.

All periods of political disquiet are necessarily favourable to eloquence, and the era of the Gracchi was especially so. Extensive political changes were now established. They had been of slow and gradual growth, and were the natural development of the Roman system; but they were changes which could not take place without the crisis being accompanied by great political convulsions. In order to understand the state of parties, of which the great leaders and principal orators were the representatives, it is necessary to explain briefly in what these changes consisted. The result of an obstinate and persevering struggle during nearly four centuries was, that the old distinction of patrician and plebeian no longer existed. Plebeians held the consulship[386] and censorship,[387] and patricians, like the Gracchi, stood forward as plebeian tribunes and champions of popular rights.

The distinctions of blood and race, therefore, were no longer regarded. Most of the old patrician families were extinct. Niebuhr believes that at this period not more than fifteen patrician "*gentes*" remained; and the individual members of those which survived, if they maintained their position at all, maintained it by personal influence. The constitutional principle which determined the difference of ranks was property. This line of demarkation between rich and poor was not an impassable one like that of birth, but it had now become

---

[383] Brut. 21.
[384] Meyer, Orat. Rom. Fragm.
[385] B. C. 149; A. U. C. 605.
[386] A. U. C. 580.
[387] A. U. C. 622.

very broad and deep, owing to the accumulation of wealth in few hands; and thus between these two orders there was as little sympathy as there had been between the patrician creditors and the plebeian debtors in the earlier times of the republic.

But besides this constitutional principle of distinction, there was another of a more aristocratic nature, which owed its erection to public opinion. Those families the members of which had held high public offices were termed *nobiles* (nobles.) Those individuals whose families had never been so distinguished were termed new men (*novi homines*.) Thus a man's ancestors were made hostages for his patriotism; and so trustworthy a pledge was hereditary merit considered for ability and fidelity in the discharge of high functions, that only in a few exceptional cases was the consulship, although open to all, conferred upon a new man. One consequence of all these changes was, that the struggle for political distinction became hotter than ever, and the strife more vehement between the competitors for public favour.

These stirring times produced many celebrated orators. Papirius Carbo, the ultra-liberal and unscrupulous colleague of Tiberius Gracchus, who united the gift of a beautiful voice to copiousness and fluency; Lepidus Porcina, who attained the perfection of Attic gentleness, and whom Tib. Gracchus took as his model; Æmilius Scaurus, whom Statius libelled as of ignoble birth; Rutilius Rufus, who was too upright to appeal to the compassion of his judges;[388] M. Junius Pennus, who met by an insulting alien act the bill of Gracchus for the enfranchisement of the Italians.

The Gracchi themselves were each in a different degree eloquent, and possessed those endowments and accidents of birth which would recommend their eloquence to their countrymen. Gentleness and kindness were the characteristics of this illustrious race. Their father, by his mild administration, attached to himself the warm affection of the Spaniards. Their mother inherited the strong mind and genius of Scipio. To a sound knowledge of Greek and Latin literature[389] and a talent for poetry, she added feminine accomplishments. She danced elegantly, more elegantly, indeed, than according to the strict notions of Roman morality a woman of character need have done. She could also sing and accompany herself upon the lute. To her care in early youth the illustrious brothers owed the development of their natural endowments, and the direction of their generous principles. Cicero tells us that he had seen the letters of this remarkable woman, which showed how much her sons were indebted to her teaching. Greek philosophers aided her in her work; and the accomplished Lælius contributed to add grace and polish to the more solid portions of her education.

Notwithstanding that the political principles which the Gracchi embraced were the same, their characters, or, more properly speaking, their temperaments, widely differed, and their style of speaking was, as might be expected, in accordance with their respective dispositions. Tiberius was cold, deliberate, sedate, reserved. The storms of passion never ruffled the calmness of his feelings. His speaking, therefore, was self-possessed and grave, as stoical as his philosophical creed. His conduct was not the result of impulse, but of a strict sense of duty. Cicero termed him *homo sanctissimus*, and his style was as chastened as his integrity was spotless. Such, if we may trust Plutarch, was the character of his oratory, for no fragments remain.

Caius, who was nine years younger than his brother, was warm, passionate, and impetuous: he was inferior to Tiberius morally, as he was intellectually his superior. His

---
[388] De Orat. 153.
[389] Sallust. Cat. 25.

impulses were generous and amiable, but he had not that unswerving rectitude of purpose which is the result of moral principle. He had, however, more genius, more creative power. His imagination, lashed by the violence of his passions, required a strong curb; but for that reason it gushed forth as from a natural fountain, and like a torrent carried all before it. On one occasion, to which Cicero alludes,[390] his look, his voice, his gestures, were so inexpressibly affecting, that even his enemies were dissolved in tears. It is said that in his calmer moments he was conscious that his vehemence was apt to offend against good taste, and employed a slave to stand near him with a pitch-pipe, in order that he might regulate his voice when passion rendered the tones unmusical. His education enabled him to rid himself of the harshness of the old school, and to gain the reputation of being the father of Roman prose. But his impetuosity made him leave unfinished that which he had well begun. "His language was noble, his sentiments wise; gravity pervaded his whole style, but his works wanted the last finishing stroke. There were many glorious beginnings, but they were not brought to perfection."[391] Several fragments remain, which confirm the correctness of Cicero's criticism—one of the most beautiful is from his speech against Popilius Lænas, which drove that blood-thirsty tyrant into voluntary exile.

Oratory began now to be studied more as an art, and to be invested with a more polished garb. The interval between the Gracchi and Cicero boasted of many distinguished names, such as those of Q. Catulus, Curio, Fimbria, Scævola, Cotta, P. Sulpicius, and the Memmii. The most illustrious names of this epoch were M. Antonius, L. Licinius Crassus, and Cicero's immediate predecessor and most formidable rival, Hortensius. Antony and Crassus, says Cicero, were the first Romans who elevated eloquence to the heights to which it had been raised by Greek genius.[392] From this complaint it may be inferred that, notwithstanding the popular prejudice which existed against Greek taste, and to which even Cicero himself sometimes conceived himself obliged to yield,[393] the leading orators had ceased to take the specimens of old Roman eloquence as their models. Cicero asserts[394] that both Antony and Crassus owed their eminence to a diligent study of Greek literature, and to the instructions of Greek professors. The former, he says, attended regularly lectures at Athens and Rhodes, and the latter spoke Greek as if it had been his mother tongue. Yet both had the narrow-minded vanity to deny their obligations: they thought their eloquence would be more popular, the one by showing contempt for the Greeks, the other by affecting not to know them.

M. ANTONIUS

M. Antonius entered public life as a pleader, and thus laid the foundation of his brilliant political career; but he was through life greater as a judicial than as a deliberative orator. He was indefatigable in preparing his case, and made every point tell: he was a great master of the pathetic, and knew the way to the hearts of the *judices*. He was not free from the prevailing fault of advocates, of being somewhat unscrupulous in his assertions; and the reason which he is said to have given for never having published any of his speeches was, lest

---

[390] Orat. iii. 56.
[391] Brut. 33.
[392] Ibid. 36.
[393] Pro Rosc. 25; pro Arch. 60; in. Verr. iv. 59.
[394] Orat. II. i.

he should be forced to deny his words. This statement, however, is refuted by Cicero.[395] Although he did not himself give his speeches to posterity, some of his most pointed expressions and favourite passages left an indelible impression on the memories of his hearers: many are preserved by Cicero, who has given us also a complete epitome of one of them.[396] In the prime of life, he fell a victim to political fury; and his bleeding head was placed upon the rostrum which was so frequently the scene of his eloquent triumphs.

L. LICINIUS CRASSUS

L. Licinius Crassus was four years younger than Antonius, having been born B. C. 140. It is not known whether he was connected with the distinguished family whose name he bore. He commenced his career at the Roman bar.[397] At the early age of twenty-one, he successfully impeached C. Carbo, and in the year B. C. 118 supported the foundation of a colony at Narbo, in Gaul. A measure so beneficial to the poorer citizens increased his popularity as well as his professional fame. He went to Asia as quæstor, and there studied under Metrodorus the rhetorician. On his way home he remained a short time at Athens, and attended the lectures of the leading professors.

Notwithstanding his knowledge of jurisprudence, and his early eminence as a pleader, the speech which established his reputation was a political one. Under the Roman judicial system, the prætor presided in court, with a certain number of assessors, (judices,) who gave their verdict like our jurymen. These were chosen from the senators. Experience proved that not only in their determination to stand by their order they were guilty of partiality, but that they had also been open to bribery. The knights constituted the nearest approach which could be found to a rich middle class. C. Gracchus, therefore, by the "*Lex Sempronia*," transferred the administration of justice to a body of three hundred men, chosen from the equestrian order. This promised to be a salutary change; but so corrupt was the whole framework of Roman society, that it did not prove effectual. The *Publicani*, who farmed the revenues of the provinces, were all Roman knights. The new judges, therefore, were as anxious to shield the peculations and extortions of their own brethren as the old had been.

In B. C. 106, L. Servilius Cæpio brought in a bill for the restoration of the judicial office to the senators. In support of this measure (the first Lex Servilia,) Crassus delivered a powerful and triumphant oration, in which he warmly espoused the cause of the senate, whom he had before as strenuously opposed on the question of the colony to Narbo. This speech was his *chef-d'œuvre*.[398] After serving the office of consul,[399] in which he seems to have mistaken his vocation by exchanging the toga for the sword, he was raised to the censorship.[400] His year of office is celebrated for the closing the schools of the Latin rhetoricians by an edict of himself and his colleague. The foundations of these schools had been laid in the ruins of the Greek schools, when the philosophers and rhetoricians were banished from Rome.[401]

---

[395] Pro Cluent. 50.
[396] De Orat. ii. 48.
[397] B. C. 122.
[398] De Orat. i. 52; Brut. 43.
[399] B. C. 95.
[400] B. C. 92.
[401] B. C. 161; A. U. C. 593.

Although the censorial power could suppress the schools, it could not put a stop to the education given there. The professors found a refuge in private mansions; and thus, protected and fostered by intelligent patrons, continued to fulfil their duties as instructors of youth. How often did literature at Rome have to seek an asylum from private patronage against the rude attacks of public prejudice! The reasons for the measure of Crassus are stated in the preamble.[402] These schools were a novelty; they were contrary to ancient institutions; they encouraged idle habits among the Roman youth. Cicero defended this arbitrary act on the ground that the professors pretended to teach subjects of which they were themselves ignorant; but Cicero could scarcely find a fault in Crassus. He thought him a model of perfection—the first of orators and jurists.[403] He saw no inconsistency in his conduct in the cases of the Narbonne colony and the Servilian law.[404] He is lavish in his praises of his wit and facetiousness, (lepor et facetiæ,[405]) and applies to his malignant and ill-natured jokes the term urbanity. The bon-mots of Crassus were by no means superior to the generality of Roman witticisms, which were deficient in point, although they were personal, caustic, and severe.[406] The grave Romans were content with a very little wit; the quality for which they looked in an oration was not playfulness, but skill in the art of ingenious tormenting. Crassus never uttered a jest equal to that of old Cato, when he said of Q. Helvidius, the glutton, whose house was on fire, "What he could not eat he has burned."[407]

His conduct with respect to the Latin schools, and his self-indulgent life in his magnificent mansion on the Palatine, prove that he had retained the narrow-mindedness of the old Romans without their temperance and self-denial, and had acquired the luxury and taste of the Greeks without their liberality. If, however, we make some allowance for partiality, Crassus deserves the favourable criticism of Cicero.[408] His style is careful and yet not laboured—it is elegant, accurate, and perspicuous. He seems to have possessed considerable powers of illustration, and great clearness in explaining and defining; his delivery was calm and self-possessed, his action sufficiently vehement, but not excessive.[409] He took especial pains with the commencement of his speech. When he was about to speak, every one was prepared to listen, and the very first words which he uttered showed him worthy of the expectation formed. No one better understood the difficult art of uniting elegance with brevity.

From amongst the crowd of orators which were then flourishing in the last days of expiring Roman liberty, Cicero selected Crassus to be the representative of his sentiments in his imaginary conversation in the *de Oratore*. He felt that their tastes were congenial. In this most captivating essay, he introduces his readers to a distinguished literary circle, men who united activity in public life with a taste for refined leisure. Antony, Crassus, Scævola, Cotta, and Sulpicius, met at Tusculum to talk of the politics of the day. For this especial purpose they had come, and all day long they ceased not to converse on these grave matters. They spoke not of lighter matters until they reclined at supper. Their day seemed to have been spent in the senate, their evening at Tusculum. Next day, in the serene and sunny climate of

---

[402] A. Gell. xv. ii.
[403] De Cl. Or. 143, 145.
[404] Pro Cluent. 51.
[405] De Orat. ii. 54.
[406] Cic. de Or. ii. 65; Plin. H. N. xxxv. 4.
[407] Macrobius, Sat.
[408] See Brutus, *passim*.
[409] Brutus, 158.

Frascati, a scene well fitted for the calm repose of a Platonic dialogue, Scævola proposed to imitate the Socrates of Plato, and converse, as the great philosopher did, beneath the shade of a plane-tree. Crassus assented, suggesting only that cushions would be more convenient than the grass. So the dialogue began in which Crassus is made the mouthpiece to deliver the sentiments of Cicero.

Like our own Chatham, Crassus almost died on the floor of the senate-house, and his last effort was in support of the aristocratic party. His opponent, Philippus the consul, strained his power to the utmost to insult him, and ordered his goods to be seized. His last words were worthy of him. He mourned the bereavement of the senate—that the consul, like a sacrilegious robber, should strip of its patrimony the very order of which he ought to have been a kind parent or faithful guardian. "It is useless," he continued, "to seize these: if you will silence Crassus, you must tear out his tongue, and even then my liberty shall breathe forth a refutation of thy licentiousness!" The paroxysm was too much for him; fever ensued, and in seven days he was a corpse.

We must pass over numerous names contained in the catalogue of Cicero, mentioning by the way Cotta and the two Sulpicii. Cotta's taste was pure; but his delicate lungs made his oratory too tame for his vehement countrymen. Publius Sulpicius had all the powers of a tragic actor to influence the passions, but professed that he could not write, and therefore left no specimens behind him. His reluctance to write must have been the result of reserve or of indolence, and not of inability, for nothing can be more tender and touching, and yet more philosophical, than his letter to Cicero on the death of his beloved daughter.[410] Servius, like too many orators, and even Cicero himself, at first despised an accurate knowledge of the Roman law. The great Scævola, however, rebuked him, and reminded him how disgraceful it was for one who desired the reputation of an advocate to be ignorant of law. These words excited his emulation; he ardently devoted himself to the study of jurisprudence,[411] and at length is said to have surpassed even Scævola himself.

Q. Hortensius

The last of the pre-Ciceronian orators was Hortensius. Although he was scarcely eight years senior to the greatest of all Roman orators, he cannot be considered as belonging to the same literary period, since the genius and eloquence of Cicero constitute the commencement of a new era. He was, nevertheless, his contemporary and his rival; and all that is known respecting his career is derived from the writings of Cicero.

Q. Hortensius was the son of L. Hortensius, prætor of Sicily, B. C. 97. He was born B. C. 114; and, as it was the custom that noble Roman youths should be called to the bar at an early age, he commenced his career as a pleader at nineteen, and pleaded, with applause and success, before two consuls who were excellent judges of his merits, the orator Crassus and the jurist Scævola. His first speech was in support of the province of Africa against the extortions of the governor. In his second he defended Nicomedes, king of Bithynia, against his brother, who had dethroned him. When Crassus and Antony were dead, he was left

---

[410] De Fam. iv. 5.
[411] Cic. Philip. ix. 5.

without any rival except Cotta, but he soon surpassed him.[412] The eloquence of Cotta was too languid to stand against the impetuous flow, and he thus became the acknowledged leader of the Roman bar until the star of Cicero arose. They first came in contact when Cicero pleaded the cause of Quintius, and in that oration he pays the highest possible compliment to the talents and genius of Hortensius.

His political connexion with the faction of Sulla, and his unscrupulous support of the profligate corruption which characterized that administration both at home and abroad, enlisted his legal talents in defence of the infamous Verres; but the eloquence of Cicero, together with the justice of the cause which he espoused, prevailed, and from that time forward his superiority over Hortensius was established and complete. But the admiration which Cicero entertained for his rival had ripened into friendship, which neither the fact of their being retained on opposite sides, nor even difference in politics, had power to interrupt. The only danger which ever threatened its stability was some little jealousy on the part of Cicero—a jealousy which must be attributed to his morbid temperament and susceptible disposition. But Hortensius was always a warm and affectionate friend to Cicero, and Cicero was affected with the deepest grief when he heard of the death of Hortensius.[413] The time at length arrived when identity of political sentiments drew them more closely together; and it is to this we owe the place which Hortensius so often occupies in the letters and other works of the great Roman orator.

Cicero had originally espoused the popular cause; but his zeal gradually became less ardent, and the Catilinarian conspiracy threw him entirely into the arms of the aristocratic party. At the Roman bar politics had great influence in determining the side taken by the leading advocates. They were virtually the great law officers of the party in the republic to which they belonged, and had, as it were, general retainers on their own side. Hence Hortensius generally advocated the same side with Cicero. Together they defended Rabirius, Muræna, Flaccus, Sextius, Scaurus, and Milo; but the former seems to have at once acknowledged his inferiority, and henceforward to have taken but little part in public life. In B. C. 51, he defended his nephew from a charge of bribery; but the guilt of the accused was so plain that the people hissed him when he entered the theatre.[414] The following year he died, at the age of seventy-five, and left behind him a daughter, whose eloquence is celebrated in history. An oration, of which she was the author, was read in the time of Quintilian for the sake of its own merits, and not as a mere compliment to the female sex. Q. Hortensius has been accused of corruption; and his attachment to a corrupt party, his luxurious habits, extravagant expenditure, numerous villas, and enormous wealth, make it probable that this suspicion was not unfounded. He was an easy, kind-hearted, hospitable, but self-indulgent man. His park was a complete menagerie; his fish-ponds were stocked with fish so tame that they would feed from his hand. His gardens were so carefully kept that he even watered his trees with wine. He had a taste for both poetry and painting, wrote some amatory verses, and for one picture gave 140,000 sesterces, (about 1,100*l.*) His table was sumptuous; and peacocks were seen for the first time in Rome at his banquets. His cellar was so well supplied that he left 10,000 casks of Chian wine behind him.[415]

---

[412] Brut. xcii.
[413] Ad Att. vi. 6.
[414] Ad Fam. viii. 2.
[415] Smith's Dict. of Antiq. *s. v.*

Cicero[416] tells us that the principal reason of Hortensius' early popularity and subsequent failure was, that his style of eloquence was suited to the brilliance and liveliness of youth, but not the dignity and gravity of mature age. In those days there were two parties,[417] who differed in their views as to the theory of eloquence; the one admired the oratory of the Attic rhetoricians, which was calm, polished, refined, eschewing all redundancies; the other that of the Asiatic schools, which was florid and ornate.

Cicero[418] tells us that the style of Hortensius' eloquence was Asiatic; and as the characteristic of his own eloquence is Asiatic diffuseness rather than Attic closeness, and he often seems to consider this quality of Asiatic eloquence least worthy of admiration, it is possible that Hortensius carried it to excess, perhaps even to the borders of affectation. In a youthful orator excess of ornament is pardonable, because it is natural; it gives promise of future excellence when genius becomes sobered and luxuriance retrenched.

Hortensius, a prosperous and spoilt child of nature, was a young man all his life: there was nothing to cast a gloom over his gayety; and to those of his auditors who possessed good taste, this juvenility seemed inconsistent, and threw into the shade the finish, polish, and animation which characterized his style. His delivery was probably no less unsuitable to more advanced years. We are told that Æsop and Roscius used to study his action as a lesson;[419] and that one Torquatus sneeringly called him Dionysius, who was a celebrated dancer of that day. His defence was clever: "I had rather," he said, "be that than a clumsy Torquatus." But these very anecdotes seem to imply that his delivery was somewhat foppish and theatrical.

---

[416] Brut. 95.
[417] Quint. xii.; ch. x.; Brut. Orat. ad Br. in many places.
[418] A. Gell. i. 5.
[419] A. Gell. i. 5.

Chapter 14

STUDY OF JURISPRUDENCE—EARLIEST SYSTEMATIC WORKS ON ROMAN LAW—GROUNDWORK OF THE ROMAN CIVIL LAW—EMINENT JURISTS—THE SCÆVOLÆ—ÆLIUS GALLUS—C. AQUILIUS GALLUS, A LAW REFORMER—OTHER JURISTS—GRAMMARIANS

Politics and jurisprudence were the subjects on which the Romans especially pursued independent lines of thought; but their jurisprudence was the more original of the two. Although the practical development of their political system was entirely the work of this eminently practical people, still in the theory of political science they were followers and imitators of the Greeks. But in jurisprudence, the help which they derived from Greece was very slight. The mere framework, so far as the laws of the Twelve Tables are concerned, came to them from Athens; but the complete structure was built up by their own hands; and by their skill and prudence they were the authors of a system possessing such stability, that they bequeathed it as an inheritance to modern Europe, and traces of Roman law are visible in the legal systems of the whole civilized world.

Roman jurisprudence is, of course, a subject of too great extent to be treated of as its importance deserves in a work like the present; but still it is so closely connected with eloquence that it cannot be dismissed without a few words. It has been already stated that arms, politics, and the bar were the avenues to distinction; and thus many an ambitious youth, who learned the art of war in a foreign campaign under some experienced general, occupied himself also at home in the forum. Not only was the young patrician conscious that he could not efficiently discharge his first duty to his clients without possessing sufficient ability and knowledge to defend their rights in a court of law, but this was an effectual method of showing his fitness for a public career. Eminence as a jurisconsult opened a direct path to eminence as a statesman.[420] He must be like Pollio, "*Insigne mæstis præsidium reis,*" as well as "*Consulenti curiæ.*"[421]

---

[420] Cic. Muræn. 8, 19; Off. ii. 19, 65.
[421] Hor. Od. II. i. 13.

Hence the complicated principles of jurisprudence and of the Roman constitution became a necessary part of a liberal education. The brilliant orator, indeed, did sometimes affect to look down with contempt on such black-letter and antiquarian lore, and stigmatize it as pedantry;[422] but still common sense compelled the sober-minded to acknowledge the necessity of the study. They saw that in the courts eloquence could only be considered as the handmaid to legal knowledge, even though the saying of Quintilian were true—"*Et leges ipsæ nihil valent nisi actoris idoneâ voce munitæ.*"[423] When, therefore, a Roman youth had completed his studies under his teacher of rhetoric, he not only frequented the forum in order to learn the practical application of the oratorical principles which he had acquired, and frequently took some celebrated orator as a model, but also studied the principles of jurisprudence under an eminent jurist, and attended the consultations in which they gave to their clients their expositions of law. In fact the young Roman acquired his legal knowledge in the *atrium* of the jurisconsult, somewhat in the same manner that the law student of the present day pursues his education in the chambers of a barrister. He studied the subject practically and empirically rather than in its theory and general principles.

Almost all the knowledge which we possess is derived from the labours of writers who flourished long after constitutional liberty had expired.

The earliest systematic works on Roman law were the Enchiridion or Manual of Pomponius, and the Institutes of Gaius, who flourished in the times of Hadrian and the Antonines. Both these works were for a long time lost, although numerous fragments were preserved in the Pandects or Digest of Justinian. In 1816, however, Niebuhr discovered a palimpsest MS., in which the Epistles of St. Jerome were written over the erased Institutes of Gaius. But owing to the decisions and interpretations of the great practising jurists, to the want of any system of reporting and recording, and to the numerous misunderstandings of the Roman historians respecting the laws and constitutional history of their country, the whole subject long continued in a state of confusion: new contradictory theories had been gradually introduced, and old difficulties had not been explained and reconciled. Gian Baptista Vico, in his *Scienza Nova*, was the first who dispelled the clouds of error and reduced it to a system; and his example was afterwards so successfully followed by Niebuhr, that modern students can understand the subject more clearly, and have a more comprehensive antiquarian knowledge of it, than the writers of the Augustan age.

The earliest Roman laws were the *Leges Regiæ*, which were collected and codified by Sextus Papirius, and were hence called the Papirian Code. But these were rude and unconnected—simply a collection of isolated enactments. The laws of the Twelve Tables stand next in point of antiquity. They exhibited the first attempts at regular system, and imbodied not only legislative enactments but legal principles.[424] So popular were they, that when Cicero was a child every Roman boy committed them to memory as our children learn their catechism,[425] and the great orator laments that in the course of his lifetime this practice had become obsolete. The explanation of these laws was a privilege confined to the pontifical college. This body alone prescribed the form of pleading, and published the days on which the courts were held. Hence, not only the whole practice and exposition of the law was in the hands of the patricians, but they had also the power of obstructing at their pleasure all legal

---

[422] Cic. pro Muræn.
[423] Inst. Or. xii. 7.
[424] De Orat. 44.
[425] De Leg. ii. 23.

business. But in the censorship of Appius Claudius, his secretary, Cn. Flavius, set up, at the suggestion of Appius, a Calendar in the Forum, which made known to the public the days on which legal business could be transacted. In vain the patricians endeavoured to maintain their monopoly by the invention of new formulæ, called Notes, for Tiberius Coruncanius, the first plebeian Pontifex Maximus, who was consul A. U. C. 474, opened a public school of jurisprudence, and in the middle of the next century[426] the "*Notes*" were published by Sextus Ælius Catus.

The oral traditional expositions of these laws formed the groundwork of the Roman civil law. To these were added from time to time the decrees of the people (plebiscita,) the acts of the senate (senatus-consulta,) and the prætorian edicts, which announced the principles on which each successive prætor purposed to administer the statute law.

Such were the various elements out of which the whole body of Roman law was composed; and in such early times was the subject diligently studied and expounded that the latter half of the sixth century A. U. C. was rich in jurists whose powers are celebrated in history. Besides S. Ælius Catus, already mentioned, P. Licinius Crassus, surnamed "the rich," who was consul A. U. C. 549, is mentioned by Livy[427] as learned in the pontifical law, the canon law of the ancient Romans. L. Acilius also wrote commentaries on the laws of the Twelve Tables; and to these may be added T. Manlius Torquatus, consul A. U. C. 589, S. Fabius Pictor, and another member of the same distinguished family, Q. Fabius Labeo, Cato the censor and his son Porcius Cato Licinianus, and lastly P. Cornelius Nasica, whose services as a jurist were recognised by the grant of a house at the public expense.

The most eminent jurists who adorned the next century were the Scævolæ. In their family the profession of the jurisconsult seems to have been hereditary; of so many bearing that distinguished name, it might have been said that their house was the oracle of the whole state; "Domus jurisconsulti totius oraculum civitatis."[428] Quintus, the augur, was Cicero's first instructor in the science of the law: his cousin Publius enjoyed also a high reputation; and Quintus, the son of Publius, who became Cicero's tutor after the death of his elder kinsman, combined the genius of an orator with the erudition of a jurist, and was called by his distinguished pupil "the greatest orator among jurists, and the greatest jurist among orators." The compiler of the digest also quotes as authorities M. Manilius and M. Junius Brutus.[429] Manilius is one of the characters introduced in Cicero's dialogue *de Republica*: he was consul A. U. C. 604, and is said to have been the author of seven legal treatises; but of all these, except three, Cicero denies the authority. Brutus was the son of the ambassador of that name who was employed in the war with Perseus, and left a treatise in three books on the civil law.[430]

In the next century flourished one Ælius Gallus, who was somewhat senior to Cicero, and was the author of a treatise on the signification of law terms. Several of his definitions are given by Festus, and fragments are preserved by A. Gellius,[431] and in the Digest. By some he has been considered identical with Ælius Gallus, the prefect of Egypt in the reign of

---

[426] A. U. C. 552.
[427] Lib. xxx. 1.
[428] De Or. i. 45.
[429] Dig. I. ii. 39.
[430] De Or. ii. 55.
[431] Lib. xvi. 5; Dig. L. 16, 157.

Augustus,[432] who was the friend of the geographer Strabo; but as there is little doubt that he is quoted by Varro,[433] such identity is impossible, since Varro died B. C. 28, and yet he speaks of Gallus as an aged man. Another distinguished jurist of this era was his namesake C. Aquilius Gallus. He was a pupil of Q. Mucius Scævola, and surpassed all his contemporaries in that black-letter knowledge of law, which in olden time was more highly valued than in the more brilliant days of Cicero. Learning then began to be ridiculed and lightly esteemed, and oratorical powers were more admired in proportion as the Roman mind became more alive to the refinements and beauties of language.

But Gallus was most eminent as a law reformer. The written law of Rome presented by its technicality the greatest impediments to actions on the unwritten principle of common right and equity. To obviate this he invented legal fictions, *i. e.* formulæ by which the effects of the statute could be annulled without the necessity of abrogating the statute itself. His practice must have been large, for Pliny mentions that he was the owner of a splendid palace on the Viminal Hill.[434] In B. C. 67, he served the office of prætor together with Cicero, and both before and after that he frequently sat as one of the judices. Cicero pleaded before him in the defence both of Cæcina and Cluentius.

Besides Aquilius Gallus, three of the most distinguished jurists, who were a few years senior to Cicero, owed their legal knowledge to the instructions of Mucius Scævola. These were—C. Juventius, Sextus Papirius, and L. Lucilius Balbus, the last of whom is mentioned by Cicero,[435] and his works are quoted by his eminent pupil Sulpicius Rufus.

GRAMMARIANS

Towards the conclusion of this literary period a great increase took place in the numbers of those learned men whom the Romans termed "*Litterati*,"[436] but afterwards, following the custom of the Greeks, Grammarians, (*Grammatici*.[437]) To them literature was under deep obligations. Although few of them were authors, and all of them men of acquired learning rather than of original genius, they exercised a powerful influence over the public mind as professors, lecturers, critics, and school-masters. By them the youths of the best families not only were imbued with a taste for Greek philosophy and poetry, but also were taught to appreciate the literature of their own country.

Suetonius places at the head of the class Livius Andronicus and Ennius; but their fame as poets eclipses their reputation as mere critics and commentators.

The first professed grammarian whom he mentions is Crates Mallotes, who, between the first and second Punic wars, was sent to Rome by Attalus. The unfortunate ambassador fell into an open drain and broke his leg, and beguiled the tediousness of his confinement by reading a course of philological lectures. After him C. Octavius Lampadio edited the works of

---

[432] B. C. 24, 25.
[433] De Lat. Lin. iv. 2; iv. 10; v. 7.
[434] H. N. vii. 1.
[435] De Orat. iii. 21.
[436] Cornelius Nepos ait litteratos quidem vulgo appellari eos qui aliquid diligenter et acute scienterque possint aut dicere aut scribere.
[437] Sueton. de Illust. Gram.

Nævius; Q. Vargunteius those of Ennius; and Lælius, Archelaus, Vectius, and Q. Philocomus read and explained to a circle of auditors the Satires of Lucilius.

Most of these grammarians were emancipated slaves: some were Greeks, some barbarians. Sævius Nicanor and Aurelius Opilius were freedmen: the latter had belonged to the household of some Epicurean philosopher. Cornelius Epicadus was a freedman of Sulla, and completed the Commentaries which his patron left unfinished, and Lenæus was freedman of Pompey the Great. M. Pompilius Andronicus was a Syrian; M. Antonius Gnipho, though of ingenuous birth, a Gaul. Servius Clodius, however, and L. Ælius Lanuvinus were Roman knights. Nor were the labours of these industrious scholars confined to Rome, or even to Italy; for Octavius Teucer, Siscennius Iacchus and Oppius Chares gave instructions in the province of Gallia Togata.

To the names already mentioned may be added those of L. Ælius Stilo, who accompanied L. Metellus Numidicus into exile, and Valerius Cato, who not only taught the art of poetry, but was himself a poet.

We have now traced from its infancy the rise and progress of Roman literature, and watched the gradual opening of the national intellect. The dawn has gently broken, the light has steadily increased, and is now succeeded by the noon-day brilliance of the "golden age."

Section II. The Era of Cicero and Augustus

Chapter 15

Prose the Test of the Condition of a Language—Dramatic Literature Extinct—Mimes—Difference Between Roman and Greek Mimes—Laberius—Passages from His Poetry—Matius Calvena—Mimiambi—Publius Syrus—Roman Pantomime—Its Licentiousness—Principal Actors of Pantomime

During the period upon which we are now entering, Roman literature arrived at its greatest perfection. The time at which it attained the highest point of excellence is fixed by Niebuhr[438] about A. U. C. 680, when Cicero was between thirty and forty years old. Poetry, indeed, still continued to improve, as regarded metrical structure and diction, in finish, smoothness, and harmony. There is *ex. gr.* in these respects a marked difference between the works of Lucretius and Virgil; but nevertheless the principles of language now became fixed and settled. In fact, the condition of a language must be judged of by its prose; so must likewise the state of perfection to which its literature has attained. If poetry could be with propriety assumed as the standard, the commencement of the empire of Augustus would constitute the best age of Latin literature, rather than the time when the forum echoed with the eloquence of Cicero; but in the two ages of Cicero and Augustus, taken together as forming one era, is comprehended the golden age both of poetry and prose.

Dramatic literature, however, never recovered from the trance into which it had fallen. The stage had not altogether lost that popularity which it had possessed in the days of Attius and Terence, for Æsopus and Roscius, the former the great tragedian, the latter the favourite comedian, in the time of Cicero, amassed great wealth. Æsopus lived liberally,[439] and yet bequeathed a fortune to his son, and Roscius is said to have earned daily the sum of thirty-two pounds.

---

[438] Lect. R. H. cvi.
[439] Plin. H. N. v. 72.

Notwithstanding, also, the degradation attached to the social position of an actor, both these eminent artists enjoyed the friendship of Cicero and other great men. They brought to the study of their profession industry, taste, talent, and learning, and these qualities were appreciated. Æsopus was on one occasion encored a countless number of times (*millies*)[440] by an enthusiastic audience, and Roscius was elevated by Sulla to the equestrian dignity. But although the standard Roman plays were constantly represented, dramatic literature had become extinct. No one wrote comedy at all, and the tragedies of Valgius Rufus and Asinius Pollio were only intended for reading or recitation. Nor, as has been already shown, does the Thyestes of Varus really form an exception to this statement.

The dramatic entertainments which had now taken the place of comedy and tragedy were termed mimes.

Their distinguishing appellation was derived from the Greek, but they entirely differed from those compositions to which the Greeks applied that title. The latter were written not in verse, but in prose;[441] they were dialogues, not dramatic pieces, and though they were exhibited at certain festivals, and the parts supported by actors, they were never represented on the stage. Even when Sophron, whose compositions were admired and imitated by Plato,[442] raised them to their highest degree of perfection, and made them vehicles of serious moral lessons mingling together ludicrous buffoonery with grave philosophy, their language was only a rhythmical prose, probably somewhat resembling that in which the celebrated despatch of Hippocrates[443] was written. Some idea may be formed of their nature from the fact that the idylls of Theocritus were imitated from the mimes of Sophron, and that Persius took them for his model in his peculiarly dramatic satires.[444]

The Roman mimes were laughable imitations of manners and persons. So far they combined features of comedy and farce; for comedy represents the characters of a class—farce those of individuals. Their essence was that of the modern pantomime; mimicry and burlesque dialogue were only accidentally introduced. Their coarseness and even indecency[445] gratified the love of broad humour which characterized the Roman people. They became successful rivals of comedy, and thus came to be admitted on the public stage. It is most probable that like other dramatic exhibitions, they originally grew out of the Fabulæ Atellanæ, which they afterwards superseded. But notwithstanding their indecency, their satire upon the living, and their burlesque representations of the illustrious dead, when exhibited at funeral games, they had sometimes, like the mimes of Sophron, a moral character, and abounded in shrewd wisdom and noble sentiments.[446] Schlegel asserts that there is a great affinity between the Roman mimes and the pasquinades and harlequinades of modern Italy. He conjectures that in them may be traced the germ of the *Comedie dell' Arte*, and states that the very picture of Polichinello is found in some of the frescoes of Pompeii.

After a time, when mimes became established as popular favourites, the dialogue or written part of the entertainment occupied a more prominent position, and was written in verse, like that of tragedy or comedy. In the dictatorship of Julius Cæsar, a Roman knight, named Decius Laberius, became eminent for his mimes. Respecting his merits, we have few

---

[440] Cic. pro Sen.
[441] Schlegel Lect. viii.; Müller's Dor. iv. 7, 5.
[442] Diog. Laert. iii. 18.
[443] Xen. Hell. i. 23.
[444] Müller's Dorians, Trans. ii. 374.
[445] Or. Tr. ii. 515.
[446] Cic. pro Rab. 12; de Orat. ii. 59. See also fragm. of Syrus' Mimes.

opportunities of forming a judgment, as the fragments of his writings[447] are but few and short; but Horace[448] speaks of them in unfavourable language, and finds fault with their carelessness and want of regular plan. He was born about B. C. 107,[449] and died B. C. 45, at Puteoli, (Pozzuoli.) The profession of an actor of mimes was infamous; but Laberius was a writer, not an actor. It happened, however, that P. Syrus, who had been first the slave, then the freedman and pupil of Laberius, and lastly a professional actor, challenged all his brethren to a trial of improvisatorial skill. Cæsar entreated Laberius to enter the lists, and offered him five hundred sestertia (about 4,000*l*.) Laberius did not submit to the degradation for the sake of the money, but he was afraid to refuse. The only method of retaliation in his power was sarcasm. His part was that of a slave, and when his master scourged him, he exclaimed, "Porro, Quirites, libertatem perdimus!" His words were received with a round of applause, and the audience fixed their eyes on Cæsar. On another occasion his attack on the Dictator was almost threatening:—

> Necesse est multos timeat quem multi timent.

He appears to have been always quick and ready in repartee. When, on being vanquished by his adversary Syrus, the Dictator said to him with a sneer—

> Favente tibi me victus es Laberi a Syro,

He replied with the following sad but true reflections:—

> Non possunt primi esse omnes omni in tempore,
> Summum ad gradum cum claritatis veneris
> Consistes ægre; et quum descendas decides;
> Cecidi ego, cadet qui sequitur, laus est publica.

Cæsar, however, restored to him the rank and equestrian privileges of which his act had deprived him; but still he could not recover the respect of his countrymen. As he passed the orchestra in his way to the stalls of the knights, Cicero cried out, "If we were not so crowded, I would make room for you here." Laberius replied, alluding to Cicero's lukewarmness as a political partisan, "I am astonished that you should be crowded, as you generally sit on two stools." The calm and feeling rebuke with which, in the prologue to his mime, he remonstrated against the tyranny of Cæsar, is singularly spirited and beautiful:—

> Necessitas, cujus cursus transversi impetum
> Voluerunt multi effugere, pauci potuerunt,
> Quo me detrusit pæne extremis sensibus?
> Quem nulla ambitio, nulla unquam largitio,
> Nullus timor, vis nulla, nulla auctoritas
> Movere potuit in juventa de statu;
> Ecce in senecta ut facile labefecit loco

---

[447] Bothe, Po. Sc. Lat. fragm. vol. v.
[448] Sat. i. x. 6. See also Sen. Controv., and Nieb. H. R. ii. p. 169.
[449] Hieron. Eus. Chron.

Viri excellentis mente clemente edita
Submissa placide blandiloquens oratio!
Etenim ipsi Dii negare cui nihil potuerunt,
Hominem me denegare quis possit pati?
Ergo bis tricenis actis annis sine nota
Eques Romanus lare egressus meo
Domum revertas mimus; Nimirum hoc die
Uno plus vixi mihi quam vivendum fuit
Fortuna, immoderata in bono æque atque in malo,
Si tibi erat libitum literarum laudibus
Floris cacumen nostræ famæ frangere,
Cur quum vigebam membris præviridantibus,
Satisfacere populo et tali cum poteram viro,
Non flexibilem me concurvasti ut carperes?
Nunc me quo dejicis? quid ad scenam affero?
Decorem formæ, an dignitatem corporis,
Animi virtutem, an vocis jucundæ sonum?
Ut hedera serpens vires arboreas necat,
Ita me vetustas amplexa annorum enecat,
Sepulchri similis nihil nomen retines.
O, strong Necessity! of whose swift course
So many feel, so few escape the force,
Whither, ah whither, in thy prone career,
Hast thou decreed this dying frame to bear?
Me, in my better days, nor foe, nor friend,
Nor threat, nor bribe, nor vanity could bend;
Now, lured by flattery, in my weaker age
I sink my knighthood and ascend the stage.
Yet muse not therefore—how shall man gainsay
Him whom the Deities themselves obey?
Sixty long years I've lived without disgrace
A Roman knight!—let dignity give place;
I'm Cæsar's actor now, and compass more
In one short hour than all my life before.
O Fortune! fickle source of good and ill,
If here to place me was thy sovereign will,
Why, when I'd youth and faculties to please
So great a master, and such guests as these,
Why not compel me then, malicious power,
To the hard task of this degrading hour?
Where now, in what profound abyss of shame,
Dost thou conspire with Fate to sink my name?
Whence are my hopes? What voice can age supply
To charm the ear, what grace to please the eye?
Where is the active energy and art,
The look that guides its passion to the heart?
Age creeps like ivy o'er my withered trunk,
Its bloom all blasted and its vigour shrunk;

A tomb, where nothing but a name remains
To tell the world whose ashes it contains.
Cumberland.

Another poet of this age who composed mimes was C. Matius, surnamed, from his baldness, Calvena. His mimes were termed *Mimiambi*, because he wrote in the iambic measure,[450] and he was also a translator of the Iliad as well as the author of a work on cookery. His principal merit is said to have been his skill in enriching his native language by the introduction of new words.[451] He was somewhat younger than Laberius, and enjoyed the friendship of the greatest amongst his contemporaries. His intimacy with Julius Cæsar,[452] to whom he was warmly attached,[453] and afterwards with Augustus,[454] gave him great influence;[455] but he never took much part in the political strife which imbittered his times, nor did he use his influence in order to procure his own advancement.

His retired habits and love of literary leisure saved him from seeking his happiness in the excitements of ambition. Cicero, who loved him dearly, often mentions him in his letters, and pays a compliment[456] to his learning and amiability. An interesting letter of his, which is preserved in the collection of Cicero's epistles to his friends,[457] shows that he possessed an accomplished mind and an affectionate heart. It cannot be supposed, therefore, that his *Mimiambi* were debased by the too common faults of coarseness and immodesty.

PUBLIUS SYRUS

Publius Syrus was, as his name implies, originally a Syrian slave, and took his prænomen from the master who gave him his freedom. All that is known respecting his life has already been stated in the account of Laberius. The commendations which his mimes received from the ancients, especially from Cicero,[458] Seneca,[459] and Pliny,[460] prove them to have been much read and admired. The fragments which still remain are marked by wit and neatness, and the shrewd wisdom of proverbial philosophy. Tradition has also recorded a *bon-mot* of his, which is as witty as it is severe. Seeing once an ill-tempered man, named Mucius, in low spirits, he remarked, "Either some bad fortune has happened to Mucius, or some good fortune to one of his friends." An accurate knowledge of human nature, exhibited in pointed and terse language, most probably constituted the charm of this species of scenic literature. The large collection of his proverbial sayings, entitled *P. Syri Sententiæ*, are by no means all genuine; but the nucleus around which the collection has grown by successive additions is undoubtedly his, and those which are the work of after ages are formed after the model of his apothegms.

---

[450] Pl. Ep. vi. 21.
[451] A. Gell. xv. 25.
[452] Suet. Cæs. 52.
[453] Cic. ad Fam. x. 28.
[454] Pl. H. N. xii. 2, 6.
[455] Tac. An. xii. 60.
[456] Ad Fam. vii. 15.
[457] Ibid. xi. 28.
[458] Ad Fam. xii. 18.
[459] Sen. Controv. vii. 3; Ep. 8, 94, 108.
[460] Pl. H. N. viii. 51.

The Roman pantomime differed somewhat from the mime—it was a ballet of action performed by a single dancer. It was first introduced in its complete form in the reign of Augustus: and Suidas,[461] misquoting a passage from Zosimus,[462] groundlessly attributes the invention to the emperor himself. As the mime bore some resemblance to the Atellan farces, so the pantomime resembled the histrionic performances introduced by Livius Andronicus. In both, the person who recited the words (*canticum*[463]) was different from him who represented the characters. In the pantomime, the *canticum* was sung by a chorus arrayed at the back of the stage. Until the times of the later emperors, when vice was paraded with unblushing effrontery, women never acted in pantomime; but the exhibition itself was sensual and licentious in its character,[464] and the actors of it were deservedly deemed infamous, and forbidden by Tiberius to hold any intercourse with Romans of equestrian or senatorial dignity.[465] Nero, however, outraged public decency by himself appearing in pantomime.[466] Fortunate was it for the dignity of Rome that the face of the emperor was concealed behind a mask which, unlike the performers in the mimes, the pantomimic actors always wore. The players not only exhibited the human figure in the most graceful attitudes, but represented every passion and emotion with such truth, that the spectators could without difficulty understand the story. Sometimes the scenes represented were founded upon the Greek tragic drama; but for its purifying effect was substituted the awakening of licentious passions.

These were the exhibitions which threw such discredit on the stage—which called forth the well-deserved attacks of the early Christian fathers, and caused them to declare that whoever attended them was unworthy of the name of Christians. Had the drama not been so abused, had it retained its original purity, and carried out the object attributed to it by Aristotle, they would have seen in it not a nursery of vice, but a school of virtue—not only an innocent amusement, but a powerful engine to form the taste, to improve the morals, and to purify the feelings of a people.

The principal actors of pantomime in the reign of Augustus were Bathyllus, Hylas, and Pylades. In the reign of Nero the art was practised by Latinus,[467] and Paris, who taught the emperor to dance, and subsequently was put to death by Nero when he became his rival for popular applause.[468] But those who attained the highest degree of popularity were another Latinus, and another Paris, who flourished in the reign of Domitian. Both have been immortalized in the epigrams of Martial.[469] To the former, Martial attributes the power to fascinate such stern and rigid moralists as resembled Cato, the Curii, and Fabricii. The epitaph concludes with these lines:—

> Vos me laurigeri parasitum dicite Phœbi,
> Roma sui famulum dum sciat esse Jovis.
> Say ye I gained the laurelled Phœbus' love,
> So that Rome hails me servant of her Jove.

---

[461] S. v. Ὀρχησίς.
[462] Hist. Rom. i.
[463] Pl. Ep. vii. 24.
[464] Juv. vi. 65.
[465] Tac. Ann. i. 77.
[466] Suet. Ner. 16, 26.
[467] Juv. i. 35; vi. 44.
[468] Lib. ix. 29; xi. 13.
[469] Suet. Ner. 54.

The latter, by his popularity, acquired great influence at court, but his profligacy proved his ruin. He intrigued with the empress Domitia; and Domitian consequently divorced his wife, and caused Paris to be assassinated. He has furnished a plot and a hero to Massinger's play of the "*Roman Actor.*" The simple and beautiful epitaph written to his memory by Martial is as follows:—

> Quisquis Flaminiam teris, viator,
> Noli nobile præterire marmor.
> Urbis deliciæ, salesque Nili,
> Ars et gratia, lusus et voluptas;
> Romani decus et dolor theatri,
> Atque omnes Veneres, Cupidinesque,
> Hoc sunt condita, quo Paris, sepulchro.
> Whoe'er thou art, O traveller, stay!
> Mark what proud tomb adorns the way.
> The town's delight, the wit of Nile,
> Art, grace, mirth, pleasure, sport and smile:
> The honour of the Roman stage,
> The grief and sorrow of the age:
> All Venuses and Loves lie here
> Buried in Paris' sepulchre.

Chapter 16

LUCRETIUS A POET RATHER THAN A PHILOSOPHER—HIS LIFE—EPIC STRUCTURE OF HIS POEM—VARIETY OF HIS POETRY—EXTRACTS FROM HIS POEM—ARGUMENT OF IT—THE EPICUREAN DOCTRINES CONTAINED IN IT—MORALITY OF EPICURUS AND LUCRETIUS—TESTIMONIES OF VIRGIL AND OVID—CATULLUS: HIS LIFE, CHARACTER, AND POETRY—OTHER POETS OF THIS PERIOD

LUCRETIUS CARUS (BORN B. C. 95.)

Lucretius Carus might claim a place amongst philosophers as well as poets, for his poem marks an epoch both in poetry and philosophy. But his philosophy is a mere reflexion from that of Greece, whilst his poetry is bright with the rays of original genius. A delineation, therefore, of his characteristics as a writer of the imagination, will present the more accurate idea of the place which he occupies amongst Roman authors. It was no empty boast of his, that, as a poet, he deserved the praise of originality—that he had opened a path through the territory of the muse, untrodden before by poet's foot—that he had drawn from a virgin fountain, and culled fresh flowers whence the Muse had never yet sought them to wreathe a garland for the poet's brow.[470]

Few materials exist for the compilation of his biography. From two passages[471] in his work, in which he states that his native language was Latin, it is clear that he was born within the limits of Italy. The date of his birth is generally fixed B. C. 95.[472] The prevalence of the Epicurean philosophy, and the additional popularity with which his talents invested the fashionable creed, combined to raise him to the equestrian dignity; and, consistently with his

---

[470] Lib. i. 925; iv. 1.
[471] Lib. i. 831; iii. 261.
[472] Clint. F. H.

cold and hopeless atheism—his proud disbelief in a superintending Providence—he died by his own hand in the prime of life and in the forty-fourth year of his age.[473] The story that his work was written in the lucid intervals of a madness produced by a love-potion, as well as his residence at Athens for the purpose of study, rest upon no foundation.

His poem *On the Nature of Things* is divided into six books, and is written in imitation of that of Empedocles, who is the subject of his warmest praise and admiration. Whilst its subject is philosophical and its purpose didactic, its unity of design, the one point of view from which he regards the various doctrines of the master whose principles he adopts, claims for it the rank of an epic poem.

This epic structure prevents it from being a complete and systematic survey of the whole Epicurean philosophy; but, notwithstanding this deficiency in point of comprehensiveness, the exactness and fidelity with which he represents those doctrines which he enunciates, renders him deserving of the credit of having given to his countrymen, as far as epic writing permitted, an accurate view of the philosophical system which then enjoyed the highest degree of popularity.

Although Greek philosophy furnished Lucretius with his subject, and a Greek poem served as a model, he also saw and valued the capabilities of the Latin language—he wielded at will its power of embodying the noblest thoughts, and showed how its copious and flexible properties could overcome the hard technicalities of science. Grand as were his conceptions, the language of Lucretius is not inferior to them in majesty. Without violating philosophical accuracy, he never appears to feel it a restraint to his muse: his fancy is always lively, his imagination has free scope even when his thoughts are fixed in the abstrusest theories, and engaged in the most subtle argumentation.[474]

The great beauty of the poetry of Lucretius is its variety. One might expect sublimity in the philosopher who penetrates the secrets of the natural world, and discloses to the eye of man the hidden causes of its wonderful phenomena. His object was a lofty one; for, although the irrational absurdities of the national creed drove him into the opposite evils of skepticism and unbelief, his aim was to set the intellect free from the trammels of superstition. But besides grandeur and sublimity we find the totally different poetical qualities of softness and tenderness. Rome had long known nothing but war, and was now rent by that worst and most demoralizing kind of war, civil dissension. Lucretius yearned for peace; and his prayer, that the fabled goddess of all that is beautiful in nature would heal the wounds which discord had made, is distinguished by tenderness and pathos even more than by sublimity. The whole passage is superior to the poetry of Ovid in force, although inferior in facility. His versification is not so smooth and harmonious as that of Virgil, who flourished in a period when the language had attained a higher degree of perfection, and the Roman ear was more educated, and therefore more delicately attuned, but it is never harsh and rugged, and always falls upon the ear with a swelling and sonorous melody. Virgil appreciated his excellence, and imitated not only single expressions, but almost entire verses and passages.[475]

As an example of sublimity, few passages can equal that in which he describes the prostration of human intellect under the grievous superstition, the dauntless purpose of Epicurus to free men from her oppressive rule, and to enable him to burst open the portals of

---

[473] Hier. Chron.
[474] The criticism of Cicero is unjust:—"Lucretii poemata ita sunt non multis luminibus ingenii multæ tamen artis."—Ep. ad Qu. fratr. ii. 11.
[475] See A. Gell. Noct. Att. i. 21.

Nature's treasure-house, and thus gain a victory which will place him on an equality with the inhabitants of heaven:—

> Humana ante oculos fede quom vita jaceret
> In terris, oppressa gravi sub Religione,
> Quæ caput a cœli regionibus ostendebat,
> Horribili super aspectu mortalibus instans;
> Primum Graius homo mortales tendere contra
> Est oculos ausus, primusque obsistere contra;
> Quem neque fama deûm nec fulmina nec minitanti
> Murmure compressit cœlum, sed eo magis acrem
> Irritât animi virtutem, effringere ut arcta
> Naturæ primus portarum claustra cupiret.
> Ergo vivida vis animi pervicit et extra
> Processit longe flammantia mœnia mondi,
> Atque omne immensum peragravit mente animoque;
> Unde refert nobis victor, quid possit oriri,
> Quid nequeat; finita potestas denique quoique
> Quanam sit ratione, atque alte terminus hærens.
> Quare Religio, pedibus subjecta, vicissim
> Obteritur; nos exæquat victoria cœlo.
> Lib. i. 63.

The idea which the poet here presents to the mind of his readers is of the same kind with that which pervades the writings of the Greek tragedians: it is that of the limited energies of mortals resolutely struggling with a superior and almost irresistible power.

The thrilling narrative of the plague at Athens, with all its physical and moral horrors, is one of the most heart-rending specimens of descriptive poetry. The stern rejection of all fear of death, though based upon a denial of the immortality of the soul, is a noble burst of poetical as well as philosophical enthusiasm; and the fifth book displays that perfect finish and accomplished grace which characterizes all the best Roman poets. Amongst the most affecting passages may be enumerated those which describe the early sorrows of the human race, and the grief of the bereaved animal whose young one has been slain in sacrifice.[476] Two other fine passages are the philosophical explanation of Tartarus, and the panoramic view of the tempest of human desires, seen from the rocky heights of philosophy—a glorious descriptive piece which has been imitated by Lord Bacon.

The following lines show how beautifully the poet has caught the spirit and feeling of Greek fancy, and how capable the Latin language now was of adequately expressing them:—

> Aulide quo pacto Triviai virginis aram
> Iphianassai turparunt sanguine fede
> Ductores Danaum delectei, prima virorum
> Cui simul infula, virgineos circumdata comtus,
> Ex utraque pari malarum parte profusa est;
> Et mœstum simul ante aras astare parentem

---

[476] Lib. ii. 352.

> Sensit, et hunc propter ferrum celare ministros,
> Aspectuque suo lacrumas effundere civeis;
> Muta metu, terram genibus summissa, petebat:
> Nec miseræ prodesse in tali tempore quibat,
> Quod patrio princeps donarat nomine regem
> Nam sublata virum manibus, tremebundaque, ad aras
> Deducta est; non ut, solenni more sacrorum
> Perfecto, posset claro comitari hymenæo;
> Sed, casta incerte, nubendi tempore in ipso,
> Hostia concideret mactatu mœsta parentis,
> Exitus ut classi felix faustusque daretur.
> Tantum religio potuit suadere malorum!
> By that Diana's cruel altar flowed
> With innocent and royal virgin's blood:
> Unhappy maid! with sacred ribands bound,
> Religious pride! and holy garlands crowned;
> To meet an undeserved, untimely fate,
> Led by the Grecian chiefs in pomp and state;
> She saw her father by, whose tears did flow
> In streams—the only pity he could show.
> She saw the crafty priest conceal the knife
> From him, blessed and prepared against her life!
> She saw her citizens, with weeping eyes,
> Unwillingly attend the sacrifice.
> Then, dumb with grief, her tears did pity crave,
> But 'twas beyond her father's power to save.
> In vain did innocence, youth, and beauty plead;
> In vain the first pledge of his nuptial bed;
> She fell—even now grown ripe for bridal joy—
> To bribe the gods, and buy a wind for Troy.
> So died this innocent, this royal maid:
> Such fiendish acts religion could persuade. *Creech.*

It cannot be denied that there are in the poem of Lucretius many barren wastes over which are scattered the rubbish and *débris* of a false philosophy; but even in these deserts the oases are numerous enough to prevent exhaustion and fatigue. They recur too frequently to enumerate them all. If the attempt were made, other tastes would still discover fresh examples.

The following is, in a few words, the plan and structure of the poem:—Its professed object is to emancipate mankind from the debasing effects of superstition by an exposition of the leading tenets of the Epicurean school. It is divided into six books. In the first, the poet enunciates and copiously illustrates the grand axiom of his system of the universe, together with the corollaries which necessarily arise from it. "Nothing is created out of nothing." He commences also the subject of the atomic theory. In the second book he pursues the subject of creation generally, and the various functions of animal life. The third treats of the nature of the soil. The fourth contains the theory of sensation, especially of sight; of the relation which thought bears to matter; of the passions, and especially of the influence of love, both physical and moral. The fifth book is devoted to the history of mankind. The sixth explains the phenomena of the natural world, including those of disease and death.

The following are the leading Epicurean doctrines imbodied in the poem:—There are divine beings, but they are neither the creators[477] nor the governors of the world.[478] They live in the enjoyment of perfect happiness and repose, regardless of human affairs, unaffected by man's virtues and vices, happiness or misery. Neither have they the power any more than the will to interfere in the affairs of the world, for they cannot resist the eternal laws of nature and destiny. Whilst, in deference to the innate sense which revolts at the denial of a God, he acknowledges the existence of divine beings, the proofs which he adduces as derived from his great master are weak and unsatisfactory.[479] The corollary of this disbelief in Divine Providence is practical atheism. The ideas which man entertains of God are false, because they are the mere creations of the imagination. Ignorant of the real causes which lead to natural phenomena, he conjures up these as the machinery to account for them.[480] The popular belief is groundless; and yet the poet believes that if this system is overthrown there is nothing to supply its place, and hence all worship, whether prayer or praise, is grovelling superstition.[481] The only true piety consists in calm and peaceful contemplation.[482]

To those who argue that unbelief leads to ungodliness, his answer is that what man calls religion has led to the greatest crimes.[483] He is not entirely destitute of the religious sentiment or the principle of faith, for he deifies nature[484] and has a veneration for her laws; and hence his infidelity must be viewed rather in the light of a philosophical protest against the degrading results of heathen superstition than a total rejection of the principle of religious faith.

It is here that Lucretius seems for awhile to leave the authority of Epicurus; and with the inspiration of a poet, which is hardly consistent with a total absence of veneration and faith, to forsake his cold and heartless system. Although he asserts that the phenomena of nature are the result of a combination of atoms, that these elementary particles are self-existent and eternal, he seems to invest nature with a sort of personality. The warm sensibility of the poet overcomes the cold logic of the philosopher. Dissatisfied with the ungenial idea of an abstract lifeless principle, he yearns for the maternal caresses of a being endued with energies and faculties with which he can sympathize. He therefore ascribes to nature an attribute which can only belong to an intelligent agent having ruling power. Nay, he even goes farther than this, and absolutely contradicts the dogmas of the Epicurean school. Even the works of nature are represented as instinct with life.[485] The sun is spoken of as a being who, by the warmth of his beams, vivifies all things: the earth, from whose womb all things spring, fosters and nurtures all her children. The very stars may possibly be living beings, performing their stated motions in search of their proper sustenance.[486] These are, doubtless, the fancies of the poet rather than the grave and serious belief of the philosopher; but they prove how false, hollow, and

---

[477] Lib. v. 166.
[478] Lib. vi. 378.
[479] Lib. v. 1197.
[480] Lib. vi. 75.
[481] Lib. v. 83, 1163.
[482] Lib. v. 1202.
[483] Lib. i. 81.
[484] Lib. i. 71, 147.
[485] See Ritter, iv. p. 89.
[486] Lib. v. 525.

artificial is a system which pretends to account for creation by natural causes, and how earnestly the human mind craves after the comfort and support of a personal deity.

The denial of the immortality of the soul is inferred from the destructibility of the material elements out of which it is composed. It must perish immediately that it is deprived of the protection of the body.[487] In accordance with this psychical theory, he accounts for the difference of human tempers and characters. Character results from the combination of the elementary principles:—a predominance of heat produces the choleric disposition; that of wind produces timidity; that of air a calm and equable temper.[488] But this natural constitution, the strength of the will, acted upon by education, is able, to a certain extent, to modify, though it cannot effect a complete change. Thus it is that, although moral as well as physical phenomena are produced in accordance with fixed laws, human ills result from unbridled passions, and may be remedied by philosophy.

Although, if tried by a Christian standard, the Lucretian morality is by no means pure,[489] yet even where he permits laxity he is not insensible to the moral beauty, the happy and holy results of purity and chastity.[490] Nor, notwithstanding the assertions of Cicero,[491] can the charge of immorality or of a selfish love of impure pleasure be made against Lucretius or Epicurus. The distinction which the latter drew between lawful and unlawful pleasures was severe and uncompromising. The former speaks of the hell which the wicked sensualist always carries within his own breast[492]—of the satisfaction of true wisdom,[493] and of a conscience void of offence.[494]

Again, Epicurus was a man of almost Christian gentleness. Stoical grossness and contempt of refinement revolted him; the unamiable severity of that sect was alien to his nature. He was thus driven to the opposite extreme; and although he was careful to make pure intellectual pleasure the *summum bonum*, his standard laid him open to objections from his jealous adversaries. The zeal with which many distinguished females devoted themselves to his system, and became his disciples because his doctrines and character especially recommended themselves to the female sex, made it easy for his enemies to stigmatize them as *effeminate*, instead of praising them as *feminine*. With that illiberality which refused to woman freedom of conduct and a liberal education, his adversaries calumniated the characters of his pupils, represented them as unchaste, and their instructor as licentious. Nor did they hesitate even to support these accusations by forgeries.[495]

A careless reception of their calumnies without investigation, added to the general, and perhaps wilful, misapprehension which prevailed among the Romans in the days of Cicero, led to the misrepresentations which are found in his writings. These have been handed down to after ages: and thus the doctrines taught by Epicurus have been loaded with undeserved obloquy.[496] There is, however, no doubt that Epicurism was adopted by the Romans in a corrupt form, and that it became fashionable because it was supposed to encourage

---

[487] Lib. iii. 265, 413.
[488] Lib. iii. 302.
[489] Lib. iv. 1072.
[490] Lib. v. 1012.
[491] De Fin. ii. 22.
[492] Lib. v. 1152.
[493] Lib. iii. 988.
[494] Lib. ii. 7.
[495] Diog. La. x. 3.
[496] Sen. de Benef. iv. 19.

indifferentism and sensuality. It is probable, too, that the denial of immortality contributed much to the depravation and distortion of his system. Nothing so surely demoralizes as destroying the hopes of eternity. Man cannot commune with God, or soar on high to spiritual things, unless he hopes to be spiritualized and to see God as He is. Whatever the philosopher may teach as to the true nature of happiness, man will set up his own corrupt standard, which his passions and appetites lead him to prefer: he will act on the principle "Let us eat and drink, for to-morrow we die." Still it must be confessed that the views of Epicurus respecting man's duty to God were disinterested—founded on ideas of the Divine perfections, not merely on hopes of reward.[497] His views of sensual pleasures were in accordance with his simple, frugal life, diametrically opposed to intemperance and excess. He taught by example as well as by precept, that he who would be happy must cultivate wisdom and justice, because virtue and happiness are inseparable. He attached his disciples to him by affection rather than by admiration; submitted to weakness and sickness with patient resignation; and died with a heroism which no Stoic could have surpassed.

Such was the master whom Lucretius followed, and the school to which he belonged; and though the sternness of the Roman character breathed into his protest against superstition a bolder spirit of defiance than that of the placid and resigned Greek, his teaching was equally pure and noble, and he would have proudly disdained to make philosophy a cloak for voluptuous profligacy. Poets who surpassed him in gracefulness, and who were fortunate enough to flourish when the Latin language had become more plastic, paid due honour to his greatness. Virgil celebrates the happiness of that man:—

> —— qui potuit rerum cognoscere causas,
> Atque metus omnes, et inexorabile fatum
> Subjecit pedibus, strepitumque Acherontis avari.[498]

His muse is instinct with Lucretian spirit when he describes with such graphic skill the murrain attacking the brute creation;[499] and Ovid exclaims that the sublime strains of Lucretius shall never perish until the day shall arrive when the world shall be given up to destruction.

CATULLUS (BORN B. C. 86.)

Contemporary with the great didactic poet, but nine years his junior in age, flourished C. Valerius Catullus. He was a member of a good family, residing on the Lago di Garda, in the neighbourhood of Verona,[500] and his father had the honour of frequently receiving Cæsar as his guest.[501] At an early age he went to Rome, probably for education, but his warm temperament and strong passions plunged him into the licentious excesses of the capital. During this period of his career, passed in the indulgence of pleasure and gayety, and in the midst of a dissipated society, he had no more serious occupation than the cultivation of his

---

[497] Diog. La. x.
[498] Georg. ii. 490.
[499] Georg. iii. 478.
[500] Plin. xxxvii. 6.
[501] Suet. v. Jul. 73.

literary tastes and talents. The elegant tenderness of his amatory poetry made him a favourite with the fair sex, for its licentiousness was not out of keeping with the sentiments and conversation prevalent in the Roman fashionable world. It must not be supposed that the tone of society amongst the higher classes was pure and moral, like that of Cicero and his friends, or that it was not marked by the same licentious freedom which polluted some even of their most graceful poems.

The poetry of Catullus was such as might be expected from the tenor of his life. The excuse which he made for its character was not a valid one;[502] for the line in Hadrian's epitaph on Voconius could not possibly be applied to him:—

>Lascivus versu, mente pudicus eras.[503]

His mistress, whom he addresses under the feigned name of Lesbia, was really named Clodia.[504] It has been said that she was the sister of the infamous Clodius; but there are no grounds for the assertion.

A career of extravagance and debauchery terminated in ruin, and though his fortune had been originally ample, his affairs became hopelessly embarrassed; and in order to retrieve them by colonial plunder, he accompanied Memmius, the friend of Lucretius, when he went as prætor to Bythinia. Owing, however, to the grasping meanness of his patron his expectations were disappointed. He returned home "with his purse full of cobwebs." Still he enjoyed the privilege of visiting those cities of Greece and Asia which were the most celebrated for literature and the fine arts.

When he went to Asia he visited the grave of a brother who had died in the Troad, and who was buried on the Rhætian promontory; and a poem which he addressed on the occasion to Hortalus, the dissipated son of the orator Hortensius, as well as another dedicated to Manlius, bear witness to the warmth of his fraternal affection. The former is a beautiful and touching specimen of his elegiac style:—

>Multas per gentes et multa per æquora vectus,
>Adveni has miseras frater ad inferias.
>Ut te postremo donarem munere mortis
>Et mutum nequidquam alloquerer cinerem.
>Quandoquidem fortuna mihi tete abstulit ipsum
>Has miser indigne frater adempte mihi!
>Nunc tamen interea prisco quæ more parentum
>Tradita sub tristes munera ad inferias
>Accipe fraterno multum manantia fletu
>Atque in perpetuum frater ave atque vale!

On his return to Rome he resumed his old habits, and died in the prime of life, probably B. C. 47, as that is the latest date to which allusion is made in his writings.

His works consist of numerous short fugitive pieces of a lyrical character; elegies, such as that already quoted; a secular hymn to Diana; a poem, somewhat of a dithyrambic character,

---

[502] See Carm. cxvi.
[503] Anthol. 208.
[504] Apuleius.

entitled Atys; and the Epithalamium of Peleus and Thetis, a mythological poem in heroic verse. His taste was evidently formed on a study of the Greek poets, from whom he learnt not only his beautiful hendecasyllables, but also their modes of thought and expression. He had skill and taste to adopt the materials with which his vast erudition furnished him, and to conceal his want of originality and inspiration. Some of his pieces are translations from the Greek, as, for example, the elegy on the hair of Berenice, which is taken from the Greek of Callimachus, and the celebrated ode of Sappho.[505] He was one of the most popular of the Roman poets—firstly, because he possessed those qualities which the literary society of Rome most highly valued, namely, polish and learning; and secondly, because, although he was an imitator, there is a living reality about all that he wrote—a truly Roman nationality. He did not merely disguise the inspiration of Greece in a Latin dress, but invested Roman life, and thoughts, and social habits with the ideal of Greek love and beauty. For these reasons his fame flourished as long as Rome possessed a classical literature. Two eminent men only have withheld their admiration—Horace in the golden age; Quintilian in the period of the decline. The former disparages him as a lyrical poet; the latter almost passes him over in silence. Horace was jealous of a rival who was so nearly equal to himself: he could not bear the remotest chance of his claim being disputed to be the musician of the Roman lyre;[506] and he dishonestly declared that he first adapted Æolian strains to the Roman lyre,[507] notwithstanding the Lesbian character and hendecasyllabic metres of his predecessor. Quintilian could not appreciate Catullus, because his own taste was too stiff and affected, and spoilt by the rhetorical spirit of his age.

Catullus had a talent for satire, but his satire was not inspired by a noble indignation at vice and wrong. It was the bitter resentment of a vindictive spirit: his love and his hate were both purely selfish. His language of love expresses the feelings of an impure voluptuary; his language of scorn those of a disappointed one. He gratified his irritable temper by attacking Cæsar most offensively; but the noble Roman would not crush the insect which annoyed him; and although Catullus insulted him personally by reading his lampoons in his presence, not a change passed over his countenance: he would not stoop to avenge himself: and the imperial clemency disarmed the anger of the libeller. The strong prejudice of Niebuhr in favour of Roman antiquity led him to pronounce Catullus a gigantic and extraordinary genius, equal in every respect to the lyric poets of Greece previously to the time of Sophocles; he believed him to be the greatest poet Rome ever possessed, except, perhaps, some few of the early ones; but that great man also thought that Virgil had mistaken his vocation in becoming an epic instead of a lyric poet.[508] Catullus certainly possessed great excellences and talents of the most alluring and captivating kind. No genius ever displayed itself under a greater variety of aspects. He has the playfulness and the petulance of a girl, the vivacity and simplicity of a child. He has never been surpassed in gracefulness, melody, and tenderness. No one, unless he possessed the coolness and self-command of a Cæsar, could have avoided wincing under the sharp attacks of his wit: he had passion and vehemence, but he had not the grandeur and sublimity either of Lucretius or Virgil.

Although the peculiar characteristics of his poetry are chiefly to be found in his lyric and elegiac poems, there are in his longer pieces, which are less known and less admired,

---

[505] Carm. li.
[506] Od. IV. iii. 23.
[507] Od. III. xx. 13.
[508] Lect. cvi.

passages of singular sweetness and beauty. He had not sufficient grasp and comprehensiveness of mind to conduct an epic poem. His knowledge of human nature, confined as it was to one of its phases—the development of the softer affections—did not admit of sufficient variety for so vast a work. His intellectual taste, like his moral principles, was too ill-regulated to construct a well-digested plan, necessary to the perfection of an epic poem; but wherever ingenuity and liveliness in description, or pathos in moving the affections, are required, the poetry of Catullus does not yield to that of Ovid or of Virgil.

The poem, entitled the marriage of Peleus and Thetis, bears some slight resemblance to an heroic poem. Its subject is heroic, for it imbodies a legend of the heroic age. The characters of mythology play a part in it, similar to that which they support in the poems of Homer or Virgil. But it is unconnected and deficient in unity; and the plan is far too extensive for the dimensions by which it is circumscribed. Nevertheless, with all these faults, it is pleasing on account of the luxuriance of its fancy and the brilliancy of its genius. The most beautiful passage, perhaps, is the episode relating the story of Theseus and Ariadne, which is introduced into the main body of the poem as being woven and embroidered on the hangings of the palace of Holeus. The following verses are taken from this episode,[509] and form part of the complaint of Ariadne for the perfidious desertion of Theseus:—

> Siccine discedens, neglecto numine Divûm,
> Immemor ah! devota domum perjuria portas?
> Nullane res potuit crudelis flectere mentis
> Consilium? tibi nulla fuit clementia præsto,
> Immite ut nostri vellet mitescere pectus?
> At non hæc quondam nobis promissa dedisti
> Voce; mihi non hoc miseræ sperare jubebas;
> Sed connubia læta, sed optatos hymenæos;
> Quæ cuncta aërii discerpunt irrita venti.
> Jam jam nulla viro juranti fœmina credat,
> Nulla viri speret sermones esse fideles;
> Qui, dum aliquid cupiens animus prægestit apisci,
> Nil metuunt jurare, nihil promittere parcunt;
> Sed simul ac cupidæ mentis satiata libido est,
> Dicta nihil metuere, nihil perjuria curant.
> Certe ego te in medio versantem turbine leti
> Eripui, et potius germanum amittere crevi,
> Quam tibi fallaci supremo in tempore deessem.
> Pro quo dilaceranda feris dabor, alitibusque
> Præda, neque injecta tumulabor mortua terra.
> Quænam te genuit sola sub rupe leæna?
> Quod mare conceptum spumantibus exspuit undis?
> Quæ Syrtis, quæ Scylla vorax, quæ vasta Charybdis,
> Talia qui reddis pro dulci præmia vitæ?
> Si tibi non cordi fuerant connubia nostra,
> Sæva quod horrebas prisci præcepta parentis;
> Attamen in vestras potuisti ducere sedes,

---

[509] Lib. v. 132, 166.

Quæ tibi jucundo famularer serva labore,
Candida permulcens liquidis vestigia lymphis,
Purpureave tuum consternens veste cubile.
Sed quid ego ignaris nequicquam conqueror auris,
Externata malo? quæ nullis sensibus auctæ
Nec missas audire queunt, nec reddere voces.—132–161.
And couldst thou, Theseus, from her native land
Thy Ariadne bring, then cruel so
Desert thy victim on a lonely strand?
And didst thou, perjured, dare to Athens go,
Nor dread the weight of Heaven's avenging blow?
Could naught thy heart with sacred pity touch?
Naught make thy soul the baleful plot forego
'Gainst her that loved thee? Ah! not once were such
The vows, the hopes, thy smooth professions did avouch!
Then all was truth, then did thy honeyed tongue
Of wedded faith the flattering fable weave.
All, all unto the winds of heaven are flung!
Henceforth let never listening maid believe
Protesting man. When their false hearts conceive
The selfish wish, to all but pleasure blind,
No words they spare, no oaths unuttered leave;
But when possession cloys their pampered mind,
No care have they for oaths, no words their honour bind.
For this, then, I from instant death did cover
Thy faithless bosom; and for this preferred,
Even to a brother's blood, a perjured lover;
Now to be torn by savage beast and bird,
With no due form, no decent rite, interred!
What foaming sea, what savage of the night,
In murky den thy monstrous birth conferred?
What whirlpool guides and gave thee to the light,
The welcome boon of life thus basely to requite?
What though thy royal father's stern command
The bond of marriage to our lot forbade,
Oh! safely still into thy native land
I might have gone thy happy serving maid;
There gladly washed thy snowy feet or laid
Upon thy blissful bed the purple vest.
Ah, vain appeal! upon the winds conveyed,
The heedless winds, that hear not my behest:
No words his ear can reach or penetrate his breast!

The writers of the Augustan age and their successors paid Catullus what they considered the highest compliment, when they called him *learned*. Criticism referred everything to the Greek standard. The qualities which they recognised by this epithet were those which they deemed most valuable—more so even than originality and invention—an extensive acquaintance with the materials of Greek story, an elaborate study of the poets taken as models, a scientific appreciation of the cadences and harmonies of Greek versification. They were grateful for the blessings which they were conscious of having derived from mental cultivation; and the highest praise which they could bestow was to confer upon a poet the title of a learned and accomplished man.

This period, at which prose reached its zenith, could boast of other poets, also, besides Lucretius and Catullus, whose merits were considerable although they did not satisfy the fastidious taste of the Augustan age. There flourished C. Licinius Calvus,[510] C. Helvius Cinna, Valerius Cato, Valgius, Ticida, Furius Bibaculus, and Varro Atacinus.

The first of these was a lively little man,[511] an orator as well as a poet. His speeches were elaborately modelled after those of the Attic orators; and had his poems displayed the same polish, they might have satisfied Horace[512] and his contemporaries, and thus have been preserved. As it is, the fragments which remain are so brief, that it is impossible to say whether his merits were such as to justify Niebuhr in placing him amongst the three greatest poets of his age. His poetry resembled that of Catullus in spirit and morality. It was the fashionable poetry of the day, and consisted of tender elegy, playful and sentimental epigram, licentious love-songs, and bitter personality.

Cinna,[513] besides smaller poems, was the author of an epic, entitled Smyrna; the subject is unknown: but Catullus, who was his intimate friend, praises it highly, and Virgil modestly declares that, as compared with Varius and Cinna, he himself appears a goose amongst swans.[514] Valerius Cato was a grammarian as well as a poet. His two principal poems were entitled Lydia and Diana;[515] and a fragmentary poem, to which the title *Diræ* or *Curses*[516] has been given, has been generally attributed to him on the grounds that the author pours forth his woes to a mistress named Lydia. The argument of the piece is as follows:—The estate of Cato, like that of Virgil, was confiscated and made a military colony; and smarting under a sense of wrong, he imprecates curses on his lost home. Then the theme changes: his heart softens; and in sad accents he bewails his separation from his mistress, and from all his rural pleasures. This poem was formerly believed to be the work of Virgil, but neither the language nor the poetry can be compared to those of the Mantuan bard; nor do the sentiments resemble the calmness and resignation with which he bears his misfortunes. J. Scaliger, impressed with these considerations, transferred the authorship from Virgil to Cato. But there are no sufficient grounds for determining the question.

Respecting C. Valgius Rufus all is doubt and obscurity. The grammarians quote from him; Pliny[517] speaks of his learning; Horace[518] refers to him as an elegiac poet, and expresses the greatest confidence in his critical taste and judgment. Ticida is mentioned by Suetonius as bearing testimony to the merits of Valerius Cato. Bibaculus was a bitter satirist, who spared not the feelings of his friend Cato when reduced from affluence to poverty;[519] who himself

---

[510] Cic. Brut. 82; ad Fam. xv. 21; Dial. de Or. 18; Quint. xi. 115.
[511] Cat. liv.
[512] Sat. I. x. 16.
[513] Cat. Carm. X. xcv.
[514] Ecl. 9.
[515] Suet. de Ill. Gram. 2–9.
[516] Wernsdorf, Po. Lat. Mi.
[517] H. N. xxv. 2.
[518] Od. ii. 9; Sat. I. x.
[519] Wernsdorf.

had the vanity to attempt an epic poem, and by his vulgar taste provoked the severe criticism of Horace.[520]

P. Terentius Varro Atacinus was a contemporary of Varro Reatinus; and for this reason his works have often been confounded with those of the latter. He was born B. C. 82,[521] near the river Atax in Gaul, and hence he was surnamed Atacinus, in order to distinguish him from his learned namesake, who derived his appellation from property which he possessed at Reati. Very few fragments of his works are extant,[522] although his poetry was of such a character that Virgil deemed some of his lines worthy of plagiarizing.[523] His principal work, which is not spoken of in very high terms by Quintilian,[524] is a translation of the Argonautica of Apollonius Rhodius. Besides this, he wrote two geographical poems, namely, the *Chorographia* and *Libri Navales*, a heroic poem entitled *Bellum Sequanicum*, on one of the Gallic campaigns of J. Cæsar, and also some elegies, epigrams, and saturæ.[525]

A fragment of the Chorographia is preserved by Meyer,[526] the concluding lines of which were evidently imitated by Virgil, and also the following severe epigram on Licinius:—

> Marmoreo Licinus tumulo jacet, at Cato nullo,
> Pompeius parvo; Quis putet esse Deos?
> Saxa premunt Licinum, levat altum fama Catonem,
> Pompeium tituli. Credimus esse Deos.

---

[520] Sat. II. v. 41.
[521] Hieron. in Euseb. Chron.
[522] See Meyer's Anthol. Lat.
[523] Ibid. 77, 78.
[524] Lib. x. i. 87.
[525] Hor. Sat. I. x. 46.
[526] Anthol. 77, 78.

Chapter 17

AGE OF VIRGIL FAVOURABLE TO POETRY— HIS BIRTH, EDUCATION, HABITS, ILLNESS, AND DEATH—HIS POPULARITY AND CHARACTER—HIS MINOR POEMS, THE CULEX CIRIS MORETUM COPA AND CATALECTA—HIS BUCOLICS—ITALIAN MANNERS NOT SUITED TO PASTORAL POETRY— IDYLLS OF THEOCRITUS—CLASSIFICATION OF THE BUCOLICS—SUBJECT OF THE POLLIO— HEYNE'S THEORY RESPECTING IT

P. VIRGILIUS MARO (BORN B. C. 70.)

The period at which Virgil flourished was singularly favourable both to the development and appreciation of poetical talent of the most polished and cultivated kind. The indulgent liberality of the imperial court cherished and fostered genius: the ruin of republican liberty left the intellect of the age without any other object except refinement; imagination was not harassed by the cares and realities of life. The same causes contributed to limit the range of prose composition,[527] and therefore the field was left undisputed to Virgil and Horace and their friends; and as the age of Cicero was essentially one in which prose literature flourished, so that of Augustus was the golden age of poetry. Of this age, Virgil stands forth pre-eminent amongst his contemporaries, as the representative. He exhibited all its characteristics, polish, ingenuity, and skill, and to these he superadded dignity and sublimity. The life of Virgil, commonly prefixed to his works, professes to be written by Tiberius Claudius Donatus, who lived in the fifth century. If, as Heyne thought, the groundwork is by him, it has been overlaid with fables similar to those found in the Gesta Romanorum, and owing their origin to the inventions of the dark ages. From this biography, stripped of those portions which are clearly fabulous, and from other sources, the following particulars respecting him may be derived:—

---

[527] See, on this subject, Niebuhr's Lectures on Roman History, cvi.

P. Virgilius Maro was born on the ides (the 15th) of October,[528] B. C. 70, on a small estate belonging to his father, at Andes (Pietola,) a village of Cisalpine Gaul, situated about three Roman miles from Mantua. It has been disputed whether his name was Virgilius or Vergilius. Most probably both orthographies are correct, as *Diana, Minerva, liber*, and other Latin words, were frequently written *Deana, Menerva, leber*, &c.[529]

Virgil was by birth a citizen of Mantua,[530] but not of Rome, for the full franchise was not extended to the *Transpadani* until B. C. 49, although they enjoyed the Jus Latii as early as B. C. 89. The varied stores of learning contained in the Georgics and Æneid, abundantly prove that Virgil received a liberal education. It is said that he acquired the rudiments of literature at Cremona, where he remained until he had assumed the *toga virilis*.[531] This event, if the anonymous life is to be depended upon, took place unusually early; for it is there assigned to the consulships of Pompey the Great and Licinius Crassus,[532] in the first consulship of whom he was born. From Cremona he went to Milan, and thence to Naples, where he studied Greek literature and philosophy under the direction of Parthenius, a native of Bithynia. Muretus asserts that he diligently read the history of Thucydides; but his favourite studies were medicine and mathematics—an unusual discipline to engage the attention of the future poet, but one which, by its exactness, tended to foster and mature that judgment which distinguishes his poetry. The philosophical sect to which he devoted himself was the Epicurean; and the unfortunate general, P. Quintilius Varus, to whom he addresses his sixth Eclogue,[533] studied this system together with him under Syron.

After this, it is probable that he came to Rome, but soon exchanged the bustle of the capital, for which his bashful disposition and delicate health unfitted him, for the quiet retirement of his hereditary estate. Of this he was deprived in B. C. 42, with circumstances of great hardship, when the whole neighbouring district was divided, after the battle of Philippi, amongst the victorious legionaries of Octavius and Antony. The town of Cremona had supported Brutus, and the old Republican Party, and Mantua, together with its surrounding district, suffered in consequence of its too close vicinity.[534] Asinius Pollio was at that time commander of the forces in Cisalpine Gaul. He was grinding and oppressive in his administration; but being himself an orator, poet, and historian, he patronised literary men. Congenial tastes recommended Virgil to his notice, and led him to take compassion on the poet's desolate condition. By his advice, Virgil proceeded to Rome with an introduction to Mæcenas. Through him he gained access to Octavius, and either immediately before or after the peace of Brundisium[535] his little farm was restored to him.

He now became a prosperous man, was a member of the literary society which graced the table of Mæcenas, and basked in sunshine of court favour. Horace, Virgil, Plotius, and Varius, were united by the closest bonds of friendship with Mæecenas, and accompanied him on that cheerful expedition to Brundisium,[536] when he went thither in order to negotiate a reconciliation between Octavius and Antony. Henceforth Virgil's favourite residence was

---

[528] Mart. Ep. xii. 68.
[529] See Quint. de Inst. Or.
[530] Servius.
[531] Scalig. in Euseb. Chron.
[532] B. C. 55.
[533] See v. 7.
[534] Ecl. ix. 18.
[535] B. C. 40.
[536] B. C. 38.

Naples.[537] Its sunny climate suited his pulmonary weakness far better than the low and damp banks of his native Mincius (Menzo.) He had, besides, a villa in Sicily, and when at Rome he lived in a pleasant house on the Esquiline, situated near those of his friends Mæcenas and Horace. It is difficult to say how Virgil became so rich: patrons were liberal in those days, and he doubtless owed a portion of his affluence to their munificence. The liberality of Mæcenas is well known; and Martial attributes the prosperity of Virgil to the favour of "the Tuscan knight."[538] Augustus also had great wealth at his disposal, and was profuse in the distribution of it amongst his favourites.

There is a passage in the Odes of Horace[539] which seems to hint that he engaged to a slight extent in mercantile concerns: even if this formed one source of his wealth, the love of gain (studium lucri,) and anxiety about the means of living, do not appear to have hindered him from devoting his hours of serious occupation to literary labours and the diligent use of his well-stored library, whilst his leisure was given to the delights of social intercourse, for which he was so eminently qualified by his sweet temper and amiable disposition.

The poet's term of life was not extended far beyond fifty years. He had never been healthy or robust: he sometimes spat blood, and frequently suffered from headache and indigestion.[540] Ill health was the only drawback to a life otherwise passed in calm felicity. In the year B. C. 19 he meditated a tour in Greece, intending, during the course of it, to give the final polish to his great epic poem. Greece and her classic scenes, the favourite haunts of the Muses, the time-honoured contests of Olympia, the living and breathing statues which he beheld in that home of art, evidently inspired the beautiful imagery which adorns the introduction to the third Georgic. He, however, only reached Athens: there he met Augustus, who was on his way back from Samos, and both returned together. On the occasion of this voyage, Horace wrote that tender ode[541] in which he affectionately calls him "the half of his soul:"—

> Navis quæ tibi creditum
> Debes Virgilium, finibus Atticis
> Reddas incolumem precor
> Et serves animæ dimidium meæ.

On the way he was seized with a mortal sickness, which was aggravated by the motion of the vessel, and he only lived to land at Brundisium. The powers of nature, already enfeebled, were now totally exhausted, and he expired on the 22nd of September. He was buried rather more than a mile from Naples, on the road to Puteoli (Pozzuoli.) A tomb is still pointed out to the traveller which is said to be that of the poet. Nor is this improbable; for, although it is not situated on the present high-road, it is quite possible that the original direction of the road

---

[537] Alexander, an Italian abbot, states, on the evidence of two spurious verses, that he was governor of Naples and Calabria.
[538] Ep. viii. 56.
[539] Carm. xv. 12.
[540] Hor. Sat. I. v. 49.
[541] Carm. i. 3.

may have been changed.[542] His epitaph is said to have been dictated by himself in his last moments:—

> Mantua me genuit; Calabri rapuere; tenet nunc
> Parthenope. Cecini Pascua, Rura, Duces.[543]

Virgil was deservedly popular both as a poet and as a man. His rivals in literature could not envy one so unassuming and inoffensive his well-merited success, but loved him as much as they admired his poetry. The emperor esteemed him, the people respected him. "Witness," says Tacitus,[544] "the letters of Augustus,—witness the conduct of the people itself, which, when some of his verses were recited in the theatre, rose *en masse*, and showed the same veneration for Virgil, who happened to be present among the audience, which they were wont to show to Augustus." He was exceedingly temperate in his manner of living; so pure-minded[545] and chaste in the midst of a profligate and licentious age, that the Neapolitans gave him the name of Parthenias (from παρθενος, a virgin,) unselfish, although surrounded by selfishness, kind-hearted, and sympathizing. His talents and popularity never spoiled his natural simplicity and modesty, as his moving in the polite circles of the capital never could entirely wear off his rustic shyness and unfashionable appearance.

He was constitutionally pensive and melancholy, and so distrustful of his own poems, that Augustus could not persuade him to send an unfinished portion of the Æneid to him for perusal. "As to my Æneas," he writes to the emperor,[546] when absent on his Cantabrian campaign, "if I had anything worth your reading I would send it with pleasure, but the work is only just begun, and I even blame my folly for venturing upon so vast a task. But you know that I shall apply fresh and increased diligence to carrying out my design." It was with real reluctance that he subsequently read the sixth book to the Emperor and Octavia. In his last moments he was anxious to burn the whole manuscript; and in his will he directed his executors, Varius and Tucca, either to improve it or commit it to the flames.[547] He was open-hearted and generous, but not extravagant in the expenditure of his wealth, for he bequeathed to his brother, his friends, and the Emperor, a considerable property.

It is said that Virgil's earliest poetical essay was an epic poem, the subject of which was the Roman wars; but that the impossibility of introducing Roman names in hexameter verse caused him to desist from the task almost as soon as he had commenced it. The minor poems which are still extant, were probably his first works. These are the *Culex, Ciris, Moretum, Copa,* and the shorter pieces in lyric, elegiac, and iambic metres,[548] commonly known by the name of Catalecta. The "*Culex*" (Gnat) is a bucolic poem, with something of a mock-heroic colouring, of which the argument is as follows:[549] A shepherd, overcome with the heat, falls

---

[542] There has been much discussion respecting the precise place of his burial. (See Cramer's Anc. It. ii. 174.) Addison, in opposition to the popular belief, thought it almost certain that it stood on that side of the town which looks towards Vesuvius. (Remarks on Italy, p. 164; sec. ed.)
[543] Meyer, Anthol. 95.
[544] Dial. de Caus. Corrup. El. 13.
[545] Hor. Sat. I. v. 41.
[546] Macrob. Saturn. I. *sub fine*.
[547] Plin. N. H. vii. 30.
[548] See Meyer's Anthol. 85–111.
[549] A litle noursling of the humid ayre,
    A gnat unto the sleepie shephearkd went;
    And, marking where his ey-lids twinckling rare

asleep beneath the shade of a tree, and a venomous serpent from a neighbouring marsh stealthily approaches. A gnat flies to his rescue, and stings him on the brow. The shepherd, awoke by the smart, crushes his rescuer, but sees the serpent and kills it. The ghost of the gnat appears, reproaches him with his ingratitude, and describes the adventures he has met with in the regions of the dead. The shepherd erects a monument in his honour, and indites the following epigram:—

> Parve culex, pecudum custos tibi tale merenti
> Funeris officium vitæ pro munere reddit.
> Poor insect, thou a shepherd's life didst save;
> Thou gavest a life, he gives thee but a grave.

The "*Ciris*," which some have attributed to Corn. Gallus, is the Greek legend of Scylla, who was changed into a fish, and her father Nisus into an eagle. Great use has been made by Spenser of this poem in the conversation between Britomart and her nurse Glauce, and also in Glauce's incantations.[550] The "*Moretum*," was intended to trace the employments of the agricultural labourer through the day; but it only describes the commencement of them, and the preparation of a dish of *olla podrida* of garden herbs called *moretum*. It contains an ingenious description of a cottager's kitchen garden. The "*Copa*," is an elegiac poem, not unlike in jovial spirit the scolia or drinking songs of the Greeks: it represents a female waiter at a tavern, begging for custom by a tempting display of the accommodations and comforts prepared for strangers. It describes the careless enjoyment of rural festivity: the simple luxuries of grapes and mulberries, the fragrant roses, the cheerful grasshoppers, and timid little lizards of Italy. Nor are the excitements of the dice, the joys of wine, the blandishments of love unsung. Dull care is banished far, and the enjoyment of the present hour inculcated:—

> Pereant qui crastina curant
> Mors aurem vellens Vivite, ait, venio.

Amongst the lyric poems of Virgil is a very elegant one on the villa of his instructor in philosophy, Syron.

The poems which first established his reputation were his Bucolics or Eclogues. This latter title was given them in later times, implying either that they were selections from a greater number of poems or imitations of passages selected from the works of Greek poets.[551]

The characters in Virgil's Bucolics are Italians, in all their sentiments and feelings, acting the unreal and assumed part of Sicilian shepherds. In fact, the Italians never possessed the elements of pastoral life, and therefore could not naturally furnish the poet with originals and models from which to draw his portraits and characters. They were a simple people, but their simplicity was rather Ascræan than Arcadian: the domestic habits and virtues of rural life in

---

> Shewd the two pearles, which sight unto him lent,
> Through their thin coverings appearing fayre,
> His litle needle there infixing deep,
> Warnd him awake, from death himselfe to keep.
> *Spenser.*

[550] Faery Queene, book iii. c. ii. 3. See Dunlop, iii.
[551] Spenser, adopting the incorrect orthography and etymology of Petrarch, writes the word Æglogue, and derives it from αἴγων λόγοι—tales of goats or goatherds.

Italy were not unlike those of Bœtia, as described by Hesiod. Virgil, therefore, wisely took him as his model, and produced a more natural picture of Italian manners in his Georgics than in his Eclogues. The denizens of the little towns had the manners and habits of municipal life: their cultivation was the artificial refinement of town life, and not the natural sentiments of the contemplative shepherd. Those who lived in the country were hard-working, simple-minded peasants, who gained their livelihood by the sweat of their brow—honest, plain-spoken, rough-mannered, and without a grain of sentimentality. Pastoral poetry owes its origin to, and is fostered by, solitude; its most beautiful passages are of a meditative cast. The shepherd beguiles his loneliness by communing with his own thoughts. His sorrows are not the hard struggles of life, but often self-created and imaginary, or at least exaggerated. When represented as Virgil represents them in his Bucolics, they are in masquerade, and the drama in which they form the characters is of an allegorical kind. The connexion with Italy is rather of an historical than a moral nature: we meet with numerous allusions to contemporary events, but not with exact descriptions of Italian characters and manners. As, therefore, we cannot realize the descriptions, we can neither sympathize nor admire. Menalcas and Corydon and Alexis, and the rest, are as much out of place as the gentlemen and ladies in the garb of shepherds and shepherdesses in English family pictures. Even the scenery is Sicilian, and does not truthfully describe the tame neighbourhood of Mantua. So long as it is remembered that they are imitations of the Syracusan poet, we miss their nationality, and see at once that they are untruthful and out of keeping; and Virgil suffers in our estimation because we naturally compare him with the original whom he professes to imitate, and we cannot but be aware of his inferiority: but if we can once divest ourselves of the idea of the outward form which he has chosen to adopt, and forget the personality of the characters, we can feel for the wretched outcast, exiled from a happy though humble home, and be touched by the simple narrative of their disappointed loves and child-like woes; can appreciate the delicately-veiled compliments paid by the poet to his patron; can enjoy the inventive genius and poetical power which they display; and can be elevated by the exalted sentiments which they sometimes breathe. We feel that it is all an illusion; but we willingly permit ourselves to be transported from the matter-of-fact realities of a hard and prosaic world.

Virgil in his Eclogues was too much cramped by following his Greek original to present us with true pictures of Italian country life; although the criticism of his friend Horace with justice attributes to his rural pieces delicacy of touch and graceful wit:—

> molle atque facetum
> Virgilio annuerunt gaudentes rure Camœnæ.[552]

The Idylls of Theocritus are transfusions into appropriate Greek of old popular Sicilian legends which had taken root in the country, and had become part and parcel of the national character. His subjects are not always strictly pastoral, for his characters are sometimes reapers and fishermen.[553] His language, characters, sentiments, scenery, habits, incidents, are all Sicilian, and therefore all are in perfect harmony. The characters of Theocritus have a specific individuality, and are therefore different from each other; those of Virgil are generic, the representatives of a class, and therefore there is little or no variety. But still Virgil's

---

[552] Sat. I. x. 44.
[553] Id. x. and xxi.

defects do not detract much from the enjoyment experienced in reading his Bucolic poetry. The Aminta of Tasso, the Pastor Fido of Guarini, the Calendar of Spenser, the Lycidas of Milton, the Perdita of Shakspeare, the pastorals of Drayton, Drummond, and Florian, are equally open to objection, and yet who does not admire their beauties?

The Bucolics may be arranged in two classes. Those in the first are composed entirely after the Greek model, and contain the following poems:—

I. The first, in which the poet, representing himself under the character of Tityrus, expresses his gratitude for the restoration of his property, whilst Melibœus, as an exiled Mantuan, bewails his harder fortune.

II. The second, which is generally supposed to have been the first pastoral written by him, and is principally copied from the Cyclops of Theocritus.

III. The third is an imitation of the fourth and fifth Idylls of Theocritus, and as well as the seventh, represent improvisatorial trials of musical skill between shepherds.

V. The fifth, in which two shepherds pay the last honours to a departed friend, the one singing his epitaph, the other his apotheosis. Scaliger[554] has with good reason supposed that this poem allegorized the murder and deification of Julius Cæsar. It has been often imitated by modern poets: the most beautiful imitations are Spenser's lament for Dido, Milton's Lycidas, Drayton's sixth Eclogue, and Pomfret's Elegy on Queen Mary.

VIII. The eighth, which is imitated from the second and third Idylls of Theocritus, consists of two parts; and, from the subject-matter of the second portion, is entitled "*Pharmaceutria*," (the Enchantress.) Two shepherds, Damon and Alphesibœus, rival Orpheus in their musical skill, for, whilst they sing, heifers forget to graze, lynxes are stupified, and rivers stop their course to listen. It was addressed by Virgil to his kind patron Pollio, whilst employed in his expedition to Illyricum.[555] Damon, personifying an unsuccessful lover, laments that a rival has been preferred to himself. Alphesibœus, in the character of an enchantress, goes through a formula of magical incantations in order to regain the lost affections of Daphnis. In this poem a refrain, or intercalary verse, recurs after intervals of a few lines. In the song of Damon, the refrain is—

> Incipe Mænalios mecum, mea tibia, versus.
> In that of his opponent—
> Ducite ab urbe domum, mea carmina, ducite Daphnim.

IX. In the ninth, two shepherds converse together on the troubles which have befallen their neighbourhood, and one of them is represented as conveying a present of a few kids to court the favour of the new possessor.

The second class are of a more original kind.

IV. The fourth, entitled Pollio, which is the most celebrated of them all, bears no resemblance to pastoral poetry. In the exordium, the poet invokes the Muses of Sicilian song; but he professes to attune their sylvan strain to a nobler theme. The melancholy Perusian war had been brought to a termination. The reconciliation of Anthony and Octavius had been effected by the treaty of Brundisium, and all things seemed to promise peace and prosperity. The contrast was indeed a bright one, after the havoc and desolation which war had spread

---

[554] In Euseb. Chron.
[555] B. C. 39.

through Italy. The peace ratified with Sextus Pompey at Puteoli opened the long-closed granaries of Sicily, and plenty succeeded to famine. The enthusiasm of the poet hailed the return of the fabled golden age—the reign of Saturn. The songs which the old bards of Italy professed to have learnt from the Cumæan Sibyl, and to which legendary tradition attributed a prophetical meaning, seemed to point to the new era which now dawned on the Roman empire.

The belief of the civilized world was undoubtedly at this time concentrated on the expectation of some great event, which should bring peace and happiness to mankind. The divine revelation which God's people enjoyed taught them now to expect the advent of the Messiah; whilst traditions, probably derived through corrupting channels from the true light of prophecy, taught the heathen, though more vaguely, to look for the coming of some great one. The prophetic literature of the East might have travelled to Europe; and the divine prophecies of Isaiah, and the other sacred writers, may have been incorporated by native bards in Italian legends.

Bishop Lowth even supposed that the Sibylline predictions derived their origin from a Greek version of Messianic prophecies.[556] A belief in the inspiration of the Sibyls prevailed in the early ages of Christianity, and the Emperor Constantine in one of his orations[557] quotes from them, and paraphrases Virgil's Pollio as an evidence to the truths of the Gospel.

Some of the fathers of the Church attributed to them supernatural power; and the Italian painters, acting under the patronage of the Roman Church, honoured the four Sibyls as participators in a knowledge of the Divine counsels. Ambrose[558] allows that they were inspired, but by the spirit of evil. Jerome[559] believes that this power was given to them by God as a reward for virginity; and Augustine[560] thinks that they predicted many truths concerning Jesus Christ. Justin[561] adopts a legend which would account for the similarity between the Sibylline oracles and Hebrew prophecy. He says that the Cumæan Sibyl, celebrated by Virgil, was born at Babylon, and was the daughter of Berosus, the Chaldean historian.

If Virgil, in the fourth eclogue, correctly paraphrased the Sibylline poems, two parallelisms between them and the prophecies of Isaiah are remarkably striking:[562]—

> Jam redit et Virgo, redeunt Saturnia regna;
> Jam nova progenies cœlo demittitur alto—
> Te duce, si qua manent sceleris vestigia nostri,
> Irrita perpetua solvent formidine terras—
> Pacatumque reget patriis virtutibus orbem.—v. 6.
> Behold a virgin shall conceive, and bear a son.—Is. vii. 14.

Of the increase of his government and peace there shall be no end, upon the throne of David, and upon his kingdom, to order it, and to establish it with judgment and with justice from henceforth even for ever.—Is. ix. 7.

---

[556] Præl. de Sacr. Po. He. xxi. p. 289.
[557] Orat. ad Sanctos, 19, 20; apud Euseb.
[558] In 1 Cor. ii.
[559] Adv. Jor. lib. i.
[560] Contra Faust, i. 13, 2.
[561] Orat. Paræn.
[562] See notes to Pope's Messiah.

> At tibi prima, puer, nullo munuscula cultu,
> Errantes hederas passim cum baccare tellus,
> Mixtaque ridenti colocasia fundet acantho.—v. 18.

The wilderness and the solitary place shall be glad for them; and the desert shall rejoice, and blossom as the rose.—Is. xxxv. 1.

Many theories have been proposed respecting the child to whom allusion is made in this eclogue, not one of which was satisfactory to Gibbon;[563] but the following is adopted by Heyne as the most probable. The peace of Brundisium was cemented by the marriage between Antony and Cæsar's half-sister Octavia. She was the widow of Marcellus, and appeared likely to give birth to a posthumous child. To this child yet unborn, the poet applies all the blessings promised by the Sibylline oracles, and predicts that, under his auspices, the peace and prosperity already inaugurated shall be confirmed.

VI. In the sixth, Virgil represents allegorically, under the character of Silenus the tutor of Bacchus, his own instructor Syron; and thus makes it the vehicle of a short account of the Epicurean philosophy. It was not long since the same subject had been treated of at greater length by the eloquent Lucretius; and it is said that when Cicero heard it recited by the mime Cytheris, he was so struck with admiration as to exclaim that he was "Magnæ spes altera Romæ." This eclogue is parodied by Gay in the Saturday of his Shepherd's Week.

X. The tenth can scarcely be distinguished from any other amatory poem, except that the heroic metre is not so usual in that species of poetry as the elegiac. The loves of the poet Gallus are sung; Arcadia is fixed upon as the place of his exile; and the lay is said to be set to the music of the oaten-pipe of Sicily: but this eclogue has no other claim to be entitled a bucolic poem.

One passage in this eclogue, which suggested the following beautiful lines in Milton's "*Lycidas,*" illustrates the truth that poetry often derives additional beauty from the fact of its being a successful imitation:—

> Quæ nemora aut qui vos saltus habuere, puellæ
> Naiades, indigno cum Gallus amore periret?
> Nam neque Parnassi vobis juga nam neque Pindi
> Ulla moram fecere, neque Aonia Aganippe.
> *Ecl.* x. 9.
> Where were ye, Nymphs, when the remorseless deep
> Closed o'er the head of your loved Lycidas?
> For neither were ye playing on the steep,
> Where your old bards, the famous Druids, lie,
> Nor on the shaggy top of Mona high,
> Nor yet where Deva spreads her wizard stream.
> Milton's Lycidas.

---

[563] Decl. and Fall. c. xx. vol. iii. p. 269.

Chapter 18

BEAUTY OF DIDACTIC POETRY—ELABORATE FINISH OF THE GEORGICS—ROMAN LOVE OF RURAL PURSUITS—HESIOD SUITABLE AS A MODEL—CONDITION OF ITALY—SUBJECTS TREATED OF IN THE GEORGICS—SOME STRIKING PASSAGES ENUMERATED—INFLUENCE OF ROMAN LITERATURE ON ENGLISH POETRY—SOURCES FROM WHICH THE INCIDENTS OF THE ÆNEID ARE DERIVED—CHARACTER OF ÆNEAS—CRITICISM OF NIEBUHR

 Didactic poetry is of all kinds the least inviting. As its professed object is instruction, there is no reason why its lessons should be conveyed in poetical language—its purpose, could in fact, be better attained in prose. Pretending, therefore, to poetry, it demands great skill, elaborate finish and such graces and embellishments as will conceal its dry character, and recommend it to the reader's attention.

 The beauty of a didactic poem depends only partially on the just views and correct discrimination which it evinces, and principally on the beauty of the language, the picturesque force, and pleasing character of the descriptions, and the interest that is thrown into the episodes. In fact, the accessaries are the parts most admired, and extracts brought forward as specimens of this kind of poetry are invariably of this kind. Poetry naturally deals with the beauties and terrors of external nature—with the emotions and passions, whether of a tender or violent kind—the sober practical rules of life are scarcely within its sphere. True it is that when all literature was poetical, the precepts of moral and physical philosophy, and even the dry commands of laws and institutions, were embodied in a metrical form; but when literature divides itself into poetry and prose, the subjects appropriated to each other become spontaneously separate likewise. For this reason, the Georgics of Virgil especially display his ability as a poet, his correct taste the "limæ labor," the pains which he took in polishing and correcting. In none of his poems can we form a better idea of the description which he gives of his patient toil, when he says, that "like the she-bear he brought his poetical offspring into shape by constantly licking them."[564] The majesty of the language elevates the subject, and divests it of so much of the homeliness as would be inappropriate to poetry, and yet at the same time it is not too grand or elevated.

The following criticism of Addison[565] is by no means too favourable:—"I shall conclude this poem to be the most complete, elaborate, and finished piece of all antiquity. The Æneis is of a nobler kind; but the Georgic is more perfect in its kind. The Æneis has a greater variety of beauties in it; but those of the Georgic are more exquisite. In short, the Georgic has all the perfection that can be expected in a poem written by the greatest poet, in the flower of his age, when his invention was ready, his imagination warm, his judgment settled, and all his faculties in their full vigour and maturity."

Rome offered a favourable field for a poet to undertake a poem on the labours and enjoyments of rural life. Agriculture was always there considered a liberal employment: tradition had adorned rustic manners with the attributes of simplicity and honesty, and divested them of the ideas of coarseness usually connected with them. The traditions of those ages of national freedom and greatness, to which the enthusiasm of the poet delighted to carry back the thoughts of his readers, had connected some of the noblest names of history with rural labours. Curius and Cincinnatus were called from the plough to defend and save their country; and after their task was performed they returned with delight to it again. Cato, the representative of the old and respected generation, and other illustrious men, had written on the pursuits and duties of rural life. Agriculture was never connected with ideas of debasing and illiberal gain, such as attached to trade and commerce.

The poet, moreover, had a model ready at hand, after which to construct his work. It was Greek, and therefore sure to be acceptable upon the recognised principles of taste. It described a species of rural life, hard, frugal, and industrious, very much like that led by the agriculturists of Italy. It painted a standard of morals, which even the licentious inhabitants of a luxurious capital could appreciate, though they had degenerated from it. The discriminating judgment of Virgil saw that the rural life of Italy could really be represented, in the same way in which Hesiod had painted that of Bœtia, and he wisely determined—

To sing through Roman towns Ascræan strains.

There exists, however, precisely that difference between the Georgics of Virgil and their model that might be expected. The Hesiodic poem belongs to a period when poetry was the accidental form—instruction the essential object; and, therefore, the teaching is systematic, precise, detailed, homely, sometimes coarse and unpolished. Virgil looks at his subject from the poetical point of view. His precepts are often put, not in a didactic but a descriptive form; they are unhesitatingly interrupted by digressions and episodes, more or less to the point; and out of a vast mass of materials such only are selected as are suitable to awaken the sensibilities.

The state of Italy also contributed to enlist a poet's sympathies in favour of the rural classes, and to devote his pen to the patriotic task of reviving the old agricultural tastes. War had devastated the land; the peasant population had been fearfully thinned by military conscriptions and confiscation; wide districts had been depopulated and left destitute of cultivation. Instead of the sword being beat into a ploughshare and the spear into a pruning-

---

[564] A. Gell. N. A. xvii. 10.
[565] Misc. Works, vol. i.

hook, the Italian peasant had witnessed the contrary state of things. The poet laments the sad change which now disfigured the fair face of Italy:—

> non ullus aratro
> Dignus honos, squalent abductis arva colonis,
> Et curvæ rigidum falces conflantur in ensem.
> *Geo.* i. 507.

The credit of having proposed this subject to Virgil is given to his patron Mæcenas; and, to him, consequently, the Georgics are addressed; but the poet doubtless gladly adopted the suggestion. When and where it was commenced is uncertain, but the finishing stroke was put to it at Naples[566] some time after the battle of Actium.[567] Although the "*Works and Days*" of Hesiod is professedly his pattern, still he derives his materials from other sources. Aratus supplies him with his signs of the weather, and the writers *de Re Rustica* with his practical directions. His system is indeed perfectly Italian; so much so, that many of his rules may be traced in modern Italian husbandry, just as the descriptions of implements in Hesiod are frequently found to agree with those in use in modern Greece.

The first book treats of tillage, the second of orchards; the subject of the third, which is the noblest and most spirited of them, is the care of horses and cattle; and the fourth, which is the most pleasing and interesting, describes the natural instincts as well as the management of bees.

But the great merit of the Georgics consists in their varied digressions, interesting episodes, and sublime bursts of descriptive vigour, which are interspersed throughout the poem. To quote any of them would be unnecessary, as Virgil and his translations are in every one's hands. It will be sufficient to enumerate some of the most striking. These are—

I.
The Origin of Agriculture, G. I. 125.

II.
The Storm in Harvest, I. 316.

III.
The Signs of the Weather, I. 351.

IV.
The Prodigies at the Death of Julius Cæsar, I. 466.

V.
The Battle of Pharsalia, I. 489.

VI.
The Panegyric on Italy, II. 136.

---

[566] G. iv. 560–564.
[567] G. ii. 171.

VII.
The Praises of a Country Life, II. 458.

VIII.
The Horse and Chariot Race, III. 103.

IX.
The Description of Winter in Scythia, III. 349.

X.
The Murrain of Cattle, III. 478.

XI.
The Battle of the Bees, IV. 67.

XII.
The Story of Aristæus, IV. 317.

XIII.
The Legend of Orpheus and Eurydice, IV. 453.

Roman poetry was more generally understood and more diligently studied in the most polished days of English literature, than the yet scarcely discovered stores of Greek learning. Want of originality was not considered a blemish in an age the taste of which, notwithstanding all its merits, was very artificial; whilst the exquisite polish and elegance which constitute the charm of Latin poetry, recommended it both for admiration and imitation. Hence English poets have been deeply indebted to the Romans for their most happy thoughts, and our native literature is largely imbued with a Virgilian and Horatian spirit. This circumstance adds an especial interest to a survey of Roman literature as the fountain from which welled forth so many of the streams that have fertilized our poetry.

The Georgics have been frequently taken as a model for imitation, and our descriptive poets have drawn largely from this source. Warton[568] considered Philips' "*Cyder*" the happiest imitation; "*The Seasons*" of our greatest descriptive poet, Thomson, is a thoroughly Virgilian poem. Many striking instances of Virgilian taste might be adduced, especially the thunder-storm in "*Summer*," and the praises of Great Britain, in "*Autumn*."

From the letter already quoted as preserved by Macrobius, it is clear that the Æneid was commenced when Augustus was in Spain,[569] that it occupied the whole of Virgil's subsequent life, and was not sufficiently corrected to satisfy his own fastidious taste when he died. Augustus intrusted its publication to Varius and Tucca, with strict instructions to abstain from interpolation. They are said to have transposed the second and third books, and to have omitted twenty-two lines[570] as being contradictory to another passage respecting Helen in the sixth book.[571] Hence in many early manuscripts these verses are wanting.

---

[568] See Dunlop, H. of R. L. iii. *s. v.* Virg.
[569] B. C. 27.
[570] Æn. ii. 567–589.
[571] Ibid. vi. 511.

The idea and plan of the Æneid are derived from the Homeric poems. As the wrath of Achilles is the mainspring of all the events in the Iliad, so on the anger of the offended Juno the unity of the Æneid depends, and with it all the incidents are connected. Many of the most splendid passages, picturesque images, and forcible epithets are imitations or even translations from the Iliad and Odyssey. The war with Turnus owes its grandeur and its interest to the Iliad—the wanderings of Æneas, their wild and romantic adventures to the Odyssey. Virgil's battles, though not to be compared in point of vigour with those of Homer, shine with a reflected light. His Necyia is a copy of that in the Odyssey. His similes are most of them suggested by those favourite embellishments of Homer. The shield of Æneas[572] is an imitation of that of Achilles. The storm and the speech of Æneas[573] are almost translations from the Odyssey.[574]

The thoughts thus borrowed from the great heroic poems of Greece, Virgil interwove with that ingenuity which distinguishes the Augustan school by means of the double character in which he represented his hero. The narrative of his perils by sea and land were enriched by the marvellous incidents of the Odyssey; his wars which occupy the latter books had their prototype in the Iliad. Greek tragedy, also, which depicted so frequently the subsequent fortunes of the Greek chieftains,[575]—the numerous translations which had employed the genius of Ennius, Attius, and Pacuvius—were a rich mine of poetic wealth. The second book, which is almost too crowded with a rapid succession of pathetic incidents, derived its interesting details—the untimely fate of Astyanax, the loss of Creusa, the story of Sinon, the legend of the wooden horse, the death of the aged Priam, the subsequent fortunes of Helen—from two Cyclic poems, the Sack of Troy and the little Iliad of Arctinus. For the legend of Laocoon he was indebted to the Alexandrian poet, Euphorion. The class of Cyclic poems entitled the νοστοι suggested much of the third book, especially the stories of Pyrrhus, Helenus, and Andromache. The fourth drew its fairy enchantments partly from Homer's Calypso, partly from the love adventures of Jason, Medea, and Hypsypile in the Argonautica of the Alexandrian poet, Apollonius Rhodius, which had been introduced to the Romans by the translation of Varro.

The sixth is suggested by the eleventh book of the Odyssey and the descent of Theseus in search of Pirithous in the Hesiodic poems. But notwithstanding the force and originality—the vivid word-painting which adorns this book—it is far inferior to the conceptions which Greek genius formed of the unseen world. In the Æneid the legends of the world of spirits seem but vulgar marvels and popular illusions. Tartarus and Elysium are too palpable and material to be believed; their distinctness dispels the enchantment which they were intended to produce; it is daylight instead of dim shadow. We miss the outlines, which seem gigantic from their dim and shadowy nature, the appalling grandeur to which no one since Æschylus ever attained, except the great Italian poet who has never since been equalled.

To this rich store of Greek learning Italy contributed her native legends. The adventures of Æneas in Italy—the prophecy, of which the fulfilment was discovered by Iulus—the pregnant white sow—the story of the Sibyl—the sylph-like Camilla—were native lays amalgamated with the Greek legend of Troy. Macrobius,[576] in three elaborate chapters, has

---

[572] Æn. viii. 626.
[573] Ibid. i.
[574] Book v.
[575] Macrob. Saturn. v. 13.
[576] Saturn. vi. 1, 2, 3.

shown that Virgil was deeply indebted to the old Latin poets. In the first he quotes more than seventy parallel turns of expression from Ennius, Pacuvius, Attius, Nævius, Lucilius, Lucretius, Catullus, and Varius, consisting of whole or half lines. In the second he enumerates twenty-six longer passages, which Virgil has imitated from the poems of Ennius, Attius, Lucretius, and Varius, amongst which are portions of "*The Praises of Rural Life*," and of "*The Pestilence*."[577] In the third he mentions a few (amongst them, for example, the well-known description of the horse[578]) which were taken by Virgil from the old Roman poets, having been first adopted by them from the Homeric poems. The following passages are a few of these examples of what would in modern times be considered plagiarisms, but which the ancients admitted without reluctance:—

> Qui cœlum versat stellis fulgentibus aptum.
> Ennius.
> Axem humero torquet stellis fulgentibus aptum.
> V. Æn. vi. 797.
> Est locus Hesperiam quam mortales perhibebant.
> Est locus Hesperiam Graii cognomine dicunt.
> Æn. i. 530.
> Unus homo nobis cunctando restituit rem.
> Unus qui nobis cunctando restituis rem.
> Æn. vi. 846.
> Quod per amœnam urbem leni fluit agmine flumen.
> —— arva
> Inter opima virum leni fluit agmine Tybris.
> Æn. ii. 781.
> Hei mihi qualis erat quantum mutatus ab illo.
> Hei mihi qualis erat quantum mutatus ab illo.
> Æn. ii. 274.
> —— discordia tetra
> Belli ferratos postes portasque refregit.
> Belli ferratos rupit Saturnia postes.
> Æn. vi. 622.

The variety of incidents, the consummate skill in the arrangement of them, the interest which pervades both the plot and the episodes, fully compensate for the want of originality—a defect of which none but learned readers would be aware. What sweeter specimens can be found of tender pathos than the legend of Camilla, and the episode of Nisus and Euryalus? Where is the turbulence of uncurbed passions united with womanly unselfish fondness, and queen-like generosity, painted with a more masterly hand than in the character of Dido? Where, even in the Iliad, are characters better sustained and more happily contrasted than the weak Latinus, the soldier-like Turnus, the simple-minded Evander, the feminine and retiring Lavinia, the barbarian Mezentius, who to the savageness of a wild beast joined the natural instinct, which warmed with the strongest affection for his son. The only character of which the conception is somewhat unsatisfactory is that of the hero himself: Æneas, notwithstanding

---

[577] Compare De Nat. Rer. ii. 24; vi. 136, 1143–1224; with Georg. ii. 461, 467, &c.; iii. 478, 505, 509, &c.
[578] Iliad, Z. 506; Æn. xi. 492.

his many virtues, fails of commanding the reader's sympathy or admiration. He is full of faith in the providence of God, submits himself with entire resignation to His divine will—is brave, patient, dutiful—but he is cold and heartless, and, if the expression is allowable, unchivalrous. In his war with Turnus, he is so decidedly in the wrong, and the character of his injured adversary shines with such lustre, and is adorned with such gallantry, that one is inclined to transfer to him the interest and sympathy which ought to be felt for the hero alone. This is undoubtedly a fault, but it is counterbalanced by innumerable excellences.

In personification, nothing is finer than Virgil's portraiture of Fame, except perhaps Spenser's Despair. In description, the same genius which shone forth in the Georgics, embellishes the Æneid also; and both the objects and the phenomena of nature are represented in language equally vivid and striking.

Notwithstanding the question has been much discussed, it is most probable that the opinion of Pope was correct respecting the political object of the Æneid. He affirmed that it was as much a party-piece as Dryden's Absalom and Achitophel; that its primary object was to increase the popularity of Augustus; its secondary one to flatter the vanity of his countrymen by the splendour and antiquity of their origin. Augustus is evidently typified under the character of Æneas: both were cautious and wise in council,[579] both were free from the perturbations of passion; they were cold, unfeeling, and uninteresting. Their wisdom and their policy were calculating and worldly-minded. Augustus was conscious, as his last words show, that he was acting a part; and the contrast between the sentiments and conduct of Æneas, wherever the warm impulses of affection might be supposed to have sway, likewise create an impression of insincerity. The characteristic virtue which adorns the hero of the Æneid, as the epithet "Pius" so constantly applied to him implies, was filial piety; and there was no virtue which Augustus more ostentatiously put forward than dutiful affection to Julius Cæsar who had adopted him.

Other characters which are grouped around the central figure are allegorical likewise— Cleopatra is boldly sketched as Dido, the passionate victim of unrequited love. Both displayed the noble, generous qualities, and at the same time the uncontrolled self-will of a woman, who neither had nor would acknowledge any master except the object of her affections: the fortunes of both were similar, for their brothers had become their bitterest enemies, and the fate of both alike was suicide.

Turnus, whose character, as has been already stated, is far more chivalrous and attractive than that of Æneas, probably represented the popular Antony; and as the latter violated the peace ratified at Brundisium and Tarentum, so the former is represented as treacherous to his engagements with Æneas. It has even been thought, and the view has been supported by many ingenious arguments, that Iapis is a portrait of the physician of Augustus.[580]

Virgil is especially skilful in that species of imitation which consists in the appropriate choice of words, and the assimilation of the sound to the sense. A series of dactyles expresses the rapid speed of horses, and the still more rapid flight of time:—

> Quadrupedante putrem Sonitu quatit ungula campum.
> *Æn.* viii. 591.

---

[579] Spence's Anecdotes.
[580] See, on this subject, Dunlop's Hist. iii. 151.

Sed fugit interea fugit irreparabile tempus.
Geo. iii. 284.

Dignity and majesty are represented by an unusual use of spondees:—

—— quæ Divum incedo regina.
Æn. i. 50.
—— penatibus et magnis Dîs.
Æn. viii. 679.

Accelerated motion by a corresponding change of metre:—

—— jamjam lapsura cadentique
Imminet assimilis——
Æn. vi. 602.

Effort by a hiatus:—

Ter sunt conati imponere Pelio Ossam.

Abruptness, or the fall of a heavy body, by a monosyllable:—

Insequitur cumulo præruptus aquæ mons.
Æn. i. 109.
—— procumbit humi bos.
Æn. v. 481.

Many other examples might be adduced[581] of that which, if it were an artifice, would be a very pleasing one, which rather proceeds from the natural impulses of a lively fancy and a delicately-attuned ear.

Dunlop has well observed, that Virgil's descriptions are more like landscape-painting than any by his predecessors, whether Greek or Roman, and that it is a remarkable fact that landscape-painting was first introduced in his time. Pliny, in his Natural History,[582] informs us that Ludius, who flourished in the lifetime of Augustus, invented the most delightful style of painting, compositions introducing porticoes, gardens, groves, hills, fish-ponds, rivers, and other pleasing objects, enlivened by carriages, animals, and figures. Thus, perhaps, art inspired poetry.

No one has ever attempted to disparage the reputation of Virgil as holding the highest rank amongst Roman poets, except the Emperor Caligula, J. Markland, and the great historian Niebuhr. The latter does not hesitate to say that the flourishing period of Roman poetry ceased about the time of the deaths of Cæsar and Cicero.[583] Doubtless Roman national poetry then ceased, and was succeeded by the new era of Greek taste; but still the poems of the new

---

[581] See Clarke's Homer, Il. iii. 363, note.
[582] H. N. xxxv. 10.
[583] Lect. cvi. on R. H.

school were equally majestic and pathetic, and though less natural, owed to their Greek originals incomparably greater polish, grace and sweetness.

It is difficult to understand the low opinion which Niebuhr entertained of Virgil, and the superiority which he attributes to Catullus. He not only declares that he is opposed to the adoration with which the later Romans regarded him, but he denies his fertility of genius and inventive powers. Although he acknowledges that the Æneid contains many exquisite passages, he pronounces it a complete failure, an unhappy idea from beginning to end. It is evident that he looked at the Æneid with the eye of an historian, and that his objections to it were entirely of an historical character.

Wrapped up in Roman nationality and Italian traditions, he did not forgive Virgil for adulterating this pure source of antiquarian information with Greek legends. He assumes, correctly enough, that an epic poem, in order to be successful, must be a living narrative of events known and interesting to the mass of a nation, and at the same time confesses that, whilst the ancient Italian traditions had already fallen into oblivion, Homer was at that time better known than Nævius. Surely, then, if Virgil had drawn from Italian sources exclusively, he would have omitted much that would have added interest to his poem in the opinion of his hearers, and would not have complied with the epic conditions which Niebuhr himself lays down. Besides, if the traditions of Nævius were Italian, were not many of the Greek and Italian traditions which form the framework of the Æneid identical? Nævius must have drawn largely from the Cyclic poems; and Niebuhr allows that Virgil copied these parts of his poem from Nævius.[584] He asserts his conviction that Virgil's shield of Æneas had its model in Nævius, in whose poem Æneas or some other hero had a shield representing the wars of the giants; and yet no one could doubt that the shield of Nævius must have been suggested by the Homeric and Hesiodic poems. Servius also believed that Virgil borrowed from the poem of Nævius the plan of the early books of the Æneid.[585]

Some of Virgil's minor poems are undoubtedly very beautiful;[586] but it is absurd to say that even the greatest elegance in fugitive pieces of such a stamp can outshine the noble and sublime passages interwoven throughout the whole structure of the Æneid. The dispraise of Niebuhr is as exaggerated as the fulsome compliment paid by Propertius to the genius of his fellow-countryman:—

> Cedite, Romani scriptores, cedite Graii,
> Nescio quid majus nascitur Iliade.
> *Eleg.* ii. 27.

---

[584] Introd. Lect. iv.
[585] Serv. ad Æn. i. 98; ii. 797; iii. 10.
[586] Meyer, Anthol. 85, 93, &c.

Chapter 19

The Libertini—Roman Feelings as to Commerce—Birth and Infancy of Horace—His Early Education at Rome—His Military Career—He Returns to Rome—Is Introduced to Mæcenas—Commences the Satires—Mæcenas Gives Him His Sabine Farm—His Country Life—the Epodes—Epistles—Carmen Seculare—Illness and Death

Horatius Flaccus (Born B. C. 65.)

Lyric poetry is the most subjective of all poetry, and the musician of the Roman lyre[587] was the most subjective of all Latin poets: hence a complete sketch of his life and delineation of his character may be deduced from his works. They contain the elements of an autobiography; and, whilst they constitute the most authentic source of information, convey the particulars in the most lively and engaging form.

At the period of Horace's birth the *Libertini*, or freedmen, were rapidly rising in wealth, and, therefore, in position. The Roman constitution excluded the senatorial order from commercial pursuits, and would not even permit them to own vessels of any considerable burden, lest they should be made use of in trade. The old Roman feeling was even more exclusive than the law. There were certain trades in which not only none who had any pretensions to the rank of a gentleman, but even no one who was free-born could engage without degradation. Cicero[588] considers that money-lending, manufactures, retail trade, especially in delicacies which minister to the appetite, are all sordid and illiberal. He does not even allow that the professions of medicine and architecture are honourable, except to such as are of suitable rank. Agriculture is the only method of money-making which he pronounces to be without any doubt worthy of free-born men.

---

[587] Od. IV. iii. 23.
[588] De Off. i. 42.

Devoted to the duties of public life either as soldiers or citizens, the Romans did not comprehend the dignity of labour. High-minded and unselfish as it may appear to think meanly of employments undertaken simply for the sake of profit and lucre, the political result of this pride was unmixed evil. Commerce was thus thrown into the hands of those whose fathers had been slaves, and who themselves inherited and possessed the usual vices of a slavish disposition.

The middle classes were impoverished, and, as the unavoidable consequence of a system in which social position depended upon property, were rapidly sinking into the lowest ranks of the population. Here then was a gap to be filled up—the question was by what means? Had Roman feeling permitted the free-born citizen to devote his energies to labour and the creation of capital, he would have risen in the social scale, would have occupied the place left vacant, and would have brought with him those sentiments of chivalrous freedom which there can be no doubt distinguished Rome in earlier times, and advanced her in the scale of nations. Thus the circulation would have been complete and healthy, and the national system would have received fresh life and vigour in its most important part. Instead of this, however, slaves and the sons of slaves rose to wealth: not such slaves as those who, well educated and occupying a high or, at least, a respectable position in the conquered Greek states, were appreciated by their conquerors, became their friends and intimates, because of their worth and intellectual acquirements, imbued their masters with their own refinement and taste, and were intrusted with the education of their children, but slaves who had formed the masses of degraded nations. These were driven in hordes to Rome. They swarmed in all the states of Italy and Sicily. Many of them were not deficient in ability and energy, and therefore they rose; but they had little or no moral principle. Their children intermarried with the lower classes of the citizens; their blood infected that of the higher European races which flowed in their veins; and thus the masses of Rome became a mixed race, but not mixed for the better. The character changed; but it changed because the old race had perished, and a new race with new characteristics occupied its place.

Under such circumstances, the *Libertini* became a powerful and important class, both socially and politically: they were the bankers, merchants, and tradesmen of Rome.

Of this class, the father of Horace was one of the most respectable. His business was that of a *coactor*, or agent who collected the money from purchasers of goods at public auctions. He was a man of strict integrity, content with his position, and would not have thought himself disgraced if his son had followed his own calling.[589] He had made by his industry a small fortune, sufficient to purchase an estate near Venusia (Venosa,) on the confines of Lucania and Apulia, but not sufficient to free him from the appellation of "a poor man."[590]

Here, on the 8th of December (vi'o id. Decembr.,) B. C. 65, Q. Horatius Flaccus was born; and on the banks of the obstreperous Aufidus,[591] the roar of whose waters could be heard far off,[592] Horace passed his infant years, and played and wandered in that picturesque neighbourhood. The natural beauties amidst which he was nursed, probably did much to form and foster his poetic tastes. He himself relates, in one of his finest odes,[593] an adventure which

---

[589] Sat. I. vi. 86.
[590] Ibid. I. vi. 71.
[591] Od. III. xxx. 10.
[592] Ibid. IV. ix. 2.
[593] Od. III. iv. 9.

befell him in his childhood, and which reminds the reader of the beautiful nursery ballad of the Children in the Wood:——

> Me fabulosæ Vulture in Appulo
> Altricis extra limen Apuliæ
> Ludo fatigatumque somno
> Fronde nova puerum palumbes
> Texere (mirum quod foret omnibus,
> Quicumque celsæ nidum Acherontiæ,
> Saltusque Bantinos, et arvum
> Pingue tenent humilis Ferenti,)
> Ut tuto ab atris corpore viperis
> Dormirem et ursis; ut premerer sacra
> Lauroque collataque myrto
> Non sine Dîs animosus infans.
> Fatigued with sleep and youthful toil of play,
> When on a mountain's brow reclined I lay,
> Near to my natal soil, around my head
> The fabled woodland doves a verdant foliage spread;
> Matter, be sure, of wonder most profound
> To all the gazing habitants around,
> Who dwell in Acherontia's airy glades,
> Amid the Bantian woods, or low Ferentum's meads.
> By snakes of poison black and beasts of prey,
> That thus in dewy sleep unharmed I lay;
> Laurels and myrtle were around me piled,
> Not without guardian gods, an animated child.
> Francis.

He remained amongst his native mountains until his eleventh or twelfth year, when his father, wisely wishing to secure for him the benefits of a liberal education, which the neighbouring village school of Flavius did not furnish, removed with him to Rome.[594] Thus he quitted Venusia for ever, of which place many passages in his works prove that he retained very vivid recollections.[595]

At Rome he was placed under the instruction of Orbilius Pupillus, a grammarian, who had been formerly in the army, and had migrated from Beneventum to the capital. He was celebrated as a schoolmaster, but still more for his severity, for he was commonly called the flogging Orbilius (Plagosus Orbilius.[596]) With him young Horace read in his own language the poems of Livius Andronicus and Ennius; and in the Greek, the Iliad of Homer, whose divine poetry he soon learnt to enjoy.[597]

Whilst his father took this care of his intellectual education, he enabled him by dress and a retinue of slaves to associate on terms of equality with boys far above him in rank and

---

[594] Sat. I. vi. 71.
[595] See *ex. gr.* Ep. II. 41; Od. III. vi. 37; Sat. II. ii. 112.
[596] Ep. II. i. 70.
[597] Ibid. ii. 41.

station;[598] and, what was still more important, he kept him under his own roof, and thus secured for his son the benefits of home influences, sage and prudent advice, and the watchful care of the parental eye.[599] For his father's liberality, good example, and constant attention, Horace expresses the deepest gratitude,[600] and to him he acknowledges himself indebted for all the good points of his character. The practical nature of this indulgent and devoted father's instruction—how he delighted to teach by example rather than by precept—is simply told by Horace himself[601] in one of his satires.

Before he arrived at man's estate, it is probable that he lost his wise adviser, for he never mentions his father except in connexion with the years of his boyhood. Perhaps this is the reason why, in his earlier poetry, his genial freedom so often degenerated into licentiousness, and his love of pleasure tempted him to adopt the dissolute manners of a corrupt age. His moral sense was accurate and just—he could see what was useful and approve it; he could censure the vices of his contemporaries—but he had lost that wise counsel which had hitherto preserved him pure.

Athens was at that period the university of Rome. Thither the Roman youth resorted to learn language, art, science, and philosophy:—

> Inter sylvas Academi quærere verum.[602]
> To seek for truth in Academic groves.

Horace commenced his residence there at a great political crisis, and the politics of Rome created a vivid interest in the young students at Athens. He had not lived there long, when Julius Cæsar was assassinated; and many of his fellow students, as was natural to youthful and ardent minds, zealously embraced the Republican Party. Horace, now twenty-two years of age, joined the army of Brutus, and served under him until the battle of Philippi in the rank of a military tribune.[603] He must have already become distinguished, since nothing but merit could have recommended the son of a freedman to Brutus for so high a military command. But the event proved that he had sadly mistaken his vocation, for he was totally unfit for the position either of an officer or a soldier.

With the rest of the vanquished he fled from the field of Philippi; and in a beautiful and affectionate ode[604] to Pompeius Varus, he confesses that he even threw away his shield; nor was he one of those who rallied, although his friend was carried back again into the bloody conflict of the tide of war. So at any rate he himself tells the story. It may have been, however, that his vanity prompted him to pretend a resemblance in this respect to his favourite Alcæus, or perhaps he wished to address a piece of courtly flattery to the conqueror. Varus was one of his earliest friends: together they had spent days of study and of festivity; and when troublous times had separated them, nothing can exceed the wild and tumultuous joy with which Horace looks forward to a reunion with his friend.

---

[598] Sat. I. vi. 76.
[599] Sat. I. vi.
[600] Ibid. vi.
[601] Ibid. iv. 103.
[602] Ep. II. ii. 43.
[603] Sat. I. vi.
[604] Od. II. vii.

On his return to Rome he found that his father was dead, and his patrimony confiscated.[605] In order to obtain a livelihood, he purchased a clerk's place under the quæstor.[606] For its duties he must have been totally unfit, for he hated business[607] and loved pleasure and literary ease. But on the income of this office, and the kindness of his friends, he lived a life of frugality and poverty.[608] It is possible that even then he gained some profit from his poems, for he says,[609] "Audacious poverty drove me to write verses." Perhaps when he became more prosperous, he resigned his place, for he does not mention it in the account he gives to Mæcenas of the usual, daily avocations of his careless and sauntering life.[610]

Soon, however, his fortunes began to brighten. His talents recommended him, when about twenty-four years of age, to Virgil and Varius.[611] They were then the leading poets at Rome; and Mæcenas, the polished but somewhat effeminate friend of Augustus, was the powerful patron of genius and the head of literary society. These two poets were warmly attached to Horace, whose affection for them was equally strong,[612] and to them he owed his introduction to the favourite of the emperor.[613] He felt rather timid at the interview: Mæcenas spoke to him with his usual reserved and curt manner, took no notice of him for nine months, and then sent for him and enrolled him in the number of his friends. Thenceforth Horace enjoyed uninterruptedly his friendship and intimacy—of the affectionate nature of which many evidences may be found in those poetical pieces which Horace addressed to him.

As Mæcenas rose in influence and favour with Augustus, he also procured the advancement of his friend. When he was sent by Augustus on the delicate mission of effecting a reconciliation with Anthony, Horace accompanied him;[614] and it is not impossible that his shipwreck off Cape Palinurus occurred when he was sailing with Mæcenas on his expedition against S. Pompey.

At this period of his life he commenced the composition of his first book of Satires.[615] The knowledge of human life which he had begun to acquire when he lived, as it were, upon the town, and became acquainted with the manners, habits and modes of thinking of the masses, was afterwards cultivated, refined and matured by intercourse with the best literary society. His observant mind found ample materials for satire at the table of the courtly Mæcenas, and amidst the brilliant circle by which he was surrounded. In this, his first publication, he also introduces himself to the reader's notice, draws a lively picture of his youth, and describes the life which was congenial to his tastes, and which his change of circumstances permitted him to lead.

But it must not be supposed that he wrote nothing at that time except satire. Some of his odes, which display the strength of youthful passions and the loosest morality, were probably written as separate fugitive pieces, and circulated privately amongst his friends. The ode to Canidia narrates a circumstance in the early part of his poetical career. The Epodes breathe

---

[605] Ep. II. ii. 49.
[606] Suet. in Vita.
[607] Ep. II. xiv. 17.
[608] Sat. I. vi. 114.
[609] Ep. II. ii. 51.
[610] Sat. I. vi.
[611] B. C. 41.
[612] Sat. I. v. 39.
[613] Ibid. vi. 55.
[614] Sat. I. v.
[615] According to Bentley, he composed them in the twenty-sixth, twenty-seventh, and twenty-eighth years of his age; according to Clinton, in the twenty-fifth, twenty-sixth, and twenty-seventh.

the spirit of the satirist rather than of the lyric poet; and therefore the coarsest of them[616] also may belong to the same period,[617] although the book which bears that name was not completed and published as a whole until some years subsequently.

The bitterness of some of the Epodes is more suitable to his years of adversity, and the hard struggles by which the temper is soured, than to that life of ease and comfort which patronage enabled him to lead. Then his temper resumed its wonted placidity, whilst his moral taste was refined; his Archilochian iambics became less cutting, and his ideas less gross; personal invective was laid aside, and his indignation was only aroused by the prospect of political troubles and the horrors of civil commotions.

Mæcenas accompanied his friendship with substantial favours. He gave him, or procured for him by his influence, the public grant of his Sabine farm. It was situated in a beautiful valley near Digentia (Licenza.) Being about fifteen miles from Tibur (Tivoli,) it was sufficiently near the capital to suit the fickle poet, who, when there, often regretted the luxury, and gossip, and brilliant society of Rome, and, when at Rome, sighed for the frugal table, the quiet retirement, the rural employment of his country abode. The rapid alternation of town and country life, which the possession of this estate enabled Horace to enjoy, gives a peculiar charm to his poetry. The scene is ever changing: his mind reflects the tenor of his life; simple pictures of rural life, and the elegant refinements of polished society, relieve one another, and prevent dulness and satiety. The property was neither extensive nor fertile, but it was sufficient for his moderate wants and wishes, which are so beautifully expressed in his sixth Satire—a poem which has found many modern imitators.

At Rome, Horace occupied a house on the pleasant and healthful heights of the Esquiline. Here he resided during the winter and spring, with the exception of occasional sojourns at Baiæ, or other places of fashionable resort, on the southern coast of Italy. Summer and autumn he passed at his Sabine farm, where he was a great favourite with his simple neighbours, and where he found all that he ever wished for, and even more.

> Modus agri non ita magnus,
> Hortus ubi, et tecto vicinus jugis aquæ fons,
> Et paulum silvæ super his.[618]

He coveted not his neighbour's field,[619] even though it disfigured his own. He never prayed that chance might throw in his way a buried vase of silver.[620] The calm of his life contrasted favourably with the hundred affairs—not so much his own as of other people—which tormented him at Rome;[621] the importunities of his friends that he would use his influence in their behalf with Mæcenas;[622] the growing envy to which his good fortune subjected him:[623] his only cares were to store up provisions for his frugal maintenance during the year,[624] so that he might live in sweet forgetfulness of how he lived.[625] His days were

---

[616] *Ex. gr.* viii. xi. xii.
[617] See Od. I. 16, 22.
[618] Sat. II. vi. 1.
[619] Ibid. 8.
[620] Ibid. 10.
[621] Ibid. vi. 33.
[622] Ibid. 38.
[623] Ibid. 47.
[624] Ep. I. 18.

divided between the books of the ancients,[626] the philosophy of Plato, and the lively scenes of Menander.[627]

The pleasing labours of the farm served him by way of exercise, although his town habits and awkwardness, and perhaps his short and stout figure, panting and perspiring under the heat and exertion, sometimes provoked good-humoured laughter.[628] At times, although he confessed how dangerous was the siren voice of sloth, he would spend hours of musing idleness on the margin of his favourite stream, listening to its murmurs, and to the music of the shepherd's reed as it echoed through the Arcadian glen.[629] The evenings were devoted to social converse with honest and virtuous friends, from which scandal and gossip were banished; the conversation usually turning on moral and philosophical discussion,[630] whilst its seriousness was occasionally relieved by witty anecdotes and pointed fables, of which those of the town and country mice, and of the madman who, when cured, complained that his friends had destroyed all the happiness of his dreamy life, furnish examples. At these *petits soupers*, which he called "suppers of the gods," the guests drank as much or as little as they pleased of his old wine, and enjoyed perfect freedom from the absurd laws which Roman custom permitted the chairman (*arbiter bibendi*) on such occasions to impose.

Sometimes, when the heat of summer was intense, he retired to the lofty Præneste (Palestrina,) where the climate was always cool and refreshing.[631] At some period of his life, also, he became possessed of a villa at Tibur (Tivoli,) of which the shady groves and roaring waterfalls furnished him a delightful refreshment after "the smoke, and magnificence, and noise of Rome." Here he wrote many of his satires, and thus achieved the reputation as a satirist of which he had laid the foundation already; and was enabled to boast that, though earnestly desirous of peace with the world, it were better not to provoke him; that he who dared to offend him should smart for it, and be the laughing-stock of the whole city.[632]

The composition and arrangement of the second book of Satires probably occupied the thirtieth, thirty-first, and thirty-second years of the poet's life,[633] and it was not published until the following year. This date will allow time for the expiration of more than seven or eight years since his intimacy with Mæcenas commenced.[634] The Satires were followed by the publication of the Epodes, very soon after the battle of Actium,[635] for the ninth is evidently an epinician ode on the occasion of that victory. Many of them contain noble sentiments, patriotic advice, burning indignation against the oriental self-indulgence of Antony,[636] the servility of Rome, its civil strife, and the degeneracy of the age; and remind us that, before Horace became an Epicurean and a courtier, he had fought against a tyrant in the ranks of freedom.[637] The first Epode was written just before the battle of Actium; the second and third at the period when he first exchanged the life of a fashionable man about town for that of a

---

[625] Sat. II. vi. 62.
[626] Ibid. vi. 61.
[627] Ibid. iii. 11.
[628] Ep. I. iv. 15; xx. 24; Suet. V. H.
[629] Ep. I. xiv.; Od. I. xvii.
[630] Sat. II. vi. 65.
[631] Od. III. 4.
[632] Sat. II. i. 45.
[633] Clinton, Fasti: B. C. 35, 34, 33
[634] Sat. II. vi.
[635] B. C. 31.
[636] *Ex. gr.* ix. xvi.
[637] See Ep. VII. ix.

country gentleman. We see in one the delight which he derived from the consciousness that his estate was his own; that he had no pecuniary embarrassments any longer; his anticipations of the happiness to be enjoyed in the regularly-recurring labours of rural life; in the absence of all care; in the kind-hearted anticipations of humble domestic felicity; the superiority of a healthful meal to all the luxuries that wealth could purchase. In the other, notwithstanding all these professions of sentiment, he shows that his refined urbanity is shocked by the grossness of rural habits. His delicate nose cannot endure the smell of garlic: to him it is nothing less than poison, such as Canidia or Medea might have used. It is more deadly than the malaria of Apulia, or the envenomed robe steeped in the blood of Nessus. Nay, in the same spirit Johnson said that "He who would make a pun would pick a pocket," he does not scruple to affirm that a garlic-eater would commit parricide.

The seventh Epode is a burst of indignant expostulation against the fratricidal madness which, at the bidding of an unprincipled woman, armed Romans against each other in that tragical episode, the Perugian war, when the first struggle took place between the civilians and the soldiers for political influence and power. In the Epodes the spirit is that of the satirist exaggerated. The outward form which he had modelled by a careful study of the Archilochian verse, prepared him for the cultivation of that poetry in which he stands pre-eminent. It was the state of transition through which he passed before he became a lyric poet.

With their publication concludes the first period of Horace's literary life. It was now flowing on calmly and peaceably, undisturbed by anxiety either about himself or his country. Although the civil wars were not yet ended, or the peace of the world solemnly and finally proclaimed, until the temple of Janus was closed,[638] the course of Octavius to universal empire lay plain and open before him. Rome was at his feet, and owed to him its safety and prosperity.

Public and private well-doing developed a new phase of Horace's genius. His muse soared to heights which had only been attempted by Pindar and the other Greek lyric poets. It cannot, of course, be supposed that he lived to the age of thirty-five years without having written many of those odes, which are so full of a youthful sprightliness and burning passion; but it is certain that many more were written, and the first three books published, during the period of eight years included between his thirty-fifth and forty-second years;[639] some when he was approaching, others when he had passed, his eighth lustre. In these three books it is probable that Horace intended all the products of his lyric muse should be comprised: to this purpose the last ode of the third book[640] seems to point. He considered his work done; and he was not insensible to the successful manner in which he had accomplished it. With conscious pride, and in a prophetic spirit, he exclaimed—

    Exegi monumentum ære perennius.

He intended his beloved friend and patron, Mæcenas, to be the subject of his last, as he was of his first, song. His introductory satire—the commencement of his published works—was addressed to him; the last ode in the book[641] (except that final one which proclaims his

---

[638] B. C. 29.
[639] Clinton, F. H.
[640] Lib. iii. 30.
[641] Lib. iii. 29.

task finished) is a noble farewell, breathing the language of affectionate compliment;[642] and in the introduction to his new work, the labour of his maturer years, the fruit of careful judgment respecting men and things, he states his determination to finish his career as a poet, and to devote his last verses to his patron.

A few years after the first three books of the Odes, Horace published the first book of the Epistles. Bentley assigns the appearance of these finished and elaborate compositions to B. C. 19, Clinton to B. C. 20. The *Carmen Seculare*, which appeared B. C. 17, on the occasion of the celebration of the Secular Games, and the fourth book of the Odes, which was published B. C. 13, were written at the personal request of the Emperor. He wished him to celebrate the victories gained over Vindelici by his step-sons, Tiberius and Drusus. His compliance with the wishes of Augustus was a graceful return for the regard and affection which the letters of the Emperor show that he felt for the poet.[643] The warm admiration which, these odes express, the praises which are lavished in them, upon Augustus and his step-sons Tiberius and Drusus, may seem inconsistent with the poet's former republicanism; but who could withstand the proffered friendship, the winning courtesy, the good-tempered condescension of his patron?

Besides, the experience of the past years must have forced him conscientiously to believe that the reign of Augustus was indeed a blessing to his country, and that his countrymen were totally unfit for real liberty, as they showed themselves quite content with the empty shadow of the constitution. He felt peace and repose were to be purchased by almost any sacrifice except that of honourable principle; that not only all the enjoyments of life were secured to himself to an extent equalling, if not surpassing, the wishes of his contented spirit, but that a similar measure of happiness was pretty generally diffused. He could not sympathize with political ambition, which had been the fruitful source of civil anarchy, and it was only the ambitious who had any cause to be dissatisfied. Doubtless the older he grew the stronger was the obligation which he felt to him who, by the lofty position which he had attained, had apparently prevented even the possibility of revolution or change. It is certain that the second book of the Epistles, and that addressed to the Pisos, which is commonly called the Art of Poetry, were written and published during the last years of his life; but the date cannot be exactly determined. He had long bid adieu to the excitements of politics; nor do these, his latest works, exhibit traces of his fondness for discussing questions of moral science, or for the profounder speculations of natural philosophy. He limits himself to the neutral ground of literature; and writes only as a writer whose judgment would be undisputed, because his works in their several departments had actually formed the taste of his contemporaries.

In November, B. C. 8, A. U. C. 746, Horace was seized with a sudden attack of illness, and died in the fifty-seventh year of his age. His old friend Mæcenas had expired but a few months before. They were buried near one another on the slope of the Esquiline.

His death was so sudden that he was unable to write a will; he had but just time before he expired to nominate, according to a common custom, the Emperor his heir.

Horace was never married; he was too general an admirer, and his tastes and habits were too much those of a bachelor, to appreciate the happiness of a wedded life. In this respect his feelings resembled those of the voluptuous and selfish society of his times. He was of small and slight figure,[644] but afterwards he grew corpulent.[645] The vigour which he enjoyed in

---

[642] Ep. I. i. 1–10.
[643] See Vit. Hor. Suet.
[644] Ep. I. xx.
[645] Suet. Ep. Aug. in Vita.

early youth[646] was diminished by ill health; he became prematurely gray,[647] and a passage in one of his Odes seems to imply that he was a valetudinarian at forty.[648]

---

[646] Ep. I. vii. 26; 3.
[647] Ep. I. xx.
[648] Od. II. iv. 22.

Chapter 20

Character of Horace—Descriptions of His Villa at Tivoli, and His Sabine Farm—Site of the Bandusian Fountain—The Neighbouring Scenery—Subjects of His Satires and Epistles—Beauty of His Odes—Imitations of Greek Poets—Spurious Odes—Chronological Arrangement

The life of Horace is especially instructive, as a mirror in which is reflected a faithful image of the manners of his day. He is the representative of Roman refined society, as Virgil is of the national mind. He who understands Horace and his works can picture to himself the society in which he lived and moved. One cannot sympathize with Petrarch, when he says "Se ex nullo poeta Latino evasisse meliorem quam ex Horatio," or exclaim with the devoted Mæcenas,

> Ni te visceribus meis Horati
> Plus jam diligo, tu tuum sodalem
> Ninnio videas strigosiorem—

but still it is scarcely possible not to feel an affection for him. Notwithstanding his selfish Epicureanism, he possessed those elements of character which constitute the popularity of men of the world. He was a gentleman in taste and sentiments. He would not have denied himself any gratification for the sake of others; but he would not willingly have caused any one a moment's uneasiness, nor was he ever ungrateful to those who were kind to him. He was a pleasant friend and a good-humoured associate, adroit in using the language of compliment, but not a flatterer, because he was candid and sincere. He changed his politics, but he had good cause for so doing. The circumstances of the times furnished ample justification. His morals were lax, but not worse than those of his contemporaries: all that can be said is, that he was not in advance of his age. His principles will not bear comparison with a high moral standard; but he had good qualities to compensate for his moral deficiencies. He looked at virtue and vice from a worldly, not a moral point of view. With him the former was prudence, the latter folly. Vice, therefore, provoked a sneer of derision, and not indignation at the sin or compassion for the sinner; and for the same reason he was incapable of entertaining a holy enthusiasm for virtue.

Good-tempered as a man, he nevertheless showed that he belonged to the *genus irritabile vatum*. He was jealous of his poetical reputation; not, indeed, towards his contemporaries, but towards the poets of former ages. He either could not or would not see any merit in old Roman poetry. His prejudice cannot be ascribed only to his enthusiasm for Greek literature, for he did not even appreciate the excellences which the old school of poetry had in common with the Greeks. Party spirit had somewhat to do with it, for a feud on the subject divided the literary society of the day,[649] and hence Horace took his side warmly and uncompromisingly.

But the principal cause was jealousy—unless he ignored Lucilius and Catullus, he could not claim to have been the first follower of Archilochus of whom Rome could boast; or, as the representative of Roman lyric poetry, to have first tuned his lyre to Æolian song.

The scenes in which Horace passed his life are so interesting to every reader of his works, that a few words respecting his villa at Tivoli and his Sabine farm will not be out of place here. Tibur[650] is situated on one of the spurs of the Appennines, about fifteen or sixteen miles from Rome, on the left bank of the Anio (Teverone.) The river winds gently by the town, separating it from the villa of Horace, and then, falling in a sheet of water over an escarped rock, disappears beneath a rocky cavern. Its roaring echoes are heard far and wide, and justifies 280the epithet (*resonans*,) which Horace gives to the dwelling of Albunea, the Tiburtine Sibyl. The villa commanded fine views, and a garden sloped down from it to the river's bank. From its grounds was visible the palace of Mæcenas: on the opposite shore the wooded Sabine hills sheltered it from the north; and the domain of the poet's friend, Quintilius Varus, formed its western boundary.

About fifteen miles north-east of Tibur, nestling amongst the roots of Mount Lucretilis, lay the Sabine farm. Fragments of white marble, and mosaic, which have been found there, show that, notwithstanding the simple frugality which Horace delights to describe, it was built and embellished with elegance and taste. From the mountain side, which rises behind the house, trickles a clear stream, the source of which is now called Fonte Bello, and which afterwards becomes the river Digentia (Licenza,) and waters the beautiful valley of the sloping Ustica (*Usticæ Cubantis*.) This rill, the parent of Horace's favourite river, the embellisher of that "*riant* angle of the earth," is interesting as being probably the fountain of Bandusia, "more transparent than glass,"[651] with whose fresh and sparkling waters the poet tempered his wine.

M. de Chaupy[652] assumes that the Bandusian fountain, mentioned by Horace, was situated near the birthplace of Horace, on the Lucano-Apulian border. His opinion rests on the words of a grant made by Pope Pascal II to the abbot of the Bantine monastery; and Mr. Hobhouse[653] considers this document as decisive in ascertaining its position. It is decisive as to the existence of a Bandusian fountain near Venusia; but it must be remembered that Horace never saw it after the days of his childhood, when his paternal estate passed away from him for ever, whilst he speaks of his Bandusian fountain as near him, when he

---

[649] This feud continued until the time of Persius. (See Sat I. 141, and Gifford's note.)
[650] See De Chaupy, Eustace, Milman, &c.
[651] Od. III. 13.
[652] Découverte de la Maison d'Horace, tom. iii. p. 364.
[653] Illust. to Childe Harold, p. 42.

writes, and promises to sacrifice a kid to the guardian genius of the spring. What, then, is more probable than the suggestion of Mr. Dunlop,[654] that the same pleasing recollections of his early years, which inspired him to relate his touching adventure, 281led him to "name the clearest and loveliest stream of his Sabine retreat after that fountain which lay in Apulia, and on the brink of which he had no doubt often sported in infancy?"[655] He has in one of his odes alluded to this affectionate desire to perpetuate reminiscences of home—a desire which is illustrated by the topographical nomenclature which has been adopted by colonists of every age and country.

Mr. Dennis, however, in a letter written at Licenza,[656] in sight of the pleasant shades of M. Lucretilis, although he makes no doubt of the Bandusian fountain being in the neighbourhood, does not identify it with the "Fonte Bello." He asserts that, although he has traced every streamlet in the neighbourhood, the only one which answers to the classical description is one now called "Fonte Blandusia." It rises in a narrow glen which divides the Mount Lucretilis from Ustica, which probably derives its modern name *Valle Rustica* from a corruption of the classical appellation. As you ascend the glen it contracts into a ravine with bare cliffs on either side; the streamlet with difficulty winds its way between mossy rocks (*musco circumlita saxa,*) overshadowed with dense woods which effectually exclude the heat of the blazing Dog-star. The water issues from a rock, and trickles into two successive natural basins. "The water is indeed *splendidior vitro*; nothing, not even the Thracian Hebrus, can exceed it in purity, coolness, and sweetness: 'its loquacious waters still bubble;' the very ilices still overhang the hollow rocks whence it springs."

A reference to Horace's description[657] will prove to the modern traveller through this classic region with what fidelity and accuracy the poet has described the natural features of the scenery. The mountain chain is continuous and unbroken (*continui montes,*) save by the well wooded and therefore shady valley of the Digentia, which intersects it in such a direction that—

> Veniens dextrum latus aspiciat sol,
> Lævum decedens curru fugiente vaporet.

282Another valley meets it, and on an exposed height, at the point of junction, stands Bardela, in Horace's time Mandela, and well described by him as *rugosus frigore pagus*.[658] Corn grows on the sunny field (apricum pratum) which slopes from the farm to the river: the ruins of other dwellings mark the spot occupied by five domestic hearths, and sending five honest representatives to the municipal council of the neighbourhood:—

> ——habitatum quinque focis, et
> Quinque bonos solitum Variam dimittere patres.[659]

---

[654] Hist. of Rom. Lit. iii. 213.
[655] Hist. of Rom. Lit. iii. 213.
[656] Hist. of Rom. Lit. iii. 213.
[657] Ep. I. xvi. 5. See also Eustace's Class. Tour.
[658] Ep. I. xviii. 105.
[659] Ep. I. xiv. 2.

A comparison of the truthful and descriptive verses of Horace identify the spot which he loved. Nature is the same now as it was then; but human skill and perseverance have adorned with the purple clusters of the vine that "little corner of the world" which Horace said would bear pepper and frankincense more quickly than grapes.[660]

The Satires of Horace occupy the position of the comedy of manners and the fashionable novel. They are much more appropriately described by the title *Sermones* (Discourses) which is also given to them. They are, in fact, desultory didactic essays, in which the topics are discussed just as they present themselves. In them is sketched boldly but good-humouredly a picture of Roman social life with its vices and follies. His object was (to use his own words)—

> Ut omnis
> Votivâ pateat veluti descripta tabellâ
> Vita.
> *Sat.* II. i. 32.

Vices, however, are treated as follies; and the man of wit and pleasure seldom uses a weapon more keen than the shafts of ridicule:—

> Omne vafer vitium ridenti Flaccus amico
> Tangit et admissus circum præcordia ludit.
> *Persius*, S. i. 116.
> Arch Horace, while he strove to mend,
> Probed all the foibles of his smiling friend;
> 283Played lightly round and round the peccant part,
> And won unfelt an entrance to his heart;
> Well skilled the follies of the crowd to trace,
> And sneer with gay good humour in his face.
> Gifford.[661]

There is nothing of the political bitterness of Lucilius,[662] the love of purity and honour which adorns Persius, or the burning indignation which Juvenal pours forth at the loathsome corruption of morals. Horace had been a politician and a warm champion of liberty; but the struggle was now over, both with himself and his country. Ease and tranquillity were insured to both by the new régime; and his contented temper disposed him to acquiesce in a state of things which gave Rome time to rest from the horrors of civil war, and did not interfere with the independence of the individual. Hence the circumstances of the times, as well as his own temper, rendered his satires social and not political. Lucilius wrote when the strife between nobles and people was still raging, and the latter had not as yet succumbed. He, therefore, breathed the spirit of the old Athenian comic poets whom he followed and emulated; and the war of public opinion furnished him with topics similar to those which were discussed in the republican commonwealth of Athens.

---

[660] Ep. I. xiv. 23.
[661] See also Pope's imitation of this passage, Essay on Satire, part iii.
[662] See Persius, Sat. I. 114.

Circumstances also influenced, in some degree, the tone of Horace's strictures on the habits of social life. Immoral as society was, its most salient features were luxury, frivolity, extravagance, and effeminacy. Vice had not reached that appalling height which it attained in the time of the emperor who succeeded Augustus. Deficient in moral purity, an Epicurean and a debauchee, nothing would strike him as deserving censure, except such success as would actually defeat the object which he proposed to himself—namely, the utmost enjoyment of life. The dictates of prudence, therefore, would be his highest standard and his strongest check. He saw that public morals were already deteriorated, and threatened to become worse; but 284though they were bad enough to provoke derision, they did not shock or revolt one who was, and who professed to be, a man of the world. Had Horace lived in the time of Persius or Lucilius, even his satire would probably have been pointed and severe.

Often his satires are only accidentally didactic; he contents himself with graphic delineations of character and manners, and leaves them to produce their own moral effect upon the reader. In one[663] he holds up the superstition of the Romans to ridicule by a minute narrative of the absurd ceremonies performed by Canidia and another sorceress in their incantations. In another,[664] amusingly describes the annoyance to which he was exposed by the importunities of a gossiping trifler. In the journey to Brundisium he seems to have had no view beyond entertainment; although two incidents give him an opportunity of exposing the pomposity of a municipal official and the superstitious follies of a country town.[665] In others, his subjects are the scenery and neighbouring society of his Sabine valley;[666] the way in which he is wont to spend his day when at Rome; his own autobiography;[667] a laughable trial in Asia;[668] an essay on cookery;[669] and a candid exposure of his own faults and inconsistencies. Not that he is forgetful of his moral duties as a satirist. He exposes to merited contempt the prevailing iniquities of the day. The meanness of legacy-hunting; the absurdity of pretension and foppery; the folly of an inordinate passion for amassing wealth;[670] the dangers of adultery;[671] the unfairness of uncharitably misinterpreting the conduct of others.[672]

Such are the varied subjects contained in the *Sermones* or Satires of Horace. The Epistles are still more desultory and unrestrained. Epistolary writing is especially a Roman accomplishment. The Romans thought their correspondents deserved that as much pains should be bestowed on that which was addressed to them as on that which was intended for the public eye; and, in addition to the careful polish of which Cicero 285set the example, Horace brought to the task the embellishment of poetry. In the Epistles, he lays aside the character of a moral teacher or censor. He treats his correspondent as an equal. He opens his heart unreservedly: he gives advice, but in a kind and gentle spirit, not with sneering severity. The satire is delivered *ex cathedrâ*;—the epistle with the freedom with which he would converse with an intimate friend.

---

[663] Sat. I. 8.
[664] Ibid. 9.
[665] Ibid. v.
[666] Sat. II. vi.
[667] Sat. I. vi.
[668] Ibid. vii.
[669] Sat. II. iv.
[670] Sat. I. 1.
[671] Ibid. 2.
[672] Ibid. 3.

The subjects of the first books are moral, those of the second critical. The *Ars Poetica* is but a poetical epistle addressed to the Pisos, who had been bitten by the prevailing mania for tragic poetry. The usual title claims a far greater extent of subject than the poet intended. It is not a treatise on poetry, but simply an outline of the history of the Greek drama, and the principles of criticism applicable to it. It harmonizes well with the literary subjects treated of in the second book of the Epistles, and might well be included in it. It is, indeed, longer and more elaborate: a synopsis of so extensive a subject required more careful treatment; but it is impossible to form a correct estimate of the taste and judgment which it displays, unless it is considered as nothing more than an epistle.

The versification of these compositions is more smooth than that of the Satires, but only in proportion to the superior neatness of the style generally. In neither does the metrical harmony rise to the height of poetry, properly speaking. Doubtless this was the poet's deliberate intention. It cannot be supposed that he who could so successfully introduce all the beautiful Greek lyric metres, and in some cases improve the delicacy of their structure, was incapable of reproducing the rhythm of the Greek hexameter. He felt that in subjects belonging to the prosaic realities of life, and hitherto treated with the conversational facility of the iambic measure, some appearance of negligence and even roughness could alone render the stately hexameter appropriate, and therefore tolerable. But, admirable as the Satires are for their artistic and dramatic power, and the Epistles for their correct taste, lively wit, and critical elegance, it is in his inimitable Odes that the genius of Horace as a poet is especially displayed. They have never been equalled in 286beauty of sentiment, gracefulness of language, and melody of versification. They comprehend every variety of subject suitable to the lyric muse. They rise without effort to the most elevated topics—the grandest subjects of history, the most gorgeous legends of mythology, the noblest aspirations of patriotism: they descend to the simplest joys and sorrows of every-day life. At one time they burn with indignation, at another they pour forth accents of the tenderest emotions. They present in turn every phase of the author's character: some remind us that he was a philosopher and a satirist; and although many are sensuous and self-indulgent, they are full of gentleness, kindness, and spirituality. Not only do they evince a complete mastery over the Greek metres, but also show that Horace was thoroughly imbued with the spirit of Greek poetry, and had profoundly studied Greek literature, especially the writings of Pindar and the lyric poets. Numerous as the instances are in which he has imitated them, and introduced by a happy adaptation their ideas, epithets, and phrases, his imitations are not mere plagiarisms or purple patches—they are made so completely his own, and are invested with so much novelty and originality, that, when compared with the original, we receive additional gratification from discovering the resemblance. The sentiments which are paraphrased seem improved: the expressions which are translated seem so appropriate, and harmonize so exactly with the context, that a poet, whose memory was stored with them, would have been guilty of bad taste if he had substituted any others. Greek feelings, sentiments, and imagery, are so naturally amalgamated with Roman manners, that they seem to have undergone a transmigration, and to animate a Roman form. The following are some of the most striking parallelisms:[673]—

 Sunt quos curriculo, &c.
 Carm. 1, 3, seq.

---

[673] See Prof. Anthon's Horace, Donaldson's Pindar, &c.

Ἀελλοποδων μεν τινας ευφραινουσιν ἱππων τιμαι και στεφανοι·
τους δ' εν πολυχρυσοις θαλαμοις βιοτα·
τερπεται δε και τις επ' οιδμ' αλιον
ναι θοα σως διαστειχων.
Pind. Fragm.

Jam te premet nox, fabulæque Manes,
Et domus exilis Plutonia: quo simul mearis,
Nec regna vini sortiere talis, &c.
Carm. 1, 4, 16, *seq.*
Κατθανοισα δε κεισ', ουδεποτε μναμοσυνα σεθεν
εσσετ' ουδεποτ' εις υστερον. ου γαρ πεδεχεις βροδων
των εκ Πιεριας. αλλ' αφανης κην Αιδα δομοις
φοιτασεις πεδ' αμαυρων νεκυων εκπεποταμενα.
Sapph. Fragm.

Vides, ut alta stet nive candidum
Soracte, nec jam sustineant onus
Silvæ laborantes, geluque
Flumina constiterint acuto?
Dissolve frigus, ligna super foco
Large reponens; atque benignius
Deprome quadrimum Sabina,
O Thaliarche, merum diota.
Carm. 1, 9. seq.
Υει μεν ο Ζευς, εκ δ' ορανω μεγας
χειμων · πεπαγασιν δ' υδατων ροαι.

Καββαλλε τον χειμων', επι μεν τιθεις
πυρ, εν δε κιρναις οινον αφειδεως
μελιχρον· αυταρ αμπι κορσα
μαλθακον αμπιτιθει γναφαλλον.
Alcæi Fragm.

Quem virum aut heroa lyra vel acri
Tibia sumis celebrare, Clio?
Quem Deum? cujus recinet jocosa
Nomen imago, &c.
Carm. 1, 12, seq.
Ἀναξιφορμιγγες υμνοι
τινα θεον, τιν' ηρωα, τινα δ' ανδρα κελαδησομεν.
Pind. Ol. 2, 1.
O navis, referent in mare te novi
Fluctus? O quid agis? fortiter occupa
Portum. Nonne vides, ut
Nudum remigio latus,
Et malus celeri saucius Africo
Antennæque gemant? ac sine funibus

Vix durare carinæ
Possint imperiosius
Æquor?
Carm. 1, 14, seq.
Το μεν γαρ ενθεν κυμα κυλινδεται,
Το δ' ενθεν· αμμες δ' αν το μεσσον
ναι φορημεθα συν μελαινα,
Χειμωνι μοχθευντες μεγανω καλων·
παρ μεν γαρ αντλος ιοτοπεδαν εχει,
λαιφος δε παν ζαδηλον ηδη,
και λακιδες μεγαλαι κατ αυτο
Χαλασι δ' αγκυραι ...
Alcæi Fragm.

Nullam, Vare, sacra vite prius severis arborem.
Carm. 1, 18, seq.
Μηδεν αλλο φυτευσης προτερον δενδρεον αμπελω.
Alcæi Fragm.

Vitas hinnuleo me similis, Chloe,
Quærenti pavidam montibus aviis
Matrem, non sine vano
Aurarum et silvæ metu.
Carm. 1, 23, seq.
Ατε νεβρον νεοθηλεα γαλαθηνον, ος εν υλη
Κεροεσσης απολειφθεις υπο μητρος επτοηθη.
Anacr. Fragm.

O Venus, regina Gnidi Paphique,
Sperne dilectam Cypron, &c.
Carm. 1, 30, seq.
Κυπρον ιμερταν λιποισα και Παφον περιρρυταν.
Alcman. Fragm.

Quid dedicatum poscit Apollinem
Vates? quid orat, de patera novum
Fundens liquorem? &c.
Carm. 1, 31, seq.
Τι δ' ερδων, φιλος σοι τε,
καρτεροβροντα Κρονιδα,
φιλος δε Μοισαις, Ευθυμια τε
μελων ειην, τουτ' αιτημι σε.
Pind. Fragm.

Nunc est bibendum, nunc pede libero
Pulsanda tellus, &c.
Carm. 1, 37, seq.
Νυν χρη μεθυσκειν, και τινα προς βιαν

πινειν, επειδη κατθανε Μυρσιλος.
Alcæi Fragm.

Nullus argento color est avaris
Abdito terris, inimice lamnæ
Crispe Sallusti, nisi temperato
Splendeat usu.
Carm. 2, 2, seq.
Ουκ εραμαι πολυν εν μεγαρω πλουτον κατακρυψαις εχειν
αλλ' εοντων, ευ τε παθειν και ακουσαι, φιλοις εξαρκεων.
Pind. Nem. 1, 45.

Sævius ventis agitatur ingens
Pinus.
Carm. 2, 10, 9, *seq.*
Ου θρυον ου μαλαχην ανεμος ποτε, τας δε μεγιστας,
η δρυας η πλατανους οιδε χαμαι καταγειν.
Lucian. in Anthol.

Eheu fugaces, Postume, Postume,
Labuntur anni: nec Pietas moram
Rugis et instanti Senectæ
Adferet, indomitæque Morti.
Carm. 2, 14, seq.
Ἀλλ' ολιγοχρονιον γιγνεται, ωσπερ οναρ,
ηβη τιμηεσσα· το δ' αργαλεον και αμορφον
γηρας υπερ κεφαλης αυτιχ' υπερκρεμαται.
Mimnerm. Fragm.

Quid brevi fortes jaculamur ævo
Multa?
Carm. 2, 16, 17.
—— Ω κενοι βροτων,
οι τοξον εντεινοντες ως καιρου περα.
Eurip. Suppl. 754.

—— Nihil est ab omni
Parte beatum.
Carm. 2, 16, 27.
Ουκ εστιν ουδεν δια τελους ευδαιμονουν.
Eurip. Suppl. 281.

Dulce et decorum est pro patria mori.
Carm. 3, 2, 13.
Τεθναμεναι γαρ καλον επι προμαχοισι πεσοντα
ανδρ' αγαθον περι η πατριδι μαρναμενον.
Tyrtæi Fragm.

Mors et fugacem persequitur virum.
Carm. 3, 2, 14.
Ο δ' αυ Θανατος εκιχε και τον φυγομαχον.
Simonides.

Ætas parentum, pejor avis, tulit
Nos nequiores, mox daturos
Progeniem vitiosiorem.
Carm. 3, 6, 46, *seq.*
Οιην χρυσειοι πατερες γενεην ελιποντο
Χειροτερην! υμεις δε κακωτερα τεξειεσθε.
Arati Phænom. 123.

Pulchris excubat in genis.
Carm. iv. 13, 8.
Ος εν μαλακαις παρειαις
νεανιδος εννυχευεις.
Soph. Antig. 779.

Dis miscent superis.	Ἀθανάτοις ἔμιχθεν.
	Pindar. Isthm. 2, 42.
Nube candentes humeros amictus.	Νεφέλῃ εἰλυμένος ὤμους.
	Hom. Il. ε´, 186.
Erycina ridens.	Φιλομειδὴς Ἀφροδίτη.
	Hom. Il. ν´, 424.
Officinas Cyclopum.	Ἡφαίστοιο καμίνοις.
	Callim. Fragm. 129.
Nitidum caput.	Λιπαρὰν ἔθειραν.
	Simonid. (Anth. Gr.)
Duplicis Ulixei.	Διπλοῦς ἀνήρ.
	Eurip. Rhes. 392.
Superis parem.	Δαίμονι ἶσος.
	Hom. Il. ε´, 438.
Aptum equis Argos.	Ἄργεος ἱπποβότοιο.
	Hom. Il. β´, 287.
Ditesque Mycenas.	Μυκήνας τὰς πολυχρύσους.
	Sophocl. Elect. 9.

Nil desperandum.	Ἄελπτον οὐδέν. *Eurip. Fragm.*
Deorum nuntium.	Ἄγγελον ἀθανάτων. *Hom. Hymn in Merc.* 3.
Marinæ filium Thetidis.	Παῖς ἁλίας Θέτιδος. *Eurip. Androm.* 108.
Carpe diem.	Καιρὸν λάβε. *Æsch. Sept. adv. Th.* 65.
Difficile bile.	Χόλου ἀργαλέοιο. *Hom. Il.* κ', 107.
Melior patre.	Πατέρων ἀμείνονες εὐχόμεθ' εἶναι. *Hom. Il.* δ', 405.
Mordaces solicitudines.	Γυιοβόρους μελεδῶνας. *Hesiod. Ἔργ,* 66.
Dulce ridentem.	Γελάσας ἱμέροεν. *Sappho.*
Dulce loquentem.	Ἀδὺ φωνοίσας. *Sappho.*
Funera densentur.	Θνῆσκον ἐπασσύτεροι. *Hom. Il.* α', 383.
Fulgentes oculos.	Ομματα μαρμαίροντα. *Hom. Il.* γ', 397.
Bellum lacrymosum.	Πόλεμον δακρυόεντα. *Hom. Il.* ε', 737.
Vacuum aera.	Ἐρήμας δι' αἰθέρος. *Pind. Ol.* α', 10.
Loquaces lymphæ. Fulmine caduco.	Λαλὸν ὕδωρ. Καταιβάτης κεραυνός. *Æsch. Pr. V.* 359.

Vis consili expers.	Ῥώμη ἀμαθής. *Eurip. Fragm.*
Flagitio additis damnum.	Πρὸς αἰσχύνῃ κακόν. *Eurip. Rhes.* 102.
Aquæ augur cornix.	Ὑετόμαντις κορώνη. *Euphorion.*
Lentus amor.	Βραδινὰ Ἀφροδίτα. *Sappho.*
Aquosa Ida.	Πολυπίδακος Ἴδης. *Hom. Il.* ξ′, 157.
Obliquum meditantis ictum.	Δοχμώ τ' ἀΐσσοντε. *Hom. Il.* μ′, 148.
Gelu acuto.	Χιόνος ὀξείας. *Pind. Pyth.* α′, 39.
Dulci fistula.	Γλυκὺς αὐλός. *Pind. Ol.* ι′, 114.
Testudinis aureæ.	Χρυσέα φόρμιγξ. *Pind. Pyth.* α′, 1.
Magnæ linguæ.	Μεγάλης γλώσσης. *Sophocl. Antig.* 12.
Morti atræ.	Μέλανος θανάτοιο. *Hom. Il.* β′, 834.
Aureo plectro.	Χρυσέῳ πλάκτρῳ. *Pind. Nem.* ε′, 44.
Supremum iter.	Ὑστάτην ὁδόν. *Eurip. Alcest.* 686.
Nescios fari infantes.	Νήπια τέκνα. *Hom. Il.* β′, 311.
Noctilucam.	Νυκτιλαμπής.

	Simonides.
Purpureo ore.	Πορφυρέου ἀπὸ στόματος.
	Simonides.
Mens trepidat metu.	Δειματὶ πάλλει.
	Soph. Æd. Tyr.

The two following[674] odes have been attributed to Horace, but there is no doubt that they are spurious. It was pretended that they were discovered in the Palatine Library at Rome by Pallavicini: no MS., however, of Horace, containing them, has ever yet been found:—

AD IULIUM FLORUM.
Discolor grandem gravat uva ramum
Instat Autumnus; glacialis anno
Mox Hiems volvente aderit, capillis
Horrida canis.
Jam licet Nymphas trepide fugaces
Insequi lento pede detinendas;
Et labris captæ, simulantis iram,
Oscula figi.
Jam licet vino madidos vetusto
De die lætum recitare carmen;
Flore, si te des, hilarem licebit
Sumere noctem.
Jam vide curas aquilone sparsas!
Mens viri fortis sibi constat, utrum
Serius leti citiusve tristis
Advolat aura.

AD LIBRUM SUUM.
Dulci libello nemo sodalium
Forsan meorum carior extitit;
De te merenti quid fidelis
Officium domino rependes?
Te Roma cautum territat ardua;
Depone vanos invidiæ metus;
Urbisque, fidens dignitati,
Per plateas animosus audi.
En quo furentes Eumenidum choros
Disjecit almo fulmine Jupiter!
Huic ara stabit, fama cantu
Perpetuo celebranda crescet.

---

[674] Meyer, Anthol. Rom. 114, 115.

According to Bentley, the works of Horace were written in the following chronological order:—

Satires	Book	I.	in his	26th, 27th, and 28th years.
Satires	"	II.	"	31st, 32d, and 33d years.
Epodes			"	34th and 35th years.
Odes	"	I.	"	36th, 37th, and 38th years.
Odes	"	II.	"	40th and 41st years.
Odes	"	III.	"	42d and 43d years.
Epistles	"	I.	"	46th and 47th years.
Odes	"	IV.	} "	49th, 50th and 51st years.
Secular Hymn				
Epistle to the Pisos			}	uncertain.
Epistles	"	II.		

Chapter 21

Biography of Mæcenas—His Intimacy and Influence with Augustus—His Character—Valgius Rufus—Varius—Cornelius Gallus—Biography of Tibullus—His Style—Criticism of Muretus—Propertius—Imitated the Alexandrian Poets—Æmilius Macer

C. Cilnius Mæcenas

In a literary history it is impossible to omit some account of one, who, although his attempts at poetry were very contemptible, exercised, by his good taste and munificence, a great influence upon literature, and to whom the literary men of Rome were much indebted for the use which he made of his confidential friendship with Augustus.

C. Cilnius Mæcenas was a member of an equestrian family, which, though it derived its descent from the old Etruscan kings,[675] does not appear to have produced any distinguished individuals. His birth-year is unknown, but his birth-day was the ides (13th) of April.[676] We have no information respecting the origin of his intimacy with Augustus. Probably his cultivated taste, his extensive acquaintance with Greek and Roman literature, his imperturbable temper, and love of pleasure, first recommended him as an agreeable companion to Octavius.

His good sense, activity, and energy in business, and decisive character, qualities in which his irresolute and desultory patron was signally deficient, enabled him rapidly to improve the acquaintance into intimacy. It is said by Dion Cassius[677] that Augustus obtained from Mæcenas a complete plan for the internal administration of his newly-acquired empire, and that in it were displayed sound judgment and political wisdom. It is probable that there is some exaggeration in this statement; but that, without being a great man, he was in these respects a greater man than Augustus, who, therefore, when he required his support, could lean upon him with safety. And yet his weaknesses were such as to prevent any feeling of

---
[675] Hom. Od. I. i.
[676] Od. IV. ii.
[677] Lib. lii. 14, &c.

jealousy, or appearance of superiority, from endangering his friendship with the emperor. His love of pleasure, and of the quiet and careless enjoyments of a private station, proved, as it turned out, a blessing to his country. His heart was so full of the delights of refined and intellectual society—of palaces and gardens, and wit and poetry, and collections of art and virtû—that there was no room in it for ambition. His careless and sauntering indolence was openly displayed in his lounging gait, and his toga trailing on the ground. No one could possibly suspect such a loiterer of sufficient energy or application to be a politician and an intriguer. Such being his character, tastes, and habits, he felt no temptation to abuse his influence with Augustus. He did not covet honours and office, because he knew they must bring trouble and distraction, perhaps peril with them. He exercised his power, which was undoubtedly great, to promote that luxurious, yet refined elegance, in which he himself delighted, and to secure the welfare of his literary friends. He had wealth enough to gratify his utmost wishes. Augustus, therefore, had nothing more to confer on him which he valued, except personal esteem and regard.

The confidence which the Emperor reposed in him is shown by his employing him in some affairs of great delicacy: first, in arranging a marriage with Scribonia; and, subsequently, on two occasions, in negotiating with Antony.[678] In B. C. 36, he accompanied Octavius into Sicily; but was sent back in order to undertake the administration of Rome and Italy;[679] and during the campaign at Actium,[680] Mæcenas was again vicegerent, in which capacity he crushed the conspiracy of the younger Lepidus. So unlimited was his power, that he was even intrusted with the signet of Octavius, and with authority to open, and even to alter, if necessary, all letters which he wrote to the senate during his campaign; and when the victorious general, on his return to Rome, consulted with him and Agrippa as to the expediency of re-establishing the republic, Mæcenas, in opposition to the recommendation of Agrippa, dissuaded him from taking that step. The moral influence also of Mæcenas over Augustus is very striking. So long as it continued, we see nothing of that heartless cruelty, that disregard of the happiness of others, which deformed the early life of the Emperor: if he was heartless, he at least did that as a matter of taste which a better man would have done on principle; and if he was still selfish, he sought fame and glory by the wise counsels of peace rather than by the brilliant triumphs of war: he conciliated friends instead of crushing enemies.

The intimacy between Mæcenas and the Emperor continued for at least ten years after the battle of Actium: then an estrangement commenced; and in B. C. 16, he was deprived of his official position, and Taurus was intrusted with the administration of Rome and Italy. Scandalous stories have been told about his wife Terentia and the Emperor, in order to account for the interruption of their intimacy; but no special causes are necessary to account for an event so common. The words of Tacitus[681] are a sufficient solution of the problem:— "Idque et Mæcenati acciderat; fato potentiæ, raro sempiternæ, an satias capit, aut illos, cum omnia tribuerunt, aut hos, cum jam nihil reliquum est, quod cupiant." He retained the outward appearance of the imperial friendship, although he had lost the reality. He went to court on the birth-day, but ceased to be of the Emperor's council. His life was passed in the voluptuous retirement of his palace on the Esquiline, which he had built for himself. This hill was not

---

[678] B. C. 40.
[679] Tac. Ann. vi. ii.
[680] B. C. 31.
[681] Annal. iii. 30.

generally considered wholesome: probably the fact that it had been a burial-ground[682] created a prejudice against it; but the loftiness of the site chosen, as well as of the building itself (*molem vicinam nubibus,*) and the breeze which played freely through the lovely garden with which it was surrounded, rendered it salubrious. All the most brilliant society of Rome was found at his table; and many of the best of them received still more substantial marks of his favour.[683] Virgil, Horace, Propertius, and Varius, were amongst his friends and constant associates.

Mæcenas was a low-spirited invalid;[684] latterly he could not sleep, and endeavoured in vain to procure repose by listening to soft music.[685] In his last distressing illness he generally resided at his Tiburtine villa, where the murmuring falls of the Anio invited that sleep which was denied him elsewhere. He died B. C. 8, and was buried on the Esquiline. Though married, he left no children, and bequeathed his property to the Emperor, whom he besought in his will not to forget his beloved Horace. His taste as a critic was evidently far superior to his talents as a writer. Few fragments of his writings remain; and all ancient critics are unanimous in the condemnation of his style. Augustus[686] laughed at his affected jargon of mingled Etruscan and Latin. Quintilian[687] quotes instances of his absurd inversions and transpositions; and Seneca[688] shows, by an example, its unintelligible obscurity.[689] He was a sensualist and a voluptuary,[690] and an unfaithful husband; and yet he was devotedly fond of his wife, the beautiful but ill-tempered Terentia, who had a great influence over him. He would divorce her one day only to restore her to conjugal rights on the next; and Seneca said that, though he had only one wife, he was married a thousand times. He abhorred cruelty and severity, and would not let it pass unrebuked even in the Emperor; and although he made a boast of effeminacy, he was ready to devote himself heartily to business in cases of emergency. In fact, he was a fair specimen of the man of pleasure and society: liberal, kind-hearted, clever, refined, but luxurious, self-indulgent, indolent, and volatile, with good instincts and impulses, but without principle.

C. VALGIUS RUFUS

Amongst the poets of the Augustan age, whose writings were much admired by their contemporaries, but have not stood the searching test of time, was Valgius Rufus. Of his life no records remain; but he probably belonged to that class of authors of whom Pliny says,

---

[682] Hor. Sat. i. 8, 7.
[683] Mart. viii. 56.
[684] Plin. vii. 51; Hor. C. ii. 17.
[685] Sen. de Prov. iii. 9.
[686] Suet. 26.
[687] Lib. ix. 4, 28.
[688] The three passages quoted by Quintilian show a wanton awkwardness in arrangement almost inconceivable:—
Sole et Aurora rubent plurima
Inter sacra movit aqua fraxinos:
Ne exequias quidem unus inter miserrimos
Viderem meas.
The last of these he considers especially offensive, because he seems to be trifling with a melancholy subject.
[689] Sen. Ep. 114.
[690] Tac. Ann. i. 54.

"Quibus nos in vehiculo, in balneo, inter cœnam, oblectamus otium temporis."[691] They were light and pleasing, calculated to amuse an idle half-hour, or to relieve the tedium of a journey. They answered the purpose of the railroad literature of our own days. These writers had a correct taste, and a critical discernment of poetical beauty, rather than a genius for poetical composition. Probably their personal characters had something to do with their reputation: they were members of a literary *coterie*; they lived, thought, and felt together; they defended each other against malicious criticism; and the bonds of friendship by which they were united tempted the greater poets to regard their effusions with kind but undue partiality. Valgius Rufus was a great favourite of Horace,[692] but only a few short, isolated passages are extant of his poems.[693] Quintilian[694] attributes to him a translation of the rhetorical precepts of Apollodorus. Seneca[695] mentions him by name: Pliny[696] praises his erudition. The testimony borne to his transcendent merits as an epic poet, in the Panegyric of Messala, need scarcely be trusted, because it is almost certain that this piece is spurious.[697]

VARIUS

Of L. Varius Rufus also, who was one of the constant guests at Mæcenas' table, scarcely any thing is known. Horace[698] tells us that he was unequalled in epic song, when Virgil had as yet only turned his attention to rustic poetry. The high praise bestowed upon his Thyestes by Quintilian has already been mentioned. To him, together with Virgil, we have seen that Horace owed his introduction to Augustus, and all three were of the party which accompanied Mæcenas to Brundisium. The titles of two of his poems are extant,—I. *De Morte*; II. *Panegyric on Augustus*. Of the former, four fragments are preserved by Macrobius, all of which Virgil has deemed worthy of imitation. Of the latter, two lines, containing a delicate compliment to Augustus, are extant, which Horace has introduced entire into one of his Epistles.[699] The passage by no means satisfies modern taste, which has been formed by the hexametrical rhythm of Virgil; but Seneca praises his style as free from the usual faults of Latin declamatory poetry—mere bombast on the one hand, and excessive minuteness on the other. Niebuhr conjectures that his Thyestes was too declamatory; and that, like the later Roman tragedies of Seneca and others, it was not an imitation of the Attic drama, but of the degenerate tragedies belonging to the Alexandrian period.

---

[691] Epp. iv. 14; vii. 4.
[692] Sat. I. x.; Od. ii. 9.
[693] Weichert, Poet. Lat. Rell.
[694] Lib. iii. i. 18.
[695] Ep. xli. i.
[696] H. N. xxv. 2.
[697] Tib. Op. iv. i. 180.
[698] Sat. I. x. 44.
[699] Ep. i. 16. See Schol.

C. Cornelius Gallus (Born B. C. 66 or 69.)

Gallus was more distinguished as a general than as a poet. Except a single line from one of his elegies, not a vestige of his poetry remains; for the short pieces attributed to him[700] are undoubtedly not genuine. He owes his fame, probably, to the kind verdict of his contemporaries, whose friendship and amiable affection for each other appear never to have been endangered by the slightest spark of jealousy.

Born at Frejus, of low parentage, he was a fellow-student in philosophy with Virgil[701] and Arius—a friendship thus commenced which continued through life. The patronage of Asinius Pollio[702] brought him into notice as a poet at the early age of twenty. He was one of the first to attach himself to the cause of Octavius; and, being appointed commissioner for allotting the lands to the military colonies, he had the opportunity of befriending Virgil and the plundered Mantuans. At Actium he commanded a brigade, burnt Antony's ships in the harbour of Parætonium, was one of the capturers of Cleopatra, and was rewarded by Octavius with being made first prefect of Egypt. How so valuable a servant lost the Emperor's favour is uncertain. Ovid hints that his crime was one of words, not of deeds:—

> Linguam nimio non tenuisse mero.

He was recalled, his property confiscated, and himself exiled. He had not strength of mind to bear his fall, and he committed suicide in the forty-first or forty-third year of his age.[703]

No judgment respecting his merits can be formed from the contradictory criticism of the ancients. Ovid awards to him the palm among the elegiac poets,[704] and Virgil is said to have sung his praises in his fourth Georgic, but afterwards to have omitted the passage and substituted for it the story of Aristæus; whilst Quintilian[705] applies the epithet *durior* to his versification. Perhaps the latter attached too much importance to the grace and sweetness of diction, but neglected the beauty of the sentiments; whilst the former might have been too partial in his sympathy with a fellow exile. He was the author of four books of elegies, in which, under the feigned name of Lycoris, he sings his love for his mistress Cytheris. He also translated the Greek poems of Euphorion.

Albius Tibullus

Tibullus was born of an equestrian family, probably in B. C. 54. He was a contemporary of Virgil and Horace;[706] and like them, during the troubles of the civil wars, suffered the confiscation of his paternal estate, which was situated at Pedum, near Tibur. After the

---

[700] Meyer's Anthol.
[701] Ecl. vi. 64.
[702] Cic. ad Fam. x. 32.
[703] Dion Cass. liii. 23.
[704] Trist. iv. 10, 5.
[705] Lib. x. i. 93; i. 5, 8.
[706] See Hor. Od. i. 33; Ep. i. 4.

conclusion of the struggle a portion was restored to him—small, indeed, but sufficient to satisfy his moderate wants and contented disposition.

Disinclined, as well by his love of quiet, to the labours and perils of a military life, as he was by the tenderness and softness of his character to the horrors of war, circumstances, nevertheless, forced him involuntarily to undertake a campaign. Messala was his patron, to whom he was evidently under great obligations.[707] When, therefore, he was sent by Octavia to quell an insurrection in Aquitania, Tibullus accompanied him. This campaign and the successes of Messala furnished the poet with subjects for his muse.[708] Tibullus also fully intended to continue his services to Messala in the east, during the following year; but illness compelled him to stop at Corcyra, whence he returned to Rome.[709]

The mistresses whose beauty, inconstancy, and cruelty Tibullus celebrates in his elegies were, unlike those of Horace, real persons. Delia's real name is said to have been Plautia or Plania;[710] who Nemesis was is not known. These are the only two mentioned by himself or alluded to by Ovid;[711] but Horace addresses an ode to him on his passion for a mistress whom he names Glycera. Probably he is speaking of one of Tibullus' mistresses under a feigned name, in accordance with his habitual practice, for the names introduced by him in his poems, generally speaking, bear no appearance of reality. They are, with very few exceptions, suggested by his study of Greek lyric poets. Chloris, Lycoris, Neobule, Lydia, Thaliarchus, Xanthias, Pholoe, are all Greek characters, translated to Roman scenes, and made to play an artificial part in Roman life. Cinara[712] was, perhaps, a real person, as Bassus, the Novii Mævius, and Numida, undoubtedly are. Sometimes, when his object is satire, he speaks of the subject of his irony under a name somewhat resembling the real one; as, for example, when he ridicules Mæcenas under the name of Malthinus,[713] Salvidianus Rufus under that of Nasidianus,[714] and lampoons Gratidia the sorceress as Canidia. But in the poetry of Tibullus, as in that of Catullus and Propertius, the same names are found in each of a series of poems. Apuleius[715] asserts that the real name of the Lesbia of Catullus was Clodia; that of the Cynthia of Propertius, Hostia, and that she was a native of Tivoli.

The style and tone of thought of Tibullus are, like his character, deficient in vigour and manliness, but sweet, smooth, polished, tender, and never disfigured by bad taste. He does not deserve the censure of Niebuhr, who stigmatizes him as a "disagreeable poet, because of his doleful and weeping melancholy and sentimentality, resulting from misunderstanding the ancient elegies of Mimnermus."[716]

After his return from Corcyra, Tibullus passed the remainder of his short life in the peaceful retirement of his paternal estate. He died young, shortly after Virgil, if we may trust to an epigram, ascribed to Domitius Marsus, contained in the Latin Anthologia:[717]—

> Te quoque Virgilio comitem non æqua, Tibulle,

---

[707] El. i.
[708] El. i. and iv.
[709] El. i.
[710] Nieb. Lect. cvii.
[711] Amorum iii. 9.
[712] Od. iv. 1, 3, 4, 13; Ep. i. 7, 27, 14, 33.
[713] Sat. I. ii.
[714] Sat. II. viii.
[715] Apol. p. 279.
[716] Lect. on R. H. 107.
[717] Meyer's Anthol. Vet. Lat. Ep. No. 122.

> Mors juvenem campos misit in Elysios,
> Ne foret, aut elegis molles qui fleret amores,
> Aut caneret forti regia bella pede.

The poems commonly ascribed to Tibullus consist of four books, but only two are genuine, and of these, the second was published posthumously. Two lines in the third book, which fix the date of the poet's birth in the consulship of Hirtius and Pansa,[718] have generally been considered as spurious, because such a date is inconsistent with the rest of the chronology; but Voss rejected the whole of that book; and there is no question but that the spirit and character of the elegies, as well as the harmony of the metre, are very inferior to those of the preceding poems. The same inferiority marks the fourth also, with the exception of the smaller poems, which bear the names of Sulpicia and Corinthus. These, as Niebuhr correctly observes, display greater energy and boldness than Tibullus possessed, and are the productions of some poet much superior to him.

That elegant scholar and judicious critic, Muretus,[719] has well attributed to him, as his chief characteristics, simplicity, and natural and unaffected genius:—"Illum (*i. e.* Tibullum) judices *simplicius* scripsisse quæ cogitaret; hunc (*i. e.* Propertium) diligentius cogitasse quæ scriberet. In illo *plus naturæ*, in hoc plus curæ atque industriæ perspicias."

SEXTUS AURELIUS PROPERTIUS

Very little is known respecting the life and personal history of Propertius beyond the few facts which may be gleaned from his poems. He was a native of the border country of Umbria, and was probably born not earlier than A. U. C. 703,[720] or later than 700.[721] This period will sufficiently agree with the statement of Ovid respecting their relative ages.[722] His family had not produced any distinguished member, but possessed a competent estate. Like Virgil and Tibullus, he was a sufferer by the consequences of war; for the establishment of a military colony reduced him from comfort to straitened circumstances.[723]

Like most young Romans of genius and education, he was intended for the bar;[724] but poetry had greater charms for him than severe studies, and he became nothing more than a literary man. He inhabited a house in the now fashionable quarter of the Esquiline, and was on intimate terms with Gallus, Ovid, Bassus, and Virgil. Cynthia, his amour with whom inspired so large a portion of his elegies, was not only a beautiful but an accomplished woman. She was his first love; and it appears to have been some time before she yielded to his solicitations,[725] nor was she even then always faithful to him.[726] She could write verses

---

[718] B. C. 45; A. U. C. 709.
[719] Schol. in Propert.
[720] Clinton.
[721] Niebuhr.
[722] Trist. iv. 10, 45.
[723] Trist. iv. 10, 45.
[724] Ibid. IV. i.
[725] Ibid. II. xiv. 15–18.
[726] Ibid. I. 1, 2; x. ii. 16.

and play upon the lyre,[727] and was a graceful dancer.[728] She owed to him, says Martial, her immortality; whilst he owed to his love for her the inspiration which immortalized himself:—

> Cynthia, facundi carmen juvenile Properti,
> Accepit famam nec minus illa dedit.

The date of the poet's death is unknown, but the probability is that he died young.

Although Propertius was a contemporary and friend of the Augustan poets, he may be considered as belonging to a somewhat different school of poetry. His taste, like theirs, was educated by a study of Greek literature; but the Greek poets whose works he took for his model belonged to a later age. Horace, Virgil and Tibullus imitated and tried to rival the Greek classical poets of the noblest ages: they transferred into their native tongue the ideas of Homer, Pindar, and the old lyric poets. Their taste was formed after the purest and most perfect models. Propertius, on the other hand, was content with a lower flight. He attempted nothing more than to imitate the graceful but feeble strains of the Alexandrian poets, and to become a second Callimachus or Philetas.[729] Roman perseverance in the pursuit of learning, and the spirit of investigation in the wide field of Greek literature, had raised up this new standard of taste, which was by no means an improvement upon that which had been hitherto established.

The imitations of Propertius are too studied and apparent to permit him to lay claim to great natural genius. Nature alone could give the touching tenderness of Tibullus or the facility of Ovid—in both of which, notwithstanding his grace and elegance, he is deficient. The absence of original fancy is concealed by minute attention to the outward form of the poetry which he admired. His pentameters are often inharmonious, because they adopt so continually the Greek rules of construction; awkward Greek idioms, and a studious display of his learning, which was undoubtedly great, destroy that greatest charm of style, perspicuity.

According to Quintilian,[730] the critics of his day somewhat overrated his merits, for they could scarcely decide the question of superiority between him and Tibullus. This, however, is to be expected in an age of affected rhetoric and grammatical pedantry, when nothing was considered beautiful in poetry except that which was in accordance with the arbitrary rules of cold criticism. They appreciated his correctness, and did not miss the warm heart of his rival. His poetry is not so polluted with indelicacy as that of Ovid, but still it is often sensual and licentious.

It is worthy of remark that the fourth elegy of the third book, entitled "*Arethusa to Lycotas*," deprives Ovid of the credit of being the inventor of the elegiac epistle.

ÆMILIUS MACER

The poem of Æmilius Macer is only known through two verses in the Tristia of Ovid,[731] which state that it treated of birds, serpents, and medicinal herbs:

---

[727] Ibid. I. ii. 27.
[728] Ibid. II. iii. 17.
[729] Prop. IV. i. 63.
[730] Inst. Orat. x. 1.
[731] Trist. IV. x. 33.

Sæpe suas volucres legit mihi grandior ævo
Quæque necet serpens; quæ juvet herba Macer.

He was born at Verona, and died in Asia, A. D. 16; and the passage already quoted proves that he was older than Ovid.

His poem was a paraphrase or imitation of the Theriaca of Nicander—a physician-poet, who flourished in Ætolia during the reign of Ptolemy Epiphanes. Quintilian couples his name with that of Lucretius; and awards him the praise of elegance, but adds that his style is deficient in dignity.

Chapter 22

BIRTH AND EDUCATION OF OVID—HIS RHETORICAL POWERS—ANECDOTE RELATED BY SENECA—HIS POETICAL GENIUS—SELF-INDULGENT LIFE—POPULARITY—BANISHMENT—PLACE OF HIS EXILE—EPISTLES AND OTHER WORKS—GRATIUS FALISCUS—PEDO ALBINOVANUS—AULUS SABINUS—MARCUS MANILIUS

OVIDIUS NASO (BORN B. C. 43.)

Ovid, as he himself states,[732] was born at Sulmo (Sulmone,) a town of the Peligni (Abruzzi,) ninety miles distant from Rome. The year of his birth was that in which the consuls Hirtius and Pansa fell in the field of Mutina (Modena.) His family was equestrian, and had been so for some generations. His father lived to the age of ninety; and, as his mother was then alive, it is probable that she also attained an advanced age. He had a brother exactly twelve months older than himself. Their common birthday was the first of the Quinquatria, or festival of Minerva (March 20th.)

Whilst still of tender age the two boys were sent to Rome for education, and placed under the care of eminent instructors. The elder studied eloquence, and was brought up to the bar: but he died at the early age of twenty. Ovid himself also, for a time, studied rhetoric under Arellius Fuscus and Porcius Latro, and the results of his study are visible in his poems;[733] for example, in the speeches of Ajax and Ulysses.[734]

Seneca has left an interesting account of his rhetorical powers.[735] "I remember," he says, "hearing Naso declaim, in the presence of Arellius Fuscus, of whom he was a pupil; for he was an admirer of Latro, although his style was different from his own. The style of Ovid could at that time be termed nothing else but poetry in prose: still he was so diligent as to transfer many of his sentiments into his verses. Latro had said—

---

[732] Trist. iv. 10.
[733] See Cic. Brut. 446.
[734] Metam. xiii.
[735] Controv. ii. 10.

> Mittamus arma in hostes, et petamus.

Naso wrote—

> Arma viri fortis medios mittantur in hostes
> Inde jubete peti.

He borrowed another idea from one of Latro's Suasorian orations:—

> Non vides uti immota fax torpeat et exagitata reddat ignes?
> Ovid's paraphrase of this illustration is—
> Vidi ego jactatas mota face crescere flammas,
> Et rursus, nullo concutiente, mori.
> When he was a student he was thought to declaim well."

On the affecting theme of a husband and wife, who had mutually sworn not to survive each other, Seneca asserts that he surpassed his master in wit and talent, and was only inferior in the arrangement of his topics. He then quotes a long passage, in which Ovid analyzes the principles of love, with a skill and ingenuity well worthy of one who, as a poet, made love the subject of his song, and with a purity of sentiment which, it were to be wished, had dignified the sweetness of his verses. Ovid preferred *suasoriæ* and ethical themes to *controversiæ*;[736] for all argument was irksome to him. In oratory he was very careful in the use of his words: in his poetry he was aware of his faults, but loved them too well to correct them. He then adds the following amusing and characteristic anecdote:—Being once asked by his friends to erase three lines, he consented on condition that he himself should be at liberty to make an exception in favour of three. He accordingly wrote down three which he wished to preserve; his friends those which they wished to erase. The papers were examined, and both were found to contain the same verses. Pedo Albinovanus used to say that one of these was—

> Semibovemque virum semivirumque bovem.

The other—

> Egelidum Borean, egelidumque Notum.

Hence it is apparent that judgment was not wanting, but the inclination to correct. He defended himself by saying that an occasional mole is an improver of beauty. The former of these miserable conceits is not now to be found in his poems. The latter occurs in the *Amores*, but it is usually read—

> Et gelidum Borean, egelidumque Notum;

or—

---

[736] See distinction between these in ch. viii.

Et gelidum Borean, præcipitemque Notum.[737]

The father of Ovid, who took a utilitarian view of life, is said to have discouraged the cultivation of his poetical talents, and to have stigmatized the service of the Muses as barren and unprofitable. Even Homer himself, he was wont to say, left no property behind him. Ovid endeavoured to comply with his father's wishes; he deserted Helicon, and tried to write plain prose. It was all in vain; his words spontaneously flowed into numbers, and whatever he tried to say was poetry. His natural genius and facility displayed itself when he was quite a boy; for he had not yet put on the *toga virilis*. When he assumed this badge of mature age, it was bordered with a broad purple stripe, which marked the patrician order; but being unambitious and indolent, he never took his seat in the senate, although he filled several magisterial and judicial offices.

His rank, fortune, and talents enabled him to cultivate the society of men of congenial tastes. He became acquainted with the best poets of his day. Macer and Propertius would recite their compositions to him. Ponticus and Bassus were guests at his table. He had heard the lyrics of Horace read by himself. Virgil he had only seen; and the untimely death of Tibullus prevented him from making the acquaintance of that poet. He was extremely young when his juvenile poems became very popular, and he wrote far more than he published; for he burnt whatever displeased him; and, when sentenced to exile, in disgust he committed the Metamorphoses to the flames.

He himself confesses his natural susceptibility and amorous temperament; but claims the credit of never having given occasion to any scandal. He was three times married. His first wife was unsuitable, and proved unworthy of him, and accordingly he divorced her. His second he divorced also, although no imputation rested on her virtue. From his third, whom, notwithstanding his fickleness and infidelity, he sincerely loved, he was only separated by exile. She was one of the Fabian family, and bore him one daughter.

Epicurean in his tastes, and a skeptic, if not a disbeliever in a future state, he lived a life of continual self-indulgence and intrigue. He was a universal admirer and as universal a favourite among the female sex in the voluptuous capital; for the tone of female morals was in that age low and depraved, and the women encouraged the licentiousness of the men. Although his favourite mistress, whom he celebrated under the fictitious name of Corinna, is unknown, and all the conjectures concerning her identity are groundless, there is no doubt that she was a lady of rank and fortune.

Ovid was popular as a poet, successful in society, and possessed all the enjoyments which wealth can bestow. He had a villa and estate in his native Sulmo, a house on the Capitoline hill, and suburban gardens, celebrated for their beauty. At some period of his life he travelled with Macer into Asia and Sicily; and, in his exile, recalls to mind with sorrowful pleasure the magnificent cities of the former, and the sublime scenery and classic haunts of the latter.[738] This sunny life at length came to an end. The last ray of happiness, which he speaks of as beaming on him, was the intelligence that his beloved daughter Perilla, who was twice married, made him a grandfather a second time. When his hair became tinged with white, and he had reached his fiftieth year, he incurred, by some fault or indiscretion, the anger of Augustus, and was banished to Tomi (Tomoswar or Baba.)

---

[737] Amor. II. xi. 10.
[738] Ep. ex Ponto, ii. 10.

The cause of his banishment is involved in obscurity. It was not unknown at Rome; but in his exile he refrains from alluding to it, except in dark allusions, out of fear of giving additional offence to the emperor.[739] He speaks of it as an indiscretion (*error*,) not a crime (*scelus*, *facinus*;[740]) as something which he had accidentally witnessed,[741] perhaps had indiscreetly told—a circumstance which deeply and personally affected Augustus, and inflicted a wound which he was unwilling to tear open afresh. He hints also that he fell a victim to the treachery of friends and domestics,[742] who enriched themselves by his ruin.

There have been many conjectures[743] on this difficult point. Some have imagined an intrigue with the elder Julia, the profligate daughter of Augustus; but this is scarcely consistent with the manner in which Ovid himself speaks of his fault; and besides this, Julia was banished to Pandataria eight years before. The banishment of the younger Julia to Trimerus, about the same time with that of Ovid, would make it far more probable that his fall was connected with that of this equally profligate princess. Tiraboschi supposed that he had surprised one of the royal family in some disgraceful act; and some have even imagined that he might have witnessed such conduct on the part of the Emperor himself. Dryden believed that he accidentally saw Livia in the bath; and the author of the article in the Biographie Universelle, as well as Schoell,[744] surmise that he was in some way implicated in the fortunes of Agrippa Posthumus, and thus incurred the hatred of Livia and Tiberius.

Whatever the cause may have been, the punishment was a cruel one, except for a crime of the deepest dye, and would never have been inflicted by the gentle Augustus so long as he was under the salutary influence of Mæcenas and his party. But in his old age he submitted to the baneful rule of the dark Tiberius and the implacable Livia. Any pretext, therefore, sufficed to remove one, who, from some cause or other, had excited their enmity. The alleged reason was the immorality of his writings; but they are not more immoral than those of Horace; and, besides, the worst of them had been published ten years before. Nor was the morality of the Emperor himself of such a character as to lead him to punish so severely a licentious poet in a licentious age. The exclusion of his works from the Palatine[745] library was a merited and more appropriate visitation. Nevertheless, this was made the pretext for a banishment, the misery of which was solaced by the empty mockery of the reservation of his civil rights.

Tomi was on the very frontiers of the Roman empire, inhabited by the Getæ, who were rude and uncivilized. The country itself, a barren and treeless waste, cold, damp, and marshy, producing naturally scarcely anything but wormwood, and yielding scanty crops to the unskilled toil of ignorant cultivators, was rendered still more desolate by frequent incursions of the neighbouring savage tribes, who used poisoned arrows, and offered up as sacrifices their prisoners of war.[746] Ovid, who, with all his faults, was affectionate and tender-hearted, was torn from all the voluptuous blandishments of the capital, from the sympathies of congenial spirits, who could appreciate his talents, and from the arms of his weeping wife,[747] amidst the voice of wailing and of prayer, which filled every corner of his desolate dwelling.

---

[739] Trist. IV. x. 100.
[740] Ibid. IV. x. 90, and III. i. 52.
[741] Ibid. I. ii. 107.
[742] Ibid. iv. 10, 101; Ep. ex Pont. p. ii. vii.
[743] See Class. Museum, iv. 13.
[744] Hist. Abreg. de la Lit. Rom.
[745] Trist. III. i. 65.
[746] Ex Ponto, IV. ix. 82.
[747] Trist. I. iii.

The blow fell suddenly upon him like a thunder-clap,[748] and so stupefied him that he could make no preparations for his voyage. The season of his departure was the depth of winter, and he was exposed to some peril by a tempest in the Ionian Gulf. The climate of his new abode was as inclement as that of Scythia. Not only the Danube, but even the sea near its mouth, was for some extent covered with ice: even the wine froze into blocks, and was broken in pieces before it could be used. He lived in exile only ten years; constant anxiety preyed upon his bodily health; he suffered languor, but no pain; he loathed all food; the little that he ate would not digest; sleep failed him; his body became pale and emaciated, and so he died. The Tomitæ showed their respect by erecting a tomb to his memory.

In the midst of such a contrast between the present and the past, no wonder that his complainings appear almost pitiful and unmanly, and his urgent petitions to Augustus couched in too fulsome a strain of adulation. No wonder that he painted in the most glowing colours the story of his woes and privations. Yet he was destitute neither of patience nor fortitude: he relied on the independence and immortality of genius; and although the enervating effect of a luxurious and easy life and a delicate constitution, rendered him a prey to grief, and he gradually pined away, still he had strength of mind to relieve his sorrows by devotion to the Muse, and he suffered with tranquillity and resignation. Poetry was his resource during his stormy voyage. Poetry gained him the affection and esteem of his new fellow-citizens, notwithstanding their barbarism,[749] and procured him the honour of a tomb.

All the extant poems of Ovid, with the exception of the Metamorphoses, are elegiac. It was the metre then most in vogue. All the minor poets, his contemporaries, wrote in it. One of his earliest works is the "*Amores*," a collection of elegies, most of which are addressed to his favourite mistress Corinna. Some of them, however, were composed subsequently to his Epistles and Art of Love.[750] An epigram, which is prefixed, states that there were originally five books, but that the author subsequently reduced them to the present number, three. Licentiousness disfigures these annals of his amours; but they teem with the freshness and buoyancy of youth, and sparkle with grace and ingenuity.

The twenty-one *Epistolæ Heroidum*, i. e. Epistles to and from Women of the Heroic Age, are a series of love-letters: their characteristic feature is passion; the ardour of which is sometimes interfered with by too laboured conceits and excessive refinement. They are, in fact, the most polished efforts of one whose natural indolence often disinclined him from expending that time and pains on the work of amending and correcting which distinguished Virgil. Their great merit consists in the remarkable neatness with which the sentiments are expressed, and the sweetness of the versification; their great defect is want of variety. The subject necessarily limited the topics. The range of them is confined to laments for the absence of the beloved object, the pangs of jealousy, apprehensions of inconstancy, expressions of warm affection, and descriptions of the joys and sorrows of love.

With the exception of the Metamorphoses, the Epistles have been greater favourites than any of the works of Ovid. Some were translated by Drayton and Lord Hervey. The beautiful translation, by Pope, of the epistle from Sappho to Phaon, is familiar to all; and his touching picture of the struggle between passion and principle, in the letter of Eloisa to Abelard, owes a portion of its inspiration to the Epistles of Ovid.

---

[748] Ibid. V. ii.
[749] Ex Pont. IV. ix. 97.
[750] See II. xviii. 19.

Love in the days of Ovid had nothing in it chivalrous or pure—it was carnal, sensual. The age in which he lived was morally polluted, and he was neither better nor worse than his contemporaries. Great and noble as was the character of the Roman matron, the charms of an accomplished female education were almost as rare as at Athens. She had sterling worth; but she had not often the power to fascinate those numbers who considered woman the minister to the pleasures of man. She was wise, self-sacrificing, patriotic, courageous—a devoted mother, an affectionate wife—and a man of heroic mould valued as she deserved such a partner of his fortunes. But those who sought merely the allurements of passion looked only for meretricious pleasure and sensual enjoyment. Hence grossness is the characteristic of Ovid's Art of Love. The instructions contained in the first two books, which are addressed to men, are fit only for the seducer. The blandishments in the third are suited only to the abandoned of the other sex.

The Art of Love was followed by the Remedies of Love, in one book: "Let him," he says, "who taught you to love, teach you also the cure; one hand shall inflict the wound and minister the balm. The earth produces noxious and healthful herbs; the rose is often nearest neighbour to the nettle."[751]

His Metamorphoses were just finished, and not yet corrected,[752] when his fall took place. When in his despair he burnt it, fortunately for the world some copies transpired. Afterwards he prayed that they might be preserved to remind the readers of the unhappy author. The Metamorphoses consist of fifteen books, and contain a series of mythological narratives from the earliest times to the translation of the soul of Julius Cæsar from earth to heaven, and his metamorphosis into a star. This poem is Ovid's noblest effort: it approaches as near to the epic form as is possible with so many naturally unconnected episodes. In many parts, especially his descriptions, we do not merely admire his natural facility in making verses, but picturesque truthfulness and force—the richest fancy combined with grandeur and dignity. Amongst the most beautiful portions may be enumerated the story of Phaeton, including the splendid description of the Palace of the Sun;[753] the golden age;[754] the story of Pyramus and Thisbe;[755] the cottage home and the rustic habits of Baucis and Philemon,[756] Narcissus at the fountain;[757] the powerfully sketched picture of the Cave of Sleep,[758] Dædalus and Icarus,[759] Cephalus and Procris,[760] and the soliloquy of Medea.[761] In this poem, especially, may be traced that study and learning by which the Roman poets made all the treasures of Greek literature their own. In fact, a more extensive knowledge of Greek mythology may be derived from it than from the Greeks themselves, because the books which were the sources of his information are unfortunately no longer extant.

---

[751] Rem. Am. 43.
[752] Trist. i. vi. 30.
[753] Metam. ii. i.
[754] Ibid. i. 89.
[755] Ibid. iv. 55.
[756] Ibid. viii. 628.
[757] Ibid. iii. 407.
[758] Ibid. xi. 592.
[759] Ibid. viii. 152.
[760] Ibid. vii. 661.
[761] Ibid. vii. 11.

The "*Fasti*" is an antiquarian poem on the Roman calendar. Originally it was intended to have formed twelve books, one for each month of the year, but only the first six were completed:[762]——

> Sex ego Fastorum scripsi totidemque libellos
> Cumque suo finem mense volumen habet.

It is a beautiful specimen of simple narrative in verse, and displays more than any of his works, his power of telling a story, without the slightest effort, in poetry as well as prose. As a profound study of Greek mythology and poetry had furnished the materials for his Metamorphoses and other poems, so in this he drew principally from the legends which had been preserved by the old poets and annalists of his own country.

The five books of the Tristia and the four books of the Epistles from Pontus were the outpourings of his sorrowful heart during the gloomy evening of his days. Without the brilliancy, the wit, and the genius, which beamed forth from his joyous spirit in the time of his prosperity, without the graceful and inspired querulousness of the ancient models, they are, nevertheless, conceived in the spirit of the Greek elegy—they utter the voice of complaining, and deserve the Horatian epithet of *miserabiles*.[763] It was natural to him to give utterance to his hope and despair in song: he had sported like a gay insect in the sunshine of prosperity. He was too fragile, delicate, and effeminate to bear the storm of adversity—his butterfly spirit was broken; but, with all his faults, that broken heart was capable of the tenderest emotions, and his letter to his daughter Perilla[764] is full of purity and sweetness. The carelessness of one who would not take the trouble to correct, and who was conscious of his dangerous facility, is compensated for by the commiseration which his natural complaints excite, and for the powerful descriptions which occasionally enliven the monotony inseparable from grief.

His minor poems consist of an elegiac poem, "*Nux*," in which a nut-tree bewails its hard fate and the ill treatment which it receives; a long and bitter satire, entitled Ibis, on some enemy, or, perhaps, some faithless friend; a poem on Cosmetics (Medicamina facici;[765]) another on Fishing (Halieutica;[766]) and an address of condolence to Livia Augusta. None, however, of these last three are universally admitted to be genuine. Other works which were the offspring of his prolific genius have perished. During his exile he acquired sufficient knowledge of the Getan language to write some poems in it; and these were as popular with the barbarians as his Latin works were at Rome. Lastly, he was the author of the Medea; a tragedy of which Quintilian says, that it shows of what grand works he was capable, if he had been willing to curb instead of giving reins to the luxuriance of his genius.[767] Two lines only are extant; but we can judge of the conception which he formed of the character of Medea from the epistle in the "*Heroides*," and her eminently tragic soliloquy in the Metamorphoses.

---

[762] Trist. ii. v. 549.
[763] Hor. Od. I. 33.
[764] Hor. Od. I. 33.
[765] Ar. Am. iii. 205.
[766] Plin. H. N. xxxii. 54.
[767] In. Or. x. 98.

Ovid was a voluptuary, but not a heartless one. The age in which he lived was as immoral as himself, and far more gross; he was, therefore, neither a corrupter nor a seducer. His poetry was popular, not only because of its beauty, but because it was in exact accordance with the spirit of the times. His wit was sometimes contrary to good taste, but it was not forced and unnatural. He was betrayed into the appearance, not the reality of affectation, by a luxuriance which required pruning, for which he had neither patience nor inclination. He stored himself with the learning of the ancients, and caught their inspiration; but their severe taste was to him a trammel to which he was too self-willed and self-complacent to submit. The prevalent taste for elegiac poetry pointed out the style which was suited to his caliber; for one cannot help feeling that his genius was incapable of mastering the gigantic proportions of a true epic, and, notwithstanding the favourable criticism of Quintilian, of soaring to the sublimity of tragedy.

GRATIUS FALISCUS

The Cynegetica of Gratius, commonly, though without any reason, surnamed Faliscus, may claim a place beside the Halieutica of Ovid, on account of its subject, but not on the score of genius, poetry, or language. Nothing is known respecting this author, except that Ovid speaks of him as a contemporary.[768] The poem is heroic, and consists of 536 lines: its style is hard and prosaic; it describes the weapons and arts of the chase, horses and hounds; but the science is rather Greek than Italian, and the information contained in it is principally derived from Xenophon.[769]

PEDO ALBINOVANUS

Another poet of the Ovidian age was his trusty friend, C. Pedo Albinovanus. He was of equestrian rank,[770] and, unlike most of his contemporaries, an epic poet.[771] Ovid in his Epistles from Pontus,[772] which are addressed to him, applies to him the epithet, "*Sidereus*," either because he had written an astronomical poem, or because his sublime language soared into the starry heavens. Martial speaks of him as having written epigrams which extend to the length of two pages.[773] A fragment of an epic poem, describing the voyage of Germanicus related by Tacitus, is preserved by Seneca.[774] Three elegies are usually ascribed to him; but their style is that of more modern times, and the authority for their genuineness very suspicious.

---

[768] Ep. ex Pont. iv. 16, 33.
[769] See Bernhardy, Gr. 440.
[770] Bern. 409.
[771] Quint. x. 1.
[772] Ibid. iv. 16, 6.
[773] Ep. ii. 77.
[774] Ann. ii. 23; Suasor. I.

A. Sabinus

Another contemporary of Ovid was A. Sabinus; and all that is known respecting him is derived from two passages in the works of the former poet.[775] In one of these,[776] he tells us that Sabinus wrote answers to six of the epistles of the Heroides. None of these, however, are extant. The three which profess to be written by him, entitled Ulysses to Penelope, Demophoon to Phyllis, and Paris to Œnone, are the work of Angelus Sabinus,[777] a philologer and poet of the fifteenth century.

Two other works are attributed to him by Ovid in a passage in which he speaks of his death.[778] One of these, entitled Trœzen, was probably an epic poem, of which Theseus was the hero;[779] the other, *Dierum Opus*, was a continuation of Ovid's Fasti. Other elegiac poets flourished at this period, such as Proculus and Montanus; but their poetical talents were of too commonplace a character to deserve special mention. They confer no obligation on literature, and contribute nothing towards the illustration of the literary character of their times.

M. Manilius

The astronomical and astrological poem of Manilius furnishes a series of those historical problems which have never yet been satisfactorily solved. The author has been in turn confounded with every one whom Roman records mention as bearing that name, and in all cases with equally little reason. No one knows when he flourished, where he lived, and of what place he was a native. Bentley determined that he was an Asiatic; Huet that he was a Carthaginian. Internal evidence renders it most probable that he lived in the reign of Tiberius;[780] and yet neither he nor his poem are ever mentioned by any ancient author. His work was never discovered until the beginning of the fifteenth century; probably it had never been published, but only a few copies had been made, some of which have been marvellously preserved.

The philosophical principles of the poem are those of a Stoical Pantheism. As one principle of life pervades the whole universe, there is a close connexion between things celestial and things terrestrial. In consequence of this relation, the astrologer can determine the course of the latter by observation of the heavenly bodies. Together with all the assumptions and absurdities of astrology are mingled extensive knowledge of the state of astronomical science in his day: gleams of truth shoot like meteors athwart the darkness. The subject which he has chosen is as unpromising for poetical effect and embellishment as that of Lucretius; but he does not handle it so successfully: he has neither the boldness of thought, the dignity of language, nor the imaginative grandeur which marked the old poet philosopher. The poem is incomplete; and probably owes some of its roughness and obscurity to its never having been corrected for publication.

---

[775] Ex Pont. iv. 16, 13.
[776] Amor. ii. 18, 27.
[777] Bernhardy, 451.
[778] Ep. ex Pont. iv. 16, 13.
[779] Smith's Dict. Glaser im Rhein. Mus. N. F. i. 437.
[780] Lib. i. 798–897; iv. 763.

Chapter 23

Prose Writers—Influence of Cicero upon the Language—His Converse with His Friends—His Early Life—Pleads His First Cause—Is Quæstor, Ædile, Prætor and Consul—His Exile, Return, and Provincial Administration—His Vacillating Conduct—He Delivers His Philippics—Is Proscribed and Assassinated—His Character

As oratory gave to Latin prose-writing its elegance and dignity, Cicero is not only the representative of the flourishing period of the language, but also the instrumental cause of its arriving at perfection. Circumstances may have been favourable to his influence. The national mind may have been in that stage of progress which only required a master-genius to develop it; but still it was he who gave a fixed character to the language, who showed his countrymen what eloquence especially was in its combination of the precepts of art and the principles of natural beauty; what the vigour of Latin was, and of what elegance and polish it was capable.

His age was not an age of poetry; but he paved the way for poetry by investing the language with those graces which are indispensable to its perfection. He freed it from all coarseness and harshness, and accustomed the educated classes to use language, even in their every-day conversation, which never called up gross ideas, but was fit for pure and noble sentiments. Before his time, Latin was plain-spoken, and therefore vigorous; but the penalty which was paid for this was, that it was sometimes gross and even indecent. The conversational language of the upper classes became in the days of Cicero in the highest degree refined: it admitted scarcely an offensive expression. The truth of this assertion is evident from those of his writings which are of the familiar character—from his graphic Dialogues, in which he describes the circumstances as naturally as if they really occurred; from his letters to Atticus, in which he lays open the secret thoughts of his heart to his most intimate friend, his second self. Cicero purified the language morally as well as æsthetically. It was the licentious wantonness of the poets which degraded the pleasures of the imagination by pandering to the passions at first in language delicately veiled, and then by open and disgusting sensuality.

It is difficult for us, perhaps, to whom religion comes under the aspect of revelation separate from philosophy, and who consider the philosophical investigation of moral subjects as different from the religious view of morals, to form an adequate conception of the pure and almost holy nature of the conversations of Cicero and his distinguished contemporaries. To them philosophy was the contemplation of the nature and attributes of the Supreme Being. The metaphysical analysis of the internal nature of man was the study of immortality and the evidence for another life. Cato, for example, read the Phædo of Plato in his last moments in the same serious spirit in which the Christian would read the words of inspiration. The study of ethics was that of the sanctions with which God has supported duty and enlightened the conscience. They were the highest subjects with which the mind of man could be conversant. For men to meet together, as was the habitual practice of Cicero and his friends, and pass their leisure hours in such discussions, was the same as if Christians were to make the great truths of the gospel the subjects of social converse.

Again, if we examine the character of their lighter conversations, when they turned from philosophy to literature,—it was not mere gossip on the popular literature of the day—it was not even confined to works written in their native tongue—it embraced the whole field of the literature of a foreign nation. They talked of poets, orators, philosophers, and historians, who were ancients to them as they are to us. They did not then think the subject of a foreign and ancient literature dull or pedantic. They did not consider it necessary that conversation should be trifling or frivolous in order to be entertaining.

Nor was the influence which Cicero exercised on the literature of his day merely extensive, but it was permanent. The great men of whom he was the leader and guide caught his spirit. His influence survived until external political causes destroyed eloquence, and its place was supplied by a cold and formal rhetoric: it was felt almost until the language was corrupted by the admixture of barbarisms. It may be discerned in the soldier-like plainness of Cæsar, in the Herodotean narrative of Livy, and its sweetness without its diffuseness occasionally adorns the reflective pages of Tacitus.

It is difficult in a limited space to do justice to Cicero, even as a literary man; such was his versatility of genius, such his indefatigable industry, so vast the range of subjects which he touched and adorned. Of course, therefore, it is impossible to do more than rapidly glance at the leading events of his political career, or at his public character, since his history is, in fact, a history of his stirring and critical times.

M. TULLIUS CICERO (BORN B. C. 106.)

On the banks of the noiseless and gently-flowing[781] Liris (Garigliano,) near Arpinum, the birthplace of Marius,[782] lived a Roman knight named M. Tullius Cicero. A competent

---

[781] Hor. Od. I. xxxi.
[782] Cicero, notwithstanding his opposite politics, admired Marius, to whom he was distantly related, and thought it an honour to have been born near Arpinum. He quotes a saying of Pompey's (Cic. de Leg. ii. 3,) that Arpinum had produced two citizens who had preserved Italy. Valerius Maximus thinks that Arpinum, in this respect, enjoyed a singular privilege:—Conspicuæ felicitatis Arpinum unicum, sive litterarum gloriosissimum contemptorem, sive abundantissimum fontem intueri velis.

hereditary estate enabled him to devote his time to literary pursuits. He had two sons: the elder, who bore his father's name, was born January 3rd, B. C. 106. The other, Quintus, was about four years younger. As both, and Marcus especially, displayed quick talents and a lively disposition, and gave promise of inheriting their father's taste for learning, he migrated to Rome when Marcus was about fourteen years of age. The boys were educated with their cousins, the young Aculei.[783] Q. Ælius[784] taught them grammar; learned Greeks instructed them in philosophy; and the poet Archias exercised them in the technical rules of verse, although he did not succeed in giving them the inspiration of poetry. Quintus prided himself on his poetic skill; and a poem by him, on the twelve zodiacal signs, is still extant.[785] Cicero also had in his boyhood some poetical taste; and there is great elegance in the translations from the Greek which we meet with in his works. He wrote a poem in hexameters, entitled "*Pontius Glaucus*," as a sort of juvenile exercise, which was extant in the time of Plutarch; and also when he was a young man in praise of Marius.

After assuming the toga virilis at sixteen years of age, M. T. Cicero attended the forum diligently; and, by carefully exercising himself in composition, made the eloquence of the celebrated orators whom he heard his own, whilst from the lectures and advice of Q. Mucius Scævola, he acquired the principles of Roman jurisprudence.

He served but little in the armies of his country: his only campaign[786] was made under the father of Pompey the Great in the social war. During the remainder of this period, Molo, the Rhodian rhetorician, instructed him in oratory, whilst Diodotus the Stoic, Phædrus the Epicurean, and Philo, who had presided over the New Academy at Athens, were his masters in philosophy. The various schools, the principles of which he thus imbibed, led to the eclecticism which characterizes his philosophical creed. The bloody era of the Marian and Sullan war was passed by him in study: he did not interfere in politics, and the fruits of his retirement are extant in the treatise *de Inventione Rhetorica*.

At twenty-five, he pleaded his first cause,[787] and in the following year defended S. Roscius of Ameria; but his constitution was not strong enough to bear great exertion. His friends, therefore, induced him to travel, and he determined to pass some time at Athens.[788] There was also another reason for this recommendation. His courageous defence of Roscius had provoked the enmity of Chrysogonus, a creature of Sulla, and it was therefore dangerous for him to remain at Rome. He was accompanied by his brother Quintus,[789] and found Pomponius Atticus residing there, who afterwards became his most intimate friend. From Athens he travelled to Asia and Rhodes, employing his time in the cultivation of oratory, his principal study at Athens having been philosophy. From Asia he returned to Rome[790] with improved health and an invigorated constitution; where he found a powerful rival, as an orator, in Hortensius, who was then at the zenith of his popularity.

As soon as he was old enough,[791] he was elected quæstor, and the province of Sicily was allotted to him. In the exercise of this office, the unusual mildness and integrity of his

---

[783] De Orat. ii. 1.
[784] Brut. 56.
[785] Meyer, Anthol. Rom. 66.
[786] B. C. 89.
[787] Pro Quint. B. C. 81.
[788] B. C. 79.
[789] De Fin. 5, 1.
[790] B. C. 77.
[791] B. C. 76; æt. 31.

administration endeared him to the provincials; whilst the judgment with which he regulated the supplies of corn from the granary of Rome, gained him equal credit with his fellow-countrymen. It was during his stay in Sicily that his love of antiquarianism was gratified by the discovery of the tomb of Archimedes.[792] On his return home[793] he resumed his forensic practice: and in B. C. 70 was the champion of his old friends, the Sicilians, and impeached Verres, who had been prætor of Syracuse, for oppression and maladministration. In the following year[794] he was elected curule ædile by a triumphant majority. In the celebration of the games which belonged to the province of this magistrate, he exhibited great prudence by avoiding the lavish expenditure in which so many were accustomed to indulge, whilst, at the same time, no one could accuse him of meanness and illiberality.

In the year B. C. 67, he obtained the prætorship, and notwithstanding the judicial duties of his office, defended Cluentius. Hitherto his speeches had been entirely of the judicial kind. He now for the first time distinguished himself as a deliberative orator, and supported the Manilian law which conferred upon Pompey, to the discomfiture of the aristocratic party, the command in chief of the Mithridatic war.

The great object of his ambition now was the consulship, which seemed almost inaccessible to a *new man*. As all difficulties and prejudices were on the side of the aristocratic party, his only hope of surmounting them was by warmly espousing the cause of the people.

Catiline and C. Antonius, who were his principal competitors, formed a coalition, and were supported by Cæsar and Crassus, but the influence of Pompey and the popular party prevailed; and Cicero and Antony were elected. He entered upon his office January 1, B. C. 63. At this period, perhaps, the moral qualities of his character are the highest, and his genius shines forth with the brightest splendour.

The conspiracy of Catiline was the great event of his consulship; a plot which its historian does not hesitate to dignify with the title of a war. Yet this war was crushed in an unparalleled short space of time; and a splendid triumph was gained over so formidable an enemy, by one who wore the peaceful *toga*, not the habiliments of a general. The prudence and tact of the civilian did as good service as the courage and decision of the soldier. The applause and gratitude of his fellow citizens were unbounded, and all united in hailing him the father of his country. One act alone laid him open to attack, and in fact eventually caused his ruin. There is no doubt that it was unconstitutional, although under the circumstances it was defensible, perhaps scarcely to be avoided. This act was the execution of Lentulus, Cethegus, and the other ringleaders, without sentence being passed upon them by the comitia. The senate, seeing that the danger was imminent, had invested Cicero and his colleague with power to do all that the exigencies of the state might require (*videre ne quid res publica detrimenti caperet;*) and although it was Cicero who recommended the measure and argued in its favour, it was the senate who pronounced the sentence, and assumed that, as traitors, the conspirators had forfeited their rights as citizens.

The grateful people saw this clearly; and when Metellus Celer, one of the tribunes, would have prevented Cicero from giving an account of his administration at the close of the consular year, he swore that he saved his country, and his oath was confirmed by the

---

[792] T. Q. v. 3.
[793] B. C. 74.
[794] B. C. 69.

acclamations of the multitude. This was a great triumph; and in sadder times he looked back to it with a justifiable self-complacency.[795] He now, as though his mission was accomplished, refused all public dignities except that of a senator: but he did not thus escape peril; he soon exposed himself to the implacable vengeance of a powerful and unscrupulous enemy. The infamous P. Clodius Pulcher intruded himself in female attire into the rites of the Bona Dea, which were celebrated in the house of Cæsar. Suspicion fell upon Cæsar's wife, and a divorce was the consequence.[796] Clodius was brought to trial on the charge of sacrilege, and pleaded an alibi. Cicero, however, proved his presence in Rome on the very day on which the accused asserted that he was at Interamnum.

Although the guilt of Clodius was fully established, his influence over the corrupt Roman *judices* was powerful enough to procure an acquittal. Henceforward he never could forgive Cicero, and determined to work his ruin. He caused himself to be adopted in a plebeian family; and thus becoming qualified for the tribunate was elected to that magistracy, B. C. 59. No sooner was he appointed, than he proposed a bill for the outlawry of any one who had caused the execution of a citizen without trial. Cicero at once saw that this blow was aimed against himself. He had disgusted Cæsar by his political coquetry; the false and selfish Pompey refused to aid him in his trouble; and spirit-broken, he fled to Brundisium,[797] and thence to Thessalonica. He had an interview with Pompey before his flight, but it led to no results.[798] He had sworn to help him as long as he felt that there was danger, lest he should join Cæsar's party; but when he saw that his foes were successful, he deserted him.

In his absence his exile was decreed, and his town and country houses were given up to plunder. It cannot be denied that during his banishment he exhibited weakness and pusillanimity: his reverses had such an effect upon his mind that he was even supposed to be mad.[799] His great fault was vanity, of which defect he was himself conscious, and confessed it;[800] and disappointed vanity was the cause of his affliction. He could bear anything better than loss of popular applause; and on this occasion, more than any other, he gave grounds for the assertion, that "he bore none of his calamities like a man, except his death." Rome, however, could not forget her preserver; and in the following year he was recalled, and entered Rome in triumph, in the midst of the loud plaudits of the assembled people.[801] Still, however, he was obliged to secure the prosperity which he had recovered by political tergiversation. The measures of the triumvirate, which he had formerly attacked with the utmost virulence, he did not hesitate now to approve and defend.

After his return[802] he was appointed to a seat in the College of Augurs; a dignity which he had anxiously coveted before his exile, and to obtain which, he had offered almost any terms to Cæsar and Pompey.[803] The following year, much against his will, the province of Cilicia was assigned to him. Strictly did the accuser of Verres act up to the high and honourable principles which he professed. His was a model administration: a stop was put to corruption, wrongs were redressed, justice impartially administered. Those great occasions on which he

---

[795] In Pis. iii.; ad Fam. v. 2.
[796] B. C. 61.
[797] B. C. 58.
[798] Ad Att. x. 4.
[799] Ad Fam. x. iv. 4; ad Att. iii. 13.
[800] Pro Planco, 26.
[801] In Pis. xxii.; Post red. xv.
[802] B. C. 53.
[803] Att. ii. 5.

was compelled to act on his own responsibility, and to listen to the dictates of his beautiful soul, "*seine schöne seele*,"[804] his pure, honest, and incorruptible heart, are the bright points in Cicero's career. The emergency of the occasion overcame his constitutional timidity.

In the year B. C. 49, he returned to Rome, and finding himself in a position in which he could calmly observe the current of affairs, and determine unbiassed what part he should take in them, or whether it was his duty to take any part at all, his weak, wavering, vacillating temper again got the mastery over him. He would not do anything dishonest, but he was not chivalrous enough to spurn at once that which was dishonourable. Cæsar and Pompey were now at open war, and he could not make up his mind which to join.[805] He felt, probably, that the energy, ability, and firmness of Cæsar, would be crowned with success; and yet his friends, his party, and his own heart were with Pompey, and he dreaded the scorn which would be heaped upon him if he forsook his political opinions. His were not the stern, unyielding principles of a Cato; but the fear of what men would say of him made him anxious and miserable. The struggle was a long one between caution and honour, but at length honour overcame caution. He made his decision, and went to the camp of Pompey; but he could never rally his spirits, or feel sanguine as to the result. He immediately saw that Pharsalia decided the question for ever, and consequently hastened to Brundisium, where he awaited the return of the conqueror. It was a long time to remain in suspense; but at last the generous Cæsar relieved him from it by a full and free pardon.

And now again his character rose higher, and his good qualities had room to display themselves. There were no longer equally balanced parties to revive the discord which formerly distracted his mind, nor were the circumstances of the times such as to demand his active interference in the cause of his country; but he was as great in the exercise of his contemplative faculties as he had been in the brightest period of his political life. The same faults may, perhaps, be discerned in his philosophical speculations: the same indecision which rendered him incapable of being a statesman or a patriot caused him to adopt in philosophy a skeptical eclecticism. Truth was to him as variable as political honesty; but he is always the advocate and supporter of resignation, and fortitude, and purity, and virtue.

He had hitherto suffered as a public man: he was now bowed down by domestic affliction. A quarrel with his wife Terentia ended in a divorce:[806] such was the facility with which at Rome the nuptial tie could be severed. His second wife was his own ward—a young lady of large fortune; but disparity of years and temper prevented this connexion from lasting long. In B. C. 45 he lost his daughter Tullia. The blow was overwhelming: he sought in vain to soothe his grief in the woody solitudes of his maritime villa at Astura, and it was long before the bereaved father found consolation in philosophy.

The political crisis which ensued upon the assassination of Cæsar alarmed him for his own personal safety: he therefore meditated a voyage to Greece; but being wind-bound at Rhegium, the hopes of an accommodation between Antony and the senate (a hope destined not to be realized) induced him to return. Antony now left Rome, and Cicero delivered that torrent of indignant and eloquent invective—his twelve Philippic orations.[807] He was again the popular idol—crowds of applauding and admiring fellow-citizens attended him to the Forum in a kind of triumphant procession, as they had on his return from exile. But soon the

---

[804] Niebuhr.
[805] See Letters to Att. *passim*.
[806] B. C. 46.
[807] B. C. 43.

second triumvirate was formed. Each member readily gave up friends to satisfy the vengeance of his colleagues, and Octavius sacrificed Cicero.

The story of his death is a brief and sad one. He was enjoying the literary retirement of his Tusculan villa when his friends warned him of his approaching fate. He was too great a philosopher to fear death; but too high-principled and resigned to the Divine will to commit suicide. Still he scarcely thought life worth preserving: "I will die," he said, "in my fatherland, which I have so often saved." However, at the entreaty of his brother, to whom he was affectionately attached, he endeavoured to escape. He first went across the country to Astura, and there embarked. The weather was tempestuous, and as he suffered much from sea-sickness, he again landed at Gaëta. A treacherous freedman betrayed him, and as he was being carried in a litter he was overtaken by his pursuers. He would not permit his attendants to make any resistance; but patiently and courageously submitted to the sword of the assassins, who cut off his head and hands and carried them to Antony. A savage joy sparkled in the eyes of the triumvir at the sight of these bloody trophies. His wife, Fulvia, gloated with inhuman delight upon the pallid features, and in petty spite pierced with a needle that once eloquent tongue. The head and hands were fixed upon the rostrum which had so often witnessed his unequalled eloquence. All that passed by bewailed his death, and gave vent to their affectionate feelings.

Although it is impossible to be blind to the numerous faults of Cicero, few men have been more maligned and misrepresented, and the judgment of antiquity has been, upon the whole, generally unfavourable. He was vain, vacillating, inconstant, constitutionally timid, and the victim of a morbid sensibility; but he was candid, truthful, just, generous, pure-minded, and warm-hearted. His amiability, acted upon by timidity, led him to set too high a value on public esteem and favour; and this weakened his moral sense and his instinctive love of virtue. That he possessed heroism is proved by his defence of Roscius, although the favourite of the terrible Sulla was his adversary. He was not entirely destitute of decision, or he would not so promptly have expressed his approbation of Cæsar's assassins as tyrannicides. He had resolution to strive against his over-sensitiveness, and wisdom to see that mental occupation was its best remedy; for in the midst of the distractions and anxieties of that eventful and critical year which preceded the consulship of Hirtius and Pansa an almost incredible number of works proceeded from his pen.[808]

There are many circumstances to account for his political inconsistency and indecision. He had an early predilection for the aristocratic party; but he saw that they were narrow-minded and behind their age. All the patricians, except Sulla and his small party, were on the popular side. He was proud of his connexion with Marius; and his friend Sulpicius Rufus, whom he greatly admired, joined the Marians. For these reasons, Cicero was inconsistent as a politician. Again, during periods of revolutionary turbulence, moderate men are detested by both sides; and yet it was impossible for a philosophic temper, which could calmly and dispassionately weigh the merits and demerits of both, to sympathize warmly with either. Cicero saw that both were wrong: he was too temperate to approve, too honest to pretend a zeal which he did not feel, and, therefore, he was undecided.

Again, having a large benevolence, and a firm faith in virtue, he was unconscious of guile himself, and thought no evil of others. He therefore mistook flattery for sincerity, and

---

[808] He wrote during that year the *De Officiis*, *De Divinatione*, *De Fato*, *Topica*, and the lost treatise *De Gloria*, besides a vast number of Letters.

compliments for kindness. He was vain; but vanity is a weakness not inconsistent with great minds, and in the case of Cicero it was fed by the unanimous voice of public approbation.

As an advocate his delight was to defend, not to accuse.[809] In three only of his twenty-four orations did he undertake the office of an accuser.

Gentle, sympathizing, and affectionate, he lived as a patriot and died as a philosopher.

---

[809] Pro Muræna, 3.

Chapter 24

CICERO NO HISTORIAN—HIS ORATORICAL STYLE DEFENDED—ITS PRINCIPAL CHARM—OBSERVATIONS ON HIS FORENSIC ORATION—HIS ORATORY ESSENTIALLY JUDICIAL—POLITICAL ORATIONS—RHETORICAL TREATISES—THE OBJECT OF HIS PHILOSOPHICAL WORKS—CHARACTERISTICS OF ROMAN PHILOSOPHICAL LITERATURE—PHILOSOPHY OF CICERO—HIS POLITICAL WORKS—LETTERS—HIS CORRESPONDENTS—VARRO

Such were the life and character of Cicero. The place which he occupies in a history of Roman literature is that of an orator and philosopher. It has been already stated that he had some taste for poetry: in fact, without imagination he could scarcely have been so eminent as an orator; but though the power which he wielded over prose was irresistible, he had not fancy enough to give a poetical character to the language.

Nor had he, notwithstanding the versatility of his talents, any taste for historical investigation. He delighted to read the Greek historians, for the same purpose for which he studied the Attic orators, merely as an instrument of intellectual cultivation; but he was ignorant of Roman history, because he took no interest in original research. His countrymen[810] expected from him an historical work, but he was unfit for the task. It is plain from his "Republic," how little he knew as an antiquarian.

The greatest praise of an orator's style is to say that he was successful. The end and object of oratory is to convince and persuade—to rivet the attention of the hearer, and to gain a mastery over the minds of men. If, therefore, any who study the speeches of Cicero in the closet find faults in his style, they must remember the very faults themselves were suited to the object which he was carrying into execution. During the process of raising the public taste

---

[810] De Leg., introduction.

to the highest standard, he carried his hearers with him: he was not too much in advance; he did not aim his shafts too high; they hit the head and heart. Senate, judges, people understood his arguments, and felt his passionate appeals. Compared with the dignified energy and majestic vigour of the Athenian orator, the Asiatic exuberance of some of his orations may be fatiguing to the sober and chastened taste of the modern classical scholar; but in order to form a just appreciation, he must transport himself mentally to the excitements of the thronged Forum—to the senate composed, not of aged, venerable men, but statesmen and warriors in the prime of life, maddened with the party spirit of revolutionary times—to the presence of the jury of judices, as numerous as a deliberative assembly, whose office was not merely calmly to give their verdict of guilty or not guilty, but who were invested as representatives of the sovereign people with the prerogative of pardoning or condemning.

Viewed in this light, his most florid passages will appear free from affectation—the natural flow of a speaker carried away with the torrent of his enthusiasm. The melodious rise and fall of his periods are not the result of studied effect, but of a true and musical ear. Undoubtedly, amongst his earlier orations, are to be found passages somewhat too declamatory and inconsistent with the principles which he afterwards laid down when his taste was more matured, and when he undertook to write scientifically on the theory of eloquence. Nor must it be concealed that some of the staid and stern Romans of his own days were daring enough, notwithstanding his popularity and success, to find the same fault with him. "Suorum temporum homines," says Quintilian, "incessere audebant eum ut tumidiorem et Asianum[811] et redundantem et in repetitionibus nimium et in salibus aliquando frigidum et in compositione fractum et exsultantem et pene viro molliorem."

But it is not only the brilliance and variety of expression, and the finely-modulated periods, which constituted the principal charm of Ciceronian oratory, and rendered it so effective. Its effectiveness was mainly owing to the great orator's knowledge of the human heart, and of the national peculiarities of his countrymen. Its charm was owing to his extensive acquaintance with the stores of literature and philosophy, which his sprightly wit moulded at will, to the varied learning which his unpedantic mind made so pleasant and popular, to his fund of illustration at once interesting and convincing. Even if his knowledge, because it spread over so wide a surface, was superficial, in this case profoundness was unnecessary.

In a work like the present it is only possible to devote a few brief observations to the most important of his numerous orations, in which, according to the criticism of Quintilian, he combined the force of Demosthenes, the copiousness of Plato, and the elegance of Isocrates. Knowledge of law, far superior to that possessed by the great orators of the day,[812] distinguishes his earliest extant oration, the defence of P. Quinctius.[813] Hortensius was the defendant's counsel. Nævius, the defendant, who had unjustly possessed himself of the

---

[811] Poverty and barrenness were most probably instrumental in producing the diffuseness and exuberance of the Asiatic and Rhodian schools. Their literature and philosophy were deficient in matter, and they sought to hide this defect by the external ornaments of language. For a long time Athens, strong in her pure classic taste, successfully resisted this influence; and in the time of Cicero the tastes of the two schools were in direct opposition. But the flowers of rhetoric are captivating: another generation saw the supremacy of rhetoric at Rome; and the days of Petronius Arbiter (Satyr. book ii.) witnessed the migration of Asiatic taste to Athens.

[812] Cicero tells us (de Orat. i. 57, 58) that Galba, Antony, and Sulpicius were ignorant of jurisprudence; that the chief requisites were elegance, wit, pathos, &c. For legal knowledge they trusted to jurisconsults. In the oration *pro Muræna*, even he himself sneers at a technical knowledge of law.

[813] Delivered B. C. 81.

property of the plaintiff's deceased brother, was a deserter from the Marians, and therefore a protégé of Sylla; but, notwithstanding these disadvantages, Cicero gained his cause. In the masterly defence of S. Roscius,[814] Cicero again defied Sulla. His client was accused of parricide: there was not a shadow of proof, and Cicero saved the life of an innocent man. The noble enthusiasm with which he inveighs against tyranny in this oration strikingly contrasts with the language, full of sweetness, in which he describes Roman rural life. The passage on parricide was too glowing and Asiatic for the taste of his maturer years, and he did not hesitate to make it the subject of severe criticism.[815] Passing over speeches of less interest, we come to the six celebrated Verrian orations. Of these chefs-d'œuvre the first only was delivered.[816] The others were merely published; for the voluntary exile of the criminal rendered further pleading unnecessary. The first is entitled "Divinatio," i. e., an inquiry as to who should have the right of prosecuting: Cæcilius, who had been quæstor to the accused, claimed this privilege, wishing to make the suit a friendly one, and thus quash the proceedings. Nothing can surpass the ironical and sarcastic exposure of this fraudulent attempt to defeat the ends of justice. The noble passages in the succeeding orations of the series are well known; the sketch of the wicked proconsul's antecedent career; the graceful eulogy of that province, in the welfare of which Cicero himself felt so warm an interest; the tasteful description of the statues and antiquities which tempted the more than Roman cupidity of Verres; the interesting history of ancient art which accompanies it; the burst of pathetic indignation with which he paints the horrible tortures to which not only the provincials, but even Roman citizens, were exposed. Transports of joy pervaded the whole of Sicily at Cicero's success; and the Sicilians caused a medal to be struck with this inscription—"Prostrato Verre Trinacria." The oration for Fonteius[817] is a skilful defence of an unpopular governor; that in defence of Cluentius[818] is one of the most remarkable causes célèbres of antiquity; and the complicated scene of villany which Cicero's forcible and soul-harrowing language paints, makes one shudder with horror, whilst we are struck with admiration at the clearness of intellect with which he unravels the web of guilt woven by Oppianicus and Sassia. This remarkable oration has been analyzed by Dr. Blair.[819]

Again, passing over other forensic orations, we come to that on which he had evidently expended all his resources of art, taste, and skill—the speech for the poet Archias.[820] If possible it is even too elaborate and polished for so graceful a theme. Although the object of the advocate was simply to establish the right of his client to Roman citizenship, the genius of the poet of Antioch furnished an opportunity not to be neglected for digressing into the fields of literature, and for pronouncing a truly academical eulogium on poetry. It is satisfactory to the admirers of Cicero to find that the attack which has been made on the genuineness of this pleasing oration is groundless and unwarrantable.[821]

The oration pro Cælio[822] is the most entertaining in the whole collection. It contains a rich fund of anecdote, seasoned with witty observations; a knowledge of human nature

---

[814] B. C. 80.
[815] De Orat.
[816] B. C. 70.
[817] B. C. 69.
[818] B. C. 66.
[819] Belles Lettres, Lect. xxviii.
[820] B. C. 61.
[821] Schröter. Leips. 1818.
[822] B. C. 56.

illustrated in a piquant and humorous style, expressed in a tone of most gentlemanlike yet playful eloquence, and interspersed with passages of great beauty. It presents a marked contrast to the coarse personal abuse which defaces the otherwise powerful invective against L. Piso, which was delivered in the following year.[823]

The list, though many more marvellous specimens are omitted, must be closed with the oration in defence of T. Annius Milo. On this occasion Cicero lost his wonted self-possession. When the court opened, Pompey was presiding on the bench, and he had caused the Forum to be occupied with soldiers. The sight, added, perhaps, to the consciousness that he was advocating a bad cause, struck Cicero with alarm; his voice trembled, his tongue refused to give utterance to the conceptions which he had formed. The judges were unmoved; and Milo remained in his self-imposed exile at Marseilles. When Cicero left the court his courage and calmness returned. He penned the oration which is now extant. He had little or no proof or evidence to offer, and therefore, as an argumentative work, it is unconvincing; but for force, pathos, and the externals of eloquence, it deserves to be reckoned amongst his most wonderful efforts. When the exiled Milo read it, he is said to have exclaimed, "O, Cicero, if you had pleaded so, I should not be eating such capital fish here!" The author himself and his contemporaries thought this his finest oration; probably its deficiencies were concealed by its eloquence and ingenuity. It appears that the oration which he actually delivered was taken down in writing by reporters, and was extant in the time of Asconius Pedianus, the most ancient commentator on Cicero's orations.[824] Its feebleness proved the correctness of the judgment of antiquity.

The oratory of Cicero was essentially judicial: he was himself conscious that his talents lay in that direction, and he saw that in that field was the best opportunity for displaying oratorical power. Even his political orations are rather judicial than deliberative. He was not born for a politician. He possessed not that analytical character of mind which penetrates into the remote causes of human action, nor the synthetical power which enables a man to follow them out to their farthest consequences; he had not that comprehensive grasp of mind which can dismiss at once all points of minor importance and useless speculation, and, seizing all the salient points, can bring them to bear together upon questions of practical expediency. Of the three qualities necessary for a statesman he possessed only two, honesty and patriotism: he had not political wisdom.

Hence, in the finest specimens of his political harangues, his Catilinarians and Philippics, and that in support of the Manilian law, we look in vain for the calm, practical weighing of the subject which is necessary in addressing a deliberative assembly. This was not the habit of his mind. He was only lashed to action by circumstances of great emergency; but even then he is still an advocate—all is excitement, personal feeling, and party spirit: he deals in invective and panegyric, and the denunciation of the enemies of his country; and the parts which especially call forth our admiration differ in nothing from those which we admire in his judicial orations. Nevertheless, so irresistible was the influence which he exercised upon the minds of his hearers, that all his political speeches were triumphs. His panegyric on Pompey,[825] in the speech for the Manilian law, carried his appointment as commander-in-chief of the armies of the East. The consequence of the oration de Provinciis Consularibus

---

[823] B. C. 55.
[824] Born about B. C. 2.
[825] B. C. 56.

continued to Cæsar his administration of Gaul. He crushed in Catiline one of the most formidable traitors that had ever menaced the safety of the republic. Antony's fall followed the complete exposure of his debauchery in private life, and the factiousness of his public career.[826]

Of the Catilinarians, the first and fourth were delivered in the senate, the second and third in the presence of the people. Every one knows the burst of indignation which the consul, rising in his place, aims at the audacious conspirator who dared to pollute with his presence the temple of the deity, and the most august assembly of the Roman people. In less than twenty-four hours Catiline had left Rome, and the conspiracy had become a war. In four words Cicero announced this to the assembled Romans the day after he had addressed the senate. The third is a piece of self-complacent but pardonable egotism. Success has overwhelmed him—he sees that all eyes are turned upon himself—he is the hero of his own story; still he demands no reward but the approbation of his fellow-citizens, and reminds them that to the gods alone their gratitude is due.

Two days pass away, and after Cæsar and Cicero had spoken, Cicero again addresses the senate, and recommends that measure which was the beginning of his troubles, the condemnation of the conspirators. The zeal of the senate made the act their own, but Cicero paid the penalty. The position which Cicero occupies on this occasion invests his speech with more dignity than is displayed in any of the preceding. He is the chief magistrate of the republic, performing the duty of pronouncing a capital sentence on the guilty. The excitement of the crisis is subsiding; and he has the more composure, because he knows that he carries with him the sympathies of the senate and people.

The Philippics, so named after the orations of Demosthenes, are fourteen in number. Cicero commenced his attack[827] upon the object of his implacable hatred with a defence of the laws of Cæsar, which Antony wished to repeal. He followed it up with the celebrated second oration, in which he demolished the character of Antony; a speech which Juvenal pronounced to be his chef-d'œuvre, but which Niebuhr thought was undeserving of being so highly exalted. He delivered the remaining twelve in the course of the succeeding year; they were the last monuments of his eloquence; he never spoke again. The fourteenth is a brilliant panegyric, but nothing more; the gallant army of Octavius received their deserved applause; but in this political crisis the orator could not discern or even catch a glimpse of the future destinies of his country.

In his rhetorical works, Cicero left a legacy of practical instruction to posterity. The treatise "De Inventione," although it displays genius, is merely interesting as the juvenile production of a future great man; and the author himself alludes to it as a rude and unfinished production.[828] Of the Rhetorical Hand-Book, in four sections, addressed to Herennius, it is unnecessary to speak, as it is now universally pronounced spurious.[829] The De Oratore, Brutus sive de claris Oratoribus, and Orator ad M. Brutum,[830] are the result of his matured experience. They form together one series; the principles are first laid down; their developments are carried out and illustrated; and lastly, in the Orator, he places before the eyes of Brutus the model of ideal perfection. In his treatment of this subject, he shows a mind

---

[826] Phil. ii.
[827] Phil. i.; B. C. 44.
[828] De Orat. i. 2.
[829] For the arguments on this point see Smith's Dict. i. 726.
[830] B. C. 55, 46, 45.

imbued with the spirit of Plato: he invests it with dramatic interest, and transports the reader into the scene which he so graphically describes. The conversation contained in the first of these works has been already described. The scene of the second is laid on the lawn of Cicero's palace at Rome: Cicero, Atticus and M. Brutus are the dramatis personæ; and their taste receives inspiration from a statue of Plato which adorns the garden. In the third, Cicero himself, at the request of M. Brutus, paints, as Plato would have done, the portrait of a faultless orator.

Three more short treatises must be added—(1.) The dialogue, De Partitione Oratoria,[831] an elementary book, written for his son. (2.) The De Optimo Genere Oratorum,[832] a short preface to a translation of the Greek oration, De Corona. (3.) The Topica,[833] i. e., a treatise on the commonplaces of judicial oratory.

PHILOSOPHY OF CICERO

Cicero somewhat arrogantly claims the credit of being the first to awaken a taste for philosophy, and to illuminate the darkness in which it lay hid by the light of Roman letters.[834] He did not confess the obligations under which he lay to his predecessors, because he never could forget that he was an orator.[835] He could not deny that some of them thought justly; but he denied that they possessed the power of expressing what they thought. He felt that there was nothing in the philosophical writings already existing to tempt his countrymen to study the subject: they were dry, unadorned, unpolished. It required an orator to array philosophy in an enticing garb. He proposed, therefore, to assuage his anxieties—to seek repose from the harassing cares of politics[836]—by rendering his countrymen independent of Greek philosophical literature.

This was all he proposed to himself: it was all that his predecessor had attempted; nor did he pretend to originality. The periods which he devoted to the task, and to which all philosophical works belong, were those during which he was excluded from political life. The first of these was the triumvirate of Cæsar, Pompey, and Crassus; the second was coincident with the dictatorship of Cæsar and the consulship of Antony. Not only did his contemplative spirit delight in such studies, but, whilst all the avenues to distinction were closed against him, his ambition sought this road to fame, and his patriotism urged him to take this method of benefiting his country. But as he was not the first who introduced philosophy to the Romans, it will be necessary briefly to sketch its progress up to the time at which his labours commenced.

Roman philosophy was neither the result of original investigation nor the gradual development of the Greek system. It arose rather from a study of ancient philosophical literature than from an examination of philosophical principles. The Roman intellect did not possess the power of abstraction in a sufficiently high degree for research, nor was the Latin language capable of representing satisfactorily abstract thoughts. Cicero was quite aware of

---

[831] B. C. 47.
[832] B. C. 46.
[833] B. C. 45.
[834] Tusc. i. 3. See also ii. 2.
[835] De Off. i. 1.
[836] De Div. II. ii.

the poverty of its scientific nomenclature, as compared with that of Greece. In one treatise,[837] he writes,—"Equidem soleo etiam, quod uno Græci, si aliter non possum, idem pluribus verbis exprimere." Pliny[838] and Seneca[839] assert the same fact. "Magis damnabis," writes the latter, "angustias Romanas si scieris unam syllabam esse, quam mutare non possim. Quæ hæc sit quæris? τὸ ὄν." The practical character also of the people prompted them to take advantage of the material already furnished by others, and to select such doctrines as it approved, without regard to their relation to each other.

The Roman philosopher, therefore, or rather (to speak more correctly) philosophical student, did not throw himself into the speculations of his age, pursue them contemporaneously, or deduce from them fresh results. He went back to the earlier ages of Greek philosophy, studied, commented on, and explained the works of the best authors, and adopted some of their doctrines as fixed scholastic dogmas. Consequently, the spirit in which philosophical study was pursued by the Romans was a literary and not a scientific one. A taste for literature had been awakened, and philosophy was considered only as one species of literature, although its importance was recognised as bearing upon the practical duties, the highest interests and happiness of man. The practical view which Cicero took of philosophy, and the extensive influence which he attributed to it, is manifest from numerous passages in his works,[840] and is imbodied in the following beautiful apostrophe in the Tusculan Disputations:[841] "O vitæ Philosophia dux! O virtutis indagatrix, expultrixque vitiorum! Quid non modo nos, sed omnino vita hominum sine te esse potuisset? Tu urbes peperisti; tu dissipatos homines in societatem vitæ convocasti; tu eos inter se primo domiciliis, deinde conjugiis, tum literarum et vocum communione junxisti; tu inventrix legum, tu magistra morum et disciplinæ fuisti; ad te confugimus, a te opem petimus; tibi nos, ut antea magna ex parte, sic nunc penitus totosque tradimus."

It is plain, therefore, that the chief characteristics of Roman philosophy would be—(1.) Learning, for it consisted in bringing together doctrines and opinions scattered over a wide field; (2,) Generally speaking, an ethical purpose and object, for Romans would be little inclined to value any subject of study which had no ultimate reference to man's political and social relations; (3,) Eclecticism; for although there were certain schools, such as the Epicurean and Stoic, which were evidently favourites, the dogmas of different teachers were collected and combined together often without regard to consistency.

The defects of such a system are fatal to its claim to be considered philosophical; for the scientific connexion of its parts is lost sight of, and results are presented independent of the chain of causes and effects by which they are connected with principles. Such a system must necessarily be illogical and inconsequential. Even the liberality which adopts the principle, "Nullius jurare in verba magistri," and which, therefore, appears to be its chief merit, was absurd; and the willingness with which all views were readily admitted led to skepticism, or doubt whether such a thing as absolute truth had a real existence.

Greek philosophy was probably first introduced into Rome by the Achæan exiles, of whom Polybius was one.[842] The embassy of Carneades the Academic, Diogenes the Stoic,

---

[837] De Fin. iii. 2.
[838] Epist. iv. 18.
[839] Ibid. lviii.
[840] *Ex. gr.* De Div. ii. 1; Brut. 93.
[841] See also T. D. ii. 4; x. b. v. ii.
[842] A. U. C. 592; Gell. N. A. xv. 2.

and Critolaus the Peripatetic, followed six years afterwards. In vain the stern M. Porcius Cato caused their dismissal; for some of the most illustrious and accomplished Romans, such as Africanus, Lælius, and Furius, had already profited by their lectures and instructions.[843] Whilst the educated Romans were gaining an historical insight into the doctrines of these schools, the Stoic Panætius, who was entertained in the household of Scipio Africanus, was unfolding the mysterious and transcendental doctrines of the great object of his veneration, Plato. But although the Romans could appreciate the majestic dignity and poetical beauty of his style, they were not equal to the task of penetrating his hidden meaning; they were, therefore, content to take upon trust the glosses and commentaries of his expositors. These inclined to the New Academy rather than to the Old: in its skeptical spirit they compared and balanced opposing probabilities; and went no farther than recommending the adoption of opinions upon which they could not pronounce with certainty. Neither did the Peripatetic doctrines meet with much favour, although the works of Aristotle had been brought to Rome by the dictator Sulla, partly, as Cicero says, because of the vastness of the subjects treated, partly because they seemed incapable of satisfactory proof to unskilled and inexperienced minds.[844]

The philosophical system which first arrested the attention of the Romans, and gained an influence over their minds, was the Epicurean.[845] But it is somewhat remarkable that, although this philosophy was in its general character ethical, a people so eminently practical in their turn of mind should have especially devoted themselves to the study of the physical speculations of this school.[846] The only apparent exception to this statement is Catius, but even his principal works, although he wrote one, "*de Summo Bono*," are on the physical nature of things.[847]

Cicero accounts for the popularity of Epicureanism by saying that it was easy—that it appealed to the blandishments of pleasure; and that its first professors, Amafanius and Rabirius, used none of the refinements of art or subtleties or dialectic, but clothed their discussions in a homely and popular style, suited to the simple and unlearned. There were many successors to Amafanius; and the doctrines which they taught rapidly spread over the whole of Italy. Many illustrious statesmen, also, were amongst the believers in this fashionable creed; of whom the best known are C. Cassius, the fellow-conspirator of Brutus, and T. Pomponius Atticus, the friend of Cicero. All the monuments and records, however, of the Epicurean philosophy, which were published in Latin, have perished, with the exception of the immortal work of T. Lucretius Carus, "*De Naturâ Rerum*."

Nor was Stoicism, the severe principles of which were in harmony with the stern old Roman virtues, without distinguished disciples; such as were the unflinching M. Brutus, the learned Terentius Varro, the jurist Scævola, the unbending Cato of Utica, and the magnificent Lucullus—a Stoic in creed, though not in life and conduct. The part which Cicero's character qualified him to perform in the philosophical instruction of his countrymen was scarcely that of a guide: he could give them a lively interest in the subject, and reveal to them the discoveries and speculations of others, but he could not mould and form their belief, and train them in the work of original investigation. Not being himself devoutly attached to any system

---

[843] Cic. de Or. ii. 37.
[844] Tusc. iv. 3.
[845] Ritter, H. of Ph. vol. iv. xii. 2, note.
[846] Tusc. iv. 3.
[847] Ac. Post. I. 2.

of philosophical belief, he would be cautious of offending the philosophical prejudices of others. He loved learning, but his temper was undecided and vacillating: whilst, therefore, he delighted in accumulating stores of Greek erudition, the tendency of his mind was, in the midst of a variety of inconsistent doctrines, to leave the conclusion undetermined. Although he listened to various instructors—Phædrus the Epicurean, Diodotus the Stoic, and Philo the Academician—he found the eclecticism of the latter more congenial to his taste. Its preference of probability to certainty suited one who shrunk from the responsibility of deciding.

It is this personality, as it were, which gives a special interest to the Ciceronian philosophy. The reflexion of his personal character which pervades it rescues it from the imputation of being a mere transcript of his Greek originals. Cicero brings everything as much as possible to a practical standard. If the question arises between the study of morals and politics and that of physics or metaphysics, he decides in favour of the former, on the grounds that the latter transcends the capacities of the human intellect;[848] that in morals and politics we are under obligations from which in physics we are free; that we are bound to tear ourselves from these abstract studies at the call of duty to our country or our fellow-creatures, even if we were able to count the stars or measure the magnitude of the universe.[849] In the didactic method which he pursues he bears in mind that he is dealing not with contemplative philosophers, or minds that have been logically trained, but with statesmen and men of the world; he does not therefore claim too much, or make his lessons too hard, and is always ready to sacrifice scientific system to a method of popular instruction. His object seems to be to recommend the subject—to smoothe difficulties, and illustrate obscurities. He evidently admires the exalted purity of Stoical morality; and the principles of that sect are those which he endeavours to impress upon his son.[850] His only fear is that their system is impracticable.[851]

Cicero believed in the existence of one supreme Creator and Governor of the universe, and also in His spiritual nature;[852] but his belief is rather the result of instinctive conviction, than of the proofs derived from philosophy; for as to them, he is, as on other points, uncertain and wavering. He disbelieved the popular mythical religion; but, uncertain as to what was the truth, he would not have that disturbed which he looked upon as a political engine.[853] Amidst the doubtful and conflicting reasons, respecting the human soul and man's eternal destiny, there is no doubt that, although he finds no satisfactory proof, he is a believer in immortality.[854] It is unnecessary to pursue the subject of his philosophical creed any further, because it is not a system, but only a collection of precepts, not of investigations. Its materials are borrowed, its illustrations alone novel. But, nevertheless, the study of Cicero's philosophical works is invaluable, in order to understand the minds of those who came after him. It must not be forgotten, that not only all Roman philosophy after his time, but a great part of that of the middle ages, was Greek philosophy filtered through Latin, and mainly founded on that of Cicero. Cicero's works on speculative philosophy generally consist of— (1.) *The Academics*, or a history and defence of the belief of the New Academy. (2.) The *De*

---

[848] De Rep. i. 18, 19.
[849] De Off. i. 43.
[850] De Off. i. 43.
[851] De Fin. iv. 9.
[852] Tusc. i. 27, 28.
[853] De Leg. ii. 13.
[854] De Sen. 21.

Finibus Bonorum et Malorum, dialogues on the supreme good, the end of all moral action. (3.) *The Tusculanæ Disputationes*, containing five independent treatises on the fear of death, the endurance of pain, the power of wisdom over sorrow, the morbid passions, the relation of virtue to happiness. In these treatises Stoicism predominates, although opinions are adduced from the whole range of Greek philosophy. (4.) *Paradoxa*, in which the six celebrated Stoical paradoxies are touched upon in a light and amusing manner. (5.) A dialogue in praise of philosophy, named after Hortensius. (6.) Translations of the Timæus and Protagoras of Plato. Of these last three treatises only a few fragments remain.

His moral philosophy comprehends—(1.) The *De Officiis*, a Stoical treatise on moral obligations, addressed to his son Marcus, at that time a student at Athens. (2.) The unequalled little essays on Friendship and Old Age. A few words also are preserved of two books on Glory, addressed to Atticus; and one which he wrote on the Alleviation of Grief when bereaved of his beloved daughter.[855] He left one theological work in three parts: the first part is on the "*Nature of the Gods;*" the second on the "*Science of Divination;*" the third on "*Fate,*" of which an inconsiderable fragment is extant. His office of augur probably suggested to him the composition of these treatises.

His political works are two in number—the *De Republica*[856] and *De Legibus*; both are imperfect. The remains of the former are only fragmentary; of the latter, three out of six books are extant, and those not entire. Nevertheless, sufficient of both remains to enable us to form some estimate of their philosophical character. Although he does not profess originality, but confesses that they are imitations of the two treatises of Plato, which bear the same name, still they are more inductive than any of his other treatises. His purpose is, like that of Plato, to give in the one an ideal republic, and in the other a sketch of a model legislation; but the novelty of the treatment consists in their principles being derived from the Roman constitution and the Roman laws.

The questions which he proposes to answer are, what is the best government and the best code: but the limits within which he confines himself are the institutions of his country. In the Republic he first discusses, like the Greek philosophers, the merits and demerits of the three pure forms of government; and upon the whole decides in favour of monarchy[857] as the best. With Aristotle[858] he agrees that all the pure forms are liable to degenerate,[859] and comes to the conclusion that the idea of a perfect polity is a combination of all three.[860] In order to prove and illustrate his theory, he investigates, though it must be confessed in a meager and imperfect manner, the constitutional history of Rome, and discovers the monarchical element in the consulship, the aristocratic in the senate, and the popular in the assembly of the people and the tribunitial authority.

The Romans continued jealously to preserve the shadow of their constitution even after they had surrendered the substance. Nominally, the titles and offices of the old republic never perished—the Emperor was in name nothing more than (Imperator) the commander-in-chief of the armies of the republic, but in him all power centred: he was absolute, autocratic, the

---

[855] B. C. 45.
[856] B. C. 54.
[857] Lib. i. 26, 35, 45; ii. 23.
[858] Ethics.
[859] Lib. i. 27, 28; ii. 39.
[860] Lib. i. 29, 35, 45.

chief of a military despotism.[861] Cicero, as the treatise *De Legibus* plainly shows, saw, with approbation, that this state of things was rapidly coming to pass; that the people were not fitted to be trusted with liberty, and yet that they would be contented with its semblance and name.

The method which he pursues, is, firstly, to treat the subject in the abstract, and to investigate the nature of law; and, secondly, to propose an ideal code, limited by the principles of Roman jurisprudence. Thus Cicero's polity and code were not Utopian—the models on which they were formed had a real tangible existence. His was the system of a practical man, as the Roman constitution was that of a practical people. It was not like Greek liberty, the realization of one single idea; it was like that of England, the growth of ages, the development of a long train of circumstances, and expedients, and experiments, and emergencies. Cicero prudently acquiesced in the ruin of liberty as a stern necessity; but he evidently thought that Rome had attained the zenith of its national greatness immediately before the agitations of the Gracchi.

Both these works are written in the engaging form of dialogues. In the one, Scipio Æmilianus, Lælius, Scævola, and others, meet together in the Latin holidays (Feriæ Latinæ,) and discuss the question of government. In the other, the writer himself, with his brother Quintus and Atticus, converse on jurisprudence whilst they saunter on a little islet near Arpinum at the confluence of the Liris and Fibrena.

We must, lastly, contemplate Cicero as a correspondent. This intercourse of congenial minds separated from one another, and induced by the force of circumstances to digest and arrange their thoughts in their communication, forms one of the most delightful and interesting, and at the same time one of the most characteristic, portions of Roman literature. A Roman thought that whenever he put pen to paper it was his duty, to a certain extent, to avoid carelessness and offences against good taste, and to bestow upon his friend some portion of that elaborate attention which, as an author, he would devote to the public eye. In fact the letter-writer was almost addressing the same persons as the author; for the latter wrote for the approbation of his friends, the circle of intimates in which he lived: the approbation of the public was a secondary object. The Greeks were not writers of letters: the few which we possess were mere written messages, containing such necessary information as the interruption of intercourse demanded. There was no interchange of hopes and fears, thoughts, sentiments, and feelings.

The extent of Cicero's correspondence is almost incredible: even those epistles which remain form a very voluminous collection—more than eight hundred are extant. The letters to his friends and acquaintances (ad Familiares) occupy sixteen books; those to Atticus sixteen more; and we have besides three books of letters to Quintus, and one to Brutus; but the authenticity of this last collection is somewhat doubtful. It is quite clear that none of them were intended for publication, as those of Pliny and Seneca were. They are elegant without stiffness, the natural outpourings of a mind which could not give birth to an ungraceful idea. When speaking of the perilous and critical politics of the day, more or less restraint and reserve are apparent, according to the intimacy with the person whom he is addressing, but no attempt at pompous display. His style is so simple that the reader forgets that Cicero ever wrote or delivered an oration. There is the eloquence of the heart, not of the rhetoric school. Every subject is touched upon which could interest the statesman, the man of letters, the

---

[861] See Tac. Annal. I.

admirer of the fine arts, or the man of the world. The writer reveals in them his own motives, his secret springs of actions, his loves, his hatreds, his strength, his weakness. They extend over more than a quarter of a century, the most interesting period of his own life, and one of the most critical in the history of his country. The letters to Quintus are those of an elder brother to one who stood in great need of good advice. Although Quintus was not deserving of his brother's affection, M. Cicero was warmly attached to him, and took an interest in his welfare. Quintus was proprætor of Asia, and not fitted for the office; and Cicero was not sparing in his admonitions, though he offered them with kindness and delicacy. The details of his family concerns form not the least interesting portion of this correspondence. There is, as might be expected, more reserve in the letters *ad Familiares* than in those addressed to Atticus. They are written to a variety of correspondents, of every shade and complexion of opinions, many of them mere acquaintances, not intimate friends; but whilst, for this reason, less historically valuable, they are the most pleasing of the collection, on account of the exquisite elegance of their style. They are models of pure Latinity. In the letters to Atticus, on the other hand, he lays bare the secrets of his heart; he trusts his life in his hands; he is not only his friend but his confidant, his second self. Were it not for the letters of Cicero, we should have had but a superficial knowledge of this period of Roman history, as well as of the inner life of Roman society.

An elegant poetic compliment paid to Cicero by Laurea Tullus, one of his freedmen, has been preserved by Pliny.[862] The subject of it is a medicinal spring in the neighbourhood of the Academy.

> Quo tua Romanæ vindex clarissime linguæ
> Silva loco melius surgere jussa viret
> Atque Academiæ celebratam nomine villam
> Nunc reparat cultu sub potiore Vetus:
> Hic etiam adparent lymphæ non ante repertæ
> Languida quæ infuso lumina rore levant.
> Nimirum locus ipse sui Ciceronis honori
> Hoc dedit hac fontes cum patefecit opes
> Ut quoniam totum legitur sine fine per orbem
> Sint plures oculis quæ medeantur, aquæ.
> Father of eloquence in Rome,
> The groves that once pertained to thee
> Now with a fresher verdure bloom
> Around thy famed Academy.
> Vetus at length this favoured seat
> Hath with a tasteful care restored;
> And newly at thy loved retreat
> A gushing fount its stream has poured.
> These waters cure an aching sight;
> And thus the spring that bursts to view
> Through future ages shall requite
> The fame this spot from Tully drew. *Elton.*

---

[862] See Meyer's Anthol. 67.

The correspondents of Cicero included a number of eminent men. Atticus was the least interesting, for his politic caution rendered him unstable and insincere; but there was Cassius the tyrannicide; the Stoical Cato of Utica; Cæcina, the warm partisan of Pompey; the orator Cælius Rufus; Hirtius and Oppius, the literary friends of Cæsar; Lucceius the historian; Matius the mimiambic poet; and that patron of arts and letters,[863] C. Asinius Pollio.

Pollio was a scion of a distinguished house, and was born at Rome B. C. 76.[864] Even as a youth he was distinguished for wit and sprightliness;[865] and at the age of twenty-two was the prosecutor of C. Cato. He was with Cæsar at the Rubicon, at Pharsalia, in Africa, and in Spain; and was finally intrusted with the conduct of the war in that province against Sextus Pompey. On the establishment of the first triumvirate, Pollio, after some hesitation, sent in his adhesion; and Antony intrusted him with the administration of Gallia Transpadana, including the allotment of the confiscated lands among the veteran soldiers. He thus had opportunity of protecting Virgil and saving his property. In B. C. 40, Octavian and Antony were reconciled at Brundisium by his mediation. A successful campaign in Illyria concluded his military career with the glories of a triumph,[866] and he then retired from public life to his villa at Tusculum, and devoted himself to study. He enjoyed life to the last, and died in his eightieth year. He left three children, one of whom, Asinius Gallus,[867] wrote a comparison between his father and Cicero, which was answered by the Emperor Claudius.[868]

In oratory, poetry, and history, Pollio enjoyed a high reputation among contemporary critics, and yet none of his works have survived. The solution of this difficulty may, perhaps, be found in the following circumstances:—1. His patronage of literary men rendered him popular, and drew from the critics a somewhat partial verdict. His kindness caused Horace to extol[869] him, and Virgil to address to him his most remarkable eclogue.[870] 2. His taste was formed before the new literary school commenced. He had always a profound admiration for the old writers, and frequently quoted them. His style probably appeared antiquated and pedantic, and, therefore, never became generally popular. A later writer[871] says, that he was so harsh and dry as to appear to have reproduced the style of Attius and Pacuvius, not only in his tragedies, but also in his orations. Quintilian observes,[872] that he seemed to belong to the pre-Ciceronian period. Niebuhr, who could only form his opinion upon the slight fragments preserved by Seneca, for the three letters in Cicero's collection[873] are only despatches, affirms that he seems to stand between two distinct generations,[874] namely, the literary periods of Cicero and Virgil. His great work was a history of the civil wars, in seventeen books. He pretended to be a critic, but his criticism was fastidious and somewhat ill-natured. He found blemishes in Cicero, inaccuracies in Cæsar, pedantry in Sallust, and provincialism (Patavinitas) in Livy. The correctness of his judgment respecting the charming narratives of the great historian has been assumed from generation to generation, yet no one can discover

---

[863] Hor. Od. ii. 1.
[864] Hieron. in Eus. Ch.
[865] Catull. xii. 1.
[866] B. C. 39.
[867] Tac. Ann. i. 12.
[868] Plin. Ep. vii. 4; Suet. Cl. 41.
[869] Sat. I. x.; Carm. ii. 1.
[870] Ecl. iii. 86; viii.
[871] Dial. de Orat. 21.
[872] Lib. x. i. 113.
[873] Ad. Fam. x. 31, 32, 33.
[874] Lect. R. H. cvi.

in what this *Pativinity* consists. It was easier to find fault than to write correctly; for, whilst all the labours of the critic have perished, Cicero, Cæsar, Sallust, and Livy are immortal. Vehemence and passion developed his character.

Still he was one of the greatest benefactors to the literature of his country; more especially as he was the first to found a public library. Books had already been brought to Rome, and collections formed. Æmilius Paulus had a library—Lucullus had one also, to which he allowed learned men to have access. Sulla enriched Rome with the plunder of the Athenian libraries; and in his time Tyrannis the grammarian was the possessor of three thousand volumes. Julius Cæsar employed the learned Varro to collect books with a view to a national collection, but death put a stop to his intentions.[875] Pollio expended the spoils of Dalmatia in founding a temple to Liberty in the Aventine, and furnishing it with a library, the nucleus of which were the collections of Sulla and Varro. After this time, the work was carried on by imperial munificence. Augustus founded the Octavian library in the temple of Juno, and the Palatine in the palace. Tiberius augmented the latter. Vespasian placed one in the temple of Peace. Trajan formed the Ulpian; Domitian the Capitoline; Hadrian a magnificent one at his own villa; and in the reign of Constantine the number of public libraries exceeded twenty.

M. TERENTIUS VARRO REATINUS (BORN B. C. 116.)

On an ancient medal is represented the effigy of Julius Cæsar bearing a book in one hand and a sword in the other,[876] with the legend "Ex utroque Cæsar." This device represents the genius of many a distinguished citizen of the republic, and that of Varro amongst the number, for he was a soldier, and at the same time the most learned of his countrymen. He was born[877] at Reate (Rieti,) a Sabine town situated in the Tempe of Italy, in the neighbourhood of the celebrated cascade of Terni. Ælius Stilo, the antiquarian, was the instructor of his earlier years,[878] and from him he derived his thirst for knowledge, and his ardent devotion to original investigation. He subsequently studied philosophy under Antiochus, a professor of the Academic school.[879] In politics he was warmly attached to the party of Pompey, under whom he served in the Piratic and Mithridatic wars. He was also one of his three *Legati* in Spain, and did not resign his command until the towns in the south of that province eagerly submitted to Cæsar. After the battle of Pharsalia, he experienced the clemency of the conqueror, but not soon enough to save his villa from being attacked and plundered.[880]

Cæsar appreciated Varro's extensive learning and intrusted to him the formation of the great public library.[881] Henceforth he shunned the perils of political life,[882] and in the retirement of his villas devoted himself zealously to the pursuit of literature. Nevertheless he could not escape the unrelenting persecution of political party; for in that proscription to

---

[875] Plin. H. N. vii. 3; xxxv. 2.
[876] See Exc. in Delph. Cic.
[877] B. C. 116.
[878] Cic. Brut. i. 56.
[879] Cic. Acad. iii. 12.
[880] Cic. Phil. ii. 18.
[881] Cæs. B. G. i. 38; ii. 17.
[882] Cic. ad Fam. ix. 13.

which Cicero fell a victim, his name was in the list until it was erased by Antony.[883] Although he was seventy years old, his industry was unabated, and he continued his literary labours until his death, which took place in the eighty-ninth year of his age.[884] Varro was a man of ponderous erudition and unwearied industry,[885] without a spark of taste and genius. No Roman author wrote so much as he did, no one read so much except Pliny; yet, notwithstanding all this practice and study, he never acquired an agreeable style. He dissected and anatomized the Latin language with all the powers of critical analysis; but he was never imbued with its elegant polish or its nervous eloquence.

Wherever, as in the case of his treatise on agriculture, he had access to sound information and good authority, his habits of arrangement, the clearness with which he classified, and the careful judgment with which he adduced his facts, render his works valuable. Few men have possessed greater powers of combining and systematizing: his mind was, as it were, full of compartments, in which each species of knowledge had its proper place, but it was nothing more. Whenever he left the beaten track of other men's discoveries, and indulged in free conjecture or original thought, as in his grammatical works, his learning seems to desert him; and etymology, which has tempted so many mere conjecturers to go astray, led him also into absurdity.

One of his works, *Antiquitates Divinarum Rerum*, acquires a peculiar interest from the fact of its having been the storehouse from which St. Augustine, who was a great admirer of his learning, derived much of his treatise *De Civitate Dei*. How this laborious compilation was lost it is impossible to say. We can only lament the accident which deprives us of the work to which especially the author owes his reputation. In the treatise, which together with this forms one work, namely, *Antiquitates Rerum Humanarum*, he investigated the early history and chronology of Rome,[886] and fixed the date of the building of the city in the year B. C. 753, a date which is now commonly received by the best historians.[887]

A catalogue of his numerous books and tracts on almost every subject which then engaged the attention of literary men—on history, biography, geography, philosophy, criticism, and morals—would be uninteresting, but his principal works were as follows:—

I.
De Re Rustica, Libri III.

II.
De Lingua Latina, Libri XXIV., of which only six are extant, and these in a mutilated condition.

III.
Antiquitates Rerum Humanarum, Libri XXV. *Antiquitates Rerum Divinarum, Libri* XVI.

---

[883] B. C. 43.
[884] Plin. N. H. xxix. 4.
[885] Quint. x. i. 95.
[886] See Meyer's Anthol. 78.
[887] Meyer, Anthol. Rom. 34–51.

IV.

Saturæ, partly in prose, partly in verse; consisting of moral essays and dialogues, exposing the vices and follies of the day, and teaching their lessons rather in a light and amusing than a didactic form.

V.

Poems, of which eighteen short epigrams of no great merit are extant.

Chapter 25

Roman Historical Literature—Principal Historians—Lucceius—Lucullus—Cornelius Nepos—Opinions of the Genuineness of the Works Which Bear His Name—Biography of J. Cæsar—His Commentaries—Their Style and Language—His Modesty Overrated—Other Works—Character of Cæsar

Historical Writers

In historical composition alone can the Romans lay claim to originality; and in their historical literature especially is exhibited a faithful transcript of their mind and character. History at once gratified their patriotism, and its investigations were in accordance with their love of the real and practical. Thus those natural powers which had been elicited and cultivated by an acquaintance with Greek literature were applied with a naïve simplicity to the narration of events, and embellished them with all the graces of a refined style. The practical good sense and political wisdom which the Roman social system was admirably adapted to nurture found food for reflection: their shrewd insight into character, and their searching scrutiny into the human heart gave them a power over their materials; and hence they were enabled in this department of literature to emulate, not merely imitate, the Greeks, and to be their rivals, and sometimes their superiors. The elegant simplicity of Cæsar is as attractive as that of Herodotus; not one of the Greek historians surpasses Livy in talent for the picturesque, and in the charm with which he invests his spirited and living stories; whilst for condensation of thought, terseness of expression, and political and philosophical acumen, Tacitus is not inferior to Thucydides.

The subjects which historical investigation furnished were so peculiarly national, so congenial to the character of the mind of the Romans, that they seem to have cast aside their Greek originals, and to have struck out an independent line for themselves.

The catalogue of Roman historians is a proud one. At the head of it stand the four great names of Cæsar, Sallust, Livy, and Tacitus; all of whom, except the last, belong to the

Augustan age. It comprehends those of Cornelius Nepos, Trogus Pompeius, Cremutius Cordus, Aufidius Bassus, and Sallust, in the golden age; Velleius Paterculus, Valerius Maximus, Q. Curtius, Suetonius, and Florus, in the succeeding one; nor must L. Lucceius and L. Licinius Lucullus be passed over without mention.

L. LUCCEIUS

L. Lucceius, the friend and correspondent of Cicero,[888] was an orator who espoused the party of J. Cæsar, and relying on his influence, became, together with him, a candidate for the consulship.[889] Being unsuccessful, he quitted politics for the calm enjoyment of a literary life. His right to be called an historian is founded on his having commenced a history of the Social and Civil Wars, but it was never completed or published. Cicero[890] entreats him to speak of the events which he was recording, as well as of his own character and conduct, with partiality; it is, therefore, impossible to trust the encomiums which accompany this request, as they were probably dictated by a wish to purchase his favourable opinion. The period of his retirement from public affairs was not of long duration, for he afterwards again engaged in the civil strife which agitated Rome, and joined the party of Pompey, who held him in high estimation.[891] On his downfall he shared with other Pompeians the clemency of the dictator.

L. LICINIUS LUCULLUS

L. Licinius Lucullus,[892] the illustrious but luxurious conqueror of Mithridates, did not disdain to devote his leisure to the composition of history, although his works are not of such merit as to claim for him a distinguished position among the historians of 357his country. The stirring events of the Social War tempted him to record them.[893] Part of his enormous wealth he had expended on a magnificent library: to the poet Archias he was a kind friend;[894] and his patronage was liberally granted to literary men, especially to those philosophers who held the doctrines of his favourite Academy. Like most of those who combined with a love of literature a life of activity in the public service of his country, he was an orator of no mean abilities.[895] His love of Greek, and his habits of intercourse with Greek philosophers, led him to write his history in the Greek language, and to select and transcribe extracts from the histories of Cælius Antipater and Polybius.

---

[888] See ad Att. i. 3, 5, 10, 11, 14.
[889] B. C. 60.
[890] Ad Fam. v. 12; xv. 21, 6.
[891] Ad Att. ix. 1.
[892] Consul, B. C. 74.
[893] Ad Att. i. 19.
[894] Cio. pro Arch.
[895] Cic. Brut. 62.

CORNELIUS NEPOS

Cornelius Nepos was a contemporary of Catullus, and lived until the sixth year of the reign of Augustus.[896] Ausonius says that he was a Gaul,[897] Catullus that he was an Italian.[898] Both are probably right, as the prevailing opinion is, that he was born either at Verona, or the neighbouring village of Hostilia in Cisalpine Gaul. Besides Catullus, he reckoned Cicero[899] and Atticus amongst the number of his friends.[900] These circumstances constitute all that is known respecting his personal history.

All his works which are mentioned by the ancients are unfortunately lost; but respecting the genuineness of that with which every scholar is familiar from his childhood, strong doubts have been entertained. His lost works were, (1.) Three books of Chronicles, or a short abridgment of Universal History. They are mentioned by A. Gellius,[901] and allusion is made to them by Catullus.[902] (2.) Five books of anecdotes styled "*Libri Exemplorum*,"[903] and also entitled "*The Book of C. Nepos de Viris illustribus*." (3.) A Life of Cicero,[904] and a collection of Letters addressed to him.[905] (4.) "*De Historicis*," or Memoirs of Historians.[906] 358The work now extant which bears his name is entitled "*The Lives of Eminent Generals*." But besides the biographies of twenty generals, it contains short accounts of some celebrated monarchs, lives of Hamilcar and Hannibal, and also of Cato and Atticus. The Proëmium of the book is addressed to one Atticus, and to the first edition was prefixed a dedication to the Emperor Theodosius, from which it appeared that the author's name was Probus. These biographical sketches continued to be ascribed to this unknown author until the latter half of the sixteenth century.

At that time the celebrated scholar Lambinus, Regius Professor of Belles Lettres at Paris, argued from the purity of the style that it was a work of classical antiquity, and, from a passage in the life of Cato, that the Atticus, to whom it was dedicated, was the well-known correspondent of Cicero, and the author no other than Cornelius Nepos. The argument derived from the Latinity is unanswerable; that, however, from the life of Cato is a "*petitio principii*," inasmuch as there is no more evidence in favour of the life of Cato having been written by Nepos, than the other biographies. The life of Atticus, which is a complete model of biographical composition, is ascribed to him by name in some of the best MSS. Of the rest nothing more can be affirmed with certainty, than that they are a work, or the epitome of a work, belonging to the Augustan age.

The strongest evidence which exists in favour of the authorship of C. Nepos, is that Jerome Magius, a contemporary of Lambinus, who also published an annotated edition of the "*Vitæ Illustrium Imperatorum*," found a MS. with the following conclusion: "Completum est opus Æmilii Probi Cornelii Nepotis." These words would seem to assert the authorship of

---

[896] Ad Att. i. 19; Liv. iv. 23; x. 9.
[897] Hieron. Chron. Euseb.
[898] Præf. Epigr. i. 3.
[899] Gell. xv. 28.
[900] Cic. ad Att. xvi. 5.
[901] Lib. xvii. 21, 3.
[902] Lib. i. 3.
[903] A. Gell. vii. 18; xxi. 8.
[904] Ibid. xv. 28.
[905] Lactant. Inst. Div. iii. 15.
[906] C. Nep. Vit. Dion. 3.

Nepos, and at the same time to admit that Probus was the editor or epitomator, and thus support the theory of Lambinus, without accusing Probus of a literary forgery.

C. Julius Cæsar (Born B. C. 100.)

To give a biographical account of Cæsar would be, in fact, nothing less than to trace the contemporary history of Rome; for 359Roman history had now become the history of those master-minds who seized upon, or were invested by their countrymen with, supreme power. Although the rapid and energetic talents of Cæsar never permitted him to lose a day, his active devotion to the truly Roman employments of politics and war, left him little time for sedentary occupations. His literary biography, therefore, will necessarily occupy but a short space, compared with the other great events of his career.

C. Julius Cæsar was descended from a family of the Julian *gens*, one of the oldest among the patrician families of Rome, of which all but a very few had by this time become extinct. The Cæsar family was not only of patrician descent, but numbered amongst its members, during the century which preceded the birth of the Dictator, many who had served curule offices with great distinction. He was born on the 4th of the ides of July (the 12th,) B. C. 100, and attached himself, both by politics and by matrimonial connexion to the popular party: his good taste, great tact, and pleasing manners, contributed, together with his talents, to insure his popularity. He became a soldier in the nineteenth year of his age; and hence his works display all the best qualities which are fostered by a military education, and which therefore characterize the military profession—frankness, simplicity, and brevity. He served his first campaign at the conclusion of the first Mithridatic war, during which he was present at the siege and capture of Mitylene,[907] and received the honour of a civic crown for saving the life of a citizen.

His earliest literary triumph was as an orator. Cn. Dolabella was suspected of oppressive extortion in the administration of his province of Macedonia, and Cæsar came forward as his accuser. The celebrated Hortensius was the advocate for the accused; and although Cæsar did not gain his cause, the skill and eloquence which he displayed as a pleader gave promise of his becoming hereafter a consummate orator. The following year he increased his reputation by taking up the cause of the province of Achaia against C. Antonius, who was accused of the same crime as Dolabella; but he was again unsuccessful in the result.

360He subsequently sailed for Rhodes, in order to pursue the study of oratory under the direction of Apollonius Molon,[908] who was not only a teacher of rhetoric, but also an able and eloquent pleader in the courts of law. Cicero[909] bears testimony to his being a skilful instructor and an eloquent speaker, and received instruction from him when he came to Rome as an ambassador from Rhodes.[910] Cæsar, on his voyage, was captured by pirates; but after he was ransomed, he carried his intention into effect, and placed himself for a short time under the tuition of Molon. After his return to Rome,[911] a proposition was made to recall from exile those of the party of Lepidus, who had joined Sertorius, and he spoke in favour of the

---
[907] B. C. 80.
[908] Suet. Cæs. 4; Cic. Att. ii. 1.
[909] Brut. 91.
[910] B. C. 81.
[911] B. C. 70.

measure. Two years subsequently he delivered funeral orations in praise of his wife Cornelia, who was the daughter of Cinna, and his aunt Julia, the widow of Marius.

The Catilinarian conspiracy, in which, without reason, he was suspected of having been concerned, furnished him with another opportunity of displaying his ability as an orator. His speech in the senate on the celebrated nones of December, would probably have saved the lives of the conspirators, had not Cato's influence prevailed. Cæsar pleaded that it was unconstitutional to put Roman citizens to death by the vote of the senate, without a trial; but his arguments were overruled, and the measure which subsequently led to the fall and assassination of Cicero was carried. The following year,[912] when Metellus made this a subject of accusation against Cicero, Cæsar again supported the same view with his eloquence, but was unsuccessful.

Great, therefore, although it is said that his talents as an orator were, he never appears to have convinced his hearers. This may have been owing, not to deficiency in skill, but to the unfortunate nature of the causes which he took in hand, or to the superior powers of his opponents, for there is no doubt that his manner of speaking was most engaging and popular. Tacitus speaks of him not only as the greatest of authors,[913] but also as rivalling the most accomplished orators;[914] whilst Suetonius praises 361his eloquence, and quotes the testimony of Cicero himself in support of his favourable criticism.[915]

Hitherto, with the exception of his first campaign, the life of Cæsar was of a civil complexion. His literary eminence took the colouring of the public occupations in which he was engaged. Like a true Roman, literature was subordinate to public duty, and his taste was directed into the channel which was most akin to, and identified with, his life. His intellectual vigour, however, demanded employment as well as his practical talents for business; and for this reason, as has been seen, he devoted himself to the study of oratory; and the principal works which as yet obtain for him a place in a history of Roman literature are merely orations.

His next official appointment opened to him a new field for thought. In B. C. 63 he obtained the office of Pontifex Maximus, and examined so diligently into the history and nature of the Roman belief in augury, of which he was the official guardian, that his investigations were published in a work consisting of at least sixteen books (*Libri Auspiciorum*.[916]) In order to fit himself for discharging the duties of his office he studied astronomy, and even wrote a treatise on that science,[917] entitled "*de Astris*", and a poem somewhat resembling the Phenomena of Aratus. His knowledge of this science enabled him, with the aid of the Alexandrian astronomers, to carry into effect some years[918] afterwards the reformation of the calendar.

The works above mentioned are philosophically and scientifically valueless, but curious and interesting; but we have now to view Cæsar in that capacity which was the foundation of his literary reputation. He obtained the province of Hispania Ulterior;[919] and at this post his career as a military commander began. As had been the case during his previous career, so

---

[912] B. C. 62.
[913] Germ. 28.
[914] Annal. xiii. 3.
[915] Suet. v. Jul. 55.
[916] See Macr. Sat. i. 16.
[917] Ibid.
[918] B. C. 46.
[919] B. C. 61.

now the almost incessant demands on his thoughts and time did not divert him from literary pursuits, but determined the channel in which his tastes should seek satisfaction, and furnished the subject for his pen. He had evidently an ardent love for literature for its 362own sake. It was not the paltry ambition of showing that he could achieve success, and, even superiority, in everything which he chose to undertake, although his versatility of talent was such as to encourage him to expect success, but a real attachment to literary employment. Hence whatever leisure his duties as a military commander permitted him to enjoy was devoted, as to a labour of love, to the composition of his Memoirs or Commentaries of the Gallic and Civil Wars.

His comprehensive and liberal mind was also convinced of the embarrassing technicalities which impeded the administration of the Roman law. Its interpretation was confined to a few who had studied its pedantic mysteries; and the laws which regulated the *dies fasti* and *nefasti* had originally placed its administration in the hands of the priests and patricians. Appius Claudius had already commenced the work of demolishing the fences which to the people at large were impregnable; and Cæsar entertained the grand design of reducing its principles and practice to a regular code.[920] His views he imbodied in a treatise,[921] which, as is often the case with pamphlets, perished when the object ceased to exist for which it was intended.

It is said that he also contemplated a complete survey and map of the Roman Empire.[922] But his greatest benefaction, perhaps, to the cause of Roman literature was the establishment of a public library.[923] The spoils of Italy, collected by Asinius Pollio, furnished the materials, just as the museums of Paris were enriched by the great modern conqueror from the plunder of Europe; but it was, nevertheless, a great and patriotic work; and he enhanced its utility by intrusting the collection and arrangement of it to the learned Varro as librarian.

Besides the works already named, Cæsar left behind him various letters, some of which are extant amongst those of Cicero; orations, of which, if the panegyrics of Cicero, Tacitus, and Quintilian[924] are not exaggerated, it is deeply to be regretted that the titles are alone preserved;[925] a short treatise or pamphlet, 363called *Anticato*; a work on the analogy of the Latin language; a collection of apothegms; and a few poems.

These are the grounds on which the claims of the great conqueror to literary fame rest in the various capacities of orator, historian, antiquarian, philosopher, grammarian, and poet; but by far the most important of his works is his "*Commentaries.*" These have fortunately come down to us in a tolerably perfect state, although much still remains to be done before we can be said to possess an accurate edition.[926] Seven books contain the history of seven years of the Gallic war, and three carry the history of the civil war down to the commencement of the Alexandrine. These are the works of Cæsar himself. The eighth book, "*De Bello Gallico,*" which completes the subject, and the three supplemental books of the work, "*De Bello Civili,*" which contain the Alexandrine, African, and Spanish wars, have been variously ascribed to the friends of Cæsar, A. Hirtius, C. Oppius, and even to Pansa. The claims of the latter, however, are entirely groundless. The marked similarity between the style of the eighth book

---

[920] Suet. V. Jul. 44.
[921] A. Gell. i. 22.
[922] Merivale's H. of R. ii. 422.
[923] Suet. 44; Plin. H. N. vii. 31.
[924] Cic. Brut. 72; Tac. Ann. xiii. 3; Quint. x. i. 114.
[925] Meyer, Fr. Or. Rom. p. 404.
[926] Nieb. Lect. R. H. xcv.

of the Gallic war and that of the Alexandrine war proves that they were written by the same author; and from the elegance and purity of the Latinity, and the confidential footing on which the author must have been with Cæsar, there is a probability, almost amounting to a certainty, that the History of the Alexandrine War must be the work of A. Hirtius. It may also be remarked that this opinion is in unison with that of Suetonius.[927]

Hirtius was the only one of the three who united in himself both these important qualifications. C. Oppius was indeed equally in the confidence of Cæsar; he was his inseparable companion.[928] But, nevertheless, Oppius was not so highly educated 364as Hirtius. Niebuhr, therefore, is probably correct in attributing to him, "without hesitation,"[929] the book on the African war. The intelligence and information displayed in it are worthy of the sensible soldier and confidential friend, with whom he corresponded in cipher, and whom he intrusted with writing the introduction to his defence in the "*Anticato*;" whilst the inferiority of the language marks a less skilful and practised hand than that of the refined Hirtius. The book on the Spanish war is by some unknown author: it is founded on a diary kept by someone engaged in the war; but neither its language nor sentiments are those of a liberally educated person.[930] The Greek term "*Ephemerides*" has sometimes been applied to the "*Commentaries*," though Bayle[931] thought that they were different works.

These memoirs are exactly what they profess to be, and are written in the most appropriate style. Few would wish it to be other than it is. They are sketches taken on the spot, in the midst of action, whilst the mind was full: they have all the graphic power of a master-mind, and the vigorous touches of a master-hand. Take, for example, the delineation of the Gallic character, and compare it with some of the features still to be found in the mixed race, their successors, and no one can doubt of its accuracy, or of the deep and penetrating insight into human nature which generally indicates the powerful and practical intellect. Their elegance and polish is that which always mark even the least-laboured efforts of a refined and educated taste, not that which proceeds from careful emendation and correction. The "*Commentaries*" are the materials for history; notes jotted down for future historians. It is evident that no more time was spent upon them than would naturally be devoted to such a work by one who was employing the inaction of winter quarters in digesting the recollections stored up during the business of the campaign; and for this reason few faults have been found with the "*Commentaries*," even by the most fastidious critics. The very faults which may be justly found with the style of Cæsar are such as reflect the man himself. The majesty of his character principally consists in the imperturbable calmness and equability of his temper. He had no sudden bursts of energy, and alternations of passion and inactivity: the elevation of his character was a high one, but it was a level table-land. This calmness and equability pervades his writings, and for this reason they have been thought to want life and energy; whereas in reality they are only deficient in contrast, and light and shade. The uniformity of his active character is interesting as one great element of his success; but the uniformity of style may perhaps be thought by some readers to diminish the interest with which his work is read.

---

[927] See Dodwell's Dissert. in Cæs. Ed. Var.
[928] The friendship which existed between these great men furnishes an anecdote (Suet. V. J. C. 72) characteristic of the most amiable feature in Cæsar's character, his devoted and hearty attachment to those whom he loved. Once, when they were journeying together, they reached a cottage, in which only one room was to be procured; Oppius was ill, and Cæsar gave up the room to his sick friend, whilst he bivouacked in the open air.
[929] Lect. R. H. xcv.
[930] See Niebuhr, Lect. R. H.
[931] Smith's Dict. in loco.

The simple beauty of his language is, as Cicero says, statuesque rather than picturesque. Simple, severe, naked—"omni ornatu orationis tanquam veste detracto;" and whilst, like a statue, it conveys the idea of perfect and well-proportioned beauty, it banishes all thoughts of human passion. It was this perfect calm propriety, perhaps this absence of all ornamental display, which prevented him from being a successful orator, and his orations from surviving, although he had every external qualification for a speaker[932]—a fine voice, graceful action, a noble and majestic appearance, and a frank and brilliant delivery.

The very few instances of doubtful Latinity which a hypercritical spirit may detect are scarcely blemishes, and fewer than might have been expected from the observation of Hirtius,[933] "Ceteri quam bene atque emendate, nos etiam, quam facile ac celeriter eos perscripserit, scimus." When A. Pollio[934] called his "*Commentaries*" hasty, his criticism was fair; but he was scarcely just in blaming the writer for inaccuracy and credulity. These faults, so far as they existed, were due to circumstances, not to himself. His observing mind wished to collect information with respect to the foreign lands which were the field of his exploits, and the habits of the inhabitants, quite as much as to describe his own tactics and victories. He naturally accepted the accounts given him, even when he had no means of testing their veracity. He is, therefore, not to blame for recording those which subsequent discoveries have shown to be untrue.

His digressions of this character yield in interest to no portion 366of his work; and though some of his accounts of the Gauls and Germans are incorrect, many were subsequently confirmed by the investigations of Tacitus. The only quality in the character of Cæsar which has been sometimes exaggerated is modesty. He does not, indeed, add to his own reputation by detracting from the merits of those who served under him. He is honest, generous, and candid, not only towards them, but also towards his brave barbarian enemies. Nor is he guilty of egotism in the strict literal sense of the term. This, however, is scarcely enough to warrant the eulogy which some have founded upon it. He has too good taste to recount his successes with pretension and arrogance; but he has evidently no objection to be the hero of his own tale. He skilfully veils his selfish, unpatriotic, and ambitious motives; and his object evidently is to leave such memoirs, that future historians may be able to hand down the most favourable character of Cæsar to posterity.

Though himself is his subject, his memoirs are not confessions. Not a record of a weakness appears, nor even of a defect, except that which the Romans would readily forgive, cruelty. His savage waste of human life he recounts with perfect self-complacency. Vanity was his crowning error in his career as a statesman; and though hidden by the reserve with which he speaks of himself, it sometimes discovers itself in the historian.

The "*Commentaries*" of Cæsar have sometimes been compared with the work of the great soldier historian of Greece, Xenophon. Both are eminently simple and unaffected; but there the parallel ends. The severe contempt of ornament which characterizes the stern Roman is totally unlike the mellifluous sweetness of the Attic writer.

The "*Anticatones*"[935] were two books in answer to Cicero's panegyric of Cato, which he had written immediately after the philosopher's death. Hirtius first, at the request of Cæsar, wrote a reply, and sent it to Cicero from Narbonne. Although he denied the justice of Cicero's

---

[932] Brut. 71, 72, 75.
[933] Præf. to book viii.
[934] Suet. 56.
[935] Juv. vi. 338; Suet. 56; Gell. iv. 16; Cic. Div. ii. 9.

eulogium, he secured the good-will of the orator himself by liberal commendations.[936] This prepared the way for Cæsar's own pamphlet.

367His philological work, *de Analogia*, or *de Ratione Latine Loquendi*, is commended by Cicero[937] for its extreme accuracy, and was held in high estimation by the Roman grammarians. Probably, in liveliness and originality, it was far superior to any of their works. Wonderful to say, it was written during the difficulties and occupations of a journey across the Alps. From the quotations from it, in the writings of the grammarians, we learn that he proposed that the letter V should be written ꟻ, to mark its connection with the Greek digamma; and that the new orthography, which substituted *lacrimæ* for *lucrumæ*, *maximus* for *maxumus*, &c., was established by his authority.

The "*Apophthegmata*" is said to have been a collection of wise and witty sayings by himself and others, although it is remarkable not a single witty saying of Cæsar is on record.[938] He began it early in life, and was continually making additions to it.

His poetical attempts consisted of a tragedy entitled "*Œdipus*;" a short piece, the subject of which was the praises of Hercules (both of these, as well as the Apophthegmata, were suppressed by Augustus;[939]) "*Iter*," an account of his march into Spain; the astronomical poem already mentioned; and some epigrams, of which three are extant, although their authenticity is somewhat doubtful.[940]

The character of Cæsar is full of inconsistencies; but they are the inconsistencies which are natural to man, and are sometimes found in men of a strong will and commanding talents who are destitute of moral principle. His faults and excellences, his capability and talents, were the result of his natural powers—not of pains or study. He was one of the greatest as well as one of 368the worst men who ever lived. He was an Epicurean in faith, and yet he had all the superstition which so often accompanies infidelity. His habitual humanity and clemency towards his fellow-citizens were interrupted by instances of stern and pitiless cruelty. He shed tears at the assassination of Pompey, and yet could massacre the Usipetes and the Tenchteri, and acted like a savage barbarian towards his chivalrous foe Vercingetorix. He delighted in the pure and refined pleasures of literature, and his intimate associates were men of taste and genius; and yet he was the slave of his sensual passions, and indulged in the grossest profligacy. He was candid, friendly, confiding, generous; but he was attracted by brilliant talents, and the qualities of the head, rather than the affections of the heart. The mainspring of his conduct as a general and a statesman exhibits a strong will and perfect self-reliance; and in like manner he owes the energy of his style of writing, and the persuasive force of his oratory, to the influence of no other minds: they are the natural fruit of clear perceptions, a penetrating intellect, an observing mind capable of taking a wide and comprehensive view of its subject. Men of varied acquirements and extensive knowledge, but of pedantic taste, are said to talk like books; the writings of Cæsar, on the contrary, are like

---

[936] Ad Att. xii. 40, 41, 44, 45; xiii. 37, 40, 48, 50.
[937] Cic. Brut. 72.
[938] See Nieb. L. R. H. xcv.; Suet. 66; Cic. ad Fam. ix. 16.
[939] Meyer's Lat. Anthol. 68, 69, 70.
[940] A. Gellius tells us (xvii. 9) that he was the author of Letters to Oppius, written in cipher, of which he gives the following interesting description:—"Erat conventum inter eos clandestinum de commutando situ literarum ut inscriptio quidem alia alius locum et nomen teneret sed in legendo locus cuique suus et potestas restitueretur." Suetonius (Vit. Cæs. 56) describes in the same way the nature of the cipher which he used, and illustrates it by saying that he used to put *d* for *a*, and so forth.

lively and unconstrained conversation: they have all the reality which constitutes the great charm of his character.

He was above affectation, for his was a mind born to lead the age in which he lived, not to think with others merely in deference to established usage and custom; and although his natural vanity and self-confidence led him to set his own character in the most favourable light, his vanity was honest: he had no intention willfully to deceive. His wonderful memory fitted him for the task of faithfully recording the events in which he himself was an actor; and his power of attention and abstraction, which enabled him to write, converse, and dictate at the same time, shows how valuable must be a work on which were concentrated at once all the energies of his penetrating mind.

Chapter 26

LIFE OF SALLUST—HIS INSINCERITY—HIS HISTORICAL WORKS—HE WAS A BITTER OPPONENT OF THE NEW ARISTOCRACY—PROFLIGACY OF THAT ORDER—HIS STYLE COMPARED WITH THAT OF THUCYDIDES—HIS VALUE AS AN HISTORIAN—TROGUS POMPEIUS—HIS HISTORIÆ PHILIPPICÆ

C. SALLUSTIUS CRISPUS (BORN B. C. 85.)

C. Sallustius Crispus was fifteen years junior to Cæsar: he was born at Amiternum[941] in the territory of the Sabines, A. U. C. 669, B. C. 85. He was a member of a plebeian family; but, having served the offices of tribune and quæstor, attained senatorial rank. In A. U. C. 704, he was expelled from the senate[942] by the censors Ap. Claudius Pulcher and L. Calpurnius Piso.[943] It is said that, although he was "a most severe censurer of the licentiousness of others,"[944] he was a profligate man himself, and that the scandal of an intrigue with Fausta, the daughter of Sulla and the wife of Milo, was the cause of his degradation.

Through the influence of Cæsar, whose party he espoused, he was restored to his rank, and subsequently became prætor. He accompanied his patron in the African war, and was made governor of Numidia. Whilst in that capacity, he accumulated by rapacity and extortion enormous wealth,[945] which he lavished on expensive but tasteful luxury. The gardens on the Quirinal which bore his name were celebrated for their beauty; and beneath their alleys, and porticoes, surrounded by the choicest works of art, he avoided the tumultuous scenes of civil strife which ushered in the empire, and devoted his retirement to composing the historical records which survived him. His death took place B. C. 35.

---

[941] Matth. H. L.
[942] Heind. on Hor. Sat. p. 40.
[943] Dion. Cas. xi. 63.
[944] Macrob. Saturn. ii. 9.
[945] Dion. xliii. 9.

Those who have wished to defend the character of Sallust from the charges of immorality, to which allusion has been made, have attributed them to the groundless calumnies of Lenæus, a freedman of Cæsar's great rival Pompey. It is not improbable that his faults may have been exaggerated by the malevolence of party-spirit in those factious times; but there are no sentiments in his works which can constitute a defence of him. If an historian is distinguished by a high moral tone of feeling, this quality cannot but show itself in his writings without intention or design. But in Sallust there is always an affectation and pretence of morality without the reality. His philosophical reflections at the commencement of the Jugurthine and Catilinarian wars are empty, cold, and heartless. There is a display of commonplace sentiment, and an expressed admiration of the old Roman virtue of bygone days, but no appearance of sincerity. The language may be pointed enough to produce an effect upon the ear, but the sentiments always fail to probe the recesses of the heart. Sallust lived in an immoral and corrupt age; and though, perhaps, he was not amongst the worst of his contemporaries, he had not sufficient strength of principle to resist the force of example and temptation.

It is almost certain that, as a provincial governor, Sallust was not more unscrupulous than others of his class; but wealth such as he possessed could not have been acquired except by extortion and maladministration. As a politician, he was equally unsatisfactory: he was a mere partisan of Cæsar, and therefore, a strenuous opponent of the higher classes as supporters of Pompey; but he was not an honest champion of popular rights, nor was he capable of understanding the meaning of patriotism. If, however, we make some allowance for the political bias of Sallust, which is evident throughout his works, his histories have not only the charms of the historical romance, but are also valuable political studies. His characters are vigorously and naturally drawn, as though he not only personally knew them, but accurately understood them. The more his histories are read the more will it be discovered that he always writes with an object. He eschews the very idea of a mere dry chronicle of facts, and uses his facts as the means of enforcing a great political lesson.

For this reason, like Thucydides, whom he evidently took as his model, not only in style but in the use of his materials, his speeches are his own compositions. Even when he had an opportunity, as in the case of Cæsar's and Cato's speeches in the "*Bellum Catilinarium*," he contented himself with giving the substance of them, clothed it in his own language, and imbodied in them his own sentiments. According to his own statement, there is one exception to his practice in this respect. He asserts that the speech of Memmius, the tribune of the people,[946] is the very one which he delivered. If this be really the case, it is a most valuable example of the style in which a popular leader addressed his audience. But it is to be feared that this is not strictly and literally true: the style is indeed somewhat different from that of the other speeches, but does not exhibit freedom enough to assure us that he has actually reported it as delivered. It may be only a specimen of that consummate skill which constitutes the principal charm of Sallust's manner, and made him a complete master of composition. Sallust never attempted anything more than detached portions of Roman history. "I have determined," he says, "to write only select portions of Roman history," (carptim perscribere.[947]) He himself gives an explanation of his motives for so doing,[948] when he

---

[946] Jug. c. 30.
[947] Cat. iv.
[948] Bel. Cat. Vii.

complains of the manner in which this department of literature was neglected. Wherever a satisfactory account existed, he thought it unnecessary to travel over the same ground a second time.

His first work, reckoning according to the chronological order of events, is the Jugurthine war, which commenced B. C. 111, and ended B. C. 106. The next period, comprehending the social war and the war of Sulla, extending as far as the consulship of M. Æmilius Lepidus, B. C. 78, had already been related by Sisenna, a friend of Cicero.[949] Where Sisenna left off, the Histories of Sallust (Historiarum Libri V.) began, and continued the narrative without interruption until the prætorship of Cicero.[950] This work is unfortunately lost, with the exception of some letters and speeches, and a few fragments relating to the war of Spartacus. Niebuhr[951] considers this one of the most deplorable losses in Roman literature; less, however, on account of its historical importance, than as a perfect model of historical composition. A break of two years ensues, and then follows the "*Bellum Catilinarium*," or history of the Catilinarian conspiracy in the year of Cicero's consulship.[952]

This completes the list of those works which are undoubtedly genuine. No satisfactory opinion has been arrived at respecting the authorship of the two letters to Cæsar, "*De Republicâ Ordinandâ*;" and it is now unhesitatingly admitted, that the declamation against Cicero, must have been, as well as its counterpart, the declamation against Sallust, the work of some rhetorical writer of a later period. The subject of this imaginary disputation was naturally suggested by the known fact that Sallust was no friend to Cicero.

It has already been stated that Sallust was a bitter opponent of the principles and policy of the aristocratic party; but it must be carefully explained what is meant by that assertion. The object of his hatred was not the old patrician blood of Rome, but the new aristocracy, which had of late years been rapidly rising up and displacing it.

This new nobility was utterly corrupt; and their corruption was encouraged by the venality of the masses, whose poverty and destitution tempted them to be the tools of unscrupulous ambition. Everything at Rome, as Juvenal said in later times, had its price. Sallust adds to the severity of his strictures upon his countrymen by the force of contrast; he represents even Jugurtha as asserting that the republic itself might be bought, if a purchaser could be found; and paints the barbarian as more honest and upright than his conquerors. The ruined and abandoned associates of Catiline represented a numerous class among the younger members of the upper classes, who, by lives devoted to lawless pleasures, had become ruined, reckless, and demoralized. They were ripe for revolution, because they had nothing to lose: they could not gratify their vicious propensities without wealth; they had no principles or scruples as to the means of acquiring it; their best prospects were in anarchy, proscription, and confiscation. The debauched and ruined nobleman, and the vulgar profligate of the lowest class, forgot their mutual differences, and thus a combination was formed, the members of which were the sink and outscourings of society.

Such degenerate profligacy is an ample justification of Sallust's hatred towards the new aristocracy; and the object of all his works evidently was to place that party in the unfavourable light which it deserved. In the Jugurthine war he describes the unworthiness of the foreign policy of Rome under its maladministration. His "*Histories*," according to the

---

[949] De Leg. i. 2; Brut. 64.
[950] B. C. 66.
[951] Lect. R. H. lxxxviii.
[952] B. C. 63.

statement of Niebuhr, describe the popular resistance to the revolutionary policy of Sulla, the profligate leader of the same party; and in the *"Catilinarian war"* he paints in vivid colours the depravity of that order of society, who, bankrupt in fortune and dead to all honourable feelings, still plumed themselves on their rank and exclusiveness. Nevertheless, notwithstanding the truthfulness of the picture which Sallust draws, selfishness and not patriotism was the mainspring of his politics; and it is scarcely possible to avoid seeing that he is anxious to set himself off to the best advantage. His hollowness is that of a vain and conceited man, who measures himself by too high a standard, and appears chagrined and disappointed that others do not estimate him as highly as he does himself.

These are the blots in his character as a man and a citizen; but we must not forget his real merits as an historian. To him must be conceded the praise of having first conceived the notion of a history in the true sense of the term. He saw the lamentable defects in the abortive attempts made by his predecessors;[953] and the model was a good one which he left for his successors to follow. It is scarcely too much to suppose, that if it had not been for Sallust, Livy might not have been led to conceive his vast and comprehensive plan. He was the first Roman historian, and the guide to future historians. Again, his style, although almost ostentatiously elaborate and artificial, and not without affectation, is, upon the whole, pleasing, and almost always transparently clear. The caution of Quintilian respecting his well-known brevity ("vitanda est illa Sallustiana brevitas"[954]) is well-timed in his work, as being addressed to orators, for public speaking necessarily requires a more diffuse style; and it is probable that Quintilian would not appreciate its merits, because he himself was a rhetorician, and his taste was formed in a rhetorical age. Seneca, for the same reasons, finds similar faults, not only with Sallust, but with the favourite literature of his day. "When Sallust flourished, abrupt sentences, unexpected cadences, obscure expressions, were considered signs of a cultivated taste."[955] But the brevity of Sallust does not produce the effect of harsh or disagreeable abruptness, whilst it keeps the attention awake, and impresses the facts upon the memory. How powerful and suggestive, for example, how abundant in material for thought, are those few words in which he describes Pompey as "oris probi, animo inverecundo!" There is, however, this difference between the brevity of Sallust and that of his supposed model, Thucydides. That of the Greek historian was natural and involuntary; that of the Roman intentional and the result of imitation. Thucydides thought more quickly than he could write: his closely-packed ideas and condensed constructions, therefore, constitute a species of shorthand, by which alone he could keep pace with the rapidity of his intellect. He is, therefore, always vigorous and suggestive; and the necessities of the case make the reader readily pardon the difficulties of his style.

The brevity of Thucydides is the result of condensation; that of Sallust is elliptical expression. He gives a hint and the reader must supply the rest; whilst Thucydides only expects his readers to unfold and develop ideas which already existed in a concentrated form. Sallust requires addition; Thucydides dilution and expansion. Neither does the brevity of Sallust resemble that of Cæsar or of Tacitus: the former was straight-forward and business-like, requiring neither addition nor expansion, because he wished to make his statements as clear as they were capable of being expressed, without ornament or exaggeration. He was

---

[953] Cat. vii.
[954] Quint. I. O. x. 1.
[955] Ep. cxiv.

brief, because he never wished to say more than was absolutely necessary, and therefore his brevity is the very cause of perspicuity. The mind of Tacitus was, from its thoughtfulness and philosophical character, the very counterpart of that of Thucydides: his brevity was therefore natural and the result of the same causes.

There is one point of view in which Sallust is invaluable as an historian. He had always an object to which he wished all his facts to converge: he brought forward his facts as illustrations and developments of principles. He analyzed and exposed the motives of parties, and the secret springs which actuated the conduct of individuals, and laid bare the inner life of those great actors on the public stage, in the interesting historical scenes which he undertakes to describe.

TROGUS POMPEIUS

Trogus Pompeius was a voluminous historian of the Augustan age, whose father was private secretary to Julius Cæsar.[956] His work was of such vast extent, and embraced so great a variety of subjects, that it has even been termed by Justin, who published a large collection of extracts from it, *a Universal History*. Its title, however, "*Historiæ Philippicæ*," proves the writer's primary object was the history of the Macedonian monarchy, together with the kingdoms which arose out of it at the death of Alexander; and that all the rest of the information contained in it were digressions into which he was naturally led, and episodes incidentally introduced into the main stream of the history.

For the materials contained in his work, which consisted of forty-four books, he was indebted to the Greek historians, but especially to Theopompus of Chios,[957] from whose principal work he derived the title, "*Philippica*," as well as the practice of branching out into long and frequent digressions. It is easy to imagine over how vast an area a history of the Macedonian empire was capable of extending. The subjugation of the East by the conquests of Alexander naturally made a rapid sketch of the Assyrian, Median, and Persian empires, an appropriate introduction to the work: the connexion of Persia with Greece and Egypt furnished an opportunity of imbodying the records of Greek history, and a description of Egypt and its inhabitants. Once embarked in Greek history, the writer pursued it until it became interwoven, through the interference of Philip, with the affairs of Macedon. Alexander and his successors succeed: the campaigns of Pyrrhus bring the Romans upon the stage; Carthage and Sicily for awhile occupy the scene; and the main body of the work is completed by a sketch of the gradual consolidation of that vast empire, of which subjugated Macedonia became a province. Nor is this all—other less important nations, states, and cities are ever and anon introduced, according as they act their part in the great drama of history.

---

[956] Justin, xliii. 5.
[957] Born B. C. 378.

Chapter 27

LIFE OF LIVY—HIS OBJECT IN WRITING HIS HISTORY—ITS SPIRIT AND CHARACTER—LIVY PRECISELY SUITED TO HIS AGE—NOT WILFULLY INACCURATE—HIS POLITICAL BIAS ACCOUNTED FOR—MATERIALS WHICH HE MIGHT HAVE USED—SOURCES OF HIS HISTORY—HIS DEFECTS AS AN HISTORIAN—HIS STYLE—GRAMMARIANS—VITRUVIUS POLLIO AN AUGUSTAN WRITER—CONTENTS OF HIS WORK

T. LIVIUS PATAVINUS (BORN B. C. 59.)

The biographical records of many great literary men of Rome are most meager and unsatisfactory. Modern critics who have written their lives have drawn largely upon their own imaginations for their materials; whilst all the information to be derived from ancient writers is often comprised in a few vague allusions and notices. Some of these have been misunderstood, and from others unwarrantable deductions have been derived. These observations are particularly applicable to him who is the only illustrious Roman historian in the Augustan age.

Universal tradition assigns to Patavium (Padua) the honour of being the birthplace of Titus Livius; but notwithstanding the general belief, some doubt has been thrown upon the fact by an epigram of Martial.[958] He came to Rome during the reign of Augustus, where he resided in the enjoyment of the imperial favour and patronage.[959] He was a warm and open admirer of the ancient institutions of the country, and esteemed Pompey as one of its greatest heroes; but Augustus, with his usual liberality, did not allow political opinions to interfere with the regard which he entertained for the historian. Livy had a great admiration for oratory,

---
[958] Ep. I. 62.
[959] Tac. Ann. iv. 34.

and advised his son to study the writings of Demosthenes and Cicero.[960] At his recommendation the stupid Claudius wrote history;[961] and it has even been asserted, though on insufficient authority, that he was his instructor. His fame rapidly spread beyond the limits of Italy, for Pliny the younger[962] relates that an inhabitant of Cadiz came to Rome for the express purpose of seeing him; a fact which St. Jerome[963] expands into an assertion that many noble Gauls and Spaniards were attracted to the capital, far more by the reputation of Livy than by the splendour of the imperial city.

His great work is a history of Rome, which he modestly terms "*Annals,*" in one hundred and forty-two books, preceded by a brief but elaborately-written preface,[964] and extending from the earliest traditions to the death of Drusus.[965] Of this history thirty-five books are extant, which were discovered at different periods.[966] Of the rest we have only dry and meager epitomes, drawn up by some uncertain author, and of these two are lost.[967]

Besides his History, Livy is said[968] to have written books which professed to be philosophical, and dialogues, the subjects of which are partly philosophical, and partly historical. Late in life he returned to Patavium, and there died A. D. 18, in the seventy-seventh year of his age.[969] He left one son, and one daughter who married L. Magius, a teacher of rhetoric, of no great talent, who owed his reputation principally to his connection with the historian.[970] Livy had one great object in view in writing his History, namely, to celebrate the glories of his native country, to which he was devotedly attached. He was a patriot: his sympathy was with Pompey, called forth by the disinterestedness of that great man, and perhaps by his sad end, after having so long enjoyed universal popularity. The character of the historian would lead us to suppose that his attachment was personal rather than political, for the general spirit of his work shows that he was a man of pure mind and gentle feelings. He began his great work about nine or ten years before the Christian era, a period singularly favourable for such a design. The passages in which especially he delights to put forth his powers, and on which he dwells 379with the greatest zest, show the truth of Quintilian's well-known criticism, "that he is especially the historian of the affections, particularly of the softer sensibilities."[971] A lost battle is misery to him; he trembles at the task of relating it. Nor does he appear to have been a stern republican. He could admire enthusiastically, and describe with spirit, the noble qualities and self-devotion which the old republican freedom fostered; but his object is rather to paint the heroes, and to give graphic representations of the struggles which they maintained in defence of liberty, than to show any love of liberty in the abstract, or a predilection for any particular form of constitution. To Livy political struggles were no more than subjects for picturesque delineations, the moral of which was the elevation of national grandeur, just as successful foreign wars were the records of national glory. Hence he is a biographer quite as much as an historian: he anatomizes the

---

[960] Quint. x. i. 39.
[961] Suet. V. Cl. 41.
[962] Ep. II. 3.
[963] Nisard, ii. 405.
[964] Lib. xliii. 13.
[965] B. C. 9.
[966] See Smith's Biog. ii. 791.
[967] *Viz.*, 136 and 137.
[968] Sen. Suasor. 100.
[969] Euseb. Chron.
[970] Sen. Proem. to Controv. V.
[971] Inst. Or. x. 1.

moral nature of his heroes, and shows their inner man, and the motive springs of their noble exploits. This gives to his narratives the charm of an historical romance, and makes up for the want of accurate research and political observation. His characters stand before us objectively, like epic heroes; and thus he is "the Homer of the Roman people," whilst the charm of his narratives makes him the "Herodotus of Roman historians."

Rome was now the mistress of the world: her struggles with foreign nations had been rewarded with universal dominion; so that when the Roman Empire was spoken of, no title less comprehensive than "the world" (*orbis*) would satisfy the national vanity. The horrors of civil war had ceased, and were succeeded by an amnesty of its bitter feuds and bloody animosities. Liberty indeed had perished, but the people were no longer fit for the enjoyment of it; and it was exchanged for a mild and paternal rule, under which all the refinements of civilization were encouraged, and its subjects could enjoy undisturbed the blessings of peace and security.

Rome, therefore, had rest and breathing-time to look back into the past—to trace the successive steps by which that marvelous 380edifice, the Roman Empire, had been constructed. She could do this, too, with perfect self-complacency, for there was no symptom of decay to check her exultation, or to mar the glories which she was contemplating.

Livy, the good, the affectionate, the romantic, was precisely the popular historian for such times as these. His countrymen looked naturally for panegyric rather than for criticism. They were not in a temper to bear one who could remorselessly tear open and expose to view all the faults and blemishes which blotted the pages of their history; who could be a morose and querulous praiser of times gone by, never to return, at the expense of their present greatness and prosperity. He lived in happy times, before Rome had learnt by sad experience what the tyranny of absolutism really was. He tells his story like a bard singing his lay at a joyous and festive meeting, chequered by alternate successes and reverses, prosperity and adversity, but all tending to a happy end at last. These features of his character, and this object of his work, whilst they constitute his peculiar charm as a narrator, obviously render him less valuable as an historian. Although he was not tasteless and spiritless, like Dionysius, he was not so trustworthy. He would not be willfully inaccurate, or otherwise than truth-telling; but if the legend he was about to tell was captivating and interesting, he would not stop to inquire whether or not it was true. He would take upon trust the traditions which had been handed down from generation to generation without inquiry; and the more flattering and popular they were, the more suitable would he deem them for his purpose. Without being himself necessarily superstitious, he would see that superstitious marvels added to the embellishments of his story, and, therefore, would accept them without pronouncing upon their truth or falsehood.

Willful unfairness can never be attributed to Livy: he was prejudiced, but he was not party-spirited. He loved his country and his countrymen, and could scarcely persuade himself of the possibility of their doing wrong. He could scarcely believe anything derogatory to the national glory. When (to take a striking example,) in the case of the treaty with Porsena, there 381were two opposite stories, he was led by this partiality to ignore the well-authenticated fact of the capture of Rome, and to adopt that account which was most creditable to his countrymen.[972] Whenever Rome was false to treaties, unmerciful in victory, or unsuccessful

---

[972] See Plin. H. N. xxxiv. 39, and Tac. Hist. iii. 72.

in arms, he is always anxious to find excuses. His predilections are evidently aristocratic; and although he states the facts fairly, he wishes his reader to sympathize with the patricians.

The plebeians of the days in which he lived were not the fair representatives of that enterprising class in the early ages of the republic, who were as well born as the patricians, although of different blood; the strength and sinews of the state in its exhausting wars—dependent only upon them from stern necessity, because they were ground down to the dust by poverty, and debt, and oppression, but independently maintaining themselves by their own industry, gradually acquiring wealth, rising to the position of a middle class, winning their way perseveringly, step by step, to political privileges.

The lower orders of Rome, in the time of Livy—for the term plebeian, in its original sense, was no longer applicable—were debased and degraded; they cared not for liberty or political power, or self-government; their bosoms throbbed not with sympathy for the old plebeians, who retired to Mount Sacer, and shed their blood for their principles. It was difficult, therefore, for him not to believe that the popular leaders of old times were unprincipled men, who sought to repair their fortunes by the arts of the demagogue. In his eyes resistance to tyranny was treason and rebellion.[973] But when, as in the story of Virginia, his gentler affections were enlisted, Livy's heart warmed with a generous admiration towards the champions of the people's rights, and his political predilections gave way to his sensibilities. In treating of history almost contemporaneous, Tacitus confesses his liberality. Although it might have rendered him more acceptable at the court of his patron if he had vilified his political foes, yet even imperial favour, acting on the same side 382as political prejudice, did not tempt him to unfairness.[974] He could see and acknowledge noble qualities and disinterested patriotism, and give credit for sincere motives, even to those who differed in political opinions.

From a character such as has been described, much care is not to be expected as to the sources from which historical information was derived. Many original documents must have existed in his day, which he evidently never took the trouble to consult. A rich treasure of original monuments relating to foreign and domestic affairs were ready at hand, which might have been examined without much trouble.[975] The great Annals of the Pontifex Maximus were digested into eighty books; and these contained the names of the magistrates, all memorable events at home and abroad—even the very days on which they occurred being marked. The commentaries not only of the priests and augurs, but of the civil magistrates, were kept with exactness and regularity. There is no reason for supposing that the *Libri Lintei*[976] were lost in Livy's time, although he quotes from Licinius Macer,[977] instead of consulting them himself. Three thousand brazen tablets, on which were engraved acts of the senate and the plebeians, extending backwards (says Suetonius[978]) almost to the building of the city, existed in the Capitol until it was burnt in the reign of Vespasian. The corpus of civil law, which is known to have existed in the time of Cicero,[979] was full of antiquarian lore; and the twelve tables furnished invaluable information, not only on language, but on the manners

---

[973] See i. 50; iv. 35; vi. 27.
[974] Augustus, according to Tacitus, (Ann. iv. 3,) thought Livy so violent a Pompeian that he once forbade one of his grandsons to read his history.
[975] Cic. Or. ii. 12; Quint. x. 2, 7; Serv. in Æn. i. 373.
[976] See Arnold's Hist. of Rome.
[977] Lib. x. 38; iv. 7, 23.
[978] Vesp. 8. See also Tac. Hist. iii. 71.
[979] Or. i. 43.

and habits of bygone times. Nevertheless the fragments of the *Leges Regiæ* and the laws of the twelve tables have been more carefully examined by critics of modern times than they were by Livy, when they existed in a more perfect condition.

Lachmann[980] has satisfactorily shown that the assertions of Livy are not based upon personal investigation, but that he trusted to the annalists, and took advantage of the researches of preceding historians. This is all that he himself professes to do; and even these professions he does not always satisfactorily perform. He does not appear to have profited by the Annals of Varro or the *Origines* of Cato, a work which, according to the testimony of Cicero, must have been invaluable to an historian; and although the Archæologia of Dionysius were published about the time at which Livy commenced his history,[981] there is no evidence that he makes use of it; certainly he never acknowledges any obligation to the indefatigable researches of the Greek historian. According to his own confession,[982] Roman history is total darkness until the capture of Rome by the Gauls; and although a dim light then begins to break, a twilight period succeeds, which continues until the first Punic war. But it cannot be asserted that he prepared himself for his difficult task as he ought, or took advantage of all the means at his disposal to enlighten the obscurity in which his subject was involved. The authorities on which he principally depends for the contents of the first Decade were such as Ennius, Fab. Pictor, Cincius, and Piso. It is evident that he also consulted Greek writers. In the third, which contains the most beautiful and elaborate passages of the whole work, he follows Polybius. Nor could he, in this portion of his history, follow a safer one. The Romans, notwithstanding all their practical tendencies, did little to promote geographical science. It is amongst the Greeks that we find the most accurate and indefatigable geographers, such as were Polybius, Strabo, and Ptolemy.

Polybius prepared himself for the task of narrating the Italian campaign of Hannibal by personal inspection. Livy did nothing of the kind. The former travelled through the Alpine passes; and his authority was considered so good that Strabo implicitly followed him. It is to be lamented that, as he was writing to his countrymen, he seldom mentions the name of places; probably he thought they would not be the wiser for the enumeration of unknown barbarian names. But his accuracy in dates and distances enables us to trace Hannibal's route with correctness. These prove that the passage of Hannibal was by the Alpis Graia, the Little St. Bernard; a statement which had been made by that veracious[983] historian, Cælius Antipater, and also by Cornelius Nepos.[984] It has been since confirmed by the researches of modern travelers, such as General Melville, M. de Luc, Cramer, and Wickham. Strange to say, Livy, although following the route marked out by Polybius almost step by step, at length ends it with the Alpis Cottia (M. Genevre.) The absence of names left the fireside traveller at fault. Cæsar[985] had crossed the Alps by that pass; and, perhaps, Livy named it at a venture, as the most familiar to him. In the succeeding portions of his work, so complete is the confidence which he reposes upon the guidance of Polybius, that the fourth and fifth Decades are little more than the history of Polybius paraphrased.

---

[980] Com. de Font. Hist. Liv.
[981] *Vide* Niebuhr (Lect. on Rom. Lit. vii.,) who takes the opposite view.
[982] Lib. ii. 21; iv. 7; vi. 1.
[983] Val. Max. i. 7; ad Att. xiii. 8.
[984] V. Hann. 22. Cornelius Nepos says that the Alpis Graia derived its name from Hercules having passed by that route. Probably the real derivation of the epithet is the root of the German "Grau."
[985] Bell. Gall. i. 11.

Niebuhr,[986] from internal evidence, gives an interesting account of the manner in which it is probable that Livy wrote his history. He supposes that, like most of the ancients, he employed a secretary, who read to him from existing authorities the events of a single year. These the historian mentally arranged, and then dictated his own narrative. The work, therefore, was composed in portions; the connection of the events of one year with those of the preceding one was lost sight of, and thus they seem isolated; and the conclusion of a series of events sometimes unaccountably synchronizes with the conclusion of a year.

To his deficiencies in the habit of diligent and accurate investigation are added others which singularly disqualify him for the task of a faithful historian. He was a reader of books rather than a student of men and things; he took upon trust what other people told him, instead of acquiring knowledge in a practical manner. He was ill-acquainted with the history of foreign countries. He was not, like Cæsar, a soldier; and therefore his descriptions of military affairs are often vague and indistinct, for he did not understand the tactics which he professed to describe. He was not, like Thucydides, a politician or a philosopher; and hence the little trustworthy information which we derive from him on questions connected with constitutional changes. He did not fit himself, like Herodotus, by travelling; and thus he is often ignorant of the localities which he describes, even though they are within the limits of Italy. Hence the difficulties in the way of understanding the route of Hannibal and his army across the Alps, the battle of Thrasimene, and the defeat at the Caudine Forks. He was not a philosopher, a lawyer, or a politician: he could embrace with the eye and depict with the hand of an artist everything which was external and tangible; but he could not penetrate the secret motives which actuate the human will, nor form a clear conception of the fundamental, legal and political principles which animated the institutions, and gave rise to the peculiarities, of Roman constitutional history.

With respect to the speeches which he attributes to his principal heroes, a greater degree of accuracy cannot be expected, than is found in those of Thucydides. But they do not possess that verisimilitude which is so admirable in those of the Greek historian. As works of art they are faultless, but Livy does not keep in view the principle adhered to by Thucydides, that they should be such as the speakers were likely to have delivered on the occasions in question. His great authority, Polybius, disapproves of imaginary speeches altogether;[987] but it must be remembered that, without some oratorical display, he would not have pleased the Roman people. The speeches of Thucydides, although they bear the stamp of the writer's mind, are, to a certain extent, characteristic of the speaker, and seem inspired by the occasion. If a Spartan speaks, he is laconic; if a general, he is soldier-like; if a statesman or demagogue, he is logical or argumentative, or appeals to the feelings and passions of the Athenian people. Consistency produces variety. The speeches of Livy are pleasing and eloquent,[988] but they are always, so to speak, Livian; they are frequently not such as Romans would have spoken in times when eloquence was rude, though forcible. They partake of the rhetorical and declamatory spirit, which was already beginning to creep over Roman literature; and often, from being unsuitable to time, place, and person, diminish, instead of heightening, the dramatic effect.

---

[986] R. L. Lect. viii.
[987] Lib. ii. 56, 10.
[988] Quint. x. i. 101.

Such are the principal defects which cause us to regret that, whilst Livy charms us with his romantic narratives and almost faultless style, he is too often a fallacious guide as an historian, and gives, not intentionally or dishonestly, but from the character of his mind, and the object which he proposed to himself, a false colouring or a vague and inaccurate outline to the events which he narrates. No one can avoid relishing the liveliness, freshness, and "lactea ubertas," of Livy's fascinating style; but its principal excellence is summed up in the expression of Quintilian, "*clarissimus candor*," (brightness and lucidity.[989]) On the authority of Asinius Pollio, quoted by the same writer,[990] a certain fault has been attributed to him, termed "Patavinity," i. e., some peculiar ideas not admissible in the purest Latin, which mark the place of his nativity. So little pains do people take in the investigation of truth, and so ready are they to take upon trust what their predecessors have believed before them, that generation after generation have assumed that Livy's clear, eloquent, and transparent style is disfigured by what we term provincialisms.[991] The penetrating mind of Niebuhr finds no ground for believing the story. If there is any truth in it, he supposes the criticism must have applied to his speaking, and not to his writing.[992] His style is always classical, even in the later decades: though prolix and tautologous, it is invariably marked by idiomatic purity and grammatical accuracy.

GRAMMARIANS

The grammarians may be passed over with little more notice than the simple mention of their names, because, although they 387contributed to the stock of their country's literature, they added little or nothing to its literary reputation. The most conspicuous amongst them were—Atteius Philologus, a freedman and friend of Sallust; Staberius Eros, who taught Brutus and Cassius; Q. Cæcilius Epirota, the correspondent of Cicero; C. Julius Hyginus, a Spaniard, the friend of Ovid, and curator of the Palatine library; Verrius Flaccus, the tutor to the grandsons of Augustus; Q. Cornificius, who was augur at the same time with Cicero; and P. Nigidius Figulus, an orator and philosopher as well as a grammarian.

M. VITRUVIUS POLLIO

The distinguished name of M. Vitruvius Pollio claims a place in a catalogue of the Augustan writers. His subject, indeed, belongs to the apartment of the fine arts; but his varied acquirements and extensive knowledge, as well as the manner in which, notwithstanding some faults, he treats his subject, shed some lustre upon Roman literature, and stamp him as one of the didactic writers of his country.

Little information exists respecting this celebrated architect; and this circumstance has led to his being confounded with another professor of the same art, L. Vitruvius Cerdo. The

---

[989] Lib. x. i. 101.
[990] Lib. viii. i. 1, 5, 56.
[991] Provincialism is not an accurate term; for the worst Latin was spoken in Italy, whilst the only Latin spoken in the provinces or conquered dependencies was as polished as that of the capital.
[992] Lect. R. L. viii.

name of the latter is thus inscribed on an arch, which was his work, at Verona:[993] "*Q. Vitruvius L. L. Cerdo, Architectus.*" That Cerdo was not the author of the treatise extant under the name of Vitruvius, may be satisfactorily proved:—Firstly. The letters L. L. signify that he was Lucii Libertus (the freedman of Lucius,) whereas M. Vitruvius Pollio was born free. Secondly. The arch on which the name appears belongs to an age when the Romans had begun, in defiance of the precepts of Pollio, to neglect the principles of Greek architecture.[994]

Both the place and date of his birth are unknown. According to some authorities he was born at Verona; according to others at Formiæ;[995] but he himself asserts that he received a good liberal education; and the truth of this statement is confirmed by the 388knowledge which he displays of Greek and Roman literature, and his acquaintance with works which treat, not only of architecture, but also of polite learning and even philosophy[996]—the writings, for example, of Lucretius, Cicero, and Varro. But the great object of his studies was, undoubtedly, professional, and to this he made literature a handmaid.

Vitruvius served under Julius Cæsar in Africa as a military engineer; and was subsequently employed by one of the emperors, to whom his treatise is dedicated, in the direction and control of that department of the public service. By his favour, and the kindness of his sister, he was thus placed in a condition, if not of affluence, at least of competency. Who his imperial patron was has been disputed; but the widely extended conquests, the augmentation of the empire, the political institutions, and, moreover, the taste for architecture which Vitruvius attributes to him, renders it most probable that it was Augustus, the sovereign who found the city of bricks and left it of marble. It is clear that his work was written after the death of Julius Cæsar, and not later than that of Titus, for the former he prefixes the word Divus, whilst he does not mention the Coliseum; and, although he speaks of Vesuvius,[997] he is evidently not aware of any eruptions having taken place except in ancient times. Notwithstanding the arguments adduced by W. Newton[998] to prove that he wrote in the reign of Titus, it is now universally admitted that Vitruvius was a writer of the Augustan age. The inferiority of his style to that of his contemporaries, its occasional obscurity and want of method, the not unfrequent occurrence of inelegant, and even barbarous expressions, notwithstanding his classical education, may be accounted for by what has already been stated respecting the professional object of all his studies. He himself claims indulgence on this score,[999] and states that he writes as an architect, and not as a literary man. So much of its difficulty as arises from conciseness he considers a matter for boasting rather than apology.

In forming an estimate of the Latinity of an author like Vitruvius, 389it must not be forgotten that our taste is formed by authority and by a study of the best models. Novelty is exceptional, and therefore displeases. But technical subjects render not only the introduction of new terms necessary, but even, owing to the poverty of language, awkward periphrases and obscure phraseology. Nevertheless, upon the whole, the language of Vitruvius is vigorous, his descriptions bold, and seem the work of a true and correct hand, and a practised draughtsman.

His work consists of ten books, in which he treats of the whole subject in a systematic and orderly manner.

---

[993] Orell. Ins. Lat. 4145.
[994] See Smith's Dict. of Biogr. sub. v.
[995] Lib. vi. Præf. and Vita Vitr. ed. Bipont.
[996] Lib. vi. Præf. and Vita Vitr. ed. Bipont.
[997] Lib. ii. 6.
[998] Life and Trans. of Vitr. 1791.
[999] See his Preface.

The following are its principal contents:—A general view of the science and of the education suitable to an architect; the choice of sites; the arrangement of the buildings and fortifications of a city;[1000] an interesting essay on the earliest human dwellings, building materials,[1001] temples, altars,[1002] forums, basilicæ, treasuries, jails, court-houses, baths, palæstræ, harbours, theatres, together with their acoustic principles, and the theory of musical sounds and harmonies.[1003] Private dwellings, both in town and country;[1004] decoration;[1005] water, and the means of supply;[1006] chronometrical instruments;[1007] surveying[1008] and engineering, both civil and military.

His work is valuable as a conspectus of the principles of Greek architectural taste and beauty, of which he was a devoted admirer, and from which he would not willingly have permitted any deviation. But he was evidently deficient in the knowledge of the principles of Greek architectural construction.[1009] His taste was pure, too pure probably for the Romans; for, notwithstanding his theoretical excellence, we have no evidence of his being employed, practically, as an architect, except in the case of the Basilica,[1010] at Colonia Julia Fanestris, now Fano, near Ancona.

[1000] Lib. i.
[1001] Lib. ii.
[1002] Lib. iii. and iv.
[1003] Lib. v.
[1004] Lib. vi.
[1005] Lib. vii.
[1006] Lib. viii.
[1007] Lib. ix.
[1008] Lib. x.
[1009] See Philolog. Museum, vol. i. p. 536.
[1010] Lib. v. i. 13.

Section III. Era of the Decline

Chapter 28

Decline of Roman Literature—It Became Declamatory—Biography of Phædrus—Genuineness of His Fables—Moral and Political Lessons Inculcated in Them—Specimens of Fables—Fables Suggested by Historical Events—Sejanus and Tiberius—Epoch Unfavourable to Literature—Ingenuity of Phædrus—Superiority of Æsop—The Style of Phædrus Classical

With the death of Augustus[1011] commenced the decline of Roman literature, and only three illustrious names, Phædrus, Persius, and Lucan, rescue the first years of this period from the charge of a corrupt and vitiated taste. After awhile, indeed, political circumstances again became more favourable—the dangers which paralyzed genius and talent, and prevented their free exercise under Tiberius and his tyrannical successors, diminished, and a more liberal system of administration ensued under Vespasian and Titus. Juvenal and Tacitus then stood forth as the representatives of the old Roman independence; vigour of thought communicated itself to the language; a taste for the sublime and beautiful to a certain extent revived, although it did not attain to the perfection which shed a lustre over the Augustan age.

The characteristic of the first literature of this epoch was declamation and rhetoric. As liberty declined, true natural eloquence gradually decayed. When it is no longer necessary or even possible to persuade or convince the people, that eloquence which calms the passions, wins the affections, or appeals to common sense and the reasoning powers, has no opportunity for exercise. Its object is a new one—namely, to please and attract an audience who listen in a mere critical spirit: the weapons which it makes use of are novelty and ingenuity; novelty soon becomes strangeness, and strangeness exaggeration; whilst ingenuity implies unnatural study and a display of pedantic erudition—the aiming at startling and striking effects—and at length ends in affectation.

[1011] A. D. 14.

If this was the prevailing false taste under the immediate successors of Augustus, it is not surprising that it affected poetry as well as prose; and that the principal talent of the poet lay in florid and diffuse descriptions, whilst his chief fault was a style overladen with ornament. The tragedies ascribed to Seneca are theatrical declamations; the satires of Persius are philosophical declamations; whilst the poems of Lucan and Silius Italicus, though epic in form, are nothing more than descriptive poems, and their style is rather rhetorical than poetical.

PHÆDRUS

Fable had been long known and popular amongst the Romans before the time of Phædrus. Livy could not have attributed the well-known one to Menenius Agrippa, unless it had been a familiar tradition of long standing. Fables amused the guests of Horace, and furnished subjects to those of Ovid. In this, as in other fields of literature, Rome was an imitator of Greece; but nevertheless the Roman fabulist struck out a new line for himself, and in his hands fable became, not only a moral instructor, but a severe political satirist. Phædrus, the originator and only author of Roman fable, flourished on the common confines of the golden and the silver age. His mode of thought, as well as the events which suggested both his original illustrations and his adaptations of the Æsopean stories, belong to that epoch of transition. His works are, as it were, isolated: he has no contemporaries. Although he was born in the reign of Augustus, he wrote when the Augustan age had passed away. Nevertheless his solitary voice was lifted up when those of the poet, the historian, and the philosopher were silenced.

Phædrus, like Horace, is his own biographer; and the only knowledge which we have respecting his life is furnished by his Fables. In the prologue to the third book he informs us that he was a native of Thrace: "I," he says, "to whom my mother gave birth on the Pierian hill—

Ego quem Pierio mater enixa est jugo."

And, again, he exclaims, "Why should I, who am nearer to lettered Greece, desert for slothful indolence the honour of my fatherland, when Thrace can reckon up her poets, and Apollo is the parent of Linus, the muse of Orpheus, who by his song endowed rocks with motion, tamed the wild beasts, and stopped the rapid Hebrus with welcome delay?—

Ego literatæ qui sum propior Græciæ,
Cur somno inerti deseram patriæ decus;
Threïssa cum gens numeret auctores suos,
Linoque Apollo sit parens, Musa Orpheo
Qui saxa cantu movit, et domuit feras,
Hebrique tenuit impetus dulci morâ?"

From the title, "*Augusti Libertus*," prefixed to his fables, it is clear that he adds one more distinguished name to that list of freedmen, who were celebrated in the annals of literature. Although, in the preface to his work, he modestly terms himself only a translator of Æsop,

> Æsopus auctor quam materiam repperit
> Hanc ego polivi versibus senariis,[1012]

still, for many of his fables, he deserves the credit of originality. Probably he enlarged and extended his original plan; for he afterwards speaks of simply adopting the style and not the matter of the Æsopean fable.[1013]

He does not appear to have gained much fame or popularity; for he is only twice mentioned by ancient authorities, namely, by Martial[1014] and Seneca.[1015] The latter, writing to Polybius, a favourite freedman of Claudius, encourages him to enter upon the field which Phædrus already occupied, asserting that fables in the style of Æsop constituted a work hitherto unattempted by Roman genius (*intentatum Romanis ingeniis opus*.) Either, therefore, the fables of Phædrus were little known and appreciated, or Seneca purposely concealed from the Emperor's favourite the fact of their existence, in order to flatter him with the hopes of his thus becoming the first Roman writer in his style. The persecution to which literary men were subject under the worst Emperors, of which Phædrus hints obscurely that he was a victim[1016]—the perils to which he would have been exposed by strictures upon persons in power, which, concealed under the veil of fiction, appear now dark and enigmatical, but which might have spoken plainly to the consciences of the actors themselves—probably rendered it a wise precaution to conceal his works during his lifetime; hence they would be little known, except to a chosen few, and the few copies made of them would account for the rarity of the extant manuscripts.

Owing to the deficiency of ancient testimony, the genuineness of the Fables has been disputed; but the purity of style, and the natural allusions to contemporary events render it almost certain that they belong to the age in which they were supposed to have been written. No one but a contemporary could have written the fable commencing—

> Narrabo memoria quod factum est mea.[1017]

The prologue to the third book evidently speaks of the author's own calamities; and the way in which the name of Sejanus is connected with the event, hints, although obscurely, that that prime minister of tyranny was the author of his sufferings. It is scarcely probable that he would have ventured to attack Sejanus during his lifetime. It may, therefore, be assumed that Phædrus lived beyond the eighteenth year of the reign of Tiberius, in which year Sejanus died.

The original manuscript followed in the early editions of Phædrus was discovered in the tenth century: it contained ninety-seven fables, divided into five books. But N. Perotto, an archbishop of Manfredonia, in the fifteenth century, published a miscellaneous collection of Latin fables, and amongst them were thirty-two new fables attributed to Phædrus, which were not found in the older editions. These were at first supposed to have been written by Perotto himself; but the manifest inferiority of some poems known to be the work of the archbishop,

---

[1012] Prol. lib. i.
[1013] Prol. lib. iii.
[1014] Lib. iii. 20.
[1015] Cons. ad Polybium, 27.
[1016] Prol. lib. iii.
[1017] Lib. iii. 40.

and the Augustan purity of style which marks the newly-discovered fables, leave little doubt of their genuineness. Consequently, they were published by Angelo Mai as supplementary to those which had already appeared.

The circumstances of the times in which he lived suggested the moral and prudential lessons which his fables inculcated. The bane of Rome, under the empire, was the public informer (*delator*,) as the sycophant had been the pest of Athens. Life and conduct, private as well as public, were exposed to a complete system of espionage: no one was safe from this formidable inquisition; a man's familiar associate might be in secret his bitterest enemy. But the principal victims were the rich: they were marked out for destruction, in order that the confiscation of their property might glut the avarice of the Emperor and the informers. For this reason, Phædrus himself professes always to have seen the peril of acquiring wealth—

> Periculosum semper reputavi lucrum.

And we cannot be surprised that the danger of riches, and the comparative safety of obscurity and poverty, should sometimes form the moral of his fables.

That of the Mules and the Thieves, which is entirely his own, teaches this lesson:—

> Muli gravati sarcinis ibant duo;
> Unus ferebat fiscos cum pecuniâ,
> Alter tumentes multo saccos hordeo.
> Ille, onere dives, celsâ cervice eminet,
> Clarumque collo jactat tintinnabulum;
> Comes quieto sequitur et placido gradu.
> Subito latrones ex insidiis advolant,
> Interque cædem ferro mulum sauciant,
> Diripiunt nummos, negligunt vile hordeum.
> Spoliatus igitur cum casus fleret suos,
> Equidem, inquit alter, me contemptum gaudeo,
> Nam nihil amisi nec sum læsus vulnere.
> Hoc argumento tuta est hominum tenuitas;
> Magnæ periclo sunt opes obnoxiæ.[1018]

"Two mules, laden with heavy burdens, were journeying together: one carried bags of money; the other, sacks filled with barley. The former, proud of his rich load, carried his head high, and made the bell on his neck sound merrily; his companion followed with quiet and gentle paces. On a sudden, some thieves rush from an ambuscade, wound the treasure-mule, strip him of his money-bags, but leave untouched the worthless barley. When, therefore, the sufferer bewailed his sad case—'For my part,' replied his companion, 'I rejoice that I was treated with contempt; for I have no wounds, and have lost nothing.' The subject of this fable proves that poverty is safe, whilst great wealth is exposed to peril."

The fable of the Man and the Ass teaches a salutary lesson to another class of wealthy men, namely, those favourites of the emperor and his creatures, who owed their wealth to plunder and confiscation. Every day's experience proved that those who battened on the spoils of the oppressed one day, became themselves the victims of the same tyrannical system

---
[1018] Lib. ii. 7.

the next. Like that of the prime minister, Sejanus himself, the sun of their prosperity was destined to set, and their ill-gotten spoil to enrich others as unworthy as themselves. Those fortunes were indeed built upon a rotten foundation, which the same system had power to raise up and to overthrow:—

> Quidam immolasset verrem quum sancto Herculi,
> Cui pro salute votum debebat sua,
> Asello jussit reliquias poni hordei.
> Quas aspernatus ille sic locutus est:
> Tuum libenter prorsus appeterem cibum
> Nisi, qui nutritus illo est, jugulatus foret.
> Majorem turbam punitorum reperies;
> Paucis temeritas est bono, multis malo.[1019]

"A man who had sacrificed a boar to Hercules, which he had vowed as a thank-offering for his recovery from sickness, ordered the remains of the barley to be given to his ass. The ass rejected it with scorn, and said, 'I would gladly eat of the food you give me, had not he who was fattened on it had his throat cut.'

"You will find that the majority of those who grow rich by violence and rapine are punished; audacity succeeds with few, but ruins many."

The continued succession of tyrannical emperors must have taught their oppressed subjects that they had nothing to hope for from a change of those who wore the purple. This truth is imbodied in the fable of the old Peasant and his Ass:——

> In principatu commutando civium
> Nil, præter domini nomen, mutant pauperes.
> Id esse verum parva hæc fabula indicat.
> Asellum in prato timidus pascebat senex.
> Is, hostium clamore subito territus,
> Suadebat asino fugere, ne possent capi.
> At ille lentus; quæso, num binas mihi
> Clitellas impositurum victorem putas?
> Senex negavit. Ergo quid refert mea
> Cui serviam, clitellas dum portem meas?[1020]

"In a change of princes the poor change nothing but the name of their master. The truth of this is shown by the following little fable. A timid old man was feeding his ass in a meadow. Alarmed by the shouts of an advancing enemy he urged the ass to fly for fear they should be taken prisoners. But the ass loitered, and said, 'Pray, do you think that the conqueror will put two pack-saddles on my back?' 'No,' replied the old man. 'What, then, does it matter to me in whose service I am, so long as I have to carry my load?'"

The well known fable of the Wolf and the Lamb (i. 1) illustrates the unscrupulousness of the informers; and that of the Wolf and the House-dog (iii. 7) teaches how preferable is

---

[1019] Lib. v. 4.
[1020] Lib. i. 15.

liberty, even under the greatest privations, to luxury and comfort purchased by submission to the caprices of a master.

Of such a kind were the moral and political lessons which Phædrus enforced in the attractive garb of fables. They were of a general character, suggested by the evils of the times in which he lived.

Another class were suggested by historical events: they were nevertheless severe satirical strictures on individuals. Two may be pointed out as examples which are evidently directed against Tiberius and Sejanus. These are—The Frogs demanding a King, (i. 2;) and the Frogs and the Sun, (i. 6.) Neither of the fables are original; they are apposite applications of two by Æsop.

The Romans,[1021] like the frogs in the first of these fables, had exchanged their liberty for the slavery of the empire. In Tiberius, now an imbecile dotard, wholly given up to sensual indulgence in his retreat at Capreæ, they had a perfect King Log. He was utterly careless of the sufferings of his subjects and the administration of his kingdom.

To his odious minister, Sejanus, he intrusted the toils of government, to which his own indolence indisposed him. All tyranny and cruelty were ascribed to the ministers; whilst the effeminate debauchery of the Emperor rendered him, even in that demoralized age, an object of contempt and insult rather than of abhorrence and fear. L. Sejanus, a kinsman of Ælius,[1022] employed bald-headed persons, and children with their heads shaved, in the procession of the Floral games, in order to hold up to scorn and derision the bald-headed Emperor, and he dared not take notice of the insult. The infamous Fulcinius Trio in his last will declared that Tiberius had become childish in his old age, and that his continued retirement was nothing else but exile.[1023] Pacuvianus was the author of pasquinades against the Emperor. In the same way Phædrus describes the frogs as treating "King Log" with scorn, and as defiling him in the most offensive manner.

But after the death of Sejanus a change took place in the Emperor's conduct, though not in his character. He left Capreæ for a time, and took up his abode in the Vatican, close to the very walls of Rome. He now gave vent to his savage disposition, and displayed the temper of the water-snake in the fable. His natural cruelty was equalled by his activity. "His sharp tooth seized his unresisting victims one after the other: in vain they fly from death; fear prevents them from uttering a word in defence or expostulation." No longer a vast expanse of sea and land intervened between the tyrant and his victims. There was nothing to delay the pompous and verbose missives of his bloody purposes: his rescripts could reach the consuls the same day, or at least after the interval of a night: he could behold, as it were, with his own eyes, the reeking hands of the executioners, and the waves of blood which deluged every dwelling.[1024] Vengeance not only fell on the guilty Sejanus and his unoffending family, the vilest and the noblest blood of Rome alike flowed at the tyrant's command. The fable of the Frogs and the Sun was a covert attack upon the ambitious designs of Sejanus. It is sufficiently short to be quoted:

[1021] See Nisard, Etudes sur les Poëtes Latins, tom. i. 9.
[1022] Dion. Cass. lviii. 19.
[1023] Tac. Ann. vi. 38.
[1024] Hæc Tiberius non mari, ut olim, divisus, neque per longinquos nuntios accipiebat, sed urbem juxta; eodem ut die, vel noctis interjectu, literis consulum rescriberet; quasi aspiciens undantem per domos sanguinem, aut manus carnificum.—*Tac. Ann.* vi. 39.

Uxorem quandam Sol quum vellet ducere,
Clamorem Ranæ sustulere ad sidera.
Convicio permotus, quærit Jupiter
Causam querelæ. Quædam tum stagni incola,
Nunc, inquit, omnes unus exurit lacus
Cogitque miseras arida sede emori;
Quidnam futurum est, si creârit liberos?[1025]

"Once upon a time the Sun determined to marry; and the Frogs raised a cry of alarm to Heaven. Jupiter, moved by their complaints, asked the cause of them. One of the denizens of the pond answered:—'Now the Sun by himself dries up all the lakes, and causes us to die a miserable death in our parched-up dwellings. What then will become of us if he has children?'"

Now let us examine the application. The fawning yet ambitious Sejanus had always aspired to ally himself with the imperial family. The first attempt which he made to accomplish his design was procuring the betrothal of his daughter to Drusus, the son of Claudius, afterwards emperor. This prince died young, and consequently the marriage never took place;[1026] but this first opened the eyes of the Romans to the audacious projects of the favourite. Later in his career,[1027] he, by a similar step, endeavoured to pave his way to the imperial purple. He seduced Livilla, the sister of the amiable Germanicus, poisoned her husband, divorced his own wife, and asked the sanction of Tiberius to his marriage with the widow of the murdered man. The emperor, with his usual finesse and dissimulation, refused. The demand awoke the suspicions of the court, and was a commencement of that coolness between Sejanus and his patron which eventually ended in the fall of the latter. The influence of Sejanus alone was sufficiently baneful; what would it be if multiplied by a race of princes descended from him? The mere probability of such an event naturally filled Rome with alarm and consternation; and this Phædrus endeavoured to encourage by a fable, which, if it had not some such object as this, would scarcely be intelligible.

The quotations which have been given from the fables of Phædrus are sufficient, as examples of his ingenuity in imitation and adaptation, as well as of his original genius, whenever he trusts to his powers of invention. Some of his pieces, although, like the rest, they are entitled fables, are, in fact, narratives of real events, and show that he possessed a charming talent for telling anecdotes, besides skill as a fabulist in the proper sense of the term. His style has great merits: it combines the simple neatness and graceful elegance of the golden age with the vigour and terseness of the silver one. Phædrus has the facility of Ovid, and the brevity of Tacitus. Thus standing in the epoch between two literary periods, he, as far as the humble nature of his walk admits, unites the excellencies of both. Between the age of Horace and Juvenal, Cicero and Tacitus, there was a gap, and a long one, not less than half a century: it was a period in which Roman genius was slumbering. Phædrus proves that that sleep was not the sleep of death. Tacitus has partially accounted for this cold and dark interval. He tells us[1028]—"that although the affairs of the ancient Roman republic, whether in prosperity or in adversity, were related by illustrious writers—and even the times of Augustus

---

[1025] Lib. i. 6.
[1026] Suet. Vit. Claud. 27.
[1027] A. D. 23.
[1028] Tac. Ann. I. i.

were not deficient in historians of talent and genius—nevertheless the gradual growth of a spirit of adulation deterred all who were qualified for the task from attempting it. Fear, during the lifetime of Tiberius, Caius, Claudius, and Nero, and hatred, still fresh after their deaths, rendered all accounts of their reigns false."

It was thus, according to him, fear and hatred, and a spirit of flattery, that silenced the voice of history. Doubtless what he says of history applies with equal force to poetry, and oratory likewise. The same cause which crushed political liberty rendered the truthfulness of the historian fraught with danger, and all poetry, except it spoke the language of adulation, treason; a crime which was no longer one against the majesty of the people, but was transferred to the person of the emperor. The very term παρρησια (boldness of speech) was a word, the utterance of which was as perilous as to speak of liberty.[1029] The danger had scarcely passed away when Juvenal, notwithstanding his fearless spirit, wrote:—

> Unde illa priorum
> Scribendi quodcunque animo flagrante liberet,
> Simplicitas, cujus non audeo dicere nomen.
> *Juv.* i. 153.
> Where the plain times, the simple, when our sires
> Enjoyed a freedom which I dare not name,
> And gave the public sin to public shame,
> Heedless who smiled or frowned.
> Gifford.

But there was a negative as well as a positive cause, the withdrawal of patronage. Literature, in order to flourish, requires the genial sunshine of human sympathy: it needs either the patronage of the great or the favour of the people. In Greece it enjoyed the latter in the highest possible degree; in Rome, from the time of the Scipios to that of Augustus, it was fostered by the former. Immediately after his death patronage was withdrawn, and there was not public support to supply its place. Tiberius was first a soldier; then a dark and reserved politician; lastly, a blood-thirsty and superstitious sensualist. The enjoyments of Gaius Caligula were the extravagancies of a madman, although he was responsible for his moral insanity, because he had, by vicious indulgence, been the destroyer of his moral principle; and not only did he not encourage literature, but he even hated Homer and Virgil. Lastly, the stupid and dozing Claudius wrote books[1030] as stupid as himself, and was at once the butt and tool of his courtiers. It was not, therefore, until the reign of Nero that literature revived; for, though the bloodiest of tyrants, he had an ambition to excel in refinement, and had a taste for art and poetry.

In the construction of his fables, Phædrus displays observation and ingenuity. Nothing escapes his watchful eye which can be turned to account in his little poems. A rude sketch in charcoal on the wall of a low tavern[1031] suggested to him the idea of the Battle between the Rats and the Weasels. His animals are grouped, and put in attitudes, just as a painter would arrange them. His accurate eye has noted and registered the habits of the brute creation, and he has adapted them to the delivery of noble and wise sentiments with the utmost ingenuity.

[1029] *Vide* Suet. Vit. Calig. 27.
[1030] Suet. Claud. 42.
[1031] Lib. iv. 6.

But there his genius stops. He is deficient in imagination. He makes his animals the vehicles of his wisdom; but he does not throw himself into them, or identify himself with them. The true poet is lost in his characters: carried away by the enthusiasm of an inspired imagination, his spirit is transfused into his heroes;—you forget his existence. The characters of Phædrus look and act like animals, but talk like human beings: the moralist and the philosopher can always be detected speaking under their mask and in their disguise.

In this consists the great superiority of Æsop to his Roman imitator. His brutes are a superior race, but they are still brutes. The reader could almost fancy that the fabulist had lived amongst them as one of themselves—had adopted their modes of life, and had conversed with them in their own language. In Phædrus we have human sentiments translated into the language of beasts—in Æsop we have beasts giving utterance to such sentiments as would be naturally theirs, if they were placed in the position of men. Skilful adaptation and happy delineation are the triumphs of ingenuity and observation: the creative power is that of the imagination.

The style of Phædrus, notwithstanding a few provincialisms,[1032] is pure and classical. He does not often indulge in the use of metaphors, but the few which are met with are striking and appropriate. He is not entirely free from some of that far-fetched affectation which characterizes the decline of Roman literature. But his fault is exaggerated conciseness, and the concentration of many ideas within a brief space, rather than the rhetorical ornament which now began to be admired and popular. His endeavour after brevity led him to use abstract substantives far more profusely than is consistent with the practice of the best classical writers. These faults, however, do not interfere with that clearness and simplicity, which, quite as much as the subjects, have rendered the fables of Phædrus a popular book for the young student, and please even those who have the opportunity of comparing his iambics with the liveliness of Gay, the politeness of Florian, the philosophy of Lessing, the sweetness of Cowper, and the unequalled versatility of La Fontaine.

[1032] See lib. i. 2, 9; ii. 7, 8; iii. 6, 9.

Chapter 29

Dramatic Literature in the Augustan Age—Revival under Nero—Defects of the Tragedies Attributed to Seneca—Internal Evidence of Their Authorship—Seneca the Philosopher a Stoic—Inconsistent and Unstable—The Sentiments of His Philosophical Works Found in His Tragedies—Parallel Passages Compared—French School of Tragic Poets

Of Roman tragedy in its earliest period, so far as the fragments of it which remain allow a judgment to be formed, an account has already been given; and if circumstances forbade it to flourish then, still less can it be expected that the boldness and independence of Greek tragedy would be found under the empire.

Nevertheless, there were not wanting some imitators of Greece in this noblest branch of Greek poetry, however unsuitable it was to the genius of the Roman people, and unlikely to be appreciated by them.

But their productions were rather literary than dramatic; they were intended to be read, not acted. They were poems composed in a dramatic form, because Athens had set the example of that form to her devoted imitators. Although, therefore, they contain noble philosophical sentiments, lively descriptions, vigorous conceptions and delineations of character, and passages full of tenderness and pathos, they are deficient in dramatic effect, and positively offend against those laws of good taste, which, not arbitrarily assumed, but founded on the principles of the human mind, regulated the Athenian stage.

We have seen that, in the Augustan age, a few writers attained some excellence in tragedy, at least in the opinion of ancient critics. Besides Ovid and Varius, whose tragedies have been already mentioned, Asinius Pollio acquired a high reputation as a tragic poet, and Virgil[1033] declares that he is the only one worthy of being compared with Sophocles:—

[1033] Ecl. viii. 10.

> Sola Sophocleo tua carmina digna cothurno.

On the revival of letters under that professor of a love of poetry,[1034] the tyrant Nero, dramatic literature reappeared, and perfect specimens are extant in the ten tragedies attributed to Seneca. Various and opposite opinions have been entertained respecting their merits; but there can be no doubt that the genius of the author never can grasp in their wholeness the characters which he attempts to copy; they are distorted images of the Greek originals; the awful and shadowy grandeur of the god-like heroes of Æschylus stand forth in corporeal vastness, and appear childish and unnatural, like the giants of a story-book. The marvels of Greek tragedy and Greek mythology, though merely the unreal conceptions of the imagination, do not appear exaggerated, because the connexion between the theory and the result, the causes and the effects, is so skilfully maintained; but in these Roman tragedies the legends of Greece appear extravagant and absurd: they are as unreal, and therefore seem as affected, as the classical garb in which English poetry was arrayed in the age of Anne. The Greeks believed in the gods and heroes whose agency and exploits constituted the machinery of tragedy—the Romans did not; and thus we cannot sympathize with them, because we see that they are insincere. The style, moreover, of the tragedies, which bear the name of Seneca, is spoiled by that inflated language and redundancy of ornament, the constant effect of which is, as Aristotle observes, frigidity. They bear the visible marks of an age in which genius had given place to an artificial and scholastic rhetoric; and the author seems to have been striving not for tragic pathos so much as brilliant declamation. In the female characters, especially, the Roman tragic poet fails; for, although he can understand heroism, he is unable to accomplish that most difficult of all tasks, the combining it with feminine delicacy. Perhaps the best and noblest of his country-women did not furnish him with such ideals. The Roman matron was the counterpart of her warlike lord. The Lucretias, Porcias, Cornelias, Arrias, though devoted and affectionate, were of sterner mould than Antigone and Deianira.

The tragedies which bear the name of Seneca have been attributed to L. Annæus Seneca, the philosopher, as early as the time of Quintilian,[1035] who quotes as Seneca's a verse from the Medea. The improbability of this being the case is also diminished by the fact that both Tacitus[1036] and Pliny the younger[1037] speak of him as a poet. Nevertheless, their authorship has been considered a very doubtful question. A passage in an epigram of Martial, in which he speaks of Cordova as the birthplace of two Senecas and one Lucan—

> Duosque Senecas unicumque Lucanum
> Facunda loquitur Corduba[1038]—

has been interpreted as implying that Seneca the philosopher was a different person from Seneca the tragedian. There can, however, be scarcely any doubt that he was speaking of M. Annæus Seneca the rhetorician, and his son Lucius the philosopher. Sidonius Apollinaris,[1039] the son-in-law of the Emperor Flavius Avitus, and Bishop of Clermont,[1040] in the last years of

---

[1034] Tac. Ann. xiv. 52.
[1035] Inst. Or. ix. 2, 9.
[1036] Annal. xiv.
[1037] Epist. v.
[1038] Lib. i. Ep. 6.
[1039] Bernhardy, Grund. p. 373.
[1040] A. D. 472.

the Roman Empire, unhesitatingly draws a distinction between them. He enumerates three members of the Cordovan family:—

> Quorum unus colit hispidum Platonem,
> Incassumque suum monet Neronem,
> Orchestram quatit alter Euripidis
> Pictum fæcibus Æschylum sequutus,
> Aut plaustris solitum sonare Thespim
> Pugnam tertius ille Gallicanam
> Dixit Cæsaris.
> *Carm.* ix. 231.

But, notwithstanding the celebrity which Sidonius enjoyed as a poet at the imperial court, his opinion is of no authority when weighed against the internal evidence derived from the tragedies themselves. This renders it almost morally certain, that they are the work of no other writer than Seneca the philosopher.

Although the Romans, as being imitators of the Greeks, and not original thinkers, were eclectics in philosophy, their favourite doctrines were those of the Stoics. They suited the rigid sternness of their character: they imbodied that spirit of self-devotion and self-denial with which the Roman patriot, in the old times of simple republican virtue, threw himself into his public duties; and Seneca, with all his faults, was a real Roman: with all his finesse and artful policy, he retained, in the midst of a debased age and a profligate court, a large portion of the old Roman character. In life and in death his was a true specimen of the Stoic creed.

Still he was by no means a consistent man: his theory was perfect, but his practice often fell short of it. The lessons of morality contained in his philosophical works are excellent, and persuasively enforced, and wear an appearance of honesty and sincerity; but, nevertheless, in his philosophy, as well as in his life, we can discover that his moral principles were unstable and wavering. These two features can be traced in his tragedies: they abound in philosophical dogmas and moral sentiments, and they display the same Stoicism mingled with occasional habits of inconsistency. Suicide is painted in the most attractive colours: death is met not only with courage, but with the same indifference with which Seneca himself, together with other victims of imperial tyranny, met it in his own day. It is not welcomed, as in the Greek tragedians, as a relief from the burden of earthly sorrows; but there is a manifest departure from the Greek model: the natural beauty of that model is violated, and the features of the original character sacrificed to Stoical coldness and want of feeling.

But not only are these tragedies filled with philosophical reflections; even the sentiments enunciated in the acknowledged works of Seneca, in his Essays and Epistles, are transferred to them, and the peculiar turns of expression used by the philosopher are repeated by the poet. A brilliant French author[1041] has ingeniously brought together and compared parallel passages, which illustrate this similarity of sentiment and style. A few of these are sufficient as examples. Two in the "*Phœnissæ*," in which Œdipus insists on "the liberty of dying," imbody the same doctrine as two others, one in the epistles to Lucilius, the other in the treatise on Providence.

[1041] Nisard, Etudes, tom. i. 88, *et seq.*

He (says Œdipus) who compels one who is unwilling to die does the same as he who hinders one who is eager for death; nay, I consider the latter treats me the worse of the two. I had rather that death were forced upon me than that the privilege of dying should be torn from me.

> Qui cogit mori
> Nolentem, in æquo est, quique properantem impedit.
> Nec tamen in æquo est; alterum gravius reor,
> Malo imperari quam eripi mortem mihi.
> Phœnis. 98.

And again the same favourite sentiment appears:—

I cannot be prevented from dying; of what availeth all that care of thine? Death is everywhere. Most wisely has God provided for this. There is no one who cannot rob a man of life, but no one can rob him of death; to this a thousand roads are open.

> Morte prohiberi haud queo.
> Quid ista tandem cura proficit tua?
> Ubique mors est. Optime hoc *cavit* Deus.
> Eripere vitam nemo non homini potest;
> *At nemo mortem*; mille ad hanc aditus *patent*.
> Phœnis. 156.

With these are compared the following sentences of the philosopher, in which not only the doctrines, but also the language in which they are expressed, are so strikingly parallel as scarcely to admit of a doubt that the authors are identical:—

To live under compulsion is an evil; but there is no compulsion to live under compulsion. Many roads to liberty lie open on all sides, short and easy. Let us thank God that no one can be retained in life.

And, again, Divine Providence is represented as declaring to mankind:—

Before all things I have provided that no one should detain you against your will—an exit is open to you.

Malum est in necessitate vivere, sed in necessitate vivere necessitas nulla est. *Patent* undique ad libertatem *viæ multæ*, breves, faciles. Agamus Deo gratias, quod nemo in vitâ teneri potest.—Ep. xii.

Ante omnia *cavi*, ne quis vos teneret invitos, patet exitus.
De Provident. vi.

How exactly in accordance with these sentiments, whether expressed in poetry or prose, is the closing scene of Seneca's life; the almost business-like way in which he entered upon the road which was appointed to lead him from the dominion of necessity to the enjoyment of liberty—the imperturbable coolness with which he could contemplate the death of his wife, whom he loved with the greatest affection![1042] How calculated, moreover, were they to engage the sympathies of his contemporaries! It was an age in which, amidst its various corruptions, the only virtue which survived was the knowing how to meet death with a courageous spirit, in which many of the best and the noblest willingly died by their own hands at the imperial mandate, in order to save their name from infamy, and the inheritance of their children from confiscation.

Again, an awful belief in destiny, and the hopeless, yet patient, struggle of a great and good man against this all-ruling power, is the mainspring of Greek tragedy. This is not transferred into the imitations of the Romans. Its place is supplied by the stern fatalism of the Stoics. The principle of destiny entertained by the Greek poets is a mythological, even a religious one: it is the irresistible will of God. God is at the commencement of the chain of causes and effects by which the event is brought about which God has ordained; his inspired prophets have power to foretell, and mortals cannot resist or avoid. It is rather predestination than destiny. The doctrine implies an intelligent agent, not a mere abstract principle.

The fatalism of the Stoics, on the other hand, is the doctrine of practical necessity. It ignores the almighty power of the Supreme Being, although it does not deny his existence. It strips him of his attributes as the moral Governor of the universe. These doctrines are found both in the philosopher and tragic poet. Translate the subjoined prose passage into the conventional language of poetry, adopt as a mere matter of embellishment the fables of Greek mythology, personify the Stoical principle of necessity by the Greek Fates, and it becomes the Chorus in the Latin tragedy Œdipus. Both these passages are quoted by Nisard:—

> *Nihil cogor nihil patior invitus*; nec servio Deo, sed assentior; eo quidem magis, quod scio *omnia certa* et in æternum dicta lege decurrere. *Fata nos ducunt*, et quantum cuique restat, *prima nascentium hora disposuit. Causa pendet ex causa*; privata ac publica *longus ordo* rerum trahit. Ideo fortiter omne ferendum est; quia non, ut putamus, incidunt cuncta, sed veniunt. Olim constitutum est quid gaudeas, quid fleas; et quamvis magna videatur varietate singulorum vita distingui, summa in unum venit; accepimus peritura perituri.

De Provid. v.

I am neither compelled to do or to suffer anything against my will. I am not a slave to God, but I bow to his will. The more so because I know that all things are fixed and proceed according to an everlasting law. Destiny is our guide, and the hour of our birth has disposed all the remainder of our lives. Each cause depends upon a preceding one; a long chain of circumstances links together all things, both public and private. Therefore we must bear all things with fortitude, since all things *come to pass*, and do not, as we suppose, *happen*. Our joys or sorrows have been determined long ago; and although a great variety of items distinguishes the lives of individuals, the sum total is the same. Perishable creatures ourselves, that which we have received is perishable likewise.

A comparison of the above with the following passage exhibits a similarity which could only have proceeded from the same mind and the same pen; for it is to be remembered, that

---

[1042] Tac. Ann. xv. 63.

though the Romans were imitators of the Greeks, they did not copy one another; and throughout the whole field of Roman literature no example could be found of a poet transferring to his works the exact sentiments, tone of thought, and turn of expression of another Latin author:—

> Fatis agimur, cedite fatis:
> Non sollicitæ possunt curæ
> Mutare rati stamina fusi.
> Quicquid patimur, mortale genus,
> Quicquid facimus, venit ex alto;
> Servatque suæ decreta colus
> Lachesis, dura revoluta manu.
> Omnia certo tramite vadunt
> Primusque dies dedit extremum.
> Non illa Deo vertisse licet
> Quæ nexa suis currunt causis.
> It cuique ratus, prece non ulla
> Mobilis, ordo.
> Œdip. 980.

We are led by destiny—yield then to its power. Anxious care cannot change the thread spun by the distaff of the Fates. Whatever we mortals do or suffer comes from on high; and Lachesis observes the decrees of the wheel which revolves beneath her pitiless hand. All things proceed in a fixed path, and the first day of life has determined the last. God has not power to change the chain of causes and effects. Each has its fixed order, which no prayers can alter.

Even the philosophical inconsistencies[1043] traceable in the prose treatises are repeated in the tragedies. In one letter[1044] he affirms his belief that the soul of Scipio Africanus has ascended into heaven as a reward of his virtue and piety; in another[1045] he asserts the gloomy doctrine that death is annihilation: "Mors est non esse." In like manner in the "*Troades*" the Chorus declares that the happy Priam wanders amongst pious souls in the "safe Elysian shades;"[1046] and yet, with an inconsistency which the Letters of the philosopher alone account for, another passage in the same tragedy declares that the spirit vanishes like smoke, that after death is nothingness, and death itself is nothing.[1047]

On such internal evidence as this rests the probability, almost amounting to certainty, that Seneca the philosopher, and the author of the ten tragedies, are one and the same.[1048]

[1043] See Nisard.
[1044] lxxxvi.
[1045] liv.
[1046] v. 156.
[1047] v. 393.
[1048] Of the closeness with which Seneca imitated the Greek tragic poets, the two following passages will serve as specimens:—
Animam senilem mollis exsolvit sopor.
Œdip. 788.
Σμικρὰ παλαιὰ σώματ' εὐνάζει ῥοπή.
Quis eluet me Tanais.
Hippolyt. 715.
Οἴμαι γὰρ οὔτ' ἂν Ἴστρον, οὔτε Φᾶσιν ἂν

Notwithstanding their false rhetorical taste, and the absence of all ideal and creative genius, the tragedies of Seneca found many admirers and imitators in modern times. The French school of tragic poets took them for their model: Corneille evidently considered them the ideal of tragedy, and Racine servilely imitated them. Their philosophy captivated an age which thought that nothing was so sublime as heathen philosophy; and yet that same age derived its notions of ancient philosophy from the Romans instead of from the original Greek sources; and its poetical taste, as far as it was classical, was formed on a study of Roman dramatic literature, before the excellence of the Attic drama was sufficiently known to be appreciated.

νίψαι καθαρμῷ....
Œd. Tyr. 1227.

Chapter 30

BIOGRAPHY OF PERSIUS—HIS SCHOOLBOY DAYS—HIS FRIENDS—HIS PURITY AND MODESTY—HIS DEFECTS AS A SATIRIST—SUBJECTS OF HIS SATIRES—OBSCURITY OF HIS STYLE—COMPARED WITH HORACE—BIOGRAPHY OF JUVENAL—CORRUPTION OF ROMAN MORALS—CRITICAL OBSERVATIONS OF THE SATIRES—THEIR HISTORICAL VALUE—STYLE OF JUVENAL—HE WAS THE LAST OF ROMAN SATIRISTS

AULUS PERSIUS FLACCUS (BORN A. D. 34.)

Roman satire subsequently to Horace is represented by Aulus Persius Flaccus and Decimus Junius Juvenalis. Persius was a member of an equestrian family, and was born, according to the Eusebian Chronicle, A. D. 34, at Volaterræ in Etruria. He was related to the best families in Italy, and numbered amongst his kindred Arria, the noble-minded wife of Pætus. His father died when he was six years old, and his mother, Fulvia Sisenna, married a second time a Roman knight named Fusius. In a few years she was again a widow. Persius received his elementary education at his native town; but at twelve years of age he was brought to Rome, and went through the usual course of grammar and rhetoric, under Remmius Palæmon[1049] and Virginius Flavus.[1050] The former of these was, like so many men of letters, a freedman, and the son of a slave. He was, according to Suetonius,[1051] a man of profligate morals, but gifted with great fluency of speech, and a prodigious memory. He was rather a versifier than a poet, and, like so many modern Italians, possessed the talent of improvising. He was prosperous as a schoolmaster, considering the very small pittance which the members of that profession usually earned, for his school brought him in forty sestertia

---

[1049] Juv. vi. 451; vii. 219.
[1050] Suet. Pers. Vit.
[1051] De Illust. Gram. 23.

per annum (about 325*l.*[1052]) Virginius Flavus is only known as the author of a treatise on Rhetoric.

Persius himself gives[1053] an amusing picture of his schoolboy idleness, his love of play, and his tricks to escape the hated declamation which, in Roman schools, formed a weekly exercise:[1054]—

> Sæpe oculos, memini, tangebam parvus olivo,
> Grandia si nollem morituri verba Catonis
> Discere non sano multum laudanda magistro,
> Quæ pater adductis sudans audiret amicis.
> Jure; etenim id summum, quid dexter senio ferret,
> Scire erat in voto; damnosa canicula quantum
> Raderet; angustæ collo non fallier orcæ;
> Neu quis callidior buxum torquere flagello.
> Oft, I remember yet, my sight to spoil,
> Oft, when a boy, I bleared my eyes with oil:
> What time I wished my studies to decline,
> Nor make great Cato's dying speeches mine;
> Speeches my master to the skies had raised,
> Poor pedagogue! unknowing what he praised;
> And which my sire, suspense 'twixt hope and fear,
> With venial pride, had brought his friends to hear.
> For then, alas! 'twas my supreme delight
> To study chances, and compute aright
> What sum the lucky dice would yield in play,
> And what the fatal aces sweep away;
> Anxious no rival candidate for fame
> Should hit the long-necked jar with nicer aim;
> Nor, while the whirling top beguiled the eye,
> With happier skill the sounding scourge apply.
> Gifford.

At sixteen, Persius attached himself to the Stoic philosopher Annæus Cornutus, by whom he was imbued with the stern philosophical principles which occupy so prominent a place in his Satires. The friendship which he formed thus early in life continued until the day of his death. The young Lucan was also one of his intimate associates, whose philosophical and poetical tastes were similar to his own, and who had a profound admiration for his writings. He was acquainted with Seneca, but had no very great regard either for him or his works. Cæsius Bassus, to whom he addressed his sixth Satire, was also one of his intimates.[1055] It redounds greatly to his honour that he enjoyed the friendship of Pætus Thrasea, one of the noblest examples of Roman virtue.[1056] Persius died prematurely of a disease in the stomach, at

---

[1052] Ruperti in Juv. vii.
[1053] Sat. iii. 44.
[1054] Quint. I. O. ii. 7; x. 5.
[1055] Quintilian (I. O. x. 96) pronounces the lyric poetry of Bassus inferior only to that of Horace; but only two lines of his poems are extant. He was destroyed by the same eruption in which Pliny the elder perished.
[1056] Tac. Ann. xvi. 21.

the age of twenty-eight. He left a large fortune to his mother and sister; and his library, consisting of seven hundred volumes, together with a considerable pecuniary legacy, to his beloved tutor, Cornutus. The philosopher, however, disinterestedly gave up the money to the sister of his deceased friend.

Pure in mind and chaste in life, Persius was free from the corrupt taint of an immoral age. He exhibited all the self-denial, the control of the passions, and the stern uncompromising principles of the philosophy which he admired, but not its hypocrisy. Stoicism was not, in his case, as in that of so many others, a cloak for vice and profligacy.

Although Lucretius was, to a certain extent, his model, he does not attack vice with the biting severity of the old satirist. He rather adopts the caustic irony of the old Greek comedy, as more in accordance with that style of attack which he himself terms—

petulanti splene cachinno.[1057]

Nor do we find in his writings the fiery ardour, the enthusiastic indignation, which burn in the verses of Juvenal; but this resulted from the tenderness of his heart and the gentleness of his disposition, and not from any disqualification for the duties of a moral instructor, such as weak moral principle, or irresolute timidity.

Although he must have been conscious that the dangerous times during which his short life was passed rendered caution necessary, still it is far more probable that his purity of mind and kindliness of heart disinclined him to portray vice in its hideous and loathsome forms, and to indulge in bitterness of invective which prevalent enormities of his times deserved. It may be questioned whether obscenities like those of Juvenal, notwithstanding purity of intention, best promote the interests of virtue. It is to be feared that often the passions are excited and the human heart rendered more corrupt by descriptions of vice, whilst the moral lesson is disregarded.

Persius evidently believed that reserve and silence, or those abominations which make the pure-minded shudder with horror, and call up a blush upon the cheek of innocence, would more safely maintain the dignity and purity of virtue, than the divesting himself of that virgin modesty (*virgineus ille pudor*) which constituted the great charm of his character. His uprightness and love of virtue are shown by the uncompromising severity with which he rebukes sins of not so deep a die; and the heart which was capable of being moulded by his example, and influenced by his purity, would have shrunk from the fearful crimes which defile the pages of Juvenal.

The greatest defect in Persius, as a satirist, is, that the philosophy in which he was educated rendered him too indifferent to the affairs which were going on in the world around him. Politics had little interest for him: he lived within himself a meditative life; wealth and splendour he despised. His contemplative habits led him to criticise, as his favourite subjects, false taste in poetry and empty pretensions to philosophy. His modest and retiring nature found little sympathy with the passions, the tumults, the business, or the pleasures which agitated Rome. He was more a student of the closet than a man of the world. Horace mingled in the society of the profligate; he considered them as fools; and laughed their folly to scorn. Juvenal looked down upon the corruption of the age from an eminence, where, involved in his virtue, he was safe from moral pollution, and punished it like an avenging deity. Persius, pure

---

[1057] Sat. i. 12.

in heart and passionless by education, whilst he lashes wickedness in the abstract, almost ignores its existence, and modestly shrinks from laying bare the secret pollutions of the human heart, and from probing its vileness to the bottom. The amiability, and above all the disinterestedness, which characterize his Satires, fully account for the popularity which they attained immediately on their publication by Cornutus, and the panegyrics of which he was the subject in later times. "Persius," writes Quintilian,[1058] "multum et veræ gloriæ, quamvis uno libro meruit." Many of the early Christian writers thought that his merits fully compensated for the obscurity of his style; and Gifford[1059] observes, "The virtue he recommends he practised in the fullest extent; and, at an age when few have acquired a determinate character, he left behind him an established reputation for genius, learning, and worth."

The works of Persius are comprised within the compass of six Satires, containing, in all, about 650 lines. And from the expression of Quintilian, already cited, and supported by a passage of Martial, there is reason to suppose that all he wrote is now extant. To his Satires is prefixed a short but spirited introduction in choliambics, *i. e.* lame iambics, in which, for the iambus in the sixth place, there is substituted a spondee.

This proëmium bears but little relation to his work; but he was accustomed to similar irrelevancy in the parabases of the old Attic comedy, which he had studied. In his first Satire he exposes and accounts for the false and immoral taste which affected poetry and forensic eloquence, attacks the coxcombry of public recitation, and parodies the style of contemporary writers, in language which our ignorance of them prevents us from appreciating. In the second, which is a congratulatory address to his dear friend Macrinus on his birthday, he imbodies the subject-matter of the second Alcibiades of Plato;[1060] a dialogue which Juvenal also had in view in the composition of his tenth Satire. In this poem, the degrading ideas which men have formed respecting the Deity, the consequent selfishness and even impiety of their prayers, are followed by sentiments on the true nature of prayer, which even a Christian can read with admiration:—

>	Quin damus id superis, de magna quod dare lance
>	Non possit magni Messalæ lippa propago;
>	Compositum jus fasque animo sanctosque recessus
>	Mentis et incoctum generoso pectus honesto:
>	Hæc cedo, ut admoveam templis, et farre litabo.[1061]
>	No, let me bring the immortals what the race
>	Of great Messala, now depraved and base,
>	On their huge charger cannot,—bring a mind
>	Where legal and where moral sense are joined
>	With the pure essence; holy thoughts that dwell
>	In the soul's most retired and sacred cell;
>	A bosom dyed in honour's noblest grain—
>	Deep-dyed;—with these let me approach the fane,
>	And Heaven will hear the humble prayer I make,

[1058] Lib. x. 1.
[1059] Trans. of Juv. and Pers. vol. i. p. lxvii. Introd.
[1060] See Spect. No. 207.
[1061] Sat. ii. 71.

Though all my offering be a barley-cake.

In the third, he endeavours to shame the ingenuous youth out of an idle aversion to the pursuit of wisdom, and contrasts the enjoyments of a well-regulated mind with ignorance and sensuality: the picture which he draws of the fate of the sensualist is very powerful:—

> Turgidus hic epulis atque albo ventre lavatur,
> Gutture sulfureas lente exhalante mephites;
> Sed tremor inter vina subit, calidumque trientem
> Excutit e manibus; dentes crepuere retecti;
> Uncta cadunt laxis tunc pulmentaria labris.
> Hinc tuba, candelæ; tandemque beatulus, alto
> Compositus lecto, crassisque lutatus amomis,
> In portam rigidos calces extendit; at illum
> Hesterni capite induto subiere Quirites.[1062]
> Now to the bath, full gorged with luscious fare,
> See the pale wretch his bloated carcass bear;
> While from his lungs, that faintly play by fits,
> His gasping throat sulphureous steam emits!
> Cold shiverings seize him, as for wine he calls,
> His grasp betrays him, and the goblet falls!
> From his loose teeth the lip, convulsed, withdraws,
> And the rich cates drop through his listless jaws.
> Then trumpets, torches come, in solemn state;
> And my fine youth, so confident of late,
> Stretched on a splendid bier and essenced o'er,
> Lies, a stiff corpse, heels foremost at the door;
> Romans of yesterday, with covered head,
> Shoulder him to the pyre, and—all is said. *Gifford.*

One more quotation must be made from this noble Satire, which is alluded to by St. Augustine,[1063] and in which Persius enunciates the sublime truth, that the most fearful punishment which can befall the profligate is the consciousness of what they have lost in rejecting virtue:—

> Magne pater divûm, sævos punire tyrannos
> Haud alia ratione velis, quum dira libido
> Moverit ingenium ferventi tincta veneno;
> Virtutem videant intabescantque relicta![1064]
> Dread sire of gods! when lust's envenomed stings
> Stir the fierce natures of tyrannic kings—
> When storms of rage within their bosoms roll,
> And call in thunder for thy just control—
> O, then relax the bolt, suspend the blow,

[1062] Sat. iii. 98.
[1063] De Civ. Dei, v.
[1064] Sat. iii. 35.

> And thus, and thus alone, thy vengeance show.
> In all her charms, set Virtue in their eye,
> And let them see their loss, despair, and—die. *Gifford.*

In the fourth Satire, Nero is represented in the character of Alcibiades; and **Plato**'s first Dialogue, which bears the name of the Athenian Libertine, furnished the foundation and many of the sentiments.

The fifth is the most elaborate of all the **poet**'s works. It is addressed to Cornutus, and is in the form of a dialogue between the philosopher and his pupil. The style is more finished than usual, and more adorned with the graces of poetry; his amiable nature beams forth in all the warmth of a grateful heart; and although he does not display any original philosophical research, he exhibits great learning, and an accurate acquaintance with the Stoic philosophy.

If the fifth Satire is the most elaborate, the sixth is, without doubt, the most delightful of the works of Persius. It is addressed to his dear friend Cæsius Bassus, and overflows with kindness of heart. The poet speaks of the duties of contentment, and of ministering to the distresses of others; the hatefulness of envy; the meanness of avarice, beneath whatever disguise it may be veiled; his own determination to use and not abuse his fortune; whilst there may be traced through the whole a foreboding, yet a cheerful one, that his weary course will soon be run, and that his heir will soon succeed to his possessions.[1065]

Such was the character of Persius as mirrored in his little volume. The gloomy sullenness of Stoicism was not able to destroy the natural amiability and placid cheerfulness of his temper. Its darkness affected his style, but not his disposition. The fault which has been universally found with the style of Persius, is difficulty and obscurity. This would be the natural consequence of his Stoical education. The Stoics were proverbially obscure and dark in their teaching; and Persius, who had not imbibed all the profoundness of their philosophy, had still caught their language and their manner of expression, and whilst he was infected by their faults he acquired also their picturesqueness and liveliness of illustration. Nor does it appear that his style was considered obscure enough by his contemporaries to interfere with its popularity. It is probable that his obscurity is not absolute, but only relative to the knowledge of the language possessed in modern times. His was the conversational Latin of the days in which he lived; and as a great change had taken place from the Latin of Cicero and Livy to that of Tacitus and Seneca, doubtless the conversational Latin of Horace, and even of Juvenal, would differ from that of Persius. If this be the case, the Satires of Persius constitute the only example of this Latin, and we have no other by a comparison of which we can explain and illustrate his modes of expression. Whatever, therefore, is unusual becomes at once a source of difficulty and obscurity.[1066] The short description which Persius represents his preceptor as giving of his style, supports this assertion:—

> Verba togæ sequeris junctura callidus acri
> Ac teres modico, pallentes radere mores
> Doctus et ingenuo culpam defigere ludo.[1067]
> Confined to common life, thy numbers flow,
> And neither soar too high, nor sink too low;

[1065] See especially ver. 61.
[1066] See this argument quoted by Gifford, ii. xlvii., from H. Frere, v. 14.
[1067] Sat. v. 14.

There strength and ease in graceful union meet,
Though polished, subtle, and though poignant, sweet;
Yet powerful to abash the front of crime,
And crimson error's cheek with sportive rhyme.
Gifford.

As the *toga* had, since the time of Augustus, been only worn by the higher orders, whilst the common people were content with the *tunica*, it is clear that the words *verba togæ* signify the language of polished society. One cause, therefore, of the difficulty of the style of Persius may be our want of familiarity with the conversational Latin used in his time by the superior classes. Excessive subtlety may have been mistaken for refinement; and an affectation of philosophy, and an enigmatical style, may cause obscurity to us which was quite intelligible to his contemporaries.

It is evident that Persius had carefully studied, and was quite well acquainted with, the Satires of Horace; but the influence which Horace produced upon his mind went no further than to impress upon his memory certain phrases which he reproduced in a more perplexed form, more in unison with the fashionable Latin of his day. The expression of Horace—

—— naso suspendis *adunco*
Ignotos,[1068]

becomes, in the Satires of Persius—

Excusso populum suspendere naso.[1069]
Si vis me flere, dolendum est
Primum ipse tibi ——,[1070]

becomes, when paraphrased by his imitator—

Plorabit qui me volet incurvasse querela.[1071]

The simplicity of Horace in the words—

Totus teres atque rotundus
Externi ne quid valeat per læve morari,[1072]

is exchanged for the more involved phrase—

Ut per læve severos
Effundat junctura ungues.[1073]

[1068] Sat. I. vi. 5.
[1069] Ibid. i. 118.
[1070] A. P. 102.
[1071] Sat. i. 91.
[1072] Ibid. II. vii. 87.
[1073] Ibid. i. 65.

He adopts Horace's wish,[1074] preserving every idea in the passage—

>—— O si
> Sub rastro crepet argenti mihi seria dextro
> Herculæ.[1075]

Horace's acquirements in geometry—

> Scilicet ut possem curvo dignoscere rectum,[1076]

are thus awkwardly rendered—

>—— rectum discernis, ubi inter
> Curva subit.[1077]

And, not to multiply examples which, whilst they show that Persius was an admirer of Horace, prove that what was pure, natural inspiration in the latter, required effort in the former. The idea of Horace—

> Clamant periisse *pudorem*
> Cuncti pene patres,[1078]

is exchanged by Persius for the forced metaphor——

> Exclamet Melicerta perisse
> *Frontem* de rebus.[1079]

Rhetorical affectation infected all the literature of this age; we can scarcely, therefore, be surprised to find that it is one of the characteristics of the Satires of Persius. The age of public recitation had already begun, of which Juvenal speaks some years later. When in one place he describes the ardour and enthusiasm which pervaded Rome, on the announcement of a new work by a popular author[1080]—

> Curritur ad vocem jucundam et carmen amicæ
> Thebaidos lætam fecit cum Statius urbem
> Promisitque diem!
> When Statius fixed a morning to recite
> His Thebaid to the town with what delight
> They flocked to him!

[1074] Sat. II. vi. 10.
[1075] Ibid. ii. 10.
[1076] Ep. II. ii. 4.
[1077] Sat. iv. 12.
[1078] Ep. II. i. 80.
[1079] Sat. v. 10, 3.
[1080] Ibid. vii. 82.

In another,[1081] like Horace, he complains of the annoyance of these recitations; and in a third,[1082] he considers it one of the causes which rendered the most desolate and solitary country-place preferable to Rome.

The style of writing, therefore, suitable to this practice, was a declamatory one, as the practice itself was in accordance with the oratorical tastes of the Roman people.

JUVENAL

Decimus Junius Juvenalis, according to the few lines of biography generally attributed to Suetonius, was the son, or the adopted son, of a wealthy freedman. He amused himself with rhetoric and declamation until middle life; but having, on one occasion, written a short satire upon Paris, the pantomime, he was tempted to apply himself to this species of writing. After some time he recited his piece with such success to a large audience, that he inserted it in one of his later compositions.[1083] He thus exposed himself to the enmity of the court, because his lines were supposed figuratively to apply to an actor who was a court favourite, and he was exiled to Egypt, under pretence of being appointed to the command of a cohort. There in a short time he died of grief at the age of eighty.

The time of his birth is unknown, but he must have flourished in the reign of Domitian, towards the close of the first century after Christ; and it is generally assumed that he was either born, or resided, at the Volscian town which subsequently gave birth to the eminent schoolman, Thomas Aquinas.[1084] Thus the greater portion of the life of Juvenal was passed during a period of political horror and misery. The short reign of Vespasian was doubtless a blessing to Rome, but it was only a brief temporary respite: the dark period of the last ten Cæsars saw the utter moral degradation of the people, and the bloodiest tyranny and oppression on the part of their rulers. If, which is most probable, he lived to see the reigns of Nerva, Trajan, and Hadrian, the spirits of the noble-minded satirist must have revived at seeing again a promise of national glory and prosperity. In the period gone by, rich as it was in material for his pen, it was fatally perilous to give utterance to his burning indignation; but an opportunity, not to be lost, was then offered when emperors ruled, who were distinguished for ability and virtue, when justice and the laws were constitutionally administered, and the empire, wisely governed, enjoyed security and tranquillity.

The picture of Roman manners, as painted by the glowing pencil of Juvenal, is truly appalling. The fabric of society was in ruins. The popular religion was rejected with scorn, and its place was not occupied even by the creed of natural religion. Nothing remained but the empty pomp, pageant and ceremonial. The administration of the state was a mass of corruption: freedmen and foreigners, full of artful cunning, but destitute of principle, had the ear of the sovereign, and filled their coffers with bribes and confiscation. The grave and decent reserve which was characteristic of every Roman, in olden times, was thrown off even by the higher classes; and emperors took a public part in scenes of folly and profligacy, and exposed themselves as charioteers, as dancers, and as actors. Nothing was respected but

---

[1081] Sat. i. 2–13.
[1082] Ibid. iii. 9.
[1083] Ibid. vii. 90, 91.
[1084] Ibid. iii. 319.

wealth—nothing provoked contempt but poverty.[1085] A vote was only valued for its worth in money; that people, whose power was once absolute, would now sell their souls for bread and the Circensian games.

Players and dancers had all honours and offices at their disposal. The city swarmed with informers who made the rich their prey: every man feared even his most intimate friend. To be noble, virtuous, innocent, was no protection: the only bond of friendship was to be an accomplice in crime. Philosophy was a cheat, and moral teaching an hypocrisy. The moralists "preached like Curii, but lived like bacchanals."[1086] The very teacher would do his best to corrupt his pupil: the guardian would defraud his ward. Luxury and extravagance brought men to ruin, which they sought to repair by flattering the childless, legacy-hunting, and gambling; and even patricians would cringe for a morsel of bread. The higher classes were selfish and cruel, grinding and insolent to their inferiors and dependants.[1087] Gluttony was so disgusting that six thousand sesterces (50*l.*) would be given for a mullet; and the glutton would artificially relieve his stomach of its load, in order to prepare for another meal.[1088] Crimes which cannot be named were common: men, for the worst of purposes, endeavoured to make themselves look like women; and even an emperor personated a female, and was given in marriage to one of his Greek favourites.[1089] The streets of Rome were as dangerous as the Pomptine marshes or the Italian forests, from constant robbery, assault, and assassination.

The morals of the female sex were as depraved as those of men: ladies of noble and royal blood would have lovers in their pay, and when they had lost the attraction of personal charms, would supply their place by the temptation of gold. One empress publicly celebrated her nuptials with an adulterer in the absence of her lord; another gratified her wantonness by prostitution. Even those who were not so profligate aped the manners and habits of men, and would even meet in mock combat; and there was no public amusement so immoral or so cruel as not to be disgraced by the presence of the female sex. Licentiousness led to murder; and poisoning by women was as common as it was in France and Italy in the sixteenth century.[1090]

Times like these would even have shocked the urbane and gentle Horace. Had he then lived, he would probably have thought such vice beyond ridicule, and his tone might have approached more nearly to the thundering indignation of Juvenal. "Society in the age of Horace was becoming corrupt; in that of Juvenal it was in a state of putrefaction."[1091]

In this period of moral dearth the fountains of genius and literature were dried up. The orator dared not impeach the corrupt politician, or defend the victim of tyranny, when every one thought the best way to secure his own safety was by trampling on the fallen favourite, now Cæsar's enemy.[1092] The historian dared not utter his real sentiments. Poetry grew cold without the genial, fostering encouragement of noble and affectionate hearts. There was criticism, grammar, declamation, panegyric and verse-writing, but not oratory, history, or poetry. Juvenal, though himself not free from the declamatory affectation of the day, attacked

---

[1085] Sat. iii. 137, 148.
[1086] Sat. ii. 1.
[1087] Ibid. i. and v.
[1088] Ibid. ii.
[1089] Tac. Ann. xv. 38. See also Juv. S. ii.
[1090] Sat. vi.
[1091] Nisard, vol. i. 461.
[1092] Sat. vii.

the false literary taste of his contemporaries as unsparingly as he did their depraved morality. From Sejanus to Cluvienus he allowed no one to escape.

But noble as Juvenal's hatred of vice must be allowed to be, and fearless as are his denunciations, we look in vain throughout his poetry for indications of an amiable and kind-hearted disposition. He was not one to recall the lost and erring to a love of virtue, or to inspire a pure and enthusiastic taste for literature. His prejudices were violent; he could see nothing good in a Greek or a freedman: he hated the new aristocracy with as bitter a hatred as Sallust. As a critic he is ill-natured; as a moralist he is stern and misanthrophic. Mark, for example, the gloomy bitterness with which he speaks of old age,[1093] and contrast it with the bright side of the picture, as drawn by the gentle Cicero in his incomparable treatise.

Deficient, however, as he was in the softer affections, his sixteen Satires exhibit an enlightened, truthful, and comprehensive view of Roman manners, and of the inevitable result of such corruption. Those whose moral taste was utterly destroyed would read and listen without profit, but they could not but tremble: his words are truth. The conclusion of the thirteenth Satire is almost Christian. It is unnecessary to quote from an author who is in every scholar's memory: it would even occupy too much space to make a fair selection from so many fine passages. The eleventh Satire is the most pleasing, and most partaking of the playfulness of Horace. The seventh displays the greatest versatility and the richest fund of anecdote. The twelfth is the most amiable. The description of the origin of civil society in the conclusion of the fifteenth is full of sound sense and just sentiments; whilst the way in which he speaks of the insane bigotry of the Egyptians, exhibits his power of combining pleasantry with dignity. But the two finest Satires are those[1094] which our own Johnson has thought worthy of imitation: one of which (the tenth) Bishop Burnet, in his Pastoral Charge, recommended to his clergy; and the noblest passage in them is that which describes the fall of the infamous Sejanus.[1095] Few men could be so well adapted to transfer the spirit of Juvenal into English as Dr. Johnson. He had the same rude, plain-spoken, uncompromising hatred of vice; and, though not unamiable, did his best to conceal what amiability he possessed under a forbidding exterior. He was not without gayety and sprightliness; but he concealed it under that stateliness and declamatory grandeur which he attributes to Juvenal.

The historical value of Juvenal's Satires must not be forgotten. Tacitus lived in the same perilous times as he did; and when they had come to an end, and it was not unsafe to speak, he wrote their public history. Juvenal illustrates that history by displaying the social inner life of the Romans.[1096] Their works are parallel, and each forms a commentary upon the other. When such were the lives of individuals, one cannot wonder at the fate of the nation.

The style of Juvenal is, generally speaking, the reflex of his mind: his views were strong and clear: his style is vigorous and lucid also. His morals were pure in the midst of a debased age: his language shines forth in classic elegance in the midst of specimens of declining and degenerate taste. His style is declamatory, but it is not artificially rhetorical. He could not restrain himself from following the example of Lucilius: he could not dam up the torrent of

---

[1093] Sat. x. *sub fin.*
[1094] Ibid. iii. and x.
[1095] Ibid. x. 56–67.
[1096] The authorities from which we derive our knowledge of the inner life and social habits and affections of the Romans are:—(1.) Ancient monuments. (2.) Cicero's speeches and letters; Horace and the elegiac poets. (3.) The later classic poets, such as Juvenal, Martial, Statius. (4.) Gellius, Petronius, Seneca, Suetonius, the two Plinys. (5.) The grammarians. (6.) Greek authors, such as Plutarch, Lucian, Athenæus, &c. See, on this subject, Bekker's Gallus—Preface.

his vehement and natural eloquence. Whether his subject is noble or disgusting, his word-painting is perfect: we feel his sublimity—we shudder at his fidelity. The nature of the subject causes his language to be frequently gross and offensive; but his object always is to lay bare the deformity of vice, and to render it loathsome. He never indulges in indecency, in order to pander to a corrupt taste or to gratify a prurient imagination. For this reason his pages are less dangerous than those of more elegant and less indecent writers, who throw a veil over indelicacy, whilst they leave those qualities which blind the moral vision and inflame the passions. It must be remembered, also, that neither the dress, manners, nor conversation of ancient Rome were so decent and modest as those of modern times; and, therefore, Roman taste would not be so shocked by plain speaking as would be the case in an age of greater social refinement. Juvenal closes the list of Roman satirists, properly speaking: the satirical spirit animates the piquant epigrams of his friend Martial; but their purpose is not moral or didactic: they sting the individual, and render him an object of scorn and disgust, but they do not hold up vice itself to ridicule and detestation.

Chapter 31

Biography of Lucan—Inscription to His Memory—Sentiments Expressed in the Pharsalia—Lucan An Unequal Poet—Faults and Merits of the Pharsalia—Characteristics of His Age—Difficulties of Historical Poetry—Lucan a Descriptive Poet—Specimens of His Poetry—Biography of Silius Italicus—His Character by Pliny—His Poem Dull and Tedious—His Description of the Alps

M. Annæus Lucanus (Born A. D. 39.)

At the head of the epic poets who flourished during the silver age stands Lucan. He was a member of the same family as the Senecas, for the same rhetorician of that name was his grandfather, and the Stoic philosopher his uncle. Another of his uncles, also, L. Junius Gallio, is mentioned in the Eusebian Chronicle as a celebrated rhetorician. This Gallio derived his surname from being the adopted son of Jun. Gallio, who, by some, is supposed to have been the proconsul of Achaia, mentioned in the Acts of the Apostles.[1097]

The father of Lucan, M. Annæus Mela, was a Roman knight, who made a large fortune as a collector of the imperial revenue. He is supposed by some to have been identical with the geographer Pomponius Mela, who was the author of a brief description, in three books, of the coasts of Europe, Asia, and Africa. The style of this writer is concise, as is suitable to a mere sketch or abridgment; and his matter, although derived from other sources, and not from personal observation, is accurate and interesting. The poet was born at Corduba (Cordova,) on the beautiful banks of the Bætis (Guadalquiver.) His birthplace is thus elegantly alluded to by Statius, in a poem addressed to his widow, on the anniversary of his birth:—

[1097] Ch. viii. v. 12.

> Vatis Apollinei magno memorabilis ortu
> Lux redit, Aonidum turba favete sacris.
> Hæc meruit, cum te terris Lucane dedisset
> Mixtus Castaliæ Bætis ut esset aquæ.
> Stat. Genethl.

Pliny tells us that on his infant lips, as on those of Hesiod, a swarm of bees settled, and thus gave presage of his poetical career; a tale which owes its origin entirely to the Greek tradition. Much which rests upon no foundation has been mixed up with the extant lives of Lucan; for example, the favour shown to him, whilst a child, by Nero; his consequent elevation in his boyhood to the rank of a senator; and his defeat of the emperor in a poetical contest at the quinquennial games, instituted by the latter, in which no one entered with any other view than that their royal antagonist might have the credit of a mock victory.[1098] The enmity of the jealous emperor can be accounted for without having recourse to so insane a competition.

It is probable that Lucan was very young when he came to Rome; that his literary reputation was soon established; and that Nero, who could not bear the idea of a rival, forbade him to recite his poems, which was now the common mode of publication. Nor was he content with silencing him as a poet, but also would not allow him to plead as an advocate.[1099] Smarting under this provocation he hastily joined a conspiracy against the emperor's life, and signalized himself by the bitterness of his hatred against his powerful enemy. The ringleader of this plot was Piso,[1100] a tragic poet of some talent, a skilful orator, and a munificent man. But he was deficient in decision and infirm of purpose: the plot therefore failed. When Lucan's passion cooled he as quickly repented, and was pardoned on condition of pointing out his confederates. In the vain hope of saving himself from the monster's vengeance, he actually impeached his mother. The upright historian contrasts this stain on the poet's character with the courage which Epicharis displayed. This noble woman was incapable of treason. Tacitus describes the resolution with which she scorned the question.[1101] "The scourge, the flames, the rage of the executioners, who tortured her the more savagely, lest they should be scorned by a woman, were powerless to extort a false confession." Lucan never received the reward which he purchased by treachery. The warrant for his death was issued, and he caused his veins to be cut asunder. As the stream of his life's blood flowed away, he repeated from his own poem the description of a soldier expiring from his wounds.[1102] He died in the twenty-seventh year of his age; and the following inscription to his memory has been attributed to Nero:—

> M. Annæo Lucano Cordubensi Poetæ
> Beneficio Neronis. Fama servata.

The sentiments contained in the Pharsalia, so far as he dared express them, breathe a love of freedom, and an attachment to the old Roman republicanism. Although the imperial

---

[1098] Suet. V. Neron. 12.
[1099] Tac. Ann. xv. 49.
[1100] Tac. Ann. xv. 48.
[1101] Ibid. 57.
[1102] Ibid. iii. 635, or v. 811.

patronage which he at first enjoyed, and, perhaps, the better promise of the commencement of Nero's reign, tempted him to indulge in courtly flattery; still, even at that time, his praises of liberty evidently came from the heart. As the poem proceeds his sentiments become more exalted; his virtuous indignation gradually rises, until it pours forth a torrent of burning satire on the inhuman tyrant. This poem, the only one of his works which survives, is an epic in ten books; its subject, the civil war between Cæsar and Pompey. It bears evident marks of having been left unfinished, and of not having received the last touches from the hand of the author. It was preceded by four other shorter poems—the first on the Death of Hector; the second on the Visit of Orpheus to the Infernal Regions; the third, on the Burning of Rome; the fourth addressed to his wife Polla Argentaria. He also wrote some prose works; and Martial attributes to him some poems on lighter subjects.[1103]

Lucan is an unequal poet: his Pharsalia is defaced with great faults and blemishes; but at the same time it possesses peculiar beauties. Its subject is a noble one and full of historic interest, and is treated with spirit, brilliance, and animation. Its arrangement is that of annals, and therefore it wants the unity of an epic poem: it has not the connectedness of history, because the poet naturally selected only the most striking and romantic incidents; and yet, notwithstanding these defects in the plan, the historical pictures themselves are beautifully drawn. The characters of Cæsar and Pompey, for example, are master-pieces. Again, some passages have neither the dignity of prose nor the melody of poetry; whilst others are scarcely inferior to any written by the best Latin poets. This inequality has caused the great diversity of opinions which have been held by critics respecting the merits of Lucan. Some have unjustly depreciated him; others, as groundlessly, have lauded him to the skies. Quintilian commended his ardent enthusiasm and lucidity of expression,[1104] but qualified his praise by adding, that he would be admired by orators rather than by poets. Corneille preferred him to Virgil, of whom he was obviously a warm admirer. His poem furnishes materials and reason for this diversity of judgment; but it may safely be asserted that his faults are due to the age in which he lived, whilst his beauties were the fruits and developments of his own native genius. His principal merit is originality: although he was not great enough to lead the taste of the age, and to rise superior to its false principles, he did not condescend to be a servile imitator even of those poets whose reputation was firmly established. There are many parallelisms between his poetry and that of Virgil, but they are the parallelisms of a student, not of a plagiarist.

Without adopting the unauthorized assumptions, found in some of his biographies, that he was educated under the immediate superintendence of his uncle Seneca, that Remmius Palæmon taught him grammar, Virginius Flaccus rhetoric, and Cornutus philosophy, it is clear that his taste was formed and his talents drawn out in an age, the characteristics of which were pedantic erudition, inflated rhetoric, and dogmatic philosophy. It is clear, also, that even though Seneca was not his tutor, still the conceit and affectation which dimmed the transcendent abilities of the philosopher, exercised a baneful influence over the literary taste of his contemporaries. In the midst of these influences Lucan was educated, and for that reason his poem is disfigured by commonplace maxims, pompous diction, an affectation of learning, a rhetorical exuberance which outstripped its subjects, and therefore produces the effect of frigidity. In a poem, the characters and events of which are historical, the real is in

---

[1103] Ep. i. 61.
[1104] x. i. 90.

too strong contrast to the ideal, hence the effect of both is marred. The fidelity expected of the historian circumscribes the creative power of the poet. To the poet who constructs his work out of the materials of epochs which are beyond the reach of history, the whole field of the past is open. The only limits within which he must restrain his genius are those of the probable: within these bounds he may conjure up the most magnificent ideal forms; he may use the most gorgeous imagery, the most supernatural machinery: the whole wears an air of historic truth; as there are no realities with which his ideal can be compared and tested, truth never appears to be violated.

But in history, almost contemporaneous with the age of the poet, every circumstance is recorded, every character well known and estimated. If an act of bravery is exaggerated into one of superhuman heroism, or one who is known to have been a man, although a great man, recast in the heroic mould, we are struck at once with the falsehood: and therefore the poet cannot venture on such efforts of genius. In a train of events, which the page of history enables us to trace from the beginning to the end, no difficulties can occur deserving of supernatural machinery, no *dignus vindice nodus*; and thus, in the place of the Olympian Pantheon of Homer and Virgil, Lucan can only deify the popular but unpoetical principle of chance, and personify Fortune.

This position may appear inconsistent with the charm which confessedly belongs to the modern historical romance; but then it is to be remembered, that the interest we take in the historical portions is purely historical, enlivened by the events grouping themselves round the hero: in fact, the interest of biography is united with that of history. The strictest accuracy, therefore, in matters which fall within the range of history is perfectly compatible. The romantic interest depends on the inner or social life of the characters—which forms no part of history—in which, as there is no standard of comparison, the imagination of the poet is quite free and unfettered. But this is totally different from the plan on which such a poem as the Pharsalia is constructed. The vision of the genius of Rome which appeared to Cæsar at the fatal Rubicon, those which haunt the slumbers of the Cæsareans in the plundered camp of Pompey, and the dream of Pompey, in which the secrets of the infernal regions are laid open by the shade of his departed wife Julia, are the nearest approaches to that invisible world which the imagination of Homer disclosed, and which Virgil reproduced;[1105] but these are only isolated passages.

It is impossible to be at once an historian and a poet: in the one character the author must restrain the flights of his imagination; in the other, he must sacrifice truth. Nor is there any doubt of which character we demand the conservation, when matters of history are concerned. We desiderate truth: we wish moot points to be settled and doubts solved. All imaginative pictures we look upon as interruptions, and cast them aside as warping the judgment and giving prejudiced views. Hence, our admiration of Lucan is called forth, not by considering his poem as an epic, but for the sake of isolated scenes, such as the naval victory off Marseilles; splendid descriptions, such as that of the cruelties of Marius and Sulla; felicitous comparisons, that, for example, of Pompey to an aged oak; and the epigrammatic terseness which gives force, as well as beauty, to his sayings. In a single line, for instance—

>Pauperiorque fuit tunc primum Cæsare Roma—

[1105] Lib. iii.

he describes the wealth and avarice of the conqueror, and in the well-known verse—

Victrix causa Diis placuit sed victa Catoni—

he depicts the disinterestedness of Cato. To this may be added, that the subject of the Pharsalia is, although a period of the deepest historical interest, ill adapted to poetry. Events so nearly contemporary were fitter for history and panegyric than for poetry; and although they give scope for descriptive power and bold imagery, they are deficient in that mysterious and romantic character which is required for an epic poem. His imagination was rich—his enthusiasm refused to be curbed. They were such as we might suppose would be nurtured by the warm and sunny climate of Spain. His sentiments often exhibit that chivalrous tone which distinguishes the Spanish poets of modern times. We may discern the nobleness, the liberality, the courage, which once marked the high-born Spanish gentleman; and the grave and thoughtful wisdom which makes Spanish literature so rich in proverbs, and which peeps out even from under the unreal conventionalisms of the contemporary Roman philosophy.

Description forms the principal feature in the poetry of Lucan; it occupies more than one half of the Pharsalia; so that it might almost as appropriately be termed a descriptive as an epic poem. Description, in fact, constitutes one of the characteristic features of Roman literature in its decline, because poetry had more than ever become an art, and the epoch one of erudition; and thus a treasure of imagery was stored up suitable for descriptive embellishment. The finest parts of Persius are descriptive: even Martial, brief though his pieces are, delights in it; and facility in this department is the strong point of Silius Italicus, and the sole merit of Valerius Flaccus. Owing to the enthusiasm with which Lucan throws himself into this kind of writing, he abounds in minute detail. He reminds one of the descriptive talent possessed in so eminent a degree by our own Thomson. Not a feature escapes his notice, whether it suggest ideas of the beautiful, the sublime, or the terrible. He is not content, as Virgil is, with a sketch—with broad lights and shadows; he delights in a finished picture; he possesses the power of placing his subject strongly before the eyes, leaving little or nothing for the imagination to supply. He omits no means of attaining descriptive truth;[1106] the inward state of feeling, the character of each passion, is presented, not so much in its moral and psychical as in its physical developments; that which is internal is exhibited in its external symptoms, with the hand of a painter and the skill of the physiognomist. Virgil sketches, Lucan paints; the latter describes physically—the former philosophically. The following passages, which describe the passage of the Rubicon and the death of Pompey, are noble specimens of Lucan's style:—

> Jam gelidas Cæsar cursu superaverat Alpes,
> Ingentesque animo motus, bellumque futurum
> Ceperat. Ut ventum est parvi Rubiconis ad undas,
> Ingens visa duci patriæ trepidantis imago,
> Clara per obscuram vultu mœstissima noctem
> Turrigero canos effundens vertice crines,
> Cæsarie lacera, nudisque adstare lacertis,
> Et gemitu permixta loqui! Quo tenditis ultra?

[1106] *E. g.* v. 165.

Quo fertis mea signa, viri? Si jure venitis,
Si cives, huc usque licet. Tunc perculit horror
Membra ducis, riguere comæ, gressumque coercens
Languor in extrema tenuit vestigia ripa.

Cæsar ut adversam superato gurgite ripam
Attigit, Hesperiæ vetitis et constitit arvis,
Hic, ait, hic, pacem, temerataque jura relinquo;
Te, Fortuna, sequor; procul hinc jam fœdera sunto.
Credidimus fatis, utendum est judice bello.
Now Cæsar, marching swift with winged haste,

The summits of the frozen Alps had past;
With vast events and enterprises fraught,
And future wars revolving in his thought.
Now near the banks of Rubicon he stood;
When lo! as he surveyed the narrow flood,
Amidst the dusky horrors of the night,
A wondrous vision stood confessed to sight.
Her awful head Rome's reverend image reared,
Trembling and sad the matron form appeared;
A towering crown her hoary temples bound,
And her torn tresses rudely hung around;
Her naked arms uplifted ere she spoke,
Then, groaning, thus the mournful silence broke:
Presumptuous men! oh, whither do you run?
Oh, whither bear you these my ensigns on?
If friends to right, if citizens of Rome,
Here to your utmost barrier are you come.
She said; and sunk within the closing shade.
Astonishment and dread the chief invade;
Stiff rose his starting hair; he stood dismayed,
And on the bank his slackening steps were stayed.

The leader now had passed the torrent o'er,
And reached fair Italy's forbidden shore;
Then rearing on the hostile bank his head,
Here farewell peace and injured laws! he said:
Since faith is broke, and leagues are set aside,
Henceforth thou, goddess Fortune, art my bride!
Let fate and war the great event decide. *Rowe.*
Jam venerat horæ
Terminus extremæ, Phariamque ablatus in alnum
Perdiderat jam jura sui. Tum stringere ferrum
Regia monstra parant. Ut vidit cominus enses
Involvit vultus; atque indignatus apertum
Fortunæ præbere caput, tunc lumina pressit,
Continuitque animam, ne quas effundere voces

Posset et æternam fletu corrumpere famam.
At postquam mucrone latus funestus Achillas
Perfodit, nullo gemitu consensit ad ictum.
Now in the boat defenceless Pompey sat,
Surrounded and abandoned to his fate.
Nor long they hold him in their power aboard,
E'en every villain drew his ruthless sword:
The chief perceived their purpose soon, and spread
His Roman gown, with patience, o'er his head;
And when the cursed Achillas pierced his breast,
His rising indignation close repressed.
No signs, no groans, his dignity profaned,
No tear his still unsullied glory stained.
Unmoved and firm he fixed him on his seat,
And died, as when he lived and conquered, great.

C. SILIUS ITALICUS

C. Silius Italicus was born in the reign of Tiberius, A. D. 25. The place of his birth is unknown. His surname, Italicus, has led some to suppose that he was a native of Italica, in Spain. But it is not probable that, if this were the case, his friend and fellow-courtier Martial, when he compared his eloquence to that of Cicero, and his poetry to that of Virgil,[1107] called him the glory of the Castalian sisters,[1108] and felicitated him on his political honours, would have forgotten to claim him as a countryman. Others, with somewhat more show of reason, have imagined that his birthplace was the city of Corfinium, in Pelignia, which was called Italica,[1109] because it was the head-quarters of the confederates in the social war; whilst Stephens mentions a little town in Sicily, of the same name, which might have been his native place.[1110]

Silius was celebrated as an advocate; but in that age of affected and rhetorical display, a high reputation does not prove that his eloquence, although it might have displayed a similar elegance of language, was more lively and stirring than his poetry. He was consul A. D. 68; an office which was also filled by his son,[1111] and by another member of his family.[1112] He was afterwards proconsul of Asia; the duties of which lucrative office he appears to have performed with credit to himself. He was very wealthy; and, as he grew old, retired from the perils of public life to enjoy his affluence, and the retirement of literary ease in his numerous villas. One cannot be surprised that an orator and a poet especially delighted in the house of Virgil, near Naples, and the Academy of Cicero, of both which he was the fortunate possessor. He lived to the age of seventy-five, and then starved himself to death, because he could not bear the pain of disease. "I have just been informed," writes Pliny the Younger, to

---

[1107] Lib. vii. 63.
[1108] See also iv. 14; vi. 64; viii. 66; ix. 86; xi. 49–51.
[1109] Strabo, Geog. v. 167.
[1110] See notes to Plin. Ep. ed. Var.
[1111] Mart. Ep. viii. 66.
[1112] Suet. v. Octav. 101.

his friend Caninius,[1113] "that Silius Italicus has put an end to his existence by starvation, at his Neapolitan villa. He had an incurable carbuncle, from the annoyance of which he took refuge in death, with a firm and irrevocable constancy. He enjoyed happiness and prosperity to his dying day, if we except the loss of the younger of his two sons; but the elder and superior one survived him in the enjoyment of prosperity, and even of consular rank. The belief that he had voluntarily come forward as a public accuser injured his reputation in the reign of Nero; but, as a friend of Vitellius, his conduct was wise and his behaviour courteous. His career in the proconsulate of Asia was an honourable one, for he washed out the stain of his former activity by a praiseworthy abstinence from public affairs. He had no influence with the great; but then he was safe from envy. All courted him, and were assiduous in paying their respects to him; and as ill health confined him to his bed, his chamber was thronged with visitors, beyond what might have been expected from his rank and station. Whenever he could spare time for writing, he passed it in learned conversation. His poems display elaborate care rather than genius: sometimes he invited criticism by recitations. Yielding to the suggestion of advancing years, he at length retired from Rome, and resided in Campania; nor had the accession of a new emperor (Trajan) power to entice him from his retirement. High praise to the monarch under whose rule he was free to act so!—high praise to him who had courage to use that freedom! His love of virtù caused in him a reprehensible passion for buying: he was the possessor of more than one villa in the same localities; and he so delighted in the newest purchase as to neglect that which he inhabited before. He had a vast collection of books, besides statues and busts, which he not only possessed, but almost worshipped. He kept Virgil's birthday more religiously than his own, and had more busts of him than any one else, especially at Naples, where he was in the habit of visiting his tomb, as if it were a temple. In this tranquil retirement he exceeded his seventy-fifth year, his constitution being delicate rather than weakly. As he was the last consul made by Nero, so he died the last of those whom he had made. It is also worthy of remark that the consul, in whose year of office Nero died, died the last of Nero's consuls. When I call this to mind, I feel compassion for human frailty: for what is so brief as the longest span of human life!"

Little interest attaches to the biography of one who owed a life of uninterrupted prosperity to his being the favourite and intimate of two emperors; the one, a blood-thirsty tyrant—the other, a gross sensualist.[1114] His ponderous work survives—the dullest and most tedious poem in the Latin language. Its title is "*Punica:*" it consists of seventeen books, and contains a history in heroic verse of the second Punic war. The Æneid of Virgil was his model, and the narrative of Livy furnished his materials. Niebuhr states that he read through the whole of his works with great care, and that he was quite convinced that he had taken every thing from Livy, of whose work his is only a paraphrase.[1115] The criticism of Pliny the Younger is, upon the whole, just: "*Scribebat carmina majori cura quam ingenio;*" for, although it is impossible to read his poem with pleasure as a whole, his versification is harmonious, and will often, in point of smoothness, bear comparison with that of Virgil. The following passage is quoted by C. Barthius as one of the most favourable specimens of his sentiments and style; and Cellarius, whose praise is extravagantly fulsome, gives it the epithet of "Aurea:"—

[1113] Ep. iii. 7.
[1114] Nero and Vitellius.
[1115] Introd. Lect. on R. H. viii.

Ipsa quidem virtus sibimet pulcherrima merces;
Dulce tamen venit ad manes quem gloria vitæ
Durat apud superos, nec edunt oblivia laudem.

Some of his episodes, if considered as separate pieces, will repay the trouble of perusal; and the following passage, which Addison thought worthy of translation, may be taken as a fair specimen of his descriptive powers:—

THE ALPS.
Cuncta gelu canâque æternum grandine tecta,
Atque ævi glaciem cohibent: riget ardua montis
Ætherii facies, surgentique obvia Phœbo
Duratas nescit flammis mollire pruinas.
Quantum Tartareus regni pallentis hiatus
Ad manes imos atque atræ stagna paludis
A supera tellure patet; tam longa per auras
Erigitur tellus et cœlum intercipit umbrà.
Nullum ver usquam, nullique æstatis honores;
Sola jugis habitat diris sedesque tuetur
Perpetuas deformis hyems: illa undique nubes
Huc atras agit et mixtos cum grandine nimbos.
Nam cuncti flatus ventique furentia regna
Alpinâ posuere domo caligat in altis
Obtutus saxis, abeuntque in nubila montes.
Stiff with eternal ice, and hid in snow,
That fell a thousand centuries ago,
The mountain stands; nor can the rising sun
Unfix her frosts and teach them how to run:
Deep as the dark infernal waters lie
From the bright regions of the cheerful sky,
So far the proud ascending rocks invade
Heaven's upper realms, and cast a dreadful shade.
No spring, no summer, on the mountain seen,
Smiles with gay fruits or with delightful green,
But hoary winter, unadorned and bare,
Dwells in the dire retreat and freezes there,
There she assembles all her blackest storms,
And the rude hail or rattling tempests forms;
Thither the loud tumultuous winds resort,
And on the mountain keep their boisterous court,
That in thick showers her rocky summit shrouds,
And darkens all the broken view with clouds. *Addison.*

Chapter 32

C. VALERIUS FLACCUS—FAULTS OF THE ARGONAUTICA—PAPINIUS STATIUS—BEAUTY OF HIS MINOR POEMS—INCAPABLE OF EPIC POETRY—DOMITIAN—EPIGRAM—MARTIAL—HIS BIOGRAPHY—PROFLIGACY OF THE AGE IN WHICH HE LIVED—IMPURITY OF HIS WRITINGS—FAVOURABLE SPECIMENS OF HIS POETRY

C. VALERIUS FLACCUS

C. Valerius Flaccus flourished in the reign of Vespasian; and, according to an epigram of Martial, in which the poet advises his friend to leave the Muses for the drier but more profitable profession of a pleader, he was born at Patavium[1116] (Padua.) The frequent addition of the surnames Setinus Balbus have caused it to be supposed that he was a native of Setia, in Campania (Sezzo;) but it is impossible to form any satisfactory conjecture as to their signification, and the statement of Martial is too definite to admit of a doubt. Quintilian[1117] asserts that, when he wrote, V. Flaccus had *lately* died: he was, therefore, probably cut off prematurely about A. D. 88.

His only poem which is extant is entitled "*Argonautica*," and is an imitation, and, in some parts, a translation, of the Greek poem of Apollonius Rhodius on the same subject. It is addressed to the Emperor, and in the proëmium he pays a compliment to Domitian on his poetry, and to Titus on his victories over the Jews.

He evidently did not live to complete his original design: even the eighth book is unfinished; and, from the events still remaining to be related, he probably planned an epic poem of the same length as that of Virgil, whose style and versification he endeavoured to imitate. An Italian poet, John Baptista Pius, continued the subject, by an addition to the eighth book, and by subjoining two more, the incidents of which were partly borrowed from Apollonius.

[1116] Lib. i. 62, 77.
[1117] Inst. Orat. x. i. 90.

Of his merits Quintilian speaks favourably in the passage already alluded to, and says, that in him literature had sustained a severe loss. The severer criticism of Scaliger is more precise and more judicious:—"Immaturâ morte præreptus acerbum item poëma suum nobis reliquit. Est autem omnino duriusculus, penitus vero nudus Gratiarum comitate." The defects of the Argonautica are, in fact, rather of a negative than a positive character. There are no glaring faults or blemishes; none of the affectation or rhetorical artifices which belong to the period of the decline. There may be a little occasional hardness, and a few awkward expressions and paraphrases, but there is no bombast to outrage good taste, and no unmetrical cadences to offend the ear. But there is no genius, no inspiration, no thrilling fervour, no thoughts that breathe or words that burn. He never rises above a dead level. Every thing is in accordance with decent and direct propriety. He has some talent as a descriptive poet: his versification is harmonious, and he attains to those superficial excellencies which are found in the prize poem of a pains-taking, ingenious, and well-educated scholar. Virgil was an imitator: that is, his taste, like Roman taste, universally was formed and trained by imitation; but his spirit disdained these trammels, and soared to originality. V. Flaccus is scarcely ever original except when he is commonplace: he imitates Virgil successfully, as far as the outward graces of style are concerned; but in the charm of natural simplicity, he always falls short of his great original.

P. PAPINIUS STATIUS (BORN A. D. 61.)

Towards the middle of the first century of the Christian era,[1118] there arrived at Rome, from Naples, a grammarian, named P. Papinius Statius. He opened a school, and soon became so celebrated as a public instructor, that he became tutor to the young Domitian, whose favour and affection continued after he became emperor. Some of his fame was also founded on gaining, in his boyhood, the prize in many public contests of poetry. Every year between the age of thirteen and nineteen, he is said to have been crowned. These contests were partly of an improvisatorial character; and in an age when public readings and recitations were in vogue, and were the means which poets had of gaining fame and patronage, success of this kind was highly valued. The subject of one of his poems is said to have been the conflagration of the Capitol, during the struggle between the Vitellians and the supporters of Vespasian.[1119] Statius, however, seems to have possessed no higher degree of poetical power than a happy facility in versification, for he died[1120] and left no works which have stood the test of time.

A son, however, inherited poetical talents of the same kind, but of a far higher order than those of his father, and although, for a long time, he was entirely dependent upon his works for the means of living, and, notwithstanding thunders of applause, must starve, unless he can sell his play to the manager Paris,[1121] the sunshine of imperial favour, which his father had enjoyed, shone upon him.[1122] He purchased patronage, however, at the expense of grossly flattering the tyrant. This son, who bore the same name as his father, was the author of the Silvæ, Thebaid, and Achilleid. He was born A. D. 61, and died in the prime of life, A. D. 95,

---

[1118] A. D. 39.
[1119] Silv. v. iii.
[1120] A. D. 86.
[1121] Juv. vii. 82.
[1122] Silv. iv. 2.

at Naples, his native city. As no interesting particulars are recorded respecting his life, and as he is never mentioned by any classical author except Juvenal,[1123] it is impossible to say how the opinion arose which was entertained by his admirer Dante, and others, that he was in secret a defender of the Christians, and also himself a believer.[1124]

He was a true Italian in the character of his genius. He had a thorough perception of the beauties of nature. His Silvæ are full of truthful pictures. He possessed ready facility in versification, which was surpassed by no poet of classic antiquity except Ovid, and that improvisatorial power for which his countrymen in the present day are so often celebrated. As long as he was content to be a poet on a small scale he was eminently successful. His Sylvæ contain many poetical incidents which might stand by themselves as perfect fugitive pieces,—brief effusions, suggested by statues[1125] and buildings,[1126] verses of compliment[1127] and delicate flattery,[1128] or condolence[1129] or congratulation. It matters not how light or trifling the subject, he can raise it and adorn it. He writes with equal beauty on the tree of his friend Atedius;[1130] the death of a parrot; of the emperor's lion;[1131] the locks of Flavius Earinus;[1132] the rude freedom of the Saturnalia.[1133] It is in these unpretending poems that we see his natural and unaffected elegance, his harmonious ear, and his truthfulness of perception. But the case is totally different when the subject is above him.[1134] He had neither grasp of mind, nor vigour of imagination, to fit him for the task of an epic poet; and, hence, his great work, the Thebaid, and his other unfinished epic, the Achilleid, are complete failures.

In his minor poems he seems to trust to the natural powers of his genius; he never strains at producing effect, nor is he too solicitous about exact finish and laborious polish. Although not improvisatorial, they partake of that character, and have all its freshness combined with the advantage of written and corrected performances. His thoughts are inspired by his subject; and its reality, which he was capable of appreciating, gives a life to his compositions. But the principal fault in his Silvæ is too great a display of Greek learning. Every page is full of mythological allusions, which sometimes render his graceful verses dry and wearisome, and must have rendered them acceptable to those only who were well versed in Greek literature: they never could have been universally popular. The qualities which recommended his Silvæ do not adorn his epic poetry. His imaginary heroes do not inspire and warm his imagination: he is not affected by their personality in the same way in which he is by the lawns and groves, and sun, and forests, and skies of Italy.

For this deficiency he attempts to compensate by extravagant bombast, totally out of keeping with the action of the poem, and by an attention to the theoretical principles of art, and an elaborate finish which must have cost him many hours of toil. Yet this perseverance is thrown away, and the effect produced by the contrast between the action and essence of the

---

[1123] Lib. vii. 82.
[1124] *Vide* Vita Gyraldi, Dial. iv. de Poet. Lat.
[1125] Lib. I. i. 3, 5.
[1126] Lib. ii. 2.
[1127] Ibid. ii. 7.
[1128] Ibid. i. 2.
[1129] Ibid. ii. 6; iii. 3.
[1130] Silv. ii. 5.
[1131] Ibid. 3.
[1132] Ibid. 4.
[1133] Ibid. iii. 4.
[1134] Silv. J. 6; iv. 9.

poem, and the language in which it is externally clothed, produces an effect contrary to that which was intended.

He was a skilful draughtsman, a gorgeous colourist, a pleasing landscape-painter, and a diligent student of the rules of art; but his genius could not rise to the highest departments of art—he could not give the mind or the *morale* to those characters whose external features he was so apt in delineating. He owes the estimation in which he is held as an epic poet not to his absolute but his relative merit. He was the best of the heroic poets of his day. Statius, notwithstanding his defects, was evidently a profound student as well as an admirer of the Homeric poems; and there are two points in which he has proved himself a successful imitator. These are his battles and his similes. His descriptions of the former are stirring and dramatic, and some of his similes will bear comparison with the best Latin specimens of this kind of illustration. When it is remembered that no epic poet has approached more nearly to Homer in the use of the simile than Dante, and that he equals the Greek bard in sublime and picturesque description, it may easily be imagined that these were the qualities in the poems of Statius which especially called forth his admiration.

A few words only are necessary to describe the nature and subject-matter of the poems of Statius. The Silvæ consist of thirty-two separate pieces. They are all hexametrical, with the exception of four in hendecasyllabics,[1135] one in Alcaic,[1136] and one in Sapphic metre.[1137] Each of the five books in which these poems are arranged has a prose dedication to some friend prefixed; the first being addressed to the poet Stella, the common friend of himself and Martial.[1138] The title Silvæ was given to these poems, on account of the very quality which constitutes their especial charm. They are the rude materials of thought, springing up spontaneously in all their wild luxuriance from the rich natural soil of the poet's imagination, unpruned, untrimmed, ignorant of that cultivated art which an affected and artificial age thought necessary to constitute a finished poem. "Such extemporaneous performances as these," says Quintilian, "are called Silvæ: the author subsequently re-examines and corrects his effusions."[1139] The Thebaid is comprised in twelve books, and its subject is the ancient Greek legends respecting the war of the Seven against Thebes. The composition of this work preceded the publication of the Silvæ. Achilleid was intended, doubtless, to embrace all the exploits of Achilles, but only two books were completed.

DOMITIAN

A paraphrase of the Phænomena of Aratus belongs to this age. It has been ascribed to Germanicus, but its real author was Domitian, who, as well as Nero, wrote verses.[1140] As far as language and versification are concerned, it is not without merit; but the subject is unsuitable to poetry.[1141] Domitian had taste, although his talents did not deserve the adulatory

---

[1135] Lib. i. 6; ii. 7; iv. 3, 9.
[1136] Ibid. iv. 5.
[1137] Ibid. 7.
[1138] See Epig. vi. 21.
[1139] I. O. x. 3.
[1140] See a passage from Nero's Troica, in Meyer's Anthol.
[1141] Nevertheless, Aratus enjoyed a large share of popularity. Cæsar and Cicero translated his works; Virgil and Manilius borrowed from them; Ovid and Maximus Tyrius compared him with Homer; and St. Paul was

commendations of Quintilian;[1142] but he encouraged learned men: and to his encouragement we owe those distinguished contemporary writers who, for one generation, arrested the downward progress of Roman literature.

Epigram

The Greek Epigram was originally, as the word implies, simply an inscription. It was therefore short and concise; its metre elegiac, as especially suited to the periodic structure of the sentiment, and its characteristic qualities, terseness and neatness. So long as it retained this character it was free from bitterness; and the principal element of success in this species of composition was tact rather than genius, and a cultivated taste rather than poetical inspiration. Not only were Catullus, Virgil, and Ovid epigrammatists, but some Roman *literati*, arrived at mediocrity, or even excellence, in epigram, who were not capable of becoming great poets. Julius Cæsar wrote one on Terence, and perhaps the following neatly-turned lines; although they have been ascribed to Augustus and Germanicus:—

> Thrax puer astricto glacie dum ludit in Hebro
> Pondere concretas frigore rupit aquas;
> Dumque imæ partes rapido traherentur ab amne,
> Abscidit tenerum lubrica testa caput.
> Orba quod inventum mater dum conderet urna,
> Hoc peperi flammis, cetera, dixit, aquis.

Lutatius Catulus was the author of a quatrain on Roscius the comedian; and the Anthology, amongst numerous others, contains one by Augustus,[1143] and four of no merit by Mæcenas,[1144] together with those beautiful lines addressed by Hadrian to his soul, which Pope has imitated in his "Dying Christian:"—

> Animula vagula blandula,
> Hospes comesque corporis,
> Quæ nunc abibis in loca?
> Pallidula rigida nudula
> Nec ut soles dabis jocos.

To the original characteristics of epigram the Romans added that which constitutes an epigram in the modern sense of the term, pointedness either in jest or earnest, and the bitterness of personal satire. Common sense, shrewdness, and an acute observation of human nature were thus superadded to Greek gracefulness and elegance; and the same nation which reduced the wild and unpremeditated sarcasms of the Greek stage into the symmetrical form of satire, produced also the epigram as written by the pen of Martial. The same characteristics

---

acquainted with his Phenomena, and quotes from it (Acts xvii. 28.) There is an English translation of his works by Dr. Lamb.

[1142] Lib. iv. i. 2; x. i. 19.
[1143] See Meyer's Anthol.
[1144] Anthol. 52, 80, 81–84.

of the Roman mind which mark satire are visible also in epigram. Epigram is the concentration of satire. The desultory vagueness which is allowable in the latter, the variety of subjects, which are touched upon with irregular and unrestrained freedom, are, in the former, limited and defined. One idea is selected, and to this all the powers of the writer's acute mind are directed, and made to converge as to a point. It is not often that the harmless elements of Greek wit, such as the pun, or the pleasantry by surprise or unexpected turn (although these sometimes occur,[1145]) are found in the Roman epigram. Smartness is generally connected with severity. The same bitter spirit which dictated the Archilochian epodes of Horace, which breathes throughout the indignant lines of Juvenal, points the shafts of Martial. The blows, however, which he aimed at vice could not be deadly, because he had no faith in virtue, and because he delighted to grovel in the impurity which he described.

M. VALERIUS MARTIALIS (BORN A. D. 43.)

All that is known of the life of Martial is derived from his own works; and this is but little, for he says nothing of his early years, and did not begin to write until the reign of Domitian. Of his parents he undutifully tells us that they were fools for teaching him to read.[1146] He was born at Bilbilis, a Spanish town in the province of Tarragon,[1147] of the position of which nothing is known for certain, except that its site was an elevated one,[1148] overlooking the river Salo, which flowed round its walls. It appears to have prided itself on its manufactures in gold and iron;[1149] to have been particularly famous for its arms;[1150] and to have been one of the Roman colonies dignified with the title of Augusta.[1151] As Vespasian had conferred on the poet's native town, in common with the rest of Spain, the *jus Latii*,[1152] Martial was by birth a Roman citizen; and in the days of his popularity obtained this privilege for many of his friends.[1153] His birthday was March 1,[1154] A. D. 43, the third year of the reign of Claudius.

In the twenty-second year of his age, the twelfth year of the reign of Nero,[1155] he migrated to Rome. He was a great favourite of Titus and Domitian, by whom the "*jus trium liberorum*" was conferred upon him,[1156] together with the rank of a Roman knight,[1157] and the honorary title of tribune.[1158] In the reign of the latter he was appointed to the office of court poet, and received a pension from the imperial treasury.[1159] Hence during the latter part of his residence in Rome it is almost certain that, although not rich, he enjoyed a competency. He

---

[1145] Lib. ix. 13; v. 33; iv. 65; v. 25, is something like an acrostic.
[1146] Lib. ix. Ep. 74.
[1147] *Vide* Nisard, Etudes, i. 335.
[1148] Lib. i. 50.
[1149] Lib. xii. 18.
[1150] Lib. x. 103.
[1151] Ibid.
[1152] Plin. iii. 3.
[1153] Lib. iii. 94.
[1154] Lib. x. 24.
[1155] A. D. 65.
[1156] Lib. iii. 94.
[1157] Lib. v. 13.
[1158] Lib. iii. 94.
[1159] Nisard, 337.

had a house in the city, and a little villa at Nomentum given him by Domitian.[1160] Nevertheless, he is constantly complaining of his poverty, and thinks that every one grows rich but himself. He laments that poets receive nothing but compliments for their verses, whilst lawyers, and even common criers, gain an ample maintenance:—that "Minerva was a better patron than Apollo; a fuller stream of wealth flowed through the Forum than from the fountain of Helicon, or the channel of Permessus."[1161] He complains that he spends all he has, and either borrows money from his friends, or takes to another the presents he has given him, and querulously asks him to purchase them back again.[1162] The roof of his villa lets in the rain; and when his friend Stella sends him some tiles to mend it he reproaches him for not sending also a toga to protect the poor inmate.[1163]

All this may have proceeded from the discontented feelings which poets and literary men so often indulge at seeing genius unrewarded, and affluence attending talents which, although if not so high an order, are of more general utility. Perhaps, too, though not absolutely poor, he was straitened in his circumstances, considering his social position and the demands which this entailed upon him. During thirty-five years he lived at Rome the life of a flatterer, and a dependant,[1164] and then returned to his native town.[1165] As Horace, when in his quiet country retirement, sometimes regrets the enjoyments of the capital, although when at Rome he sighs for the pleasures of rural life, so Martial, when at Rome, longed for Bilbilis, and when he returned to Bilbilis regretted Rome. At this late period of his life he married a Spanish lady, named Marcella, whose property was amply sufficient to maintain him in affluence. Her estate he considers a little kingdom; her gardens he would not exchange for those of Alcinous; he praises her bowers, groves, fountains, streamlets, fish-ponds, and meadows; and tells us the climate is so genial that the olive-grounds are green in January, and the roses blow twice in the year, like those of Pæstum.[1166] His wife he praises for her rare genius and sweet manners; he tells her that no one could discover her provincial origin; that her equal could not be found amongst the most elegant ladies in the capital; and when inclined to forget Rome she alone is all that Rome ever was to him:—

> Tu desiderium dominæ mihi mitius urbis
> Esse jubes; Romam tu mihi sola facis.[1167]

But, notwithstanding the delicate compliment which he pays to his rich wife—a compliment dictated probably more by his habit of courtly flattery than by sincerity of affection—he evidently pined for Rome. He was fitted for crowds and not for solitude: his spirit was not pure enough to commune with itself. His delight had been so long to study the human heart in its worst developments, to drag forth to public view its blackest plague-spots, that he would miss the foul models which he had so long studied. Provincial life was therefore utter dulness to him; his only enjoyment was to reproduce the results of his observations on the life of the capital. Combining in himself the apparently inconsistent

---

[1160] Lib. vii. 36.
[1161] Lib. i. 77.
[1162] Lib. vii. 16.
[1163] Lib. vii. 35.
[1164] Lib. xii. 31.
[1165] A. D. 100.
[1166] Lib. xii. 31.
[1167] Lib. xii. 21.

characters of the flatterer and the satirist, he needed great men to whom he might look up for patronage and approbation, as well as moral wounds to probe and subjects to anatomize. Rome alone supplied these; and when he lost them he lost the intellectual food necessary for his existence. The absence of his accustomed pursuits, and the irremediable void thus created, is evident in many of his epigrams.

The time of his death is uncertain, as the date of Pliny's elegant epistle to Priscus, in which it is mentioned, cannot be determined.[1168] But as it is probable that the eleventh book of his Epigrams was published in the year in which he left Rome for Bilbilis, and as he apologizes in the dedication of his twelfth book to Priscus for his obstinate indolence during a period of three years, his death cannot have taken place before A. D. 104. It is, however, generally supposed that his life was not prolonged much beyond this date. His death may have been hastened by his distaste for a provincial life, and by the malice and envy of his new neighbours.[1169]

According to his own account, in an epigram,[1170] in which he contrasts himself with an effeminate fop, his appearance was rough and unpolished, his shaggy hair refused to curl, his cheeks were well-whiskered, and his voice was louder than the roar of a lioness.[1171] It is impossible to believe the assertion which he makes respecting his own moral character, namely, that although his verses are licentious his life was virtuous,

> Lasciva est nobis pagina, vita proba est.[1172]

—although, measured by the corrupt standard of morals which disgraced the age in which he lived, he was probably not worse than most of his contemporaries. The fearful profligacy which his powerful pen describes in such hideous terms spread through Rome its loathsome infection. As no language is strong enough to denounce the impurities of his age—impurities, in the description of which, the poet evidently revels with a cynical delight—so they were not merely creatures of a prurient imagination, but had a real existence.

It may be said in extenuation of his crime, that the prevalence of vice produced the obscenity of the poet; but no more can be said in defence of works in which the characters of vice are emblazoned in such shameless and unnatural deformity. Had he lived in better times, his talents, of which no doubt can be entertained, might have been devoted to a purer object; as it was, his moral taste must have been thoroughly depraved not to have turned with loathing and disgust from the contemplation of such subjects, instead of voluntarily seeking them; for "out of the abundance of the heart the mouth speaketh." In Martial we observe that paradoxical but still not unusual combination of varied wit, poetical imagination, and a happy power of graceful expression, not only with strong sensual passions, but with a delight in vice in its most hateful forms and attributes.

Although the new feature which Martial added to the Greek epigram is such as has been described, and although his pages are polluted and defiled, not all his poems are spiteful or obscene. Amidst some obscurity of style and want of finish, many are redolent of Greek

---

[1168] Lib. xii. 21.
[1169] Præf. ad lib. xii.
[1170] Lib. x. 65.
[1171] There are two readings of the line to which allusion is here made, viz.:—
 Nobis filia fortius loquetur, and
 Non nobis lea fortius loquetur.The latter is the one adopted.
[1172] Lib. i. 5.

sweetness and elegance. Here and there are pleasing descriptions of the beauties of nature;[1173] and, setting aside those which are evidently dictated by the spirit of flattery, many are kind-hearted, as well as complimentary. The few lines which were intended to accompany such trifling offerings of friendship as the poet could afford to give, and which, doubtless, rendered a flower or a toy doubly acceptable, are equal in neatness to many of the Greek Anthology. When he sends a rose to Apollinaris, it is accompanied by the following elegant lines:—

> I felix rosa, mollibusque sertis
> Nostri cinge comas Apollinaris;
> Quas tu nectere candidas sed olim,
> Sic te semper amet Venus, memento.[1174]

Go, happy rose, and with thy delicate garlands wreathe the locks of my Apollinaris; and remember, so may Venus ever love thee! to entwine them when gray: but may it be long ere that time comes.

The fourteenth book contains numerous ingenious couplets, sent, together with pencases, dice, tablets, toothpicks, and other little presents, at the Saturnalian festival.

In so vast a collection of pieces it is natural to expect that there would be great inequality, and that some of his wit would be commonplace and puerile. That such was the case, he himself confesses more than once;[1175] and in one place he states that this inequality constitutes one of the merits of his work.[1176]

He knew that his works were appreciated, not only at Rome, but also throughout the empire:—

> Toto notus in orbe Martialis
> Argutis epigrammaton libellis;[1177]

and this consciousness is some excuse for the vanity which occasionally shows itself,[1178] and which does not hesitate to account blemishes as beauties.

The following are favourable specimens of his poetry:—

> Indignas premeret pestis cum tabida fauces,
> Inque ipsos vultus serperet atra lues;
> Siccis ipse genis flentes hortatus amicos
> Decrevit Stygios Festus adire lacus.
> Nec tamen obscuro pia polluit ora veneno,
> Aut torsit lenta tristia fata fame;
> Sanctam Romana vitam sed morte peregit,
> Dimisitque animam nobiliore via.
> Hanc mortem fatis magni præferre Catonis
> Fama potest; hujus Cæsar amicus erat.

[1173] For example, lib. iii. 48.
[1174] Lib. vii. 88.
[1175] Lib. vii. 89.
[1176] Lib. i. 12; vii. 30.
[1177] Lib. i. 1.
[1178] Lib. x. 100; i. 54; iv. 46.

When the dire quinsey choked his noble breath,
And o'er his face the blackening venom stole,
Festus disdained to wait a lingering death,
Cheered his sad friends, and freed his dauntless soul.
Nor meager famine's slowly-wasting force,
Nor hemlock's gradual chillness he endured;
But closed his life a truly Roman course,
And with one blow his liberty secured.
The Fates gave Cato a less glorious end,
For Cæsar was his foe, Festus was Cæsar's friend.[1179]
Hodgson.

Casta suo gladium cum traderet Arria Pæto
Quem de visceribus traxerat ipsa suis,
Si qua fides, vulnus, quod feci, non dolet, inquit;
Sed quod tu facies, hoc mihi, Pæte, dolet.
When Arria to her Pætus gave the steel,
Which from her bleeding side did newly part;
"From my own stroke," she said, "no pain I feel,
But, ah! thy wound will stab me to the heart."
Dum nos blanda tenent jucundi stagna Lucrini
Et quæ pumiceis fontibus antra calent,
Tu colis Argivi regnum Faustine coloni
Quo te bis decimus ducit ab urbe lapis.
Horrida sed fervent Nemeæi pectora monstri
Nec satis est Baias igne calere suo.
Ergo sacri fontes et littora sacra valete
Nympharum pariter Nereidumque domus!
Herculeos colles gelida vos vincite bruma,
Nunc Tiburtinis cedite frigoribus.
While near the Lucrine lake, consumed to death,
I draw the sultry air and gasp for breath,
Where streams of sulphur raise a stifling heat,
And thro' the pores of the warm pumice sweat;
You taste the cooling breeze where, nearer home,
The twentieth pillar marks the mile from Rome.
And now the Sun to the bright Lion turns,
And Baia with redoubled fury burns;
Then briny seas and tasteful springs, farewell,
Where fountain Nymphs confused with Naiads dwell.
In winter you may all the world despise,
But now 'tis Tivoli that bears the prize.
Addison.

[1179] Martial generally condemns suicide; for instance, "Fortiter ille facit qui miser esse potest," and "Hunc volo laudari, qui sine morte potest." But, see epigram on death of Otho (Lib. vi. 32.)

Chapter 33

AUFIDIUS BASSUS AND CREMUTIUS CORDUS—VELLEIUS PATERCULUS—CHARACTER OF HIS WORKS—VALERIUS MAXIMUS—CORNELIUS TACITUS—AGE OF TRAJAN—BIOGRAPHY OF TACITUS—HIS EXTANT WORKS ENUMERATED—AGRICOLA—GERMANY—HISTORIES—TRADITIONS RESPECTING THE JEWS—ANNALS—OBJECT OF TACITUS—HIS CHARACTER—HIS STYLE

The earliest prose writers belonging to this epoch were Aufidius Bassus and Cremutius Cordus. The former wrote a history of the German and civil wars, which was continued by the elder Pliny; of the latter only a few fragments have been preserved by Seneca.[1180] They were published in the reign of Tiberius; and it is evident that they contained a history of the civil wars, for his praise of Brutus and Cassius was made the pretext for his impeachment. It is also clear that he treated of contemporary events; for the real cause of the emperor's hostility was an attack which he made upon the favourite Sejanus. In vain he tendered an apology; and seeing there was no hope of escape he starved himself to death.[1181] His histories were publicly burned, but his daughter, to whom Seneca addressed his "*Consolatio*," concealed some copies, and afterwards published them, with the approbation of Caligula.[1182]

M. VELLEIUS PATERCULUS

Together with these flourished M. Velleius Paterculus. He was a soldier of equestrian family, served his first campaign in Asia, and subsequently, after passing through the various steps of promotion, acted as *legatus* to Tiberius in Germany. His services recommended him to the favour of the prince, on whose accession he was made prætor, and proved himself a

---

[1180] Suasor. vii.
[1181] A. D. 25; Tac. Ann. iv. 34.
[1182] Suet. Calig. 16.

stanch supporter of him and his favourite minister Sejanus. In the fall of that unworthy man,[1183] Paterculus was involved, and was most probably put to death.

The short historical work by which he is known as an author is a history of Rome, and of the nations connected with the foundation of the imperial city, in two books. It is dedicated to M. Vinucius, consul; and as it carries on the history to the death of Livia, the mother of Tiberius, in the year of his consulate,[1184] it must have been finished, perhaps almost entirely written within that year. Assuming that it was wise to undertake the task of comprising within such narrow limits events extending over so large a field, it is not unskilfully performed. The most striking events are selected and told in a lively and interesting manner; but he had one fault fatal to his character as an historian, who professed to treat of his own times. He is partial, prejudiced, and adulatory. He had not courage to be a Thucydides or a Sallust. The perilous nature of the times, and the personal obligations under which he was to the emperor, made him a courtier, and from this one-sided point of view he viewed contemporary history.

He was, however, a man of lively talents though of superficial education: his taste was formed after the model of the Augustan writers, especially Sallust, of whose style, so far as the outward form, he was an imitator. But although he was one of the earliest writers of the so called silver age, his language shows signs of degeneracy. It is, at times, overstrained and unnatural; there is the usual affectation of rhetorical effect, and an unnecessary use of uncommon words and constructions; still, whenever he keeps his model in view, he is scarcely inferior to him in conciseness and perspicuity. The first book of his history is in a very imperfect state; in fact, the commencement is entirely lost. Only one manuscript of it has been discovered, and even this is now nowhere to be found.

VALERIUS MAXIMUS

Valerius Maximus can scarcely be termed an historian, although the subject of which he treated is historical. His work is neither one of original research, nor is it a connected abridgment of the investigation of his predecessors. It is a collection of anecdotes, entitled *Dictorum Factorumque Memorabilium*, Libri IX. His object is a moral one; namely, to illustrate, by examples, the beauty of virtue and the deformity of vice; but he is influenced in the selection less by historical truth than by the striking and interesting character of the narrative. The arrangement of the anecdotes resembles that of a commonplace book, rather than of history, the only principle observed being, that anecdotes of Romans and foreigners are kept distinct from one another.

Nothing is known, for certain, respecting his personal history. He himself states[1185] that he accompanied Sextus Pompeius into Asia; and, from a comparison of different passages, it is probable that, like Velleius Paterculus, he flourished and wrote during the reign of Tiberius. His style is prolix and declamatory, and characterized by awkward affectation and involved obscurity.

[1183] A. D. 31.
[1184] A. D. 30.
[1185] Lib. ii. 6, 8.

C. Cornelius Tacitus

For the reasons already stated, Rome, for a long period, could boast of no historian; but, under the genial and fostering influence of the Emperor Trajan,[1186] not only the fine arts, especially architecture, flourished, but also literature revived. The choice of Nerva could not have fallen on a better successor to his short reign. He was a Spaniard, but his native town was a flourishing Roman colony: the whole country round about it had experienced the effects of Roman civilization, and the language of all the towns in the south of Spain was Latin. The glories of war and the duties of peace divided his attention. By the former, he gave employment to his vast armies; by the latter he refined the tastes and improved the character of his people. No better testimony can be desired than the correspondence between him and Pliny to the mildness and wisdom of his domestic and foreign administration. The influence, also, of his empress, Plotina, and his sister, Marciana, exercised a beneficial influence upon Roman society; for they were the first ladies of the imperial court who by their example checked the shameless licentiousness which had long prevailed amongst women of the higher classes. The same taste and execution which are visible in the bas-reliefs on the column of Trajan adorn the literature of his age, as illustrated by its two great lights, Tacitus and the younger Pliny. There is not the rich, graceful ornament which invests with such a charm the writers of the golden age; but the absence of these qualities is amply compensated by dignity, gravity, honesty and truthfulness. There is a solidity in the style of Tacitus which makes amends for its difficulty, and justifies the intense admiration with which he was regarded by Pliny. Truthfulness beams throughout the writings of these two great contemporaries; and incorruptible virtue is as visible in the pages of Tacitus as benevolence is in the letters of Pliny. They mutually influenced each other's character and principles: their tastes and pursuits were similar: they loved each other dearly; corresponded regularly, corrected each other's works, and accepted patiently and gratefully each other's criticisms. If, however, on all occasions, their observations were such as appear in the letters of Pliny, it is probable that their mutual regard, and the unbounded admiration which Pliny entertained for the superior genius of his friend caused them to be rather laudatory than severe.

The exact date of the birth of Tacitus is not known; but from one of the many letters extant, addressed to him by Pliny,[1187] it may be inferred that the former was not more than one or two years senior to his friend. In it he reminds him that in years they are almost equals, and adds that he himself was a young man when Tacitus had already obtained a brilliant reputation. There is a tradition which assigns the birth of Tacitus to the year of Nero's accession; but as Pliny the Younger was born A. D. 61, and Nero assumed the imperial purple A. D. 54, this date would make the difference in age between him and Pliny too great to be consistent with the expressions of the latter. Tacitus was of equestrian rank, and was procurator of Belgic Gaul in the reigns of Vespasian and Titus, from whom, as well as from Domitian, he received many marks of esteem. In A. D. 78, he married the daughter of C. Julius Agricola. He was one of the fifteen commissioners appointed for the celebration of the Ludi Seculares, A. D. 88, and was also prætor the same year. In A. D. 97, he served the office of consul. To this magistracy he was elected in order to supply the place of Virginius Rufus, who had died during his year of office, and over him Tacitus pronounced the funeral oration.

[1186] A. D. 98.
[1187] Plin. Ep. vii. 20.

In A. D. 99, he was associated by the Senate with Pliny[1188] in the impeachment of Marius Priscus, proconsul of Africa, for maladministration of his province; and his friend Pliny praises his reply to the acute subtleties of Salvius Liberalis, the advocate of Marius, as distinguished, not only for oratorical power, but for that which he considers the most remarkable quality of his style, *gravity*. His words are, "Respondit Corn. Tacitus eloquentissime et quod eximie orationi ejus inest, σεμνως."[1189] It is not known when Tacitus died, nor whether he left any descendants; but there can be no doubt that he survived the accession of Hadrian.[1190]

The works of Tacitus which are extant, are:—(1.) A Life of his father-in-law, Agricola. (2.) A tract on the Manners and Nations of Germany. (3.) A small portion of a voluminous work, entitled Histories. (4.) About two-thirds of another historical work, entitled Annals. (5.) A dialogue on the Decline of Eloquence is also ascribed to him; and although doubts have been entertained of its genuineness, they do not rest upon any strong foundation. It is impossible to do more than approximate to the dates at which each work of Tacitus was composed. The imminent peril of writing or speaking plainly on events or individuals renders it almost certain that none of them could have been published before the accession of Trajan. Niebuhr[1191] entertains no doubt that the first edition of the Life of Agricola was published towards the end of Domitian's reign, and that, subsequently, it was revised and an introduction prefixed. But is it not more probable that, although the work was then written, it was not published until after revision?

Great as were the moral worth and the amiable gentleness of Agricola, his courage as a soldier, his skill and decision as a general, his prudence and caution as a politician, and, therefore, however deserving he may be of the pleasing light in which his character is portrayed, still the life of Tacitus is a panegyric rather than a biography. The near relation in which Tacitus stood to him, the affectionate admiration which Agricola must necessarily have commanded from one who knew him so well, unfitted him for the work of an impartial biographer. The fine points of Agricola's character outshine all its other features; but we cannot suppose that he had no defects, no weaknesses. These, however, do not appear in the little work of Tacitus. His son-in-law either could not or would not see them. Still the brief sketch is a beautiful specimen of the vigour and force of expression with which this greatest painter of antiquity could throw off any portrait which he attempted. Even if the likeness be somewhat flattered, the qualities which the writer possessed, his insight into character, his pathetic power, and his affectionate heart, render this short piece one of the most attractive biographies extant.[1192]

With what simple pathos does he tell us of the obligation which Agricola, like so many other great men, owed to the educating care of his pure-minded, prudent, and indulgent mother, and the gratitude with which he was wont constantly to speak of that obligation! With what affection does he speak of one bound to him, not only by the ties of affinity, but by the stronger ties of a congenial temper and disposition! In his reflections on his death, there is no affected attempt at dramatic display. The few words devoted to so mournful a subject simply breathe the overwhelming sense of bereavement, unassuaged by the consolation of being

---

[1188] Plin. Ep. ii. 1.
[1189] Ep. II. xi.
[1190] A. D. 117.
[1191] Lect. R. H. cxix.
[1192] Agric. 4.

present at his last moments. "Happy wert thou, Agricola, not only because thy life was glorious, but because thy death was well-timed! All who heard thy last words bear witness to the constancy with which thou didst welcome death as though thou wert determined manfully to acquit the emperor of being the cause. But the bitterness of thy daughter's sorrow and mine for the loss of a parent is enhanced by the reflection, that it did not fall to our lot to watch over thy declining health, to solace thy failing strength, to enjoy thy last looks, thy last embraces. Faithfully would we have listened to thy parting words and wishes, and imprinted them deeply on our memories. This was our chief sorrow, our most painful wound. Owing to our long absence from Rome, thou hadst been lost to us four years before. Doubtless, O best of parents! enough, and more than enough, of honour was paid to thee by the assiduous attention of thy affectionate wife; still the last offices were paid thee amidst too few tears, and thine eyes were conscious that some loved object was absent just as their light was dimmed for ever." To this tribute of dutiful affection, succeed sentiments of noble resignation, joined with a humble conviction of the transitory nature of human talents, and an earnest looking-for of immortality. To us, the biography of Agricola is especially interesting, because Britain was the scene of his glory as a military commander, and of his success in civil administration. His army first penetrated beyond the Friths of Forth and Clyde into the Highlands of Scotland, and his fleet first circumnavigated the northern extremities of the British island.

The treatise on the geography, manners and nations of Germany (*De Situ Moribus et Populus Germaniæ*) is but little longer than the Life of Agricola. The information contained in it is exactly of that character which might be expected, considering the sources from which it was derived. Tacitus was never in Germany, and therefore his knowledge was collected from those who had visited it for the purposes either of war or commerce. Hence his geographical descriptions are often vague and inaccurate; a mixture of the marvellous shows that some of his narratives consist in mere travellers' tales, whilst the salient points and characteristic features of the national manners bear the impress of truth, and are supported by the well-known habits and institutions of Teutonic nations.

He tells of their bards, and explains the etymology of the term by the word Barditum, which signified the recitation of their songs.[1193] He hints at wild legends and dark superstitions with which the German imagination still loves to people the dark recesses of their forests.[1194] He describes their pure and unmixed race, and, consequently, the universal prevalence of the national features—blue eyes, red or sandy hair, and stalwart and gigantic frames.[1195] According to his account, their political constitutions were elective monarchies, but the monarch was always of noble birth and his power limited;[1196] and all matters of importance were debated by the estate of the people.[1197] In the solemn permission accorded to a German youth to bear arms, and his investiture with lance and shield, is seen the origin of knighthood;[1198] and in the sanctity of the marriage-tie, the chastity of the female sex, their social influence, and the respect paid to them—the rarity of adultery and its severe punishment, and the total absence of polygamy—we recognise the germ of the distinguishing

---

[1193] Cap. iii.
[1194] Cap. ix., xxxix., xl., xliii.
[1195] Cap. iv.
[1196] Cap. vii.
[1197] Cap. xi.
[1198] Cap. xiii.

characteristics of chivalry.[1199] They were hospitable and constant to their hereditary friendships, but stern in perpetuating family feuds;[1200] passionately fond of gambling, and strict in their regard for debts of honour;[1201] inveterate drinkers, and their favourite potation was beer;[1202] they could not consult on important matters without a convivial meeting;[1203] if they quarrelled over their cups, they had recourse rarely to words, usually to blows.[1204] Their slaves were in the condition of serfs or villains, and paid to the lord a fixed rent in corn, or cattle, or manufactures.[1205] They reckoned their time by nights instead of days,[1206] just as we are accustomed to use the expressions se'nnight and fortnight.

After having sketched the manners and customs of the nation as a whole he proceeds to treat of each tribe separately.[1207] In speaking of our forefathers, the *Angli*, who inhabited part of the modern territory of Sleswick Holstein, and whose name is still retained in the district of Angeln, one word which he uses is an English one. The Angli, he says, together with the conterminous tribes, worship Herthus, *i. e.* Terra.[1208] Even in these early times he mentions the naval superiority of the Suiones, who were the ancestors of the Normans and Sea-kings. With these he affirms that the continent of Europe terminates, and all beyond is a motionless and frozen ocean.[1209] Truth in these distant climes mingles with fable. Daylight continues after the sun has set, but a hissing noise is heard as his blazing orb plunges into the sea, and the forms of the gods, and the radiant glories which surround their heads, are visible.[1210] The list of marvels ends with fabulous beings, whose bodies and limbs are those of wild beasts, whilst their heads and faces are human.

The earliest historical work of Tacitus is his "*Historiæ*," of which only four books and a portion of the fifth are extant. Their contents extend from the second consulship of Galba[1211] to the commencement of the siege of Jerusalem. The original work concluded with the death of Domitian.[1212] He purposed also, if his life had been spared, to add the reigns of Nerva and Trajan, as the employment of his old age. "The materials for which," he says, "are more plentiful and trustworthy, because of the unusual felicity of an age in which men were allowed to think as they pleased, and to give utterance to what they thought."[1213] It is plain from the word Divus (the deified) being prefixed to the name of Nerva, and not to that of Trajan, in the passage above quoted, that this work was written after Trajan had put on the imperial purple.[1214]

According to St. Jerome it originally consisted of thirty books; and the minuteness with which each event is recorded in the portion extant renders it highly probable that the original work was as extensive as this assertion would imply. The object which he proposed to

---

[1199] Cap. xviii., xix.
[1200] Cap. xxi.
[1201] Cap. xxiv.
[1202] Cap. xxiii.
[1203] Cap. xxii.
[1204] Cap. xxii.
[1205] Cap. xxv.
[1206] Cap. xi.
[1207] From cap. xxviii.
[1208] Cap. xl.
[1209] Cap. xlv.
[1210] Cap. xlvi.
[1211] A. D. 69.
[1212] A. D. 96.
[1213] Hist i. 1.
[1214] A. D. 117.

himself was worthy of his penetrating mind, from the searching gaze of which even the hypocrisy and dissimulation of a Tiberius were powerless to veil the foul darkness of his crafty nature. He intended "to investigate the political state of the commonwealth, the feelings of its armies, the sentiments of the provinces, the elements of its strength and weakness, the causes and reasons for each phænomenon."[1215] The principal fault which diminishes the value of his history as a record of events, is his too great readiness to accept evidence unhesitatingly, and to record popular rumours without taking sufficient pains to examine into their truth. Still these blots are but few, scattered over a vast field of faithful history. Perhaps the most lamentable instance is presented in his incorrect account of the history, constitution, and manners of the Jewish people. Wanting either the opportunity or the inclination to consult the sacred books of the nation, he mixes up vague traditions of their early history with the fables of Pagan mythology; and, like the Greeks and Romans, gives names to imaginary patriarchs, taken from localities connected with their history.

According to his account the Jews originally inhabited Crete,[1216] and from Mount Ida, in that Island, received the name of Idæi, which afterwards became corrupted into Judæi. From Crete, when Saturn was expelled by Jove, they took refuge in Egypt; and thence under two leaders, Juda and Hierosolymus, again migrated to the neighbouring country of Palestine. A second tradition attributes to them an Assyrian origin; a third an Æthiopian; a fourth asserts that they were descended from the Solymi which Homer celebrated in his poems.[1217]

The next tradition which he mentions approaches nearer to the true one. Egypt being afflicted with a plague, the king Bocchoris, by the advice of the oracle of Ammon, purged his kingdom of them, and under the guidance of Moses they began their wanderings. When they were dying on their way for want of water, their leader followed a herd of wild asses, by which he was led to a copious well of water. Thus was their drought relieved; and, after journeying six days, they obtained possession of the land in which they built their capital and temple. Moses introduced new religious rites contrary to those of other nations. He set up the image of an ass in the Holy of Holies—a statement which afterwards Tacitus virtually contradicts by saying that they allow no images in their temples,[1218] that they preferred taking up arms to admitting the statue of Caligula into the temple;[1219] and that when Pompey took Jerusalem,[1220] he found no image of any deity, and the sanctuary empty. He adds, that they sacrifice rams in order to show contempt to Jupiter Ammon, and oxen, because, under that form, Apis was worshipped by the Egyptians; that they abstain from pork in remembrance of their having been afflicted with leprosy, to which that animal is subject, and eat unleavened bread as a memorial of their once having stolen food. On the seventh day, which terminated their wanderings, they do no work, and in like manner the seventh year they devote to idleness. This Sabbath, some assert that they keep holy in honour of Saturn. They believe in the immortality of the soul, and in future rewards and punishments, and embalm their dead like the Egyptians. Such are the various traditions respecting the Jews which Tacitus incorporates in his Histories.

[1215] Hist. i. 4.
[1216] Hist. v. 2.
[1217] Ibid. iii.
[1218] Ibid. v.
[1219] Ibid. ix.
[1220] B. C. 62.

The Annals, which were written subsequently to the Histories, were so called, because each historical event is recorded in historical order under the year to which it belongs.[1221] They consist of sixteen books; commence with the death of Augustus,[1222] and conclude with that of Nero.[1223] The only portions extant are—the first four books, part of the fifth, the sixth, part of the eleventh, the twelfth, thirteenth, fourteenth, fifteenth, and the commencement of the sixteenth book. The Annals are rather histories of each successive emperor than of the Roman people; but this is the necessary condition of narrating the fortunes of a nation which now possessed only the bare name, and not the reality of constitutional government. The state was now the emperor; the end and object of the social system his security; and every political event must therefore be treated in relation to him.

But a history of this kind in the hands of one who had such skill in diving into the recesses of man's heart, who could read so shrewdly and delineate so vigorously human character, who possessed as a writer such picturesque and dramatic power, becomes the more interesting from its biographical nature, and its philosophical importance as a moral rather than a political study. It is not, owing to circumstances over which the author had no control, the history of a great nation, for the Romans, as a whole, were no longer great. Neither does it paint the rise, progress and development of constitutional freedom, for it had reached its zenith, had declined, become paralyzed, and finally extinct. But still there existed bright examples of heroism, and courage, and self-devotion, truly Roman, and instances not less prominent of corruption and degradation. Individuals stand out in bold relief, eminent for the noblest virtues or blackened by the basest crimes. These appear either singly or in groups upon the stage: the emperor forms the principal figure; and the moral sense of the reader is awakened to admire instances of patient suffering and determined bravery, or abject slavery and remorseless despotism.

The object of Tacitus, therefore, was not, like that of the great philosophical historian of Greece, to describe the growth of political institutions, or the implacable animosities which raged between opposite political principles—the struggles for supremacy between a class and a whole people—but the influence which the establishment of tyranny on the ruins of liberty exercised for good or for evil in bringing out the character of the individual. Rome, the imperial city, was the all-engrossing subject of his predecessors; Romans were but subordinate and accessary. Tacitus delineated the lives and deaths of individuals, and showed the relation which they bore to the fortunes of their country.

It would have been impossible to have satisfied a people whose taste had become more than ever rhetorical, without the introduction of orations. Those of Tacitus are perfect specimens of art; and probably, with the exception of Galgacus,[1224] far more true than those of other Roman historians. Still he made use of them, not only to imbody traditional accounts of what had really been said on each occasion, but to illustrate his own views of the character of the speaker, and to convey his own political opinions.

Full of sagacious observation and descriptive power, Tacitus engages the most serious attention of the reader by the gravity of his condensed and comprehensive style, as he does by the wisdom and dignity of his reflections. The purity and gravity of his sentiments remind the reader even of Christian authors.

[1221] Ann. iv. 71.
[1222] A. D. 14.
[1223] A. D. 68.
[1224] Life of Agricola.

Living amidst the influences of a corrupt age he was uncontaminated; and by his virtue and integrity, his chastened political liberality, commands our admiration as a man, whilst his love of truth is reflected in his character as an historian. Although he imitated, as well as approved, the cautious policy of his father-in-law, he was not destitute of moral firmness.

It derogates nothing from his courage that he was silent during the perilous times in which great part of his life was passed, and spoke with boldness only when the happy reign of Nerva had commenced, and the broken spirit of the nation had revived. Like the rest of his fellow-countrymen he exhibited a remarkable example of patient endurance, when the imperial jealousy made even the praise of those who were obnoxious to the tyrant treason; when it was considered a capital crime for Arulenus Rusticus to praise Pætus Thrasea, and Herennius Senecio to eulogize Priscus Helvidius.

In those fearful times he himself says, that "as old Rome had witnessed the greatest glories of liberty, so her descendants had been cast down to the lowest depths of slavery; and would have been deprived of the use of memory, as well as of language, if it were equally in man's power to forget as to be silent."[1225] In such times prudence was a duty, and daring courage would have been unavailing rashness. In his praise of Agricola, and his blame of Pætus, he enunciates the principles which regulate his own conduct—that to endanger yourself without the slightest prospect of benefiting your country is mere ostentatious ambition. "Sciant," he writes, "quibus moris illicita mirari, posse etiam sub malis principibus magnos viros esse; obsequiumque ac modestiam, si industria ac vigor adsint, eo laudis excedere quo plerique per abrupta, sed in nullum reipublicæ usum ambitiosa morte inclaruerunt."[1226] Again, "Thrasea Pætus sibi causam periculi fecit, cæteris libertatis initium non præbuit."[1227]

In the style of Tacitus the form is always subordinate to the matter; the ideas maintain their due supremacy over the language in which they are conveyed. There is none of that striving after epigrammatic terseness which savours of affectation. His brevity, like that which characterizes the style of Thucydides, is the necessary condensation of a writer whose thoughts flow more quickly than his pen can express them. Hence his sentences are suggestive of far more than they express: they are enigmatical hints of deep and hidden meaning, which keep the mind active and the attention alive, and delight the reader with the pleasures of discovery and the consciousness of difficulties overcome. Nor is this natural and unintentional brevity unsuitable to the cautious reserve with which all were tutored to speak and think of political subjects in perilous times. It is extraordinary how often a similarity between his mind and that of Thucydides inadvertently discovers itself—not only in his mode of thinking, but also in his language, even in his grammatical constructions, especially in his frequent substitution of attraction for government, in instances of condensed construction, and in the connexion of clauses grammatically different, although they are metaphysically the same.

Nor is his brevity dry or harsh—it is enlivened by copiousness, variety, and poetry. He scarcely ever repeats the same idea in the same form. No author is richer in synonymous words, or arranges with more varied skill the position of words in a sentence. As for poetic genius, his language is highly figurative; no prose writer deals more largely in prosopopœia:

[1225] Vit. Agric. ii.
[1226] Agric. 42.
[1227] Ann. xiv. 12.

his descriptions of scenery and incidents are eminently picturesque; his characters dramatic; the expression of his own sentiments and feelings as subjective as lyric poetry.

Chapter 34

C. SUETONIUS TRANQUILLUS—HIS BIOGRAPHY—SOURCES OF HIS HISTORY—HIS GREAT FAULT—Q. CURTIUS RUFUS—TIME WHEN HE FLOURISHED DOUBTFUL—HIS BIOGRAPHY OF ALEXANDER—EPITOMES OF L. ANNÆUS FLORUS—SOURCES WHENCE HE DERIVED THEM

C. SUETONIUS TRANQUILLUS

C. Suetonius Tranquillus[1228] was the son of Suetonius Lenis, who served as tribunus angusticlavus of the thirteenth legion at the battle of Bedriacum, in which the Emperor Otho was defeated by Vitellius. The time of his birth is uncertain; but from a passage at the end of his Life of Nero[1229] it may be inferred that he was born very soon after the death of that emperor, which took place A. D. 68; for in it he mentions that, when twenty years subsequent to Nero's death, a false Nero appeared, he was just arriving at manhood (*adolescens*.) The knowledge of language and rhetorical taste displayed in the remains of his works on these subjects prove that he was well instructed in these branches of a Roman liberal education: and a letter of the younger Pliny,[1230] whose intimate friend he was, speaks of him as an advocate by profession. This letter represents him as unwilling to plead a cause, which he had undertaken, because he was frightened by a dream. It is probable that this anecdote is an authentic one, because so many examples occur in his memoirs of his superstitious belief in dreams, omens, ghosts, and prodigies.[1231]

The affectionate regard which Pliny entertained for his friend was very great, and led him to form too high an estimate of his talents as a writer and an historian. On one occasion he used his influence at court to get him a tribuneship; which, however, he did not accept.[1232] On another he obtained for him, from Trajan,[1233] the "*jus trium liberorum*," although he had no

---

[1228] See A. Krause de Font. et Auctor. Suet.
[1229] Cap. 57.
[1230] Ep. I. 18.
[1231] See *e. g.* Cæs. 81; Aug. 6, 94; Tib. 14, 74; Calig. 5, 57, &c.
[1232] See Ep. III. 8.
[1233] Ep. X. 95.

children. But this privilege, as in the case of Martial, was sometimes granted under similar circumstances. In this letter, which he wrote to the Emperor, he speaks of Suetonius as a man of the greatest probity, integrity, and learning; and adds that, after the experience of a long acquaintance, the more he knows of him the more he loves him.

Subsequently Suetonius became private secretary (*Magister Epistolarum*) to Hadrian,[1234] but was deprived of the situation. Owing to the only sources of information respecting Suetonius being his own works, and the few scattered notices in the letters of Plinius Secundus, nothing more is known respecting his life.

A catalogue of his numerous writings is given by Suidas:[1235] but, with the exception of the Lives of the Twelve Cæsars, it does not contain his chief extant works. These are notices of illustrious grammarians and rhetoricians, and the lives of the poets Terence, Horace, Persius, Lucan, and Juvenal.

Niebuhr[1236] believed that the history, or rather the biography of the Cæsars was written when Suetonius was still young, before he was secretary to Hadrian, and previous to the publication of the Histories of Tacitus. If so, he neither enjoyed the opportunities of consulting the imperial records which his situation at court would have given him, nor of profiting by the accurate guidance and profound reflection of Tacitus. Krause,[1237] on the other hand, adduces many parallelisms between the language of Tacitus and Suetonius; and as Tacitus did not publish his earliest historical work before A. D. 117,[1238] assumes that Suetonius did not write his biographies until after the accession of Hadrian.

It is very difficult to determine which of these theories is the correct one; but there can be no doubt that the sources from which he derived his information are quite independent of the authority of Tacitus; and that the Lives of the Twelve Cæsars would have contained all that we find in them, even if the Annals and Histories had never been written. He does not only trust to the works of the Roman historians, but his exact quotations from acts of the senate and people, edicts, fasti, and orations, and the use which he makes of annals and inscriptions, prove that he was a man of diligent research, and that he examined original documents for himself.

Again, as a writer of biographical memoirs rather than of regular history, and fond of anecdote and scandal, he availed himself largely of such private letters of Emperors and their dependants as fell in his way, of testamentary documents, and of the information he could collect in conversation. Many of the lives which he wrote were those of his contemporaries. Some of the events recorded were passing under the eyes of the public, and were matters of notoriety. He himself asserts in three several places[1239] that he received some of the accounts which he gives from the testimony of eye-witnesses. The more secret habits of the Emperors, either truly told or exaggerated by an appetite for scandal, would ooze out. Anecdotes of the reigning Emperor's private life would be eagerly sought for, and be the favourite topic of gossip in all circles of Roman society. Nor would he have any difficulty in procuring copious stores of information respecting those Emperors who reigned before he was born from those of his contemporaries who were a generation older than himself, and who were spectators of,

---

[1234] Spart. L. of Had. c. ii.
[1235] S. v. Τράγκυλλος.
[1236] Lect. R. H. cxvi. note.
[1237] De Suet. Fontibus. Berl. 1831.
[1238] Ann. ii. 61.
[1239] Cal. 19; Nero, 29; Tit. 3.

or actors in, many of the scenes which he describes. As a biographer, there is no reason to doubt his honesty and veracity; he is industrious and careful; he indulges neither in ornament of style nor in romantic exaggeration; the picture which he draws is a terrible one, but it is fully supported by the contemporary authority of Juvenal and Tacitus. Nevertheless, his mind was not of that comprehensive and philosophical character which would qualify him for taking an enlarged view of political affairs, or for the work of an historian. He has no definite plan formed in his mind, without which an historian can never hope to make his work a complete whole; he wanders at will from one subject to another, just as the idea seizes him, and is by no means careful of committing offences against chronological order.

Niebuhr accuses him of inconsistency in the character which he draws and the praise which he bestows on Vespasian:[1240] but adds what may, in some sort, be considered a defence, namely, that Vespasian was, negatively speaking, a good, upright, and just man, and that the dark side of his character must be considered in reference to the fearful times in which he reigned. He also mentions, as an example of his deficiencies as an historian, the bad accounts which he has left of his own times, especially of the anarchy which followed Nero's death, and the commencement of the reign of Vespasian. But in his praise it may be said that Suetonius has formed a just estimate of his own powers in undertaking to be a biographer and not an historian; and it is scarcely fair to criticise severely his unfitness for a task to which he made no pretensions.

One great fault pollutes his pages. The dark pictures which he draws of the most profligate Emperors, the disgusting annals of their unheard-of crimes, are dwelt upon as though he took pleasure in the description, and loved to wallow in the mire of the foulest debauchery. Truth, perhaps, required that they should not have been passed over in silence, but they might have been lightly touched, and not painted in detail with revolting faithfulness. He is often brief, sometimes obscure: in such passages of his narrative we would have gladly welcomed both brevity and obscurity.

Q. CURTIUS RUFUS

The doubts which have always been entertained respecting the time when the biographer of Alexander the Great flourished, and which no investigations have been sufficient to dissipate, render it impossible to pass him by unnoticed, although he may, perhaps, belong to an age beyond the chronological limits of this work. The purity of his style has, in the opinion of some critics, entitled him to a place among the writers of the silver age; whilst Niebuhr, judging by the internal evidence, thinks that he must have lived as late as the reign of Caracalla or Septimius Severus.

No valid argument, however, can be based upon his style, because it is evidently artificial: it is, indeed, infected with a love of declamatory ornament; it is sometimes more like poetry than prose; it abounds in metaphors, and therefore proves that he lived in a rhetorical age; but it is upon the whole an imitation of the Latinity of Livy. This rhetorical character of his style gives some value to the opinion of F. A. Wolf, that he was the Q. Curtius Rufus mentioned by Suetonius in his treatise on Illustrious Orators. If so, he was probably a contemporary.

[1240] Lib. cxvi.

With respect to internal evidence, reference has been made to two passages as containing allusions to his times. (1.) Multis ergo casibus defuncta (sc. Tyrus,) nunc tamen longa pace cuncta refovente, sub tutela Romanæ mansuetudinis acquiescit.[1241] (2.) Proinde jure meritoque P. R. salutem se principi suo debere profitetur, qui noctis, quam pæne supremam habuimus, novum sidus illuxit, hujus hercule, non solis ortus, lucem caliganti reddidit mundo, cum sine suo capite discordia membra trepidarent.[1242] The former has been considered descriptive of many periods in Roman history: although Niebuhr[1243] makes the unqualified assertion, that it has no meaning, unless it alludes to the times of Septimius Severus and Caracalla. The latter is equally vague: Niebuhr thinks it might refer to Aurelian: Gibbon considers that it alluded to Gordian. But to how many Emperors might a spirit of eulogistic flattery make it applicable! Upon the whole, it is most probable that he lived towards the close of the first century.

The biography of Alexander is deeply interesting; for, although Curtius evidently disdains historic reality, his hero always seems to have a living existence: it is a romance rather than a history. He never loses an opportunity by the colouring which he gives to historical facts of elevating the Macedonian conqueror to a superhuman standard. He has no inclination to weigh the merits of conflicting historical testimonies: he selects that which supports his partial predilections; nor are his talents for story-telling checked by a profound knowledge of either tactics or geography, or other objective historical materials, for correct details in which he is too frequently negligent.[1244] His florid and ornamented style is suitable to the imaginary orations which are introduced in the narrative, and which constitute the most striking portions of the work. The sources from which he derived his information are various, the principal one being the account of Alexander's exploits by the Greek historian Clitarchus, who accompanied the Macedonian conqueror in his Asiatic expedition. He is, however, by no means a servile follower; for in one instance he does not hesitate to accuse him of inaccuracy. They were, however, kindred spirits: both would sacrifice truth to romantic interest; both indulged in the same tale-telling tendency. His work originally consisted of ten books. Two of these are lost, and their places have been supplied, in a very inferior manner, by Cellarius and Freinsheim. Even in the eight books which are extant, an hiatus of more or less extent occasionally occurs.

L. ANNÆUS FLORUS

Brief as the epitomes are which bear the name of L. Annæus Florus, the style is characterized by the rhetorical spirit of the age to which they belong. They are diffuse and declamatory, and their author is rather the panegyrist of his countrymen than the grave and sober narrator of the most important events contained in their history. This short summary, entitled "*Rerum Romanarum*, Libri IV.," or "*Epitome de Gestis Romanorum*," is a well-arranged compilation from the authorities extant; but it is probable that, like all other Roman historians except Velleius Paterculus, he derived his materials principally from Livy. Such a dry skeleton of history, however, must be uninteresting. Who the author was is by no means

---

[1241] Book iv. 20.
[1242] Book x. 9.
[1243] Lect. R. H. cxxviii.
[1244] Lect. R. H. cxxviii.

certain. Some have supposed him to be the same with Annæus Florus, who wrote three trochaic verses to Hadrian. Titze[1245] imagines that it is the work of two authors, one a contemporary of Horace,[1246] the other belonging to a later literary period.

It is generally assumed that the author[1247] of the Epitomes was either a Spaniard or a Gaul; and, if we may consider the introduction to the work as genuine, he lived in the reign of Trajan.

[1245] Anthol. Lat. ii. 97, Burm. or 212 Meyer. Titze ed. Flor. Prag. 1819.

[1246] Ep. i. 3; ii. 2.

[1247] Matth. 284.

Chapter 35

M. ANNÆUS SENECA—HIS CONTROVERSY AND SUASORIÆ—L. ANNÆUS SENECA—TUTOR TO NERO—HIS ENORMOUS FORTUNE—HIS DEATH AND CHARACTER—INCONSISTENCIES IN HIS PHILOSOPHY—A FAVOURITE WITH EARLY CHRISTIAN WRITERS—HIS EPISTLES—WORK ON NATURAL PHENOMENA—APOCOLOCYNTOSIS—HIS STYLE

M. ANNÆUS SENECA

The family of the Senecas exercised a remarkable influence over literature; they may, in fact, be said to have given the tone to the taste of their age.

M. Annæus Seneca was born at Corduba (Cordova.) The precise date of his birth is unknown; but Clinton places it about B. C. 61. This is not improbable, for he asserts[1248] that he had heard all the eminent orators except Cicero, and that he might have enjoyed that privilege also if the civil wars had not compelled him to remain in his native country. After this hinderance was removed by the accession of Augustus he came to Rome, and, as a professional rhetorician, amassed a considerable fortune. Subsequently he returned to Cordova, and married Helvia, by whom he had three sons, of whom L. Annæus Seneca, the philosopher, was the eldest.

He left behind him two works, the composition of which was the employment of his old age. They are the results of his long and successful experience as a teacher of rhetoric, the gleanings of his commonplace book, the stores accumulated by his astonishing memory, which enabled him to repeat two thousand unconnected words after once hearing them, and to report literally any orations which he had heard delivered. They are valuable as showing how a hollow and artificial system, based upon the recollection of stock-passages and commonplaces, had supplanted the natural promptings of true eloquence. They explain the

---

[1248] Præf. ad Controv. i. 67.

principles and practice of instruction in the popular schools of rhetoric, the means by which the absence of natural endowments could be compensated. They exhibit wit, learning, ingenuity, and taste to select and admire the best literary specimens of earlier periods; but it is plain that matter was now subordinate to form—that the orator was content to borrow the phraseology of his predecessors in which to clothe sentiments which he could neither feel nor understand. The ear still yearned for the language of sincerity, although the heart no longer throbbed with the ardour of patriotism. It is this want of conformity of ideas to words which causes the coldness of a declamatory and florid style. It is a mere representation of warmth: it disappoints like a mere painted fire.

The first work of M. Seneca was entitled *Controversiæ*: it was divided into ten books, of which, with the exception of fragments, only the first, second, seventh, eighth, and tenth are extant. It contains a series of exercises or declamations in judicial oratory on fictitious cases. The imaginary causes were probably sketched out by the professor. The students composed their speeches according to the rules of rhetoric: they were then corrected, committed to memory, and recited, partly with a view to practice, partly in order to amuse an admiring audience. The cases are frequently as puerile as a schoolboy's theme, sometimes extravagant and absurd.

His other work, the *Suasoriæ*, contains exercises in deliberative oratory. The subjects of them are taken from the historians and poets: they are as harmless as tyranny could desire: there is no danger that languid patriotism should revive, or the empire be menaced, by such uninteresting discussions. Nor were they confined to mere students. Public recitations had, since the days of Juvenal, been one of the crying nuisances of the times. The poets began it, the rhetoricians followed, and the most absurd trash was listened to with patience, being ushered into popular notice by partial flatterers or hired claqueurs.

L. ANNÆUS SENECA

L. Seneca was born at his father's native town about the commencement of the Christian era. He was brought to Rome when very young, and there studied rhetoric and philosophy. He soon displayed great talents as a pleader; and by his success is said to have provoked the jealousy of Caligula. In the reign of Claudius he was accused by the infamous Messalina of improper intimacy with Julia, the emperor's niece, and was accordingly banished to Corsica.[1249] He solaced his exile with the study of the Stoic philosophy; and although its severe precepts exercised no moral influence over his conduct, he not only professed himself a Stoic, but sincerely imagined that he was one. Eight years afterwards Agrippina caused his recall,[1250] in order to make him tutor to her son Nero.

His pupil was naturally vicious; and Seneca, though wise and prudent, was too unscrupulous a man of the world to attempt the correction of his propensities, or to instil into him high principles. After the accession of Nero,[1251] Seneca endeavoured to arrest his depraved career; but it was too late: all he could do was to put into his mouth specious words of clemency and mercy. He saw how dangerous was the unprincipled ambition of Agrippina;

[1249] A. D. 41.
[1250] Tac. Ann. xii. 8.
[1251] Ibid. xiii. 2.

and dreadful though it was to sanction parricide, there was scarcely any other course to be pursued, except the consenting to her death. When the deed was done, he had the pitiful meanness to screen the murderer by a falsehood. He wrote a letter, which Nero sent to the senate, accusing his mother of treason, and asserting that she had committed suicide.[1252]

Seneca had by usury and legacy-hunting, amassed one of those enormous fortunes, of which so many instances are met with in Roman history. This had already exposed him to envy,[1253] and caused his temporary banishment to the Balearic isles.[1254] But after that Burrus was dead, who shared his influence over the Emperor, he felt the dangers of wealth, and offered his property to Nero.[1255] The Emperor refused; but Seneca retired from public life. Being now under the influence of new favourites, Nero wished to rid himself of Seneca; and although there was no evidence of his being privy to the conspiracy of Piso, it furnished a pretext for his destruction.[1256] In adversity his character shone with brighter lustre. Though he had lived ill, he could die well. His firmness was the result, not of Stoical indifference, but of Roman courage. He met the messengers of death without trembling. His noble wife Paullina determined to die with him. The veins of both were opened at the same time. The little blood which remained in his emaciated and enfeebled frame refused to flow: he suffered excruciating agony: a warm bath was applied, but in vain; and a draught of poison was equally ineffectual. At last he was suffocated by the vapour of a stove, and expired.[1257]

Seneca lived in a perilous atmosphere. The philosophy in which he believed was hollow, and, being unsuited to his court life,[1258] he thought it expedient to allow himself some relaxation from its severity. His rhetorical taste led him to overstate even his own real convictions; and hence the incongruity of his life appeared more glaring. He was not insincere; but he had not firmness to act up to the high moral standard which he proposed to himself. In his letters, and his treatise "*De Consolatione*," addressed to Polybius, he even convicts himself of this defect. He had difficult questions to decide, and had not sufficient moral principle to lead him in the right course. He was avaricious; but it was the great sin of his times. Tacitus is not blind to his weaknesses;[1259] but he estimates his character with more candour and fairness than Dio.[1260] He is neither a panegyrist nor an accuser. The education of one who was a brute rather than a man was a task to the discharge of which no one would have been equal. He, therefore, retained the influence which he had not uprightness to command by miserable and sinful expedients. He had great abilities, and some of the noble qualities of the old Romans. Had he lived in the days of the Republic he would have been a great man.

Seneca was the author of twelve ethical treatises, the best of which are entitled "*De Providentiâ*," "*De Constantiâ Sapientis*," and "*De Consolatione*." The latter was addressed to his mother Helvia, and written during his exile in Corsica. In the treatise on Providence he discusses the question why, since there is a Divine Providence, good men are liable to misfortunes. Although the difficulty is explained by the doctrine that the remedy, "*suicide*," is

---

[1252] Quint. viii. 5, 18.
[1253] Ibid. xiii. 42.
[1254] A. D. 58.
[1255] Quint. xiv. 53.
[1256] Ibid. xv. 60.
[1257] Ad. 65.
[1258] Ep. 108.
[1259] Ann. xiii.; xiv. 2.
[1260] Lib. lxi. 10.

always in man's power, it asserts the omnipresence of the Deity, and the existence of a moral Governor of the universe.

Great as are the inconsistencies in his ethical philosophy (nor could it be otherwise, as his life was always doing despite to his moral sense of right and wrong,) his views are generally clear and practical. In this he was a true Roman; he cared little for abstract speculation; he did not value, except as subordinate aids, either mental or natural philosophy. He delighted to inculcate precepts rather than investigate principles. It is for this reason that his works are not satisfactory as a whole, whilst they furnish a rich mine for quotations. The fault which pervades all Roman philosophy exists in an exaggerated form in his works: they are ethical digests of didactic precepts; but there is no system, no developement of new truths. His studies taught him that general principles are the foundations of morals, and that casuistry is the application of those principles;[1261] but the Romans were naturally inclined to be casuists rather than moralists; and in this preference Seneca went beyond all his countrymen. He writes like a teacher of youth rather than as a philosopher; he inculcates, without proof, maxims and instructions, and impresses them by repetition, as though they recommended themselves by their intrinsic truthfulness to the consciences of his hearers.

Seneca was always a favourite with Christian writers; he is in fact a better guide to others than he was to himself. Some of his sentiments are truly Christian; there is even a tradition that he was acquainted with St. Paul, and fourteen letters to that apostle have been, though without grounds, attributed to him. He may, however, unconsciously have imbibed some of the principles of Christianity. The gospel had already made great and rapid strides over the civilized world, and thoughtful minds may have been enlightened by some of the rays of divine truth dispersed through the moral atmosphere, just as we are benefited by the light of the sun, even when its disc is obscured by clouds.

His Epistles, of which there are one hundred and twenty-four, are moral essays in an epistolary form, and are the most delightful of his works. Although addressed to a disciple named Lucilius, they are evidently written for the public eye: they are rich in varied thought, and the reflections flow naturally and without effort. Letters were perhaps the most appropriate vehicle for his preceptive philosophy, because such a desultory style is best adapted to convey isolated and unconnected maxims. They contain a free and unconstrained picture of his mind. We see in them how he despised verbal subtleties,[1262] the external badges of a sect or creed, and insisted that the great end of science is to learn how to live and how to die.

In his old age he wrote seven books on questions connected with natural phenomena (*Quæstionum Naturalium*, Libri vii.) Why he did so it is impossible to say, since he had so often argued against the utility of physical studies.[1263] The declamatory praise which he bestows upon them in this work would lead us to suppose that it was a mere exercise for amusement and relaxation. But in this case he is not so inconsistent as might be supposed— he treats the subject like a moralist, and makes it the occasion of ethical reflections.[1264]

Once he indulged in the playfulness of satire. He had written a fulsome funeral oration on Claudius, which Nero delivered in the midst of laughter and derision; but for this abject flattery he afterwards made compensation by composing, as a parody on the apotheosis of the

---

[1261] Ep. 94, 95.
[1262] Ep. 45.
[1263] See *ex. gr.* Ep. 88, 106.
[1264] See L. vii. c. 30.

stupid Emperor, the *Apocolocyntosis*, or his metamorphosis into a pumpkin. The pun was good enough, but the execution miserable.

In the style of Seneca we see the result of that false declamatory taste of which the works of his father furnish specimens. Thought was subordinate to expression. The masters of rhetoric were all in all. His style is too elaborate to please; it is generally affected, often florid and bombastic: he seems always striving to produce striking effects, either by antithesis or ornament; of course he defeats his object, for there is no light and shade. There is too much sparkle and glitter, too little repose and simplicity.

Chapter 36

Pliny the Elder—His Habits Described by His Nephew—His Industry and Application—His Death in the Eruption of Vesuvius—The Eruption Described in Two Letters of Pliny the Younger—The Natural History of Pliny—Its Subjects Described—Pliny the Younger—His Affectionf for His Guardian—His Panegyric, Letters, and Despatches—That Concerning the Christians—The Answer

C. Plinius Secundus

Pliny the Elder was born A. D. 23, either at Verona[1265] or Novo-Comum[1266] (Como.) As he possessed estates at the latter town, and his nephew, the younger Pliny, whom he adopted, was undoubtedly born there, it was most probably the family residence and the place of the elder Pliny's nativity. He was educated at Rome; and serving Claudius in Germany, employed the opportunities which this campaign afforded him in travelling. Afterwards he returned to Rome and practised at the bar; filled different civil offices, amongst them that of augur, and was subsequently appointed procurator in Spain.[1267]

Some interesting particulars respecting his life and habits are contained in a letter of the younger Pliny to his friend Macer,[1268] illustrative of his studies, his temper, his thirst for knowledge, and his strict economy of time. The letter is also valuable for another reason—namely, as giving a catalogue of all the writings of his uncle. "It is a great satisfaction to me," he writes, "that you so constantly and diligently read my uncle's works, that you wish to

---
[1265] Anon. Life.
[1266] Suet. Vit.; Hieron. Eus. Chron.
[1267] Matth. H. of L. *s. V.*
[1268] Ep. iii. 5.

possess them all, and ask me for a list of them. I will therefore perform the duty of an index; and will also tell you the order in which they were written." He then subjoins the following titles:—(1.) The Art of using the Javelin on Horseback; composed when he was commander of cavalry in Germany. (2.) The Life of his friend Pomponius Secundus. (3.) A History of all the Wars, twenty in number, which the Romans had carried on with the Germans. This was commenced during his German campaign, in obedience to the suggestions of a dream:— "There appeared to him whilst sleeping the shade of Drusus; commended his memory to his care, and besought him to rescue it from undeserved oblivion." In accordance with his superstitious and credulous temper, he obeyed the call of his supernatural visitant. (4.) A treatise on Eloquence, entitled "*Studiosus*," in three books, but subdivided, on account of its length, into six volumes. In it he traces the education of an orator from the very cradle. (5.) Eight books on Grammatical Ambiguity, which he wrote during the reign of Nero, a period when imperial tyranny rendered studies of a freer kind too perilous. (6.) Thirty books in continuation of the History of Aufidius Bassus, dedicated to the Emperor Titus.[1269] (7.) Thirty-seven books on Natural History—a work, not only, as Pliny the Younger describes it, as full of variety as Nature herself, but, as will be shown hereafter, a treasure-house of the arts, as well as of natural objects.

"You will wonder," he continues, "how a man occupied with official business could have completed so many volumes filled with such minute information. You will be still more surprised to learn that he practised sometimes as a pleader; that he died in his fifty-sixth year; and that the intermediate time was distracted and interrupted by the friendship of princes and most important public affairs. But he was a man of vigorous intellect, incredible application, and unwearied activity. Immediately after the festival of the Vulcanalia (August 23d,) he used to begin to study in the dead of the night; in the winter at one o'clock in the morning, at the latest at two, often at midnight. No one ever slept so little—sometimes he would snatch a brief interval of sleep in the midst of his studies. Before dawn he would wait upon the Emperor, for he also used the night for transacting business. Thence he proceeded to the discharge of his official duties; and whatever time remained he devoted to study.

"After a light and frugal meal, which, according to the old fashion, he partook of by day, he would in summer, if he had any leisure time, recline in the sun whilst a book was read to him, from which he took notes and made extracts. In fact, he never read any book without making extracts; for he used to say that no book was so bad but that some profit could be derived from it. After sunset he generally took a cold bath, then a slight repast, and afterwards slept for a very short time. When he awoke, as if it were a new day, he studied till supper; during which a book was read, on which he made annotations as the reading proceeded. I remember that one of his friends interrupted the reader, because he had mispronounced a word, and compelled him to repeat it; upon which my uncle asked, 'Did you understand him?' and when he answered in the affirmative, he continued—'Why did you interrupt him? we have lost more than ten lines;'—so frugal was he of his time. In summer he rose from the supper-table by daylight, in winter at nightfall; and this custom was a law to him.

"These were his habits amidst the toils and bustle of a town-life. In the retirement of the country the bath was the only interruption to his studies. But only the bath itself, for whilst he was rubbed and wiped dry, he either dictated to an amanuensis or had a book read to him. On journeys, as he was then relieved from all other cares, study was the only employment of his

---

[1269] See Præf. to N. H.

leisure. He had a precis-writer at his side, with books and tablets, who in the winter wore gloves, so that his master's studies might not be interrupted by the severity of the cold. For the same reason, when at Rome, he always used a sedan. I remember once having been chid by him for walking: 'You might,' said he, 'avoid wasting all this time.' For he thought all time was lost which was not devoted to study. By this intense application he completed so many volumes, and bequeathed to me, besides, one hundred and sixty rolls of commentaries, written in the smallest possible hand and on both sides. He used to say that when he was procurator in Spain, he was offered for a portion of them 400,000 sesterces (about 3,200*l*.) by Lartius Licinius.... I cannot help laughing when people call me studious, for, compared with him, I am the idlest fellow in the world."

Pliny perished a martyr to the cause of science, in the terrible eruption of Vesuvius, which took place in the first year of the reign of Titus.[1270] Had he been as ardent an original observer in all other respects, instead of a mere plodding student, and collector, and transcriber of other men's observations, his works would have been less voluminous, but more valuable. The eruption in which he perished was the first of which there is any record in history. It is probable that none of any consequence had occurred before; and that the lava had never before devastated the smiling slopes and green vineyards which Martial has described.[1271] The circumstances of his death are thus described by his nephew[1272] in two letters to Tacitus:—"He was at Misenum, in command of the fleet. On the 24th of August, about one o'clock P. M., my mother pointed out to him a cloud of unusual size and appearance. He had lain in the sunshine, bathed, and taken refreshment, and was now studying. He forthwith asked for his shoes; and ascended an eminence from which he could best see the phenomenon. The distance was too great to know for certain from what mountain the cloud arose, but it was afterwards ascertained to be Vesuvius. Its form resembled that of a pine tree more than anything else. It rose into the air in the form of a tall trunk, and then diffused itself like spreading branches. The reason of this I take to be that it was at first carried upwards by a fresh current of air, which as it grew older and weaker was unable to support it, or perhaps its own gravity caused it to vanish in a horizontal direction. Sometimes it was white, sometimes solid and spotted, according to the quantity of earth and ashes which it threw up.

"The phenomenon appeared to him, as a learned man, deserving of closer investigation. He ordered a light galley to be fitted out, and gave me permission to accompany him. I replied that I preferred studying, and as it chanced he himself had given me something to write. Just as he was leaving the house with his note-book in his hand, the troops stationed at Retina, a village at the foot of the mountain, from which there was no escape except by sea, alarmed by the imminent peril they were in, sent to entreat him to rescue them. Notwithstanding this circumstance his determination was unaltered; but the task which he had commenced with earnestness he went through with the greatest resolution.

"He launched some quadriremes, and embarked for the purpose of assisting, not Retina only, but others; for the beauty of the coast had attracted a large population. He hastened to the spot whence others were flying, and steered a direct course to the point of danger, so fearlessly that he observed all the phases and forms of that sad calamity, and dictated his

---

[1270] A. D. 79.
[1271] Ep. iv. 43.
[1272] Ep. vi. 16, 20.

remarks on them to his secretary. Soon ashes fell on the decks, and the nearer he approached the hotter and thicker they became. With them were mingled scorched and blackened pumice-stones, and stones split by fire. Now the sudden reflux of the sea, and the fragments of the volcano which covered the coast, presented an obstacle to his progress, and he hesitated for awhile whether he should not return. At length, when his sailing-master recommended him to do so, he exclaimed, 'Fortune favours the brave—steer for the villa of Pomponianus.'

"This was situated at Stabiæ, and was divided from the coast near Vesuvius by an inlet or gulf formed by the sea. His friend, although danger was not yet imminent, yet, as it was within sight, and would be very near if it increased, had put his baggage on board of a ship, and had determined on flight if the wind, which was then contrary, should lull. A fair wind carried my uncle thither. He embraced his trembling friend, consoled and encouraged him. In order to assuage his fears by showing his own unconcern, he caused himself to be carried to a bath: after bathing, he sat down to supper with cheerfulness, or, what is almost the same thing, with the appearance of it. Meanwhile from many parts of the volcano broad flames burst forth: the blaze was reflected from the sky, and the glare and brightness were enhanced by the darkness of the night. He, to soothe the alarm of Pomponianus, endeavoured to persuade him that what he saw was only the burning villages which the country people had deserted in their consternation. He then retired to rest and slept soundly; for his snoring, which on account of his broad chest was deep and resonant, was heard by those who were watching at the door.

"Soon the court through which there was access to his apartment was so choked with cinders and pumice that longer delay would have rendered escape impossible. He was awakened; and went to Pomponianus and the rest, who had sat up all night. They then held a consultation whether they should remain in the house or go into the open fields. For repeated shocks of an earthquake made the houses rock to and fro, and seemed to move them from their foundations; whilst in the air the fall of half-burnt pumice, though light, menaced danger. After balancing the two dangers, he chose the latter course: with him, however, it was a comparison of reasons, with others of fears. They tied cushions over their heads with towels, to protect them from the falling stones. Although it was now day elsewhere, the darkness here was denser than the darkest night, broken only by torches and lights of different kinds. They next walked out to the coast to see whether the sea was calm enough to venture upon it, but it was still a waste of stormy waters. Then he spread a linen cloth and lay down upon it, asked for two or three draughts of cold water; and, afterwards, flames, and that sulphureous smell which is the forerunner of them, put his companions to flight and aroused him.

"He arose by the assistance of two slaves, and immediately fell down dead, suffocated as I imagine by the dense vapour, and the functions of his stomach being disordered, which were naturally weak, and liable to obstructions and difficulty of digestion. On the morning of the third day after his body was found entire, uninjured, and in the clothes in which he died: its appearance was rather that of sleep than death."

Pliny the Younger was left with his mother at Misenum; and in another letter he gives an account of the appearance of the eruption at that place:[1273]—

"After my uncle's departure, I spent some time in study (for that was my object in remaining behind:) I then bathed and supped, and had some broken and restless sleep. For

---

[1273] Ep. vi. 20.

many days previously shocks of an earthquake had been felt; but they caused less alarm because they are usual in Campania; but on that night they were so violent that it was thought they would not only shake but overturn everything. My mother burst into my bed-chamber—I was just rising in order to arouse her, in case she should be asleep. We sat down in the court which divided the house from the sea. I know not whether to call this courage or imprudence, for I was only in my eighteenth year. I asked for a volume of Livy, and began to read it leisurely and to make extracts.

"Well! a friend of my uncle came in who had lately arrived from Spain, and when he saw us sitting together, and me reading, he rebuked his patience and my 'insouciance.' Still I was not the less for that absorbed in my book. It was now seven o'clock, and the dawn broke faintly and languidly. The surrounding buildings were tottering; and the space in which we were, being limited in extent, there was great reason to fear their fall. We then resolved to leave town. The populace followed in alarm.

"When at a sufficient distance from the buildings we halted, and witnessed many a wonderful and alarming phenomenon. The carriages which we had ordered to be brought out, although the ground was very level, rolled in different directions, and even stones placed under the wheels could not stop them. The sea ebbed and seemed to be repelled by the earthquake. The coast certainly had advanced, and detained many marine animals on dry land. On the other side of the heavens hung a dark and awful cloud, riven by wreathed and quivering lines of fiery vapour, in long flashes resembling lightning, but larger. Then our friend from Spain exclaimed, with eagerness and vehemence, 'If your relative lives, he doubtless wishes your safety; if he has perished, he wished you to survive him. Why then do you delay to escape?' Our answer was, 'We will not think of our own safety so long as we are uncertain of his.' Without any more delay he hurried off, and was soon beyond the reach of danger. Soon the cloud descended to the earth, and brooded over the sea; it shrouded Capreæ, and hid from our eyes the promontory of Misenum. My mother besought, entreated, nay, commanded me to fly by all means; she felt that, weighed down by years and infirmity, she should die contented if she had not been the cause of my death. I, on the other hand, persisted that I would not seek safety except with her. I took her by the hand and forced her to go forward. She obeyed reluctantly, and blamed herself for delaying me. Ashes now began to fall, though as yet in small quantities. I looked back; behind us was thick darkness, which poured over the earth like a torrent. 'Let us turn aside from the road,' said I, 'whilst we can see, for fear we should be thrown down and trampled under foot by the crowd in the darkness.' We had scarce time to [think about it] [sit down] when we were enveloped in darkness, not like that of a moonless night, or clouds, but like that of a room shut up when the lights are extinguished. Then were heard the shrieks of women, the wailings of infants, the shouts of men; some were calling for their parents, others for their children, others for their wives, whom they could only recognise by their voices. Some bewailed their own misfortune, others that of their family; some even from the fear of death prayed for death. Many lifted up their hands to the gods; still more believed that there were no gods, and that the last eternal night had overwhelmed the world. There were not wanting some to increase the real danger by fictitious and imaginary terrors; and some brought word that the conflagration was at Misenum: the false intelligence met with credence. By degrees the light returned; but it seemed to us not the return of day, but the indication that the fire was approaching. Its progress, however, was arrested at some distance: again darkness succeeded with showers of ashes. Every now and then we got up and shook them off from us, otherwise we should have been overwhelmed and bruised by their weight. I might boast that not a groan or unmanly expression escaped me in the midst of my dangers, were it not that my firmness was founded on the consolatory belief that all mankind was involved, together with myself, in one common ruin. At length the darkness cleared up, and dispersed like smoke or mist. Real daylight succeeded; even the sun shone forth, but with a lurid light as when eclipsed. The aspect of everything which met our astonished eyes was changed: ashes covered the ground like a deep snow. We returned to Misenum, and refreshed ourselves, and passed an anxious night in alternate hopes and fears: the latter, however, predominated. The earthquake still continued; and many, in a state of frenzy, made a mockery of their own and their neighbours' misfortunes by terrific prophecies." The above letters, though long, have been quoted because they detail, in the most interesting manner, the circumstances of the elder Pliny's death, and at the same time illustrate the simple and graphic power of the nephew's pen.

The Natural Philosophy of Pliny is, to say the least, an unequalled monument of studious diligence and persevering industry. It consists of thirty-seven books, and contains, according to his own account,[1274] 20,000 facts (as he believed them to be) connected with nature and art: the result, not of original research, but, as he honestly confessed, culled from the labours of other men. It must, however, be allowed that the confused arrangement is owing partly to the indefinite state of science, and the consequent mingling together of branches which are separate and distinct.[1275]

Owing to the extent and variety of his reading, his credulous love of the marvellous, and his want of judgment in comparing and selecting, he does not present us with a correct view of the degree of truth to which science had attained in his own age. He does not show how one age had corrected the errors of a preceding one; but reproduces errors, evidently obsolete and inconsistent with facts and theories which had grown up afterwards and replaced them.

With him mythological traditions appear to have almost the same authority as modern discoveries. The earth teems with monsters, not miracles, or exceptions to the regular order of nature, but specimens of her ingenuity. In his theory of the universe he assumes such causes and principles as lead him to admit, without question, the existence of prodigies, however impossible they may be. They are wonderful because unusual; but they are effects which might result from the natural causes which he believed to be in operation. His theory, that Nature acted not only by regular laws but often by actual interferences, (for this was the character of his pantheism, ii. 5, 7,)—his belief that the various germs of created things were scattered in profusion throughout the universe, and accidentally mingling in confusion produced monstrous forms, (3)—prepared him to consider nothing incredible (xi. 3;) and his temper inclined him to go further, and to admit almost every thing which was credible as true.[1276]

Deficient as the work is in scientific value and philosophical arrangement, the author evidently wished to stamp it with a character of practical utility. It is an encyclopædia of the knowledge which could be brought together from different sources; and for such a work there are two important requisites—facility of reference, and the citation of authorities. With this view the whole is preceded by a summary, and to each book is added a table of contents, together with the names of authors to whom he is indebted.

[1274] See Proem. 17.
[1275] Proem. 16, 17.
[1276] See book ii.

The work commences with the theory of the universe;[1277] the history and science of astronomy; meteorological phenomena; and the geological changes which have taken place on the earth by volcanic and aqueous action. Geography, both physical and political, occupy the four next books.[1278] Here truth and error are mingled in dire confusion. Accounts which are based solely on the traditions of remote antiquity are given side by side with the results of modern investigation, and yet no distinction is drawn as to authenticity; and, owing to his confusing together such different accounts, measurements and distances are generally wrong.

But in the zoological division of the work, which next follows,[1279] he gives unrestrained scope to his credulity and love of the marvellous. He tells of men whose feet were turned backwards; of others whose feet were so large as to shade them when they lay in the sun. He describes beings in whom both sexes were united; others in whom a change of sex had taken place; others without mouths, who fed on the fragrance of fruits and flowers.[1280] Such are some of the marvels of the human race recorded by him. Amongst the lower animals he enumerates horned horses furnished with wings;[1281] the Mantichora, with the face of a man, three rows of teeth, a lion's body, and a scorpion's tail;[1282] the unicorn with a stag's head, a horse's body, the feet of an elephant, and the tail of a boar;[1283] the basilisk, whose very glance is fatal. The seas are peopled not only with sea-goats and sea-elephants, but with real Nereids and Tritons.[1284] Mice, according to his account, produce their young by licking each other; and fire produces an insect (pyralis) which cannot live except in the midst of the flames.

Sixteen books[1285] are devoted to botany, both general and medical; and the medicinal properties of the human frame, and of other animal substances, as well as of different waters, are next discussed.[1286] An account of minerals and metals concludes the work; and this portion embraces an account of their various uses in the fine arts, intermingled with interesting anecdotes and histories of art and artists. This is the most valuable as well as the most pleasing section of the work.

He was pre-eminently a collector of stories and anecdotes and supposed facts, and he was only accidentally a naturalist, because natural history furnished the most extensive variety of marvellous and curious materials. The naturalist, Cuvier,[1287] observed his want of judgment, his credulity, his defective arrangement, and the inappropriate nature of his observations. Notwithstanding all these faults this elaborate work contains many valuable truths, much entertaining information, and the style in which it is written is, when not too florid, full of vigour and expression. The philosophical belief can scarcely be considered that of any particular school, although tinctured by the prevalent Stoicism of the day; but its pervading character is querulous and melancholy. Believing that nature is an all-powerful principle, and the world or universe itself, instinct with Deity, he saw more of evil than of good in the Divine dispensations; and the result was a gloomy and discontented pantheism.

[1277] Book ii.
[1278] Books iii.-vi.
[1279] Books vii.-xi.
[1280] Book vii. 4.
[1281] Book viii. 30.
[1282] Book viii. 30.
[1283] Book viii. 31.
[1284] Book viii. 33.
[1285] Books xii.-xxvii.
[1286] Books xxviii.-xxxii.
[1287] Biogr. Un. art. Plin.

Pliny the Younger (Born A. D. 61.)

C. Plinius Cæcilius Secundus was sister's son to the elder Pliny. Most of the information which we possess respecting his life and character is derived from his letters. He was born at Novo-Comum, on the Lake Larius (Como;) and as he was in his eighteenth year[1288] at the time of the eruption of Vesuvius, which took place A. D. 79, the date of his birth must have been A. D. 61.

On the death of his father, C. Cæcilius, he was adopted by his uncle, and therefore took the name of Plinius. He was educated under the guardianship of Virginius Rufus, who felt for him the affection of a parent. The regard was evidently mutual. "I loved him," writes Pliny to Voconius,[1289] with that tenderness which so frequently adorns his letters, especially those to his wife Calphurnia, "as much as I admired him;" and he thus concludes his letter: "I had wished to write to you on many other subjects, but my thoughts are fully occupied on this one subject of contemplation. I see, I think of no one but Virginius. In fancy I seem to hear his voice, to address him, to hold him in my arms. We may perhaps have, and shall continue to have, men equal to him in virtue, but no one equal to him in glory." In belles-lettres and eloquence[1290] he attended constantly the lectures of Quintilian and Nicetes Sacerdos, of whom favourable mention is made by Seneca.[1291]

Under the care of such tutors and such an uncle, his literary tastes were cultivated early, and before he had completed his fifteenth year he gave proof of his love of poetry, by writing what he modestly says *was called* a Greek tragedy. This taste for poetry remained to him in after life: once when weather-bound at the island of Icaria, he celebrated the event in an elegiac poem. He wrote hexameters, of which he gives a short specimen, and also a birth-day ode in hendecasyllables, and he tells us he wrote with quickness and facility.[1292]

He was called to the bar in his nineteenth year, and attained great celebrity as a pleader.[1293] He stood high in favour with Trajan; and filled with distinction high offices, both military and civil. He was military tribune in Syria; and besides being prætor and consul at home, he served as procurator of the province of Bithynia abroad. He was gentle, liberal, refined, and benevolent; and his zeal for the interests of literature, and his wish that the youths of Como might not be forced to resort to Milan for education, but might owe that blessing to their native place,[1294] led him to offer help in founding a school, in forming a public library, and in establishing exhibitions for ingenuous students.[1295] He thought with justice, such acts of munificence nobler than gaudy spectacles and barbarous shows of gladiators.

His works consist of a Panegyric on Trajan and a collection of Letters in ten books. The Panegyric is a piece of courtly flattery, for the fulsomeness of which the only defence which can be made, is the cringing and fawning manners of his times. It was written and delivered in the year in which he was consul.[1296] The Letters are very valuable, not only for the insight which they give into his own character, but also into the manners and modes of thought of his

---

[1288] Ep. vi. 20.
[1289] Ep. ii. 1.
[1290] Ep. vi. 6.
[1291] Sen. Suasor. I.
[1292] Ep. vii. 4.
[1293] Ep. v. 8.
[1294] Ep. iv. 13.
[1295] Ep. i. 8.
[1296] A. D. 100.

illustrious contemporaries, as well as the politics of the day. Many of them bear evident marks of having been expressly intended for publication. This of course detracts from their value as fresh and truthful exponents of the writer's thoughts, which all letters ought to be; but they are most delightful to read, and for liveliness, descriptive power, elegance and simplicity of style, are scarcely inferior to those of Cicero, whom he evidently took for his model.

The tenth book, which consists of his despatches to Trajan, together with the Emperor's rescripts, will be read with the greatest interest; and the notices of public affairs contained in them are most valuable to the historian. The despatch respecting the Christians, written from Bithynia, A. D. 104, and the Emperor's answer,[1297] are well worthy of transcription; both because reference is so often made to them, and because they throw light upon the marvellous and rapid propagation of the gospel; the manners of the early Christians; the treatment to which their constancy exposed them, even under favourable circumstances, and the severe jealousy with which even a governor of mild and gentle temper thought it his duty to regard them. "It is my constant practice, sire, to refer to you all subjects on which I entertain doubt. For who is better able to direct my hesitation or to instruct my ignorance? I have never been present at the trials of Christians, and therefore I do not know in what way, or to what extent, it is usual to question or to punish them. I have also felt no small difficulty in deciding whether age should make any difference, or whether those of the tenderest and those of mature years should be treated alike; whether pardon should be accorded to repentance, or whether, where a man has once been a Christian, recantation should profit him; whether, if the name of Christian does not imply criminality, still the crimes peculiarly belonging to the name should be punished. Meanwhile, in the case of those against whom informations have been laid before me, I have pursued the following line of conduct. I have put to them, personally, the question whether they were Christians. If they confessed, I interrogated them a second and third time, and threatened them with punishment. If they still persevered, I ordered their commitment; for I had no doubt whatever that, whatever they confessed, at any rate dogged and inflexible obstinacy deserved to be punished. There were others who displayed similar madness; but, as they were Roman citizens, I ordered them to be sent back to the city. Soon persecution itself, as is generally the case, caused the crime to spread, and it appeared in new forms. An anonymous information was laid against a large number of persons, but they deny that they are, or ever have been, Christians. As they invoked the gods, repeating the form after me, and offered prayers, together with incense and wine, to your image, which I had ordered to be brought, together with those of the deities, and besides cursed Christ, whilst those who are true Christians, it is said, cannot be compelled to do any one of these things, I thought it right to set them at liberty. Others, when accused by an informer, confessed that they were Christians, and soon after denied the fact; they said they had been, but had ceased to be, some three, some more, not a few even twenty years previously. All these worshipped your image and those of the gods, and cursed Christ. But they affirmed that the sum total of their fault or their error was, that they were accustomed to assemble on a fixed day before dawn, and sing an antiphonal hymn to Christ as God: that they bound themselves by an oath, not to the commission of any wickedness, but to abstain from theft, robbery, and adultery; never to break a promise, or to deny a deposit when it was demanded back. When these ceremonies were concluded, it was their custom to depart, and

---

[1297] Ep. x. 97 and 98.

again assemble together to take food harmlessly and in common. That after my proclamation, in which, in obedience to your command, I had forbidden associations, they had desisted from this practice. For these reasons I the more thought it necessary to investigate the real truth, by putting to the torture two maidens, who were called deaconesses; but I discovered nothing but a perverse and excessive superstition. I have therefore deferred taking cognizance of the matter until I had consulted you. For it seemed to me a case requiring advice, especially on account of the number of those in peril. For many of every age, sex, and rank, are and will continue to be called in question. The infection, in fact, has spread not only through the cities, but also through the villages and open country; but it seems that its progress can be arrested. At any rate, it is clear that the temples which were almost deserted begin to be frequented; and solemn sacrifices, which had been long intermitted, are again performed, and victims are being sold everywhere, for which up to this time a purchaser could rarely be found. It is therefore easy to conceive that crowds might be reclaimed if an opportunity for repentance were given."

Trajan to Pliny

"In sifting the cases of those who have been indicted on the charge of Christianity, you have adopted, my dear Secundus, the right course of proceeding; for no certain rule can be laid down which will meet all cases. They must not be sought after, but if they are informed against and convicted, they must be punished; with this proviso, however, that if any one denies that he is a Christian, and proves the point by offering prayers to our deities, notwithstanding the suspicions under which he has laboured, he shall be pardoned on his repentance. On no account should any anonymous charge be attended to, for it would be the worst possible precedent, and is inconsistent with the habits of our times."

Pliny's accurate and judicious mind, his political and administrative prudence, his taste for the beautiful, his power of description, his unrivalled neatness, his skill in investing with a peculiar interest every subject he takes in hand, may be amply proved by a perusal of his Letters. His touches are neither too many nor too few. A mere note of thanks for a present of thrushes[1298] shows as much skill, in its way, as his numerous elaborate despatches to the Emperor.[1299] His brief biographical notice of Silius Italicus contains, in a few short sentences, all that can be said favourably of the life and character of his correspondent. The sympathy which he felt for his friends, as well as the delicacy of his panegyric, are exhibited in the few lines which he penned to Germinius on the death of the wife of Macrinus;[1300] his honesty in the case of the inheritance of Pomponia;[1301] his legal skill in passages too numerous to specify; his descriptive power in the narrative of the eruption of Vesuvius,[1302] in which his uncle perished; and in the full and minute description of his villa, its rooms, furniture, works of art, garden, and surrounding scenery.

[1298] Ep. v. ii.
[1299] Lib. x.
[1300] Ep. viii. 5.
[1301] Ep. v. i.
[1302] Ep. vi. 20.

Chapter 37

M. Fabius Quintilianus—His Biography—His Institutiones Oratoriæ—His Views on Education—Division of His Subjects into Five Parts—Review of Greek and Roman Literature—Completeness of His Great Work—His Other Works—His Disposition—Grief for the Loss of His Son

M. Fabius Quintilianus

In this peculiarly rhetorical age, the most distinguished teacher of rhetoric was M. Fabius Quintilianus. He attempted to restore a purer and more classical taste; and although to a certain extent he was successful, the effect which he produced was only temporary. He was, like Martial, a Spaniard, born[1303] at Calagurris, the modern Calahorra.[1304] At an early age he came to Rome, and had the advantage of hearing the celebrated orators Domitius Afer and Julius Africanus, whose eloquence he considered superior to that of their contemporaries.[1305] How long he remained at Rome is uncertain; but he appears to have gone back to his native country, and then returned to the capital together with the Emperor Galba.

Although he practised as a pleader, he was far more eminent as an instructor. Domitian intrusted to him the education of his two great-nephews;[1306] and the younger Pliny was also one of his pupils.[1307] The Emperor's favour conferred on him that reward to which Juvenal alludes in the following lines:—

> Si Fortuna volet fies de rhetore consul;[1308]

[1303] A. D. 40.
[1304] Auson. Profess. i. 7.
[1305] Inst. Or. i. 138.
[1306] I. O. iv. Proem.
[1307] Pl. Ep. ii. 14.*
[1308] Sat. vii. 197. Another professor of rhetoric, Ausonius, was also elevated to the consulship by the Emperor Gratian, A. D. 379.

and besides this he held one of the professorships which were endowed by Vespasian with 100,000 sestertia per annum (800*l*.[1309]) He thus formed an exception to the larger number of instructors and grammarians who swarmed in Rome, who, depending on the fees of their pupils, earned a precarious subsistence,[1310] and was even able to purchase estates and accumulate property.

But though more fortunate than many deserving members of his profession, he was not esteemed a wealthy man by the rich and luxurious Romans of his day; for his grateful pupil, Pliny, when he presented him with 400*l*. towards his daughter's portion, spoke of him as a man of moderate means.[1311] His expressions are:—"Te porro, animo beatissimum, modicum facultatibus scio." The probability is that he was twice married. His first wife died at the early age of nineteen, leaving two sons, of whom death bereaved him in a few years.[1312] For the instruction of the elder of these, who survived his younger brother for but a short time, he wrote his great work. His second wife was the daughter of one Tutilius, and the fruit of this marriage was an only daughter who married Nonius Celer, and to whom the liberal present of Pliny was made. For twenty years he discharged the duties of his professorship, and then retired from active life; and died, as is generally supposed, about A. D. 118. His countryman, Martial,[1313] speaks of him as the glory of the Roman bar, and the head of his profession as an instructor:—

> Quintiliane, vagæ moderator summe juventæ,
> Gloria Romanæ, Quintiliane, togæ.[1314]

Quintilian's great work is entitled *Institutiones Oratoriæ*, or a complete instruction in the art of oratory: and in it he shows himself far superior to Cicero as a teacher, although he was inferior to him as an orator. The rhetorical works of the great orator will not, in point of fulness and completeness, bear a comparison with the elaborate treatise of Quintilian. When engaged in its composition he had retired from the duties of a public professor, and was only occupied, as he himself states,[1315] with his duties as tutor to the great-nephew of Domitian. He professes to have undertaken the task reluctantly, and at the earnest solicitations of his friends. He thought that the ground was already pre-occupied, both by Greek and Latin writers of eminence. But seeing how wide the field was, and that such a work must treat of all those qualifications without which no one can be an orator, he complied with their entreaties, and dedicated his book to his friend Marcellus Victorius, as a token of his regard, and a useful contribution towards the education of his son. Two rhetorical treatises had already appeared under his name, but not published by himself. One consisted of a lecture which occupied two days in delivery; the other a longer course: and both had been taken down in notes, and given to the public, as he says, by his excellent but too partial pupils: (boni juvenes, sed nimium amantes mei.[1316])

[1309] Suet. Vesp. 18.
[1310] Juv. vii. 186.
[1311] Ep. vi. 32.
[1312] I. O. vi. Proem.
[1313] Epig. i. 62.
[1314] Epig. ii. 90.
[1315] I. O. Proem. iv.
[1316] I. O. Proem. I.

On the Institutiones he professes to have expended the greatest pains and labour. He traces the progress of the orator from the very cradle until he arrives at perfection.[1317] He speaks of the importance of earliest impressions, of the parental, especially the maternal care, and illustrates this by the example of Cornelia, to whom the Gracchi owed their eminence; and brings forward, as instances of female eloquence, the daughters of Lælius and Hortensius. He believes that education must commence, and the tastes be formed, and the moral character be impressed, even in infancy. The choice, therefore, of a nurse is, in his opinion, as important, as of early companions, pedagogues, and instructors.

Both on account of the positive good to be acquired, and the evil resulting from the corrupt state of Roman society which the boy would thus avoid, he prefers a school to a home education.[1318] As we consider the classical languages the best preparation for the study of the vernacular tongue,[1319] so he lays down as an axiom that education in Greek literature should precede Latin. Grammar[1320] is to be the foundation of education, together with its subdivisions, declension, construction,[1321] orthography,[1322] the use of words,[1323] rhythm, metre, the beauties and faults of style,[1324] reading,[1325] delivery, action;[1326] and to these are to be added music and geometry.[1327]

Primary education being completed, the young student is to be transferred to the care of the rhetorician.[1328] The choice of a proper instructor,[1329] as well as his duties and character,[1330] are described; the necessary exercises, the reading and study of orations and histories are recommended,[1331] and the nature, principles, objects, and utility of oratory are accurately investigated. In the third book, after a short notice of the principal writers on rhetoric,[1332] he divides his subject into five parts,[1333] namely, invention, arrangement, style, memory, both natural and artificial, and delivery or action. Closely following Aristotle, he then discusses the three kinds of oratory, the demonstrative, deliberative, and judicial.[1334] In the fourth, he treats of the physical divisions of all orations, namely, the exordium,[1335] the narration,[1336] excursions or digressions,[1337] the question proposed,[1338] the division of topics.[1339] In that part of his treatise which discusses the next division, namely, proofs, Aristotle is his chief guide, as meeting, in his opinion, the universal assent of all mankind.

[1317] Lib. i. i.
[1318] Cap. ii.
[1319] Cap. i.
[1320] Cap. i.
[1321] Cap. iii.
[1322] Cap. vi.
[1323] Cap. vii.
[1324] Cap. v.
[1325] Cap. viii.
[1326] Cap. xi.
[1327] Cap. x.
[1328] Lib. ii. i.
[1329] Cap. iii.
[1330] Cap. ii.
[1331] Cap. iv. and v.
[1332] Cap. xiii. *ad fin.*
[1333] Lib. i. ii.
[1334] Cap. iii. *ad fin.*
[1335] Lib. iv. i.
[1336] Cap. ii.
[1337] Cap. iii. iv.
[1338] Cap. v.
[1339] Lib. v. i.-xiv.

The sixth book analyzes the peroration, and also discusses the passions,[1340] moral habits,[1341] ridicule,[1342] and other topics, which complete the subject of invention. The seventh treats of arrangement and its kindred topics; the eighth and ninth of style and its essential qualities, such as perspicuity,[1343] ornament[1344] tropes,[1345] amplification,[1346] figures of speech.[1347]

Facility, or as we, in common with the Romans, frequently term it, "*copia verborum*,"[1348] is the next division of the subject; and as original invention has already occupied so large a portion of his work, he now endeavours to guide the student in imitating the excellencies of the best Greek and Latin writers; and tells him that the next duty, in point of importance, is to profit by the inventions of others.[1349] A wide field is thus opened before him, affording an opportunity for the display of his extensive learning, his critical taste, his penetrating discrimination, and his great power of illustration.[1350]

He passes over in rapid review the whole history of Greek and Roman literature. His remarks, though brief, are clear and decided, and are marked with an attractive beauty and sound judgment, which have stood the test of ages, and recommend themselves to all who have been distinguished for pure classical taste. So adroit is he in catching the leading features, that the portraits of great authors of antiquity, though only sketches and outlines, stand forth in bold and tangible shape, each exhibiting marked and distinct characteristics. There are few specimens of criticism so attractive, so suggestive, and which lay such hold on the memory, as this portion of the Institutions of Quintilian. Other subjects are also briefly handled in the tenth book, such as the necessity of pains and elaborate corrections, in order to form a polished style.[1351] The choice of materials,[1352] original thought,[1353] the means of acquiring and perfecting a habit of extemporaneous speaking.[1354]

The eleventh book is devoted to the subjects of appropriateness, memory,[1355] and delivery.[1356]

The twelfth opens with what the author designates[1357] as the most grave and important portion of the whole work, well worthy of the dignified character of true Roman virtue. Its subject is the high moral qualifications necessary for a perfect orator.[1358] Talent, wisdom, learning, eloquence are nothing, if the mind is distracted and torn asunder by vicious thoughts and depraved passions.[1359] The orator, therefore, must learn studies by what his moral

---

[1340] Cap. i.
[1341] Cap. ii.
[1342] Cap. iii.
[1343] Cap. ii.
[1344] Cap. iii.
[1345] Cap. vi.
[1346] Cap. iv.
[1347] Lib. ix. i. ii. iii.
[1348] Lib. x. i.
[1349] Lib. x. ii.
[1350] Lib. x. i. and lib. xii. x. xi.
[1351] Lib. iii. iv.
[1352] Cap. v.
[1353] Cap. vi.
[1354] Cap. vii.
[1355] Lib. xi. i.
[1356] Cap. ii. iii.
[1357] *Vide* Proem.
[1358] Cap. i.
[1359] Cap. i.

character can alone be formed;[1360] he must possess that firmness of principle which will cause him fearlessly to practise what he knows. "Neque erit perfectus orator nisi qui honeste dicere et sciet et audebit."

A knowledge of history[1361] and the principles of jurisprudence,[1362] he also considers indispensably necessary, notwithstanding the slighting way in which Cicero speaks of the antiquarian learning of the jurisconsults. Some practical rules[1363] are also added as to the time of commencing practice in the courts, the rules to be observed in undertaking causes,[1364] and the cautions to be attended to in preparing and pleading them.[1365] He deprecates the undertaking such important duties early, although the call to the bar at Rome took place as soon as the manly gown was assumed: tradition spoke of boys clothed with the prætexta pleading. Cæsar Augustus, at twelve years old, publicly pronounced a eulogy on his grandmother, as did Tiberius at the early age of nine over the body of his deceased father.[1366]

Enough has been said to show the fulness and completeness with which Quintilian has exhausted his subject, and left, as a monument of his taste and genius, a text-book of the science and art of nations, as well as a masterly sketch of the eloquence of antiquity.

There have been attributed to Quintilian, besides his great work, nineteen declamations or judicial speeches relating to imaginary suits; also one hundred and forty-five sketches of orations, the remains of a larger collection, consisting of three hundred and eighty-eight. But there is no evidence in favour of their being his, and their style seems to show that they were the work of different authors and different ages. Neither is there any good reason for considering that the treatise on the Causes of Corrupt Eloquence is the same as that to which he alludes in the proëmium to the sixth and the conclusion of the eighth book[1367] of the Institutions. Indeed, the almost unanimous opinion of scholars assigns it to Tacitus. His works were discovered by Poggius, together with those of Silius Italicus and L. Valerius Flaccus, in the monastery of St. Gall, twenty miles from Constance, during the sitting of the celebrated ecclesiastical council.

The disposition of Quintilian was as affectionate and tender as his genius was brilliant, and his taste pure. Few passages throughout the whole range of Latin literature can be compared to that in which he mourns the loss of his wife and children. It is the touching eloquence of one who could not write otherwise than gracefully; and if he murmurs at the divine decrees, it must be remembered that his dearest hopes were blighted, and that he had not the hopes, the consolation, or the teaching of a Christian. "I had a son," he says, "whose eminent genius deserved a father's anxious diligence. I thought that if—which I might fairly have expected and wished for—death had removed me from him, I could have left him, as the best inheritance, a father's instructions. But by a second blow, a second bereavement, I have lost the object of my highest hopes, the only comfort of my declining years. What shall I do now? Of what use can I suppose myself to be, as the gods have cast me off? It happened that when I commenced my book on the Causes of Corrupt Eloquence, I was stricken by a similar blow. It would surely have been best then to have flung upon the funeral pile—which was

---

[1360] Cap. ii.
[1361] Lib. iv.
[1362] Lib. iii.
[1363] Cap. vi.
[1364] Cap. vii.
[1365] Cap. viii. ix.
[1366] Suet. v. Ti.
[1367] Lib. viii. 6.

destined prematurely to consume all that bound me to life—my unlucky work, and the ill-starred fruits of all my toils, and not to have wearied with new cares a life to which I so unnaturally clung. For what tender parent would pardon me if I were able to study any longer, and not hate my firmness of mind, if I, who survived all my dear ones, could find any employment for my tongue except to accuse the gods, and to protest that no Providence looks down upon the affairs of men? If I cannot say this in reference to my own case, to which no objection can be made except that I survive, at least I can with reference to theirs—condemned to an unmerited and untimely grave.

"Their mother had before been torn from me, who had given birth to two sons before she had completed her nineteenth year; and though her death was a cruel blow to me, to her it was a happy one. To me the affliction was so crushing, that fortune could no longer restore me to happiness. For not only did the exercise of every feminine virtue render her husband's grief incurable, but, compared with my own age, she was but a girl, and therefore her loss may be accounted as that of a child. Still, my children survived, and were my joy and comfort, and she since I survived (a thing unnatural, although she wished it,) escaped by a precipitate flight the agonies of grief. In my younger son, who died at five years old, I lost one light of my eyes. I have no ambition to make much of my misfortunes, or to exaggerate the reasons which I have for sorrow; would that I had means of assuaging it! But how can I conceal his lovely countenance, his endearing talk, his sparkling wit, and (what I feel can scarcely be believed) his calm and deep solidity of mind? Had he been another's child he would have won my love. But insidious fortune, in order to inflict on me severer anguish, made him more affectionate to me than to his nurses, his grandmother, who brought him up, and all who usually gain the attachment of children of that age.

"Thankful therefore do I feel for that sorrow in which but a few months before I was plunged by the loss of his matchless, his inestimable mother; for my lot was less a subject for tears than hers was for rejoicing. One only hope, support, and consolation, had remained in my Quintilian. He had not, like my younger son, just put forth his early blossoms, but entering on his tenth year had shown mature and well-set fruit. I swear by my misfortunes, by the consciousness of my unhappiness, by those departed spirits, the deities who preside over my grief, that in him I discerned such vigour of intellect, not only in the acquisition of learning (and yet in all my extensive experience I never saw it surpassed,) such a zeal for study, which, as his tutors can testify, never required pressing, but also such uprightness, filial affection, refinement, and generosity, as furnished grounds for apprehending the thunder-stroke which has fallen. For it is generally observed that a precocious maturity too quickly perishes; and there is I know not what envious power which deflowers our brightest hopes, lest we soar higher than human beings are permitted to soar. He possessed also those gifts which are accidental—a clear and melodious voice, a sweet pronunciation, a correct enunciation of every letter both in Greek and Latin. Such promise did he give of future excellence; but he possessed also the far higher qualities of constancy, earnestness, and firmness to bear sorrow and to resist fear. With what admiration did his physicians contemplate the patience with which he endured a malady of eight months' duration! What consolation did he administer to me in his last moments! When life and intellect began to fail, his wandering mind dwelt on literature alone. O! dearest object of my disappointed hopes! could I behold thy glazing eyes, thy fleeting breath? Could I embrace thy cold and lifeless form, and live to drink again the common air? Well do I deserve these agonizing thoughts, these tortures which I endure!"

Chapter 38

A. Cornelius Celsus—His Merits—Cicero Medicorum—Scribonius Largus Designatianus—Pomponius Mela—L. Junius Moderatus Columella—S. Julius Frontinus—Decline of Taste in the Silver Age—Foreign Influence on Roman Literature—Conclusion

Such were the principal writers who adorned and illustrated the literature of the silver age: it remains only to speak briefly of those whose works, although of minor interest, must not be passed over without notice.

Aurelius Cornelius Celsus

Celsus was the author of many works on various subjects, of which one, in eight books, on Medicine, is now extant. The place of his birth and the age at which he flourished are unknown, but he probably lived in the reign of Tiberius. He was a man of comprehensive, almost encyclopædic knowledge, and wrote on philosophy, rhetoric, agriculture, and even strategy. It has been doubted whether he ever practised medicine, or was only theoretically acquainted with the subject; but the independence of his views, the practical as well as the scientific nature of his instructions, are inconsistent with any hypothesis except that he had himself patiently watched the phenomena of morbid action and experimented upon its treatment. Above all, his knowledge of surgery, and his clear exposition of surgical operations, necessarily imply that practical experience and reality of knowledge which never could have been acquired from books.

If we compare the masterly handling of the subject by Celsus with the history of medicine by Pliny,[1368] it is easy to distinguish the man of practical and experimental science from the collector and transcriber of others' views. His manual of medicine embraces the

---

[1368] H. N. xxix.

following subjects: Diet,[1369] Pathology,[1370] Therapeutics,[1371] Surgery;[1372] and without entering into its peculiar merits, a task which could only be performed satisfactorily by a professional writer, the highest testimony is borne to its merits by the fact of its being used as a text-book even in the present advanced state of medical science.

The study of medicine has a tendency to predispose the mind for general scientific investigations in other departments not immediately connected with it. Hence the medical profession has numbered amongst its members many men of general scientific attainments; and Celsus was an example of this versatility. The taste of the age in which he lived turned his attention also to polite literature; and to this may be ascribed the Augustan purity of his style, which gained for him the appellation of "Cicero Medicorum."

SCRIBONIUS LARGUS DESIGNATIANUS

The "Cicero of physicians" was followed by Scribonius, an obsequious court physician, in the reign of Claudius. He was the author of several works, one of which, a large collection of prescriptions, is extant. In the language of impious flattery, he calls the imbecile emperor a god. He is said to have accompanied him in his expedition to Britain.

POMPONIUS MELA

Pomponius Mela may be considered as the representative of the Roman geographers. He was a native of Tingentera, a town in Spain, and lived in the reign of Claudius. His treatise is entitled, "*De Situ Orbis, Libri iii.*" It is systematic and learned. The stores of information derived from the Greek geographers are interspersed with entertaining myths and lively descriptions. The knowledge, however, contained in it is all taken from books: it is an epitome of former treatises, and is not enriched by the discoveries of more recent travellers. The simplicity of the style, and the almost Augustan purity of the Latinity, prevent even so bare a skeleton and list of facts from being dry and uninteresting.

L. JUNIUS MODERATUS COLUMELLA

The didactic work of Columella gives, in smooth and fluent, though somewhat too diffuse, a style, the fullest and completest information on practical agriculture amongst the Romans, in the first century of the Christian era. Pliny is the only classical author who mentions him; but he refers to him as a competent authority. Columella himself informs us

---

[1369] Cap. i. ii.
[1370] Cap. iii. iv.
[1371] Cap. v. vi.
[1372] Cap. vii. viii.

that he was born at Gades (Cadiz,[1373]) and resided at Rome,[1374] but had travelled in Syria and Cilicia.[1375] It is generally supposed that he died and was buried at Tarentum.

His work, "*De Re Rusticâ*," is divided into twelve books. It treats of all subjects connected with the choice and management of a farm,[1376] the arrangement of farm buildings,[1377] the propagation and rearing of stock,[1378] the cultivation of fruit trees,[1379] and household economy.[1380] A calendar is attached to the eleventh book, pointing out the cosmical risings and settings of the constellations, which marked the successive seasons for various labours and other practical points of rustic astronomy. The tenth book, the subject of which is horticulture, is in hexameters. It never rises quite to the height of poetry: it is rather metrical prose, characterized, like the rest of his work, by fluency, and also expressed in correct versification. The reason which he gives for this variation from his plan is, that it is intended as supplementary to the Georgics of Virgil, and that in so doing he is following the great poet's own recommendations. In his preface to his friend Silvinus he thus expresses his intention:—"Postulatio tua pervicit ut poeticis numeris explerem Georgici carminis omissas partes, quas tamen et ipse Virgilius significaverat posteris se memorandas relinquere."

SEXTUS JULIUS FRONTINUS

Sex. Jul. Frontinus deserves a place amongst Roman classical writers as the author of two works, both of which are still extant. The first, entitled, "*Stratagematicon, Libri iv.*," was a treatise on military tactics. The form in which he has enunciated his doctrines is that of precepts and anecdotes of celebrated military commanders. In this way the necessary preparations for a battle, the stratagems resorted to in fighting, the rules for conducting sieges, and the means of maintaining discipline in an army, are explained and illustrated in a straightforward and soldier-like style.

As the object which he had in view in adducing his anecdotes is scientific illustration rather than historic truth, he is not very particular as to the sources from which his examples are derived. It is interesting, however, to the antiquarian, if not of practical utility to the tactician, as displaying the theory and practice of ancient warfare. This subject had in early times been treated of by Cato and Cincius, and afterwards by Hyginus in a treatise on Field Fortification (*de Castrametatione*,) and also in the epitome of Vegetius.

His other work, which has descended to modern times in a perfect state, is a descriptive architectural treatise, in two books, on those wonderful monuments of Roman art, the aqueducts. But besides these, fragments remain of other works, which assign Frontinus an important place in the estimation of the student of Roman history. These are treatises on surveying, and the laws and customs relating to landed property. They were partly of a scientific, partly of a jurisprudential character, and are to be found amongst the works of the *Agri-mensores*, or *Rei Agrariæ Scriptores*. The difficulty and obscurity of everything

---

[1373] Lib. x. 185.
[1374] Præf. 20.
[1375] Lib. ii. 10.
[1376] Lib. ii.
[1377] Lib. i.
[1378] Lib. vi. vii. viii. ix.
[1379] Lib. iii. iv. v.
[1380] Lib. xii.

connected with Roman agrarian institutions is well known; and every fragment relating to them is valuable, because of the probability of its throwing light upon so important a subject. Niebuhr[1381] saw their value, and pronounced that "the fragments of Frontinus were the only work amongst the *Agri-mensores* which can be counted a part of classical literature, or which was composed with any legal knowledge." These fragments, therefore, may be taken as a favourable specimen of this class of writers, amongst whom were Siculus Flaccus, Argenius Urbicus, and Hyginus (Grammaticus.)

Of the life of Frontinus himself very few facts are known. He was city prætor in the reign of Vespasian,[1382] and succeeded Cerealis as governor of Britain. He made a successful campaign against the Silures[1383] (S. Wales,) and was succeeded by Agricola, A. D. 78. He was subsequently *curator aquarum*,[1384] an office which probably suggested the composition of his practical manual on aqueducts. He also had a seat in the college of augurs, in which, after his death,[1385] he was succeeded by the younger Pliny.

With this third epoch a history of Roman classical literature comes to a close. In the silver age taste had gradually but surely declined; and although the Roman language and literature shone forth for a time with classic radiance in the writings of Persius, Juvenal, Quintilian, Tacitus, and the Plinies, nothing could arrest its fall. In vain emperors endeavoured to encourage learning by pecuniary rewards and salaried professorships: it languished together with the death of constitutional freedom, the extinction of patriotism, and the decay of the national spirit. Poetry had become declamation. History had degenerated either into fulsome panegyric, or the fleshless skeletons of epitomes; and at length Romans seemed to disdain the use of their native tongue—that tongue which laborious pains had brought to such a height of polish and perfection, and wrote in Greek, as they had in the infancy of the national literature, when Latin was too rude and imperfect to imbody the ideas which they had derived from their Greek instructors.

The Emperor Hadrian resided long at Athens, and became imbued with a taste and admiration for Greek; and thus the literature of Rome became Hellenized. From this epoch the term Classical can no longer be applied to it, for it did not retain its purity. To Greek influence succeeded the still more corrupting one of foreign nations. Even with the death of Nerva the uninterrupted succession of emperors of Roman or Italian birth ceased. Trajan himself was a Spaniard; and after him not only barbarians of every European race, but even Orientals and Africans were invested with the imperial purple. The empire also over which they ruled was an unwieldy mass of heterogeneous materials. The literary influence of the capital was not felt in the distant portions of the Roman dominions. Schools were established in the very heart of nations just emerging from barbarism—at Burdegala (Bourdeaux,) Lugdunum (Lyons,) and Augusta Trevirorum (Treves;) and, although the blessings of civilization and intellectual culture were thus distributed far and wide, still literary taste, as it filtered through the minds of foreigners, became corrupted, and the language of the imperial city, exposed to the infectious contact of barbarous idioms, lost its purity.[1386]

[1381] See Smith's Dict. of Antiq. *s. v.*
[1382] A. D. 70.
[1383] Tac. Agric.
[1384] De Ag. I.
[1385] About A. D. 106.
[1386] Macrobius.

The Latin authors of this period were numerous, and many of them were Christians; but few had taste to appreciate and imitate the literature of the Augustan age. The brightest stars which illuminated the darkness were A. Gellius, L. Apuleius, T. Petronius Arbiter, the learned author of the Saturnalia; the Christian ethical philosopher, L. Cœlius Lactantius; and that poet, in whom the graceful imagination of classical antiquity seems to have revived, the flattering and courtly Claudian.

Chronological Table

B. C.	A. U. C.	Literary Chronology.	Civil Chronology.
		First Era.	
753–510	1–244	Chant of the Arvalian Brotherhood; Saturnian measure; Salian hymn; Pontifical annals; Libri Lintei.	Regal period.
449	305	Laws of the Twelve Tables; the so-called Leges Regiæ.	The Decemvirs deposed.
390	364	- - -	Rome taken by Gauls.
364	390	Stage-players sent for from Etruria.	The year following the death of Camillus.
326–304	428–450	The Tiburtine inscription -	Second Samnite War.
280	474	Appius Claudius Cæcus; Ti. Coruncanius.	The year following the arrival of Pyrrhus.
264	490	- - -	Commencement of first Punic war.
260	494	The Columna Rostrata; epitaphs on the Scipios.	Fifth year of the first Punic war.
241	513	- - -	Conclusion of the first Punic war.
240	514	Livius Andronicus.	
239	515	Birth of Ennius.	
235	519	Cnæus Nævius flourished.	The Temple of Janus closed for the second time.
227	527	Birth of Plautus; funeral oration of Q. Metellus.	
219	535	Q. Fabius Pictor; L. Cincius Alimentus; birth of Pacuvius	

Chronological Table (Continued)

B. C.	A. U. C.	Literary Chronology.	Civil Chronology.
204	550	Ennius brought to Rome; Corn. Cethegus; P. Licinius Crassus.	
201	553	Speech of Fabius Cunctator; Sextus Ælius Catus.	Conclusion of second Punic war.
195	559	M. Porcius Cato consul; Licinius Tegula.	
186	568	Senatus-consultum respecting the Bacchanals.	The year following the condemnation of L. Scipio.
516184 570		Cæcilius Statius flourished; he died A. U. C. 586; death of Plautus.	Censorship of M. Porcius Cato.
183	571	- - -	Deaths of Hannibal and Scipio Africanus.
181	573	The (so-called) books of Numa found.	
179	575	- - -	Accession of Perseus.
170	584	Attius born.	
168	586	- - -	Defeat of Perseus at Pydna.
166	588	Terence exhibits the Andrian; Sp. Carvilius; C. Sulpicius Gallus; Lavinius Luscius; T. Manlius Torquatus.	
155	599	The three Attic philosophers visit Rome; C. Acilius Glabrio; Crates Mallotes.	
154	600	M. Pacuvius; Scipio Æmilianus; Lælius.	
150	604	L. Afranius; S. Sulpicius Galba.	
148	606	Birth of C. Lucilius; Cassius Hemina; A. Postumius Albinus	Second year of the third Punic war.
146	608	- - -	End of third Punic war; Carthage and Corinth taken.
138	616	L. Attius flourished; Q. F. M. Servilianus; C. Fannius; Vennonius; C. Sempronius	Dec. Jun. Brutus consul.
133	621	M. Junius Brutus; P. Mucius Scævola; L. Cælius Antipater; Cn. S. and A. Gellii; L. Calpurnius Piso Frugi; Papirius Carbo; Lepidus Porcina; Ælius Tubero.	Murder of Tib. Gracchus; Numantia taken.
129	625	- - -	Death of Scipio Æmilianus; æt. 56.
123	631	C. Sempronius Gracchus; Sextus Turpilius; C. Lucilius flourished; Lævius; (?) C. Junius Gracchanus; M. Julius Pennus.	
119	635	L. Licinius Crassus accuses Carbo; M. Antonius (born B. C. 144.)	

Chronological Table

B. C.	A. U. C.	Literary Chronology.	Civil Chronology.
113	641	- - -	War begun with the Cimbri.
517111	643	- - -	First year of Jugurthine war.
109	645	Publius Sempronius Asellio; M. Æmilius Scaurus; P. Rutilius Rufus; Q. Lutatius Catulus.	
106	648	Birth of Cicero	Birth of Cn. Pompeius.
100	654	L. Ælius Stilo	Birth of Julius Cæsar.
95	659	Cotta; the Sulpicii; Hortensius; Q. Mucius Scævola; Lucretius born.	
91	663	Death of the orator Crassus.	
90	664	C. Licinius Macer; Q. Claudius Quadrigarius; Q. Valerius Antias; L. Lucullus; Sulla; Plotius Gallus.	Commencement of the Social war.
87	667	M. Antonius killed; Catullus born.	Massacres by Cinna and Marius.
86	668	Birth of Sallust	Death of Marius.
84	670	Attius probably died about this time, and Latin acting tragedy disappeared; L. Cornelius Sisenna.	
82	672	Births of Varro Atacinus and Licinius Calvus Valerius Cato.	Sulla's proscription.
78	676	Commencement of Sallust's history.	Death of Sulla.
76	678	Birth of Asinius Pollio.	

Second Era.

B. C.	A. U. C.	Literary Chronology.	Civil Chronology.
74	680	Roman prose literature arrived at its greatest perfection; Cicero twenty-two years of age.	Third Mithridatic war began.
72	682	- - -	Murder of Sertorius.
71	683	- - -	Defeat of Spartacus.
70	684	Cicero accuses Verres; Virgil born.	
67	687	C. Aquilius Gallus; C. Juventius; Sext. Papirius; L. Lucilius Balbus.	Pompey, entrusted with the war against the Pirates.
65	689	Birth of Horace	First Catilinarian conspiracy.
63	691	Pomponius Atticus; M. Terentius Varro Reatinus; L. Lueceius; Nigidius Figulus; Orbilius came to Rome in the fiftieth year of his age (Suet. de Ill. Gram. 9;) Q. Cornificius.	Consulship of Cicero; birth of Augustus; Jerusalem taken by Pompey.

Chronological Table (Continued)

B. C.	A. U. C.	Literary Chronology.	Civil Chronology.
61	693	Oration for Archias	Acquittal of Clodius.
60	694	- - -	First triumvirate.
59	695	Birth of T. Livius.	
55	699	- - -	Cæsar's first invasion of Britain.
54	700	Julius Cæsar; Lucretius Carus; C. Val. Catullus; Æsopus; Q. Roscius; Licinius Calvus; Helvius Cinna; Ticida; Bibaculus; Varro Atacinus; Cornelius Nepos; A. Hirtius; C. Oppius; S. Sulpicius Rufus.	Cæsar's second invasion of Britain.
52	702	Death of Lucretius.	
49	705	D. Laberius; C. Matius; P. Syrus.	J. Cæsar appointed Dictator.
48	706	- - -	Battle of Pharsalia; murder of Pompey.
46	708	- - -	Cæsar reforms the calendar.
44	710	C. Sallustius Crispus; Atteius Philologus; Asinius Pollio.	Murder of Julius Cæsar.
43	711	Death of Cicero; Valgius Rufus; birth of Ovid; death of Laberius.	Second triumvirate formed.
42	712	Horace at Philippi.	
40	714	- - -	Treaty of Brundisium.
34	720	Death of Sallust.	
32	722	Death of Atticus.	War declared against Antony.
31	723	Virgilius Maro (born B. C. 70;) Mæcenas; Horatius Flaccus; L. Varius; Albius Tibullus; Cornelius Gallus; Plotius Tucca; Bathyllus; Pylades; Trogus Pompeius.	Battle of Actium.
29	725	- - -	The three triumphs of Octavius; temple of Janus closed.
28	726	Palatine library founded; death of Varro.	
27	727	- - -	Octavius receives the title of Augustus.
25	729	J. Hyginus; S. Aurelius Propertius; Æmilius Macer; Ovidius Naso; Gratius Faliscus; Pedo Albinovanus; A. Sabinus; T. Livius; Ateius Capito; Vitruvius; Q. Cæcilius Epirota.	
19	735	Death of Virgil.	
18	734	Death of Tibullus.	

Chronological Table

B. C.	A. U. C.	Literary Chronology.	Civil Chronology.
17	737	Carmen seculare of Horatius;	Ludi sæculares. Porcius Latro.
15	739	- - -	Tiberius and Drusus conquer the Vindelici.
9	745	History of Livy terminates.	
8	746	Death of Horace	The month Sextilis named Augustus.
4	750	- - -	Birth of our Lord Jesus Christ.

A. D.			
4	758	Death of Asinius Pollio.	
9	763	Exile of Ovid	Defeat of Quintilius Varus.
14	767	- - -	Death of Augustus.

		Third Era.	
16	769	T. Phædrus	Sejanus the imperial favourite.
18	771	C. Asinius Gallus; deaths of Ovid and Livy; Valerius Maximus.	
23	776	Birth of C. Plinius Secundus.	Murder of Drusus.
25	778	Birth of Silius Italicus; death of Cremutius Cordus; M. Annæus Seneca; A. Cornelius Celsus; Arellius Fuscus; Valerius Maximus.	
30	783	Velleius Paterculus writes his history.	
31	784	- - -	Fall of Sejanus.
34	787	A. Persius Flaccus born.	
37	790	- - -	Death of Tiberius.
40	793	Lucan brought to Rome.	
41	794	Exile of Seneca	Caligula assassinated; Claudius emperor.
43	796	Birth of Martial; Pomponius Mela; L. Junius Columella; Remmius Fannius Palæmon.	Expedition of Claudius to Britain.
49	802	Recall of Seneca.	
54	807	L. Annæus Seneca; M. Annæus Lucanus; Cornutus; Persius; Cæsius Bassus; C. Silius Italicus; Q. Curtius Rufus.	Accession of Nero.
52059	812	- - -	Murder of Agrippina.
61	814	Pliny the Younger born	Boadicea conquered by Suetonius Paullinus.

Chronological Table (Continued)

B. C.	A. U. C.	Literary Chronology.	Civil Chronology.
62	815	Death of Persius.	
65	818	Deaths of Seneca and Lucan.	
66	819	Martial came to Rome.	
69	822	- - -	Accession of Vespasian.
70	823	Saleius Bassus; C. Valerius Flaccus.	Jerusalem taken by Titus.
74	827	The dialogue *De Oratoribus* supposed to have been written.	
77	830	C. Plinius Secundus Major flourished.	
78	831	- - -	Agricola Governor of Britain.
79	832	Death of Pliny the Elder	Destruction of Herculaneum and Pompeii.
80	833	- - -	The Coliseum built.
81	834	- - -	Accession of Domitian.
90	843	M. F. Quintilianus; the Philosophers expelled by Domitian; Papinius Statius; Martialis.	
93	846	- - -	Death of Agricola.
96	849	- - -	Assassination of Domitian.
98	851	C. Cornelius Tacitus; C. Plinius Minor; Julius Frontinus; Suetonius Tranquillus; Annæus Florus; Julius Obsequens; D. Junius Juvenalis.	Accession of Trajan.
104	857	Pliny's letter respecting the Christians.	
117	870	- - -	Accession of Hadrian.
138	891	S. Pomponius; Gaius	Accession of Antoninus Pius.
161	914	L. Appuleius; Minucius Felix; Tertullian.	Accession of M. Aurelius.

INDEX

A

Æmilianus, Scipio, 83, 239, 368
Æsopus, 135, 136, 275, 370
Afranius, L., 78, 368
Africanus, Scipio, vi, 41, 48, 49, 52, 76, 111, 115, 117, 236, 288, 368
Agricola, ix, 323, 325, 326, 327, 330, 331, 364, 372
Agricola Governor of Britain, 372
Agrippina, 340, 371
Albinus, A. Postumius, 110, 368
Alimentus, L. Cincius, vi, 97, 100, 367
Andrian, 44, 67, 70, 71, 368
Andronicus, Livius, v, 27, 31, 36, 37, 38, 48, 86, 130, 140, 179, 367
Antias, Q. Valerius, 112, 369
Antipater, L. Cælius, 111, 368
Antonius, M., vi, 115, 120, 131, 368, 369
Appuleius, L., 372
Archias, 4, 223, 231, 246, 370
Asellio, Publius Sempronius, 111, 369
Atacinus, Varro, 94, 154, 155, 369, 370
Attic philosophers, 368
Atticus, 37, 39, 66, 79, 109, 221, 234, 238, 239, 241, 247, 370
Atticus, Pomponius, 223, 236, 369
Attius, L., vi, 89, 368
Augustus, vi, vii, xii, xiii, 22, 31, 32, 86, 98, 130, 133, 135, 139, 140, 157, 159, 160, 170, 173, 174, 181, 185, 191, 201, 202, 203, 204, 213, 214, 215, 242, 247, 253, 261, 264, 267, 268, 273, 274, 279, 280, 297, 317, 330, 339, 359, 369, 370, 371
Aurelius, M., 372

B

Bacchanals, 22, 368
Balbus, L. Lucilius, 130, 369

Bassus, Cæsius, 292, 296, 371
Bassus, Saleius, 372
Bathyllus, 140, 370
Battle of Actium, 370
Battle of Pharsalia, 169, 370
Bibaculus, 154, 370
Boadicea, 371
books of Numa, 368
Britain, 4, 170, 327, 362, 364, 371
Brutus consul, 368
Brutus, M. Junius, 129, 368

C

C. Plinius Minor, 372
C. Plinius Secundus, 345, 371, 372
C. Plinius Secundus Major, 372
Cæcilius Statius, 53, 60, 65, 67, 368
Cæcus, Appius Claudius, vi, 115, 116, 367
Cæsar reforms the calendar, 370
Cæsar, Julius, 4, 136, 139, 163, 169, 173, 180, 216, 242, 248, 259, 268, 317, 369, 370
Caligula, 174, 280, 323, 329, 340, 371
Calvus, Licinius, 154, 369, 370
Camillus, 367
Capito, Ateius, 370
Carbo, 121, 368
Carbo, Papirius, 119, 368
Carmen secular, 371
Carthage, 6, 33, 43, 66, 104, 107, 110, 259, 368
Carus, Lucretius, 143, 236, 370
Cato, M. Porcius, 102, 236, 368
Catullus, vii, xiii, 143, 149, 150, 151, 152, 153, 154, 172, 175, 188, 206, 247, 317, 369
Catullus, C. Val., 370
Catulus, Q. Lutatius, 112, 369
Catus, Sextus Ælius, 129, 368
Celsus, A. Cornelius, ix, 361, 371

Chant of the Arvalian Brotherhood, 367
Christians, ix, 54, 68, 140, 222, 315, 345, 353, 365, 372
Cicero, vi, vii, ix, xii, xiii, 4, 6, 20, 23, 26, 31, 32, 33, 37, 38, 39, 41, 42, 43, 44, 45, 48, 51, 52, 56, 61, 63, 65, 66, 70, 78, 79, 80, 86, 87, 89, 90, 91, 93, 99, 100, 103, 105, 110, 111, 112, 113, 114, 115, 116, 117, 118, 119, 120, 121, 122, 123, 124, 125, 128, 129, 130, 133, 135, 136, 137, 139, 144, 148, 150, 157, 165, 174, 177, 191, 221, 222, 223, 224, 225, 226, 227, 228, 229, 230, 231, 232, 233, 234, 235, 236, 237, 239, 240, 241, 243, 246, 247, 248, 249, 250, 252, 253, 257, 262, 264, 265, 267, 268, 279, 296, 301, 309, 316, 339, 353, 356, 359, 361, 362, 369, 370
Cimbri, 369
Cinna, 91, 154, 249, 369
Cinna, Helvius, 154, 370
Claudius, 41, 99, 101, 116, 129, 157, 241, 250, 255, 262, 275, 279, 280, 318, 340, 342, 345, 362, 371
Claudius emperor, 371
Clodius, 40, 131, 150, 225, 370
Cn. Pompeius, 369
Cn. S. and A. Gellii, 368
Coliseum, 268, 372
Columella, L. Junius, 371
Cordus, Cremutius, ix, 246, 323, 371
Corinth, 368
Corn. Cethegus, 116, 368
Cornificius, Q., 267, 369
Cornutus, 292, 294, 296, 305, 371
Coruncanius, Ti., 367
Cotta, 57, 120, 122, 123, 124, 369
Crassus, vi, 120, 121, 122, 123, 158, 224, 234, 369
Crassus, L. Licinius, 115, 120, 121, 368
Crassus, P. Licinius, 129, 368
Crispus, C. Sallustius, 255, 370
Cunctator, Fabius, 117, 368

D

De Oratoribus, 372
Decemvirs deposed, 367
Domitian, viii, xii, 140, 141, 242, 299, 313, 314, 316, 318, 325, 326, 328, 355, 356, 372
Drusus, 185, 262, 279, 346, 371

E

Ennius, v, xii, 6, 22, 25, 26, 39, 42, 43, 45, 47, 48, 49, 50, 51, 52, 57, 59, 60, 65, 66, 81, 86, 87, 92, 116, 130, 131, 171, 172, 179, 265, 367, 368

Epirota, Q. Cæcilius, 267, 370
epitaphs on the Scipios, 367
Etruria, 7, 8, 15, 34, 36, 291, 367
Exile of Ovid, 371

F

Faliscus, Gratius, vii, 211, 218, 370
Fannius, C., 71, 75, 111, 368
first Punic war, 27, 31, 50, 100, 107, 265, 367
first triumvirate, 241
Flaccus, A. Persius, 371
Flaccus, C. Valerius, viii, 313, 372
Flaccus, Horatius, 177, 178, 370
Florus, Annæus, ix, 333, 336, 372
Frontinus, Julius, ix, 361, 363, 372
Fuscus, Arellius, 211, 371

G

Gaius, 11, 20, 128, 280, 372
Galba, S. Sulpicius, 104, 368
Gallus, C. Aquilius, vi, 127, 130, 369
Gallus, C. Asinius, 371
Gallus, C. Sulpicius, 368
Gallus, Cornelius, vii, 201, 205, 370
Gallus, Plotius, 369
Glabrio, C. Acilius, vi, 97, 101, 368
Gracchanus, C. Junius, 368
Gracchus, C. Sempronius, 368
Gracchus, Tib., 119, 368

H

Hadrian, 4, 28, 31, 128, 150, 242, 299, 317, 326, 334, 337, 364, 372
Hannibal, 21, 48, 100, 101, 107, 117, 247, 265, 266, 368
Hemina, Cassius, vi, 107, 110, 368
Herculaneum, 372
Hirtius, A., 250, 370
History of Livy, 371
Horace, vi, vii, viii, xiii, 5, 9, 26, 29, 34, 39, 42, 44, 45, 49, 55, 59, 60, 66, 84, 86, 89, 92, 93, 94, 137, 151, 154, 157, 158, 159, 162, 177, 178, 179, 180, 181, 182, 183, 184, 185, 187, 188, 189, 190, 191, 192, 199, 200, 203, 204, 205, 206, 208, 213, 214, 241, 274, 279, 291, 292, 293, 296, 297, 298, 299, 300, 301, 318, 319, 334, 337, 369, 370, 371
Horatius, 20, 82, 177, 178, 370, 371
Hortensius, vi, 6, 115, 120, 123, 124, 125, 150, 223, 230, 238, 248, 357, 369

I

invasion of Britain, 370
Italicus, C. Silius, 309, 371
Italicus, Silius, viii, 274, 303, 307, 310, 354, 359, 371

J

J. Hyginus, 109, 370
Jerusalem, 328, 329, 369, 372
Jugurthine war, 257, 369
Juvenalis, D. Junius, 372
Juventius, C., 130, 369

L

Laberius, vi, 135, 136, 137, 139, 370
Laberius, D., 370
Lælius, xii, 49, 66, 68, 69, 87, 88, 93, 98, 118, 119, 131, 236, 239, 357, 368
Lævius, vi, 89, 95, 368
Latin acting tragedy, 369
Latro, Porcius, 211, 371
Lavinius Luscius, 79, 368
Laws of the Twelve Tables, 367
Lintei, Libri, 33, 264, 367
Livius, T., 261, 370
Livy, v, viii, xiii, 7, 8, 13, 20, 22, 25, 26, 32, 33, 36, 37, 39, 52, 99, 101, 103, 105, 111, 112, 113, 114, 116, 117, 129, 222, 241, 245, 258, 261, 262, 263, 264, 265, 266, 267, 274, 296, 310, 335, 336, 349, 371
Lord Jesus Christ, 371
Lucan, viii, 273, 274, 284, 292, 303, 304, 305, 306, 307, 334, 371, 372
Lucanus, M. Annæus, 303, 371
Lucilius, C., 92, 368
Lucullus, L., 369
Ludi sæculares, 371
Lueceius, L., 369

M

Macer, Æmilius, vii, 201, 208, 370
Macer, C. Licinius, 112, 369
Mallotes, Crates, 130, 368
Manlius Torquatus, T., 129, 368
Marius, 40, 91, 222, 227, 249, 306, 326, 369
Martial, ix, xii, xiii, 103, 140, 141, 159, 208, 218, 261, 275, 284, 294, 301, 302, 305, 307, 309, 313, 316, 317, 318, 319, 320, 322, 334, 347, 355, 356, 371, 372
Martialis, 318, 321, 372
Matius, C., 139, 370
Maximus, Valerius, ix, 89, 103, 222, 246, 323, 324, 371
Mela, Pomponius, ix, 303, 361, 362, 371
Metellus, Q., 116, 367
Minucius Felix, 372

N

Nævius, Cnæus, 367
Nepos, Cornelius, vi, viii, 48, 65, 68, 107, 130, 245, 246, 247, 265, 370
Nero, viii, ix, 83, 140, 280, 283, 284, 296, 304, 305, 310, 316, 318, 325, 330, 333, 334, 335, 339, 340, 341, 342, 346, 371
Nigidius Figulus, 267, 369
Numantia, 93, 111, 368

O

Obsequens, Julius, 372
Octavius, 75, 81, 130, 131, 158, 163, 184, 201, 202, 205, 227, 233, 370
Oppius, C., 250, 251, 370
Orbilius, 44, 179, 369
Ovid, vii, xiii, 45, 86, 143, 144, 149, 152, 205, 206, 207, 208, 209, 211, 212, 213, 214, 215, 216, 218, 219, 267, 274, 279, 283, 315, 316, 317, 370, 371
Ovidius Naso, 211, 370

P

Pacuvius, vi, 66, 81, 83, 86, 87, 89, 171, 172, 241, 367
Pacuvius, M., 87, 88, 368
Palæmon, Remmius Fannius, 371
Palatine library, 267, 370
Paterculus, Velleius, ix, 246, 323, 324, 336, 371
Paullinus, Suetonius, 371
Pedo Albinovanus, vii, 211, 212, 218, 370
Perseus, 76, 88, 102, 129, 368
Persius, viii, 83, 87, 88, 92, 94, 136, 188, 190, 191, 273, 274, 291, 292, 293, 294, 295, 296, 297, 298, 307, 334, 364, 371, 372
Phædrus, T., 371
Philippi, 158, 180, 370
Philologus, Atteius, 267, 370
Pictor, Q. Fabius, vi, 97, 99, 367
Piso Frugi, L. Calpurnius, 111, 368

Pius, Antoninus, 372
Plautus, vi, xii, 6, 7, 22, 23, 42, 53, 54, 57, 58, 59, 60, 61, 62, 64, 65, 72, 78, 102, 367, 368
Pliny the Elder, ix, 345, 372
Pliny the Younger, ix, 309, 310, 325, 345, 346, 348, 352, 371
Pollio, Asinius, 86, 136, 158, 205, 241, 250, 267, 283, 369, 370, 371
Pompeii, 136, 372
Pompeius, Trogus, viii, 246, 255, 259, 370
Pompey, 40, 91, 93, 131, 158, 164, 181, 222, 223, 224, 225, 226, 232, 234, 241, 242, 246, 253, 256, 258, 261, 262, 305, 306, 307, 309, 329, 369, 370
Pomponius, S., 372
Pontifical annals, 367
Porcina, Lepidus, 119, 368
Propertius, S. Aurelius, 370
Punic war, 100, 111, 116, 130, 310, 368
Pydna, 368
Pylades, 88, 140, 370
Pyrrhus, 116, 171, 259, 367

Q

Q. Curtius Rufus, ix, 333, 335, 371
Quadrigarius, Q. Claudius, 112, 369
Quintilianus, M. F., 372

R

Recall of Seneca, 371
Regal period, 367
Regiæ, Leges, 20, 128, 265, 367
Roman prose literature, 369
Rome, vi, vii, xi, xii, xiii, 3, 4, 5, 6, 8, 9, 13, 18, 22, 23, 27, 29, 31, 33, 35, 37, 40, 42, 43, 48, 49, 59, 60, 61, 65, 66, 69, 81, 82, 83, 84, 85, 86, 87, 89, 91, 92, 94, 100, 101, 102, 103, 104, 105, 107, 108, 110, 111, 112, 115, 116, 117, 121, 124, 130,131, 140, 144, 149, 150, 151, 158, 159, 168, 177, 178, 179, 180, 181, 182, 183, 184, 188, 190, 191, 199, 201, 202, 206, 211, 214, 217, 223, 224, 225, 226, 230, 233, 234, 235, 238, 239, 240, 241, 242, 243, 246, 248, 257, 261, 262, 263, 264, 265, 274, 276, 278, 279, 280, 291, 293, 298, 299, 300, 302, 304, 305, 306, 308, 310, 314, 318, 319, 320, 321, 322, 324, 325, 327, 330, 331, 339, 340, 345, 347, 355, 356, 359, 363, 364, 367, 368, 369, 371, 372
Rome taken by Gauls, 367
Roscius, Q., 370
Rostrata, Columna, 22, 23, 367
Rufus, P. Rutilius, 112, 369
Rufus, S. Sulpicius, 370
Rufus, Valgius, vii, 136, 154, 201, 203, 370

S

Sabinus, A., 219, 370
Salian hymn, 19, 26, 367
Sallust, viii, xii, 113, 119, 241, 245, 255, 256, 257, 258, 259, 267, 301, 324, 369, 370
Saturnian measure, 19, 45, 367
Scævola, P. Mucius, 368
Scævola, Q. Mucius, 130, 223, 369
Scaurus, M. Æmilius, 112, 369
Scipio, L., 21, 368
second Punic War, 37, 66
Second Samnite War, 367
Second triumvirate, 370
Sejanus, viii, 273, 275, 277, 278, 279, 301, 323, 324, 371
Sempronius, C., 111, 368
Senatus-consultum, 21, 22, 368
Seneca, vii, viii, xiii, 81, 83, 86, 139, 203, 204, 211, 212, 218, 235, 239, 241, 258, 274, 275, 283, 284, 285, 286, 288, 289, 292, 296, 301, 305, 323, 340, 341, 342, 343, 352, 371, 372
Seneca, L. Annæus, ix, 284, 339, 340, 371
Seneca, M. Annæus, ix, 284, 339, 371
Sertorius, 248, 369
Servilianus, Q. F. M., 368
Sext. Papirius, 369
Sextilis, 371
Sisenna, L. Cornelius, 113, 369
Social war, 369
Sp. Carvilius, 368
Spartacus, 257, 369
Statius, Papinius, viii, 313, 314, 372
Stilo, L. Ælius, 131, 369
Sulla, 91, 98, 99, 112, 113, 124, 131, 136, 223, 227, 231, 236, 242, 255, 257, 258, 306, 369
Sulpicii, 123, 369
Syrus, P., 137, 370

T

Tacitus, C. Cornelius, 325, 372
Tegula, Licinius, 79, 368
temple of Janus, 184, 370
Terence, vi, xii, 6, 44, 52, 53, 55, 56, 57, 58, 60, 65, 66, 67, 68, 69, 70, 71, 72, 75, 76, 78, 79, 80, 87, 92, 102, 105, 135, 317, 334, 368
Tertullian, 372

Third Mithridatic war, 369
third Punic war, 368
three triumphs of Octavius, 370
Tiberius, viii, 22, 83, 119, 129, 140, 157, 185, 214, 219, 242, 273, 275, 278, 279, 280, 309, 323, 324, 329, 359, 361, 371
Tibullus, vii, xii, 201, 205, 206, 207, 208, 213, 370
Tibullus, Albius, 205, 370
Tiburtine inscription, 21, 367
Ticida, 154, 370
Titus, 60, 261, 268, 273, 313, 318, 325, 346, 347, 372
Trajan, ix, 5, 83, 242, 299, 310, 323, 325, 326, 328, 333, 337, 352, 353, 354, 364, 372
Tranquillus, Suetonius, ix, 333, 372
Treaty of Brundisium, 370
Tubero, Ælius, 113, 368
Tucca, Plotius, 370
Turpilius, Sextus, 80, 368

V

Valerius Cato, Licinius Calvus, 369
Varius, L., 204, 370
Varro Reatinus, M. Terentius, 242, 369
Vennonius, 111, 368
Verres, 42, 124, 224, 225, 231, 369
Vespasian, 83, 242, 264, 273, 299, 313, 314, 318, 325, 335, 356, 364, 372
Vindelici, 185, 371
Virgil, vii, xii, xiii, 5, 26, 42, 43, 45, 50, 51, 57, 86, 109, 135, 143, 144, 149, 151, 152, 154, 155, 157, 158, 160, 161, 162, 163, 164, 165, 167, 168, 169, 170, 171, 172, 173, 174, 175, 181, 187, 203, 204, 205, 206, 207, 208, 213, 215, 241, 280, 283, 305, 306, 307, 309, 310, 313, 314, 316, 317, 363, 369, 370
Vitruvius, viii, 261, 267, 268, 370

Related Nova Publications

Art and Music: Past, Present and Future Perspectives

Editors: Angla Lear and Min Street

Series: Fine Arts, Music and Literature

Book Description: In *Art and Music: Past, Present and Future Perspectives*, the authors begin by arguing that this question only yields a satisfying answer if we look at contextual conditions, both of production and of reception.

Softcover ISBN: 978-1-53614-113-9
Retail Price: $82

Exploring Art and Literature: Interpretations, Perspectives and Influences

Editor: Aron Medrano

Series: Fine Arts, Music and Literature

Book Description: In this compilation, the authors suggest a temporal model interpretation for the stele from the Scythian ¡°Senior¡± Trekhbratnyi barrow (IV¨CIII centuries BC).

Hardcover ISBN: 978-1-53613-531-2
Retail Price: $325

To see complete list of Nova publications, please visit our website at www.novapublishers.com